Economic Analysis and Law

A comprehensive presentation of the use of economics in judicial decisions, the book is structured to provide all the foundational concepts that are important for the application of economics to the development and interpretation of statutes that emanate from economic conditions.

The diversity of the economic field defines the scope of the book and its relevance to the study of law and rule adjudication. Beyond the positive dimensions of law and economics, the book evaluates the normative aspects of law and economics when laws are imprecise, and markets are inefficient. The ethical scope of transactions and rule adjudication are further considered in the context of professional ethics and the rationale for ethical considerations in the practice of law and economics. It presents a unique analysis of law, finance, and economics, by taking a look at the intricate quantitative requirements that are essential for scientific knowledge in the courtroom and the international dimensions of the practice of law and economics beyond municipal frontiers. It alerts entrepreneurs to risk exposures in the global economy and provides foundational information for readers who are also interested in international law and economics, and the essence and interpretations of international conventions appertaining to money, expropriation, the environment, and investments in international financial markets.

This book is a useful reference for both undergraduate and graduate students who are interested in law and economics, forensic economics, corporate white-collar crime, and legal studies. It is also valuable for certificate programs for paralegals who wish to have a basic understanding of economic and financial concepts.

Christopher E.S. Warburton is an international economist who currently teaches economics at East Stroudsburg University in Pennsylvania, USA.

Economic Analysis and Law

The Economics of the Courtroom

CHRISTOPHER E.S. WARBURTON

LONDON AND NEW YORK

First published 2021
by Routledge
2 Park Square, Milton Park, Abingdon, Oxon OX14 4RN

and by Routledge
52 Vanderbilt Avenue, New York, NY 10017

Routledge is an imprint of the Taylor & Francis Group, an informa business

© 2021 Christopher E.S. Warburton

The right of Christopher E.S. Warburton to be identified as author of this work has been asserted by him in accordance with sections 77 and 78 of the Copyright, Designs and Patents Act 1988.

All rights reserved. No part of this book may be reprinted or reproduced or utilised in any form or by any electronic, mechanical, or other means, now known or hereafter invented, including photocopying and recording, or in any information storage or retrieval system, without permission in writing from the publishers.

Trademark notice: Product or corporate names may be trademarks or registered trademarks, and are used only for identification and explanation without intent to infringe.

British Library Cataloguing-in-Publication Data
A catalogue record for this book is available from the British Library

Library of Congress Cataloging-in-Publication Data
Names: Warburton, Christopher E. S., author.
Title: Economic analysis and law: the economics of the courtroom / Christopher E.S. Warburton.
Description: Abingdon, Oxon ; New York, NY : Routledge, 2020. | Includes bibliographical references and index.
Identifiers: LCCN 2020004623 (print) | LCCN 2020004624 (ebook) |
Subjects: LCSH: Law and economics. | Forensic economics. |
Law–Economic aspects–United States.
Classification: LCC K487.E3 W37 2020 (print) |
LCC K487.E3 (ebook) | DDC 343.07–dc23
LC record available at https://lccn.loc.gov/2020004623
LC ebook record available at https://lccn.loc.gov/2020004624

ISBN: 978-0-367-36119-8 (hbk)
ISBN: 978-0-367-36120-4 (pbk)
ISBN: 978-0-429-34396-4 (ebk)

Typeset in Avenir, Bell and Bembo
by Newgen Publishing UK

Visit the eResources: www.routledge.com/9780367361204

To my family—Conrad, Denise, and Nabia Warburton

CONTENTS

List of figures   xi
List of tables   xiii

INTRODUCTION   1

1 MICROECONOMIC FOUNDATION   7
    1.1 Microeconomic foundation   8
    1.2 Normative versus positive law and economics   10
    1.3 Economic models and markets   13
    1.4 Market transactions and consumer class action litigation   21
    1.5 Economic and judicial interpretations of consumer responsiveness to price changes   24
        1.5 (A) US labor market and the Civil Rights Act of 1964   27
        1.5 (B) US labor law and economics of discrimination   30
    1.6 Production cost and consumer welfare   36

2 MACROECONOMICS IN FORENSIC ECONOMICS   51
    2.1 Aggregate economic performance (the business cycle)   52
    2.2 Forensic implications of (international) unemployment   55
    2.3 Nominal and real interest rates   59
    2.4 The inflation factor   62
    2.5 Interest rates and inflation in courts of law   67
    2.6 Open macroeconomics and exchange rate law   73

3 CORPORATE FINANCIAL ANALYSIS AND INVESTMENT LAW   89
    3.1 The interface of corporate finance and real economic performance   90
    3.2 Laws of the Security and Exchange Commission   93
        3.2 (A) Financial statements   96
        3.2 (B) The income statement   97
        3.2 (C) The balance sheet   100
        3.2 (D) The statement of cash flow   105
    3.3 Financial statements and securities regulation   109
    3.4 Applications of SEC law   115
        3.4 (A) Securities trade and extraterritorial jurisdiction   117
        3.4 (B) The principal-agent problem   120
        3.4 (C) A case of abusive managerial discretion? *Dodge v. Ford Motor Company* (204 Mich. 459 170 N.W. 668 (1919))   129
            3.4 (C) (I) Managerial economics in *Dodge v. Ford*   131
            3.4 (C) (II) Normative economics in *Dodge v. Ford*   134
    3.5 The principal-agent struggle for control of public corporations   136

4	**INNOVATION AND EXPROPRIATION OF CREATIVE RIGHTS**	**159**
	4.1 Innovation and human rights	160
	4.2 Ethical lapses and costs of IP expropriation	164
	4.3 The economic consequences of innovation	168
	4.4 Intellectual property law	175
5	**ECONOMETRICS FOR THE COURTROOM**	**193**
	5.1 Federal rules of evidence and scientific requirements (the *Daubert Standard*)	194
	5.2 The structure of data	195
	5.3 Sampling strategies	197
	5.4 Forecasting economic value	198
	5.5 Ordinary least squares (OLS)	207
	5.5 (A) Time value of money	217
	5.5 (B) Future value of money	217
	5.5 (C) Present value of money	220
	5.5 (D) Litigating the discount rate	223
	5.5 (E) Annuities and amortization	228
	5.5 (F) The net present value (NPV) of money	232
	5.6 Putting it all together: the *Mooresville Honda Case* and work life expectancy	235
	5.7 Chi square analysis	238
	5.8 The intrinsic value of public companies	244
6	**TAX AVOIDANCE AND EVASION**	**273**
	6.1 Types of taxpayers	273
	6.2 The economics and laws of taxation	275
	6.3 The US tax gap	287
	6.4 Theories of tax avoidance and evasion	289
	6.5 The tax court system of the US	300
	6.6 Tax flight and the Foreign Account Tax Compliance Act (FATCA)	305
7	**US ANTITRUST LAW AND ENFORCEMENT**	**315**
	7.1 The evolution of US antitrust law	315
	7.1 (A) The Sherman Act (1890)	317
	7.1 (B) The Clayton Act (1914)	319
	7.1 (C) The Federal Trade Commission (FTC) Act (1914)	321
	7.1 (D) The Robinson–Patman Act (1936)	322
	7.1 (E) The Wheller-Lea Act (1938)	324
	7.1 (F) The Cellar-Kefauver Act (1950)	327
	7.1 (G) The Williams Act (1968)	331
	7.1 (H) The Hart-Scott-Rodino (HSR) Act (1976)	333
	7.2 The development of mergers and acquisitions (merger waves)	336

7.3	Measuring market concentration: the Herfindahl-Hirschman and Lerner indices		341
7.4	Innovation, tying, and monopolization: antitrust law and the *Microsoft Case*		346
7.5	Estimating antitrust damages		349

8 INTERNATIONAL ECONOMICS IN INTERNATIONAL COURTS OF LAW 363

8.1	The sources of international law			363
8.2	Trade theories as foundations of international trade law			369
8.3	Trade restrictions with partial equilibrium analysis (subsidies and tariffs)			379
8.4	International trade law			388
	8.4 (A)	Infant industry protection (Art. XIII)		390
	8.4 (B)	Dumping (Art. VI, Anti-Dumping Agreement, and Agreement to Implement)		390
	8.4 (C)	Balance of payments stability and quantitative restrictions (Art. XII)		395
	8.4 (D)	Non-discrimination, quotas, and exemptions (Arts. I, XIII and XIV)		396
	8.4 (E)	Regional Trade Agreements (RTAs) (Arts. XXIV and I)		397
	8.4 (F)	Agreement on Subsidies and Countervailing Measures (SCM) (Art. XVI and SCM)		398
8.5	The WTO's Dispute Settlement Understanding (DSU)			402
8.6	Applications of economic law to trade disputes			408
	8.6 (A)	Export subsidy		409
	8.6 (B)	Dumping		414
	8.6 (C)	Discriminatory market access		419
8.7	Monetary economics and international law: the confiscatory effects of currency devaluation or manipulation of value			425
8.8	Customary and conventional monetary law			434
	8.8 (A)	The limits of monetary "sovereignty": contractual monetary arrangements		435
		8.8 (A) (I)	Obligations regarding exchange arrangements (Art. IV)	436
		8.8 (A) (II)	Surveillance over exchange arrangements (Art. IV § 3)	437
		8.8 (A) (III)	Waiver conditions (Art.V § 4)	437
		8.8 (A) (IV)	Ineligibility to use the Fund's general resources (Art.V § 5)	437
		8.8 (A) (V)	Interpretation of the Articles of Agreement (Art. XXIX)	438
8.9	Applications of monetary law: no contrived confiscation			438
8.10	Long-term foreign investment and foreign investment laws			439
	8.10 (A)	The international law of Foreign Direct Investment (FDI)		442

	8.10 (B)	National treatment (OECD Guidelines: Declaration II. 4)	443
	8.10 (C)	International investment incentives and disincentives (OECD Guidelines: Declaration IV. 1–3)	443
	8.10 (D)	Concepts and principles	444
	8.10 (E)	General policies (OECD Guidelines II)	445
	8.10 (F)	Disclosure (OECD Guidelines III)	446
	8.10 (G)	Human rights (OECD Guidelines IV)	446
	8.10 (H)	Environment (OECD Guidelines V)	446
	8.10 (I)	Combating bribery, bribe solicitation and extortion (OECD Guidelines VII)	447
	8.10 (J)	Consumer interests (OECD Guidelines VIII)	447
	8.10 (K)	The taking of foreign property (international law of expropriation and confiscation)	448
8.11	The Aminoil Case (*Government of Kuwait v. American Independent Oil Company*, 1982)		450
	8.11 (A)	The laws governing the arbitration	452
	8.11 (B)	Sovereignty over national resources and nationalization	453
	8.11 (C)	Fair and equitable treatment (FET)	455
	8.11 (D)	Good business (oilfield) practices	455
	8.11 (E)	The gold clause and asset (currency) price stability or convertibility	456
	8.11 (F)	Business valuation and compensation	457

Table of cases	476
Index	481

FIGURES

1.1	A consumption function	15
1.2	Market demand	17
1.3	Market supply	18
1.4	Change in market demand and supply	19
1.5	Economic surplus and efficiency loss	20
1.6	Frequently targeted products (FTP) for class action litigation	22
1.7	Total Settlement Fund Value by settlement year ($m)	23
1.8	Characteristics of consumer class action settlements without a reported settlement fund value	24
1.9	Price elasticity and inelasticity of demand	26
1.10	Charge statistics with the EEOC FY1997 to FY2017	30
1.11	Illegal disutility in employment and compensation	31
1.12	The Occupational Segregation Model	32
1.13	Median weekly earnings, by level of education and gender, 2017 (female percent of male income in parenthesis)	35
1.14	Earnings ratio male-female (1979–2015)	36
1.15	Output and per unit cost in the long run	38
1.16	The competitive and monopolistic market structures	39
2.1	The business cycle	53
2.2	Total unemployment (% of labor force, 2000–2019)	56
2.3	Daily five-year forward inflation rates (October 2014–October 2019)	62
2.4	Three-month Treasury bill secondary market rate (%) (January 1950–October 2019)	63
2.5	Inflation in Germany, US, and the UK: annual percent of consumer prices (2000–2018)	65
2.6	Inflation in Eurozone, US, and the UK: annual percent of consumer prices (2000–2018)	65
3.1	Enron: price per share $90.75 (August 23, 2000) to $1 (November 28, 2001)	123
3.2	Bear Stearns: price per share $159 (March 19, 2007) to $2 per share (March 17, 2008)	126
3.3	Lehman Brothers Holding—market capitalization, 1994–2008 ($billions)	127
3.4	Elasticity and total revenue	132
3.5	Economies of scale and long-run per unit cost of production	133
4.1	Estimated annual cost of intellectual property theft from the US ($b)	163
4.2	Innovation, productivity, and economic growth	170
5.1	Data trends and stationarity	199
5.2	Components of time series data	201
5.3	Excel's moving average function	204
5.4	Regression in Excel	204
5.5	Personal disposable income (PDI) and white-collar crime (WCC)	209
5.6	Dummy variable regression (ANOVA and ANCOVA) models	213

5.7	The HP 10bII+ financial calculator	218
5.8	The future value of a dollar	221
5.9	The present value of a dollar	222
5.10	Future value with Excel	231
5.11	Net present value and IRR with Excel	233
5.12	The internal rate of return	234
6.1	Maximum capital gains and individual income tax rate; tax years 1954–2018	277
6.2	OECD and US tax-to-GDP ratio (2000–2017)	279
6.3	OECD and US corporate tax receipt as a percentage of GDP (2000–2016)	279
6.4	US proposed discretionary spending in 2020 ($1.43 trillion)	286
6.5	US total proposed mandatory spending in 2020 ($2.84 trillion)	286
6.6	US tax gap (1985–2010) (US$ billion)	290
6.7	Individual and corporate income taxes, 1934–2015 (as percentage of total federal revenue)	291
6.8	Tax revenue as a percentage of GDP (2007–2017)	292
6.9	The Tax Laffer curve	293
7.1	Merger filings and transactions (2008–2017)	336
7.2a	Formal actions by US antitrust authorities (2015–2016)	340
7.2b	Court challenges (2015–2016)	341
7.3	The HHI and levels of concentration	343
7.4	Output and per unit cost in the long run	345
7.5	Efficient allocations versus efficiency loss	352
8.1	Cost of producing and consuming manufacturing goods	372
8.2	Comparative cost of manufactures and farm products in the US and Mexico	378
8.3	US–Mexico agricultural exports and imports (US$b, 1975–2016 estimates)	379
8.4	Tariff (without loss of generality)	380
8.5	Trade creation and diversion	383
8.6	Dumping under competitive and imperfect conditions	384
8.7	The discriminating price-maker	385
8.8	Import and export subsidies (Good M)	398
8.9	Boeing v. Airbus commercial aircraft orders (1974–2006)	409
8.10	Influential determinants of exchange rate	428
8.11	The fixed exchange rate under the classical gold standard	429
8.12	The relationship between money supply and interest rate	431
8.13	Money supply, exchange rate, interest rate, and national income	432
8.14	Monetary policy and exchange rate adjustment	433
8.15	FDI inflows by economies and region, 2016–2018 (US$b)	441

TABLES

1.1	Price elasticity coefficients and their meanings	26
1.2	Occupation by gender and pay (full-time employment, 2016)	34
1.3	Short-run costs ($)	37
2.1	US unemployment by industry (%, 2000–2019)	58
2.2	Pre- and post-judgment rates in Alaska (1997–2019)	73
2.3	Exchange rate arrangements (2010–2018)	74
2.4	Exchange rates (January 1999–January 2018)	78
3.1	Capital adequacy requirements (US$m)	124
3.2a	Lehman's reported gross leverage ratios (2003–2007)	128
3.2b	Goldman Sachs Group Inc leverage ratios (February 26, 2008 and June 26, 2015)	129
4.1	Estimated international economic losses due to counterfeiting and piracy (US$b, unless otherwise stated)	167
4.2	Growth rate of patents and trademarks applications (2017–2018)	171
4.3	Forms of federal intellectual property protection	176
4.4	US intellectual property protections and sanctions	178
5.1	US educational attainment of the population 18 years and over (thousands of civilian non-institutionalized population, 1st Grade through Ph.D.)	196
5.2	Monthly sales of US motor vehicle and parts dealers (2013–2015, $b)	205
5.3	Evaluating forecasts ($b)	206
5.4	ANOVA and ANCOVA results (p-value in parenthesis)	212
5.5	US inflation rates	225
5.6	Amortization schedule	229
5.7	Future value interest factors	232
5.8	Net present value with financial calculator and Excel (cells in parenthesis)	233
5.9	Venires of district judges in Boston (1966–1968)	242
5.10	Expected free cash flow of ABC	248
A5.1	Future Value Interest Factors for a dollar	258
A5.2	Present Value Interest Factors for a dollar	259
A5.3	Future Value Interest Factors for a dollar ordinary annuity	261
A5.4	Present Value Interest Factors for a dollar annuity	263
A5.5	Normal distribution table	266
A5.6	The chi square (X^2) distribution	268
A5.7	Regression data	270
6.1	Marginal tax rates (MTR) and tax brackets for $800 (Revenue Act of 1862)	278
6.2	Marginal tax rates (MTR) and tax brackets (Tax Cuts and Jobs Act of 2018)	280
6.3	MACRS depreciation schedules by allowable recovery period	281
6.4	MACRS depreciation schedules and asset description	282
6.5a	Narrative approach: first year tax multipliers	283
6.5b	Narrative approach: first year spending multipliers	284

6.6	Tax gap estimates for tax years 2006 and 2008–2010 and decomposition of change (money amounts are in billions of US$)	287
6.7	Average annual GDP growth (2007–2017)	292
7.1	Antitrust enforcement 1952 to March 1961	330
7.2	US antitrust laws	331
7.3	The HHI and size of market concentration	342
8.1	Applied tariff rates of major traders in 1913 and 1925: all products (percentage)	387
8.2	Rulings of the panels and appellate body	413
8.3	Determinants of exchange rates	427
8.4	Inward FDI rates of return, 2010–2018 (%)	441

INTRODUCTION

This book is not a textbook of law; rather, it is an economics text that shows the interaction of law and economics, and how economics has helped to shape legislative and judicial decisions. More precisely, it also shows how law and judicial decisions are contingent on perceptions of economic theories and models, and how the interaction of law and economics shape the evolution of national and international jurisprudence. As such, this book has been written to assist students of law and practitioners who may want to delve deeper into the intricacies of economic theories and models that are inevitably going to show up in courts of law. Accordingly, the book presents a unique interface of law and economics that is essential to understand legislative and judicial decisions in domestic and international courts of law.

The contents of the book are deliberately exhaustive to provide maximum exposure to the central concepts that will be encountered in microeconomics, financial economics, macroeconomics, econometrics, and international economics. More often than not, economic concepts are interrelated or interdependent; this reality has been integral to the rendition of this book. The fundamental aspects of municipal and international law, which constitute the bulk of this work, have been derived from pedagogical work, reputable scholarly research and writings, and examination of written laws and judicial decisions. All the reputable sources of information have been exhaustively referenced with clarifying notes as and when necessary. I make the assumption that some students, lawyers, and judges are already very familiar and comfortable with the relevant or applicable laws. In effect, the contribution of this work to the legal and pedagogical professions is its application of economic theories and models to legislative and judicial decisions that may not always reflect precise and apparent economic meanings.

In Chapter 1, I look at the microeconomic foundation for understanding some of the contending philosophical positions in legislating and interpreting laws. These positions are circumscribed by subterranean notions of positive and normative economics, and perceptions of the decisions that could lead to efficient allocation of economic resources and efficient markets. Philosophical schools of law and economics include public choice theory, institutional law and economics, the new institutional economics, social norms and law and economics, as well as the New Haven School and Austrian law and economics. Nicholas Mercuro (2009) presents a comprehensive analysis of these schools of thought.

The diversity of thought presupposes conflicting and overlapping theories of economic occurrences and the interpretation of economic models. The orientation of Chapter 1 is not to subscribe to any of these schools of thought but to present economic theories, models, and data for an understanding of economic laws, fundamental fairness (equity) when interpreting laws, and the economic implications of unbalanced legal and judicial decisions. By so doing, I venture into concepts of market failures, income distribution, price movements, and the resulting losses that are associated with price changes. The chapter brings out frictions in the marketplace and how consumers concertedly deal with the issue of market failure and degradation of human welfare when businesses behave badly in the marketplace. Against this backdrop are the economic drivers (concepts) that configure the political, legal, and judicial landscapes of societies. Invariably, equity (what is reasonable and just, *ex aequo et bono*) is not an alien concept to some economists and judges.

Accordingly, Chapter 1 lays the foundation for an understanding of the basic micro concepts that underpin legal theories and judicial decisions. The chapter is also critical for understanding some of the foundational concepts in economics that will be referenced in subsequent chapters. While the chapter presents some of the most primordial theories of economics, some of the most consequential theories can be found in macroeconomics. This is because policy makers and judges are usually interested in aggregational concepts: for example, the common good. Additionally, variables that have general, widespread or national appeal are more attractive to legislatures and triers of facts. Chapter 2 addresses the judicial implications and value of aggregate (macroeconomic) variables.

Macroeconomic variables are integrally related to various court decisions and they impinge on matters that affect the future value of awards that are usually discounted to the present. The forensic literature is replete with controversies over the value of the appropriate discount rate and how it should be determined. The vagaries of the debates have forced some states or countries to legislate the discount rate. Beyond the litigation of the discount rate, the appropriate financial instruments for establishing the appropriate rate(s) are also called into question. There seems to be a consensus that safe and long-term instruments that are issued by governments should be the benchmark.

Other indicators of general economic performance like unemployment, inflation, and industry-specific attributes have become valuable indicators of aggregate performance when projecting and generating reasonable awards in courts of law. Of course, there are occasions when awards can be subject to taxation. While taxes are dealt with more extensively in Chapter 6, the concept of taxation is integral to macroeconomic performance; not only in terms of how awards should be taxed, but in terms of how businesses make decisions that affect employment interest rate and inflation. Taxes contribute to macroeconomic stabilization or destabilization with multiplier effects. Macroeconomic outcomes are influenced by public policies, but they can be exogenously determined by shocks (sudden but temporary disruptions). Therefore, the chapter provides background information about policy choices and how the choices impact the value of critical macroeconomic variables that are so valuable to triers of facts in courts of law.

A basic open macro identity incorporates the global economy; in this regard, exchange rates and net exports are significant components of overall economic performance. Awards may also be paid in domestic or foreign currencies and judicial decisions are also sensitive to currency valuations and timing. Chapter 2 also provides a background to currency valuation and changes in the international monetary and financial system that impinge on choice of exchange rates and the volatility of these rates. The bifurcated legal theory of breach and award dates and some drawbacks are presented in the chapter. In effect, the chapter provides a foundation for understanding the essential macroeconomic variables that are routinely explored and utilized in courts of law all over the world. Definitions, measurements, limitations, and applications of macroeconomic variables to judicial decisions will be encountered in Chapter 2.

I take a look at financial variables and the legal environment for the operations of businesses, including international exposures, in Chapter 3. The chapter provides extensive financial literacy for students and practitioners who are not very well exposed to the financial theories and models that are essential for understanding financial problems and judicial decisions in the field of finance. The scope of this chapter is very extensive; it presents salient aspects of the laws of the US Securities and Exchange Commission (SEC), financial statements, deceptive financial practices and the consequences of such practices, the conduct and effects test in the extraterritorial application of SEC law, the principal-agent problem, and discussions of abusive managerial decisions. Invariably, though the performance of the financial sector is usually given undue or residual consideration in the appraisal of the real sector, the financial and real sectors are highly integrated. Therefore, in meaningful ways, Chapter 3 cannot be isolated from Chapter 2. Chapter 4 considers the importance of intellectual property to economic growth and development.

Since intellectual property contributes tremendously to economic growth and development, it is incumbent upon nations to protect the integrity of creative rights. Technological innovation has heightened the urgency of the protection of intellectual property rights. These rights are freely debated in courts of law, but they have value that is less conspicuous in the fight to protect inventions and meaningful intellectual ingenuity in courts of law. Chapter 4 addresses the economic implications of expropriation of creative rights. In this chapter, I present economic models from the economic literature to show why innovation is critical to economic growth and development; but the chapter also presents the psychological and sociological (ethical) deficiencies of intellectual theft that is pervasively missing from the discussions of the social malaise.

Most often, the human right element is also missing from the debates of intellectual property rights. The chapter additionally presents the complementary aspects of ethical lapses and violations of fundamental human rights. However, the legal and economic implications of intellectual property theft have not been made subsidiary. The chapter presents and examines some of the laws and cases of intellectual theft in various parts of the world, and the inconvenient resolutions that are associated with intellectual property theft in courts of law. Supporting data on national losses and the consequences of international intellectual theft are presented in the chapter. The chapter is followed by a methodological chapter.

In Chapter 5, I present various economic measurements and the theories underlying the measurements (econometrics) that are routinely used in courts of law. The chapter is intended to provide a foundation for those who are not very proficient in estimating methodologies and economic theories. In the US, the role of science was elevated in courtrooms after the celebrated US Supreme Court case of *Daubert v. Merrell Dow Pharmaceuticals* (1993). US courts, invariably in other parts of the world as well, can now call on experts to provide testimony in their areas of expertise. In economics, scientific evidence involves an understanding of economic theories and calculations or estimations.

The content of the chapter presents an opportunity for readers who are unfamiliar with some of the intricacies of economic models to understand the structure of data, sampling strategies, detrending data to obtain stationarity for forecasting, using a financial calculator to determine present value, regression analysis or the ordinary least squares estimating methodology, and the intrinsic value of public corporations. It is noteworthy that very advanced econometric techniques are beyond the scope of this work. However, references have been made to additional sources from which such techniques can be obtained for those who are interested in very advanced work; for example, I have not dealt with uses of vector autoregression techniques for forecasting in this work.

Historically, the payment of taxes has been a very thorny issue. Individuals and businesses who are less willing to fulfill their civic duties find ways and means to avoid or evade the payment of taxes. The difference between avoidance and evasion is a legal technicality but the outcomes are identical. That is, lawyers and judges spend a lot of time trying to figure out the intention for not paying taxes or for defeating the purpose of a tax, but the economic consequence remains the loss of revenue to finance public investments and social obligations of government when the determination is either avoidance or evasion. Chapter 6 deals with the issue of tax avoidance and evasion (outright violation of tax law).

In many ways, Chapters 2 and 6 are complementary when overall economic performance is taken into consideration. Chapter 6 is much more specialized to include tax laws, tax gaps, the socio-economic theories behind tax evasion or avoidance, the effects of safe havens that are available for tax flight, the multiplier effects of fiscal policies, and some of the worldwide efforts that are being made to minimize tax evasion or avoidance. The legal dimension of the chapter incorporates efforts to determine whether individuals and businesses are actually evading or avoiding the payment of taxes in some parts of the world.

Chapters 4 and 7 follow the interdependent nature of Chapters 2 and 6. In Chapter 4, I alluded to intellectual property rights and the economic implications. If it was not very apparent that the rewards of intellectual property are contingent on competition (see the Schumpeterian theory), Chapter 7 is a consummation of Chapter 4. Antitrust (anti-merger/combination) laws are intended to promote competition to foster innovation and improvement of the welfare of consumers. Conspiring to charge higher prices (without efficiency gains), prevents competition, disincentivizes innovation, and degrades aggregate welfare. Chapter 7 presents the evolution of US antitrust laws and provides examples of enforcement measures. The chapter examines some of the tests that are used to ascertain violations of US antitrust laws, including the Herfindahl-Hirschman Index (HHI), the *per se* rule, and the rule of reason.

Contemporary US laws minimize the agglomeration effects of mergers by proactively evaluating the legitimacy of mergers. The evolution of mergers in the light of changing global economic conditions and realities is discussed in Chapter 7. Since illegal combinations impose cost to societies—generally considered to be deadweight loss in economics—there are punitive damages for foisting illegal combinations upon societies. In the US, laws permit for trebling damages, but economists and judges are yet to arrive at a persuasive conclusion on how societal loss can be estimated as a deadweight loss in pecuniary terms. The chapter identifies the major US antitrust laws, including Sherman, Robinson-Patman, Clayton, Wheller-Lea, Cellar-Kefauver, and Williams.

The final chapter of this book is dedicated to the interaction of international economics and international law. Pointedly, it discusses the role of economic theories in international courts of law. Therefore, the chapter evaluates international judicial decisions in the context of the economic theories and principles that have helped to shape those decisions over several years. Three areas are of particular interest: (i) natural resources and international trade, (ii) international monetary arrangements and the confiscatory and destabilizing effects of unilateral currency valuation, and (iii) transnational international investments and illegal expropriations.

The chapter introduces the sources of international law and emphasizes the widely held view of peacefully resolving international disputes. The Dispute Settlement Understanding (DSU) and the Dispute Settlement Mechanism (DSM) of the World Trade Organization (WTO) are discussed in the context of peacefully resolving international economic disputes and some notable pacific settlements. Accordingly, various cases involving international trade theories and investments are presented in Chapter 8.

This book is a comprehensive presentation of the uses of economics in legislative and judicial decisions. Consequently, this book has been structured to provide economic concepts with far-reaching cognitive implications for law and rule adjudication. The essential areas of economics that will be considered include microeconomics, macroeconomics, finance, econometrics, and international economics. The intricate combination of the branches of economics presents a pedagogical advantage for confronting the practical and worldwide challenges of law and economics in courts of law.

1

CHAPTER 1
MICROECONOMIC FOUNDATION

> It is somewhat surprising that so conspicuous a truth as the interaction of economics and law should have waited so long for recognition—a recognition by no means universal. Some of those who question it maintain the independence and self-sufficiency of law, while others maintain that of economics. In reality law and economics are ever and everywhere complementary and mutually determinative.
> (Berolzheimer, 1912, p. 23)

LEARNING OBJECTIVES

LO 1 Present the basic microeconomic theories that apply to law and judicial rulings.
LO 2 Discuss the relevance of equity to economic and judicial decisions.
LO 3 Provide a foundational basis for an understanding of economic models and markets in law and judicial decisions.
LO 4 Introduce the concepts of market failures and efficiency loss (the deadweight loss) for an assessment of damages.
LO 5 Discuss the economic legal implications of market failures and consumer responses.
LO 6 Present the meaning and uses of elasticities in law and economics.
LO 7 Discuss the concepts of labor market, economics of discrimination, and judicial responses.
LO 8 Introduce the concepts of production cost, market structure for antitrust litigation, and the limits of price regulation.

This work is not a presentation of the philosophical legal, political, and economic arguments in the literature. Rather, it presents economic theories without the subjective ideological persuasions or schools of thought in the literature.[1] The schools of thought provide a valuable analytical framework for analyzing and understanding the way and manner in which economics have been co-opted into the legislative and judicial branches of government to facilitate governance in a polarized or fractious system. Consequently, the thrust of this presentation is to let the economic theories and models stand independently without political corruption or interpretation. This work should not be construed as an extension of the philosophical dichotomy that has characterized the subject matter of law and economics for quite some time. It basically presents economic theories and models and show how these models are alluded to and applied in courts of law. In the process, the legislative arm of government becomes an intermediating agent in the spectrum of economics and rule adjudication.

What are the economic drivers (concepts) that configure the political, legal, and judicial landscapes of society? Why is economics so ubiquitous? Why are the drivers so susceptible to competing philosophical persuasions that define laws and the interpretation of laws? Law and Economics is often defined as the interface of welfare and microeconomics with law and legal institutions; essentially because economics have shaped the formation, structure, processes, and of legal institutions. I use "jurisprudential microeconomics" in this chapter to mean the application of microeconomic theories to law and judicial decisions. Judicial decisions are naturally based on laws, precedents, and equity (what is reasonable and just, *ex aequo et bono*). Therefore, legislatures are intermediating institutions between the adoption of viable economic theories and judicial interpretation of law and economics.[2]

This chapter lays the foundation for an understanding of the basic micro concepts that underpin legal theories and judicial decisions in subsequent chapters. While the discipline of microeconomics plays a dominant role in legal disputes, an understanding of macroeconomics or macro variables is just as important as an understanding of the micro variables. The next chapter will be devoted to the macro variables and their relevance to law and rule adjudication.

1.1 MICROECONOMIC FOUNDATION

The relevance of economics to law was heightened by a sense of realism, which replaced the "edifice of doctrinalism."[3] Melding *stare decisis*, dissenting opinions, and complementary disciplines like sociology, psychology, and economics, the realists systematically redefined American jurisprudence by integrating relevant disciplines to the study of law in order to make informed legal decisions. That is, lawyers and judges were to be informed by the law, humanities, and social sciences of the day by being outward-oriented to meet policy challenges.[4]

The era of the realists brought gender, race, and economics into the circuits of law. The law of the courts became important to issues of sexuality, power, and individual rights. The practical and pedagogical aspects of law entered a critical phase.

The earlier traditions, especially within the Chicago school of thought, focused on neoclassical economics and eventually the competitive market as a trajectory for efficient outcomes. It was believed that less government intervention, fewer redistributive policies, reliance on voluntary exchange with reliance on the common law for mediating conflicts, and the promotion of private enterprise would facilitate a more efficient allocation of resources. It became fashionable to conduct empirical cost-benefit analysis of judicial decisions.

Mercuro (2009) outlines the defining characteristics of the Chicago approach to law and economics that was essentially microeconomic or price theoretic. Some basic economic theories were subsumed: (i) individuals maximize their self-interests, (ii) individuals respond to market and non-market incentives (probabilities of being caught in the conduct of a crime or cost benefit analysis), (iii) *ex ante* thinking (effects of changes in legal rules on future behavior), (iv) the efficiency of legal rules and legal outcomes, (v) common law can be conceptualized as promoting efficient resource allocation, (vi) whether regulation or law enhances or reduces efficiency, and (vii) market efficiencies (remedies) rather than policy intervention, generate optimum social welfare.[5]

Principles of economics have helped to shape political (non-market) decisions (public choice theory) like voting rules, voter behavior, and party politics. Most of the focus has been on the implementation of law through political processes rather than the role of the judiciary.[6] The methods and tools of economics are used to explain or explore how politics and government work. An endogenous or feedback relationship should be expected in public choice theory. Econometrics explains political behavior and politicians react to the empirical conclusions of econometrics. While the judiciary is not directly incorporated into the public choice methodology, the judiciary responds to decisions that are made by law makers and the enforcers of law.

In effect, economics have far-reaching institutional implications. Policy makers state their economic theories in order to win elections and move on to enact such policies when they do not renege on their promises. Butler underscores the role of economics in public policy in terms of cost-benefit analysis. However, he relates the efficacy of economics to the contingency of rational behavior and impartiality, the combination of which is exceedingly difficult to find in politics. Politics is not bereft of the abnormal principal-agent problem, or profit-seeking activities, which is at times a euphemism for corrupt behavior.

Rent-seekers aspire to persuade policymakers to implement or alter laws and/or regulations that benefit them rather than the larger population or society. In effect, they transfer wealth from society to themselves and impose costs on societies because of resource misallocation. Directly unproductive profit-seeking activities (DUP) became prevalent in the 1980s after an upsurge of lobbying to prevent competition for a larger share of industrial or import licenses and enactment of laws that created monopolistic barriers to trade while utilizing resources to evade price regulations.[7]

Rents retard the flow of resources by creating information and mobility asymmetries. They can be found in private markets for goods, factor markets, asset markets, and political markets. "Within the political arena, [the] legal changes may result in special privileges, monopoly positions, and other forms of transfers granted to certain individuals or groups through the aegis of the State."[8] The rents are actually the wasted resources that are used to acquire or maintain these privileged positions. As such, public officials may not always seek the interest of voters or those they are supposed to represent. Voters may also vote against their own interests and conflicting interests improperly define societal interests.[9]

Profit-seeking and related activities challenge the market-oriented theory of economic analysis that had been pioneered by the Chicago school. The emerging issues became the winning interests that give effect to law. Whose interests were being supported for legislation? The changing phenomenon gave rise to institutional economics and institutional law and economics, and the institutional environment of the New Institutional Economics created the framework within which human interaction took place. The environment provided the "rules of the game" (the fundamental political, legal, and social ground rules) which, in effect, are the "institutional background constraints under which individuals in society [made] choices."[10]

The New Haven School situated welfare in the center of the discussions of law and economics. Normative issues are generally subdued by notions of competitive markets and market efficiency. The New Haven transformation forced judges and legal scholars to examine the roles of Congress, agencies, and the courts. The economic justification for public policy became of interest, and courts were encouraged to play a greater role in the policymaking system to enhance societal welfare. Market failures induced the call for a greater role of government in markets. The normative dimension of the school incorporated both productive and allocative efficiencies, with distributive connotations. The New Haven School is credited with shaping the evolution of tort law and economics.

1.2 NORMATIVE VERSUS POSITIVE LAW AND ECONOMICS

The evolution of the various schools of thought under the realist tradition opened the way for further normative considerations in law and the judicial interpretations of law. Judges have been long familiar with equity as a source of law and the law books are replete with judge-made (common) laws. Some of the theories that have been discussed in the previous section have been variously adopted to shape political and legal processes. Components of these theories have evident political biases and they represent ongoing societal conflicts over the appropriate way to articulate and represent the economic and legal interests of constituent contestants.

Theories of justice tend to be shaped by this reality, which is not always a close approximation of pristine economic theories and models. That is, the utility of some economic theories and models is contingent on the interpretations of the theories and models and the circumstances that lead to their adoption.

The previous section prefaced two diametrical economic concepts: (i) positive economics (largely based on theories, models, and data), and (ii) normative economics, which is a highly subjective and value-based perception of good or evil, and fair or unfair. However, it is usually a mistaken proposition to think that the two areas are estranged and unrelated to each other. Issues of equity affect national prosperity.[11] That is, the state of equity also impacts the real and financial sectors that generate data for positive economics or analysis via consumption and investment channels.

Normative economics prescribe what an economy should look like or what policies should be adopted to accomplish a subjective goal. In effect, it essentially appraises the desirability of policies and their fair or unfair effects on society. Accordingly, it is a welfare-oriented approach to economics that is related to policy choices and the effects of public policies on society, especially the poor and marginalized who are usually voiceless. So, what is the proper role of government? While normative economics looks at what ought to be the case, positive economics takes a look at what actually exists. As such, positive economics does not thrive on suppositions. It directly explains how an economy operates with the aid of economic methodology that is based on actual information or data.

The judicial impact of normative and positive economics ultimately depends on what type of law and economics a judge practices.[12] Mindful of the propensity to exacerbate activism, Levmore (1997) suggests, with some precaution, that skilled judges will be forgiven and even encouraged to make normative use of ideas about law and economics, and that all judges might be encouraged to use law and economics to appreciate the value of the rules and practices that we have inherited (*stare decisis*).

The positive dimension of law is closely aligned with economic analysis of law, with a strong belief that efficiency is the predominant factor that configures the rules, procedures, and institutions of the common law. Efficiency is seen as a defensible criterion in the context of judicial decision-making because in the absence of academic and political consensus, "justice" considerations introduce unacceptable ambiguity into the judicial process.[13] Positivists tend to apply the natural sciences to legal theory. This approach probably started around the 1820s and was pioneered by the Chicago school.[14]

On the normative side, the Yale school of law and economics advances the argument that there is a larger need for legal intervention to correct the adverse manifestations of market failures. Distributional concerns are central to the normative thought. Rather than relying on market efficiency, the normative school proposes normative formulations of what laws ought to be in the pursuit of justice and fairness via the legal system. Efficiency is not conceived as the ultimate end of a legal system.[15] This approach to law is closely akin to the natural precepts of law that imposes moral obligation (natural law) on society, including rule adjudication.

Prefacing his analysis with Shakespeare's *The Merchant of Venice*, Stake (1991) makes a case for status efficiency in judicial rulings. That is, unfair contracts that demand a pound of flesh cannot be enforceable without rational thought. Alternatively, rule adjudication cannot be limited to deterrent incentives; suggesting that economic models can offer a comprehensive normative or positive theory of judicial behavior only when they take status effects into consideration.

Judicial decisions are classified into two broad categories: (i) status effects, and (ii) incentive effects. Status effects emanate from resolutions of disputes, which define things like rights, immunities, duties, and liabilities, and the effects of resolutions on the disputants. On the other hand, incentive effects are the behavioral changes (deterrents) that the resolutions are intended to generate on nondisputants. The distinction between status and incentive effects of judicial decisions is further defined in terms of rule and act utilitarianism.[16] However, status effects often lead to incentive effects.[17]

Beyond the incentive effects, the external effects (efficiencies or opportunity cost) of contract enforcement on disputants are worth considering in rule adjudication. In Stake's Shylock analogy, the pound of flesh might mean certain death for Antonio when as a matter of fact, Antonio could have committed his life to a greater good. More so, the pound of flesh is of no marginal value to Antonio. Should judicial decision consider equity without being draconian?

When circumstances change in fundamental ways, *clausula rebus sic stantibus*, an agreement may be nullified.[18] The doctrine of changed circumstances holds that:

> [i]njunctive relief against the violation of the obligations arising out of a covenant cannot be secured "if conditions have so changed since the making of the promise as to make it impossible longer to secure in a substantial degree the benefits intended to be secured by the performance of the promise."[19]

Stake notes that status effects of a court's application of the doctrine include ordinary distributional effects and efficient consequences. The distributional effects involve counterbalancing wealth transfer and the efficiency effects of the potential to increase subsequent gains. Who values an asset more highly? Who has the ability to increase the returns on an asset? These efficiency questions also elicit value judgments by triers of facts. Yet neither status nor incentive effects are considered to carry greater normative weight; except that some transactional compensation for economic losses could have inefficient outcomes. Positive hypotheses do not necessarily lack status effects. Courts hearing housing cases often require that the actions be reasonably conducted in good faith and not arbitrary or capricious.[20]

Normative economics and law have coalesced in judicial analysis of antitrust cases in the 1970s and beyond.[21] The monopolistic market structure will be discussed later in this chapter and in Chapter 7. The antitrust cases involve the impact of market and non-market (equity) effects on consumers. The US Supreme Court's decision in *Eastman Kodak Co. v. Image Technical Services, Inc.* (504 U.S. 451 (1992)) is one of the earlier cases to validate the existence of market imperfections involving information asymmetry, high switching costs, and tying arrangements.[22] Notwithstanding, antitrust cases tend to show disagreements over the most appropriate way to ensure consumer welfare.

Do distributional allocations generate normative and efficient outcomes? Pareto tried to tackle the problem unsuccessfully but influentially by defining the capacity to satisfy needs (*ophélimité*), which should be distinguished from utility.[23] In law, the cost of compensating all losers is rather prohibitive, and changing legal rules to satisfy Pareto efficiency is naturally unfeasible. Pareto is *status quo* dependent (changing the welfare of some while presuming the invariant welfare of others without compensation). Invariably, the rationale for compensating losers can only be meaningful when the losers become victims of cryptic (unfair) laws that ultimately necessitate the imposition of questionable equity. The Kaldor-Hicks compensation or wealth maximization test somewhat refined Pareto's prognosis by proposing (legal) changes or redistributive tax policies that will compensate losers without immiserizing gainers; but compensation tests are not without price and real income challenges or deficiencies.

Economists incorporate detrimental price changes into the calculus of equitable compensation. That is, price changes will produce undesirable outcomes when subsequent price variations are inaccurately conceptualized and factored into distributional settlements. Therefore, the issue of articulating and measuring fairness becomes a challenging mathematical proposition rather than a conceptual one. Hence, the concept of transferring resources in such a way that no one is a victim seems to be easier said than convincingly estimated. The mathematical hurdle has made it difficult for welfare models to gain popularity in some circles, not because of ideological preconceptions but rather as the result of a combination of several practical reasons. These reasons include the general tendency to undertake a two-step optimization in the design of policies, and the difficulties of identifying an objective criterion for assessing interpersonal utility and diminishing marginal utility effects (Parisi & Klick, 2004, pp. 441–2).

Of course, inequity is also an ocular phenomenon and some legal scholars have called for the use of interpersonal utility in judicial decisions.

> There is a way to extend the economic approach to cases in which there are no incentive effects and no status efficiencies. By factoring interpersonal utility into the model, the theory can be applied to cases in which the only status effects relate to wealth.
>
> (Stake, 1991, p. 1447)[24]

Though the use of interpersonal utility can be objectionable (on the ground that it is impossible to ascertain the superiority of one person's utility to someone else's), the practical relevance of interpersonal utility to conflict resolution is ultimately contingent on circumstances and the assumptions that are being made. Pointedly, an inadequate measure of a concept does not necessarily make the concept spurious.

1.3 ECONOMIC MODELS AND MARKETS

Economic models are formal presentations of economic theories in illustrative and/or mathematical forms. A functional relationship is generally subsumed in such models; meaning that there is generally an interest in correlative relationships when causative relationships cannot be convincingly established. Models are judged by their theoretical value, efficiencies (margins of errors), consistencies, assumptions, and applicability. The rule of thumb is that "less is more"; meaning that models should not be superfluous and vain.

Implicitly, it is unnecessary to include extraneous variables in model specifications. This fundamental principle is generally referred to as "Ockham's razor."[25]

It is worth detecting some traps (fallacies) when constructing economic models: (i) the *post hoc ergo propter hoc* (the idea that the occurrence of an event is the result of an unrelated anteceding event), and (ii) compositional (generalization) fallacies (using an isolated event to make unwarranted generalizations). If the Whigs win an election and the stock market does well, it is an *ergo* fallacy to argue that the stock market performed well because of the Whigs winning an election. Similarly, if John starts *microdosing* after gainful employment, the employment may not necessarily be responsible for John's *microdosing* behavior. If Janet is 22 years old and she decides to rob a bank, that does not mean that 22-year-old females are predisposed to robbing banks; to state otherwise is a compositional fallacy. Variables, samples, data, and model estimation will be discussed in Chapter 5.

Apart from specifying economic models, the results of economic models must be interpreted carefully in line with the operationalization of variables and the regularity conditions or assumptions. Economists are not likely to analyze the behavior or performance of all variables at the same time. Such an analysis is impractical, and it produces confounding, questionable, and imprecise results. Therefore, the empirical challenge is generally to pay attention to one variable at a time without simultaneously disturbing the other variables of interest.

The *ceteris paribus* assumption is a regularity condition that facilitates an analysis of the relationship between two variables while holding the values of other variables constant. Researchers can use advanced models to introduce a unit shock to an endogenous variable and then examine the reactions (responses) of other variables to the unit shock (see vector autoregressive models with impulse responses). Alternatively, researchers can simultaneously track the relationship between two or more variables to check for a long-run relationship and make projections.[26]

A very simple example of an economic model is a consumption function, which states that consumption is a function of disposable income. That is, consumption depends on disposable income. This statement can be represented in the form of an equation and an illustration:

$$C = a + \alpha I_D + \varepsilon; \tag{1.1}$$

where C is for consumption, a is for autonomous consumption, α is for the marginal propensity to consume (MPC), I_D is for disposable income (income after taxes), and ε is for all the other variables that have been omitted from the model (an error expression, which is assumed to be normally distributed with zero mean and unit (constant) variance). The MPC is the slope of a consumption function which indicates the amount by which consumption is going to change when disposable income (I_D) goes up or down by one unit of a currency, say a dollar or pound. Regression will be discussed more fully in Chapter 5.

The model is based on economic theory, and researchers must have a reasonable understanding of the theories that they are modeling to have a *prima facie* knowledge about the interactions of the variables. One would naturally expect disposable income to have a positive effect on consumption; implying that increases in disposable income will contribute to increases in consumption of a good. Therefore, the slope is traditionally presumed to be positive. However, there are times when consumers will buy less of a good when they have an increase in disposable income. The negative relationship suggests that the good must be of an inferior quality; so that consumers prefer to buy less of the good and more of something else after an increase in disposable income.

The intercept expression a is for consumption when disposable income is zero, since we expect people to consume something even when they do not have income. Therefore, a normal consumption function cannot go through the origin of a graph. The equation is in actual fact a linear equation that shows the formula for a straight line without the stochastic error expression. Typically, economists will evaluate the significance of variables in such a function by examining the t-statistic or probability value (p-value). These analyses will be pursued further in Chapter 5.

Equation 1.1 can be graphically illustrated as Figure 1.1.

The consumption function (Figure 1.1) shows that a 100 dollar increase in disposable income increases consumption by $10, or a dollar increase in disposable income increases consumption by 10 cents. Without testing for the significance of the increase in disposable income or evaluating price increases (inflation), we assume that disposable income must have a significant effect on consumption. The relationship between the two variables will not be so straightforward if other variables are considered simultaneously. The *ceteris paribus* assumption enables us to track the relationship between consumption and disposable income without extraneous considerations. The graph typifies a visual (ocular) relationship between consumption and disposable income and its slope (MPC) is positive.

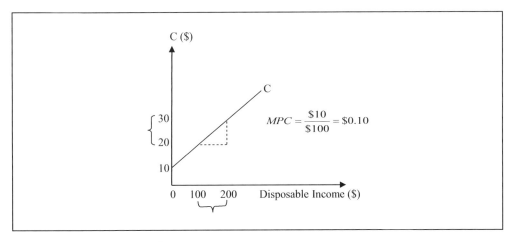

Figure 1.1 A consumption function

A considerable amount of judicial conflicts will involve market transactions or conflicts between buyers and sellers.

Markets are forums in which buyers and sellers interact. The forums can be physical or electronic. A lot of consumers purchase products electronically, or from physical locations and they are exposed to fraud and undesirable market activities that decrease their welfare. It is important to understand consumer behavior and the factors that are most likely to influence the purchasing decisions of consumers. It is also important to understand the behavior of sellers and the factors that will influence the ability of sellers to make products available in markets and the prices that they will be willing to accept under normal circumstances. The competitive market is the preferred environment of market interaction and US laws are generally intended to promote and validate competition to increase human welfare.

Chapter 7 deals with the laws that are intended to promote competition (antitrust laws) and the penalties that are imposed for violating the competitive preconditions for market transactions. Some key concepts in this chapter, which will be explored in subsequent chapters, include: consumer surplus, producer surplus, the competitive price, elasticity, conspiracy, monopolization of trade, and the deadweight loss to society. Therefore, this chapter lays the foundation for an understanding of significant economic concepts in dispute resolution.

In the aggregate, rational consumers react to price changes in a predictable way and in so doing they increase or decrease their surplus in the marketplace. First, consider the law of demand which tracks the behavior of rational consumers in a marketplace. Building on our *ceteris paribus* discussion earlier on, the law simply states that as price falls, consumers espouse a willingness and ability to buy or consume more of a product or service and vice versa.

The law presumes that the other factors that affect demand are not changing in tandem with price. As such, the law precludes ambiguities that will complicate and nullify the analysis. For example, if disposable income is falling while price is also falling, the law of demand cannot be validated on its own accord. Similarly, if consumers do not have preference for a good, they are not likely to buy more of it even when the price is falling.

Economic laws have precise meaning in economics. They are the results of years of testing and empirical validation. They emanate from hypothesis (an unproven but testable assertion), theories, multiple tests, and widespread acceptability after decades or centuries of empirical inquiry. Therefore, economic laws cannot be debunked easily; they are different from hypotheses and theories. The law of demand shows that the market demand (summation of demand for a particular good or service) curve is downward sloping or negatively sloped. A market demand curve represents an inverse or indirect relationship between price and consumption when the values of other factors are presumed to be invariant. When price falls, consumers are prone to buy more because of real income and substitution effects. Declining marginal utility will also cause consumers to buy more when price falls. Marginal utility declines as consumers buy more of a good.

Figure 1.2 shows two market demand curves with lower and higher prices (Panels (a) and (b) respectively). When the price of the good is $20 per unit, consumer surplus (the difference between what consumers are willing to pay ($50) and what they actually pay ($20), shaded area) is greater. When the price goes up to $30 per unit, consumer surplus becomes smaller and areas L and W are lost. Using the formula for calculating the area of a triangle ((base*height)/2), consumer surplus can be estimated.

The theory of consumer surplus needs further discussion because it is not instantly revealing. The $50 price tag is confounding. Why would anyone pay $50 for a good that is not available? Consumers would be willing to pay a positive amount for zero output if they want to retain the option of consuming the good at a future date even though they are choosing not to consume the good today.[27] Therefore, the concept of consumer surplus has an intertemporal dimension to it that is based on surveys. The loss of consumer surplus is very important for antitrust litigation cases.

The demand curve can shift outwards or inwards because of changes in the variables that were originally presumed to be invariant. In effect, we can now introduce an additional demand curve after relaxing the *ceteris paribus* assumption. The new demand curve, which might show an increase (shift to the right) or decrease in demand (shift to the left), should be considered a change in demand rather than a change in quantity demanded (Panel (b)). This is because consumers can now afford to buy more or less at each of the original prices, depending on whether they are having a positive or negative change in the other factors—apart from the price of the good in question—that affect consumption. Figure 1.2 Panel (b) does not show two or more demand curves because only the price of the good in question has increased. It shows a change in quantity demanded and not a change in demand.

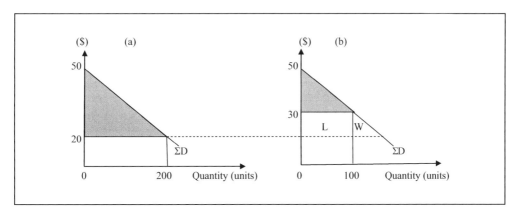

Figure 1.2 Market demand

Changes in demand will shift the demand curve to the right or to the left when the *ceteris paribus* assumption is relaxed. For example, an increase in disposable income will shift the demand curve to the right. A decrease in disposable income will have the opposite effect. This is because consumers will be able to buy more or less at each of the series of original prices. Changes in prices of related goods (substitutes and complements) will also have similar effects. Although we are referring to prices, we are not referring to the price of the good in question. Complementary goods are jointly demanded (an increase in the consumption of one good, say coffee, leads to an increase in the consumption of another good, say sugar, when the goods are complementary). Substitute goods are replacement goods. Buying more of one, say Pepsi, because of a price change means buying less of another good, say Coca Cola. Therefore, we should expect the demand curve of a substitute good to shift to the right when the price of its counterpart increases.

Unlike the demand curve, the supply curve captures the behavior of sellers or producers who receive payments for offering their goods and services in markets. The supply curve is upward sloping (positively sloped) and increases in price will cause a concomitant increase in producer surplus; see Figure 1.3. An increase in the price from $20 to $30 actually increases producer surplus. The producer surplus is the difference between an inducement cost (price) and the price that obtains in the market.

Like the market demand curves, the market supply curves also subsume a comparable assumption that the values of other variables affecting supply are presumed to be invariant (*ceteris paribus*). These variables are directly related to the cost of production or the conditions that will increase or decrease supply; for example, resource cost (cost for using land, labor, and capital), the number of sellers, time horizon, weather or climatic conditions, taxes and subsidies, technological innovation (application of science to production), and the regulatory environment. Changes that are favorable to the increase in production or supply, other than the price of a good/service in question, will shift the supply curve to the right. Alternatively, changes that adversely affect the production or supply of a good/service will cause a leftward shift of the supply curve.

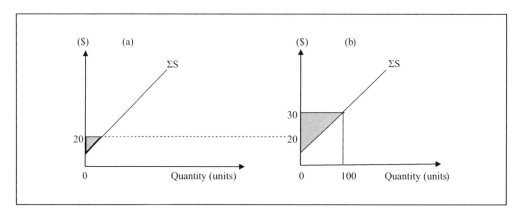

Figure 1.3 Market supply

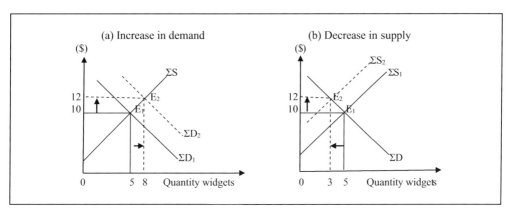

Figure 1.4 Change in market demand and supply

Figure 1.4 shows the market for widgets. It is a market because the buyers (consumers) of widgets (ΣD) are now interacting with the sellers (suppliers) of widgets (ΣS). In effect, markets are forums in which buyers and sellers interact for all types of goods, services, and assets; broadly defined as real and financial markets. The left Panel (a) shows an increase in market demand for a stationary market supply that is sensitive to price and output changes. If the market supply was not sensitive to price changes the price would be invariant regardless of the quantity demanded (a horizontal supply curve). On the contrary, if the supply was insensitive to output changes the supply curve would be vertical; meaning that price will vary when quantity is constant. Analogous arguments can be made for demand.

As a result of an increase in demand, which is a change in demand and not a change in quantity demanded, the price and quantity increase simultaneously. On the contrary, when there is a decrease in market supply, the quantity of widgets supplied falls from 5 to 3 units and the price increases from $10 per unit to $12 per unit. The intersection of the demand and supply curves indicates some kind of agreement (equilibrium) in the marketplace between willing buyers and sellers of widgets. The concept of equilibrium is important for a variety of reasons.

Equilibrium is generally an indicator of efficiency in law and economics; where efficiency means the production of what society wants at the least possible cost. In economics, efficiency has productive and allocative components. Market efficiency also means lack of coercion in economic transactions. Buyers and sellers are freely and willingly making transactional decisions based on all available information without deception or fraud. These preconditions make it less likely to have undesirable frictions (disequilibria) in the marketplace; except on occasions of economic shocks (sudden but temporary and unanticipated disruptions, which may or may not be desirable).

Equilibrium is therefore a manifestation of stability and fairness in the marketplace. Equilibrium connotes fair prices and the required amount of societal resources that should be allocated to the production of goods and services; especially when scarce economic resources have alternative uses (opportunity costs that are associated with their allocations and use).[28] However, market equilibrium and efficiency must be used with some amount of precaution. Market equilibrium assumes that there is productive efficiency, but it does not precisely show productive efficiency. This concept will be discussed under market structure.

Economic surplus is derived from fair (market) prices and the efficient allocation of resources. Price distortions by whatever mechanism are distortionary and they lead to inefficiencies that are costly to societies. That is, price distortions generate efficiency losses; consider Figure 1.5.

In Panel (a), economic surplus (ES), the combination of consumer and producer surpluses, is greater because the market is in equilibrium and P_E is the market (fair) that consumers and sellers are willing to accept. Economic resources are efficiently allocated and there is no noticeable efficiency loss. Panel (b) shows the effect of a price distortion or disequilibrium. Consumers actually lose triangle L and transfer surplus over to producers, but society collectively loses L and W.

A number of non-economic factors or disturbances can be responsible for the price distortion. Some of these factors may include illegal infractions in the marketplace that have to be arbitrated in courts of law to determine the appropriate damages that are associated with the illegal price increase (P_1). Very prominent reasons for price distortion include false advertising or misrepresentation, product liability, and inadequate warning information. The reasons that have been identified collectively cause information asymmetry in the marketplace, which further leads to an adverse selection that corrupts market interactions of buyers and sellers. The corruption generates inefficiencies that cause market failures and efficiency losses that are equivalent to triangles L and W in Figure 1.5 Panel (b). Areas L and W are collectively known as the deadweight loss which will be further discussed in Chapter 7 as part of the effects of antitrust behavior. Although individuals may seek damages in courts of law because of violations that regulate

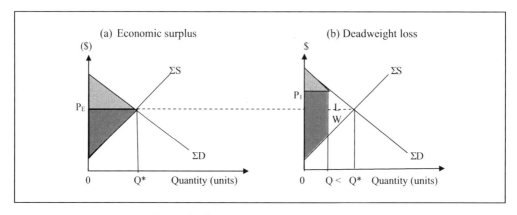

Figure 1.5 Economic surplus and efficiency loss

commerce, consumers may also bring about class action suit as a group when there are significant violations of the laws that regulate commerce.

1.4 MARKET TRANSACTIONS AND CONSUMER CLASS ACTION LITIGATION

When prices are illegally distorted, market equilibrium can be forged at a higher or lower level. Consider Figure 1.4 Panel (a); the shift of the demand curve causes equilibrium (E_2) at a higher price ($12) for the greater quantity (8 units) demanded. This outcome may be the result of false advertising or fraud in the marketplace. In effect, consumers are not making informed decisions that are based on fair or appropriate information (there is misinformation). Therefore, the equilibrium cannot be considered a desirable outcome of balanced information in the marketplace; it is contrived or fraudulent, and it cannot be considered an indicator or measurement of market efficiency.

Over the years, consumers have taken action as a group (class) against sellers who have misbehaved in the marketplace. "A class action is a procedure by which a large group of entities—that is, a 'class'—may challenge a defendant's allegedly unlawful conduct in a single lawsuit, rather than through numerous, separate suits initiated by individual plaintiffs" (Lewis & Freeman, 2018, p. 2).[29] In general, courts have emphasized the efficiency effects of pursuing socially desirable lawsuits; for example, the Supreme Court observed that a "principal purpose" of class actions is to advance "the efficiency and economy of litigation."[30]

At the same time, however, class actions can occasionally subject defendants to costly or abusive litigation because it can be cheaper to settle the disputes (with or without merit) than pursuing them in courts of law. Additionally, class attorneys may not always act in the best interests of the class members. At the same time, class action serves to protect defendants from repeated and possibly inconsistent adjudications.[31] Class action suits permit thousands or millions of people to aggregate their claims and defendants can face prohibitive costs if they decide not to settle a case.

The intricacies or complexities of consumer complaints as a class has generated Federal Rules of Civil Procedure to mitigate contending risks or abuses. The Federal Rule of Civil Procedure 23 establishes prerequisites that a federal class action must satisfy, and the Rule subjects claims to scrutiny and mandatory certification by courts of law.[32] A court may not certify a class action unless each of the four mandatory requirements is satisfied.

Some consumer products have featured prominently in class action litigations; for example, food marketing class actions increased from about 20 in 2008 to over 425 active cases in federal courts in 2015 and 2016. Research shows that about 120 new food class actions were filed in or removed to federal court in 2015. Filings increased in 2016, with over 170 new food class actions filed in or removed to federal court.[33] Figure 1.6 shows categories of food products that have been targeted for class action.

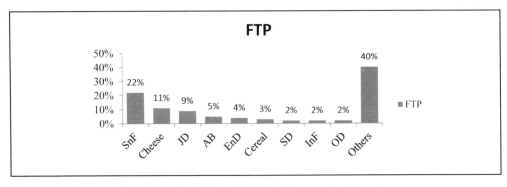

Figure 1.6 Frequently targeted products (FTP) for class action litigation
Source: Silverman and Muehlberger (2017, p. 7).
Notes: Federal and Identified State Class Actions Active in 2015–2016).
SnF = snack food, JD = juice/juice drinks, AB = alcoholic beverages, EnD = energy drinks,
SD = soft drinks, InF = infant food, and OD = other drinks.

Silverman and Muehlberger reveal that some of the products tend to have some generic attributes such as trans-fats (partially hydrogenated oils—PHOs), product liability, and false advertising.[34] Some class action lawyers are targeting products that contain fats known as trans-fats. Courts have found that federal law preempts lawsuits that conflict with Food and Drug Administration (FDA) regulations that require products with a nominal amount of PHOs to be labeled 0 percent trans-fat. But the FDA's recent policy phasing out trans-fats has led to another flurry of lawsuits, even though the agency gave manufacturers till 2018 to change their products.

Food class action litigation has been reported to cut across a spectrum of products that are found in the supermarket.[35] The suits generally involve claims that can be associated with one or more of ten main categories: (i) natural, (ii) slack fill, (iii) origin, (iv) specific health claim, (v) healthy foods, (vi) looks healthy, (vii) evaporated cane juice when white sugar is involved, (viii) trans-fat, (ix) processing, and (x) other representations.[36]

The findings of Plancich, Augustson, and Magoronga (2014) affirm the problem of information asymmetry in the marketplace. Between January 1, 2010 and December 31, 2013, they examined 479 consumer class actions for which either a preliminary settlement was reached, or the final settlement approved by a judge. Their class action study focused on situations in which consumers had purchased a product or service from the defendant(s) with complaints of at least one of the following types of allegations: (i) false advertising/misrepresentation, (ii) product liability, (iii) inadequate information/warning, (iv) fraud, and (v) antitrust.[37]

Consumer class action settlements also increased between 2010 and 2013 for all the aforementioned categories. In this instance, settling defendants came from very diverse industries, including banking/finance, cosmetics/pharmaceuticals, and retail. The banking/finance sector is reported to have both the most cases settled and also roughly half of the aggregate settlement dollars, driven by the $7.25 billion Visa/Mastercard settlement noted above.[38]

It was discovered that more than ten percent of the aggregate settlement funds were related to the motor vehicle industry. When

> the two large settlements are excluded, the settlements become more evenly distributed across industries, although five industries—banking/finance, building materials/industrial products, business/consumer services, cosmetics/pharmaceuticals and electronics—had more than 10 percent of aggregate settlement dollars each. Two industries—entertainment/social media and telecommunications—accounted for a relatively small share, with less than 1 percent of aggregate settlements in each.
> (Plancich, Augustson, & Magoronga, 2014, p. 6)

Figures 1.7 and 1.8 show total settlement fund value for the settlement years 2010–2013, and reported and unreported settlement values of the most common allegations respectively.

Fraud turned out to be the most common allegation. Limiting their study to the 321 cases with a reported settlement fund value, Plancich et al. found that fraud remains the most common allegation followed by antitrust cases. While most of the cases settled had allegations of fraud or false advertising, they found that most of the settlement dollars—56 percent of the total—were related to antitrust cases.[39] Also, certain product/allegation pairs show a relatively frequent presence in consumer class action litigation.

Drugs and food show high complementarity and cases of false advertising/misrepresentation were associated with drugs and food. Other products with complementarity like automotive products, building materials, and electronics registered a high presence of product liability. The financial industry, checking accounts and loans, mortgages or insurance products, espoused fraudulent activities.[40] Fraud cases constitute the highest percentage of cases with reported settlement value, while product liability constitutes the highest percentage of cases with unreported settlement fund value.

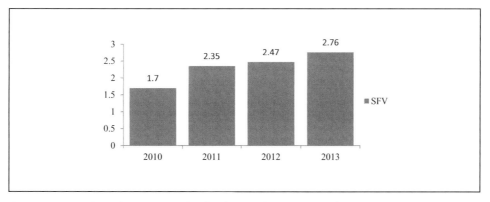

Figure 1.7 Total Settlement Fund Value by settlement year ($m)
Source: Plancich et al. (2014, p.4).

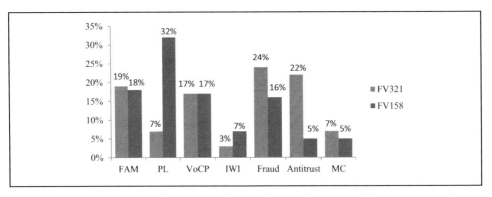

Figure 1.8 Characteristics of consumer class action settlements without a reported settlement fund value
Source: Plancich et al. (2014, p. 16).
Notes: FAM = False advertising/misrepresentation, PL = Product liability, VoCP = Violation of consumer privacy, IWI = Inadequate warning information [information asymmetry], MC = Multiple categories, FV321 = Cases with reported settlement fund value (321), FV158 = Cases with unreported settlement fund value (158).

Transactional violations and class action litigations manifest inherent problems with the efficient market hypothesis. They also raise questions about the compensation of society for injurious market transactions and negative externalities. Not all the victims of injuries can be recipients of class action awards even when violators are severely punished. In fact, it is not unusual for attorneys to derive skewed benefits from class action suits. Apart from not knowing how compensation should be distributed for societal loss, one of the problems with estimating societal loss (DWL) is the lack of knowledge about the precise slope of the demand curve. The elasticity of demand or the responsiveness of consumers to price changes can be helpful. Elasticity tracks the percentage change in quantity demanded relative to the percentage change in price over a range of the demand curve. Of course, estimating price elasticities of demand is more of an academic exercise than a contemporaneous judicial response to the problem.

1.5 ECONOMIC AND JUDICIAL INTERPRETATIONS OF CONSUMER RESPONSIVENESS TO PRICE CHANGES

A DWL occurs when there is a reduction in economic surplus (see Figure 1.5 Panel (b)). Price elasticity of demand is measured by estimating the percentage change in quantity demanded relative to the percentage change in the price of the same good.

$$\eta_D = \left(\frac{dQ}{dP}\right) \star \left(\frac{P}{Q}\right); \qquad (1.2)$$

where P is for price and Q is for quantity. Point elasticity is also a useful estimating mechanism for continuous rather than discrete data. Invariably, data for prices and quantities are usually in continuous (dollars and cents) rather than discrete form (dollars or cents). By taking the double log of a demand function, point elasticity estimates price elasticity of demand with relative ease.

The double log specification will be further discussed in Chapter 5, but as a matter of introduction, and in keeping with the theme of this chapter, consider the following specification:

$$\ln Q_W = \beta_0 - \beta_W \ln P_W; \qquad (1.3)$$

where Q_W is the quantity of widgets demanded and P_W is the price of widgets. It can be shown that β_W, the price coefficient, is an elasticity coefficient. Taking the derivative of Equation 1.3 gives:

$$\frac{1}{Q_W} dQ_W = \beta_W \star \frac{1}{P_W} dP_W \qquad (1.4)$$

$$\beta_W = \frac{dQ_W}{dP_W} \star \frac{P_W}{Q_W} \qquad (1.5)$$

Equation 1.5 is theoretically identical to Equation 1.2. It is noteworthy that β_0 is a constant and that a constant does not change.

The discrete form of elasticity, which is of the midpoint or arc variety, is provided below:

$$\eta_D = \frac{\%\Delta Q_{Dx}}{\%\Delta P_x} = \left(\frac{Q_2 - Q_1}{Q_2 + Q_1}\right)_x \star \left(\frac{P_2 + P_1}{P_2 - P_1}\right)_x \qquad (1.6)$$

The absolute value of the coefficients tells us whether total revenue (TR, or $P \star Q$) will rise or fall when price changes by 1 percent (incrementally). A table should helpfully convey the thought.

When consumers are very responsive to price changes ($\eta_D > 1$), increases in prices will lead to a reduction in total revenue. Consumers generally have options when they are very sensitive to price changes. On the contrary, consumers do not have much of an option when demand is price inelastic. Therefore, increases in prices will increase total revenue

Table 1.1 Price elasticity coefficients and their meanings

Coefficient (η_D)	Interpretation	Revenue effect of price change
$\eta_D = 1$	Unit elastic	Unchanged
$\eta_D > 1$	Elastic	P↑ TR↓
$\eta_D < 1$	Inelastic	P↑ TR↑
$\eta_D = 0$	Perfectly inelastic	P↑ TR↑
		P↓TR↓

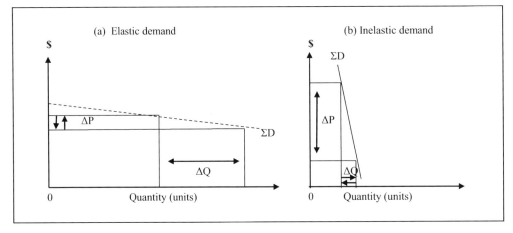

Figure 1.9 Price elasticity and inelasticity of demand

and reduce consumer welfare. The typical goods in this category are extensively considered to be essential, and litigation is usually centered on essential products with high prices, product quality, and fraudulent advertising. This observation does not mean that all cases have merit. Some lawyers shop around for class action cases.

Figure 1.9 illustrates the concept of consumer responsiveness to price changes. A very small change in price causes a very large change in quantity demanded in Panel (a). Alternatively, a very large change in price causes a very small change in quantity demanded because consumers do not have much of an option. Consumers may be responsive to price changes for various reasons, including the amount of disposable income that should be expended after a price change, their taste or preference for the good, the necessity of consuming the good, substitutability of goods, and the timeframe within which they have to make adjustments.

Elasticity can also be useful to determine the relationship between products—the substitutability or complementarity—and market share in antitrust cases. The cross-price elasticity can be estimated to determine the relationships of products. Implicitly, the negative or positive sign of the cross-price elasticity coefficient will indicate whether the goods are replacement (substitute) goods (positive coefficient) or complementary goods that are jointly consumed (negative coefficient):

$$\eta_{DY,PX} = \left(\frac{dQ_Y}{dP_X}\right) \star \left(\frac{P_X}{Q_Y}\right) \tag{1.7}$$

Intuitively, if consumers are buying more of an interchangeable good when the price of its counterpart is rising, then there is *prima facie* evidence that the positive coefficient suggests that products are replacement goods. If the price and quantity are moving in opposite directions, then a price increase is negatively impacting the consumption of the two goods that are jointly consumed.

However, the findings emanating from the estimation of elasticity can be sensitive to the timing of economic transactions. Past incidents of substitutability may not accurately reflect the consequences of prospective transactions or mergers and the effects of prospective transactions on consumers. The determination of market share, with the aid of elasticity coefficients, is just a way of estimating market power. Courts will defer to alternative measures that are superior when they are available.

The *DuPont Cellophane Case* has been an intriguing example of the use of cross-price elasticity in judicial adjudication of evidence. The government alleged that DuPont had a monopoly over cellophane (where it had a market share of 75 percent) in violation of the Sherman Act, §2. However, the defendant argued that it only participated in the flexible packing materials market (where it had a market share of 20 percent).

The Supreme Court used a reasonable interchangeability test (cross-price elasticity) to ascertain the relationship of the goods in the market, and it found that cellophane was sufficiently interchangeable with Pliofilm, greaseproof paper, glassnine, waxed paper, and foil. The test actually shows direction, which may suffice for its purpose, but not strength. Some have argued that the ruling made insufficient valuation of the prospective outcome (Cellophane fallacy). Antitrust law will be revisited in Chapter 7. The next section takes a look at US labor law and the economics of discrimination.

1.5 (A) US LABOR MARKET AND THE CIVIL RIGHTS ACT OF 1964

Discrimination is the practice of according people inferior treatment in hiring, occupational access, education and training, promotion, wage rate, or working conditions on the basis of race, gender, ethnicity, or national origin. Discrimination is an awful human right violation that has to be proven in courts of law. Discrimination in the labor market may take several forms, but two forms are particularly notorious and common in labor relations: race and gender discrimination. The probability of young attorneys dealing with such cases is exceedingly high. Title VII of the Civil Rights Act (1964) prohibits discrimination in all forms, except in cases of exemptions including national security, seniority, use of controlled substances, and the Indian Reservations. The relevant law (unlawful employment practices) for this section can be found in 42 U.S.C.§2000e:

(a) Employer practices
   It shall be an unlawful employment practice for an employer
   (1) to fail or refuse to hire or to discharge any individual, or otherwise to discriminate against any individual with respect to his compensation, terms, conditions, or privileges of employment, because of such individual's race, color, religion, sex, or national origin; or
   (2) to limit, segregate, or classify his employees or applicants for employment in any way which would deprive or tend to deprive any individual of employment opportunities or otherwise adversely affect his status as an employee, because of such individual's race, color, religion, sex, or national origin.
(b) Employment agency practices
   It shall be an unlawful employment practice for an employment agency to fail or refuse to refer for employment, or otherwise to discriminate against, any individual because of his race, color, religion, sex, or national origin, or to classify or refer for employment any individual on the basis of his race, color, religion, sex, or national origin.
(c) Labor organization practices
   It shall be an unlawful employment practice for a labor organization
   (1) to exclude or to expel from its membership, or otherwise to discriminate against, any individual because of his race, color, religion, sex, or national origin; or
   (2) to limit, segregate, or classify its membership or applicants for membership, or to classify or fail or refuse to refer for employment any individual, in any way which would deprive or tend to deprive any individual of employment opportunities, or would limit such employment opportunities or otherwise adversely affect his status as an employee or as an applicant for employment, because of such individual's race, color, religion, sex, or national origin; or
   (3) to cause or attempt to cause an employer to discriminate against an individual in violation of this section.
(d) Training programs
   It shall be an unlawful employment practice for any employer, labor organization, or joint labor-management committee controlling apprenticeship or other training or retraining, including on-the-job training programs to discriminate against any individual because of his race, color, religion, sex, or national origin in admission to, or employment in, any program established to provide apprenticeship or other training.
(e) Businesses or enterprises with personnel qualified on basis of religion, sex, or national origin; educational institutions with personnel of particular religion ….
(k) Burden of proof in disparate impact cases
   (1) (A) An unlawful employment practice based on disparate impact is established under this subchapter only if
      (i) a complaining party demonstrates that a respondent uses a particular employment practice that causes a disparate impact on the basis of race, color, religion, sex, or national origin and the respondent fails to demonstrate that the challenged practice is job related for the position in question and consistent with business necessity; or

(ii) the complaining party makes the demonstration described in subparagraph (C) with respect to an alternative employment practice and the respondent refuses to adopt such alternative employment practice.
(B) (i) With respect to demonstrating that a particular employment practice causes a disparate impact as described in subparagraph (A)(i), the complaining party shall demonstrate that each particular challenged employment practice causes a disparate impact, except that if the complaining party can demonstrate to the court that the elements of a respondent's decision-making process are not capable of separation for analysis, the decision-making process may be analyzed as one employment practice.
(ii) If the respondent demonstrates that a specific employment practice does not cause the disparate impact, the respondent shall not be required to demonstrate that such practice is required by business necessity.
(C) The demonstration referred to by subparagraph (A)(ii) shall be in accordance with the law as it existed on June 4, 1989, with respect to the concept of "alternative employment practice."
(2) A demonstration that an employment practice is required by business necessity may not be used as a defense against a claim of intentional discrimination under this subchapter.

(42 U.S.C.§2000e)

Section 2000e-4 establishes the Equal Employment Opportunity Commission (EEOC), which has the primary duty for enforcing the civil rights laws of the US. Over the years, the Commission has brought successful charges, but it has also been riddled with allegations of corruption. In very simple terms, corruption is usually defined as the abuse of public authority for private gain that is costly to society. Corruption is a surreptitious (covert) offense with overt manifestations (acts) that espouse cooperative malfeasance in the forms of willful negligence, intentional omissions, bribery, conflicts of interest, biased misrepresentations of facts, perjury, collusion, and price-fixing.

Social scientists have tried to identify various sources of corruption. Some have surprisingly rationalized the benefits of malfeasance in economic activity (see the grease hypothesis), but Ashforth and Anand (2003) identify three sources that contribute to the normalization of corruption in an organization or institution: (i) institutionalization (the process by which corruption is enacted [adopted] as a routine course of business without careful thought), (ii) rationalization (the process by which corrupt individuals use social metrics or occurrences to justify their own behavior), and (iii) socialization (the process by which newcomers are taught to comport or conform with corrupt practices).[41] Intransigent workers are expeditiously ostracized. In selecting winners and losers, some corrupt employers are not prosecuted to the full extent of the law, especially when EEOC corruption converges with judicial corruption.[42]

Notably, corruption distorts the validity of labor discrimination data, and the data must be viewed or used with precaution because of the noisy elements. Figure 1.10 shows the number of charges filed, which is not prone to too much error, barring the disincentives

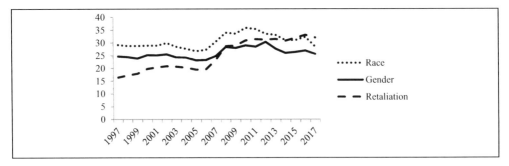

Figure 1.10 Charge statistics with the EEOC FY1997 to FY2017
Source: www.eeoc.gov.
Note: Charge statistics do not include charges filed with state or local Fair Employment Practices Agencies. Retaliation charges are for Title VII only.

and inabilities to file the charges. A cursory view of the data suggests that though the US population increased between 1997 and 2017 (20 years), the number of charges filed for race discrimination in 2017 is less than the number filed in 1997. Race relations in the workplace must have improved exponentially or a considerable amount of people preferred to file state or local charges. Charges for gender discrimination edge above that of the 1997 data by less than 1,000 complaints. Only retaliation shows a discernible trend between 1997 and 2017.

1.5 (B) US LABOR LAW AND ECONOMICS OF DISCRIMINATION

Discrimination is the practice of according people inferior treatment in hiring, occupational access, education and training, promotion, wage rate, or working conditions on the basis of race, gender, ethnicity, or national origin. Discrimination may be based on an illegal preference or taste, which an employer is willing to pay for at the expense of societal income. That is, society is paying for the misbehavior of an employer in pecuniary and psychological (non-economic) forms. The amount of the cost, which is presumed to be a disutility parameter, is a fixed amount of money for a blatant display or surreptitious concealment of prejudice (bias) that does not vary with the job performance or potential.

Accordingly, when one employee is paid more than another because of prejudice, or when one group of people is unfairly alienated from the job market for discriminatory reasons, the wage rate and the number of the endangered group will be affected in one way or another. Consequently, if Caucasian employees are illegally preferred to colored employees, then the wage rates or salaries of Caucasian employees will reflect an illegal disutility parameter (social cost). It must be highlighted that the wage disparity is not based on job performance. The wage of the Caucasian employee (W_K) will then be a function of the wage of the colored employee (W_C) plus the disutility parameter:

MICROECONOMIC FOUNDATION

$$W_K = W_C + d \rightarrow Wc = W_K - d. \tag{1.8}$$

Therefore, d is an illegal wage premium accruing to the employment of the Caucasian employee. Explicitly, a prejudiced employer will only employ employees of color only if the wage rate of the colored employees is sufficiently below that of the Caucasian employee in order to accommodate the disutility parameter:

$$Wc = W_K - d. \tag{1.9}$$

When employers do not accommodate the illegal disutility parameter, d, compensation of employees will be based on job performance (productivity) and experience, and the disutility parameter will be equal to zero.

$$W_K = W_C - 0 \tag{1.10}$$

The disutility parameter can be endogenized as a cost coefficient:[43]

$$W_K = W_C(1+d). \tag{1.11}$$

Even though it costs the employer W_C per hour to hire a colored employee, the discriminating employer acts as if it costs $W_C(1+d)$. Implicitly, the disutility coefficient is integrated into the work performance of the colored employee to enhance the premium earned by the Caucasian employee.

The disutility coefficient has additional implications. It discourages the employment of victims of discrimination and depresses the wage rate of the colored employees below the market value (see Figure 1.11). A racially prejudiced Caucasian employer who decides not to employ people of color will demand fewer colored employees ($D_{CE(1)}$ to $D_{CE(2)}$) and reduce the wage rate of the colored employee from $W^\star$ to W_2 because of the illegal disutility cost.[44]

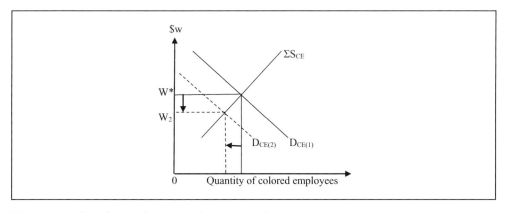

Figure 1.11 Illegal disutility in employment and compensation

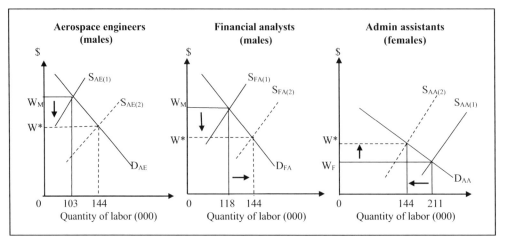

Figure 1.12 The Occupational Segregation Model
Note: See also Table 1.2.

Discrimination also leads to occupational segregation—the bunching of women, African Americans, and certain ethnic groups into less desirable lower-paying occupations. Statistics indicate that women are disproportionately concentrated in a limited number of occupations such as teaching, nursing, and secretarial work; for example, less educated people are crowded into low-paying jobs, but more Hispanics can be found in agricultural and cleaning jobs. Immigration issues and lack of upward mobility are also determinative of job choices in the low-skilled market (the negative self-selection syndrome).

Does occupational segregation (discrimination) impact wage disparities? With some regularity conditions, Figure 1.12 provides a somewhat revealing response to the question. Assume that there are 432,000 people in the labor force for a given period of time, of which 221,000 are men. Further assume that 103,000 men are aerospace engineers, 118,000 men are financial analysts, and 211,000 females are administrative assistants. When females are not significantly employed (crowded out) in the aerospace and financial sectors for a variety of reasons, they will be clustered in the low-paying market for administrative assistants. Of course, the same analogy can be made to race discrimination.

Wages are higher in the aerospace and financial markets because of the required skills, asymmetric opportunities, and the limited number of workers that are employable in those markets. A lot of females are in the low-paying administrative assistant market, because of the relatively low skill requirement and the greater number of female workers who are employable in that market and who cannot be absorbed into the other markets with higher wages.

Better enforcement of labor laws, opportunities for upward mobility, and less unfavorable working preconditions will generate better acquisition of human capital to increase employment in the higher paying markets. Wages will fall in the aerospace and financial markets as more people become available to work in those markets. The wages of administrative assistants will rise as a result of the reduction in the supply of administrative assistants and redistribution of employees in the labor force (say, 144,000 in each market). Wage inequality will not be eliminated because of skill asymmetries, preferences, and experience (*inter alia*), but the variation in wage disparity will be reduced. There is an improvement in the allocation of labor (efficiency), because the skills of administrative assistants can be better utilized to increase output in the other markets while at the same time increasing the earnings of the assistants; especially when the assistants are also capable of being financial analysts rather than engineers in the short-run.

When laws are enacted to prevent discrimination in any society, courts of law must appropriately interpret the laws (adjudicate conflicts) without biases, and the executive arm of government must ensure the enforcement of the laws if the laws are going to be effective (have any meaningful or deterrent effect). Judicial failures will magnify the problem and the accompanying societal cost.

> An efficient allocation of labor is realized when workers are being directed to their highest valued uses. Labor is being allocated efficiently when society obtains the largest amount of domestic output from the given amount of labor available [say, 432,000 people from the previous model]. Stated technically, available labor is efficiently allocated when its value of marginal product or VMP—the dollar value to society of its marginal product—is the same in all alternative employments.[45]

Table 1.2 is indicative of some amount of bunching (clustered employment). It is a random compilation of the number of males and females in a variety of jobs (30) and the amount of money that males and females are paid in each occupation. I must note that the data do not control for experience, variations in education, productivity, or skill set. Estimation of the data and some regularity conditions will be further discussed in Chapter 5. The men and women are randomly selected full-time employees from an interactive visualization database of the US Department of Labor that lists over 300 occupations. Annual earnings are also provided for all occupations. The positive sign indicates that more females are employed in a particular occupation.

For a considerable amount of the jobs, including: registered nurses, customer service representatives, human resources managers, and budget analysts, though more females are employed, males receive a higher pay. For higher paying jobs like aerospace engineers, actuaries, chief executives, economists, and financial analysts, more males are employed with higher pay. The data do not shed light on the underlying reasons for pay discrepancies, but lack of opportunity and discrimination (employment segregation)

Table 1.2 Occupation by gender and pay (full-time employment, 2016)*

	Male ($)	Female ($)	Male	Female
Registered nurses	70,952	64,413	281,048	2,036,445+
Secretarial and administration assistants	42,411	36,929	118,739	2,107,852+
Elementary and middle school teachers	53,096	50,021	530,970	1,867,475+
Customer service representatives	36,744	32,893	624,476	1,158,158+
First-line supervisors of retail sales workers	46,343	33,778	1,537,529+	1,140,049
Nursing, psychiatric, and home health aides	29,503	25,706	174,528	1,081,522+
Accountants and auditors	76,129	57,370	656,553	972,271+
Office clerks general	39,885	33,492	145,063	696,284+
Human resources managers	77,463	70,342	143,842	225,676+
Book-keeping, accounting, and auditing clerk	42,013	38,665	105,920	723,611+
Actuaries	125,465	92,500	17,769+	7,428
Aerospace engineers	104,133	91,982	102,611+	12,345
Agricultural and food science technicians	48,340	40,927	16,564+	11,104
Appraisers and assessors of real estate	62,298	50,291	50,409+	23,281
Architectural and engineering managers	130,300	130,255	131,956+	12,856
Automotive service technicians and managers	36,695	28,342	717,661+	8,776
Biological scientists	65,122	56,853	35,893+	29,218
Biological technicians	50,495	44,796	8,401+	7,815
Budget analysts	75,399	68,955	16,123	26,287+
Chemical engineers	101,626	84,137	46,688+	11,124
Chemists and material scientists	75,433	63,426	49,013+	28,010
Chief executives	141,108	103,564	813,898+	254,360
Civil engineers	89,218	75,052	271,698+	39,309
Computer programmers	87,064	80,528	293,334+	77,178
Credit analysts	58,520	51,419	12,589	13,793+
Designers	60,035	46,516	328,481+	300,384
Economists	111,514	103,723	15,164+	6,583

(continued)

Table 1.2 Cont.

	Male ($)	Female ($)	Male	Female
Electricians	51,289	50,082	635,090+	12,832
Financial analysts	93,203	73,427	117,808+	77,124
Insurance underwriters	73,389	56,465	36,949	61,245+
Σ			**8,036,767**	**13,030,395**

Data Source: US Department of Labor; https://dol.gov/wb/occupations_interactive.htm.
Notes: The positive sign denotes a greater number of men or women in an occupation.
* Dummy variable = male, and employees = males and females combined. There are two pages of data, but the variables must be labeled at the top of the data only once before estimation. Non-numeric values within the data will not be estimated by Excel or any software. It is important to note that for an equal number of observations, the number of women exceeds the number of men in the sample.

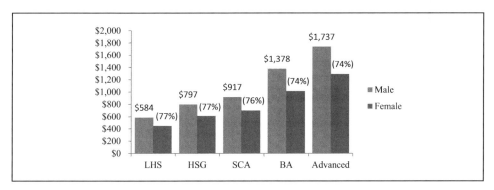

Figure 1.13 Median weekly earnings, by level of education and gender, 2017 (female percent of male income in parenthesis)
Source: U.S. Bureau of Labor Statistics (2018, usual weekly earnings of wage and salary workers, fourth quarter 2017. Economic News Release USDL-18–0079).
Notes: LHS = Less than high school education, HSG= High School graduate, SCA = Some College or Associate degree, BA = Bachelor's degree, and Advanced = Advanced degree.

cannot be discounted without further inquiry. Figures 1.13 and 1.14 are illustrative of the required precaution. Males earn more than females for all the categories of education in Figure 1.13. Therefore, wage disparities cannot be convincingly explained in terms of levels of education. Figure 1.14 shows that the earnings ratio increased between 1979 and 2015, but almost stabilized or increased slowly after 1997.

In 2018, the women-to-men earnings ratio varied by race and ethnicity. White women earned 82.2 percent as much as their male counterparts, compared with black women (86.9 percent), Asian women (77.1 percent), and Hispanic women (86.0 percent).[46]

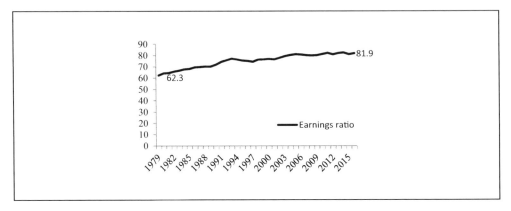

Figure 1.14 Earnings ratio male-female (1979–2015)
Source: US Census Bureau.

1.6 PRODUCTION COST AND CONSUMER WELFARE

The market forces of demand and supply partly explain the story of efficient allocation of economic resources. The concept of the cost of production is not fully integrated into the price mechanism. Costs of production are important for characterizing market structure and the timeframe of production. Therefore, they say a lot about resource allocation in the short and long run, and whether firms have the capacity to make adjustments to output. In the final analysis, however, control over price or market power has more explanatory power over market structure. This section is important for understanding some of the key arguments in Chapter 7; especially the concepts that appertain to the benefits of the competitive structure rather than the monopolistic structure.

Costs can be decomposed into two broad temporal categories: (i) short-run costs, and (ii) long-run costs. The short run is defined in terms of the ability of entrepreneurs to vary some costs or inputs, and capital is presumed to be invariant. This limitation means that the productivity of labor is susceptible to diminishing returns. In the long run all inputs are variable, and production is not amenable to diminishing returns. Consequently, production time periods are defined by the actual variability of factor inputs rather than a calendar period.

Entrepreneurs have fixed, variable, and total costs in the short run; where the total cost (TC) is a combination of the fixed cost (FC) and variable cost (VC):

$$TC = FC + VC \qquad (1.12)$$

Fixed cost exists even when output is zero. In effect, it is the type of cost that does not vary with output. Entrepreneurs do not have control over fixed costs like rental and interest payments. Variable costs vary with output and they are costs that entrepreneurs can regulate or control; for example, entrepreneurs can determine how many workers to hire and pay and the profitable cost mixing capital and labor. The change in total cost is indicative of the marginal cost (MC), which is closely associated with a change in the variable cost when there is a fixed cost.

$$MC = \frac{\Delta TC}{\Delta Q} \text{ or } \frac{dTC}{dQ} \tag{1.13}$$

To get per unit costs, we divide Equation 1.12 by Q (output):

$$\frac{TC}{Q} = \frac{FC}{Q} + \frac{VC}{Q} \text{ or ATC = AFC+AVC} \tag{1.14}$$

Average total cost (ATC) = Average Fixed Cost (AFC) + Average Variable Cost (AVC).[47]

Table 1.3 gives a hypothetical and numerical representation of the costs and their estimation.

When quantity (output) is zero, only fixed cost is incurred, and total cost is representative of the fixed cost for producing nothing. No variable cost is incurred when output is zero. The total cost is a summation of the variable and fixed costs, and the marginal cost reflects incremental changes in the total and variable costs as output changes incrementally (by one unit). An extension of the MC and the per unit costs will reveal that they are "u-shaped" because of the fixed cost and diminishing returns. That is, they fall and then increase as output increases.

In the long run when all inputs are variable, firms vary capital and the decision to vary capital is contingent on the long-run total per unit cost (ATC). Entrepreneurs deal with scales of production. This concept is important for some of the merger arguments in Chapter 7; specifically, the efficiencies to be derived when firms combine their assets. Three scales of production are worth noting: (i) economies of scale, (ii) constant returns to scale, and (iii) diseconomies of scale; Figure 1.15 provides an illustrative representation of the long-run average cost (LRAC) curve, which will be further discussed in Chapter 7.

Table 1.3 Short-run costs ($)

Output (Q)	Fixed cost	Variable cost	Total cost	Marginal cost	Average fixed cost	Average variable cost	Average total cost
0	40	0	40	0	0	0	0
1	40	30	70	30	40	20	70
2	40	40	80	10	20	20	40
3	40	55	95	15	13.33	18.33	31.67

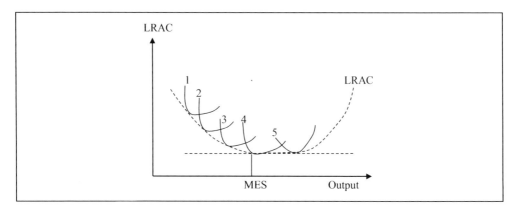

Figure 1.15 Output and per unit cost in the long run

From plant size 1 to plant size 4, the firm enjoys economies of scale; meaning that per unit cost falls as the firm expands production and adds new facilities or plants. Economies of scale are exhausted with the addition of the fourth facility, which provides the firm's minimum efficient scale (MES). The addition of the fifth plant does not alter the long-run per unit cost, but further expansions or additions will cause inefficiencies (diseconomies). The long-run per unit cost will increase if another plant size is added. Convincing arguments cannot be made for bringing more subsidiaries or plants into the scale of operations.

The production costs can be used to assess the profitability of firms. In combination with per unit prices of goods and types of product (already discussed), the costs can provide information about market power or the ability of sellers to determine prices at or above the market rate. The perfectly competitive and monopolistic models should suffice for the analysis here. Other models, such as the monopolistically competitive and oligopolistic models, will not be discussed here; part of Chapter 7 will be devoted to the oligopolistic pricing decisions.

The competitive market is preferred because of its efficient allocation of resources and welfare-enhancing effect on consumers. Figure 1.16 is illustrative of the advantages.

All businesses operate to maximize profit (π), which is the positive difference between total revenue (TR) and total cost (TC). That is, π = TR−TC; where total revenue is the product of per unit price (P) and quantity sold (Q) or TR = P★Q. Panel (a) shows that a competitor is a price-taker. The price line is perfectly elastic, and the marginal revenue (MR) or change in total revenue is the same as the price and average revenue because price is invariant. In effect, the competitor does not have market power. The competitor is incapable of singularly influencing the market price because there are many buyers and sellers.

MICROECONOMIC FOUNDATION

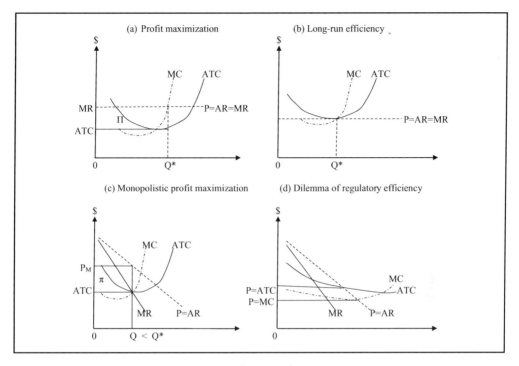

Figure 1.16 The competitive and monopolistic market structures

Since the competitive market is not restrictive (people are free to enter and leave), there are opportunities for profit in the short run. Accordingly, competitors make profit in the short run. However, profits dissipate as more competitors participate in the market. This transformation provides assurances for a fairer price and better resource allocation in the long run. At least two outcomes must be notable: (i) the price is equal to the marginal cost (allocative efficiency), and (ii) the price is also equal to the minimum per unit cost (ATC) (productive efficiency); see Figure 1.16 Panel (b). The two conditions cannot be attained under monopolistic conditions (see Figure 1.16 Panel (d)). Also, it should be recalled from Figure 1.2 Panel (b) that consumer surplus becomes smaller when price increases (d = deterioration of consumer welfare).

Unlike the competitor, the monopolist is a price-maker. He/she has control over the price of his/her product since he/she is the only seller of the product. Monopoly rights may arise because of patents, copyrights, trademarks, legislation, or natural and prime-mover advantages that confer cost advantages. These barriers to entry restrict entry into markets with unique products. Actually, more often than not, unique products have variations; but these variations may be limited by geographic delineations that make monopolies a virtual reality. Therefore, the monopolistic competitive model approximates market reality on a more general scale.

Since monopolists charge prices above their marginal revenues, it is impractical for the per unit price to be equal to the marginal revenue of the monopolist. Panel (c) shows that the monopoly price (P_M) is not equal to the marginal revenue (MR) of the monopolist (compare Panels (a) and (c)). Notably, it is not feasible to attain efficient outcomes in this type of market structure. However, there is a chance that consumers can benefit from extensive economies of scale when part of the cost benefits that are derived from productive efficiencies are transferred over to consumers. Can the monopolist be regulated to achieve productive and allocative efficiencies?

Recall that no regulation is required to attain productive and allocative efficiencies in Panel (b). Yet the same situation cannot be applied to the monopolist, because the monopolist has market power. Some amount of policy intervention will be required to derive efficiencies, and policy must be conceptualized in terms of allocation or production; meaning that it is impossible to achieve both productive and allocative efficiencies (P = minimum ATC and MC) (see Panel (d)). The concepts of "reasonableness" and property rights come into play.

The monopolist cannot possibly continue to produce without significant subsidy if the price is set so low that it is below the per unit cost of production. The "fair" price, which is generally conceived of as a per unit cost, is not enough to generate profit for reinvestment and enjoyment of private property. In the 1890s, the US Supreme Court dealt with the regulatory dilemma. The case that went to the Supreme Court in the 1890s concerned the interaction of property rights and the fair price for freight. The case was also known as the "Maximum Freight Case."

In the 1890s, the Nebraska legislature used its authority to establish maximum rates for the transportation of passengers and freight on railroads. The language of the 1893 statute authorized the imposition of "reasonable" maximum rates. The classification of the statute states:

> The classification established by this act shall be known as the "Nebraska Classification." Freights shall be billed at the actual weight unless otherwise directed in the classification—twenty thousand pounds shall be a carload, and all excessive weights shall be at the same rate per hundred pounds, except in carloads of light and bulky articles, and unless otherwise specified in the classification. When the classification makes an article "released" or "owner's risk," the same at carrier's risk will be the next highest rate higher, unless otherwise provided in the classification. Articles rated first class, "released" or "owner's risk," if taken at "carrier's risk," will be 1 1/2 times first class unless otherwise provided in the classification. All articles carried according to this classification at "owner's risk" of fire, leakage, damage or breakage must be so receipted for by agents of the railroad, and so considered by owners and shippers. Signing a release contract by a shipper shall not release the railroad company for loss or damages caused by carelessness or negligence of its employees.[48]

Three classes of Massachusetts residents challenged the constitutionality of the law to protect their 14th Amendment rights:

All persons born or naturalized in the United States, and subject to the jurisdiction thereof, are citizens of the United States and of the state wherein they reside. No state shall make or enforce any law which shall abridge the privileges or immunities of citizens of the United States; nor shall any state deprive any person of life, liberty, or property, without due process of law; nor deny to any person within its jurisdiction the equal protection of the laws.

(§1)[49]

The suits were brought July 28, 1893, and they involved the constitutionality of an act of the Legislature of Nebraska approved by the Governor April 12, 1893, and which took effect August 1, 1893. They arose over the intent to:

[R]egulate railroads, to classify freights, to fix reasonable maximum rates to be charged for the transportation of freights upon each of the railroads in the State of Nebraska, and to provide penalties for the violation of this act.

(Smyth v. Ames, 169 U.S. 466 (1898))

The appellees in the first case were the plaintiffs included citizens of Massachusetts and stockholders of the Union Pacific Railway Company who sued on behalf of themselves and all others similarly situated.[50] Evidently, the statute made provision for reasonable impositions.

The Supreme Court found that the schedule of railroad tariffs enacted by Nebraska was repugnant to the US Constitution, and it defined the constitutional limits of governmental power to set railroad and utility rates. The court held that regulated industries were constitutionally entitled to earn a "fair return" on the "fair value" of the enterprise. Under the fair value rule a governmental authority was required to determine a "rate base," which was the present value of the enterprise's assets, and to allow the enterprise to charge rates sufficient to earn a normal return on that value.[51] The court further alluded to the reasonableness provision within the statute:

The grant to the Legislature in the Constitution of Nebraska of the power to establish maximum rates for the transportation of passengers and freight on railroads in that state has reference to "reasonable" maximum rates, as the words strongly imply that it was not intended to give a power to fix maximum rates without regard to their reasonableness, and as it cannot be admitted that the power granted may be exerted in derogation of rights secured by the Constitution of the United States, and that the judiciary may not, when its jurisdiction is properly invoked, protect those rights.[52]

What is fairness or fair value? The court maintained that:

The basis of all calculations as to the reasonableness of rates to be charged by a corporation maintaining a highway under legislative sanction must be the fair value of the property being used by it for the convenience of the public, and in order to ascertain that value, the original cost of construction, the amount expended in permanent improvements, the amount and market value of its bonds and stock, the present as compared with the original cost of construction, the probable earning capacity of the property under particular rates prescribed by statute, and the sum required to meet operating expenses, are all matters for consideration, and are to be given such weight as maybe just and right in each case. What the company is entitled to ask is a fair return upon the value of that which it employs for the public convenience, and on the other hand, what the public is entitled to demand is that no more be exacted from it for the use of a public highway than the services rendered by it are reasonably worth.[53]

The Supreme Court unanimously found the law to be unconstitutional. The court found that a tax should be in the public interest but that it should still give companies enough revenue to pay for operating expenses and stock dividends.[54] The case reveals that regulatory prices can have confiscatory and legal problems that violate property and investment rights. The next chapter will examine jurisprudential macroeconomics.

CHAPTER SUMMARY

- This chapter lays the foundation for an understanding of the basic micro concepts that underpin legal theories and judicial decisions in the subsequent chapters.
- Principles of economics have helped to shape political (non-market) decisions (public choice theory) like voting rules, voter behavior, and party politics. Most of the focus has been on the implementation of law through political processes rather than the role of the judiciary.
- Normative economics prescribe what an economy should look like or what policies should be adopted to accomplish subjective goals. The normative school of law argues that there is a need for legal intervention to correct the adverse manifestations of market (economic) failures.
- Economic models are formal presentations of economic theories in illustrative and/or mathematical forms. A functional relationship is generally subsumed in such models; meaning that there is generally an interest in correlative relationships when causative relationships cannot be convincingly established. It is worth detecting some traps (fallacies) when constructing economic models.
- Price increases decrease consumer surplus and welfare. On the contrary, prices increases increase producer surplus. Consumers are not making informed decisions when prices are contrived or fraudulent and consumers may file class action suits.
- "A class action is a procedure by which a large group of entities—that is, a 'class'— may challenge a defendant's allegedly unlawful conduct in a single lawsuit, rather than through numerous, separate suits initiated by individual plaintiffs."
- Class action suits must satisfy the requirements of the Federal Rule of Civil Procedure 23: numerosity, commonality, typicality, and adequacy. Class action suits must be certified by courts of law.
- Consumers are sensitive to price changes when they have options, and cross-price elasticity indicates the relationship between two different categories of products.

- The Civil Rights Act of 1964 prohibits employment discrimination, but some employers continue to promote illegal discrimination in labor markets. Illegal employment discrimination increases income inequality and poverty.
- There are noticeable institutional failures when it comes to enforcing civil rights laws.
- The competitive market structure is a model of allocative and productive efficiencies. Only one of the two efficiencies can be obtained in the monopolistic markets. Price regulation must be reasonable at all times.

KEY WORDS

• Adequacy	• Economic models	• Normative
• *Ceteris paribus*	• Elasticity	• Numerosity
• Civil rights	• Equilibrium	• Ockham's razor
• Class action suit	• Fraud	• Producer surplus
• Commonality	• Jurisprudential	• Product liability
• Consumer surplus	• Long run	• Short run
• Cross-price elasticity	• Market structure	• *Stare decisis*
• Deadweight loss	• Market failure	• Total revenue
• Earnings ratio	• Microeconomics	• Typicality

CHAPTER QUESTIONS

1. Why do markets fail? Discuss the importance of equity in economic and judicial decisions.
2. Suppose consumers are willing to pay $60 for a good, what will be the consumer surplus if the pay $20 for 100 units? What will be the reduction in consumer surplus, if consumers reduce their consumption of the good by 50 units because of a $20 increase in the price?
3. What is a class action suit? Discuss the conditions for bringing about a class action suit in a US court of law. Why is it that certain products have been targeted for class action suits? Are the suits frivolous? Why?
4. What is the price elasticity of demand? Imagine that the market demand function for packets of blue cheese is specified as follows:

$$Q_{DC} = 20 - 6P_C;$$

where Q_{DC} is for the quantity of blue cheese packets demanded and P_C is for the price of blue cheese per packet. Evaluate the function when price is $2 per packet and explain why consumers may or may not be sensitive to changes in the price of blue cheese.

Hint: $|\eta_D| = \left(\dfrac{dQ}{dP}\right) * \left(\dfrac{P}{Q}\right) \rightarrow \dfrac{dQ}{dP} = -6\dfrac{P?}{Q?} \leq \text{ or } \geq 1?$

5. Suppose the cheese function is alternatively specified as:

    $Q_{DC} = 20 - 6P_C + 2P_Y$,

    where P_Y is for the per unit price of yellow butter. Explain how this information will help you to generate a legal brief about the relationship between blue cheese and yellow butter.

6. What is discrimination? With reference to the Civil Rights Act of 1964, explain why employment discrimination is illegal. What are the economic implications of employment discrimination? To what extent have the US enforcement agencies and the courts successfully dealt with the issue of "modern" employment discrimination? Why do some employers engage in discriminatory employment?
7. Why is the perfectly competitive mode a model of efficiency? How have the courts dealt with market inefficiencies or failures and price regulation?

NOTES

1. These philosophical schools of law and economics include public choice theory, institutional law and economics, the new institutional economics, social norms and law and economics, as well as the New Haven school and Austrian law and economics; see Mercuro (2009). The diversity of thought presupposes conflicting and overlapping theories of economic occurrences and the interpretation of economic models. The orientation of this chapter is not to subscribe to any of these schools of thought but to present economic theories, models, and data for an understanding of economic laws and fundamental fairness when interpreting laws with economic implications.
2. See also Marshall (2008, p.307).
3. Doctrinaires were inward-looking and they utilized a scientific approach to the study and application of law by excluding extraneous disciplines. The concept flourished from the mid-nineteenth century to the mid-twentieth century; see Mercuro (2009, pp. 64–68).
4. Ibid.
5. See Pareto optimality and the Kaldor-Hicks compensation test. "A legal change is efficiency-enhancing if the winners could (conceptually) compensate the losers (to make the latter whole once again) and still remain gainers" (Mercuro, 2009, p. 77; see also p. 78).
6. Ibid.
7. See Bhagwati (1982, p. 988).
8. See Mercuro (2009, p. 84).
9. In effect, the catallactic approach, which is to take individual decision-makers as the basic unit of analysis to view both politics and the political processes, may suffer from some inherent deficiencies. Invariably, the challenge is not unique. It characterizes

a broad swath of empirical work that relies on surveys. The positive public choice theorists, unlike the catallactic, attempt to develop logical, descriptive, consistent theories that link individual behavior to collective action (Mercuro, 2009, p. 80).

10 Ibid., p. 93. An *institutional arrangement* is considered to be a specific arrangement among economic units that governs the ways in which the units can cooperate or compete; see Mercuro (2009) for discussions about the New Institutional Economics in the late 1960s and 1970s, social norms, and the New Haven and Austrian schools.
11 Caplan and Miller examine the underlying variables that shape beliefs about normative and positive economics. They find that variables like education, income, and job security are invariant drivers of the beliefs about normative and positive economics.
12 See Levmore (1997, p. 129).
13 Parisi and Klick (2004, p. 434). Beyond the natural and positive dimensions, doctrinalism examined judicial opinions to discern the fundamental doctrines of law.
14 Mercuro (2009, p. 63).
15 Ibid., p. 435.
16 Rule utilitarianism ensures that rules safeguard the utility of society (aggregate utility). Act utilitarianism maximizes the utility of an individual. Even though all individuals will not be appeased by rules, the greatest good for the greatest number is the targeted objective. See the debtor's prison, rule against perpetuities, and servitudes after neighborhood changes in Stake (1991).
17 Ibid., p. 1451.
18 See also the Vienna Convention on the Law of Treaties (1969).
19 Stake (1991, p. 1457).
20 See *Rhue v. Cheyenne Homes*, 168 Colo. 6, 9, 449 P.2d 361, 363 (1969); see also Stake (1991, p. 1469).
21 See Jacobs (1995, p. 220).
22 "Plaintiffs in *Kodak*, independent service organizations (ISOs) that repaired and maintained Kodak copying and micrographic equipment, alleged that Kodak violated §§ 1 and 2 of the Sherman Act by unlawfully tying the sale of service to the sale of replacement parts and by monopolizing and attempting to monopolize the service market for Kodak equipment" (Berman & Knight, 2008, op. cit., pp. 246–247).
23 See Kurtz (2017, p. 92); the concept of falling marginal utility of income and collective or societal utility did not make too much sense to Pareto. Additionally, the concept of interpersonal utility (comparing one person's utility to another) is not straightforward. Which utility is superior? See also the Scitovsky paradox in Brent (1996, p. 34).
24 On the condition that judges or juries are willing to make interpersonal comparisons of utility for maximization purposes, and that they believe people have the same declining marginal utility of wealth (or risk profiles); one would predict a bias for the poor and against the rich (ibid).
25 William Ockham, sometimes spelt "Occam," was a fourteenth-century Franciscan friar who argued that when there are two competing theories that make the same predictions, the simpler one is the better alternative.
26 See Diebold (2008, Chapter 11); see also Warburton (2018) and cointegration models.
27 See Brent (2017, p. 18).
28 Scarcity is a relative concept. Economic resources are scarce relative to human wants. Since human wants are unlimited, there cannot be an infinite amount of resources to

satisfy the unlimited wants of humans. This economizing problem necessitates the need to make choices that generate sacrificed (foregone) alternatives (opportunity costs).
29 See also *Eubank v. Pella Corp.*, 753 F.3d 718, 719 (7th Cir. 2014).
30 *Gen. Tel. Co. of Sw. v. Falcon*, 457 U.S. 147, 159 (1982); *Am. Pipe & Constr. Co. v. Utah*, 414 U.S. 538, 553 (1974); see also Lewis and Freeman (2018, p. 3).
31 *United States Parole Comm'n v. Geraghty*, 445 U.S. 388, 402–03 (1980). See also *Bell v. PNC Bank, N.A.*, 800 F.3d 360, 379 (7th Cir. 2015) (observing that certification works in the defendants' favor by providing a single proceeding in which to adjudicate the claims that will bind all class members); see Lewis and Freeman (2018, p. 4).
32 Federal Rules of Civil Procedure, Title IV, Rule 23. "Class Actions: (a) Prerequisites. One or more members of a class may sue or be sued as representative parties on behalf of all members only if: (1) the class is so numerous that joinder of all members is impracticable [numerosity]; (2) there are questions of law or fact common to the class [commonality]; (3) the claims or defenses of the representative parties are typical of the claims or defenses of the class [typicality]; and (4) the representative parties will fairly and adequately protect the interests of the class [adequacy]. … (c) At an early practicable time after a person sues or is sued as a class representative, the court must determine by order whether to certify the action as a class action." See Lewis and Freeman (2018) for further reading about class action requirements.
33 See Silverman and Muehlberger (2017, p. 1).
34 Federal law preempts lawsuits that conflict with the FDA regulations and the FDA has slowly phased out trans fats. Manufacturers were given until 2018 to change their products (Silverman & Muehlberger, 2017, op. cit., p. 3).
35 From jarred cucumbers to tater tots. Orange juice, cereal, frozen breakfast foods, instant oatmeal, pasta, Parmesan cheese, yogurt, soup, tuna fish, hummus, salad dressing, bread crumbs, olive oil, and iced tea are among the items on a very long list for plaintiffs' lawyers who are shopping for a class action. Snack foods, such as protein and granola bars, chips, and brownie mix, are particularly popular for lawsuits (op. cit., p.5). And when lawyers check out at the supermarket, some head to the liquor store where they scan for products they think might lead a highly gullible consumer to believe a product is completely "handmade" or go to a coffee shop where they sue over the amount of ice in iced coffee.
36 See *Kane v. Chobani, LLC*, 645 Fed. Appx. 593 (9th Cir. 2016), [natural] and *Ebner v. Fresh, Inc.*, No. 13-56644, 2016 WL 5389307, at *6 (9th Cir. Sept. 27, 2016) [slack fill]; see also Silverman and Muehlberger (2017, p. 6 & pp. 49–62) for additional cases.
37
"[T]he aggregate settlement value in many cases was not reported because the total size of the settlement would ultimately depend heavily on the number and value of individual claims that emerged during the claim process and/or the total value of the settlement fund was not capped" (Plancich et al., 2014, p. 3).
38 See Pancich et al. (2014, p. 6).
39 Ibid.
40 Plancich et al., 2014, op. cit., p. 13. The complementarity of the goods coincided with industry complementarity. For example, 37 percent and 34 percent of the defendants named in false advertising/misrepresentation cases were in the cosmetics/

pharmaceuticals and food products industries, respectively; 24 percent of the defendants named in violation of consumer privacy cases were in the retail industry; and 57 percent of the defendants named in fraud cases were in the banking/finance industry. Violation of consumer privacy was associated with retail. It is believed that settlements without a reported value were relatively likely to be associated with allegations related to product liability (p. 16).
41 See also Ashforth and Anand (2003, p. 3).
42 See Warburton (2019).
43 See Borjas (2016, p. 365).
44 Illegal disutility is contingent on several biases (innate and acquired). However, it is rather difficult to validate the view that people are born with (innate) biases. Rather, over a period of time, people acquire biases because of association and experience, be it by parenting, peer association, insecurity, inadvertence, or unchecked impulses. Victims of discrimination may be judged collectively on the basis of specific attributes such as gender, or data generalizations about costs and benefits that are associated with the employment or provision of services for specific groups. Employers may look at generalized data on gender, age, education, and work experience to make hiring decisions that may not necessarily be well-informed. Profiling consists of a fallacy of generalization.
45 See McConnell, Brue, and Macpherson (2003, p. 175).
46 See News Release of the Bureau of Labor Statistics, October 16, 2018.
47 Implicitly, TC = ATC*Q, FC = AFC*Q, and VC = AVC*Q. Also, ATC-AVC = AFC, and ATC-AFC = AVC.
48 See https://supreme.justia.com/cases/federal/us/169/466/.
49 See https://law.cornell.edu/constitution/amendmentxiv.
50 In the first case the defendants were the Union Pacific Railway Company; the St. Joseph & Grand Island Railroad Company, the Omaha & Republican Valley Railroad Company, and the Kansas City & Omaha Railroad Company, corporations of Nebraska under the control of the Union Pacific Railway Company; certain persons, citizens of Nebraska, who hold the offices, respectively, of attorney general, secretary of state, auditor of public accounts, state treasurer, and commissioner of public lands and buildings, and constitute the state board of transportation; and James C. Dahlman, Joseph W. Edgerton, and Gilbert L. Laws, citizens of Nebraska, and secretaries of that board. By a supplemental bill in the same suit, certain persons, receivers of the Union Pacific Railway Company, were made defendants; see https://caselaw.findlaw.com/ for other appellees and defendants.
51 See http://oxfordreference.com.
52 See https://supreme.justia.com/cases/federal/us/169/466/.
53 Ibid.
54 Over time, knowledge of finance has evolved and some have argued that enterprise value must be derived from rates, but also because of the intricate administrative requirements to determine the value of utility assets; see http://oxfordreference.com.

FURTHER READING

Ashforth, B. E., & Anand, V. (2003). The normalization of corruption in organizations. *Research in Organizational Behavior, 25,* 1–52.

Baye, M. R., & Prince, J. T. (2017). *Managerial economics and business strategy*. New York: McGraw-Hill.
Berman, K., & Knight, J. (2008). *Financial intelligence for entrepreneurs*. Boston, MA: Harvard Business Press.
Berolzheimer, F. (1912, 1968). *The world's legal philosophies*. Boston: Boston Book Company, Rothman Reprints.
Bhagwati, J. N. (1982). Directly unproductive profit-seeking activities. *Journal of Political Economy, 90*(5), 988–1002.
Borjas, G. (2016). *Labor economics* (7th ed.). New York: McGraw-Hill.
Brent, R. J. (1996). *Applied cost–benefit analysis*. Cheltenham, UK: Edward Elgar.
Brent R. J. (2017). *Advanced introduction to cost–benefit analysis*. Cheltenham, UK: Edward Elgar.
Butler, E. (2012). *Public choice—A primer*. London: Institute of Economic Affairs.
Caplan, B., & Miller, S. (2012). Positive versus normative economics: What's the connection? Evidence from the Survey of Americans and Economists on the Economy and the General Social Survey. *Public Choice, 150*(1), 241–261.
Coase, R. H. (1988). *The firm, the market, and the law*. Chicago, IL: University of Chicago Press.
Diebold, F. X. (2008). *Elements of forecasting*. Mason, OH: South-Western, Cengage Learning.
Jacobs, M. S. (1995). An essay on the normative foundations of antitrust economics. *North Carolina Law Review, 74*(1), 219–266.
Kurtz, H. D. (2017). *Economic thought: A brief history*. New York: Columbia University Press.
Levmore, S. (1997). Judges and economics: Normative, positive, and experiential perspectives. *Harvard Journal of Law & Public Policy, 21*(1), 129–133.
Lewis, K. M., & Freeman, W. C. (2018, April). *Class action lawsuits: A legal overview for the 115th Congress*. Congressional Research Service, R 45159, Retrieved from www.crs.gov.
McConnell, C. R., Brue, S. L., & Flynn, S. M. (2012). *Economics*. New York: McGraw-Hill.
McConnell, C. R., Brue, S. L., & Macpherson, D. A. (2003). *Contemporary labor economics*. New York: McGraw-Hill.
Marshall, K. S. (Ed.) (2008). *The economics of antitrust injury and firm specific damages*. Tuscon, AZ: Lawyers and Judges.
Mercuro, N. (2009). The jurisprudential niche occupied by law and economics. *Journal of Jurisprudence, 2*, 61–109.
Mercuro, N., & Medema, S. G. (2006). *Economics and the law: From Posner to post-modernism and beyond* (2nd ed.). Princeton, NJ: Princeton University Press.
Parisi, F., & Klick, J. (2004). Functional law and economics: The search for value-neutral principles of law making. *Chicago-Kent Law Review, 79*, 431–450.
Plancich, S., Augustson, A., & Magoronga, W. (2014, July). Consumer class action settlements: 2010–2013: Settlement increasing, with focus on privacy. National Economic Research Association. Retrieved from NERA.com.
Schilit, H. M., & Perler, J. (2010). *Financial shenanigans: How to detect accounting gimmicks and fraud in financial reports*. New York: McGraw-Hill.
Schmidt, S. J. (2005). *Econometrics*. New York: McGraw-Hill.
Silverman, C., & Muehlberger, J. (2017, February). *The food court: Trends in food and beverage class action litigation*. Washington, DC: US Chamber Institute for Legal Reform.

Skeel Jr., D. A. (1997). Public choice and the future of public choice influenced legal scholarship. *Vanderbilt Law Review, 50*, 647–648.

Stake, J. E. (1991). Status and incentive aspects of judicial decisions. *Georgetown Law Journal, 79*, 1447–1497.

Warburton, C. E. S. (2018). Covered interest parity and frictions in currency and money markets: Analysis of British Pound and Dollar for the period 1999–2006. *Applied Econometrics and International Development, 18*(1), 55–72.

Warburton, C. E. S. (2019). Human capital and unequal opportunities among social groups in the US. *Regional and Sectoral Economic Studies, 19*(1), 5–28

2

CHAPTER 2
MACROECONOMICS IN FORENSIC ECONOMICS

LEARNING OBJECTIVES

LO 1 To have a basic understanding of the overall economy.
LO 2 To learn how macroeconomic variables affect decisions in courts of law.
LO 3 To know how the value of macroeconomic variables are computed.
LO 4 Introduce the concepts of market failures and efficiency loss (the deadweight loss) for an assessment of damages.
LO 5 To understand the behavior of exchange rates when awards are to be determined in foreign currencies.

Macroeconomic variables affect financial markets and assets. Finance is usually considered to be a subsidiary category of economics. Therefore, when economists consider macroeconomic variables, financial markets and variables are usually given residual considerations. Evidently, the financial variables are not given prime consideration in the notional or real computation of national income or gross domestic product (GDP). This is partly because primary and secondary asset transactions in financial markets are not considered to be quantifiable contributions to newly created tangible goods and services.

Financial transactions are seen as exchanges that generate wealth without observably new and tangible results. Ironically, the service sector is not given residual consideration though tangible output cannot be counted in such a sector. Yet macroeconomic conditions and policies create an environment for wealth creation in which consumers and investors can consume final goods and services. More so, financial disturbances and adverse frictions in financial markets have systemic consequences that eclipse the real sector. Accordingly, macroeconomic variables like inflation, unemployment, interest rate (the creation of liquidity or the lack thereof), taxes, and exchange rates will not be given discriminatory considerations in this chapter.

Macroeconomic variables are integrally related to various court decisions since they impinge on matters of the appropriate discount rate, the aggregate performance of an economy, projected inflation for compensation on investments, the manner in which firms raise capital and taxes, and exchange rate determination. Macroeconomic variables have universal appeal and implications for macroeconomic policies and judicial settlements. Some of these variables are substantively dealt with in later chapters of this book. Accordingly, this chapter will not only discuss the relevant macroeconomic variables as a foundation for forensic and legal decisions, it will also highlight the foundations for understanding some subsequent economic and legal concepts in this book.

2.1 AGGREGATE ECONOMIC PERFORMANCE (THE BUSINESS CYCLE)

Over the years, economists have provided various theories for occurrences of the business cycle.

Schumpeter attributed the business cycle to innovation, diffusion of knowledge, and the dissipation of the returns to useful innovation. National economies perform well during periods of booming innovation, but the profitable effects of innovation dissipate until new ideas generate innovation, which are implicitly useful. Schumpeter estimated cycles to be about nine to ten years long, but later added the concept of "long wave," which spans approximately 50 years. By investigating output, employment, and capital stock through World War I, he discovered three long waves of expansion that could be associated with technological breakthroughs.

The Russian statistician, Kondratiev/Kondratieff (1892–1938), studying European prices, wages, and interest rates, found long upward and downward trends in economic activity that can be associated with technological changes (Kurz, 2017, p.117). Kondratiev noticed significant economic changes that can be linked to various innovations: (i) the steam engine (1787–1842), (ii) the railway (1843–1897), and (iii) electrification (1897–c.1940); to these could be added autos and petrochemicals (1930–1970), and information technology in the post-1970s.

Some have associated the cycle to imprudent financial activities and misguided public policies in capitalist systems with well-developed financial markets. For example, Hyman Minsky alluded to the relaxation of "survival constraints" (Merhling, 1999, p. 141) (the propensity for cash outflows to exceed inflows) and the destabilizing consequences of fragile finance as capitalist systems take on investments to foster growth into distant hinterlands of economic prosperity. Robust finance often gives way to fragile finance for economic growth, but when cash commitments become too overpowering, the system seizes up under the overwhelming weight of risk aversion and reluctance of financial institutions to extend credit—a lifeline of the capitalist system. However, Minsky, like Bagehot, noted that hypothecated capital must be sufficient to avoid the crippling results of risk aversion, which has been considered more recently to be a "Minsky moment."[1] "Upward instability" is inherent in the growth of capitalist economies.

Karl Marx had a different view of the business cycle. He conceptualized economic performance in terms of inventory accumulation (a glut of unsold commodities), which is the result of overinvestment and low wages (inadequate consumption) that he attributed to the exploitation of workers and a superstructure that reinforced the fundamental tenets of market capitalism. In periods of deficient demand, production is cut back, prices fall, profit disappears, unemployment soars, and capital accumulation is halted. In matters of deficient absorption, Marx was not entirely in disagreement with John Maynard Keynes.

In *The General Theory of Employment, Interest, and Money* (1935), Keynes highlighted the economic consequences of deficient demand during the recessionary period and argued in favor of stimulative policies with multiplier effects. Today, deficit spending is characteristic of public policies that target the return to full employment when unemployment increases and national output falls below acceptable levels. Ludwig von Mises, Hayek, and fervent supporters of market efficiency see some fundamental threats to the overall operations of the economy when policy makers make misguided monetary policies that trigger inflation and volatility of economic performance. Figure 2.1 provides a fundamental representation of the business cycle, which tracks the relationship between the level of economic activity and the progression of time.

The relationship significantly shows that economic performance can be volatile; meaning that probabilistic legal theories that seek compensation in employment-related issues cannot convincingly ignore the overall potential economic performance; in particular, as they relate to certain industries. Accordingly, the business cycle has important forensic implications for unemployment compensation when employment laws are inadvertently or flagrantly violated.

Though the cycle has four segments, two of which (peaks and troughs) may be less obvious segments, five phases are discernible: (i) peak, (ii) recession, (iii) trough (turning point), (iv) recovery, and (v) expansion (see Figure 2.1). In the US, a dating committee of the National Bureau of Economic Research (NBER) makes a determination as to when a recession begins or ends. Prior to 2013, the NBER finds that there have been 33 business cycles in the US since 1854, with the average recession lasting for about 16 months. Since

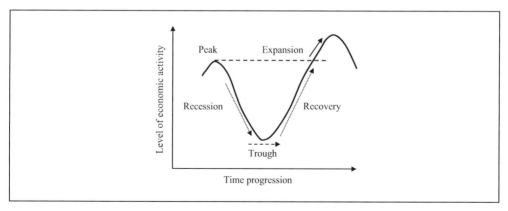

Figure 2.1 The business cycle
Source: Baumohl (2013, p. 21).

World War II, there have been 11 complete business cycles, with recessions averaging about 11 months in duration (Baumohl, 2013, p. 21). Periods of recessions theoretically reflect unemployment; a state in which the economy is not operating at full capacity or absorbing all those who are willing to work.

Unemployment may run from 5 to 27 weeks or more in the US. The gloomy days of unemployment are indicative of the fact that workers are being laid off, mostly because of inadequate aggregate absorption. Unemployment may generate accompanying social problems such as crime and substance abuse, as some of the unemployed become penniless and despondent. In the US, the unemployment rate is measured as the percentage of the civilian labor force that is unemployed; where the workforce or labor force (L) is defined as anyone who is 16 years or older who may be employed (E) or unemployed (U); $L=U+E$, or $L-U=E$.

People in the military, prisons, mental hospitals, and nursing homes are excluded from the labor force statistic. Information about monthly job numbers in the US is obtained from two notable outlets: (i) household surveys, and (ii) payroll survey, which is contingent on information provided by companies about changes in staffing conditions.

The undulatory or vacillating pattern of the business cycle generally mirrors patterns of unemployment and employment. For example, in the US, the unemployment rate fell to about 4 percent during the period of expansion in the 1990s. The unemployment rate soared to about 25 percent during the Great Depression of the twentieth century and to about 10 percent during the later days of the Great Recession of the twenty-first century. After the Great Recession, the unemployment rate declined to about 5 percent. According to the September 2011 jobs report, while employment increased by more than 100,000 people, the unemployment rate picture remained unchanged and the number of people who were "involuntary part-time employees" increased in September. Those considered as "long-term unemployed," defined as workers who have been unemployed for more than 27 weeks, represented 44.6 percent of the unemployed. The average workweek remained at similar levels, to be 34.3 hours for all workers and 33.5 hours for non-supervisory production workers (Tranfa-Abboud, 2012, p. 6).

Notwithstanding this somewhat tidy pattern of ebb and flow, economic expansions do not always reflect periods of rising employment; for example, between 1990–1991 and 2001, during periods of expansion, unemployment continued to rise. This positively correlative relationship describes an unusual phenomenon that is widely characterized as "jobless recovery."

The reasons for jobless recovery may not always be very evident, but technological innovation or the infusion of capital into production, increasing levels of productivity, and lagging indicators of unemployment can be very good candidates for explaining the unusual phenomenon. Since 1990, three recessions have been followed by a period of jobless recovery (Krugman & Wells, 2018, p. 216). Consequently, the use of unemployment data as an adjudicative instrument for judicial decisions must proceed with some amount of precaution. Of course, this caveat is tempered by industry-oriented forensic considerations. Unemployment rates must be studied with precaution for other reasons; especially when people are underemployed and utilizing their skills and natural abilities below their full capacity for underpayment, and when they are actually unemployed but considered to be discouraged (not looking for work for a given amount of time). Unemployment may be classified as frictional (when people are between jobs or searching for work), structural (when changes in the economy render some skills obsolete or less appealing), seasonal (when seasonal changes affect the level of unemployment), and cyclical (when a downturn in economic activity causes people to lose their jobs).[2] Economists estimate that unemployment has a natural rate, which is the normal rate of unemployment that consists of frictional and structural unemployment.

The natural rate of unemployment changes over time and is not sacrosanct. Therefore, actual unemployment is the combination of frictional and structural unemployment by theoretical definition. The Congressional Budget Office (CBO), the independent agency that conducts budget and economic analyses for Congress, estimates that the US natural rate of unemployment was 5.3 percent in 1950, 6.3 percent by the end of the 1970s, and 5 percent by 2017 (Krugman & Wells, 2018, p. 223). There is an implicit relationship between unemployment and inflation. Excessive employment induces demand-pull inflation or excessive consumption beyond productive capacity; but inflation can also be induced by the rising cost of production or factor cost. The unemployment rate for which inflation does not change over time (the estimated long-run inflation rate) is usually considered to be the nonaccelerating inflation rate of unemployment.

2.2 FORENSIC IMPLICATIONS OF (INTERNATIONAL) UNEMPLOYMENT

Global unemployment data suggest that there can be a pattern of symmetric shock across various countries. The unemployment rate of the US and UK is virtually invariant after 2012. All the countries show adverse unemployment levels during the Great Recession (2008–2010). Some studies have investigated the potential reasons for the surprisingly different labor market performance of the United States, Canada, Germany, and several other Organization for Economic Cooperation and Development (OECD) countries during and after the Great Recession of 2008–2009.[3] Hoffman and Lemieux (2014) find that while unemployment rates did not change substantially in Germany, they increased and remained at relatively high levels in the US and increased moderately in Canada. Domestic and international comparative studies have shown that inter-sectoral industrial differences can account for variations in unemployment data. In the US, a distinguishing attribute was the relatively poor performance of the construction industry during the recessionary period. However, Hoffman and Lemieux also find that cross-country differences are consistent with Okun's theory that link GDP growth to employment performance. Figure 2.2 shows the trajectory of total unemployment for the US, UK, and Canada. Though there are variations in the levels of unemployment, partly as a result of

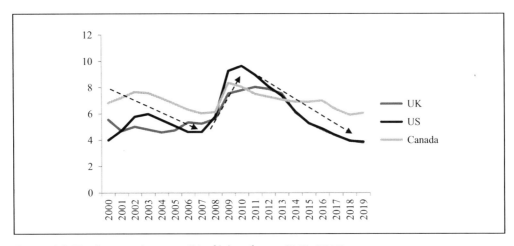

Figure 2.2 Total unemployment (% of labor force, 2000–2019)
Data Source: World Bank's *World Development Indicators* (2019).
Note: Modeled International Labor Organization (ILO) estimates; unemployment refers to the share of the labor force that is without work but available for and seeking employment.

the impact and magnitude of sectoral shocks, the data typify some amount of symmetry in the general direction of overall economic performance or trends. These trends facilitate broader forensic projections that must also take industry variations into consideration. More often than not, forensic projections are territorially limited with implicit assumptions of labor immobility and problems with extraterritorial legal accommodations. Actually, international comparisons and extraterritorial issues may be redundant when international business cycles are highly synchronized or well-coordinated. Yet it is unclear why labor is presumed to be so immobile without international considerations.

One of the main findings of Hoffman and Lemieux is that the US unemployment rate would have been more similar to unemployment rates of Canada, Germany and most other major OECD economies had employment remained stable in the construction sector during both the boom and bust phases of the US housing boom.[4] The synchronization of the business cycle gives the forensic theory of general economic conditions an international appeal. Table 2.1 reveals corroborative evidence in support of the distortionary effect of an adverse sectoral shock. While the manufacturing, transportation and utilities, and financial sectors show relatively low levels of volatility (as measured by their standard deviations), the construction industry reports a higher level of volatility for the period 2000 to 2019. Ironically, of the industries that have been considered in the US sample, the financial industry has the least amount of unemployment volatility. Data for approximately 20 years show that unemployment in the construction industry had the most amount of variability, which can be attributed to the mortgage-backed crisis and construction shock of 2008. The forensic implications of the variations will be substantively explored later.

Legal and illegal termination increases the level of unemployment or underemployment, and wrongfully terminated employees may require compensation or restitution even when employment agencies and courts are corrupt and dysfunctional. Employees may also be injured when they are deliberately deprived of due promotion, or when they suffer physical injury in job related or unrelated matters. The objective of a lost compensation analysis is to provide an estimate of a compensatory amount that would make a plaintiff whole, or in other words, that would restore the plaintiff's pre-incident earnings-related conditions. It is the role of the economic expert to provide an estimate of the compensatory amount that would satisfy this objective. Lost compensation analyses are not "one size fits all." Jurisdiction, type of claim, and employment and economic data are factors that play a key role in the design of the lost compensation model that fits the case.

The economic models that are designed for cases of compensation in courts of law almost always require the use of macroeconomic variables to determine: (i) the period of alleged lost compensation, (ii) compensation structure and potential increases in compensation, (iii) fringe benefits, (iv) eligibility for bonuses, stock options, and other forms of compensation, (v) tax liability, (vi) the probability of continued employment and compensation, (vii) potential or actual considerations mitigating employment and compensation, and (viii) disability benefits in personal injury claims.[5]

Recall that the employment fortunes of some workers are tied to the business cycle (see Figure 2.1). Therefore, it is not certain that some workers will be persistently or permanently employed under all circumstances. Accordingly, the probability that some workers could face periods of unemployment or underemployment is an important factor in estimating lost wages and/or other compensation. Therefore, any "analysis that involves the estimation of lost compensation, whether due to a wrongful termination claim, a claim of personal injury, or a wrongful death matter, needs to incorporate the probability that expected earnings may not have occurred" (Tranfa-Abboud, 2012, p. 5). A very good probabilistic indicator of employment and the duration of employment is the pattern of the business cycle (macroeconomic performance), with a subset consideration of the performance of specific industries.

The cycles generally reveal the amount of jobs that are shed and required to reverse recessionary trends. In effect, compensatory models for lost wages that ignore employment volatility or the probability of unemployment will reflect an exaggerated bias. Therefore, it is not unreasonable to factor economic trends into the consideration of compensations. Duration of trends varies, but trends generally seem to last from about three to five years or more. When it comes to estimating economic damages that incorporate risks, some scholars have suggested the minimum duration of three years.[6] Apparently, not all jobs are sensitive to the business cycle, which is why industry-specific analysis is becoming highly imperative.

Data availability and econometric challenges make the measurement of risky unemployment a nonlinear projection. The options include attrition rates in specific industries, average rate of unemployment over a 30-year span, which is capable of

Table 2.1 US unemployment by industry (%, 2000–2019)*

	Manufacturing	Construction	Transportation and utilities	Financial activities
2000	3.5	6.3	3.4	2.4
2001	5.2	7.1	4.2	2.9
2002	6.7	9.2	4.9	3.6
2003	6.6	9.3	5.3	3.5
2004	5.6	8.4	4.4	3.6
2005	4.9	7.5	4.2	2.9
2006	4.2	6.7	4.0	2.7
2007	4.3	7.4	3.9	3.0
2008	5.8	10.6	5.1	4.0
2009	12.1	19.1	8.9	6.4
2010	10.6	20.6	8.4	6.9
2011	9.0	16.4	8.2	6.4
2012	7.3	13.8	6.9	5.1
2013	6.6	11.3	6.6	4.5
2014	4.9	8.9	5.7	4.0
2015	4.3	7.3	4.4	2.6
2016	4.3	6.3	4.2	2.7
2017	3.6	6.0	4.1	2.4
2018	3.3	5.1	3.4	2.2
2019	3.0	4.4	3.6	2.1
Mean	**5.8**	**9.6**	**5.2**	**3.7**
SD	**2.4**	**4.5**	**1.7**	**1.5**
Max	**12.1**	**20.6**	**8.9**	**6.9**
Min	**3.0**	**4.4**	**3.4**	**2.3**

Data Source: The Federal Reserve Bank of St. Louis (FRED).
Notes:
* Author's computation of annual averages from monthly data. Data for 2019 is from January to October. SD is for standard deviation, Max is for maximum value for approximately 20 years and Min is for minimum values for the same proximate time period. All data are for private wage and salaried workers, and not seasonally adjusted.

analyzing and smoothing potential trends for forecasts, and a disregard of the business cycle as an indicator of pre-incident earnings.

The most reliable way of dealing with these empirical shortcomings is to critically study the historical peculiarities of industries, while fully acknowledging that noisy disturbances are distortionary temporary occurrences; that is, such disturbances do not provide long-lasting conditions for empirical analysis though they can provide some information that is relevant to decisions in the immediate period. Longer time horizons, which are more realistic indicators of time trends, can provide more valuable information for econometric analysis. Compensatory decisions can hardly be made without considerations of interest rate and inflation. These variables are discussed in subsequent sections.

2.3 NOMINAL AND REAL INTEREST RATES

Interest rate is broadly considered to be the cost of borrowing money. Borrowing may straddle assorted periods. In economics, short-term instruments mature in one year or less; conversely, longer-term instruments mature after one year and the interest rates also reflect the attributes that are associated with the maturity of financial instruments. In economics, the rates that are generally considered to be the cost of borrowing money can be modified in courts of law under a legal theory known as the "coerced loan theory." The theory holds that when defendants do not immediately compensate plaintiffs for injuries, the defendants coercively extract loans from the plaintiffs to amounts that are comparable or equivalent to the pecuniary injuries that are inflicted on plaintiffs. The legal theory does not have universal application or appeal for prejudgment, but it underscores an important economic principle that credit imposes a cost on borrowers.

The cost of credit can be annualized in the form of annual percentage rate (APR) or an effective annual rate (EAR), which corrects for tardiness in repayment of loans or credit. Depending on the financial arguments that are made, the APR can be specified as:

$$r = \frac{2 \star n \star I}{P(N+1)}; \qquad (2.1)$$

where P is for the principal, I is for finance charges, n is for the number of annualized payments, and N is for the total amount of payments that are associated with the maturity of a loan. Aforesaid, the formulation is obviously contingent on the type of financial information that is provided for which a solution is sought; the EAR takes an obvious departure:

$$EAR = \left(1 + \frac{i/100}{12}\right)^{12} - 1; \qquad (2.2)$$

where $i/100$ presents the interest rate in decimal form when it is not so stated. Costs of credit can be adjusted for inflation, taxes, and productivity (as and when appropriate) in courts of law. Interest rates are tricky because they are driven by economic conditions and expectations.

Interest rate can be classified into short-term and long-term as well as nominal and real. Short-term rates like Treasury bills and commercial paper, which are otherwise known as money market rates, are applied to investments and loans that mature in one year or less. On the contrary, long-term rates apply to investments and loans with longer maturities. A thorny issue in forensic economics is the rate that must be applied to compensate for inflation. The rate that takes inflation into consideration is generally known as the real interest rate. Predicting inflation has never been an exact science because inflation is driven by a number of elusive factors. However, inflation can be forecasted with some regularity conditions to obtain reasonable or scientific estimates. The real rate of inflation can be specified as the difference between the nominal interest rate (i) and the expected rate of inflation (π^e); ($r = i - \pi^e$). Implicitly, the nominal rate is the sum of the real rate and the percentage of expected inflation.[7]

Interest rates are time-sensitive, and courts of law are aware of the sensitivity of interest rates to the progression of time. Long-term rates that carry very little or no risk have been a very significant jurisprudential benchmark for compensation in the UK and the US. Expectations theory suggests that the interest rate on long-term assets that are risk-free will approximate the average value that investors expect to occur over the life of long-term assets that have very little risk exposure; that is, if investors expect 2 percent to be the average value of interest over the next 5 years, risk-free assets with comparable maturity will also provide a return of 2 percent. The relevant assumption is that buyers do not discriminate on the basis of the maturity of the assets; the assets are perfect substitutes (Mishkin, 2019, p. 127).

In countries with autonomous central banks, monetary policy is critical to establishing the value of short- and long-term interest rates. The banks normally target the rate of inflation, and long-term instruments that incorporate inflation targets become attractive instruments for judicial compensation that is sensitive to inflation. Since the effects of inflation and unemployment cannot be isolated from monetary policy, it is instructive to see how monetary policies have shaped the concept and awareness of inflation. The Taylor rule has been an influential monetary policy rule that targets short-term interest rate to obtain price stability and full employment.[8]

Wicksell (1898) observes that

> If prices rise, the rate of interest is to be raised; and if prices fall, the rate of interest is to be lowered; and the rate of interest is henceforth to be maintained at its new level until a further movement in prices calls for a further change in one direction or the other.

The rule, which has interest rate as an important instrument, has been considered to be reactive and less appealing; probably because of the omission of real economic activity.[9]

> To be useful in practice, policy rules must be simple and transparent to communicate, implement, and verify. This requires a clear choice of what should serve as the policy instrument—for example the money supply, m, or the short-term interest rate, i—and clear guidance as to how any other information necessary to implement the rule—for

instance, recent readings or forecasts of inflation and economy activity— should be used to adjust the policy instrument

(Orphanides, 2007, p. 3).

Milton Friedman's *k-percent* rule suggests that a central bank must maintain a constant growth of the money supply. The rule, which has an interesting parallel to Hume's specie flow mechanism, relates the growth of money and velocity to inflation and the growth of output:

$$\Delta m + \Delta v = \pi + \Delta q \qquad (2.3)$$

where $\pi \equiv \Delta p$ is the rate of inflation and $p, m, v,$ and q are the logarithms of the price level, money stock, money velocity, and real output respectively. Selecting the constant growth of money, k, to correspond to the sum of a desired inflation target, $\pi\star$, and the economy's potential growth rate, $\Delta q\star$, and adjusting for any secular trend in the velocity of money, $\Delta v\star$, suggests a simple rule that can achieve, on average, the desired inflation target, $\pi\star$ (Orphanides, 2007, p. 3):

$$\Delta m = \pi\star + \Delta q\star - \Delta v\star \qquad (2.4)$$

Orphanides notes that an advantage of a constant money growth rule is that very little information is required to implement it. If velocity does not exhibit a secular trend, the only required element for calibrating the rule is the economy's natural growth of output. The monetary rule proposed by John Taylor (1993) has been relatively more consequential. Taylor's rule shows that an autonomous central bank can target the nominal interest rate based on deviations of inflation and output from their targeted levels:

$$i_t = \pi_t + \rho + \theta_\pi(\pi_t - \pi_t^*) + \theta_Y(Y_t - \bar{Y}_t); \qquad (2.5)$$

where π_t^* is a central bank's target for the inflation rate, $\theta\pi$ and θ_Y are policy parameters that indicate how a central bank can adjust its interest rate target to changing economic conditions of inflation and output; larger deviations of the parameters from their targets can induce central banks to be more aggressive in their responses to the deviations. The Fed's targeted inflation rate, π_t^*, is usually presumed to be 2 percent (see also Figure 2.1).[10]

An important empirical estimation of monetary rules, designed to identify simple reactive interest rate rules that would deliver satisfactory economic performance for price stability and economic stability across a range of competing estimated models, was published by the Brookings Institution (Bryant, Hooper, & Mann, 1993).[11] The Brookings project examined rules that set deviations of the short-term nominal interest rate, i, from some baseline path, i★, in proportion to deviations of target variables z, from their targets, z★:

$$i - i\star = \theta(z - z\star). \qquad (2.6)$$

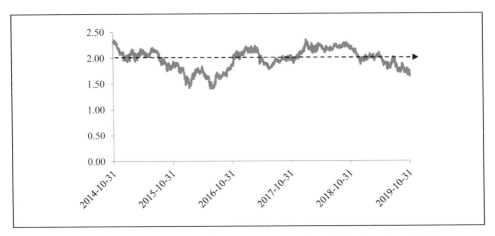

Figure 2.3 Daily five-year forward inflation rates (October 2014–October 2019)
Data Source: Federal Reserve Bank of St. Louis.
Note: Five-year forward expected inflation rates (not seasonally adjusted).

Orphanides notes that the collective findings pointed to two alternatives as the most promising in delivering satisfactory economic performance across models. One targeted nominal income, while the other targeted inflation and real output:

$$i - i^\star = \theta\pi(\pi - \pi^*) + \theta q (q - q^\star) \tag{2.7}$$

Taylor's hypothetical and representative policy rule highlighted the economic relevance of the Brookings project:

$$i = 2 + \pi + 0.5(\pi - 2) + 0.5(q - q^\star). \tag{2.8}$$

The parameterization is believed to have aptly simulated the Fed's policy in the late 1980s and early 1990s.[12] The 2 percent expected inflation rate tends to hold reasonably well over an extended period of time (see also Figure 2.1). However, Orphanides notes that at the zero bound, (see Figure 2.4, 2008/2009 to 2016) the stance of monetary policy can no longer be measured or communicated with a short-term interest rate instrument.

2.4 THE INFLATION FACTOR

Inflation is a sustained increase in the general price level, but monetary policy, which has been discussed in the previous section, could reverse or stabilize the direction of escalating prices. Macroeconomists think that there are two main drivers of inflation: (i) excessive demand (demand-pull inflation), and (ii) increasing cost of production (cost-push inflation). In some countries where banks are not autonomous, excessive liquidity or unchecked increases in the money supply can quickly lead to hyperinflation, which is inflation of about 40 percent per month (Reinhart & Rogoff, 2009, p. 5).

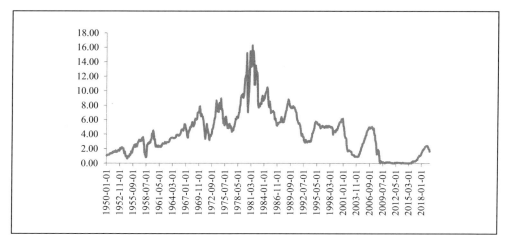

Figure 2.4 Three-month Treasury bill secondary market rate (%) (January 1950–October 2019)
Source: Federal Reserve Bank of St. Louis.
Note: Not seasonally adjusted. This rate generally moves with the expected rate of inflation. Falling and rising rates usually coincide with recessionary and expansionary periods respectively.

Fixed weight indices are popular measures of inflation all over the world. These indices include the consumer price index (CPI), and the producer price index (PPI). These indices are referred to as "fixed" because the weights of their components are generally determined in a base or reference period until the relevant sample is revised. The CPI estimates the prices that are paid by consumers at the retail level over a period of time. Some consumer goods like food and energy have very volatile prices; others, excluding food and energy, tend to be relatively stable and are used to compute "core" inflation. The CPI is the most popular measure of price inflation in the retail of goods and services, and it is currently released on a monthly basis by the Bureau of Labor Statistics (BLS). Changes in the CPI alter the benefits of millions of Social Security recipients and low-income people who receive food stamps. Judges refer to the CPI to compute alimony and child-support payments. The effects of inflation can be characterized as ubiquitous (Baumohl, 2013, p. 305). Major categories of the CPI are housing, food and beverages, transportation, medical care, apparel, recreation, education and communication, and other goods and services; each category having its own weight in the computation of the CPI.

The CPI has international appeal. It is also used as an indicator of inflation in Germany, which is Europe's largest economy. The German CPI is released on a monthly basis by the German Federal Statistics Office. The level of inflation in Germany can have external impact on the growth of the European economy and the monetary policies of the European Central Bank (ECB). All autonomous central banks pay proactive attention to the destabilizing growth of aggregate prices. Therefore, if the rate of inflation is disturbingly increasing in Germany, the ECB will be compelled to pay attention to the surge in prices. Analogously, the Bank of England will not ignore inflationary pressures in the UK. Germany's CPI has also caught the attention of international investors for several decades; especially after its unpleasant experience with hyperinflation of the 1940s.

The German CPI measures the average change in prices for all goods and services that are bought by households for the purpose of consumption. In the middle of the month, about 560 price collectors, working out of state government offices across the country, will collect prices on a basket of 750 specific goods and services. Approximately, 400,000 prices are obtained each month, including taxes (value-added and excise) and price discounts (such as sales or rebates) (Baumohl, 2013, p. 369). Actually, the Eurozone (euro area) has a syndicated inflation report, the Harmonized Index of Consumer Prices (HICP), which is the official report of inflation in the member countries. The members produced an inflation report based on standardized measurements of inflation, for which the Financial Statistics Office provides another version of an inflation report that is not significantly different from the national definition (Baumohl, 2013, p. 370).

Like other consumer price indices, the HICP is consumption oriented, but it provides valuable enabling information. The ECB relies on information about consumer spending and prices to make monetary policy for the Eurozone countries. One of the main objectives of the ECB is price stability and that was a significant precondition for Germany to become part of the Eurozone. The prices measured by the HICP come from the prices of representative goods from urban and rural pricing patterns. The index tracks the prices of goods such as coffee, tobacco, meat, fruit, household appliances, cars, pharmaceuticals, electricity, clothing and many other widely used products. Owner-occupied housing costs are excluded from the HICP. The HICP is also used as the basis of the Monetary Union Index of Consumer Prices (MUICP), an aggregate measure of consumer inflation.[13]

The record of inflation in the US and UK, depicted in Figures 2.5 and 2.6 are somewhat pertinent to the unemployment illustration of Figure 2.1. Inflation tends to rise as unemployment falls. The illustrations also show that the countries are somewhat exposed to drivers of symmetric shocks in the global economy; that is, prices tend to move in a general direction for the countries that have been considered. The information data reinforces theoretical notions about general economic conditions that are not just peculiar to particular countries even though some judicial decisions about economic conditions are surprisingly limited to geographic delineations and industries.

Between 2000 and 2008, inflation in the US, as measured by consumption prices, was relatively high compared to the UK and Germany. However, after 2008—the period of the housing crisis that persisted for over five years—consumer price inflation in the US plummeted precipitously. US inflation has traditionally surpassed that of Germany, but has been occasionally lower than that of the UK. Figure 2.6 mirrors a similar story, except that consumer price inflation in the UK was lower than that of the Eurozone countries from 2000 to 2008. Very reasonable arguments can be made that consumer price inflation in Germany and monetary policies of the ECB have facilitated relative price stability and comparatively lower levels of inflation (compared to the US and UK) after 2013.

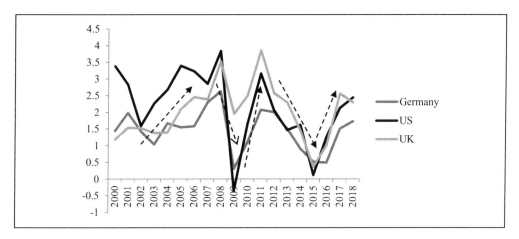

Figure 2.5 Inflation in Germany, US, and the UK: annual percent of consumer prices (2000–2018)
Data Source: World Bank's *World Development Indicators* (2019).

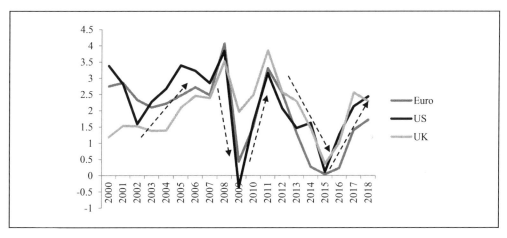

Figure 2.6 Inflation in Eurozone, US, and the UK: annual percent of consumer prices (2000–2018)
Data Source: World Bank's *World Development Indicators* (2019).

Unlike the CPI, the PPI estimates the prices that are paid by producers at three different levels: (i) raw/crude materials, (ii) intermediate materials, and (iii) finished goods. Indices such as the CPI and PPI with a fixed basket of goods are considered to be a *Laspeyres* index, while those with changing baskets are considered to be a *Paasche index*. The implicit price deflator, which is the ratio of nominal to real GDP, is a *Paasche index*. It is a broader measure of inflation, but it is released less frequently. The weights of the goods and services are equal to the quantities of the current period for which the implicit deflator is computed.

The accuracy of implicit deflators is contingent on the velocity of price increases or decreases. As improvements in technology decrease prices, price deflators may not necessarily reflect an accurate trajectory of aggregate prices. The combination of *Laspeyres* and *Paasche* indices can be used to estimate chained price indices. The chained index (CI) uses a previous year's weights to estimate inflation. Accordingly, it is a methodology that links the current rate of inflation to data of a previous year:

$$CI = \frac{q_{1t} * p_{1t} + q_{2t} * p_{2t} + \ldots q_{nt} * p_{nt}}{q_{1t} * p_{1t-1} + q_{2t} * p_{2t-1} + \ldots + q_{nt} * p_{nt-1}}; \quad (2.9)$$

where q is for quantities and p is for prices of the respective goods with the corresponding lag indicators (t-1) for the prices of previous years. However, the components of constant dollar (real) GDP no longer sum up to total GDP (Evans, 2004, p. 74). The unemployment rate at which inflation does not change is known as the nonaccelerating inflation rate of unemployment (NAIRU). Inflation adversely impacts investors in fixed income markets when they are not compensated by the real rate of interest. Therefore, courts of law will appropriately pay attention to increasing levels of prices when plaintiffs must be made whole because of injuries and loss of purchasing power.

Depending on the types of arguments to be made and tolerable judicial tradition, other measures of inflation can be instructive. In the US, the employment cost index (ECI) is another indicator of inflation for a very specific purpose. It is the most comprehensive measure of labor cost, but courts are not generally inclined to use it as a measure of inflation. The ECI is released on a quarterly basis by the BLS. The ECI is a proactive indicator of inflation rather than a reactive (*ex post facto*) measurement of inflation. In effect, it can be considered a potential harbinger of inflation. The ECI estimates the cost of labor, which is the greatest component of the variable costs of companies.

> Labor-related outlays on wages, salaries, and fringe benefits (such as vacations, health insurance, and Social Security) account for more than 70% of the cost of making a product. Employees make up such a huge proportion of operating expenses that any significant acceleration in compensation can quickly cut into corporate profits and pressure companies to pass on these additional costs to consumers in the form of higher prices.
>
> (Baumohl, 2013, p. 323)

The danger of employment related inflation is that it can quickly become inertial. As retailers increase prices, a corresponding snowball effect is that workers will require higher wages to offset the cost of inflation in order to salvage the dwindling value of nominal income. Job-related actions and reactions can set off detrimental inflationary spirals. However, prices increases can be tempered by the willingness and ability of firms to absorb some of the cost pressures without transmitting the pressures to consumers. Like most if not all indices, the ECI relies on surveys of private and public sectors. Notably, wage-related issues and employment conditions can proactively influence the monetary policies of autonomous banks.

2.5 INTEREST RATES AND INFLATION IN COURTS OF LAW

Courts of law are generally interested in the appropriate value of interest rate and inflation when economic losses have been incurred in personal injury and wrongful death cases. Accordingly, the macroeconomic variables have a very long-lasting presence in courts of law. The legal issues routinely involve the type of interest rate that should be used and the appropriate measurement of inflation as and when necessary.

In 1916 the US Supreme Court in *Kelly v. Chesapeake & Ohio* established the legal principals "that when future payments or other pecuniary benefits are to be anticipated, the verdict should be made on the basis of their present value only" (Strangways et al., 2014, p. 491) and that the interest to be used should be based on "the best and safest" investment (Strangways et al., 2014, p. 491). Safest instruments are assets with very low probability of default, and US Treasuries have traditionally met that requirement. Financial instruments that adjust for inflation can also be very good proxies of the real interest rate, which was discussed in the previous section. Treasury Inflation Protected Securities (TIPS), which were first issued in the US in 1997, and similarly situated securities in Europe, have been very good candidates to deal with the issue of real interest rate and inflation. Of course, the selection of instruments has not been a spontaneous revelation and there have been long and acrimonious debates about desirable assets. Some people who are risk-averse might demonstrate affinity for risk-free securities; on the contrary, others who are risk-loving will welcome greater returns for their sophisticated risky decisions in financial markets. But courts must ultimately make a decision to not undercompensate or overcompensate litigants. Some states set a fixed prejudgment interest rate by statute, but others tie the rate to an established index (see Philips & Freeman, 2001).

The attractiveness of inflation indexed securities is that they eliminate the arduous task of forecasting inflation with precision; these categories of financial assets protect investors from unanticipated inflation, but taxes complicate their usefulness. The combination of inflation and taxation complicate the analysis of the appropriate discount rate for judicial awards. Taxes will be discussed in Chapter 6, in the context of avoidance and evasion. Though there is some amount of controversy over what should be the appropriate discount rate, with some tolerance for divergent risk profiles, the traditional view has shown strong preference for "risk-free" rates ever since the Supreme Court ruling in *Kelly v. Chesapeake & Ohio Railway Co.* (1916). The court based its decision on a legal principle that verdicts involving future pecuniary payments should be based on present value only.[14]

Since investments can be exposed to multiple risks, such as exchange rate risk, default risk, inflation risk, and market risk, there are other financial risks that courts have dealt with; notably inflation. Since the magnitude of inflation can be unanticipated, unanticipated inflation (λ) is the difference or discrepancy between actual (π) and forecasted inflation (π^e). The inflation discrepancy (λ) can be conveniently denoted as:

$$\lambda = \pi - \pi^e \qquad (2.10)$$

Equation 2.10 shows that when actual inflation increasingly deviates from the expected level of inflation, the inflation discrepancy will get larger. The discrepancy can also be enlarged if projected forecasts are increasingly biased downwards. Invariably, the direction of forecast errors can easily overcompensate or undercompensate litigants.

Strangways et al. (2014) underscore the importance inflationary pressures in the landmark case of *Jones & Laughlin v. Pfeifer* (1983).[15] While the Supreme Court alluded to the controlling law of the case, it highlighted the importance of discounting lump sum awards in an inflationary environment. The Supreme Court considered several methodologies utilized by US Federal Courts and other common law countries to account for inflation and a fair discount rate. *Pfeifer* reaffirmed the preference for the best and safest investment and by so doing extended the precedential value of *Kelly v. Chesapeake & Ohio Railway Co.* (1916). The court ruled:

> Once it is assumed that the injured worker would definitely have worked for a specific term of years, he is entitled to a risk-free stream of future income to replace his lost wages; therefore, the discount rate should not reflect the market's premium for investors who are willing to accept some risk of default.
>
> (*Jones & Laughlin v. Pfeifer*, 1983, p. 537)[16]

The court further noted that the calculation of present value should be based on two elements: (i) projected income that a worker would have earned, and (ii) "the appropriate discount rate, reflecting the safest available investment" (*Jones & Laughlin v. Pfeifer*, 1983, pp. 537–538).[17]

Unsurprisingly, the court also acknowledged the ubiquitous presence of inflation that had been a permanent feature of the US economy for decades, noting that the existence of inflation must be recognized in the process of calculating equitable awards. The computation of inflation was considered to be a second stage of the discounting formulation, with recognition of the fact that expected inflation affects market rates of return.

> If a lender knows that his loan is to be repaid a year later with dollars that are less valuable than those he has advanced, he will charge an interest rate that is high enough both to compensate him for the temporary use of the loan proceeds and also to make up for their shrinkage in value.
>
> (*Jones & Laughlin v. Pfeifer*, 1983, pp. 538–539)[18]

In macroeconomic terms, the court was alluding to the Fisherian equation of nominal interest rate (i), which incorporates a real (r) rate and expected inflation (π^e); where $i = r + \pi^e$. Recall that the empirical evidence, including the Taylor Rule, has reasonably estimated the real interest rate to be about 2 percent (see Figure 2.3). The default real interest rate has been two percent, dating as far back as 1980. In *Doca v. Marina Mercante*

Nicaraguense (1980), the court ruled that trial judges may use a real interest rate of 2 percent. In many ways, *Pfeifer* minimized the vagaries of expected inflation, which had included speculative wage inflation (also recall the discussion of the ECI in the previous section). Notwithstanding, the United Kingdom, Canada, and Australia have shown tolerance for the use of real interest rates or growth rates of real wages (Strangways et al., 2014, p. 87). Invariably, no economy can claim to be permanently immune from the corrosive effects of inflation.

Pfeifer opened the door for competing but limited methodologies to estimate inflation for judicial awards. Three methodologies gained judicial recognition: (i) the nominal (or market) interest rate, (ii) the real interest rate (or below market rate), and (iii) the total offset methods. However, market estimations with wage projections were discouraged. The court did not impose a methodology but conceded that a rate between 1 and 3 percent is not objectionable. Trial judges have used real interest rate of 2 percent when there is no convincing evidence to persuade them otherwise (see *McCrann v. United States Lines, Inc.* (1986) and *Ammar v. United States* (2003)).

Some courts have been open to rates that are below markets rates, but establishing rules for such rates have been rather imprecise. TIPS have provided very good alternatives to imprecise measurements of inflation. Strangways et al. (2014) find that assets that are indexed to inflation have some international recognition; for example:

> In Hong Kong the claimant in personal injury litigation should be assumed to invest the lump sum award in low-risk investment vehicles. Under the linked exchange rate system we believe the average real rate of return from U.S. Treasury inflation-indexed securities is an appropriate yardstick for the determination of the discount rate in Hong Kong.[19]

Inflation protected securities are issued in several countries, including Canada and the UK, and in countries with reliable governments and stable democracies they are guaranteed by central governments with a track record of credibility. In the US, coupon payments are adjusted by unadjusted percentage changes in the CPI. Accordingly, projected inflation is built into these securities with very low probability of default (default risk). In *Wells v. Wells* (1999), the British House of Lords held that discount rate should be assessed on the assumption that the claimant will invest in Index Linked Government Securities (ILGS), which were first issued in 1981 and comparable to the TIPS.[20] The Damage Act of 1996 had authorized the Lord Chancellor to issue a declaration prescribing the appropriate discount rate that should be used by courts in the UK to discount damage awards. Between 1999 and June 2000, the discount rate hovered around 2.5 percent in Britain. The discount rate remained at 2.5 percent until 2017 but has been substantially reduced to below 1 percent at the time of this writing. The change should not be entirely surprising. Consider Figures 2.5 and 2.6. Between 2011 and 2015, consumer price inflation plummeted steeply; thereafter prices returned to a steep rise until 2017. Curiously, this pattern is not peculiar to the UK, which means that more information should be desired beyond the threat of inflation. Lewis (2012) observes that the law is intended to make the rate more stable to avoid frequent changes.

Canada also uses the real rate for the purpose of discounting awards to the present. However, Rotstein (2013) notes that provinces individually determine the discount rate.

> Seven of the provinces (Ontario, British Columbia, Nova Scotia, Saskatchewan, Manitoba, New Brunswick, and Prince Edward Island) have prescribed specific rates to be used for discounting pecuniary losses. In six of the provinces the discount rate is between 2.5% and 3.5%.
>
> (Rotstein, 2013)[21]

A two-tier approach was adopted in Ontario (2000), which sets one rate for the first 15-year period following the date of trial and a different rate for all later years (Dionne, 2011). The discount rate for the first 15 years is equal to the average interest rate on long-term Canadian Government Bonds. While there is no guarantee that the real interest rate will perpetually hover around 2 to 3 percent, the literature reveals that the rate has hovered around 2 to 3% in the common law countries for a very long period of time dating back to the 1980s. However, introducing taxes into the legal discussion complicates the discounting arguments.

First, consider a pre-tax multiplier. Knoll and Colon (2005) show that courts most often assess the final award by first calculating a multiplier (denoted by m), which, when applied to the original judgment (J), produces the final judgment (PV):

$$PV = J \star m; \text{ where } m = \left(1 + \frac{r_m}{n}\right)^{nT}; \qquad (2.11)$$

where r_m is the prejudgment interest rate, n is the number of compounding periods in a year, and T is the prejudgment period in years. Accordingly, setting the multiplier entails three tasks: (i) setting the prejudgment interest rate (r_m), (ii) calculating the prejudgment period (T), and (iii) determining the frequency with which interest is compounded (n) (the formula assumes that prejudgment interest will be compounded. Although interest in commercial settings is always compounded, courts sometimes award prejudgment interest using simple interest, which is the traditional common law rule. They argue that courts should, however, award compound prejudgment interest).

The term structure of interest rates shows the time dynamics of interest payments on an asset until the time of maturity (yield). Aforesaid, long-term rates interest rates usually vary with the duration of an investment. The longer-term interest rates usually exceed short-term rates and when a reversal occurs, that is usually considered to be an inverse yield, reflecting the pessimism of investors in the current period. The two-percent rule is generally considered to be consistent with long-term rates and expectations theory. Notably, the application of ten one-year rates that are compounded to the present will give a different result from a ten-year rate, with the ten-year rate reflecting a higher value (Knoll & Colon, 2005, p. 16). In contradistinction, the mutual settlement of disputes favorably considers short-term rates, which implicitly suggests that the use of long-term rates discourages the incentive to settle. An interesting proposition by Knoll and Colon (2005) is that the risk element need not be an inherent consideration since prejudgment rates are set *ex post facto* with knowledge of all available information; meaning that courts should use floating variable rates that exclude premium for interest rate risk.[22]

Discounting and tax considerations have raised an issue of timing since plaintiffs do not pay tax on prejudgment interest until the award date; meaning that plaintiffs are able to defer the tax payments on their earnings to the award date (compared to receiving compensation immediately at the time of injury and investing the proceeds in taxable bonds). Knoll and Colon (2005) adjust the multiplier for tax payments. They argue that to make adjustments for the benefit of deferral, courts should compound prejudgment interest at the product of defendant's cost of unsecured borrowing, denominated by one minus the plaintiff's tax rate over the prejudgment period on the award date.[23] When courts take into account the tax on prejudgment interest, their multiplier, denoted by m_{AT} becomes:

$$m_{AT} = \frac{\left(1+\frac{r_m^{AT}}{n}\right)^{nT} - 1}{1-t_r} + 1; \qquad (2.12)$$

where t_T is the tax rate in year T and r_m^{AT} is the mean after-tax interest rate, with $r_i = r_i(1-t)$.

In their estimation, courts might also need to adjust the multiplier to reflect the tax treatment of the original judgment. Equations (2.11) and (2.12) implicitly assume that the plaintiff would not have paid any taxes if the defendant had immediately compensated the plaintiffs; so that the plaintiff could have invested the entire payment. If, however, the plaintiff had to pay taxes on any payment received from the defendant, then the plaintiff would have been able to invest only the after-tax amount, which would have limited interest earnings. Therefore, they argue that when the original judgment is taxable, the multiplier (m_{AT}), can be modified to be m'_{AT}:

$$m'_{AT} = \frac{(1-t_o)\left(1+\frac{r_m^{AT}}{n}\right)^{nT}}{1-t_r} \qquad (2.13)$$

where t_T and r_m^{AT} are as defined in Equation (2.12) and t_o is the tax rate at the time of injury. Multipliers calculated using Equation (2.12) will usually exceed those calculated using Equation (2.13).[24]

Incidences of taxation modify award multipliers (the present value interest factor). Further, they argue that the applicable multiplier should be contingent on a plaintiff's tax status and the taxability of the award. When plaintiffs are exempted from taxation, courts should use Equation (2.11). However, when plaintiffs have tax liabilities on taxable interest income, they propose that courts should use either Equation (2.12) or Equation (2.13). If the award is also taxable, they observe that Equation (2.13) gives the correct multiplier. On the other hand, if the award is not taxable, then Equation (2.12) gives the correct multiplier. In general, the award is taxable if it compensates the plaintiff for lost income, but not if it compensates for an otherwise deductible loss. Strangways et al. (2014) highlight the mixture of taxes and inflation.

Taxing of interest income on TIPS is comprised of two components. The first is a tax on the annual cash interest received. As expected, income taxes on the periodic interest payments reduce the real rate of return. The standard expression to adjust for taxes is $r = i(1-t)$, in which r denotes the real after-tax rate of return if the security is held to maturity, i denotes the coupon (real) interest rate used to calculate interest payments, and t denotes the marginal tax rate on interest income. If inflation is stable for the life of the security, the inflation rate which makes the rate of return equal to zero depends on the real pre-tax interest rate on the bond and the tax rate:

$$\pi = \frac{r(t-1)}{r-tr-t}; \tag{2.14}$$

where π denotes the inflation rate, r denotes the pre-tax real interest rate of TIPS, and t denotes the marginal tax rate on interest and increase in principal.

Macroeconomic theories of inflation and taxation have some consistency with judicial theories of compensation. The use of net income (income after taxes) in courts of law prevents overcompensation in cases where taxes have to be paid. Invariably, not all awards are taxable and nontaxable awards cannot be subjected to discounting methodologies that are designed for taxable awards. Accordingly, discount rates incorporating after-tax rates must be relevant to the discounting algorithms of net income or taxable awards.

In the US, interest rate litigation is also extended to post-judgment. Interest is allowed on most judgment awards entered in the federal courts from the date of judgment until the awards are paid (post-judgment). Judgments generally fall under one of three statutes: (i) 28 U.S.C. 1961, which governs civil and bankruptcy adversary judgment interest; (ii) 18 U.S.C. 3612 (f)(2), which governs criminal judgments or sentences; and (iii) 40 U.S.C. 3116, which governs deficiency judgments in condemnation proceedings. Under each of the aforementioned statutes, the rate of interest used in calculating the amount of post-judgment interest is the weekly average one-year constant maturity (nominal) Treasury yield, published by the Federal Reserve System.

Prior to December 21, 2000, the rate of interest allowed under the statutes cited above was based on the coupon issue yield equivalent (as determined by the Secretary of the

Table 2.2 Pre- and post-judgment rates in Alaska (1997–2019)

Year	Federal reserve discount rate on January 2	Pre- and post-judgment interest rate for judgment entered that year
1997*	5%	8%
1998	5%	8%
1999	4.5%	7.5%
2000	5%	8%
2001	6%	9%
2002	1.25%	4.25%
2003	0.75%	3.75%
2004	2%	5%
2005	3.25%	6.25%
2006	5.25%	8.25%
2007	6.25%	9.25%
2008	4.75%	7.75%
2009–2010	0.5%	3.5%
2011–2015	0.75%	3.75%
2016	1%	4%
2017	1.25%	4.25%
2018	2%	5%
2019	3%	N/A

Source: Public Courts Alaska.
Note:
* After the August 7, 1997 effective date of the current interest rate law (§§ 18 and 55 Ch 26 SLA 1997).

Treasury) of the average accepted auction price for the last auction of 52 week t- bills settled immediately preceding entry of the judgment. The way the rate is used differs under each of the cited statutes, so those sections should be reviewed to determine how to apply it to any particular judgment.[25]

Some states actually legislate pre- and post-judgment rates for awards; for example, see the Alaskan schedule in Table 2.2.

2.6 OPEN MACROECONOMICS AND EXCHANGE RATE LAW

Exchange rates are determinative in specific periods, but they can be volatile over a period of time; that is, the value of exchange rates can be determined on a particular date,

Table 2.3 Exchange rate arrangements (2010–2018)*

Type	2010	2011	2012	2013	2014	2015	2016	2017	2018
Hard peg	13.2	13.2	13.2	13.1	13.1	12.6	13	12.5	12.5
Currency board	6.9	6.3	6.3	6.3	6.3	5.8	5.7	5.7	5.7
Soft peg	39.7	43.2	39.5	42.9	43.5	47.1	39.6	42.2	46.4
Conventional	23.3	22.6	22.6	23.6	23.0	23.0	22.9	22.4	22.4
Crawling peg	1.6	1.6	1.6	1.0	1.0	1.6	1.6	1.6	1.6
Floating	36	34.7	34.7	34	34	35.1	37	35.9	34.4
Free floating	15.9	15.8	16.3	15.7	15.2	15.7	16.1	16.1	16.1
Residual	11.1	8.9	12.6	9.9	9.4	5.2	10.4	9.4	6.8

Source: IMF's *Annual Report on Exchange Arrangements and Exchange Restrictions* (AREAER) (2018, p. 8).
Note:
* Percent of IMF members as of April 30 includes 189 member countries and three territories: Aruba and Curaçao and Sint Maarten (all in the Kingdom of the Netherlands) and Hong Kong SAR (China). Hard peg includes no separate legal tender; soft peg consists of conventional peg, stabilized arrangement, crawl-like arrangements, and pegged rates within horizontal bands; floating rates are classified into floating and free floating.[26]

but the value cannot be presumed to be sacrosanct as time changes. Uncertainty of the value of currencies was heightened after the movement from the fixed exchange rate to the flexible and/or managed exchange rate systems; especially after the collapse of the Bretton Woods system in 1971. The global economy now has a variety of exchange rate arrangements (see Table 2.3).

Exchange arrangements fall into four general categories: (i) hard pegs, which minimize the variability of the value of the pegged currencies, (ii) soft pegs, which are relatively variable pegs, (iii) floating rates, which are susceptible to a considerable amount of volatility, and (iv) residually managed rates. A considerable amount of countries have consistently shown a preference for soft pegs.

A currency board is a *de jure* exchange rate arrangement or an explicit legislative commitment to exchange a domestic currency for a specified amount of foreign currency at a fixed rate. The issuing authorities normally issue restrictions that will enable them to fulfill their exchange commitment to enhance the international credibility of their monetary and financial system. The legislative commitment ensures that the domestic currency is fully backed by foreign assets and the traditional functions of a central bank, including that of a lender-of-last-resort, is eliminated. Banking flexibility is contingent on the degree of legislative strictness.

In the case of stabilized arrangement, a spot market exchange rate is maintained within a margin of 2 percent for six months or more, which is not floating.

The required margin of stability can be met either with respect to a single currency or a basket of currencies, where the anchor currency or the basket is ascertained or confirmed using statistical techniques. Classification as a stabilized arrangement requires that the statistical criteria are met and that the exchange rate remains stable as a result of official action (including structural market rigidities). The classification does not imply a policy commitment on the part of the country authorities.

(International Monetary Fund, 2018).

Floating exchange rates are largely determined by the market forces of demand and supply for a currency. As such the rate is hardly ascertainable or predictable.

In particular, an exchange rate that satisfies the statistical criteria for a stabilized or a crawl-like arrangement will be classified as such unless it is clear that the stability of the exchange rate is not the result of official actions. Foreign exchange market intervention may be either direct or indirect, and such intervention serves to moderate the rate of change and prevent undue fluctuations in the exchange rate, but policies targeting a specific level of the exchange rate are incompatible with floating. Indicators for managing the rate are broadly judgmental (e.g., balance of payments position, international reserves, parallel market developments). Floating arrangements may exhibit more or less exchange rate volatility, depending on the size of the shocks affecting the economy.

(AREAER) (IMF, 2018, p. 46)

Crawling pegs require *de jure* affirmation and the exchange rates are adjusted incrementally.

The currency is adjusted in small amounts at a fixed rate or in response to changes in selected quantitative indicators, such as past inflation differentials vis-à-vis major trading partners or differentials between the inflation target and expected inflation in major trading partners. The rate of crawl can be set to generate inflation-adjusted changes in the exchange rate (backward looking) or set at a prehdetermined fixed rate and/or below the projected inflation differentials (forward looking). The rules and parameters of the arrangement are public or notified to the IMF.

(AREAER) (IMF, 2018, p. 45)[27]

Exchange rates are ratios of the value of currencies, usually the value of the domestic currency relative to a foreign currency or a basket of foreign currencies, such as the Special Drawing Rights (SDRs). SDRs are supplementary foreign exchange reserve assets or unit of account, defined and maintained by the International Monetary Fund (IMF).[28] The SDR is a synthetic currency unit that is occasionally referred to as "paper gold," because it augmented the gold supply of the 1970s. Therefore, an exchange rate indicates the amount of foreign currencies that can be fetched by a domestic currency over a period of time.

The assorted classifications of exchange rates partly indicate why the value of currencies can be volatile. Disputes over the value of currencies have macro and civil (tort) implications. This chapter will focus on the civil implications. In the US, civil infractions are dealt with in civil courts of original jurisdiction, from which escalation can take place to higher levels of adjudication; other cases fall in the realm of international disputes that involve autonomous states. However, apart from international trade, the international environment does not have well-developed tribunals to deal with currency issues among individuals or private citizens. States may however act on behalf of their citizens. Cases involving macro stability and exchange rates and international trade will be dealt with in Chapter 8.

In open macroeconomics, exchange rates play a critical role through the net exports channel, the channel that deals with exports and imports of goods, services, and assets. It is presumed that exports will increase relative to imports, *ceteris paribus*, when the value of a currency depreciates or is being devalued. For several years, this theory significantly guided the multilateral and supranational policy of the IMF for conditional (short-term) lending, which is based on the Articles of Agreement of the IMF. In actual fact, the economic disturbances that destabilized exchange rate alignments in the post-1970s—long after the Articles of Agreement were ratified—are contingent on a host of other refractory and exogenous factors, including restrictive trade policies abroad and local government corruption that are generally unsuitable for parameterized exchange rate models.

On the civil side, courts of law are periodically or occasionally conflicted over the appropriate exchange rate that must be used in cases involving two or more currencies. Two competing theories serve as reference points for awards: (i) the date of breach, and (ii) the date of award. Evidently, the intertemporal variability of the value of exchange rates is hardly taken into consideration. In actual fact, currencies can have wild intertemporal swings between the date of breach and the date of award. Can there be a general principle that can be used to smooth exchange rate variability without punishing plaintiffs or defendants? In this book, I argue that considerations must be given to the weighted value of exchange rates from the date of infraction to the award date in order to smooth exchange rate volatility for fairer conversion rates and judicial compensation.

Decisions involving civil cases, which are susceptible to municipal laws and extraterritorial jurisdiction, are contingent on the plurality of municipal laws, though customary international laws occasionally inform judicial decisions. Aforesaid, unlike the provisions for international trade dispute resolutions, there has not been a well-developed international forum for handling civil cases that appertain to currency valuation. The International Court of Justice (ICJ) constitutes a forum, but only if states are willing to submit disputes to the competence of the court. The IMF deals with the stabilization of the value of currencies so that adverse public policies, including manipulative devices, will not pose a threat to global macroeconomic and financial stability. Consequently, civil currency cases are riddled with issues of extraterritoriality (national autonomy), currency conversion rates, and plurality of laws.

A theory that is conspicuously utilized to resolve currency dispute in the US is based on a restatement of conflict laws, which stipulates choice of law considerations. The appropriate law is based on the law of the country that has the most significant interest in the issue or case at hand. The state, where the conduct or injury occurred is not necessarily the state most concerned with the judgment for damages resulting from a tort. The relevant factors that are considered in determining the relationship of a state to an action are the needs of the interstate and international systems, the policies of the forum, the policies of other interested states, a state's justifiable expectations, certainty, predictability, uniformity, and ease of application of the governing law (Egan, 1982, p. 172).

Since exchange rate is a tricky phenomenon, and loss of value or realization of gain cannot be ascertained in specific periods that are detached from the real effects of exchange rate volatility, compensation must straddle all periods for which injury is inflicted. Of course, the contractual date must be the initial condition, but when injury goes beyond the contractual date *ex post facto*, injury cannot be cured by limitations to a contractual date; that is, transitional volatility of exchange rates, which may result in loss or gain, must be accounted for in order for justice to produce wholesome effects. The foregoing argument is independent of whether some currencies, like convertible currencies, have a low degree of variability (see Table 2.4).

Consider an American firm that has to be compensated in US dollars; further, imagine that the contract was denominated in euros and that an effective pecuniary contractual breach occurred in 2010. The breach date principle suggests that the conversion rate should have been $1.36 (€0.74). However, the US dollar would have been worth $1.18 (€0.85) if the judgment was rendered in 2018 or if the judgment criterion is the controlling law. Clearly, the rates are bifurcated with losses for the American firm when the breach date is utilized and overcompensation for the American firm when the judgment date is preferred. The intertemporal controversy can be avoided if a general conversion principle considers the volatility of asset value between the two periods. One of such theories is the weighted value of the assets ($1.23 or €0.85) that endogenizes the magnitude of volatility in asset valuation; realizing that the American company suffered injury at a time when the dollar was both weak and strong from 2010 to 2018.

Notably, with very low standard deviations or degree of variability (0.17 and 0.19), the convertible currencies under review (for a given time period) are not as volatile as one might generally presume. Yet the size of compensation is apparently material when large sums of money are at issue; for example, a 20 cents gain on every dollar for a $1m award will amount to $200,000; on the contrary a 20 cents gain on every dollar for $100 will amount to $20. Evidently, courts can be open to a conversion rule of general application (*Competex v. LaBow*). Accordingly, the weighted average of exchange rates from the date

Table 2.4 Exchange rates (January 1999–January 2018)*

Year	US ($)/€	US ($)/CAD($)	US ($)/£
1999	1.0653	1.4858	1.6172
2000	0.9232	1.4855	1.5156
2001	0.8952	1.5487	1.4396
2002	0.9454	1.5704	1.5025
2003	1.1321	1.4008	1.6347
2004	1.2438	1.3017	1.8330
2005	1.2449	1.2115	1.8204
2006	1.2563	1.1340	1.8434
2007	1.3711	1.0734	2.0020
2008	1.4726	1.0660	1.8545
2009	1.3935	1.1412	1.5661
2010	1.3261	1.0298	1.5452
2011	1.3931	0.9887	1.6043
2012	1.2859	0.9995	1.5853
2013	1.3281	1.0300	1.5642
2014	1.3297	1.1043	1.6484
2015	1.1096	1.2791	1.5284
2016	1.1072	1.3243	1.3555
2017	1.1301	1.2984	1.2890
2018	1.1817	1.2957	1.3363
Mean	1.2100	1.2400	1.6000
SD	0.1700	0.1900	0.1900
Maximum Appreciation	0.9000	0.9900	1.29[φ]
Minimum Depreciation	1.4700	1.5700	2.0000
Weighted Mean ($\bar{x}_w$)	1.23	1.27	1.63

Data Source: Federal Reserve Bank of St. Louis (FRED).
Notes:
* Not seasonally adjusted. [φ] Notwithstanding the appreciation, the US dollar remained overvalued relative to the British pound. $\bar{x} = \sum_{i=1}^{n} w_i x_i$.

of infraction to judgment day—with penalties for delay thereafter—provides an attractive alternative to mitigate unsettling conversion and volatility issues.

Courts in the United States express money judgments for damages in dollars, but they generally ignore fluctuations in the value of the dollar between the time of injury or breach and the time of judgment. The courts generally use either the conversion rate available as of the date of injury or the date of judgment. Most federal and state courts faced with the foreign currency conversion issue have adopted the two-rule doctrine established by the Supreme Court in *Hicks v. Guinness* (269 U.S. 71 (1925)) and *Die Deutsche Bank Filiale Nurnberg v. Humphrey* (272 U.S. 517 (1926)). The two-rule doctrine dictates the proper use of either the breach date or the judgment date for conversion of damages into United States dollars (Egan, 1982, p. 166).

The breach date rule requires conversion of a foreign currency judgment at the exchange rate available on the date of the injury, while the judgment date rule sets the conversion rate as of the date of final judgment. The benchmarks have been tied to the definitions, functions, or perceptions of money. The jurisprudential characterization of money is bifurcated; money is conceptualized as a commodity (implicitly, medium of exchange) or measure of money. In economics, the definition of money is wholesome with functions that are more variegated to include store of value, unit of account, and standard of deferred payment; where the latter can be associated with the coercive loan theory. The dichotomous representation of the monetary theory suggests that the value of money fluctuates when it is used as a commodity in the market place (for a breach date) but not when it is used as a measure of value (for the judgment date).[29] Ironically, the value of currency is fixed, but prices are settled on a daily basis until contracts are fulfilled in commodity markets.

Since a convertible currency, like United States dollars, operates as money in the US where it is issued, it is presumed that the claim for foreign money cannot fluctuate with exchange rates involving the US dollar. The judgment date rule is an attempt to limit the value of recovery that a foreign court would have awarded a plaintiff, but the weighted value of exchange rates is capable of mooting such a concern. In actual fact, relative to the options or controversies of the 1920s, the competing dates have been whittled down after a long history of precedents with international appeal.[30] In the 1920s, the Court of Appeal in England, in *Di Ferdinando v. Sinton, Smits & Co.*, a suit for breach of contract of carriage and conversion, laid down the rule that the correct rate to apply was the rate prevailing on the date the breach of contract and conversion took place.[31] In *Di Ferdinando*, the trial court fixed the damages as the market value of the goods at the place—Italy, and time (February 10, 1919)—set by the contract for delivery; and the amount so fixed was 48,000 Italian lire, though the value of the lire had increased since the date of breach and conversion (Gluck, 1922, p. 220). The earlier cases relied on the presumption that there was no difference in principle between a contract and tort action, even when there were prospective or continuing damages.

Egan notes that the Supreme Court followed a nineteenth-century "vested rights" (territoriality autonomy) choice of law theory in *Hicks and Humphrey*. Under the vested rights theory, the function of money in the country where the breach occurred is determinative. For example, the breach of a foreign money contract in the United States creates a claim for a fixed value of dollars as of the date of the breach; gains or losses from volatility are foreclosed. However, under the doctrine of territorial autonomy, the law of a nation does not operate directly beyond its territorial limits and a domestic court is not expected to apply domestic law to a foreign right, since a foreign law determines the existence and extent of an obligation. Thus, the US can enforce but not alter rights created by foreign laws. Pointedly, the vested rights theory requires a determination of which country's law should govern the cause of action and the governing law determines whether a currency acts as a commodity or as money.[32]

Applications of extraterritorial laws to foreign currency awards have limitations. Applications of foreign laws are inadmissible when they are contrary to the policies of a state (forum state) and the *situs* of an action or court. "A forum court could refuse to enforce a foreign claim if the forum court had a policy against foreign laws that are different but do not conflict with the law of the forum" (Egan, 1982, p. 175). The local-law theory supports the authority of local jurisdiction or forums to establish rights and remedies for all cases. There is a presumption that foreign states and forum courts must be able to create comparable rights under extraterritorial laws. Under the local-law theory, a United States court would use the judgment date rule only when the court found it appropriate to fashion a remedy similar to the remedy created by the foreign law.[33] Yet without considerations of volatility, inflation, and alternative forms of investments in which money can serve as a store of value, such decisions may have confiscatory and prejudicial effects. Additionally, the local law has no clearly defined parameters for determining the controlling state or forum law.

Not all courts and jurisdictions, including the US, have shown a preference for local currencies. In *Miliangos v. George Frank Ltd.* (1975) the House of Lords overruled centuries of English common law requiring all judicial awards be denominated in pounds sterling (Beal, 2014, p. 120). In the 1970s, English precedent showed a strong preference to the breach date rule and conversion into pound sterling. However, the devaluation of the pound sterling relative to the Swiss franc (the contractual currency) created the specter of a colossal loss (£28,000) between the breach date and the judgment date (Beal, 2014, p. 221). The realignment of exchange rate and the specter of a colossal loss induced Lord Wilberforce to adopt a rule that would allow for foreign currency awards; analogously, money as a measure of value.[34] The House of Lords was strongly persuaded and motivated by the desire to formulate a rule that would not disadvantage plaintiffs in times of the depreciation (market-based decline in value) or devaluation (policy-based reduction in value) of the pound. However, Beal observes that the majority decisions in the House of Lords did not address the potential that the new rule might be detrimental to injured parties in times of an appreciation or revaluation of the pound (Beal, 2014, p. 122).

The *Miliangos* rule had far-reaching implications. The reasoning of Lord Wilberforce has been extended to cases in which the loss of currency value could be felt in the most profound way that is indicative of the loss. *Miliangos* has caught the attention of US courts and law makers. The Uniform Foreign Money Claims Act (UFMCA) was created by the National Conference of Commissioners on Uniform State Law (NCCUSL) in 1989. The UFMCA facilitates international business transactions by allowing courts in the United States to accept or render judgments that are denominated in foreign currencies and fair conversion rates. The Act, which has been enacted in several states of the US, suggests that the home currency rule could not be granted satisfactory and universal application. The UFMCA legitimizes judgments and arbitration awards in foreign currency and presents a countervailing weight to the discretion of courts and the home currency rule that has been legitimized by the Coinage Act of 1792. UFMCA also gives debtors the option of using the payment date as a conversion date, which is a departure from the contractual theory of commodity money. The Coinage Act, which was subsequently repealed, laid a foundation for award in foreign currency and judicial discretion.[35]

Beal (1998) found that as in *Miliangos*, one of the primary concerns of courts in the US has been the potential unfairness of the breach-day rule. In *Competex v. LaBow* (613 F. Supp. 332 (1985)), he noted that the

> Second Circuit undertook a broad examination of the breach-day rule, concluding that the rule goes beyond the intended purpose of making the plaintiff whole and promotes gamesmanship by the creditor who is effectively given the option to choose the exchange rate most beneficial to him.
> (Beal, 1998, p. 124)

The court expressed a preference for "a conversion rule of general application that is neutral between the parties with respect to currency fluctuation"; noting that apart from currency rule and breach-day rule, a judgment day rule can also be acceptable.

In *Competex*, the Second Court expressed disfavor with Restatement proposals but approved of the Restatement's provisions by allowing for both foreign judgments and the use of a payment-day conversion rule in US courts. The area of contention surrounded comment of the Restatement, which requires courts to choose the currency conversion rate most favorable to the plaintiff:[36]

> [I]f the foreign currency has depreciated since the injury or breach, judgment should be given at the rate of exchange applicable on the date of injury or breach; if the foreign currency has appreciated since injury or breach, judgment should be given at the rate of exchange applicable on the date of judgment or the date of payment.
> (Beal, 1998, p. 125)

By controlling for some measure of asset devaluation, the British and American courts have realized that there is fairness, with varying degrees of intensity, in recognizing that there can be adverse currency depreciation for which plaintiffs must be compensated.

> The once well established precept that a U.S. court may only award judgments in dollars no longer holds force as doctrine. The recent federal court decisions in In Re Oil Spill by the Amoco Cadiz and *Mitsui & Co. v. Oceantrawl Corp.*, granting judgments in foreign currencies, indicate a willingness by courts to look beyond the doctrines of the past and formulate rules better suited to trans-national legal disputes. Numerous states have seen fit to reject the home-currency rule, which requires that all awards be denominated in dollars, by adopting statutes that require judgments to be awarded in foreign currency.
> (Beal, 1998, pp. 101–102)

The multiplicity of international exchange rate arrangements (see Table 2.3) and the scope of international business operations in the contemporary (integrated) global economy require satisfactory currency awards in litigation for the robust flow of capital and investment. Accordingly, numerous nations in Europe have now responded to the pressure that has been created by floating regimes by adopting rules that are equivalent to the foreign currency rule or payment-day rule. Not surprisingly, a substantial amount of commentators have now conceded that the traditional home-currency rule is antiquated and incapable of satisfying the needs of international commerce and litigation. Not all court awards may be determined by domestic currencies, and currency valuation over time poses a unique forensic challenge for equitable awards in international disputes or contractual cases with different international currencies.

CHAPTER SUMMARY

- Macroeconomic variables are integrally related to various court decisions since they impinge on matters of the appropriate discount rate, the aggregate performance of an economy, projected inflation for compensation on investments, the manner in which firms raise capital, taxes, and exchange rate determination.
- Macroeconomic variables have universal appeal and implications for macroeconomic policies and judicial settlements.
- Global unemployment data suggest that there can be a pattern of symmetric shock across various countries.
- Courts of law are generally interested in the appropriate value of interest rate and inflation when economic losses have been incurred in personal injury and wrongful death cases. Accordingly, the macroeconomic variables have a very long-lasting presence in courts of law. The legal issues routinely involve the type of interest rate that should be used and the appropriate measurement of inflation as and when necessary.
- Courts in the United States express money judgments for damages in dollars, but they generally ignore fluctuations in the value of the dollar between the time of injury or breach and the time of judgment. The courts generally use either the conversion rate available as of the date of injury or the date of judgment.

KEY WORDS

• Breach date	• Gross domestic product	• Present value
• Business cycle	• Inflation	• Recession
• Consumer Price Index	• Special Drawing Rights	• Nominal interest rate
• Fiscal policy	• Real interest rate	• Macroeconomics
• Fixed exchange rate	• Judgment date	• Monetary policy

CHAPTER QUESTIONS

1. Examine the data for unemployment in various industries of your country. Is the unemployment rate similar across industries? How have the courts determined

unemployment compensation in your country? Are the courts sensitive to industry unemployment rate? Why?
2. What is the difference between nominal and real interest rate? With reference to specific cases explain how the courts have determined the discount rate in your country. Should the courts use rate on safest investments? Why?
3. What is inflation? How have courts determined the appropriate measure of inflation for judicial decisions? Should awards be adjusted for inflation? Why?
4. What is the importance of exchange rates in judicial awards? Explain the difference between the breach date and the judgment date. Should plaintiffs be compensated for exchange rate volatility? Why? How will you control for exchange rate volatility?

NOTES

1 For further insights into the relevant discussions of Walter Bagehot and Minsky, see Warburton (2018a, pp. 104–114). A comprehensive analysis of Minsky's work can be found in Merhling's "The Vision of Hyman P. Minsky" (1999). The expression, "Minsky moment," which gained attraction and significance during the Great Recession of 2007/2008, has been widely credited to the former Managing Director at Pacific Investment Management Company (PIMCO), Paul McCulley.
2 Frictional unemployment is a level of unemployment that ensures the continuous flow of workers in the job markets. Symptoms of structural unemployment show that more people are seeking jobs in a particular sector or industry than the industry or sector could absorb because of dynamic needs.
3 See the work of Hoffman and Lemieux (2014).
4 Op. cit., p. 2. See Tranfa-Abboud (2012) for US industry variations, see also Hoffman and Lemieux (2014, p. 32) for international comparisons and changes in employment by sectorial shares from 2000 to 2010.
5 For a fuller discussion of the identified compensatory variables see Tranfa-Abboud (2012, pp. 5–6). Compensation is also contingent on territorial and legal jurisdictions, general economic conditions, and pre-incident considerations (trends and probabilities of economic occurrences).
6 See Tranfa-Abboud (2012, p. 6).
7 Mankiw observes that the formula for the real interest rate is an approximation of the form: $\sqrt[n]{x_1 * x_2 * x_3...x_n}$, which is a more accurate mathematical representation. The difference between the nominal rate and expected inflation is somewhat representative of the real rate when, r, i, and π^e are relatively small or approximately less than 20 percent (Mankiw, 2019, p. 112).
8 Various proposals have been suggested to obtain price stability and full employment (economic growth); see for example, Wicksell (1898), Simons (1936), Cooper and Fischer (1972), and McCallum (1988, 1993).
9 See Orphanides' (2007) discussion of the rule.
10 Since the targeted inflation rate is presumed to be constant, its time subscript is rather redundant, but it is retained to analyze policy when the Fed changes its value (Mankiw, 2019, p. 440).
11 See Orphanides (2007, p.6).
12 Ibid.
13 See Hayes (2019).

14 In contradistinction to the legal theory of the court, some capital market-oriented views show a preference for corporate bonds and common stocks as appropriate assets for discounting rewards; see Breeden and Brush (2008) and Albrecht (2012).
15 *Pfeifer* was a personal injury case that was brought in a Pennsylvania Federal Court under the Longshoremen's and Harbor Workers Compensation Act (LHWCA). The District Court found in favor of the plaintiff's injury claim and calculation of the award, which applied Pennsylvania's "total offset approach." The Third Circuit affirmed, but the Supreme Court reversed, finding error solely on the ground that an injury claim under LHWCA should be governed by federal maritime rather than state law (Strangways et al., 2014, p. 73).
16 Ibid.
17 Ibid.
18 Ibid.
19 See Chan and Chan (2003, p. 22); cited in Strangways et al. (2014, p. 77).
20 Loc. cit.
21 Op. cit. p. 78.
22 Coerced loan theory, the judicial theory that implies that plaintiffs are offering defendants a loan when plaintiffs are not compensated in a timely manner for injuries, suggests that prejudgment rates should be based on unsecured borrowing, which is usually about 200 to 300 basis points below the prime rate. The presumption is made that only creditworthy borrowers could issue commercial paper. However, Losey, Mass, and Li (2002) observe that such rates do not account for bankruptcies and the probabilities of default.
23 See Knoll and Colon (2005, p. 24).
24 Ibid.
25 See www.uscourts.gov. "Effective October 11, 2016 the Federal Reserve Board ceased publication of the following interest rates on its Selected Interest Rates (H.15) statistical release: Eurodollar deposits, corporate bonds, state and local bonds, and conventional mortgages. The interest rate swaps continued to be published for two more weeks and was discontinued on October 31, 2016." At the time of this writing, the Board continues to publish the following interest rates in the H.15 release: federal funds (effective), commercial paper, bank prime loan, discount window primary credit, and US Treasury securities. A list of sources for the discontinued data is available at: http://federalreserve.gov/releases/h15/h15_technical_qa.htm.
26 An exchange rate is characterized as free floating if intervention occurs in exceptional circumstance with the objective of addressing disorderly market conditions. Further, the authorities must have provided information or data confirming that intervention has been limited to at most three instances in the previous six months, each lasting no more than three business days. "If the information or data required are not available to the IMF staff, the arrangement will be classified as floating. Detailed data on intervention or official foreign exchange transactions will not be requested routinely from member countries, but only when other information available to IMF staff is insufficient to resolve uncertainties about the appropriate classification" (see AREAER) (IMF, 2018, p. 46).
27 For classification as a crawl-like arrangement, the exchange rate must remain within a narrow margin of 2 percent relative to a statistically identified trend for six months or more (with the exception of a specified number of outliers) and the exchange rate arrangement cannot be considered as floating (AREAER) (IMF, 2018, p. 45).

28 The SDR was created by the IMF in 1969 to supplement the official reserves of member countries. SDR is usually allocated to the members of the IMF on the basis of the sizes of their economies to stabilize current account balances *inter alia*. At the time of this writing, the value of the SDR is based on a basket of five currencies—the US dollar, the euro, the Chinese renminbi, the Japanese yen, and the British pound sterling. The IMF reports that the collapse of the Bretton Woods system in 1973 and the shift of major currencies to floating exchange rate regimes lessened the reliance on the SDR as a global reserve asset.

29 See Egan (1982, pp. 167–8). The commodity concept has been related to commodity contracts and trade in commodity markets, which makes the rules for breach of contract to deliver a commodity applicable to contractual dealings in a foreign currency for preferential breach dates.

30 In the 1920s, similar questions arose over currency of awards and dates of conversion. If one was entitled to recover an amount expressed in foreign currency from suit in the US, questions arose as to what currency and conversion date should be applied to an action in the United States. The options were evidently multifarious: (i) the date of execution or payment of the judgment, (ii) the date of judgment or verdict, (iii) the date of commencement of the suit; or if a contract, (iv) the date of the obligation to pay a liquidated amount, or (v) the date of breach of contract, or (vi) the date the damages are ascertainable, where the damages are unliquidated; or if a tort, (vii) the date the amount of damages is ascertainable, or (viii) the date of the tort. The controversy was also rooted in cases of the eighteenth and nineteenth centuries, *Cowan v. McCutchen* (1870) 43 Miss. 207; *Rawlings v. Duvall* (Md. 1797) 4 Har. & McH. 1 (lease); see Gluck (1922, p. 218).

31 See Gluck (1922, p. 217 fn); *Di Ferdinando v. Sitmon, Smis & Co.* (C. of App., July 12, 1920).

32 Egan, op. cit., pp. 170–2. Current choice of law theories ascertains the governing law by evaluating the facts of a case to determine the jurisdiction that has the most significant relationship to an action.

33 Egan, op. cit., p. 176.

34 The early English cases had been *sui generis*. The Gold Standard and the fixed exchange rate regime had given the pound sterling an aura of stability. The collapse of the Gold Standard and Bretton Woods altered the realities of exchange rates.

35 In *Mitsui & Co. v. Oceantrawl Corp.*, the court rendered an award in yen and concluded that it was not prevented from awarding a foreign money judgment. The court based its authority for non-dollar award on the repeal of the Coinage Act of 1792 and the *Amoco Cadiz* decision; see Beal (2014, p. 131).

36 The Court saw RESTATEMENT as a "more extreme rule of creditor's preference" and the court felt it allowed the creditor to speculate without facing risk. However, British courts have exercised deference to the plaintiff when determining the proper currency for judgment and they do not automatically accept that a foreign currency is appropriate if it would disadvantage the plaintiff (Beal, 2014, p. 126).

FURTHER READING

Albrecht, G. R. (2012). A review of the three arguments used to justify including a risk-premium in the discount factor. *Journal of Legal Economics*, 18(2), 1–15.

Baumohl, B. (2013). *The secrets of economic indicators: Hidden clues to future economic trends and investment opportunities* (3rd ed.). Upper Saddle River, NJ: FT Press.

Beal, C. (2014). Foreign currency judgments: A new option for United States courts. *University of Pennsylvania Journal of International Economic Law, 19*(1), 101–140.

Bernanke, B. S. (2013). *The Federal Reserve and the financial crisis*. Princeton, NJ: Princeton University Press.

Breeden, C. H., & Brush, B. C. (2008). The plaintiff as victim and investor: Prudent investing and the calculation of economic damages. *Journal of Legal Economics, 14*(3), 15–41.

Bryant, R. C., Hooper, P., & Mann, C. (Eds.). (1993). *Evaluating policy regimes: New research in empirical macroeconomics*. Washington, DC: Brookings.

Chan, W. S., & Chan, F. W. H. (2003). On selection of the discount rate for actuarial assessment of damages in personal injury litigation in Hong Kong. *Law, Probability, and Risk, 2*, 15–24.

Chen, N.-F. (1991). Financial investment opportunities and the macroeconomy. *Journal of Finance, 46*, 529–554.

Cooper, J. P., & Fischer, S. (1972). Simulations of monetary rules in the FRB-MITPenn model. *Journal of Money, Credit and Banking, 4*(2), 384–396.

Dionne, M. (2011). Opinion letter to Mr. Stephen Cavanagh. Canadian Institute of Actuaries. Retrieved from http://actuaries.ca/members/publications/ 2011/211068e.pdf

Egan, T. J. (1982). Conversion of judgments measured in foreign currencies. *Washington and Lee Law Review, 39*(1), 164–184.

Evans, M. K. (2004). *Macroeconomics for managers*. Oxford, UK: Blackwell Publishing.

Fama, E. F., & French, K. R. (1989). Business conditions and expected returns on stocks and bonds. *Journal of Financial Economics, 25*, 23–49.

Friedman, M. (1960). *A program for monetary stability*. New York: Fordham University Press.

Gilchrist, S., & Zakrajšek, E. (2011). *Credit spreads and business cycle fluctuations*. Working Paper 17021, National Bureau of Economic Research.

Gluck, E. (1922). The rate of exchange in the law of damages. *Columbia Law Review, 22*(3), 217–250.

Hayes, A. (2019, July 16). Harmonized index of consumer prices. Investopedia. Retrieved from https://investopedia.com/terms/h/hicp.asp. Accessed November 4, 2019.

Hoffman, F., & Lemieux, T. (2014). *Unemployment in the Great Recession: A comparison of Germany, Canada, and the United States*. NBER Working Paper Series/w20694.

International Monetary Fund (2018). *Annual report on exchange arrangements and exchange restrictions*. Washington, DC: International Monetary Fund.

Knoll, M. S., & Colon, J. M. (2005). The calculation of prejudgment interest. Working Paper: 06-21. Retrieved from https://papers.ssrn.com/sol3/papers.cfm?abstract_id=732765. Accessed November 4, 2019. *University of Pennsylvania Law School*, 1–35.

Krugman, P., & Wells, R. (2018). *Macroeconomics* (5th ed.). New York: Worth Publishers.

Kurz, H. D. (2017). *Economic thought: A brief history*. New York: Columbia University Press.

Lewis, A. (2012). Discount rates. *Journal of Personal Injury Law, 2012*(1), 40.

Losey, R. L., Mass, M., & Li, J. (2002). Prejudgment interest: The long and the short of it. *Journal of Forensic Economics, 15*(1), 57–70.

McCallum, B. T. (1988). *Robustness properties of a rule for monetary policy*. Carnegie Rochester Conference Series on Public Policy 29, Autumn, 173–203.

McCallum, B. T. (1993). Specification and analysis of a monetary policy rule for Japan. *Bank of Japan Monetary and Economic Studies*, November, 1–45.

Mankiw, G. N. (2019). *Macroeconomics* (10th ed.). New York: Worth Publishers.

Merhling, P. (1999). The vision of Hyman P. Minsky. *Journal of Economic Behavior and Organization, 39*, 129–158.

Mishkin, F. S. (2019). *The economics of money, banking and financial markets* (12th ed.). New York: Pearson.

Orphanides, A. (2007). Taylor rules. Retrieved from http://SSRN.com. Accessed November 4, 2019.

Philips, J. R., & Freeman, N. W. (2001). Interest as damages. In R. Weil, D. G. Lentz, & E. A. Evans (Eds.), *Litigation services handbook: The role of the financial expert* (3rd ed. 2001 & Supp. 2005). Hoboken, NJ: Wiley.

Reinhart, C. M., & Rogoff, K. S. (2009). *This time is different: Eight centuries of financial folly*. Princeton, NJ: Princeton University Press.

Rotstein, R. LLP. (2013). Rule 53.09(1) Discount rates applicable in 2013. Retrieved from http://richrotstein.com/pdf/thediscountrate.pdf.

Samy de Castro, A. (2016). *Judicial indicators and business cycles in Brazil*. Research Gate Working Paper. Retrieved from http://SSRN.com. Accessed November 4, 2019.

Scholes, M. R., Wolfson, M. A., & Erickson, M. (2005) *Taxes and business strategy* (3rd ed.). Upper Saddle River, NJ: Prentice Hall.

Simons, H. C. (1936). Rules vs authorities in monetary policy. *Journal of Political Economy*, 44(1), 1–30.

Stock, J. H., & Watson, M. W. (1989). New indexes of coincident and leading economic indicators. In *NBER Macroeconomics Annual 1989* (Vol. 4, pp. 351–409). National Bureau of Economic Research.

Strangways, R., Rubin, B. L., & Zugelder, M. (2014). Using TIPS to discount to present value. *Journal of Forensic Economics*, 25(1), 71–89.

Taylor, J. B. (1993). *Discretion versus policy rules in practice*. Carnegie-Rochester Conference Series on Public Policy 39, December, 195–214.

Tranfa-Abboud, J. V. (2012). Compensatory damages in lost wages claims: The relevance of unemployment trends adjustments. *Employee Relations Law Journal*, 1–16.

Warburton, C. E. S. (2018a). *The development of international monetary policy*. Oxon, UK: Routledge.

Warburton, C. E. S. (2018b). Covered interest parity and frictions in currency and money markets. *Applied Econometrics and Development*, 18(1), 55–72.

Weil, R. L. (1995). Compensation for the passage of time. In R. Weil, P. B. Frank, C. W. Hughes, & M. J. Wagner (Eds.), *Litigation services handbook: The role of the accountant as expert* (2nd ed., Ch. 37). Hoboken, NJ: Wiley.

Whale, L. (2017). Legal update: Contractual disputes, foreign currencies, and the plummeting Pound. Retrieved from www.kingsleynapley.co.uk. Accessed November 5, 2019.

Wicksell, K. (1898). *Interest and prices*. (1936 translation from the German by R. F. Kahn.) London: Macmillan.

Woodford, M. (2003). *Interest and prices: Foundations of a theory of monetary policy*. Princeton, NJ: Princeton University Press.

Yardeni, E. (2018). *Predicting the markets: A professional autobiography*. Brookville, NY: YRI Press.

CHAPTER 3
CORPORATE FINANCIAL ANALYSIS AND INVESTMENT LAW

LEARNING OBJECTIVES

LO 1 To understand the importance of finance in law and investment.
LO 2 To learn how to read and use financial statements for use in courts of law.
LO 3 To detect fraud in financial statements.
LO 4 Understand the spirit and intent of securities law and extraterritorial jurisdiction.
LO 5 Develop familiarity with the principal-agent problem.
LO 6 Implement ethical decisions in financial transactions and avoid abusive managerial discretion.

Finance is a subsidiary category of economics and macroeconomic performance is contingent on the performance of financial markets and businesses *inter alia*. Finance, including the intertemporal financial decisions that are made by individuals, households, and governments, has everything to do with the acquisition, management, and use of (relatively scarce) financial assets (resources). An international genre of finance (open macroeconomics) incorporates trade, balance of payments accounting, transactions in international financial markets, and macroeconomic stabilization policies (fiscal and monetary) that impinge on government revenue, unemployment, money supply, interest rates, and exchange rates. Invariably, transactions in international financial markets are also accounted for in the balance of payments positions of nations (recall the relevant discussions of inventory accumulation, the business cycle, and unemployment in Chapter 2). Some significant international exposures will be discussed in Chapter 8.

There are various forms of business organizations, such as sole proprietor, partnerships, limited liability companies (LLCs), and corporations. However, corporations may be closed or open (public). Closed corporations do not have the same transparent obligations as public corporations, especially because they do not raise capital from the public. As such, public corporations have peremptory obligations to be transparent and straightforward in their financial dealings (transactions) with the public; meaning that their business transactions and financial statements must conform to lawful standards that also exemplify good (ethical) intentions. This chapter addresses some of the pressing economic and legal obligations of corporations, including their impact on a national economy, transparency requirements, reporting obligations, dividend payments, and the economic and legal consequences of financial irregularities (shenanigans). The overarching objective is to present the interdependence of the financial and real sectors and investment law in relation to purchase and sale of securities.

3.1 THE INTERFACE OF CORPORATE FINANCE AND REAL ECONOMIC PERFORMANCE

The performance of financial markets is highly dependent on the performance of the real economies at home and abroad; especially because of the fact that the values that are created in financial markets are tied to employment, aggregate consumption (cum-consumer confidence), disposable income, and investor confidence. Financial markets will perform poorly if and when the macro variables that have been listed collapse. Positive correlation can be found between industrial production and stock prices, because industrial production is normally symbolic of economic growth and, implicitly, corporate profits. Therefore, financial markets are sensitive to jobs report. Notwithstanding, expansions cannot last forever since aggregate economies go through cycles of growth and downturns.

Business inventories are affiliated with economic cycles. Business inventories are unsold assets or assets that are yet to be sold. They constitute unsold raw materials and finished products and they can be found in the stockrooms of manufacturers, wholesalers, and retailers. Accordingly, the buoyancy (or lack thereof) of an economy can determine whether businesses accumulate inventories to detrimental levels. Consequently, the real sector can be both a symptom and a cause of an economic downturn via unemployment and consumption channels. Alternatively, business production can be linked to consumption and the propensities to consume. Since the stock of inventory can be very tricky, businesses generally try to avoid wild swings by analyzing their inventory-to-sales (I/S) ratio. Inventory-to-sales ratios are variable and related to the genre of goods that are being produced. Baumohl (2013) finds that a general rule of thumb is for the I/S ratio to be about one-and-a-half months. However, automakers routinely prefer an I/S ratio of two. Invariably, disparities in preferences can be associated with the turnaround times for effective production.[1] The ratios can pertinently excite investment or dissuade investors' interest in some firms or industries.

Of course, the linchpin between the real and financial sectors is the availability and use of liquidity. The capitalist system that has evolved since the Industrial Revolution of the eighteenth century is highly dependent on liquidity. Too often, liquidity is taken for granted, but the true operation of the financial system is intrinsically related to perceptions of trust and risks; even when it comes to the provision of liquidity. There are various types of financial risks, but four are particularly noteworthy: (i) market risk, (ii) default/credit risk, (iii) exchange rate risk, and (iv) inflation risk. Market risk is systematic risk that is not peculiar to any industry. As such, it is very difficult to hedge against since its effects are pervasive but might somehow be mitigated by territorial geography. Default risk is real, and it is a function of the probability of defaults. Exchange rate risk is contingent on the volatility of the value of a domestic currency to that of a foreign currency; meaning that a domestic currency is susceptible to loss of contractual value when it depreciates in relation to a foreign currency. Sustained increases in the general price level of a nation reduce the notional values of assets, including saving.

Market and default risks have garnered considerable interests in the day-to-day operations of financial markets, and they have caused episodic havoc. Invariably, such risks impinge on the performance of the real and financial sectors. Therefore, laws have been promulgated over the years to ensure the mitigation of unwanted or undesirable risks while promoting the smooth operations of financial markets. Some of the most insightful renditions of default risks and their implications for the performance of aggregate economies can be found in the writings of Hyman Minsky (1999).

In the 1950s, for example, Minsky argued that financial conditions generate investments, which further generate business cycles. Disagreeing with Schumpeter's creative destruction and dissipation of the effects of innovation, Minsky emphasized that financial commitments are the major cause for economic cycles or instability in advanced capitalist systems; that is, systems with well-established markets that are permitted to operate without undue restrictions. The "logic of finance" is discernible in systems with well-established rules and markets in which the acquisition and direction of cash flows can be transparently evaluated. Minsky's central themes involved the survival constraint and the consequences of the breach of the survival constraint.

The basic survival constraint requires that cash inflows exceed cash outflows or commitment for capital accumulation and finance operates along the spectrum of fragile and robust.[2] Finance is "fragile" when cash outflows exceed cash inflows, thereby imposing a danger of default. Implicitly, fragile finance (a state of social constraint) is symptomatic of a default risk and an exposure to systematic (market) risk when fragility is pervasive. In effect, it is the type of finance that can cause a breakdown in coherence (stability). "Robust finance" refers to states in which commitments are relatively light compared to cash inflows, so that the danger of incoherence is relatively remote (slight). Capital is important when assets can be sold or hypothecated (serve as collateral); more pointedly, assets have appealing intertemporal market value.

Individuals and businesses with assets can gain access to current purchasing power in excess of current cash flows, possibly far in excess of current cash flows. The exposure to excess cash flows, which generates commitments, manifests a double-edged or duplicitous quality; the prospect of financing economic growth and the risk of killing economic growth when commitments are exorbitant and unaffordable. Unlike robust finance, fragile finance leaves insufficient room for expanded cash commitments. Accordingly, there must be an infrastructure to maintain the continual adjustment that is required to maintain equanimity between cash commitments and expected cash flows.[3]

Minsky's financial hypotheses presuppose that the capitalist system is intricately unstable and that upward trends (economic growth) are equally precarious when expectations about the future are imprecise or lacking any objective foundation. Therefore, by relaxing the survival constraint, incentives are created to expand investment decisions in well-developed decentralized economic systems; especially when marginal returns on investments are perceived to exceed incremental cash commitments. Invariably, economic growth is caused by debt-financed expenditures that commit cash flows out into the distant and uncertain future. So, "finance makes growth possible by providing current purchasing power to those who would use it to expand the boundaries of the system" (Merhling, 1999, p. 141).

Over the years, individuals and corporations have relaxed the survival constraint to destabilizing proportions when expected cash flows—based on unrealistic and speculative expectations—fail to materialize. The legal and economic implications of some destabilizing relaxations will be discussed subsequently (see the cases of Enron, Lehman Brothers, etc.). Evidently, the interaction of market operations and laws has a very long history with political and economic connotations, embedded in contentious notions of self-interest and the outcomes that are derived from the execution of such interests.

Thomas Hobbes (1588–1679) was less willing to trust the natural instincts of humans who are predisposed to satisfy their own interest at the expense of all others. Therefore, in 1651, he forewarned humans about the latent tendency to prosecute "the war of all against all" (*bellum omnium contra omnes*) that will inevitably make human lives "solitary, poor, nasty, brutish, and short."[4] Notably, there was an intrinsic political dimension to his conception of order and stability based on irrational human incontinence and self-interest. Some classical economists ultimately felt otherwise. With some caveats (regularity conditions), they acknowledged a role for self-interest in the marketplace. Markets became the mechanisms through which divergent interests could converge as individuals pursued their self-interests. In the eighteenth century, Adam Smith wrote:

> It is not from the benevolence of the butcher, the brewer, or the baker, that we expect our dinner, but from their regard to their own interest. We address ourselves, not to their humanity but to their self-love, and never talk to them of our own necessities but of their advantages.
>
> (Fusfeld, 2002, p. 29)

Yet, neither the relaxation of the constraint nor the stability of markets has been found to attain satisfactorily independent results. Over time, the conditions of "robust finance," which support investment and upward instability, give way to conditions of "fragile finance" in which investment is weak, growth is retarded, and the continued coherence of the system is called into question.[5] Hence, a breach of the survival constraint threatens continued economic growth when expected future cashflows fail to materialize. "Stability is destabilizing" when robust finance gives way to instability that requires prompt stability. The prospects of instability and actual instability necessitate policies to provide liquidity and regulation as proactive measures to prevent debilitating threats to the financial system and assurances for a lower bound on downward economic spirals. The financial system can become frozen when savers run on backs, investors sell their equities, and commercial banks become hesitant to provide liquidity; the symptoms of risk aversion and systematic evaporation of confidence in the financial system that is otherwise characterized as a "Minsky moment."[6]

Yet, following the proposition of Walter Bagehot, policy makers must be able to separate insolvencies from bankruptcies when firms have hypothecated capital during periods of financial seizures.[7] Minsky saw financial crises as extreme cases of shifting imbalances between cash flows and cash commitments that are usual occurrences in financially developed economies. A lawful and fundamental question is: what drives the relaxation of the survival constraint? Is the desire to invest and grow legitimate and consistent with the common good? The very fragile predicament of the capitalist economy necessitates transactional rectitude. Accurate and reliable financial statements are expected to provide a solid rung on the ladder of financial stability. Accuracy, financial prudence, balanced distribution of information, and transparency minimize fraudulent financial commitments when Minsky's survival constraint becomes amenable to relaxation. The Securities and Exchange Commission (SEC) was commissioned to ensure financial market integrity by means of lawful transparency, fair and competitive practices, and accurate dissemination of financial information.

3.2 LAWS OF THE SECURITY AND EXCHANGE COMMISSION

The SEC requires public corporations to provide accurate financial information that is transparent. SEC rules are extensive, and this book is not suitable for an exhaustive discussion of SEC laws or regulations. Rather, the presentation of SEC law will only be made relevant to the objectives of this chapter, which are limited to accuracy of information, fair and competitive practices, and transparency for the smooth operations of financial markets and macroeconomic stability.[8] Some applications of SEC laws will be discussed later in this chapter and in Chapter 7.

The SEC is a federal agency that was created by the Securities and Exchange Act of 1934. It was organized on July 2, 1934 to enforce the SEC Act of 1934 and to take over the administration of the SEC Act of 1933 from the Federal Trade Commission (FTC). The Commission provides advice to US district courts on securities matter and functions as a quasi-judicial entity in matters appertaining to its decisions in US district courts. The Exchange Act and the Securities Act constitute the primary sources of the federal securities law of the US. While the 1933 Act is primarily concerned with securities' distribution, the 1934 Act is primarily aimed at correcting abuses in outstanding securities on exchanges and in the over-the-counter (OTC) markets.[9] The amended provisions outlaw misrepresentations, manipulative and other abusive practices in securities markets, and they seek to provide just and equitable principles of trade, which will be conducive to open, fair, and orderly financial transactions in US securities markets. The 1934 Act also contains provisions that regulate some corporate practices.

Some fundamental principles of the 1934 Act are noteworthy: (i) the principle of disclosure was expanded to ensure that securities, which are trade on an exchange, are registered with the SEC. Registered companies have an obligation to provide accurate financial reports to the public; (ii) insiders (officers, directors, and 10 percent owners) who trade on listed exchanges have an obligation to regularly report their holdings of equities and transactions in all equities of the issuers with whom they are associated (insiders are also accountable to their companies for profits that are derived from sales and purchases within a six-month period); (iii) management officials of listed companies must disclose in their solicitations of proxies basic financial and material information that show the financial conditions of their companies and the results of business operations. Proxy rules specify the rights of shareholders to vote and make proposals; (iv) the SEC is granted policing rights to maintain surveillance of security trading practices on exchanges and OTC markets. Listed companies must maintain minimum capital requirements (relative to liabilities) at all times in order to prevent insolvencies. The Federal Reserve Board is granted statutory authority to regulate margin requirements; (v) the Act gives the SEC enforcement authority to elicit testimony under oath and subpoena books and records in order to develop facts to ascertain violations or compliance with the law, including the ability to obtain injunctive relief against practices that are detrimental or potentially detrimental to the smooth operations of US financial markets.

Rule 10b-5, which is the securities antifraud rule that was promulgated under the 1934 Act, is widely considered to be the bedrock of US securities regulation.

> Every securities transaction lives under its protective shade and its menacing shadow. For those who enter into securities transactions, the rule assures that relevant securities information is not purposefully false or misleading. For purveyors of securities information, it imposes standards of honesty that carry risks of heavy liability.
> (Palmiter, 2017, p. 397)

The origin of Rule 10b-5 dates back to 1942 as an effort to improve on the 1933 statute, which did not clearly establish antifraud provisions for the purchases of securities. The antifraud provisions of the 1933 Act were limited to the sale of securities; so, when fraudulent purchases were perpetrated in the 1940s, the statute was insufficient to deal with the threat.[10] The language of Rule 10b-5 is purposefully broad enough to criminalize assorted methods of fraudulent activities in US securities markets, including material omissions.

> Clause (2) of Rule 10b-5 prohibits the "[omission] to state a material fact necessary in order to make the statement made, in the light of the circumstances under which they were made, not misleading.***" The Commission "believes that, depending on the circumstances, there is a duty to correct statements made in any filing***if the statements either have become inaccurate by virtue of subsequent event, or are later discovered to have been false and misleading from the outset, and the issuer knows or should know that persons are continuing to rely on all or any material portion of the statement."
> (Coffee, Seligman, & Sale, 2007, pp. 945–6)

Information is material if it is valuable and pertinent to the investment-making decision of an investor. Therefore, an investor must not be deprived of such information *ex ante*. Accordingly, SEC rules require that filings contain "such further material information … as may be necessary to make the required statements … not misleading" (Rule 408). However, Palmiter observes that materiality balances: (i) the costs of mandated disclosure such as the information-gathering burden, the risk of investor confusion, the possibility of frivolous litigation, or the revelation of competitive secrets, (ii) the availability of the same information through unregulated channels, and (iii) the effect disclosure has on other regulatory regimes (such as environmental compliance or corporate governance).[11] Material information is intrinsically related to insider trading though insider trading law is rather inchoate.

Trading on privileged information (insider trading) has not been comprehensively defined by any statute. The offense is highly dependent on federal common law. Courts have traditionally used theories like implied duties of confidentiality to litigate insider trading cases.[12] There is a presumption that there is an obligation to disclose material information when the information is obtained in a relation of trust or fiduciary arrangement. Alternatively, the parity of information theorem, requiring abstention in the absence of disclosure, has also been applied. Criminal sanctions range from fines to imprisonment of 20 years. Fair and competitive practices impose further obligations on publicly traded firms.

Section 13(d) of the Williams Act 1968 (discussed more fully in Chapter 7) allows stockholders and targeted management to be apprised of acquisition threats. Section 13(d) requires disclosure of: (i) the name and address of the issuing firm and the type of securities to be acquired; (ii) the number of shares actually owned; (iii) the background of the filer, including any criminal information; (iv) the purpose of the transaction (acquisition or investment purposes); and (v) the source of funding to finance an acquisition.[13]

Corporations may merge when there are lawful circumstances to permit the merger and economic gains to be derived from the merger. That is, there are beneficial synergies. Suppose Xerox (X) wants to merge with or purchase Melox (M). Then the purchase is beneficial if the combined present value (PV) of X and M (XM) is greater than X+M:

$$\pi = PV_{XM} - (PV_X + PV_M) = \Delta PV_{XM} \tag{3.1}$$

Equation 3.1 is instructive because the purchaser can determine *ex ante* the value that it is looking for, given the independent value of the two firms. That is, by definition:

$$PV_{XM} = \pi + (PV_X + PV_M) \tag{3.2}$$

The real cost (R_C) of acquiring Melox is simply the cost incurred (A_C) less the independent value of Melox (PV_M):

$$R_C = A_C - PV_M \tag{3.3}$$

and the positive net present value (NPV > 0) must be NPV = $\pi - R_C$, or $\pi > A_C$. Estimating the benefits of mergers must be done with very modest projections of cash flows. Overoptimistic projections of discounted cash flow (DCF) can provide misleading results for a financial analyst or forensic economist who is trying to estimate net gain (NG):

$$NG = DCF_T - \text{cost of acquisition;} \qquad (3.4)$$

where DCF is inclusive of merger benefits. For the purposes of understanding SEC disclosure and transparency requirements, discussions of the compositions and integrity of financial statements are presented in the next section.

3.2 (A) FINANCIAL STATEMENTS

Financial statements are documented financial records of business transactions, activities, and overall financial performances. They are often audited by government agencies, accountants, firms, or qualified personnel to ensure the accuracy of reporting for tax, financing, and investment purposes. Financial statements may or may not be publicly displayed, depending on whether a company wants to raise financial resources from the public. Under the Securities and Exchange (SEC) regulations, companies that want to raise capital from the public are obligated to accurately disclose their mission or vision, financial positions, and prospects in good faith. There are two primary sources of US federal securities law: (i) The Exchange Act, and (ii) The Securities Act. These sources are augmented by regulations that are promulgated by the SEC, appertaining to both.[14] Companies that do not want to raise capital from the public (private businesses) are not obligated to make their financial statements public.

There are multiple forms of financial statements but three are very prominent: (i) the Income Statement (IS), (ii) the Balance Sheet (BS), and (iii) the statement of Cash Flow (CF). Though the statements, in isolation, provide limited financial information, an interactive analysis of the statements—in the form of financial ratios—provide much more useful information about the overall performance and prospects of businesses. Accountants are usually responsible for disseminating the financial information of businesses on a quarterly or annual basis. Fiscal years—the 12-month period that a company uses to report its financial activities for accounting purposes—may be periodized differently. While some companies may use the regular calendar period, others may use a different period; for example, some companies use a fiscal year that corresponds to that of the US Government's fiscal year (October 1 to September 30). Fiscal years provide indications of the currency or obsolescence of information.

For the sake of consistency and clarity, certain rules and procedures are strongly recommended for reporting financial statements. The rules are professionally considered to be Generally Accepted Accounting Principles (GAAP) and they govern the preparation of financial statements. The GAAP are broadly considered to be a set of objectives, conventions, and principles that are professionally important to prepare and present financial statements.[15] Public corporations must adopt the accounting practices recommended by GAAP unless there is an underlying reason for an authoritative alternative.

Label (2013) identifies three basic assumptions as the corner stone of GAAP: (i) a business is considered to be distinct (separate from its owners and other businesses), meaning that revenues and expenses of a business must be kept separate from personal expenses, (ii) a business is assumed to be a going concern,[16] and (iii) accounting records are assumed to reflect only quantifiable transactions.[17] In the final analysis, "financial statements must present relevant, reliable, understandable, sufficient, and practicably obtainable information in order to be useful."[18]

3.2 (B) THE INCOME STATEMENT

The income statement (IS) is variously described as the "profit and loss statement," the "operating statement," and "statement of earnings" or earnings statement, especially because the IS gives an indicator of whether or not a company is profitable after producing and marketing a certain line of product after tabulating and summing up all the items on the IS.[19] A conventional IS has information about the earnings (revenue or sales) of a company, costs to market the products or services that are sold (cost of goods sold) (CoGS), or cost of service (CoS), non-cash expenses, gross income, taxes, net income, earnings per share, and addition to retained earnings (ARE), the difference between net income (NI) and dividend payments (D).

Revenue, sometimes recorded as "Sales/Revenue," is the monetary value that companies receive for selling goods and services to customers for a given period of time. Income statements have a revenue recognition problem. That is, income is recognized even though cash has not been paid. Therefore, IS must be viewed with some amount of precaution. Of course, a sticky point is usually when to actually recognize revenue. The guiding principle is that revenue must have been "earned"; in which case, a company that is selling a product must have shipped the product, and a company that is providing a service must have performed the service.[20] The recognition problem provides opportunities for manipulation and fraud.

CoGS accounts for all the costs that directly contribute to the making of a product or delivery of a service, generally within the purview of accountants or bookkeepers. Unlike wages, cost of materials, and salaries, some costs—like commissions and distant contributions of plant supervisors—are not immediately apparent for inclusion in an IS. In addition to CoGS (the costs that are directly driven by production), there are operating expenses (OPEXs) (the costs that are directly associated with the operations of a business during the production process for a given period of time). OPEXs include rent, insurance, marketing, payroll, and research and development (R&D) expenditures. OPEX may also be referred to as selling (sales), general, and administrative expenses (SG&A, G&A). OPEX defines the value of the overhead of a company. Berman and Knight (2008) observe that it is misleading to dichotomize the CoGS and OPEXs into variable and fixed categories respectively; this is partly because of cross-classification and time dynamism.[21] According to a matching principle of accounting, costs are integrally matched with corresponding sales in the income statement.

Gross profit (income) is the difference between sales/revenue and CoGS or CoS. As such, it is the residual after the direct costs of production, or the provision of service have been taken into account. It must be adequate to cover operating expenses, taxes, financing cost, and net profit.[22] It is generally considered to be "the line" of demarcation between those items with relatively high variability in the short-term (above gross profit, "the line") and those items with comparatively low variability (below gross profit, "the line").[23]

Depreciation (capital consumption allowance) is one of the items below "the line" in an income statement. Depreciation is a non-cash expense, an expenditure that is recognized in the income statement without any obligation to make further payments. Therefore, it is a credit for expenditure on physical capital that spans the expected lifespan (duration) of the physical capital.[24] Allowance for depreciation permits businesses to spread the cost of acquiring physical capital over multiple years. The choice of a depreciation regime is tricky because it can affect the value of net profit or income. The length of years of depreciation is positively correlated with net income. The longer the years of depreciation, the greater the positive effect on net income. Accordingly, huge ticket items with long-lasting lifespans cannot be depreciated in one year since such depreciation can lead to negative net income. Invariably, it is unrealistic to presume that the item will be exhaustively utilized in one year. Depreciation schedules are optional, and some firms may opt for the straight-line method or the Modified Accelerated Cost Recovery System (MACRS). In the case of the straight-line method, the annual value of depreciation is based on the value of the asset and its expected duration; for example an asset that costs $20,000 and is expected to last for ten years will have an annual depreciation value of $20,000/10 or $2000 a year.[25] MACRS will be discussed in Chapter 6. Unlike the depreciation schedule for tax purposes, income tax rates are pretty regimented and lawfully specified in terms of marginal tax rates and income thresholds. Taxes will be discussed in Chapter 6.

Net profit is computed after all expenses, including taxes, interest payments, and other expenses, have been made. It is generally considered to be the bottom line of the income statement. Profits can be estimated in various ways to satisfy a specific analytical purpose; for example, there is gross profit, operating profit—otherwise known as earnings before interest and taxes (EBIT)—and net profit. Gross profit/income is the residual after a company has made payments for the direct costs of producing a product or providing a service (CoGS or CoS). Operating profit is gross profit less operating expenses, including depreciation and amortization. It is considered to be the profit from running a business. Box 3.1 provides an itemization of key items in an income statement, including the percentage of sales for Profit and Loss Inc. The percentage of sales may be used to make income projections or comparative analysis of companies that are similarly situated.

BOX 3.1 INCOME STATEMENT FOR PROFIT & LOSS INC.

12 months ending December 31, 2019 (all numbers are in millions, US$)

Profit			Percentage of sales
	Sales/Revenue	67,211.10	100
	CoGS	(54,312.50)	81
Gross	**Gross Profit**	**12,898.60**	**19**
	SG&A	(8,541.50)	13
	EBITD	4,357.10	6
	Depreciation	(598.40)	1
Operating	**EBIT**	**3,758.70**	**6**
	Interest	(102.30)	0
	EBT*	3,656.40	5
	Taxes	(930.60)	1%: 25%$^\Psi$
Net	**Net**	**2,725.80**	**4**
	ARE**	1,826.29	3%: 67%$^\Psi$

* Earnings before taxes ** Addition to retained earnings (NI−D = ARE)
Ψ Percentage of net income EBITD = Earnings before interest, taxes, & depreciation

The numbers in the income statement (Box 3.1) are the realized or actual numbers, showing the sales, revenues, and profits. There are times when companies might want to make projections (forecasts); in such instances, they might construct what are known as proforma statements for projection, or standardization for comparative analysis. The percentages for items in the income statement are conventionally taken out of total sales/revenue. Proforma statements may exclude unusual or non-recurring results. In fact, it makes sense to exclude such results since they are not likely to recur. For the balance sheet, the percentages are conventionally taken out of total assets (not total current assets) for the asset column, and total liability and shareholders' equity for the liability and equity column. The net income is generally considered to be "the bottom line."

CoGS are costs incurred for generating sales during the financial period. By the matching principle, costs are associated with revenue for the same period. The cost for generating the sales of Profit and Loss Inc., as of December 31, 2019, was $54,312.5 million ($54.3 billion). The statement provides information about the three important concepts of profit—(i) gross ($12,898.60 million), (ii) operating ($3,758.70 million), and (iii) net, "bottom line," ($2,725.80 million)—and how they are derived.

3.2 (C) THE BALANCE SHEET

The balance sheet shows the assets, debts, and net worth of a company at a particular point in time. Assets are marketable items of value that a company owns, and they can be classified into two broad categories—short- and long-term—based on their liquidity (the promptness with which they can be converted into cash without significant loss of value). Short-term assets can be converted into cash in less than a year and they are conventionally listed at the top of the asset column, which is usually on the left of the balance sheet. Long-term assets—the relatively illiquid assets—are assets that cannot be converted into cash within a year. For accounting purposes, the assets in the balance sheet are itemized at historical cost (purchase value) rather than elusive market value. Accountants prefer a stable monetary unit for consistency and comprehension even though prices might change over time.

Short-term assets include cash and short-term investments, accounts receivables, and inventories. Short-term investments can be considered cash equivalents. Accounts receivable are debts that a company hopes to collect from customers. A company may or may not be able to collect all its debts from customers. Therefore, receivables must be watched closely.[26] It gives an indicator of the amount of cash that is outstanding. Some balance sheets make provision for bad debts under total accounts receivable. Historical knowledge of bad debts and the exclusion of bad debts from receivables enable managers to conservatively estimate their pending cash inflow.

Inventories are items that are in stock, which have not been shipped out. There are three general categories of inventories: (i) finished goods, (ii) work in progress (WIP), and (iii) raw materials. Of course, service-oriented companies are not likely to have products in a warehouse and the classifications are not relevant to such companies. Since a valuation method has to be selected to determine the value of inventories, it is important to know the valuation methodology for comparative analysis and synchronization. Two methods are generally preferred: (i) first-in-first-out (FIFO), and (ii) last-in-first-out (LIFO). Changing price levels will affect both the balance sheet and income statement. During inflationary periods a firm that is using FIFO will experience increases in the value of its income and inventory. Sales will be priced at a higher value relative to historical cost and CoGs. On the contrary, companies that are using LIFO will have higher CoGS, lower net income, and lower inventory value. Therefore, financial analysts should make adjustments for differences in inventory valuation methods since such disparities have significant impact on the balance sheet and income statement.[27] A summation of the value of the current assets is provided as a portion of total assets.

Long-term assets include property plant and equipment (PPE), accumulated depreciation, goodwill, and intangibles. PPE is made up of machinery, computers, trucks, and other physical assets of a company. The item reflects the pecuniary value, at historical cost, of all the physical assets that are required to operate a business. Therefore, the market value of PPE is not readily apparent unless there is an appraisal. The conservative approach is consistent with the three assumptions of GAAP that were discussed earlier on. In effect, one of the drawbacks of the balance sheet is that assets can be undervalued.

Depreciation is the gradual reduction in the value of physical assets as a result of usage. As noted earlier on, accountants try to allocate the costs of tangible assets over the life expectancy of the assets. The life expectancy is the time period during which a company is expected to benefit from the use of a tangible asset. Recall the discussion of depreciation earlier on and the preferred method of depreciation. It is noteworthy that the measurement of depreciation in the balance sheet is not the same as that in the income statement. The balance sheet accounts for accumulated depreciation, which is cumulative depreciation of an asset up to a specific time of its life expectancy.[28] Accumulated depreciation is calculated by summing up all the charges for depreciation that have occurred since the date of purchase or commission. Since the lifespan of physical assets can be a subjective matter, the subjectivity affects the value of PPE on the balance sheet; the longer the life of an asset, the lower the depreciation, and the higher the value of PPE.

Although land is prone to erosion and degradation, its accounting value is presumed to be invariant. The declining value of land is not taken into consideration because it is presumed that the life expectancy of land is infinite. Of course, there are complications that underlie the measurement of erosion and degradation. Further, the value of land occasionally appreciates because of the market forces of demand and supply and the geographic location of land (the value that is associated with the usage of land). Goodwill is also now treated like land.

Goodwill can be considered an intangible asset. Recall that goodwill now incorporates the value of the clientele that a company is acquiring. Since the Financial Accounting Standards Board (FASB) has considered goodwill to include reputation (customer base), goodwill—like land—is not amortized.[29] Formerly, goodwill can be amortized over a longer period of time with some diminutive effects. By not amortizing goodwill, reported profits can be exaggerated and companies are incentivized to go in search of goodwill on their books, which can be distortionary and deceptive.

Intellectual property is an intangible asset—copyrights, patents, trademarks—but like a physical asset, the cost of generating innovation cannot be accounted for in a single year. Accordingly, the cost of innovation has to be amortized over a period of time for which they can generate revenue.[30] Conceptually, the changes in the values of depreciation and amortization have implications for the income statement and balance sheet.

Liabilities and equity are conventionally reported on the right-hand side of the balance sheet. Liabilities are debts, which like assets, can be classified into (current) short- and long-term categories. Short-term debts are debts that must be paid within a year and long-term debts are debts which can be paid after a year. Short-term loans, accounts payable (including dividends payable and accrued payroll) are examples of the short-term debts of a company. Accounts payable are debts to the vendors of a company, partly to build up inventory and to pay for services received.

Deferred taxes, non-convertible debts, and deferred income payments are examples of long-term liabilities. Non-convertible debentures or unsecured debts are usually the bonds of companies that cannot be converted into the securities (stocks) of the issuing companies. Because of their limitations non-convertible debentures usually have higher rates of return than convertible debts. Deferred income, which is also referred to as deferred revenue or unearned revenue, is akin to the accrual principle in the income statement. It means that a company has received payments for goods or services that it has not provided or delivered. The revenue recognition principle requires such income or payments to be recorded as liabilities until the goods or services are delivered. Revenue is recognized after the goods or services are delivered.

Owners' equity (E) is the third and final component of the balance sheet. Owners' equity is an accounting residual. It is the difference between the value of asset (A) and liabilities (L), since total assets must be equal to the combination of liabilities and equity; see Equation 3.5 for the routine financial identity:

If $A = L + E$, then by common mathematical manipulation, $E = A - L$. (3.5)

There are two categories of equity: (i) common equity, and (ii) preferred equity. Holders of common equity have voting rights for Boards of Directors (BoDs) but they are not guaranteed dividend payments and missed payments cannot be rolled over. Preferred stockholders have voting rights under extraordinary circumstances and are guaranteed fixed dividend payments like bond holders and missed payments can be rolled over. Consequently, relative to common stockholders, preferred stockholders have seniority on the claims of the profits of a public company. Notwithstanding, preferred shares may be converted into common equity under requisite arrangements or bylaws, but the interests of all equity holders are subordinated to those who hold the corporate debt (bonds) of a company. The balance sheet reports the par value of equity, which is the notional value in the charter of a public company that is assigned to its stock at inception.[31] Explicitly, the par value is not the market value of the stock of a company. It is also regarded as the contributed capital in excess of par. The additional paid-in capital is indicative of the value that was initially paid above the par value. Therefore, it is an initial public offering (IPO) concept that shows the spread of prices of the stock of a public company between inception and the present. The additional paid-in capital is computed over time to show the spread. In Box 3.2 the paid-in amount is $1,080 million.

Unlike ARE in the income statement, the concept of retained earnings in the balance sheet is an accumulated measure of retained earnings after taxes have been paid. A public company does not pay out all its profits as dividends or return on the investment of shareholders. Some amount of money is retained to finance the growth of the company or pay maturing debts. The retained earnings reflect the retained profits of the company since the inception of the business less the money that may have been spent.

While earning retention is critical to the growth of a public company, managerial decision to withhold earnings can be challenged in courts of law when the decision is based on the abusive use of managerial discretion. Managerial decisions about retained earnings and growth will be subsequently discussed in the case of *Dodge v. Ford*. However, the total equity that is reported in a balance sheet does not reflect the market value of a company because accounting principles and assumptions conservatively show preferences for historical cost or stable currency unit of measurement.

Box 3.2 presents some of the fundamental arguments and accounting principles that are important to understand the contents and meaning of the balance sheet. It is an abridged representation of a typical balance sheet. Assets are listed on the left-hand side with the most liquid assets at the top. The summation of the most liquid assets is denoted as "total current assets." Three categories have been used for the hypothetical computation: (i) cash and cash equivalents ($3,049.62 million), (ii) total accounts receivable ($500 million), and (iii) inventories ($4,716.51). The balance sheet shows that as of December 31, 2019 (a specific date), Profit and Loss Inc. had total current assets to the tune of $8,266.13 million, valued at historical cost.

The lower portion of the left-hand side of the assets column has assets that are not very liquid; these are assets that cannot quickly be converted into cash within a year without loss of value. For brevity and simplicity, three categories have also been presented: (i) PPE ($3,793.12 million), (ii) intangible assets[32] ($1,776.67 million), and (iii) other assets ($2,335.09 million).[33] The combination of total current assets and all other assets give the value for total assets ($16,171.01 million). It must be promptly noted that this value corresponds to the value of "total liabilities and shareholders' equity," which is consistent with Equation 3.5.

The liabilities of the company are conventionally listed on the right-hand side of a balance sheet, with the most liquid debts at the top; these are debts that must be paid within a year. The category is made up of Accounts Payable ($540 million). The relationship between current assets (CA) and current liabilities (CL) has significant managerial connotations. The difference between current assets and current liabilities define the working capital of a business. The working capital of a business indicates whether a firm has enough liquid resources to finance the day-to-day operations of a business. It is preferential for the differential to be significantly positive, meaning that liquid assets exceed the liabilities that are immediately due. The difference between the change in current assets and the change in current liabilities is known as net working capital. The difference between working capital and net working capital can be confusing. It must be pointed out that while working capital (WC) shows no dynamism, net working capital (NWC) shows dynamism because it considers financial results for two years. Consider Equations 3.6 and 3.7.

BOX 3.2 BALANCE SHEET FOR PROFIT & LOSS INC.

12 months ending December 31, 2019 (all numbers are in millions, US$)

Assets		%	Liabilities & Shareholders' Equity		%
Cash & cash equivalents	3,049.62	19	Accounts payable	540.00	
Cash only	1,449.07		Inc. tax	400.00	
Short-term inv.	1,600.55		Accrued payroll	140.00	
Total accts. rec.	**500.00**	3	**Total current liabilities**	**540.00**	3
Receivables	510.00		**Long-term debt**	**5,546.98**	
Bad debts	(10.00)		Non-convertible debt	3,649.84	
Inventories	**4,716.51**	29	Deferred income	1,355.10	
Finished goods	1,298.10		Deferred taxes	542.04	
Work in progress	1,684.64		**Other liabilities**	**8,004.03**	
Raw materials	1,733.78		**Total liabilities**	**14,091.01**	87
Total current assets	**8,266.13**	51	**Common equity total**	**2,080.00**	13
PPE*	**3,793.12**	23	Common stock and paid-in surplus$^\psi$	1,080.00	
Buildings	2,374.15		Retained earnings	1,000.00	
Accumulated depreciation	1,418.97		**Total shareholders' equity**	**2,080.00**	13
Intangible assets	**1,776.67**	11	**Total liabilities & shareholders' equity**	**16,171.01**	
Goodwill	1,776.67				
Other assets	**2,335.09**	14			
Total assets	**16,171.01**				

*PPE= Property, Plant & Equipment
ψ % / Total assets, and total liabilities & shareholders' equity

Common stock (1000@$1 par value)	$0.001 million
Additional paid-in capital	$1,080 million
Total paid-in capital	$1,080.001 million

$$WC_{2019} = CA_{2019} - CL_{2019}, \qquad (3.6)$$

and

$$NWC = \Delta CA_{2018/19} - \Delta CL_{2018/19}. \qquad (3.7)$$

Alternatively, the current ratio (CR), CA/CL, can be used to examine the capability of a firm to cover its immediate liabilities by its short-term convertible assets. In the hypothetical example of Profit and Loss Inc., the company has so many valuable current assets that it could cover its immediate debt 15 times:

$$CR = \frac{CA}{CL} = \frac{\$8,266.13}{\$540} = 15.31x. \qquad (3.8)$$

That is, the company has $15.31 cents for every dollar worth of current liabilities. Since inventories (I) have not been taken into consideration, the current ratio can be a misleading indicator of liquidity. Recall that inventories are part of current assets. Inventories can be disposed of rather sluggishly. To avoid the exaggerated results of the current ratio, managers, investors, or analysts might look at the quick ratio (QR), which is a much more stringent measure of liquidity:

$$QR = \frac{CA - I}{CL} = \frac{\$8,266.13 - \$4,716.51}{\$540} = 6.57x. \qquad (3.9)$$

The inclusion of inventories reduces the value of the current ratio by almost half its original value. A dollar's worth of current liabilities is now covered by about $7 worth of liquid assets; not necessarily a bad situation. There is buffer!

Long-term debt consists of non-convertible debt, deferred income, and deferred taxes ($5,546.98 million). Other liabilities (like pension payments and capital leases) amount to ($8,004.03 million). The sum of all debts—current, long-term, and other—adds up to ($14,091.01 million). Total equity (owners' equity) is $2,080 million. By combining total liabilities and total shareholders' equity, we get total liabilities and shareholders' equity (TLSE) ($16,171.01). It is noteworthy that this value TLSE denominates the percentages for proforma calculations or projections on the right-hand side.

3.2 (D) THE STATEMENT OF CASH FLOW

The statement of cash flows shows the receipts, investment, and payments of cash by a firm for a given period of time. As such, it reports actual cash transactions without the accrual principle that was previously discussed for the income statement. However, information in the statement of cash flow is significantly derived from the income statement and balance sheet. The statement of cash flow is notable for making a distinction between the accounting concept of profit and actual cash availability. Not all expenditures promptly and clearly appear in the other financial statements; for example, apart from the accrual principle, expensive purchases of capital (capital expenditures) show up incrementally in the income statement as depreciation over the perceived lifespan of an asset. Additionally, there is an investment dimension to the concept of cash. Short-term assets are considered cash equivalents. Cash may arrive to a company from one or more entities. Governments, consumers, investors, and depository institutions may be willing to provide cash to finance a business or make purchases from a company, so cash is actually bidirectional. It can flow into a business (cash inflow) or it could flow out of a business (cash outflow).

Multiple factors are responsible for the inflows and outflows of cash, and the balance sheet provides a reasonable indicator of the direction of cash flows. Notably, since cash is being used to purchase assets and pay debts, increases in assets and decreases in total liabilities and shareholders' equity are reasonable indicators that money is being spent and vice versa. Therefore, transactions with cash implication will affect inventories, fixed assets, dividend payments, and working capital. The rise and fall of the value of the aforementioned financial variables is inversely related to the direction of cash flows. The interaction of the income statement and the balance provides information about changes in net income for a given period of time and relevant changes in the balance from the end of a previous period to the end of a current period. The statement of cash flows actually summarizes the use of cash based on information that is provided in a balance sheet for two years; that is, changes in a balance sheet from the beginning of one year (end of a previous year) to the end of a current year.

The statement of cash flows tracks the movement of cash in three interrelated areas: (i) operations, (ii) investment, and (iii) financing activities. Cash flow from operations show the amount of cash that is generated from operations by analyzing net income, and depreciation of capital in the income statement, and accounts payable, inventories, and current assets in the balance sheet. Investing activities are long-term investments that require the use of cash. Such investments include the purchase of property, plants, and other assets, and increases (purchases) in goodwill and other assets in the balance sheet. The purchases are considered cash outflows. Financing activities identify increases in long-term debt (inflow), increase in note payable (an inflow) and purchase of treasury stock (an outflow). The net results are reported for each of the categories. The beginning and ending cash positions are then used to reconcile a firm's statement of cash flows.

Contents of the statement of cash flow are provided in Box 3.3. The delta symbol means change in the value of a variable, which is an increase or decrease in the value of an item relative to a starting period. Positive signs indicate cash inflows and negative signs indicate cash outflows. It has not been numerically populated because of brevity, but because one balance sheet has been presented for analytical purposes. However, the contents can be used as a worksheet to estimate the cash flow of a public company; readers are encouraged to do so. It is noteworthy that two years' worth of information is required from the balance sheets of a company of interest to derive the statement of cash flow. Additions to, and subtractions from an income statement are also made to derive the statement of cash flow.

BOX 3.3 CASH FLOWS FOR GENERIC COMPANY INC.

12 months ending December 31, 2019 (all numbers are in millions, US$)

Operating activities

  Net income

    Cash inflows

    Δ Depreciation & amortization (+)

    Δ Accounts payable (+)

    Δ Current assets (+)

    Δ Accrued income taxes (+)

    Cash outflows

    Δ Accounts receivable (−)

    Δ Inventories (−)

11. **Net cash from operations**   (I)

  Long-term investing activities

    Δ Property, plant, & equipment (PPE) (−)

    Δ Goodwill and other assets (−)

15. **Net cash used in investing activities**   (II)

    Financing activities

    Δ Long-term debt (+)

    Δ Treasury stock (−)*

    Δ Notes payable (+)

20. **Net cash from financing activities**   (III)

  Cash reconciliation

22. Net increase in cash and marketable securities   (I) + (II) + (III)

23. Cash and securities at the beginning of the year

    Cash and securities at the end of the year   (22) − (23)

Source: Parrino, Kidwell, & Bates (2015, p.66) (with modifications by author).

(+) = cash inflows; (−) = cash outflows

*Treasury stock is outstanding stock that is repurchased from stockholders by the issuing company. A treasury stock is not included in the calculation of dividends are earnings per share (EPS). Consequently, the stock is not considered to be outstanding.

This chapter has not focused on the statement of retained earnings, but it is worth noting that such a statement exists.

The interaction of the financial statements is important to glean exceedingly useful information about the operations of a public company. Interactive financial ratios provide information about the level of indebtedness (leverage or solvency), profitability, market value, and the efficiency of the management of a company. Some of these ratios have already been referenced and the bulk of them can be found in various financial texts and books. This book has not been designed to extensively delve into the ratios.[34] Notwithstanding, additional allusions to the ratios can be found in this chapter and Chapter 5.

Financial statements are so important to investors and creditors that they can become susceptible to accounting irregularities or deceptions by accountants and managers; this was particularly the case in the late 1990s. Several companies like Enron, KPMG, Bristol-Myers Squibb (BMS), and WorldCom became liable for accounting fraud that misled investors. Accounting fraud can be perpetrated on investors (domestic and international) in various ways and an exhaustive list can be found in *Financial Shenanigans*, the work of Schilit and Perler (2010). The sources of most accounting irregularities can be found in Box 3.4.

The accounting irregularities are oftentimes associated with unprofessional indiscretion, the ability to deliberately mistime entries, exaggerate financial results, push sales (channel stuffing) to reduce inventories and increase accrual income, dissemble expenditures, record loans as income, and report non-recurring events as recurring events in financial statements. These misrepresentations (deceptively attractive numbers) enhance the marketability of the securities of public companies. Apparently, Securities and Exchange

BOX 3.4 DODGY FINANCIAL ENTRIES

- Recording revenue too soon
- Recording bogus revenue
- Using one-time events as sustainable activities
- Postponing the record of expenses
- Hiding expenses or losses
- Shifting current income or revenue to a later period
- Shifting future expenses to an earlier period
- Shifting financial inflows to the operating section
- Shifting normal operating cash outflows to the investing section
- Inflating operating cash flow using acquisitions or disposals
- Boosting operating cash flow using unsustainable activities

Source: Schilit and Perler, 2010, pp. 73–252.

(SEC) regulations are designed to dissuade improper and fraudulent financial reports and punish those who engage in them. All public companies are required to periodically file financial reports with the SEC on a quarterly and annual basis. These reports, which include financial statements that have been previously discussed, are expected to accurately reflect the financial decisions, health, and prospects of public companies. Three reports are particularly instructive for reporting the financial positions of public companies: (i) the 10-K (annual report), (ii) the 10-Q (quarterly report), and (iii) the 8-K (for augmentation or material omission).

3.3 FINANCIAL STATEMENTS AND SECURITIES REGULATION

Recall that securities regulation in the US is administered by the SEC and that the SEC is a federal agency that was created by the Securities Exchange Act of 1934 to implement the provisions of the Act. The Securities Exchange Act outlaws misrepresentation, manipulation, and all abusive practices in securities markets in order to establish just and equitable principles of trade that are not based on false and privileged information. It is worth restating some fundamental principles of the securities law: (i) disclosure, (ii) equitable distribution of information, (iii) transparent proxy solicitations, (iv) dissuasion of recalcitrant trading, (v) monitoring trading practices, and (vi) enforcement.

As a general measure of disclosure and proportional distribution of information in the marketplace, all public companies are required to register with the SEC and file annual and periodic reports that disclose financial information for the investing public. Insiders (officers, directors, and 10 percent owners) make regular reports to the SEC about their holdings and transactions in all equities of an issuer with whom they are associated. Insiders must also account to their companies for profitable transactions within a six-month period. The reports that provide information to the public are of grave interest to competitors, creditors, and investors.

The 10-K is a lengthy annual report that is provided about 90 days before the end of the fiscal year of a company. The report contains information about the operations of public companies (domestic and international).[35] The 10-Q (quarterly report) is somewhat truncated but it provides valuable information about the performance of public companies in about 45 days before the end of each quarter appertaining to a company's fiscal year. Investors and creditors can expect to find information about the latest development of companies, unaudited financial results, and projected business trajectories of the companies. Material omissions in the 10-K and 10-Q must be provided in the 8-K, which amends and augments the other reports because of material omission and belated developments. The 8-K is considered an unscheduled report, but it might contain information about bankruptcies, purchase or sale of assets, and the departures or recruitment of top executives. The letter and intent of SEC rules are promulgated to have national and extraterritorial effects (see *Lep v. Itoba*). Rule 10b-5, which has been considered a "bedrock of US

> **BOX 3.5 17 CFR § 240.10B-5—RULE 10B-5**
>
> **§ 240.10B-5 EMPLOYMENT OF MANIPULATIVE AND DECEPTIVE DEVICES**
>
> It shall be unlawful for any person, directly or indirectly, by the use of any means or instrumentality of interstate commerce, or of the mails or of any facility of any national securities exchange,
>
> **(a)** To employ any device, scheme, or artifice to defraud,
> **(b)** To make any untrue statement of a material fact or to omit to state a material fact necessary in order to make the statements made, in the light of the circumstances under which they were made, not misleading, or
> **(c)** To engage in any act, practice, or course of business which operates or would operate as a fraud or deceit upon any person, in connection with the purchase or sale of any security.
>
> (Sec. 10; 48 Stat. 891; 15 U.S.C. 78j)
>
> [13 FR 8183, Dec. 22, 1948, as amended at 16 FR 7928, Aug. 11, 1951]

securities regulation," contains the central antifraud provisions of the Securities Exchange Act of 1934 (see Box 3.5).

Unlike robbery, which constitutes outright theft by violence or the use of instruments of violence, fraud is a tricky offense that can lead to results of robbery without physical harm. That is, the methodologies of economic deprivation are different, but victims of theft encounter common pecuniary and psychological effects. Fraudulent acquisition of money is just another way of robbing people without using a gun, a knife, or the physical instruments of coercion or violence. Ironically, lower-class theft ("street crimes" or "conventional robbery") of paltry sums of money tends to be treated more harshly than white-collar crimes resulting in loss of colossal sums of money and pervasive global economic havoc. Although there are many formal definitions of fraud, a succinct definition can be found in Albrecht, Albrecht, Albrecht, and Zimbelman (2009):

> Fraud is a generic term, and embraces all the multifarious means which human ingenuity can devise, which are resorted to by one individual, to get an advantage over another by false representations. No definite and invariable rule can be laid down as a general proposition in defining fraud, as it includes surprise, trickery, cunning and unfair ways by which another is cheated. The only boundaries defining it are those which limit human knavery.[36]

Thus, fraud is a deception with the following elements: misrepresentation, materiality, falsehood, intent, believability (of the misrepresentation), overt act, and injury. Therefore, it can be defined as a *misrepresentation* about a *material matter*, which is *false* and deliberately intended—recklessly or otherwise—to persuade a victim to adversely believe and *injuriously* act upon the misrepresentation.[37] Palmiter identifies five critical elements: (i) material misinformation, (ii) scienter (when a defendant knows or should have known the true state of affairs and recognized that a plaintiff might rely on misinformation), (iii) reliance on misinformation, (iv) causation (loss that can be linked to misrepresentation), and (v) damages. Courts use diverse theories to measure damages under Rule 10b-5, but punitive damages (sanctions to deter/punish criminal behavior) are unavailable under the Rule.[38]

However, courts have placed limits on who can sue and be sued for securities fraud under 10b-5. Additionally, the element of reliance (believability) has been somewhat attenuated and only actual purchasers or sellers may recover damages in a private action under Rule 10b-5.[39] Any person who makes false or misleading statements and induces others to trade to their detriment (a primary violator) can become liable under Rule 10b-5. Accordingly, privity (agreement or consent) is not required for the Rule to take effect. Officials who exert control over others (control persons) are equally liable for the dissemination of false information except when they can show that they acted in good faith and did not induce primary violators to commit violations of the rule, meaning that the control persons did not exert actual control to further the commission of a crime.[40]

The aiding and abetting violation of Rule 10b-5 is rather unsettled. Palmiter observes that until 1994, lower courts uniformly upheld aiding and abetting liability under Rule 10b-5 for secondary participants such as accountants who certified falsified financial statements, or lawyers who gave substantial legal assistance to swindlers. However, in *Central Bank of Denver v. First Interstate Bank of Denver*, 511 U.S. 164 (1994), the US Supreme Court maintain the aiding and abetting liability "[d]espite its long and seemingly established place in 10b-5 jurisprudence."[41] Since *Central Bank*, it has become unclear whether the primary violator standard extends to facilitators. Similarly, in 1994, the Supreme Court did not find liability for sham transactions (scheme liability) that facilitated securities fraud.[42] Primary violators must actually make the misrepresentation to investors or have the misrepresentation directly attributed to them.[43] The Supreme Court has also ruled that only those who make false and misleading statement can be liable for such statement under Rule 10b-5.[44]

Deception may take multifarious forms, but the elements of intent and materiality are central to an actionable liability suit. Half-truths, material omission, and injurious acquiescence when there is a duty to speak can be actionable when the materiality threshold is met. Deception can also exist when new or superseding material information is not reported to prevent financial injury when in fact there is a duty to report.[45] The Supreme Court has also held that Rule 10b-5 is also applicable to oral contracts for the sale of securities.[46]

Materiality is required to avoid a pretext for shifting culpability for losses. For the purposes of Rule 10b-5, the Supreme Court has held that: "a fact is material … if there is a substantial likelihood that a reasonable investor 'would' (not 'might') consider it as altering the 'total mix' of information in deciding whether to buy or sell."[47] Material information is information that will otherwise affect an investment decision if it was made available *ex ante*. Manipulative devices, like financial statements fraud, are equally problematic under Rule 10b-5.

Manipulative devices generate false appearance of market activity and they are most often intended to distort market prices or the prices of securities. Inaccurate financial statements and unusual price-targeting schemes via purchases and/or sales of securities to manipulate prices in securities trade can be a violation of the anti-manipulative requirement of Rule 10b-5.[48] While the duty to speak is not generally actionable under Rule 10b-5, individuals with fiduciary obligations fall into a special category. Therefore, the courts require individuals to disclose material information when individuals have a special relationship of trust and confidence with their clients.[49] Manipulative trading is separated from trading based on misappropriation of information.

In *Chiarella v. United States*, the petitioner, Chiarella, worked as a "markup man" for a financial printer involved with the announcements of corporate takeover bids. The documents that were delivered to the printer did not initially disclose the names of the target company. The petitioner cleverly made deductions from the information without specific names and purchased stocks in the target companies prior to the disclosure of the information to the public. Chiarella's profits from the purchase and sale of the stocks exceeded $30,000.[50]

Did Chiarella misappropriate and benefit from privileged information? The court ruled that "the obligation to disclose … rested upon one having the 'affirmative' duty to disclose arising from a relationship of trust and confidence between parties to a transaction."[51] Chiarella was not seen as a corporate insider who received information from target companies. As such, the court did not speculate that everyone including a seller must have a duty to report information, which will create a general duty among all participants in the marketplace to forego actions based on material nonpublic information:

> We cannot affirm petitioner's conviction without recognizing a general duty between all participants in market transactions to forgo actions based on material, nonpublic information. Formulation of such a broad duty, which departs radically from the established doctrine that duty arises from a specific relationship between two parties * * * should not be undertaken absent some explicit evidence of congressional intent.
>
> (Coffee et al., 2007, p. 1148)

The classical misappropriation (insider) theory has not exonerated all "outsiders" in the employ of entities with fiduciary duties from liability.[52]

The "misappropriation theory" holds that a person commits fraud "in connection with" a securities transaction, and thereby violates § 10(b) and Rule 10b-5, when he misappropriates confidential information for securities trading purposes, in breach of a duty owed to the source of the information. Under this theory, a fiduciary's undisclosed self-serving use of a principal's information to purchase or sell securities, in breach of a duty of loyalty and confidentiality, defrauds the principal of the exclusive use of that information ... .

The classical theory targets a corporate insider's breach of duty to shareholders with whom the insider transacts; the misappropriation theory outlaws trading on the basis of nonpublic information by a corporate "outsider" in breach of a duty owed not to the trading party, but to the source of the information.

(O'Sullivan, 2003, p. 775)

In *Securities and Exchange Commission v. Materia* (2d. Cir. 1984), the Second Circuit affirmed an injunction and disgorgement of unlawfully obtained profits where the employee of a printing company misappropriated confidential information concerning tender offers and subsequently traded on the information. "The Court found that the misappropriation of material nonpublic information by an employee, perpetrated a fraud upon the employer that was prohibited by the antifraud provisions of the Securities Exchange Act of 1934."[53] Similarly, in *US v. O'Hagan*, the conduct of a lawyer who benefited from information about his client's planned takeover bid of a target by purchasing the stock of the target was determined to be fraudulent. A fraud was consummated when the lawyer acted (traded) on the information to which he was entrusted without disclosure to his principal. The breach of duty coincided with the securities transaction and animated the essence of the Securities Exchange law (Rule 10b-5).[54] Though the person or entity defrauded is not the other party to the trade, it is the source of the nonpublic information.

In reality, "insider" and "outsider" theories are known to have complementarities. Both are induced by privileged information (riskless news) to profit from securities trade based on different sources of information.

Not every securities fraud is prosecuted exclusively under specific securities statutes. General criminal provisions such as mail fraud, wire fraud, obstruction of justice, and conspiracy to commit an offense against the United States or to defraud the United States may be applied under the general criminal provisions.[55] The mail fraud statute is situated in 18 U.S.C. § 1341 and it requires proof of four elements: (i) a scheme devised or intending to defraud or for obtaining money or property by fraudulent means, (ii) intent, (iii) materiality, and (iv) use or causing to use the mails (or private carrier) in furtherance of the fraudulent scheme.[56] The law is considered to be a low-hanging fruit because of its breadth and simplicity of proof. Mail and wire fraud are considered inchoate (transitory) offenses. Since there is no general federal attempt statute, inchoate offenses can be attacked even before criminal acts are consummated. A wire fraud case needs two elements: (i) a scheme to defraud, and (ii) the use of interstate wire communications in furtherance of the scheme.[57] Since the SEC cannot enforce the mail and wire fraud statute, which can only be enforced by the US Justice Department in a criminal prosecution, misappropriation by means of mail/wire fraud is susceptible to criminal penalties.[58]

The federal criminal code has multiple provisions that deal with obstruction of justice, including: (i) influencing or injuring an officer or juror generally (18 U.S.C. § 1503), (ii) obstruction of proceedings before departments, agencies, and committees (18 U.S.C. § 1505), (iii) tampering with a witness, victim, or an informant (18 U.S.C. § 1512), (iv) destruction, alteration, or falsification of records in federal investigations and bankruptcy (18 U.S.C. § 1519), and (v) destruction of corporate audit record (18 U.S.C. § 1520).[59]

US conspiracy statutes appear within and without the criminal code of Title 18 and they address various forms of conspiracies; for example, the conspiracy to restrain trade (15 U.S.C. § 1), and the conspiracy to monopolize trade (15 U.S.C. § 2). Like mail fraud, conspiracy is an inchoate crime. A federal conspiracy charge under 18 U.S.C. § 371 can be filed when there is an agreement and overt act.[60] Therefore, it gives prosecutors a legal foundation to disrupt or stop criminality before consummation. According to Podgor and Israel (2009), the main federal conspiracy statute, 18 U.S.C. § 371, requires proof of the following elements: (i) an agreement, (ii) an unlawful object, (iii) knowledge and intent, and (iv) an overt act.[61]

Conspiratorial agreements do not have to be written, oral or explicit; they can be inferred from the facts and circumstances of a case.[62] While it is necessary to prove beyond a reasonable doubt that the conspirators agreed on the "essential nature of the plan," it is unnecessary to prove that all the conspirators had knowledge of all the details of a plan or even of the concerted participation of all the conspirators.[63]

For a conspiracy to exist there must be at least two or more parties (plurality). The multiplicity of parties does not necessarily mean that all the conspirators will be charged. A fundamental problem with conspiracy cases is that at least two people are required to prosecute certain cases, say bribery. Additionally, can some conspirators be found guilty when others are not? The rule prohibiting inconsistent verdict is contingent on the manner in which charges are applied (severally or in unison). Further, in *US v. Powell* (S. Ct. 1984), the court held that inconsistency alone cannot suffice to reverse a decision. Instrumentality (the use of a telephone) was separated from the crime (the conspiracy to possess illicit substance) and deemed sufficient for liability. Plurality becomes moot when a statute specifically protects one of the conspirators, say a government agent. But there is no true agreement when there is not a meeting of minds. Therefore, a conspiracy must include others apart from an agent.[64]

Under the conspiracy offense provision, the violation of other civil and criminal statutes is considered unlawful object of a conspiracy (external statutory infraction); for example, conspiracy to commit mail fraud is also a violation of 18 U.S.C. § 371. An overt act is defined by the *actus reus* (guilty act), which is an extension of intent or *mens rea* (guilty mind).

> The overt act must take place during the conspiracy. For purposes of the statute of limitations for conspiracy prosecution, the time does not commence to run until the commission of the last overt act in furtherance of the conspiracy as alleged in the charging document. It is incumbent that the government prove an overt act within the statute of limitations.
>
> (Podgor & Israel, 2009, p. 51)

Notably, Racketeer Influenced and Corrupt Organizations (RICO) and money laundering statutes do not require proof of overt acts.[65]

3.4 APPLICATIONS OF SEC LAW

One of the most consequential cases in recent memory of the application of securities law to investment decisions is the case of Enron. The case has several aspects of incriminating crimes under SEC law and general statutes that include individuals and a corporation with juridical personality. The case is replete with instances of white-collar crime that cannot easily be ignored: (i) filing false statement with the SEC, (ii) obstruction of justice, (iii) mail fraud, and (iv) perjury. The grand jury charges, plea agreements, and additional information in this section can also be found in Brickey[66], 2007, pp. 243–84, O'Sullivan (2003), pp. 442–81, and Fusaro and Miller (2002), pp. 163–79.

Enron Corp. ("Enron") was an Oregon corporation with its principal place of business in Houston, Texas. For most of 2001, the company was considered the seventh largest corporation in the US because of its reported revenues. In the previous ten years, Enron evolved from a regional natural gas provider to a trader of natural gas, electricity, and other commodities, *inter alia*, with retail operations in energy and other products.

In 1991, the company adopted mark-to-market accounting practices. In contradistinction to the historical costs principle of the balance sheet that was discussed earlier, it used replacement cost to report its income and value of assets. It also engaged in off-balance sheet practices during this time. Enron expanded and created special purpose entities (SPEs) in the 1990s. In 2000, the company was regarded as the most innovative company in America and in the same year it launched EnronCredit.com (the first real time credit department for a corporation). Concomitantly, in August of the same year its stock hit an all-time high of $90 per share[67] (see also Figure 3.1).

On or about May 15, 2001, within the Southern District of Texas (the *situs* of preparation), Enron filed via electronic transmission its Form 10-Q for the first quarter of 2001, which contained deceptive and manipulative information that was willfully and unlawfully filed with the SEC. Between 1997 through 2002, Enron overstated its financial results and filed false statements with the SEC. The company omitted material information and knowingly filed information that was materially false (wire fraud and violation of 10b-5).[68] Between March 1998 and October 21, 2001, the chief financial officer, Fastow, concertedly utilized electronic means to deceive investors. Four SPEs known as "Raptors" were particularly instrumental in the deception of the public. The Raptors, which were purported to be independent entities, were used to hedge the value of some of the assets of Enron. One of the SPEs, Talon, was created in April 2000 to prevent the depreciating value of certain investments that were reported in Enron's balance sheet. It was capitalized through promissory note and Enron's own stock. The SPEs showed no respect for arm's-length principles that are required by accounting practices, and the managers conspired to enrich themselves at the expense of shareholders.

Along the path of ruin, the accounting practices of Enron enabled it to dissemble losses and exaggerate earnings to the tune of about $1.2 billion in equity.[69] On October 16, 2001, numerous charges against the company's income for the third quarter were characterized as "non-recurring" (see also Box 3.4), against the advice of Arthur Andersen. The reduction in equity was directly related to a net loss of $618 million that was previously unreported for the third quarter of 2001, but which was subsequently made known on or about October 16, 2001, via a press release by the company. The SEC, which is responsible for investigating and punishing violations of federal securities law, immediately opened up an investigation into Enron's financial activities and reports. Invariably, financial malpractices, obstinacy to not correct misinformation, and compromised internal auditing or conflicts of interest perpetrated the fraud on investors.

At the time of the Enron debacle, Arthur Andersen, LLP (Anderson), performed accounting services for Enron. The firm, which was a partnership that provided accounting and consulting services for clients within and without the US and was ranked as one of the "Big Five" accounting firms in the US, had performed accounting services for Enron since the 1980s. By Friday October 19, 2001, Enron notified Andersen that the SEC had started an inquiry into the SPEs and the involvement of Enron's chief financial officer, Andrew Fastow. The following day, the accounting firm convened a meeting to address the SEC inquiry. The partners of the accounting firm assigned to Enron engaged in a wholesale destruction of documents in Houston, Texas on October 23, 2001. Instructions were given to Andersen personnel working on the Enron audit in Portland, Oregon, Chicago, Illinois, and London to destroy documents appertaining to the Enron inquiry.[70] In 2005, the US Government brought several charges against the accounting firm and employees of Enron:

(i) Andersen, for obstruction of justice for withholding records, documents, and other objects from official proceedings and altering, destroying, mutilating, and concealing objects with the intent to impair the objects' integrity and availability for use in official proceedings, hereby violating 18 U.S.C. §§ 1512(b)(2) and 3551 *et seq.*
(ii) Richard Causey, for filing false and misleading statements with the SEC in conspiracy with Enron's senior management, in violation of Rule 10b-5.

(iii) Fastow, for conspiracy to commit wire and securities fraud in violation of Rule 10b-5 and 18 U.S.C. § 371. Recall the elements of conspiracy, including: (i) an agreement between two or more persons, (ii) a crime against the US, and (iii) an overt act committed by one of the conspirators in furtherance of the agreement.

3.4 (A) SECURITIES TRADE AND EXTRATERRITORIAL JURISDICTION

Can SEC laws have international effect? This was precisely the question confronting a United States Court of Appeals in 1995 in *Itoba Ltd. v. Lep Group PLC*. Foreign companies issue securities in the US and US investors invest abroad. Recall some of the consequences of the mortgage-backed crisis (MBS). There are differences in national savings rates, disparities in propensities to invest, and the willingness of international investors to diversify their investments. At the same time, regulatory obligations vary from country to country. However, US interstate commerce law is broad enough to include foreign transactions. Section 2(a) 7 of the 1933 securities law includes "trade or commerce in securities or any transportation or communication relating thereto ★ ★ ★ between any foreign country and any State, Territory or the District of Columbia." Section 5 of the 1933 Act prohibits the use of "any means or instruments of transportation or communication in interstate commerce."[71]

In the 1990s, Lep Group PLC was a London-based holding company with subsidiaries in several countries. It was a conglomerate that owned biotechnology services, home security systems, and freight forwarding businesses, *inter alia*. It traded in the International Stock Exchange of the United Kingdom and the Republic of Ireland. At some point, the company became interested in trading in the US securities market. It deposited about 9 percent of its 136 million shares with an American depository, which in turn issued American Depository Receipt (ADR) for each five ordinary shares of Lep on deposit. The ADRs traded in Nasdaq. Invariably, companies that traded in Nasdaq must adhere to US securities law. Accordingly, Lep was no exception.

Itoba was a wholly-owned subsidiary of ADT, a securities system company that was headquartered in Delaware. The American securities company also owned ADT, a transnational holding company—also involved with securities protection services—that was headquartered in Bermuda. ADT traded in the New York Stock Exchange (NYSE). As an expansionary matter, ADT considered acquiring the National Guardian, one of ADT's competitors in the American security market. Because ADT held shares of the London-based Lep, the parent company of the National Guardian, it implicitly held shares in the National Guardian. Ultimately, Canadian Pacific and ADT became interested in the acquisition of Lep.

Canadian Pacific recruited a London-based investment bank, S.G. Warburg, to value Lep's business operations. ADT recruited its in-house financial analyst, Nicholas Wells, to perform the financial evaluation of Lep. The London-based investment bank, S.G. Warburg, released its report in December 1989, based on information obtained from

Lep's UK annual report, Form 20-F that was filed with the SEC (December 31, 1988), Lep's shareholder register, and broker reports. The ADT analyst pursued his valuation but relied heavily on the report of the London-based investment bank. Wells frequently discussed his analyses with ADT's vice chairman and official in charge of acquisition, David Hammond.

ADT eventually decided to purchase Lep and formulated plans to increase its holdings of Lep by using Itoba, one of its offshore companies, to make anonymous purchases. Itoba's board subsequently approved of the purchase of Lep and authorized one of ADT's employees to purchase shares of Lep in the name of Itoba. During the second half of 1990, Itoba conducted a number of significant purchases on the London Stock Exchange (LSE). By November 1990, Itoba had acquired over 37 million ordinary shares of Lep for an estimated $114 million.[72]

However, before ADT could complete its planned acquisition, Lep disclosed some business reversals that reduced the market value of its shares. The share price of Lep fell by 97 percent and the value of Itoba's Lep holdings declined by $111 million. Lep wrote off approximately $522 million from its books for the fiscal year ending on December 31, 1991.[73] Did Lep—a London-based company—engage in deceptive business practice that violates US SEC law?

Itoba sued Lep and its officers in the District of Connecticut, asserting violations of Sections 10(b) and 20 of the SEC Act of 1934.

> According to Itoba, the defendants were subject to liability because they failed to disclose material matters in statements filed with the SEC. Specifically, Itoba alleged that Lep made high risk investments and engaged in speculative business ventures without informing the investing public. Itoba claimed that had these matters been properly disclosed, it would not have purchased Lep's stock at artificially inflated prices.
>
> (Coffee et al., 2007, p. 1443)

The defendants moved to dismiss the suit on the basis of subject matter jurisdiction; implying that SEC law should not have far-reaching international effect (enforcement through US courts) on foreign companies that use US securities markets to conduct business. Because the financial statements were prepared in England, Lep contended that a mere filing with the SEC should not confer subject matter jurisdiction in the US. The filing with the SEC was considered to be incidental or preparatory conduct in whatever injury may have occurred. The Appellate Court disagreed. It held that the *situs* of preparations for SEC filings should not be determinative of jurisdictional questions. "Otherwise, the protection afforded by the Securities and Exchange Act could be circumvented simply by preparing SEC filings outside of the United States. We find no support in the Act for such a result."[74]

> It is well recognized that the Securities Exchange Act is silent as to its extraterritorial application … .[75]
>
> However, in determining whether Congress intended that the "precious resources of the United States courts" be devoted to a specific transnational securities fraud claim, we are not without guidance. Two jurisdictional tests have emerged under this Court's decisions: the "**conduct test**" as announced in *Leasco Delata Processing Equip. Corp. v Maxwell*, 468 F. 2d 1326, 1336–37 (2d Cir. 1972), and the "**effects test**", as announced in *Schoenbaum*, 395 U.S. 906 * * * (1969) (in banc), cert. denied sub nom. *Manley v Schoenbaum*, 395 U.S. 906 * * * (1969). There is no requirement that these two tests be applied separately and distinctly from each other. Indeed, an admixture or combination of the two often gives a better picture of whether there is sufficient United States involvement to justify the exercise of jurisdiction by an American court. It is in this manner that we address the issue of jurisdiction in the instant case. Because we believe that the allegations are sufficient to support jurisdiction, we reverse.
>
> (Coffee et al., 2007, p. 1444)[76]

A federal court is empowered to exercise subject matter jurisdiction under the conduct test if: (i) a defendant's activities in the US were more than merely preparatory to a securities fraud conducted elsewhere (out of the US) and (ii) the fraudulent activities or culpable failures to act within the US directly cause losses (injury).[77] "Inherent in the conduct test is the principle that Congress does not want 'the United States to be used as a base for manufacturing fraudulent security devices for export, even when these are peddled only to foreigners.'"[78]

The superseding ruling of the Appellate Court rejected the ruling of the magistrate judge that ADT and Itoba did not read and rely on the SEC filing when making their acquisition decision. The firms clearly relied on the report of the London-based investment bank which also included information from the Form 20-F that Lep had filed with the SEC. Further, the companies also used their own copy of the 1988 Form 20-F. The court found no compelling reason for a party to an investment dispute—involving a public corporation—to read a misleading financial report to establish reliance; derivative reliance was considered to be a well-established basis for liability in a Rule 10b-5 action.[79]

The effects test was considered to be premised on the basic purpose of the securities law; the fair disclosure of material information (facts). Absent any public enlightenment, a material fact that is undisclosed will remain opaque, which raises an accompanying duty to report correct information or correct inaccurate information. Therefore, the effects test is based on fraud, which takes place abroad but generates adverse effects on American investors who purchase stocks that are registered and listed on an American securities exchange. The court noted:

> We believe that Congress intended the Exchange Act to have extraterritorial application in order to protect domestic investors who have purchased foreign securities on American exchanges and to protect the domestic securities market from

> the effects of improper foreign transactions in American securities. In our view, neither the usual presumption against extraterritorial application of legislation nor the specific language of Section 30 (b) show Congressional intent to preclude application of the Exchange Act to transactions regarding stocks traded in the United States which are effected outside the United States when extraterritorial application of the Act is necessary to protect American investors.
>
> (Coffee et al., 2007, p. 1448)[80]

Shareholders ultimately lose financial value when management makes bad financial decisions. Adverse managerial decisions and distrust between shareholders (principal) and management (agent) cause unsurprising struggle for control of managerial decisions by public corporations.

3.4 (B) THE PRINCIPAL-AGENT PROBLEM

A significant problem with investment and public corporations is the principal–agent relationship, when large firms try to separate ownership from control. Shareholders (principals) entrust the management of the corporations to managers (agents) who are supposed to pursue the best interest of the shareholders and management, partly because the shareholders are not constantly present or skilled enough to manage the affairs of public corporations. The shareholders can neither manage the businesses by themselves nor monitor the motives and activities of management constantly. At times, the shareholders are unable to clearly identify the reasons for bad managerial outcomes because they are separated from the business by trust in management. Therefore, the integrity of corporate governance is critically important for successful business operations. Resnick and Eun (2015) provide a very workable definition of corporate governance:

> Corporate governance can be defined as the economic, legal, and institutional framework in which corporate control and cash flow rights are distributed among shareholders, managers and other stakeholders of the company.
>
> (Eun & Resnick, 2015, p. 82)[81]

The structural arrangement of public corporations therefore creates information-asymmetric problems. Distribution of information appertaining to the operations of public corporations is not evenly distributed at all times. As such, there is a tendency for agents to renege on their obligations and pursue their own selfish interests, which are not necessarily in the best interest of the principals (shareholders). This unsettling situation creates a principal-agent problem; a situation in which the best interest of shareholders is not represented by management, because management is pursuing the self-interests that are at variance with that of the shareholders. The foundation of self-interests is usually associated with "residual control rights," which are acquired because of contractual deficiencies that incompletely specify the obligations of management.[82] Apart from pursuing their own self-interests, managers may shirk their responsibilities by not putting in the amount of time and effort that are required to successfully innovate and operate the business. They might prefer to live a life that is ostentatiously skewed towards leisure.

Principal-agent conflicts erupt when shareholders belatedly realize that management has been exploiting fiduciary trust. In the fiduciary arrangement, supervisory detachment, lack of curiosity, and inadequate managerial skill has not paid off. In many ways, the structure of public corporations creates an inherent bias that favors the management. Essentially, it is a prohibitively costly proposition for shareholders to effectively monitor the incentives, business decisions, and actions of management. However, the ignorance hypothesis is waning because institutional investors—who are very sophisticated—tend to play a very dominant role in the operations of public corporations today. With huge blocks of investments, they actually monitor managerial performance and the results of their investments more closely. They are also capable of generating consequential financial news.

Disagreements of various forms among managers and shareholders can threaten the life of a business and the equity created by the shareholders. These disagreements include: breach of contract, breach of fiduciary duty, corporate mismanagement, disagreements over the sale of assets, mergers, and similar corporate events, executive compensation claims, buyout agreements and buyout rights, issues with dividends, distributions and shareholder loans, minority shareholder oppression, misappropriation of confidential information, self-dealing, shareholder appraisal rights, shareholder class actions, shareholder derivative suits and individual suits, valuation disputes, wrongful acquisition of shares, and wrongful transfer of stock.[83] Disagreements may also be the result of flawed and incomplete contracts that give managers acquired rights or discretion to make business decisions. Failed companies, like Enron, Lehman Brothers, and Bear Stearns, are unexemplary manifestations of the effects of mismanagement and incontinence that carry heavy agency costs.

Monitoring management is integral to successful business operations, but it may be an insufficient method to maintain a successful business. In actual fact, not all the Enron shareholders were free riders (some proactively and diligently monitored the report of the management and questioned some financial results); but shareholders can be bullied into submission or they can pursue judicial remedy, in which case lawyers and judges must be familiar with the underlying economic or financial theories or problems. It might even be too late to pursue judicial remedy. In April, 2001, Enron released its financial results for the first quarter of 2001. Revenues were up 280 percent from the previous year (Fusaro & Miller, 2002, p. 109). The detailed numbers that were submitted to the SEC showed that the earnings of the company on paper were not actually translating into real cash. In April 2001, the company held an analyst conference call. One of the participants, a managing director of a firm, asked why the balance sheet—the statement that reports the assets, liabilities, and equity of Enron—was not included in a press release. The then CEO of Enron, Jeffrey Skilling, replied that the balance sheet would be released as part of the following month's filing with the SEC. The participant who was dissatisfied, if not irritated, with the response retorted prophetically: "You're the only financial institution that can't come up with a balance sheet or cash flow statement after earnings."[84] The inquiry elicited unpleasant and untoward expletives from the CEO.

Dodgy financial reporting (of the sort that is reported in Box 3.1) enabled the Enron management to deceive investors. The company improperly characterized hundreds of millions of dollars as increase rather than decrease in shareholder equity. In the first quarter of 2000, Enron recorded $85 million in earnings from a partnership vehicle that held Enron stock. The earnings were recorded as recurring though they were windfall earnings from materially false information to the investing public. At the same time losses of Enron Energy Services (EES), amounting to hundreds of millions of dollars went unreported in the first quarter of 2001.[85] In 2001, numerous charges against income were classified as "non-recurring" expenses. SPEs were used to hide the liabilities of the company.[86] SPE exposures were colossal; in one instance, about $35 million (Fusaro & Miller, 2002, p. 116). Essentially, Enron guaranteed the debts of the SPEs but kept the liabilities off its balance sheet (off-balance sheet liabilities). The liabilities should have been disclosed as "contingent liability," because of an obligation to make subsequent repayments,[87] if the management had preferred ethical accounting practices regardless of GAAP stipulations.

If the lack of transparency and obscenities were bad enough, employees (shareholders who were also stakeholders) were in a much more precarious situation. They were prevented from disposing of their toxic equities. In October 2001, Enron employees were prevented from selling the stock of Enron for about a month when the company changed its 401(k) pension plan administrator. On December 2, 2001, Enron filed for Chapter 11 bankruptcy protection and 4,000 employees lost their jobs.[88] The legal infringements will be subsequently explored in this chapter.

The lack of good (ethical) business judgment and transparency has dire consequences for the expansion of market share and the continuation of cash flows. Figure 3.1 captures the horrific consequences of the agency problem for the stakeholders and shareholders of Enron between August 23, 2000 and November 28, 2001; the stock price dropped from $90.75 to $1, leaving considerable loss of value and destruction for stakeholders and shareholders.

(A) 1996 to 2001: Enron is the darling of Wall Street; share price rises; Fortune magazine calls Enron "America's Most Innovative Company" for six consecutive years.
(B) 1999 to mid-2001: Enron executives and directors receive $1.1 billion by selling 17.3 million shares.
(C) April 17, 2001: Enron reports first quarter profits of $536 million.
(D) August 14, 2001: Jeffrey K. Skilling abruptly resigns as chief executive, citing "personal reasons." Kenneth Lay reassumes the position of CEO.
(E) August 20, 2001: Lay sells 93,000 shares for about $2 million. At the same time, he urges employees to buy company shares, sends an e-mail to employees assuring them that the company is on a solid footing, and predicts "significantly higher stock price."

CORPORATE FINANCIAL ANALYSIS

Figure 3.1 Enron: price per share $90.75 (August 23, 2000) to $1 (November 28, 2001)
Source: Douglas Linder, UMKC School of Law. "A short seller lucky enough to have sold Enron stock short at $90 per share in August 2000 … could buy it back at $60 per share in April 2001, could have made a profit of $30 per share" (Fusaro & Miller, 2002, p. 110).

(F) September 26, 2001: In an online chat with employees, Lay says that Enron stock is a good buy and that the company's accounting methods are "legal and totally appropriate."
(G) October 16, 2001: Enron reports a third-quarter loss of $618 million.
(H) October 22, 2001: The SEC opens an inquiry into Enron's accounting.
(I) December 2, 2001: Enron files for bankruptcy protection.[89]

While Enron failed because of reckless investment strategies and serious accounting irregularities, some other companies in a similar predicament (like KPMG and BMS) were able to recover and clean up their acts. The mortgage-backed crisis of 2007/2008 was different from that of the late 1990s in so far as it involved financial engineering and coordinated efforts to sell new and risky securities for personal gain while avoiding criminal liability. The mechanisms and processes for accomplishing the objectives were already in place: (i) securitization, (ii) issuance of collateralized debt obligations (CDOs), (iii) valuing asset quality, (iv) insuring assets, and (v) profiting from spreads.

Securitization involves the aggregation of assets that cannot be marketed on their own accord into a new category of securities with investment-grade appeal that can be marketed. However, the bundling of assorted assets can excite inflated levels of confidence in the securities and less discernible risks of default. Bank managers will worry about bank capital when loans are risky. They will therefore try to get rid of risky loans as fast as possible to safeguard capital when depository institutions are regulated. Loans appear

Table 3.1 Capital adequacy requirements (US$m)

Prudential Bank		Risky Bank	
Assets	**Liabilities**	**Assets**	**Liabilities**
Reserves $10	Deposits $70	Reserves $10	Deposits $80
Loans $75	Bank Capital $15	Loans $75	Bank Capital $5

on the asset side of balance sheets and depository institutions must have adequate capital to cover depreciation of asset value. Consider Prudential and Risky Banks of Table 3.1. Should both banks incur losses of $6 million in bad loans, Risky Bank will have a negative (-$1 million) bank capital while the bank capital of Prudential Bank will be reduced to a positive $11million. Banks with negative bank capital will not be permitted to continue their operations when they are properly regulated.[90] Typically, very precarious situations of inadequate bank capital can lead to bank runs, in which case the banks must be able to use reserves or increase securities on the asset side, or borrow from the Fed on the liabilities side. Banks with access to the funds of central banks are not considered to be shadow banks.

Investment banks can be obliging if they are willing to reduce the exposure of depository institutions for profits. Managers of securities firms can be equally happy if they can make handsome bonuses for peddling securities.

By the start of the twenty-first century, investment banks like Lehman Brothers and Bear Stearns played a critical role in investment banking and the sale of new securities. When it comes to securitization, investment banks can set up trusts for the purpose of buying assets that are being securitized. The trust (SPE) will purchase specialized assets from the originators, repackage the assets and sell the assets as securities to investors. Mortgage-backed securities followed a similar procedure with coordinated involvement of ratings agencies, securities firms, and insurance companies. The mortgage securitization process involved borrowers, depository institutions, SPEs, and investors. Borrowers dealt with bank originators of loans, the banks dealt with SPEs, and the SPEs dealt with investors.[91] Some investment companies prominently became shadow banks (financial intermediaries that pretended to be banks but were not regulated like banks); for example, they were not stringently scrutinized for capital adequacy and the repeal of the Glass-Steagall Act—by the Gramm-Leach-Bliley Act of November 1999—somewhat encouraged investment banks to engage in investment and commercial banking activities at the same time. Shadow banking activities consist of financial intermediation (by otherwise specialized financial intermediaries) without direct and explicit access to central bank liquidity (backstop). Financial mediation may be in the form of credit, maturity, and liquidity transformation (using short-term funds to invest in longer-term assets).[92]

The mortgage-backed crisis was infamous for the creation of tranches that were based on perceived value of mortgages and probability of default by debtors. The "senior" or top-rated tranche was perceived to have low probability of default, and therefore relatively low yield. The "mezzanine" tranche was the intermediate category with a probability of modest risk. The "toxic waste" tranche was the most vulnerable category that was associated with a very high probability of default.[93] With the encouragement of rating agencies, the toxic category assets had to be enhanced by better quality assets for better ratings (diversification) that would appeal to investors. The financial engineering took place with insufficient emphasis on the probabilities of default and loss of investor confidence in the securities, or even access to newer loans.

The National Commission on the Causes of the Financial Crisis identified five key players: (i) securities firms, (ii) CDO managers, (iii) rating agencies, (iv) investors, and (v) financial guarantors. The securities firms underwrote the CDOs by approving the selection of collateral, structuring the notes into tranches, and selling them to investors. They were more interested in generating fees and structuring securities that were marketable. CDO managers selected collateral, such as Mortgage-Backed Securities (MBS), and received fees for the value of CDOs they managed and/or performance. CDO managers received fees in the range of $600k to $1 million for deals in the senior category. Even junior tranches provided lucrative fees in the range of $750k to $1 million. In effect, the perverse incentives were irresistible.

The rating agencies provided guidance on the collateral and the structure of the CDOs (sizes, returns, and tranches).[94] Triple-A rating cajoled many investors into the ill-fated toxic MBS market. Investors based their investment on risk preferences based on ratings, and many were also institutional investors. Guarantors like American International Group (AIG) provided opportunities for credit default swaps (over-the-counter derivatives). The swaps made the CDOs very attractive and reassuring of profits. Wall Street employees made fabulous bonuses and linkages were created for a boom in other securities.

> [A]t the beginning of the 21st century, pretax profit for the five largest investment banks doubled between 2003 and 2006, from $20 billion to $43 billion; total compensation at these investment banks for their employees across the world rose from $34 billion to $61 billion.[95]

During the housing boom, investors got triple-A security protection and AIG obtained fees for providing insurance. However, in the spring of 2005 (after auditors uncovered records of manipulated earnings), AIG lost its triple-A rating. By November 2005, the reported earnings of the company were reduced by about $3.9 billion and the company stopped writing credit default swaps (CDS) in the same year.[96] About two years later, in July 2007, the values of the mortgage securities that the company had insured dropped precipitously and the company started to receive collateral calls from counterparties, especially Goldman Sachs.[97] Uncertainty pervaded the global market in 2007 and foreign institutions like Paribas came under stress. Aggregated collateral calls led to the failure of the company in 2008. The company had accumulated exposure worth $2.7 trillion of notional value in derivative markets, of which $1 trillion was with 12 major institutions.[98] Further downgrade of the AIG security and calls forced the Fed to invoke the obscure Article 13(3) in order to extend an $85 billion loan to AIG. The amount eventually reached $182 billion.[99] Under Article 13(3), the Fed provided special assistance to four firms that were deemed "too big to fail"—AIG, Bear Stearns, Citigroup, and Bank of America.[100] However, in terms of the Wall Street Houses, Bear Stearns was fifth in size. Blinder highlights its interconnectedness ("too interconnected to fail").[101]

The Financial Crisis Inquiry Report (FCIR) reveals that Bear Stearns, the smallest of the five investment banks, started its asset management business in 1985 when it established Bear Stearns Asset Management (BSAM). The company suffered prominently because of its role in the CDO trade, which it participated in with very high leverage ratios and aggressive use of the repo markets.[102] The repo markets are notable for hedge fund financing. By the end of 2006, BSAM had exposure amounting to about $18.3 billion in assets, with very little supervision by Bear Stearns.[103] Mortgage securitization became the largest component of the firm's fixed income division, the most profitable line of business that generated more than half of the firm's revenue.[104] In 2008, the firm had difficulties accessing the repo market and rumors (news) about the company's illiquidity made it difficult for the company to secure funding from the private sector. The value of the company plummeted and, after obtaining a loan of $13 billion from the Fed, the company was eventually purchased by JP Morgan for $2 a share (see Figure 3.2).

Lehman Brothers was not as lucky as Bear Stearns. On September 15, 2008, Lehman Brothers Holdings, Inc., the fourth largest US investment bank, sought Chapter 11 protection. The move initiated what has been characterized as the largest bankruptcy proceeding in US history. Beginning in 2006, like other investment banks of the time, Lehman started to invest aggressively in real estate-related assets and eventually garnered significant exposures to housing and subprime mortgages. According to Wiggins, Piontek,

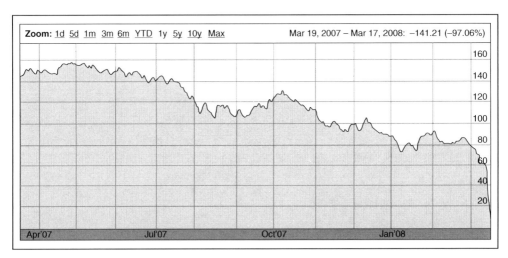

Figure 3.2 Bear Stearns: price per share $159 (March 19, 2007) to $2 per share (March 17, 2008)
Source: Phoenix Real Estate.

CORPORATE FINANCIAL ANALYSIS

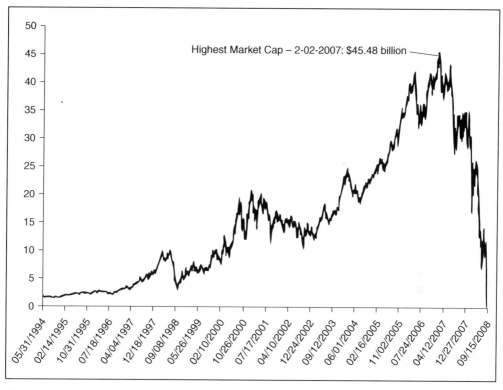

Figure 3.3 Lehman Brothers Holding—market capitalization, 1994–2008 ($billions)
Source: CRSP data; see Wiggins (2014, p. 4).

and Metrick (2014), it declared $639 billion in assets and $613 billion in debts. Of the reasons identified for the failure of the company, two are particularly noteworthy and common: (i) a highly leveraged, risk-taking business strategy supported by limited equity; and (ii) a culture of excessive risk-taking.[105]

As the MBS crisis progressed, rating agencies and analysts put pressure on the investment banks to reduce their leverage. Wiggins et al. (2014) identify two options for the reduction: (i) increase equity, or (ii) sale of assets. While the company was able to raise $6 billion in additional capital in early 2008, it preferred to sell assets. Additionally, the company significantly increased its reliance on repo transactions in 2007 and 2008, removing as much as $50 billion of assets from its balance sheet at quarter-end, which impacted its publicly reported leverage ratio.[106] The adjustment was belated and not reported under SEC disclosure requirement.

The company funded its long-term assets with short-term debt (repo agreements and commercial paper) and borrowed billions of dollars each day in the overnight market until financial institutions became disinclined to accept its collateral for borrowing. The inability to borrow short-term made it impossible for the company to meet its short-term obligations.

Table 3.2a Lehman's reported gross leverage ratios (2003–2007)

Year	2007	2006	2005	2004	2003
Leverage ratio reported*	30.7x	26.2x	24.4x	23.9x	23.7x

Source: Wiggins et al. (2014, p. 7).
Notes:
*Total assets divided by stockholders' equity.
It is estimated with some suspicion that the ratio for 2008 amounted to 25x (see Blinder, 2014, p. 121).

Figure 3.3 mirrors the effects of financing preferences (equity multipliers for Lehman) of Table 3.2a and Table 3.2b. It is much more straightforward to use the ratio of total liabilities-to-shareholders equity to determine the leverage ratio of a firm. Evidently, financial ratios are much more meaningful and revealing when they are utilized for comparative analysis; relative analyses can be intra-industrial or product-specific (for products in comparable market structures). Some firms operate in the clothing, automobile, food, pharmaceutical, and technology industries. Therefore, the markets in which firms operate must be taken into consideration when the performances of firms are comparatively evaluated.[107]

The asset/equity ratio shows the relationship of the total assets of the firm to the equity by shareholders. This ratio is an indicator of the company's leverage (via equity) used to finance the asset-generating aspect of the firm. Since there is no unique threshold for the ratio, the ratio is more valuable for comparing firms that are similarly situated. A relatively high ratio is indicative of the amount of equity (claim on wealth) that a company has absorbed to operate its business. In actual fact, the interpretation is less precise because it could also mean that the return on borrowed money (equity) is greater than the cost of raising capital. Additionally, the ratio does not say anything about asset quality or value, especially when diminishing historical cost cannot be unquestionably used to ascertain value. Implicitly, other financial indicators must be examined to determine a specific probative objective. When interest rate rises, investors lose confidence in businesses, and financial markets become jittery; high leverage ratios can create problems for public corporations. The equivocal effects of the asset-to-liability relationship were also affirmed by the financial crisis of 2007/2008. The assuming and very robust asset values quickly disintegrated into worthless financial artifacts. The Goldman Sachs' version of the leverage ratio (Table 3.2b) (total liabilities-to-shareholders equity) is indicative of the extent to which all outstanding debts can be covered by shareholders' equity. The liabilities version of the leverage ratio is a much more instructive and revealing leverage position that is less dissembling.

The leverage ratios show that the firms were highly leveraged just before the financial crisis of 2007 and 2008. In the case of Lehman Brothers, $1 worth of debt (equity) was used to generate about $31 worth of total "asset" in 2007. In 2008, the Goldman Sachs Group had about $27 worth of debt that was covered by $1 of shareholders' equity. This exposure was significantly reduced by more than half in 2015. The investment firms,

Table 3.2b Goldman Sachs Group Inc leverage ratios (February 26, 2008 and June 26, 2015)*

Year	2015	2008	Avg.
Leverage ratio reported*	8.81x	26.89x	14.57x

Source: CSI Market.com.
Note:
*Total liabilities-to-shareholders' equity.

including Bear Stearns, operated with very high leverage ratios in the run up to the financial crisis. As Blinder (2014) pointed out, a mere 2.5 percent decline in the value of assets was capable of wiping out all shareholder value.[108] Evidently, the financial crisis revealed that the asset/equity representation of leverage can be very misleading. In the final analysis, Lehman failed because it could not be purchased by Barclays, and the Fed became less tolerant of rescuing companies that had high investment in toxic assets but did not pose consequential systemic risk.

The policies that led to the demise of the formerly great companies were never sudden and dramatic. They were incremental malfeasance or misfeasance that spanned several years of mismanagement, self-interest, and incontinence. Notably, the managerial inefficiencies made the welfare of shareholders and stakeholders residual at best. Maturity transformation (obtaining short-term funds to invest in longer-term assets), excessive risk undertakings, the conflation of investment and commercial banking without adequate pecuniary backstops (shadow banking) and fraudulent or deceptive financial reports, exposed shareholders and stakeholders to grave financial peril. On occasions when management and shareholders fight over the payment of dividends, when should judges get involved in the principal–agent dispute?

3.4 (C) A CASE OF ABUSIVE MANAGERIAL DISCRETION? DODGE V. FORD MOTOR COMPANY (204 MICH. 459 170 N.W. 668 (1919))

Dodge v. Ford is controversial and instructive because it reflects a curious mixture of managerial decision and positive and normative economics (review the subject matter in Chapter 1). While the positive aspect of economics is evident and susceptible to real examination, the normative aspect is opaque and elusive when intent or motive cannot be clearly ascertained. The judicial value of the case is twofold: (i) the affirmation that courts are not surrogate managers, and (ii) that courts can rule on arbitrary and abusive use of managerial discretion. Of course, altruistic motives cannot be clearly and convincingly ascertained when there are subterranean lingering ulterior motives. In actual fact, the normative issue of stakeholder interest was not determined to have superseding consideration when it comes to the distribution of rights between shareholders and stakeholders.

Ford was a private enterprise that was owned by only a few shareholders. Henry Ford held the majority of shares. In 1916, the company was able to sell over 470,000 cars and made a profit just shy of $60 million, but the BoDs under Henry Ford's control was disinclined to issue dividends above $1.2 million.[109] John and Horace Dodge (brothers) owned 10 percent of Ford. From 1904 until 1913, the Dodge brothers built the engines for Ford vehicles and in 1914 they formed a company and began producing trucks for the government.[110] In 1917, the Dodges introduced a commercial automobile, which competed with Ford. Though Ford made a substantial amount of revenue and was full of prospects, the minority shareholders received what they believed to be inadequate dividends. Additionally, the per unit price of cars was reduced from $900 to $440 and eventually to $360.[111] The head of the company, Henry Ford, conceded that the price reductions adversely affected the profits of the business. Declining profits were juxtaposed with altruistic (normative), idiosyncratic, or arbitrary decisions to increase the welfare of as many people (stakeholders) as possible.[112]

The plaintiffs, the Dodges, were wealthy, and interested in competing in the automobile industry. Henry Ford was equally determined to stifle any form of competition against his business. The plaintiffs had received more than they invested, and Ford felt it was time to slow down dividend payments in order to expand the business and improve the welfare of stakeholders (the greatest number of people). Dissatisfied with the business decision of the management, the Dodges sued, challenging the authority of the BoDs to make business decisions that did not maximize the value of the shares of the plaintiffs. Higher dividends could have transferred financial resources from Ford to the competition. Was Ford making a business decision in his best interest to stifle competition?

The lower court disagreed with Ford's altruism to use shareholder investment for the benefit of stakeholders, ordered the company to pay $19 million, and enjoined the construction of a factory (growth or expansion of the company). However, as a matter of customary practice or law, courts have not interfered with the business judgments of BoDs. Consequently, the Michigan Supreme Court reversed the decision of the lower court to enjoin the construction of a factory. The State Supreme Court lifted the injunction because judges were never considered to be business experts with responsibilities for the business decisions and operations of corporations. After inspection and review of Ford's balance sheet and anticipated capital outlays, the court concluded that the withholding of greater dividends was an arbitrary act and ordered a supplemental dividend payment of $19 million.[113] The court telegraphed that though altruistic sentiments are laudable, they cannot supersede the interests of shareholders. Judges can neither enjoin the ability or managerial decisions of businesses to lawfully expand nor dictate the appropriate price mechanisms that are within the legal authority of managers.

CORPORATE FINANCIAL ANALYSIS

In 1919, the year of the *Dodge* decision, Henry Ford bought out the interest of the Dodge brothers in Ford for $25 million. The Dodges traded their $10,000 shares for $25 million and the reward of the State Supreme Court (supplemental payment).[114] Did the management abuse its discretion? Cox and Hazen (2003) note that:

> In most cases where dividends have been compelled, it has been shown that the directors willfully abused their discretion by withholding distributions because of an adverse interest, a wrongful purpose, or bad faith. In one case, dividends had not been declared in more than 20 years, even though the firm was profitable and its majority shareholder had awarded herself with an excessive salary and had misappropriated the company's assets.[115]

Evidently, though courts can be reluctant to make business decisions, they are less likely to accept abusive managerial discretion.

The ruling of the court must be scrutinized very carefully. The court did not outlaw the interest of stakeholders in business decisions. The court examined the proportionality of business decisions that impact shareholders and stakeholders and failed to see why the interest of shareholders must be adversely subordinated to that of stakeholders, especially in circumstances when the motives of management are ocularly contrived.

3.4 (C) (I) MANAGERIAL ECONOMICS IN *DODGE V. FORD*

Let us first review the positive economic aspects of the case. What are the underlying positive economic theories of the case? It is a case of price determination, profit v. wealth maximization, and long-term financial or economic growth of a public corporation. Evidently, firms in the automobile industry do not operate in a perfectly competitive market structure. They are price makers and they have market power. Their products are differentiated or unique, and they can increase total revenue when they are operating on the elastic segment of their market demand curve by reducing prices. Consider Figure 3.4 to understand the business decision of Ford.

Ford reduced price from $900 per unit to $360 per unit. Assume that the company was producing about 500,000 units of cars. The company could have increased its total revenue by decreasing price only if it was operating on the elastic segment ($e_d > 1$) of its market demand curve (review the concept of elasticity in Table 1.1 and the discussion of Figure 1.9 (a) and (b) in Chapter 1). Implicitly, if price had fallen below the hypothetical $450, the company would have been operating on the inelastic segment ($e_d < 1$) of its market demand curve. For the management to have attributed declining profits to price reduction and not the cost of production, it would most likely have been operating on the inelastic segment of its market demand curve. We must recall that total revenue (TR) is just one component of profit determination (see Equation 3.10); since profit is just the difference between total revenue and total cost. When TR is maximized, marginal (additional or incremental) revenue (MR, dTR/dQ) must be zero.

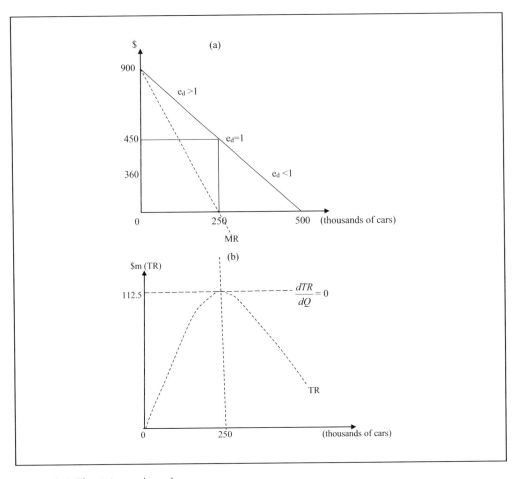

Figure 3.4 Elasticity and total revenue

$$\pi = PQ - C(Q) \tag{3.10}$$

$$\frac{d\pi}{dQ} = P - \frac{dC(Q)}{dQ} = 0 \tag{3.11}$$

$$P = \frac{dC}{dQ} = MC \tag{3.12}$$

So, why will management reduce the price of its product when the price reduction has detrimental effects on the profitability of its operations and the welfare of its shareholders? Three contending and plausible reasons can be attributed to such a pricing strategy:
(i) the management might be engaged in sporadic dumping of unwanted inventory without necessarily exposing direct nefarious intent (assuming the company is engaged in international trade) (this issue will be discussed extensively in Chapter 8 of this book),

(ii) the management might want to create a loyal clientele and project a positive corporate image by momentarily charging prices that are between the per unit cost of production and the average variable cost of production (review the cost discussion in Chapter 1), and (iii) the management might outrightly be engaged in predatory pricing to retard or prevent the prospects of formidable competition (domestic and/or international) by exploiting economies of scale and prime-mover advantage. Given the circumstances of the case, the latter two reasons seem to be more appealing. The Dodges wanted to transfer financial resources from Ford in order to compete fiercely. But what if Ford could create extensive economies of scale by producing the new factory that was not enjoined under the customary legal threshold of managerial independence? Figure 3.4 is further revealing.

By constructing a larger factory (Figure 3.5 Panel (a), plant size 2), Ford could have enjoyed some amount of economies of scale. Now in the long run, it could have increased both labor and capital and produced large quantities at a lower per unit cost of production. It also had prime-mover advantage. With Dodge lacking comparable capacity, Dodge could only have produced cars on a smaller scale because it could not have expanded labor and capital (new factory) on the same scale at the same time. It could also have faced diseconomies after expansion, partly because it was not a prime mover. Therefore, diseconomies, production at the upward sloping segment of its long-run average cost (LRAC) curve (Figure 3.5 Panel (b)), could have set in quickly to inhibit its ability to compete significantly. Alternatively, Ford could have sold his cars at lower prices because it was very well established, a tradition that it was already developing in order to squeeze Dodge out of the market. Consider the long-run per unit cost of production for both companies with different scales of production.

Extending the analysis beyond a private corporation, private and public corporations are wealth-maximizers. In economics, profit is a very static concept; it is just the difference between total revenue and total cost and nothing else. Wealth maximization and stakeholder interests add dynamism to the goals of corporations. The dynamism subsumes two important concepts: (i) growth and market share, and (ii) corporate social

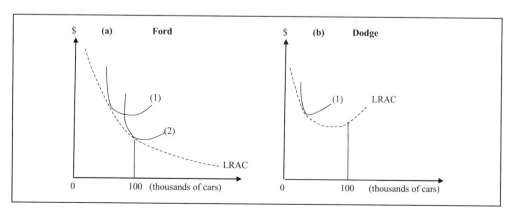

Figure 3.5 Economies of scale and long-run per unit cost of production

responsibility to stakeholders. That is, it is unrealistic to presume that corporations merely exist to maximize profit and shareholders' wealth. To facilitate growth and increase market share, managers must think about sustainable levels of economic activities. Growth can be based on internal results or assets (Equation 3.13) and revenue retention, or it can be based on external sources (a more sustainable model). Equations 3.13 and 3.14 capture the concepts of internal growth (IG) and sustainable growth (SG) of a company:

$$IG = \frac{ROA \star b}{1-(ROA \star b)} \tag{3.13}$$

$$SG = \frac{ROE \star b}{1-(ROE \star b)}; \tag{3.14}$$

where *ROA* is for return on assets (the ratio of net income to total assets), *ROE* is for return on equity (the ratio of net income to total equity), and *b* is the plowback or retention ratio:[116]

$$b = \frac{NI - D}{NI}; \tag{3.15}$$

where *NI* is for net income and *D* is for dividend payments.

The State Supreme Court of Michigan astutely stayed away from pricing and general managerial decisions but weighed in on the retention ratio (*b*) for reasons that it determined to be arbitrary and abusive. It also proffered alternative ways that can be exploited to facilitate growth of a company (the construction of a new factory). The court was clearly concerned about the inequitable payment of dividends and the arbitrariness with which revenue was withheld from shareholders in preference for stakeholders after analyzing Ford's balance sheet, Ford's projected (long-term) capital outlays, and normative arguments for subordinating the interest of shareholders to that of stakeholders.

3.4 (C) (II) NORMATIVE ECONOMICS IN *DODGE V. FORD*

Beyond the positive argument for economic growth, the decision that the retention of revenue was arbitrary is unavoidably linked to the normative arguments for withholding revenue in contradistinction to the return of shareholders after investment. The courts could not quite see why the welfare of stakeholders, which was a fundamental argument of the company to retain revenue, should gain peremptory considerations over the welfare of shareholders. If the rationale of the State Supreme Court was to suggest alternative sources of financing and equitable payment of dividends, its decision was a managerial rendition that had an impact on the prospects of economic growth of the company and the commitment of the company to stakeholders, because of abusive managerial discretion. Evidently, the court did not declare that corporations should not pay attention to stakeholders; it barely ruled on the priorities of management and the basis for prioritizing the welfare of stakeholders over that of shareholders.

Normative decisions are unavoidable in economic transactions, especially because they cannot be separated from positive outcomes and the long-run goals of corporations. Arguments that separate the interests of shareholders from that of stakeholders are based on a false premise that shareholders can maximize their welfare (wealth) without sensitivities to the interests of stakeholders. Corporations pay taxes to governments and governments can promulgate laws that reduce the profits and wealth of corporations. Employees (consumers) can become less motivated to be productive because of corporate culture and exploitative or abusive business decisions.

When companies reduce prices, they increase the real income of consumers and enhance their corporate image. More purchases increase corporate revenues. Consumers may also boycott the corporate sale of products because of labor and environmental abuses in the name of wealth maximization for shareholders. Therefore, corporations can create and retain a loyal and committed clientele as artificial bulwark against competition by engaging in rightful (normative) practices that enhance their images. That is, successful business models rely on amicable and long-lasting business relationships with stakeholders. Since the interest of shareholders and stakeholders cannot be mutually exclusive, the alienation of stakeholders is counterintuitive and self-destructive for any effort to increase wealth. Companies that ignore good (normative) practices expose themselves to fines, outrages of employees, consumers, or investors, and probable extinction in the short run.

When it comes to shareholder wealth maximization, the American Law Institute's (ALI's) Principles of Corporate Governance Project stipulate that corporations can ignore shareholder wealth maximization in order to: (i) comply with a law; (ii) make charitable contributions; and (iii) devote a "reasonable amount of resources to public welfare, humanitarian, educational, and philanthropic purposes."[117] In other words, the only exceptions permitted to abridge shareholder wealth maximization are recognizable norms that enhance stakeholder welfare.

In the contemporary global economy, some public companies are going beyond state corporate statutes (call of duty) to project a positive business image. They provide scholarships, contribute to various foundations (charities), and sponsor social events. These activities do not harm the interest of shareholders in any demonstrable way; rather they are intended to increase the market shares and project responsible and positive images of corporations. The managerial decisions and interventions that promote corporate image do not mean that the distribution of benefits (gains from trade) should be asymmetrically beneficial to stakeholders or that benefits from investments should be equally distributed; much to the contrary, responsible managerial decisions merely show that the interests of stakeholders can no longer be considered insignificant or unusually residual if corporations want to be successful in the modern economy. Pointedly, the significance of the contributions of stakeholders to the growth of public corporations can no longer be discounted or trivialized as corporations try to maximize wealth for their shareholders.

Good business practices expand consumer base, generate economies of scale, and maximize long-term wealth. Accordingly, contemporary public corporations are adopting growth models that endogenize people (stakeholders) and the environmental resources that sustain production. Henry Ford might just have been too precocious to think that his defense was omnipotent to defray ostensible intent or suspicion. One hundred years later, his business model is still committed to improvement of the welfare of people (shareholders and stakeholders):

> I believe the purpose of a company is to make people's lives better. That is how we became great in the past and it is how we will become even greater in the future.
> (William Clay Ford Jr. Executive Chairman, Ford Motor Company, 2019)

3.5 THE PRINCIPAL-AGENT STRUGGLE FOR CONTROL OF PUBLIC CORPORATIONS

Corporate managers can engage in three types of inefficiencies: (i) malfeasance, (ii) misfeasance, and (iii) nonfeasance. Malfeasance is the performance of an unlawful act as in the case of Enron. On the contrary, misfeasance is the performance of a legal act in an improper or injurious manner; for example, while the trading of toxic mortgage securities could have been done without breaking any law in some instances, the consequences were clearly injurious to shareholders and the general public. Nonfeasance is a breach of duty in a principal-agent relationship. It can also be seen as substantial neglect, or refusal (negligence) to perform a lawful duty without excuse. While malfeasance conveys the intent of an unlawful act, nonfeasance reflects deliberate apathy and a breach of trust (contract). Bainbridge (2012) notes that malfeasance and misfeasance have variously occurred in the annals of American business history. "The annals of American business corporations are replete with examples of both forms of shirking, ranging from congenital unluckiness, to incompetence, to outright theft."[118]

Therefore, it cannot be surprising that this type of distrust breeds tension between shareholders and management that morph into legal turf wars for the control of public companies. Boards have frantically fought to limit the ability of shareholders to take over companies by mounting up defenses such as "poison pills" to prevent takeovers. Also, the boards routinely fight to maintain robust executive compensation in proxy statements.[119] This book is not well suited for hosting the debate over who should be accorded primacy;[120] some form of legal compromise and due diligence (efficiency) should suffice to deal with the contention. However, courts of law have made some decisions that address the issue directly or tangentially.

As major investment banks organized teams of defense specialists to collaboratively work with management to forestall aggressive takeover bids, anti-takeover defenses became more sophisticated by the end of the 1980s.[121] Takeover hypotheses are rather dichotomous: (i) the management entrenchment hypothesis, and (ii) the shareholder interests hypothesis.

In the management hypothesis, it is asserted that stakeholders (non-participating shareholders), like employees lose value and stockholder wealth declines as financial markets re-evaluate a firm's stock when management resists takeover bids. The shareholder (convergence) hypothesis asserts that shareholder wealth increases as management undertakes measures to prevent changes in control; the interests of shareholders and management converge in such circumstances.[122]

Delaware corporate law empowers boards to resist hostile takeovers as part of the fiduciary duty of the boards. Accordingly, a target's (the company to be co-opted) board of directors has acquired broad legal authority to determine whether to merge a firm and to select a bidder or merger partner (see Box 3.6: Delaware General Corporation Law (DGCL) Title 8 § 251(b)).

Though shareholders have no explicit statutory authority to initiate merger negotiations, they are not eliminated from the process (see § 251 (c)). Merger agreements must

> be submitted to the stockholders of each constituent corporation at an annual or special meeting for the purpose of acting on the agreement. Due notice of the time, place and purpose of the meeting shall be mailed to each holder of stock, whether voting or nonvoting, of the corporation at the stockholder's address as it appears on the records of the corporation, at least 20 days prior to the date of the meeting.
> (also recall the earlier discussion of the proxy statement DEF 14A)
>
> To be sure, most mergers require shareholders approval. If the target's board rejects bidder however, the merger process comes to a halt without shareholder involvement. If the board approves a merger agreement, the shareholders become somewhat more involved, but only slightly. Shareholders have no statutory right to amend or veto specific provisions, their role being limited to approving or disapproving the merger agreement as a whole, with the statute requiring only approval by a majority of the outstanding shares.
> (Bainbridge, 2012, p. 58)[123]

Corporate law defers to boards when it comes to making very important business decisions about the operations of public companies. Corporate boards of directors (BoDs) have a legal authority to represent the interests of shareholders. The duties of BoDs include hiring and firing CEOs, setting up compensation and monitoring performance, approving major decisions of the enterprise, and ensuring that there is a convergence of interest between managers and shareholders. "The most effective means of aligning the interests of managers with those of stockholders is a well-designed compensation (pay) package that rewards managers when they do what stockholders want them to do and penalizes them when they do not."[124] As such, some corporations have management compensation plans that link compensation to the performance of the business in order to incentivize management.

BOX 3.6 DELAWARE CODE TITLE 8 § 251

MERGER OR CONSOLIDATION OF DOMESTIC CORPORATIONS

(a) Any 2 or more corporations of this State may merge into a single surviving corporation, which may be any 1 of the constituent corporations or may consolidate into a new resulting corporation formed by the consolidation, pursuant to an agreement of merger or consolidation, as the case may be, complying and approved in accordance with this section.

(b) The board of directors of each corporation which desires to merge or consolidate shall adopt a resolution approving an agreement of merger or consolidation and declaring its advisability. The agreement shall state:

(1) The terms and conditions of the merger or consolidation;

(2) The mode of carrying the same into effect;

(3) In the case of a merger, such amendments or changes in the certificate of incorporation of the surviving corporation as are desired to be effected by the merger (which amendments or changes may amend and restate the certificate of incorporation of the surviving corporation in its entirety), or, if no such amendments or changes are desired, a statement that the certificate of incorporation of the surviving corporation shall be its certificate of incorporation;

(4) In the case of a consolidation, that the certificate of incorporation of the resulting corporation shall be as is set forth in an attachment to the agreement;

(5) The manner, if any, of converting the shares of each of the constituent corporations into shares or other securities of the corporation surviving or resulting from the merger or consolidation, or of cancelling some or all of such shares, and, if any shares of any of the constituent corporations are not to remain outstanding, to be converted solely into shares or other securities of the surviving or resulting corporation or to be cancelled, the cash, property, rights or securities of any other corporation or entity which the holders of such shares are to receive in exchange for, or upon conversion of such shares and the surrender of any certificates evidencing them, which cash, property, rights or securities of any other corporation or entity may be in addition to or in lieu of shares or other securities of the surviving or resulting corporation; and

BOX 3.6 CONTINUED

MERGER OR CONSOLIDATION OF DOMESTIC CORPORATIONS

(6) Such other details or provisions as are deemed desirable, including, without limiting the generality of the foregoing, a provision for the payment of cash in lieu of the issuance or recognition of fractional shares, rights or other securities of the surviving or resulting corporation or of any other corporation or entity the shares, rights or other securities of which are to be received in the merger or consolidation, or for any other arrangement with respect thereto, consistent with §155 of this title.

The agreement so adopted shall be executed and acknowledged in accordance with §103 of this title. Any of the terms of the agreement of merger or consolidation may be made dependent upon facts ascertainable outside of such agreement, provided that the manner in which such facts shall operate upon the terms of the agreement is clearly and expressly set forth in the agreement of merger or consolidation. The term "facts," as used in the preceding sentence, includes, but is not limited to, the occurrence of any event, including a determination or action by any person or body, including the corporation.

(c) The agreement required by subsection (b) of this section shall be submitted to the stockholders of each constituent corporation at an annual or special meeting for the purpose of acting on the agreement. Due notice of the time, place and purpose of the meeting shall be mailed to each holder of stock, whether voting or nonvoting, of the corporation at the stockholder's address as it appears on the records of the corporation, at least 20 days prior to the date of the meeting. The notice shall contain a copy of the agreement or a brief summary thereof. At the meeting, the agreement shall be considered and a vote taken for its adoption or rejection. If a majority of the outstanding stock of the corporation entitled to vote thereon shall be voted for the adoption of the agreement, that fact shall be certified on the agreement by the secretary or assistant secretary of the corporation, provided that such certification on the agreement shall not be required if a certificate of merger or consolidation is filed in lieu of filing the agreement. If the agreement shall be so adopted and certified by each constituent corporation, it shall then be filed and shall become effective, in accordance with §103 of this title. In lieu of filing the agreement of merger or consolidation required by this section, the surviving or resulting corporation may file a certificate of merger or consolidation, executed in accordance with §103 of this title,... .

Over the years, there has been a presumption that the boards know much more about the goals and growth opportunities of a company than the shareholders. This argument is becoming tenuous because of the towering presence of sophisticated institutional investors in financial markets. The ignorance hypothesis may well be true until shareholders realize that things are falling apart (going horribly wrong) in Minsky moments;[125] moments that can be associated with malfeasance, misfeasance, and nonfeasance. The tenuous corporate arrangements or legal constraints create opportunities for proxy fights. A single shareholder or a group of shareholders can try to reform or take control of a public company through proxy corporate votes.

Shareholder voting occurs in two significant circumstances: (i) when the management of a public company is conducting a proxy process for the election of the BoDs, and (ii) when shareholders are seeking proxies on their own to reform or take over control of a company.[126] The concentration and form of ownership of public corporations have configured the dimensions of proxy fights. As noted earlier, institutional investors now play a significant role in stock ownership. Unlike small stock owners who have disincentives to be actively engaged (an incentive to be passive) in business decisions, institutional owners with large blocks of stocks are more proactive and watchful of stock price movements in financial markets. Hence, they are predisposed to check mismanagement (perceived or otherwise) or extend the market size of their businesses, especially when synergies are evident and beneficial.

Proxy fights occur when one group of dissidents or insurgents try to obtain seats on a firm's BoDs in order to wrest control from management or the incumbent group. The fights are usually to obtain seats on the BoDs or to contest management proposals. Because proxy contests threaten the continued employment and benefits of incumbent managers, the incumbents are not very well disposed to encourage them, and they will use defense mechanisms to prevent them. The proxy fights usually begin months ahead of the annual meetings to elect the BoDs of public corporations. The insurgents present a slate of directors and initiate campaigns among shareholders to support their slate in opposition to the incumbent managers. Dissidents and incumbents aggressively seek the votes of shareholders who have a mandate to sign and return proxy forms of preferred groups.[127]

Three defensive mechanisms are particularly noteworthy: (i) poison pills, (ii) corporate charter amendments (shark repellents), and (iii) litigation. A poison pill is a takeover defense that gives the shareholders of a target company the right to purchase additional target or bidder stock at a discount should there be a change in the control of a company. It is an obvious deterrent because it increases the cost of acquisition by diluting the bidders' existing shareholder holdings. The defensive motives can be altered under amicable circumstances when a target's BoDs permits the acquisition. Poison pills were manufactured to stop bidders or acquirers from directly negotiating a price for the sale of shares with shareholders. Instead, bidders were forced to negotiate with the BoDs. Shareholder rights plans are legally issued by the BoDs in the form of warrants or options that are attached to existing shares. The prescription of the pills can be stopped by BoDs.

Target corporations may provide various amendments to their charters to discourage acquisitions and change of managerial control. Some prominent amendments include supermajority provisions, staggered boards, fair price provisions, and dual capitalizations.[128] An amendment to a charter calling for a supermajority of shareholders will require more than the normal percentage of shareholders to approve of a takeover, say 70 to 90 percent. A staggered (classified) board consists of directors who are grouped into classes with different tenure. Classified boards are also designed to discourage takeover bids; for example, three classes of board members may serve for one, two, and three years; implying that only a third of board members may be eligible for vote in any given year. Delaware law prohibits the removal of classified members, but not unclassified members. By entrenching the positions of board members, it is uncertain whether a board might be well disposed to work in the best interest of shareholders in an aura of hostility. There has been a significant pressure to declassify boards as a result of protests by shareholder activists and some companies have moved in the direction of declassification.[129]

A fair price amendment of a charter forces the acquirer to pay minority shareholders a (fair) market price for their stock and the price may be expressed as a financial multiple, say the price-earning (P/E) ratio. The price is normally triggered after a bid is made and it ensures that no discriminatory (two-tiered) payment arrangement can be made, separating majority from minority shareholders or making a partial tender offer with an intention of acquiring the remaining shares in a subsequent merger. Accordingly, stockholders would expect to receive the maximum amount paid by the acquirer. Actually, this mechanism has become a less consequential defense in many states with corporate laws that prohibit the price discrimination.[130]

Dual capitalization involves the issuing of a new class of stock with larger voting rights. The intent may be multifarious, but it can be used as a defense mechanism against a takeover bid; for example, management can acquire stocks with larger voting rights or create a class of stocks with larger voting rights to prevent a takeover bid. Stocks with superior voting rights could have 10 to 100 votes for each share of stock.[131] Dual capitalization, equity restructuring, must be approved by shareholders, but shareholders are usually more interested in financial gains from higher dividends than in controls. Less surprisingly, equity restructuring can be blessed by shareholders.

Poison pills have gone through several transformations as bidders or raiders became cleverer over the years. Bainbridge (2012) and Gaughan (2015) identify at least three generations of poison pills. First-generation poison pills were preferred stock plans that date back to the 1980s. In an attempt to stave off Brown Foreman, each of the Lenox common stockholders was offered convertible preferred shares that were equivalent to 40 shares of Brown Foreman stock. A Brown Foreman acquisition would have severely reduced its share ownership position. The first-generation pills had inherent disadvantages.[132]

The second-generation pills adopted a flip-over immunization strategy. The flip-over poison pill permitted stockholders of target companies to purchase the shares of acquiring companies (raiders) at a steep discount, say at a two-for-one rate, should an acquisition be successful (a dilution of post-acquisition value). The second-generation pills avoided the symptoms of the adverse balance sheet effects and offered rights (options and dividends) to shareholders that were contingent on triggering conditions. Shareholders could then exercise their options if the conditions are triggered. A typical triggering event could be any of the following developments: (i) an acquisition of 20 percent of the outstanding stock by an individual partnership or corporation, and (ii) a tender offer for 30 percent or more of the target corporation's outstanding stock.[133] The potency of the second-generation pills was attenuated by the third-generation symptoms in the mid-1980s. Like the first-generation pills, the second-generation pills had side effects of their own. Gaughan (2015) notes that the second-generation pills were effective only if bidders acquired 100 percent of the target. They are ineffective if bidders are able to acquire a controlling influence that is less than 100 percent.[134]

To avoid the undesirable side effects of the second-generation poison pills, the third-generation poison pills adopted a flip-in immunization strategy. The flip-in diagnosis allowed holders of rights, excluding the acquirer, to acquire stocks in the target company at a discount, which also allowed the holders of rights to acquire stocks of the acquirer. In the process, the value of a limited amount of stock of the acquirer is also diluted. As a result, the flip-in strategy allowed the target to dilute its value with or without an acquisition and diminished the ability of raiders to have controlling influence. The right to purchase shares is available to the shareholders before a takeover is finalized (*ex ante*) and is often triggered when the acquirer attains a threshold percentage of shares of the target company (*ex post facto*). The poison pills gave shareholders a dividend of one right for each share of stock ownership, which they can redeem within a considerable period of time; ten years in some instances.[135]

Litigation proved to be a somewhat consequential defensive mechanism in the 1970s, suggesting that it is a tool but not an inevitable one. In many ways the litigation defense bears relevance to key antitrust and disclosure laws that are discussed in Chapter 7. The laws promote competition and discourage or prohibit unwarranted and inefficient consolidations. It has been observed that the litigation defense pursues four objectives: (i) a more favorable forum for dispute resolution, (ii) a preemptive measure that prevents a raider from taking judicial initiative, (iii) to retard acquisition while the target searches for a white knight,[136] and (iv) to provide psychological support for the targets management.[137]

Litigation typically starts with the request for an injunction to stop the continuation of the takeover process or the purchases of shares until the request for injunctive relief can be materially supported. In the interim, the target can create insurmountable defenses or secure a white knight. Gaughan (2015) also suggests that an injunction might give the target an opportunity to prolong negotiations and increase the offer price in order to discontinue litigation.[138] Over the years, corporate management has developed a variety of defensive mechanisms to preserve administrative control. A detailed discussion of these mechanisms can be found in the work of Bainbridge (2012). Various states have enacted legislation to prohibit unwarranted consolidations. The statutes are generally referred to as "antitakeover statutes."

The state of incorporation is also important for empirical analysis and an analysis of the economic and social obligations of public corporations. The number of shareholders residing in a state of incorporation could also be an important indicator of the juridical rights and obligations of a public corporation. Historically, various states including Delaware, Arizona, Connecticut, Georgia, Idaho, Indiana, Kentucky, Minnesota, Missouri, New Jersey, Pennsylvania, Washington, and Wisconsin have business combination acts. Delaware is rather unique for its scope of incorporation and the accommodative nature (mildness) of its corporate statute, which has been considered to represent a "mid-course compromise" between those who view hostile takeovers as destructive and those who view them as beneficial.[139] Two-thirds of all publicly-traded US companies, including more than 60% of the Fortune 500, are incorporated in Delaware. The Delaware courts have become famous for giving corporations and their shareholders maximum flexibility and predictability.[140] The state presents a rich and reliable repository of incorporations, corporate law (see for example, part of §§ 203 and 251 infra, Boxes 3.6 and 3.7),[141] and judicial decisions. The antitakeover statute has been considered the most important anti-takeover statute in the US and it has withstood constitutional challenges.[142]

The accommodative aspects of corporate law in Delaware do not actually translate into expeditious encouragement of consolidations. As Oesterle noted, the drafters of the Delaware statute designed the three-year cooling-off period primarily to block heavily leveraged acquisitions that depend on the assets of the target for repayment of the acquisition financing.[143]

The basis for regulating takeovers grew rapidly. Subramanian, Herscovici, and Barbetta (2009) report that in 1960, there were eight tender offers involving companies listed on the New York Stock Exchange. In 1966, the number rose to 107. The unprecedented and unanticipated growth in tender offers surprisingly caught the attention of state and federal regulators. Since the bids of acquirers were completely unregulated, they surreptitiously operated with impunity without disclosures; raiders especially benefited from getting toe-holds in targets.[144] The Williams Act (1968) (see Chapter 7) was intended to deal with some of the contrivances.

However, as far as defensive mechanisms are concerned, the Delaware statute has not been exhaustive. The Delaware courts have traditionally evaluated other variables, such as the behavior of targets, the intent and use of shark repellents.[145]

According to Securities Data Company (SDC) Platinum, from January 1, 1988, through December 31, 2008, there were 1,101 tender offers for Delaware targets, of which 145 (or 13 percent) were hostile (the target's board rejected the offer, but the acquirer persisted)[146] or unsolicited (i.e., the acquirer made an offer without prior negotiations

BOX 3.7 DELAWARE CODE TITLE 8 § 203

BUSINESS COMBINATIONS WITH INTERESTED STOCKHOLDERS

(a) Notwithstanding any other provisions of this chapter, a corporation shall not engage in any business combination with any interested stockholder for a period of 3 years following the time that such stockholder became an interested stockholder, unless:
  (1) Prior to such time the board of directors of the corporation approved either the business combination or the transaction which resulted in the stockholder becoming an interested stockholder;
  (2) Upon consummation of the transaction which resulted in the stockholder becoming an interested stockholder, the interested stockholder owned at least 85% of the voting stock of the corporation outstanding at the time the transaction commenced, excluding for purposes of determining the voting stock outstanding (but not the outstanding voting stock owned by the interested stockholder) those shares owned (i) by persons who are directors and also officers and (ii) employee stock plans in which employee participants do not have the right to determine confidentially whether shares held subject to the plan will be tendered in a tender or exchange offer; or
  (3) At or subsequent to such time the business combination is approved by the board of directors and authorized at an annual or special meeting of stockholders, and not by written consent, by the affirmative vote of at least 66 two-thirds% of the outstanding voting stock which is not owned by the interested stockholder.
(b) The restrictions contained in this section shall not apply if:
  (1) The corporation's original certificate of incorporation contains a provision expressly electing not to be governed by this section;
  (2) The corporation, by action of its board of directors, adopts an amendment to its bylaws within 90 days of February 2, 1988, expressly electing not to be governed by this section, which amendment shall not be further amended by the board of directors;
  (3) The corporation, by action of its stockholders, adopts an amendment to its certificate of incorporation or bylaws expressly electing not to be governed by this section; provided that, in addition to any other vote required by law, such amendment to the certificate of incorporation or bylaws must be adopted by the affirmative vote of a majority of the outstanding stock entitled to vote thereon …

with the target board). In at least 73 of the 145 hostile/unsolicited tender offers, the bidder held less than 15 percent of the target's stock prior to commencing the tender offer and sought to acquire over 85 percent. Of those 73, 29 (or 40 percent) were ultimately completed, while 43 were withdrawn. Moreover, of the 43 withdrawn, at least 23 of those targets agreed to be acquired in a white-knight type transaction (Sparks, 2010). Between January 1981 and August 1988, about 45 percent of tender offers that began and ended as "hostile" did not achieve 85 percent voting stock. However, based on empirical work, about 54.2 percent of the successful hostile tender offers achieved 85 percent during the period.[147]

CHAPTER SUMMARY

- The SEC requires public corporations to provide accurate financial information that is transparent. SEC rules are extensive, and this book is not suitable for an exhaustive discussion of SEC laws or regulations.
- Information is material if it is valuable and pertinent to the investment-making decision of an investor. Therefore, an investor must not be deprived of such information *ex ante*. Accordingly, SEC rules require that filings contain "such further material information ... as may be necessary to make the required statements ... not misleading" (Rule 408).
- Financial statements are documented financial records of business transactions, activities, and overall financial performances. They are often audited by government agencies, accountants, firms, or qualified personnel to ensure the accuracy of reporting for tax, financing, and investment purposes. Financial statements may or may not be publicly displayed, depending on whether a company wants to raise financial resources from the public.
- A significant problem with investment and public corporations is the principal-agent relationship, when large firms try to separate ownership from control.
- A federal court is empowered to exercise subject matter jurisdiction under the conduct test if: (i) a defendant's activities in the US were more than merely preparatory to a securities fraud conducted elsewhere (out of the US) and (ii) the fraudulent activities or culpable failures to act within the US directly cause losses (injury).
- For a conspiracy to exist there must be at least two or more parties (plurality). The multiplicity of parties does not necessarily mean that all the conspirators will be charged.
- *The "misappropriation theory" holds that a person commits fraud "in connection with" a securities transaction, and thereby violates § 10(b) and Rule 10b-5, when he misappropriates confidential information for securities trading purposes, in breach of a duty owed to the source of the information. Under this theory, a fiduciary's undisclosed self-serving use of a principal's information to purchase or sell securities, in breach of a duty of loyalty and confidentiality, defrauds the principal of the exclusive use of that information ...* (O'Sullivan, 2003, p. 775).

KEY WORDS

- Balance sheet
- Conduct test
- Current assets
- Current liabilities
- Effects test
- Equity
- Extraterritorial jurisdiction
- Income statement
- Insider information
- "Poison pills"
- Form 10-K
- Form 10-Q
- Principal-agent problem
- Rule 10b-5
- Leverage ratio
- Total revenue
- Managerial discretion
- Marginal revenue
- Misappropriation of information
- Return on asset
- Return on equity

CHAPTER QUESTIONS

1. What is a financial market? What are some of the factors that ensure the stability of financial markets?
2. Can outsiders misappropriate financial information? How? Critically discuss the difference between outsider misappropriation of financial information and insider trading.
3. What is Rule 10b-5? Discuss the salient provisions of the rule for financial market stability.
4. Refer to Box 3.3; select a public company of your choice and estimate the net increase in cash and marketable securities. Is the company viable? Why?
5. Can foreign securities be fraudulently traded in the US securities market? Why? Critically discuss the difference between the conduct and effects tests.
6. What is the principal-agent problem? How can investors remedy the problem?
7. Refer to the *Dodge v. Ford Case*. Identify the key arguments for and against the case of abusive managerial discretion. Is this a case that should have been decided in a court of law? Why?

NOTES

1. See Baumohl (2013, p. 163).
2. See Merhling (1999, p. 139–40).
3. Minsky's subsidiary financial classifications include "hedge," "speculative," and "ponzi." Hedge finance maintains some type of equilibrium in which cash commitments approximate cash inflows. The "speculative" variety differs from the "ponzi" in that "ponzi finance" requires principal and interest to be rolled over while "speculative finance" is limited to rolling over principal. "Ponzi finance" is a particularly precarious way of financing economic activity (Merhling, 1999, p. 140).
4. See Kurtz (2017, p. 20).
5. See Merhling (1999, p. 142).
6. A former managing director at Pacific Investment Management Company (PIMCO) characterized the seizure as a "Minsky Moment"; see Krugman (2012, p. 48).
7. See Warburton (2018, pp. 104–6).

8 See Coffee et al. (2007) and Palmiter (2017) for a comprehensive analysis of securities law.
9 See Cox and Hazen (2003, p. 737).
10 See Palmiter (2017, p. 398).
11 Op. cit., p. 81.
12 Op. cit., p. 463.
13 Disclosure of funding is important, since borrowed funds that have to be repaid could cause a resale of equity that can affect stock prices; see Gaughan (2015, p. 79); see also Chapter 5 for valuation of public companies.
14 See Bell (2019, p. 13); "The Securities Act governs the offer and sale of securities in the US, while the Exchange Act regulates the trading of securities on securities exchanges (including the NYSE and Nasdaq), ongoing periodic reporting, and tender offers."
15 See Label (2013, p. 7). Accepted rules of accounting can be found in documents issued by the American Institute of Certified Public Accountants (AICPA), the Financial Accounting Standards Board (FASB), the Internal Revenue Service (IRS), the SEC, and other regulatory bodies. The SEC first assigned the role of specifying GAAP to AICPA, but the duty was subsequently transferred over to FASB and all rulings of FASB are considered to be GAAP.
16 A going concern is an accounting classification of a business operation that indicates whether the financial resources needed to operate the business will be indefinitely available until the business can provide evidence of its inability to be operative in the short- or long-run. "Going concern" explicitly suggests that there is no foreseeable imminent bankruptcy or liquidation. The recording of assets and depreciation in separate financial statements (balance sheet and income statement respectively) is consistent with the theory of going concern; see also Label (2013, p. 15).
17 Ibid.
18 Loc. cit. A financial statement is relevant when it provides information that will enable the valuation of a firm and an understanding of how a firm is being managed. Reliable financial information is information that can be corroborated by objective evidence. Verifiable information is contingent on the sufficiency and ascertainment of a financial record or statement. A statement is understandable when it is comparable to similarly situated statements and the terms therein are consistently understood by all users. Information is quantified when it is reported numerically and information is obtainable when it can be readily accessed; see also Label (2013, pp. 15–18).
19 See Berman and Knight (2008, pp. 28–31).
20 Op. cit., p. 39. The authors provide some complicating situations for revenue recognition; partly because accounting practices differ from firm to firm.
21 Op. cit., p. 47. For example, if a supervisors' salary is included in CoGS, it may be fixed for a period of time as output changes.
22 Op. cit., p. 55.
23 Op. cit., p. 47.
24 Amortization is an analogous recognition of spending on intangible (human) capital—patents, copyrights, trademarks—and goodwill (formerly, the difference between acquired value of a business and net assets); where net assets is the difference between the market value of assets less the liabilities assumed by the acquirer. Current accounting procedures include the value of clientele that does not

deteriorate; see Berman and Knight (2008, pp. 75–6). Goodwill is reported in balance sheets.
25 MACRS has been used in the US since the Tax Reform Act of 1986. Under the MACRS of depreciation, charges for all assets, with the exception of non-farm real property, are relatively higher in the earlier years of the life of an asset.
26 Ratios like accounts receivable turnover (net income/accounts receivable) or average collection period, give investors and creditors information about the efficiency with which a company is able to collect its debts from consumers. The accounts receivable turnover provides information about the number of times a company is able to collect its debt and reissue new debt in a year, while the days' sales in receivables ratio, also known as the average collection period, enhances the turnover ratio by explicitly stating the number of days, on average, that it takes a company to collect its debt (365/receivable turnover).
27 See Parrino et al. (2015, p. 56).
28 The difference between the purchase price of an asset and its accumulated depreciation is known as its carrying value. It is presumed that a company purchases and retains an asset on the balance sheet until the salvage value corresponds to the carrying value.
29 See Berman and Knight (2008, pp. 76–77), for additional analysis of the measurement of goodwill.
30 R&D expenditures that do not lead to the creation of an asset that is likely to generate revenue are considered to be an expense. GAAP rules ordain that R&D can be amortized if the product that is being developed is technologically feasible. Therefore, a company can amortize its R&D if it decides that its R&D is technologically feasible; op. cit., p. 78.
31 See Parrino et al. (2015, p. 57); see also Berman and Knight (2008, p. 84).
32 Notice that patents, copyrights, and trademarks can be included in this category.
33 "Other assets" are listed as a separate line item because the contents of this category cannot be neatly packaged into any of the bifurcated categories of current- and long-term assets. Bond issuance cost (cost recorded as deductions from bond liability), deferred tax assets (income tax that is recoverable in the future), and prepaid expenses (expenses that have been paid for in an accounting period but for which the benefits will linger into the distant future, like insurance) are usually found in this category; see accountingtools.com for further discussions of the category.
34 Some of these ratios include profitability ratios such as: profit margin (net income/sale), return on assets (net income/total assets), and return on equity (net income/total equity); market value shares such as: earnings per share (net income/number of shares outstanding), the price-earnings ratio (price per share/earnings per share); management ratios such as days' sales in inventory (365 days/inventory turnover), where turnover is CoGS/inventory; and liquidity ratios of total debt ((TA-TE)/TA), and debt-to-equity (total debt/total equity); for a wholesome discussion of these ratios see Ross, Westerfield, and Jordan (2016, pp. 57–70); Parrino et al. (2015, pp. 89–107); Label (2013, pp. 118–36); and Berman and Knight (2008, pp. 130–53).
35 The report also includes information about marketing, research and development, competitors, legal proceedings, and financial statements.
36 In Albrecht et al. (2009, p. 7); see also *Webster's New World Dictionary* (1964) *College Edition* (p. 380). Cleveland and New York: World.
37 Author's modification of Albrecht et al. (2009, p. 7).
38 See Palmiter (2017, p. 415).

39 Ibid, 404–5.
40 Op. cit., p. 407; see also *Lustgraaf v. Behrens*, 619 F. 3d867 (8th Cir. 2010).
41 Op. cit., p. 408.
42 See *Software Toolworks Inc. Securities Litigation*, 50 F. 3d 615 (9th Cir. 1994); see also Palmiter (2017, p. 409).
43 Loc. cit.; *Wright v. Ernst & Young LLP*, 152 F. 3d 169 (2d Cir. 1998).
44 See *Janus Capital Group, Inc. v. First Derivative Traders*, 564 U.S. 135 (2011); op. cit., p. 410.
45 Op. cit., p. 415; see also discussions of Form 8-K.
46 See *Wharf (Holdings) Ltd. v. United International Holdings Inc.*, 532 U.S. 588 (2001), loc. cit.; see also Coffee et al. (2007, pp. 942–6), and the Ihlen Declaration, PCIJ, Ser. A/B. No.53 at 36 and 71 (1933). A declaration, *qua* a communication of an official character on a matter within one's province is binding beyond dispute (an advisory opinion of the PCIJ on the *Eastern Greenland-Norway* situation).
47 See *Basic, Inc. v. Levinson*, 485 U.S. 224 (1988); see also Palmiter (2017, p. 416).
48 Loc. cit. *United States v. Mulheren*, 938 F. 2d 364 (2d Cir. 1991).
49 See *Chiarella v. United States*, 445 U.S. 222 (1980); op. cit., p. 417; see also O'Sullivan (2003, pp. 757–73), and Coffee et al. (2007, pp. 1145–9).
50 See Podgor and Israel (2009, p. 86); see also Coffee et al. (2007, pp. 1146–9).
51 Loc. cit.
52 Insiders have fiduciary duty to shareholders. Outsiders have no direct fiduciary relationship to shareholders but may be employed by insiders and responsible to insiders.
53 Op. cit., p. 90.
54 See *United States v. O'Hagan*, 521 US 642 (1997); see also Palmiter (2017, p. 413), Podgor and Israel (2009, p. 91), and O'Sullivan (2003, pp. 773–88).
55 Op. cit., pp. 80–81.
56 Podgor and Israel (2009, p. 59).
57 See O'Sullivan (2003, p. 482).
58 See Palmiter (2017, p. 475).
59 Op. cit., p. 383. The conspiracy statute has an "omnibus" clause which speaks in general terms against any effort that interferes with the administration of justice: "Whoever * * * corruptly or by threats of force, or by any threatening letter or communication, influences, obstructs, or impedes or endeavors to influence, obstruct, or impede, the due administration of justice, shall be punished * * *" (O'Sullivan, 2003, p. 384).
60 See Podgor and Israel (2009, p. 40).
61 Op. cit., p. 41.
62 See *Iannelli v. US* (S. Ct. 1975); see also Podgor and Israel (2009, p. 42).
63 Loc. cit.
64 See *US v. Schmidt* (9th Cir. 1991); see also Podgor and Israel (2009, p. 47).
65 See *Salinas v. US* (S. Ct. 1997), *Whitfield v. US* (US 2005), and Podgor and Israel (2009, p. 51).
66 See also Brickey (2007, pp. 215–374) for other cases involving BMS, KPMG, ImClone, and WorldCom.
67 See Fusaro and Miller (2002, pp. 172–3).
68 See Brickey (2007, p. 260). This was a violation of 10b-5 and one of the general statutory provisions discussed earlier, for which the former executive vice president and chief accounting officer, Richard Causey, pled guilty.

69 Op. cit., p. 177.
70 Op. cit., p. 247.
71 See Coffee et al. (2007, pp. 1441–2).
72 Ibid, 1443.
73 Loc. cit.
74 Op. cit., p. 1446.
75 See *Alfadda v. Fenn*, 935 F. 2d 475, 478 (2d Cir.) (citing 15 USC § 78aa), cert. denied, 502 US 1005*** (1991).
76 The "conduct" and "effects" tests are emphasized by the author.
77 See *Bersch v. Drexel Firestone Inc.*, 519 F. 2d 974, 987 (2d Cir.), cert. denied, 423 US 1018 * * * (1975) and *Alfadda*, supra 935 F. 2d at 478.
78 Cited in Coffee et al. (2007, p. 1444).
79 Op. cit., p. 1445.
80 Op. cit., p. 1448; "The provisions of this title or of any rule or regulation thereunder shall not apply to any person insofar as he transacts a business in securities without the jurisdiction of the United States, unless he transacts such business in contravention of such rules and regulations as the Commission may prescribe as necessary or appropriate to prevent the evasion of this title" 30(b); see Palmiter (2017, pp. 625–9) for foreign exemptions.
81 Stakeholders include workers, creditors, banks, institutional investors, and even the government.
82 See Resnick and Eun (2015, p. 85). Various schemes can be deployed to transfer funds from investors; including free cash flows (FCF) (internally generated funds in excess of investment requirements). FCF represents the cash flows from operations after depreciation expenses, taxes, working capital, and investments. It is what is available for distribution among shareholders; see also the proposed mechanisms for mitigating the agency problem, including independent board of directors, overseas listing, and incentive contracts, (p. 86).
83 Some conflicts identified by Larkin and Hoffman, see www.larkinhoffman.com.
84 Top executives take turns in highlighting the financial results of companies and the growth prospects of companies during these calls. The presentations are then followed by questions and answers (Q&As), during which shareholders can ask embarrassing and impolite questions; see also Fusaro and Miller (2002, p. 110).
85 Brickey (2007), op. cit., pp. 258–9.
86 Op. cit., p. 245. The SPEs were specifically created to borrow money on behalf of Enron. The liabilities were not reflected in the balance sheet of Enron; unsurprisingly why the balance sheet of the company was hard to come by.
87 See Bodie, Kane, and Marcus (2018, p. 641).
88 Unlike Chapter 7 bankruptcy, which requires liquidation, Chapter 11 bankruptcy gives a company time to reorganize and get out of bankruptcy; see Fusaro and Miller (2002) op. cit., p. 178.
89 Linder, UMKC School of Law; see www.famous-trials.com.
90 See Levison (2014, pp.113–6), for a fuller discussion of the securitization process, its evolution, and benefits; see also Sanches (2014), and Mishkin and Eakins (2016, pp. 195–209) for general principles of bank management.
91 A very insightful and schematic representation of the securitization process can be found in the work of Sanches (2014).

92 For a comprehensive discussion of the subject matter, see Pozsar, Adrian, Ashcraft, and Boesky (2013).
93 See Blinder (2014, pp. 72–81); see also Mishkin and Eakins (2016, p. 276), and the *Financial Crisis Inquiry Report* (FCIR), pp. 127–55.
94 FCIR, pp. 130–2. The BBB rated variety of assets were held back by the investment firms during the ramp up period for subsequent release in about six to nine months.
95 Loc. cit.
96 Op. cit., pp. 141–142.
97 See Blinder (2014, pp. 132–4).
98 Loc. cit.
99 Section 13(3) of the Federal Reserve Act gives the Board of Governors and the Federal Reserve Banks authority to engage in secured discounting with any individual or business entity in distress. Credit was extended to non-bank financial firms in the 1930s. This section has been amended by Dodd Frank, Wall Street Reform and Consumer Protection Act (2010).
100 See Labonte (2016, pp. 1–2). Credit extended under Section 13(3) in 2008 was disaggregated into two broad categories: (i) broadly based facilities to address liquidity problems in specific markets, and (ii) exclusive, tailored assistance to prevent the disorderly failure of individual firms deemed too big to fail. Contrary to skeptical opposition, the Fed earned profits—more than $30 billion—under its Section 13(3) action, with more than half from AIG related returns.
101 Blinder (2014, p. 113).
102 The repo market is a money market (short term) for overnight collateralized loan transactions among institutionalized investors. Large amounts of money are traded for a very short period of time to earn attractive returns. Collateral is usually posted in the form of government bonds (risk-free securities). When the value of the collateral becomes risky and volatile in the market, the market will be exposed to great financial peril and more collateral will be required for redemption in a short period of time, since the loans are virtually rolled over on a daily basis.
103 FCIR, p. 135.
104 Blinder (2014, p. 101).
105 Wiggins (2014, p. 2); Yale Program on Financial Stability (YPFS).
106 Op. cit, pp. 6–8.
107 See the North American Industry Classification System (NAICS) for business and industry classifications.
108 Blinder (2014, p. 52).
109 Delany (2009, p. 1).
110 Loc. cit.
111 See www.casebrief.com.
112 Stakeholders are those who stand to benefit or profit from the existence of a public company apart from the shareholders; for example, creditors (from loan repayments), governments (from tax revenues), employees (from wages and healthcare benefits) and the public, including consumers who are not shareholders or employees (for the provision of vital services and responsible use of environmental resources).
113 Loc. cit.
114 Loc. cit.
115 See Cox and Hazen (2003, pp. 552–3); see also *Cole Real Estate Corp. v. Peoples Bank & Trust Co.* 310 N.E. 2d 275 (Ind. Ct. App. 1974). Evidence of personal hostility

is more likely to be exposed in closed corporations and nonpayment of dividends has been challenged much more successfully in closed corporations.
116 See Ross et al. (2016, pp. 91–113) for a comprehensive discussion of long-term financial planning and sustainable growth; see also Parrino et al. (2015, pp. 630–3).
117 See Macey (2008, p. 178).
118 Bainbridge (2012, p. 40).
119 A proxy statement is a form, Form DEF 14A (Definitive Proxy Statement) that is filed with the SEC by public corporations, delineating matters that are pending for annual or special meetings of stockholders. It is useful for evaluating the compensation of managers and potential conflicts of interest with auditors. In effect, it proactively discloses material information about the affairs of a company for shareholder votes and final approval of nominated directors. Shareholders might want an insurgent nominee in a company's board. The statement may include, but not be limited to: voting procedure, background information of a company's nominated directors, compensation of board members (including salary, bonus, non-equity compensation, stock awards, options, and deferred compensation), and any other material compensatory benefits.
120 See Carney (2009, p. 65).
121 See Gaughan (2015, p. 187). The fourth merger wave coincided with developments in the 1980s. Mergers (consolidations) are believed to have occurred in waves: (i) first wave (1897–1904), (ii) second wave (1916–1929), (iii) third wave (1965–1969), (iv) fourth wave (1984–1989), (v) fifth wave (1992–2001), and (vi) sixth wave (post-2001); op. cit., pp. 41–74. The initiation and duration of the waves have been shaped by technological innovation, changes in economic circumstances, and legislation.
122 Op. cit., p. 188; see also Bainbridge (2012, p. 47). But the AFL-CIO estimated that 500,000 jobs were lost as a direct result of takeovers between 1983 and 1987 alone. Takeovers of industrial companies can also devastate local communities. In effect, it is much better for companies to operate efficiently (a failure to reject the shareholder hypothesis).
123 See DGCL § 251(c), infra; see also Dodd and Warner (1983, p. 402).
124 See Parrino et al. (2015, p. 17).
125 The expression has been widely credited to Paul McCulley of Pimco. The moments have also been considered to be Wile E. Coyote moments; see Krugman (2012, p. 48).
126 See Coffee et al. (2007, p. 1210).
127 In the US, with very limited exception, directors are elected annually. When all shareholders cannot attend shareholder meetings, the shareholders may designate someone, usually from the management team to vote on their behalf. Votes are cast by shares and not the number of shareholders (one share, one vote). For example, John and Mary might have 40 and 60 shares respectively. If 5 directors are to be elected, John will have 40 × 5 votes = 200 votes and Mary will have 60 × 5 votes = 300 votes. Proxy votes may be cast by mail or electronically before the cut-off time, usually 24 hours. Voting may be non-cumulative (straight) or cumulative (disaggregated or "plumping"). In the non-cumulative procedure, directors are elected one at a time, and each time Mary can cast 300 votes. Evidently, those with a majority of shares have an advantage. On the other hand, cumulative voting permits owners to use up their entire voting percentage for one candidate or to spread the percentage across the number of candidates. Mary's directors may get

60 votes each or one of the directors can get 300 votes with the certainty of a seat. Cumulative voting allows minority shareholders (shareholders with a small amount of stock) to have a say in the voting process. Rule of thumb suggests that if there are N directors, then 1/N+1 percent of stock will guarantee a director a seat (see Ross et al., 2016, p. 251; Dodd & Warner, 1983, p. 403; and Engstrom & Brischetto, 1998, p. 815). Responses may include abstentions. While voting procedures are usually stipulated by state laws and corporate by-laws, SEC Rule 14a-4 regulates the proxy form, including requirements about the date of execution and the matters for action at the shareholder meeting (Coffee et al., 2007, p. 1211; see also Gaughan, 2015, p. 279).
128 See Gaughan (2015, p. 190).
129 Op. cit., p. 205; Chesapeake Energy Corp., Hewlett-Packard, and Verizon.
130 Op. cit., p. 210.
131 Op. cit., p. 211.
132 Op. cit., p. 191–3. *Inter alia*, the issuer can redeem them only after an extended period of time and they adversely impact the balance sheet of targets. The value of preferred stock can be added to long-term debt, thereby increasing the leverage profile of a company; see also Bainbridge (2012, pp. 239–45).
133 Gaughan (2015, p. 192).
134 Op. cit., p. 193.
135 Op. cit., p. 194.
136 A white knight is an entity or friend of a target that makes an amicable or favorable tender offer in competition with an initial bidder or raider. The knight may offer to buy all or part of the target, secure the employment of management, and preserve a functioning target.
137 See Lipton and Steinberger (1987); see also Gaughan (2015, p. 243).
138 See Gaughan (2015, p. 244); see also Bainbridge (2012, Chapter 7) for a fuller discussion of defensive mechanisms.
139 See Oesterle (1988, p. 880).
140 See Forbes, October 27, 2017. From about 56 percent in 1988, the percentage of Fortune 500 companies increased to more than 60 percent in 2017; see also Oesterle (1988, p. 883).
141 Section 203 was enacted between June 1987 and February 1988. Amendments were made to both sections in 2017.
142 See Subramanian et al. (2009, abstract). Further, the constitutionality of the anti-takeover statute has been upheld; partly because it gives bidders a meaningful opportunity to succeed. However, the circumstances for success are not sacrosanct and definitive. The constitutionality of Section 203 was first examined in *BNS Inc. v. Koppers Co.* (683 F. Supp. 454 (D. Del. 1988)), during which the US District Court pointed out that Section 203 does not circumvent the goals of the Williams Act even though it may give target boards a significant advantage to prevent unwanted takeovers (see Sparks, 2010).
143 Op. cit., p. 893.
144 A toe-hold is an initial step that is undertaken by a raider to gain access to privileged information to accumulate shares before embarking on more aggressive tactics to launch a hostile bid; see Gaughan (2015, pp. 250–1) for further information; see also Subramanian et al. (2009, p. 6).
145 See Oesterle, (1988, 884–5).

146 In *City Capital*, "hostile" is defined as "offers in which no merger agreement is ultimately negotiated between bidder and target" *and* in which target management did not tender their stock; see Sparks (2010).

147 See Sparks (2010), op. cit.

FURTHER READING

Albrecht, W. S., Albrecht, C. C., Albrecht, C. O., & Zimbelman, M. F. (2009). *Fraud examination* (3rd ed.). Mason, OH: South-Western, Cengage Learning.

Bainbridge, S. M. (2012). *Mergers and acquisitions* (3rd ed.). New York: Foundation Press.

Baumohl, B. (2013). *The secrets of economic indicators: Hidden clues to future economic trends and investment opportunities* (3rd ed.). Upper Saddle River, NJ: Pearson.

Baye, M. R., & Prince, J. T. (2017). *Managerial economics and business strategy* (9th ed.). New York: McGraw-Hill.

Bell, B. J. (2019). The acquisition of control of a US public company. Retrieved from https://media2.mofo.com.

Berman, K., & Knight, J. (2008). *Financial intelligence for entrepreneurs*. Boston, MA: Harvard Business Press.

Bernanke, B. (2013). *The Federal Reserve and the financial crisis*. Princeton, NJ: Princeton University Press.

Blinder, A. S. (2014). *After the music stopped: The financial crisis, the response and the work ahead*. New York: Penguin.

Bodie, Z., Kane, A., & Marcus, A. J. (2018). *Investments* (11th ed.). New York: McGraw-Hill.

Brealy, R. A., Myers, S. C., & Allen, F. (2017). *Principles of corporate finance* (12th ed.). New York: McGraw-Hill.

Brickey, K. F. (2007). *Corporate and white-collar crime: Selected cases, statutes, and documents*. New York: Wolters Kluwer.

Carney, W. J. (2009). *Essentials: Mergers and acquisitions*. New York: Wolters Kluwer.

Coffee, Jr., J. C., Seligman, J., & Sale, H. A. (2007). *Securities regulation: Cases and materials* (10th ed.). New York: Foundation Press.

Cox, J. D., & Hazen, T. L. (2003). *Corporations* (2nd ed.). New York: Aspen Publishers.

Delany, P. (2009, October). Confronting the squeeze-out of minority shareholders: Court more likely to grant relief if failure to pay dividends appears as arbitrary act or ulterior motive. *Legal Brief*, 1.

Dodd, P., & Warner, J. B. (1983). On corporate governance: A study of proxy contests. *Journal of Financial Economics*, 11, 401–438.

Engstrom, R. L., & Brischetto, R. R. (1998). Is cumulative voting too complex? Evidence from exit polls. *Stetson Law Review*, XXVII, 813–834.

FCIR: The Financial Crisis inquiry report. Public Affairs (2011). *The Financial Crisis Inquiry Report*. New York: Public Affairs.

Foerster, S. R. (2003). *Financial management: A primer*. New York: W.W. Norton.

Friedlob, G. T., & Schleifer, L. L. F. (2003). *Essentials of financial analysis*. Hoboken, NJ: Wiley.

Fusaro, P. C., & Miller, R. M. (2002). *What went wrong at Enron: Everyone's guide to the largest bankruptcy in US history*. Hoboken, NJ: Wiley.

Fusfeld, D. R. (2002). *The age of the economist* (9th ed.). Boston, MA: Pearson.

Gaughan, P. A. (2015). *Mergers, acquisitions, and corporate restructurings* (6th ed.). Hoboken, NJ: Wiley.

Gold, S. S., & Spinogatti, R. L. (2008, August). Extraterritorial applications of US securities laws. *New York Law Journal, 240*(31), 1–2.

Krugman, P. (2012). *End this depression now!* New York: WW Norton and Company.

Kurtz, H. D. (2017). *Economic thought: A brief history.* New York: Columbia University Press.

Label, W. A. (2013). *Accounting for non-accountants* (3rd ed.). Naperville, IL: Sourcebooks.

Labonte, M. (2016, January). *Federal Reserve: Emergency lending.* Congressional Research Service, 7-5700, R44185.

Levison, M. (2014). *Guide to financial markets: Why they exist and how they work.* New York: Public Affairs.

Lipton, M., & Steinberger, E. H. (1987). *Takeovers and freezeouts* (pp. 6–144). New York: Law Journal Seminar Press.

Macey, J. R. (2008). A close read of an excellent commentary on *Dodge v. Ford. Faculty Scholarship Series. 1384.* Yale Law School.

Merhling, P. (1999). The vision of Hyman P. Minsky. *Journal of Economic Behavior & Organization, 39,* 129–158.

Mishkin, F. S., & Eakins, S. G. (2016). *Financial markets and institutions* (8th ed.). Essex, England: Pearson.

Moyer, R. C., McGuigan, J. R., & Rao, R. P. (2015). *Contemporary financial management* (13th ed.). Stamford, CT: Cengage Learning.

O'Sullivan, J. R. (2003). *Federal white-collar crime* (2nd ed.). St. Paul, MN: Thomson-West.

Oesterle, A. D. (1988). Delaware's takeover statute: Of chills, pills, standstills, and who gets iced. *Delaware Journal of Corporate Law, 13,* 879–914.

Oesterle, D. A. (2006). *Mergers and acquisitions.* St, Paul, MN: Thomson-West.

Palmiter, A. R. (2017). *Securities regulation* (7th ed.). Frederick, MD: Wolters Kluwer.

Parrino, R., Kidwell, D., & Bates, T. (2015). *Fundamentals of corporate finance* (3rd ed.). Hoboken, NJ: Wiley.

Podgor, E. S., & Israel, J. H. (2009). *White collar crime in a nutshell* (4th ed.). St. Paul, MN: Thomson-West.

Pozen, R. (2010). *Too big to save? How to fix the US financial system.* Hoboken, NJ: Wiley.

Pozsar, Z., Adrian, T., Ashcraft, A., & Boesky, H. (2013). Shadow banking. *FRBNY Economic Policy Review,* December, 1–16.

Resnick, B. G., & Eun, C. S. (2015). *International financial management.* New York: McGraw-Hill.

Ross, S. A., Westerfield, R. W., & Jordan, B. D. (2016). *Fundamentals of corporate finance.* New York: McGraw-Hill.

Sanches, D. (2014). Shadow banking and the crisis of 2007–08. *Business Review, Q2,* 7–14.

Schilit, H. M., & Perler, J. (2010). *Financial shenanigans: How to detect accounting gimmicks and fraud in financial reports.* New York: McGraw-Hill.

Sparks, G. A. (2010). Delaware's antitakeover statute continues to give hostile bidders a meaningful opportunity for success. Harvard Law School Forum on Corporate Governance and Financial Regulation. Retrieved from https://corpgov.law.harvard.edu.

Subramanian, G., Herscovici, S., & Barbetta, B. (2009). *Is Delaware's antitakeover statute unconstitutional? Evidence from 1988–2008. Seminar in law and economics.* Retrieved from https://pcg.law.harvard.edu.

United States. (2011). *The financial crisis inquiry report.* New York: US Public Affairs.

Warburton, C. E. S. (2018). *The development of international monetary policy*. Oxon, UK: Routledge.
Wiggins, R. Z., Piontek, T., & Metrick, A. (2014). *The Lehman Brothers bankruptcy*. Retrieved from http://som.yale.edu/ypfs. Yale School of Management.
Wray, L. R. (2016). *Why Minsky matters*. Princeton, NJ: Princeton University Press.
Yardeni, E. (2018). *Predicting the markets*. Brookville, NY: YRI Press.

4

CHAPTER 4
INNOVATION AND EXPROPRIATION OF CREATIVE RIGHTS

LEARNING OBJECTIVES

LO 1 To realize the importance of innovation for the global economy.
LO 2 To develop ethical values as a bulwark against property theft.
LO 3 To understand the liabilities that are associated with intellectual theft.
LO 4 To be familiar with domestic and global intellectual property laws.
LO 5 To detect instances of intellectual theft in litigation.

Innovation fuels economic growth and prosperity. Consequently, when the benefits of innovation are expropriated, the incentives to innovate are endangered and economic growth and prosperity are threatened. It is a long-held principle in international law that humans are entitled to the fruits of their creativity as a matter of economic and human right. The entitlement of such a right may be statutorily limited to a specific number of years after which the knowledge and returns from innovation diffuse and dissipate. Schumpeter (1934) characterized this dynamism as a precondition for "creative destruction." Since inventions that are useful (innovation) may not last forever after they have been diffused and replicated, firms are compelled to come up with new ideas and products that will render previous innovations outdated or obsolete. Only firms that are creative will survive in a competitive environment. Notwithstanding, innovations must be induced and the conditions for innovation must be encouraging if new products are going to be created.

There is probably no area in economics that is as fraught with controversies as that which entails the rights of humans to exist. For better and worse, this area is not immune from the rewards and benefits of innovation. Consequently, the ethical connotations of innovations and economic transactions pose challenging legal and global disturbances. Obviously, not all innovations present competing theories of the abridgement of economic rights; those that do not, safeguard the rights of innovators to enjoy exclusive privileges and rights (economic and human) that are derived from their ingenuity. Accordingly, business schools and professional organizations now teach students and practitioners the importance of ethical behavior in economic transactions. Invariably, unethical expropriations of creative rights are economic misbehaviors that espouse ethical disorders (deficiencies) that are inherently harmful to the global community.

4.1 INNOVATION AND HUMAN RIGHTS

Before the United Nations Declaration of Human Rights (UNDHR, 1948), there was the Berne Convention of 1885. Among other things, the Berne Convention stipulated minimum standards to safeguard the rights of authors. Pointedly, the intellectual work of authors was protected during their life spans plus 50 additional years thereafter. The scope and language of the convention suggest that it was intended to cover virtually every kind of creative work (Trebilcock, Howse, & Eliason, 2013, p. 522). The US joined the Convention in 1988, after a considerable period of relying on unilateral measures and bilateral treaties to protect copyrights.

In areas where innovation and economics impinge on human lives, conflicts of intellectual and human rights have been detected and chronicled in terms of bifurcated perceptions. One of the most erudite analyses of this conflict has been provided by Helfer (2003). The dichotomous representation shows that innovation and human rights can either be conflictive or mutually reinforcing, with opportunities for distributing benefits based on equity. The *conflict theory* suggests that strong intellectual property protection undermines a broad spectrum of human rights obligations; especially as far as socioeconomic rights are concerned. The second approach does not legally separate the essence of innovation from human rights but concedes to the necessity of encouraging innovation while also making consumption of monopolized products available for optimal consumption and the improvement of human welfare.

In actual fact, the legally dichotomous positions have not been historically cogent and discernible. The UNDHR recognizes intellectual property as human right:

1. Everyone has the right freely to participate in the cultural life of the community, to enjoy the arts and to share in scientific advancement and its benefits.
2. Everyone has the right to the protection of the moral and material interests resulting from any scientific, literary or artistic production of which he is the author (Art. 27).

Similar clauses have been included in various conventions, for example, the International Covenant on Economic, Social and Cultural Rights (ICESCR). However, though earlier conventions like the Paris and Berne Conventions allude to property rights, the earlier conventions make no conspicuous linkage to the concepts of fundamental human rights. The Paris Convention (1883) is the principal instrument of international law that covers the protection of patents and trademarks (industrial property). The comparatively recent World Intellectual Property Organization (WIPO, 1967) was established to administer multilateral agreements on intellectual property rights, which include the Paris and Berne Conventions. WIPO attained the status of a specialized agency of the United Nations (UN) in 1974.

International trade and the rights of indigenous people (through the HIV epidemic and human rights) brought into sharper focus the jurisprudential separation or abeyance of the relationship between human rights and intellectual property rights. There were just too many distractions in the post-World War II period.[1] Prior to the World Trade Organization (WTO, 1995), an outgrowth of the Uruguay Round of talks, intellectual property rights and trade conventions under the General Agreement on Tariffs and Trade (GATT) were not robustly enforced. The Uruguay Round was launched in Punta del Este (September, 1986), but it evolved through several cities and vicissitudes.

Laxed conventions and generous patent protections in favor of developing countries forced the businesses in more advanced countries to seek new protections that will prolong their patent protection and make them more competitive and profitable in the global economy. As a result of inadequate protections in developing countries, American business interests estimated losses in the billions of dollars annually in developing countries and newly industrializing countries (NICs). The reconstituted GATT, or newly formed WTO, incorporated three significant areas: (i) agriculture and unfair non-tariff barriers, (ii) trade-related aspects of intellectual property rights (TRIPS), and (iii) a new set of rules for trade in the service sector (General Agreement on Trade in Services (GATS)). The new law imposed conditions on leaders of developing economies to set minimum standards to regulate the creation and use of several forms of intellectual property. Enabling clauses provided some mitigating considerations for relatively poorer countries.[2] However, the asymmetry of protections (benefits) and welfare gains accruing to the developing economies posed new legal and economic challenges for the less developed economies and dispute resolutions. The Dispute Settlement Understanding (DSU), which will be discussed more fully in Chapter 8, provides the principles for resolving disputes within the new framework. Foreign business enterprises and individuals occasionally expropriate the creative rights of other entities. Expropriation can take multiple forms, including: (i) piracy of books, films and videos, (ii) dilution of trademarks by opening stores to market goods and services with a particular trademark, and (iii) mass production of generic drugs with identical patented ingredients under different names.[3]

In the US, intellectual property (IP) law has four major branches, all of which are generally applicable to different types of subject matter: copyright (original artistic and literary works of authorship), patent (inventions of processes, machines, manufactures, and compositions of matter that are useful, new, and non-obvious), trademark (commercial symbols), and trade secret (confidential, commercially valuable business information) (Yeh, 2016, p. 1). Artistic and literary works are protected under the Copyright Act (17 U.S.C. 101, *et seq.*). Copyright Act gives the copyright owner the exclusive right to: (i) reproduce work, (ii) prepare derivative works of the original, (iii) distribute copies of artistic and literary work to the public, and (iv) perform or display the work publicly. Copyrighted objects may be communicated with the aid of a machine or device.[4] Common ideas and objects that are not in fixed form cannot be copyrighted.

The Patent Act (35 U.S.C. 101 *et seq.*) governs the issuance and use of patents in the US. Patents are granted for inventions of new products, processes, or organisms (known as utility patents). Additionally, patents may be granted for designs and plants. For an invention to be patentable, it must be new and "non-obvious" (involving an inventive step), and have a potential industrial or commercial application.[5] The patent provides the holder with the exclusive right to exclude others from making, using, selling, or importing into the United States the items that have been patented.

Patent right is based on the concept that inventors must be granted a temporary monopoly over their invention in order to encourage innovation and to promote the expenditure of money on research and development (R&D). Patents ensure that patent holders recoup up-front costs through a temporary monopoly over the invention. In return for the economic rents to be derived, patent holders are required to disclose the content of the patent along with test data and other information concerning their inventions. Disclosure is intended to generate further creativity by others who might want to improve on the methodologies of patented products after their expiration dates. In the US, patents are granted by the US Patent and Trademark Office (PTO) of the Department of Commerce.

Unlike patents, trademarks are service marks that are protected by state and federal laws in the US. The main federal statute is the Lanham Act of 1946 (15 U.S.C. 1051, *et seq.*). Trademarks permit sellers to use distinctive names, marks, symbols, or sounds to identify and market products, services, or companies.[6] Essentially, trademarks allow for expeditious identification of the products of sellers, with the concomitant effect of generating network externalities or undesirable taste for identifiably bad products. In effect, reputable trademarked goods may carry a premium in markets. For trademarks, distinctiveness is at a premium because a trademark must capture the consumer's imagination to be effective as generic names of commodities cannot be trademarked. Trademarks can be applied to words, logos, phrases, shapes, sounds, or colors. They can also include initials and number combinations such as IBM and 3M.[7] Slogans, design and sound marks, and colors can also be trademarked.

Geographic indicators, which are also protected by the Lanham Act, are closely related to trademarks. The indicators cover products that require reputational protection—especially agricultural goods—from specific territorial areas or geographic areas. Protective benefits are not unique to a single producer but all producers who produce products, including wines, and spirits, within a defined territorial area. The geographic indication acts to protect the quality and reputation of a distinctive product originating in a certain region; however, the benefit does not accrue to a sole producer, but rather the producers of a product originating from a particular region. Geographic protection, like trademark, can be obtained from the PTO.

A trade secret is valuable business information that is protected from dissemination to competitors. Proprietary trade secrets can be found in: research and development, secret formulae, designs, computer source code, manufacturing tools, marketing, sales, and financial and administrative data, such as customer lists and marketing plans.[8] The Uniform Trade Secret Act (UTSA) defines a trade secret as:

[A]ny type of valuable information, including a "formula, pattern, compilation, program, device, method, technique, or process," that derives independent economic value from not being generally known or readily ascertainable and is subject to reasonable efforts by the owner to maintain its secrecy.

(Uniform Trade Secret Act, § 1(4))

Trade secrets can be shared between employer and employee or customer and vendor. Invariably, not all information can be protected as a trade secret; especially when the information is: publicly known, not very valuable to a company, easily acquired, and can be duplicated.

In the US, most states have adopted the UTSA, which is a model law that was drafted by the National Conference of Commissioners on Uniform State Laws. The application for a trade secret protection is unlike that for a patent. Protection of trade secrets originates immediately with the creation of the trade secret; there is no process for applying for protection or registering trade secrets and trade secret protection does not expire until it is publicly known.[9] On the contrary, patent applicants must disclose information about their innovation to the PTO in order to acquire patents. Further, patents offer stronger protection for a limited period of time.

Human creativity has evolved over the years. In 1883, there was no internet. The development of the internet has created scope for newer technological innovation, property theft, and colossal economic losses. US losses are particularly staggering in the area of trade secrets (see Figure 4.1), where the US loses an estimated $180 billion on an annual basis. Since the advent of TRIPS in 1995, the US stance on intellectual property has evolved to include digital media and Internet Treaties. The Trade Promotion Authority (TPA), as reconstituted in June 2015 (P.L. 114–26), has broader objectives to include cyber theft, trade secrets, and proprietary information (Akhtar & Fergusson, 2019 p. 2). Intellectual property theft is a manifestation of ethical lapses around the world, compounded by inefficiencies to seriously deter and punish the misconduct.

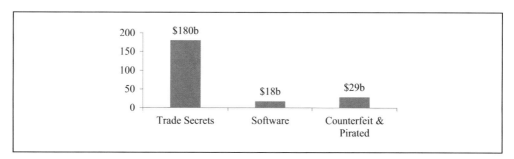

Figure 4.1 Estimated annual cost of intellectual property theft from the US ($b)
Source: US Department of State.

4.2 ETHICAL LAPSES AND COSTS OF IP EXPROPRIATION

By "ethical lapses," I refer to outright and immoral theft of intellectual property. Until there is some type of legislation that prohibits behaviors that are perceived or recognized as unethical, *ethics* is a rather nebulous concept; that is, the enactment of laws that protect the common good can clearly define acceptable behavior regardless of cultural or idiosyncratic arguments. Not surprisingly, ethics may mean different things to different people until binding laws define acceptable behaviors across international boundaries. Of course, some behaviors are instantly opprobrious. No law is required to state that illegally killing someone is unethical and unacceptable. The problem is, as the American psychologist, Kohlberg, once noted, human behaviors and moral senses evolve over time. Implicitly, laws may not be enough to combat human impulses and ethical violations in cases of arrested moral development. Laws are coercive instruments that are not always well suited for regulating all aspects of human lives when impulsive humans are unrestrained by innate impulses in sparsely regulated environments.

Over the years, scholars have wrestled with the concept of ethics and a moral sense. Boatright (2014) observes that although ethics is a complex subject matter, it can be easily understood by six familiar concepts: (i) [general] peoples' welfare ("the greatest good for the greatest number" (common good), (ii) duty (the obligation to act), (iii) recognition of rights; especially those affirmed by laws and treaties (for example, human rights, employee rights, customer rights, and shareholder rights), (iv) manifestation of a legitimate sense of fairness or justice, (v) display of honesty, and (vi) a sense of dignity.[10] In several ways, the concepts are restraining virtues that check the excesses to prefer an inordinate amount of pleasure or gain over the pain that is inflicted on others.

Fairness can be multidimensional. It can mean equity, reciprocity, and impartiality. Broadly defined, equity also implies distributive justice; meaning that people should not be getting disproportionate benefits from their investments; especially when they are stealing from others. Self-control is probably the greatest virtue (moral sense) when laws are inefficient (unenforceable) and illegal economic gains are infinite. Self-control is a reflexive attribute that is not contingent on cost-benefit analysis.[11] It attains worldwide approbation and is usually dependent on biological and environmental exposures. Wilson discovers that the development of self-control requires more parental effort than that of fairness.[12] Invariably, personality theories are revealing indicators of virtue.

> Virtue ... is a state of character lying in the mean between two extremes; temperance lies in the mean between an excess of indulgence and a deficiency of pleasure.
> (Wilson, 1993, p. 91)

A sense of duty can be positioned as close as possible to self-control.

> Duty is the disposition to honor obligations even without hope of reward or fear of punishment. One reveals himself [/herself] to be a moral person not merely by

honoring obligations but by being disposed to honor them even when it is not in his [/her] interest to do so.

(Wilson, 1993, p. 100)

Normal humans are usually aroused to act, not by warm sympathy for the plight of a victim of robbery or the calm deliberation of what justice might require, but by an outrage that someone is conspicuously flouting an obligation.[13] Accordingly, individuals and states have a responsibility to be globally dutiful.

Of the various definitions of ethics that are worthy of consideration, ethics can be defined as the principles of conduct governing an individual or group. Some will classify the subject matter as "the study of morality" (Velasquez, 2002, p. 7); where morality is understood to mean the standards that an individual or group perceive to be right or wrong or good or bad. Professional or business ethics is considered to be a specialized study of what is morally right or wrong, because the theory is applicable to business policies, institutions, and behaviors. Velasquez notes that the most influential institutions within contemporary societies may be their economic institutions, which are designed to: (i) produce the goods and services that the societies want and need, and (ii) distribute the goods and services to the various members of their societies.[14]

How do individuals develop a moral sense? In reality, the development of moral sensibilities is not an instantaneous occurrence. Psychologists have shown that moral values of restraint emanating from a sense of fairness, self-control, and duty are principles that are developed over time with very good societal reinforcements. After conducting research into human moral development for over 20 years, the American psychologist, Lawrence Kohlberg, provided an insight into the evolution of the human sense of morality. He identified three levels or stages of moral development: (i) preconventional stages, (ii) conventional stages, and (iii) postconventional, autonomous, or principled stages.[15] In fact, Kohlberg's evolutionary analysis is a paradigmatic representation of human sensibilities over time. Mental development in an arrested state can induce theft; but theft may also be induced by poverty (desperation), a sense of deprivation (lack of fairness), outright incontinence (deficient self-control), and the rapacious desire to maximize profit (lack of balance).[16]

Apparently, parenting is a necessary but insufficient moral guidepost. In the western world, some institutions pay attention to ethical issues at the undergraduate and graduate levels; mostly in law schools and graduate schools of business. In some parts of the world, formal ethical instruction is nonexistent. Parents provide moral guidance to the best of their abilities, but kids may quickly forget the moral basics without sufficient societal reinforcements of appropriate social values. The desire to earn inordinate profits and wealth at all cost is a ubiquitous problem that may be rampant in some societies.

Not surprisingly, theft of technology information has posed enormous economic threats to the furtherance of innovation and economic growth. Information technology encompasses a wide range of media activities, including the internet, wireless communication, and digitalization, which have enabled individuals and businesses to exploit destructive mechanisms that endanger communication, economic transactions, and entertainment. Apart from privacy rights that are being violated by cyber criminals, computer software, and computer codes or other types of encryption also have risk exposures. Movies, newspapers, music, and books can now be transferred from one area of the globe to another at a rapid pace via electronic media. However, almost all ethical issues that are raised by the revolutionary form of electronic communication in one way or another involve risk exposures.[17]

States can deliberately or inadvertently nurture bad impulses by reinforcing perceptions of unfairness, or they can create a bureaucratic infrastructure or apparatus to perpetuate fraud and IP theft. The intensity of theft will depend on regime types and the level of tolerance for IP theft under the deconstruction of municipal and/or international laws. There are very simple ways in which the bases for IP theft can be perceived; all of which will fail to pass the fundamental moral tests that have been previously discussed. First, illegal and unlimited personal gains can be derived from IP theft; second, IP criminals tend to have no intimate affiliation with their victims (the IP criminals do not see that IP theft destroys the common good or shared prosperity); and third, IP crimes can be committed with virtual impunity (no punishment or deterrence). Criminals generally have idiosyncratic motives and are blessed with opportunities until they are caught. What are the effects of the technological turpitude?

The economic consequences of IP theft cannot be precisely computed but the monetary values that have been estimated are staggering. Table 4.1 provides some information about international IP theft. The data, which have been facilitated by the International Chamber of Commerce (ICC), the International Trademark Association (INTA), and TECXCIPIO,[18] underscores the implications of IP theft for economic growth and long-term foreign direct investment (FDI). In all categories of IP theft, the societal implications are severe.

The pecuniary costs of cybercrime can be classified under three broad headings: (i) proactive, (ii) the directly and indirectly consequential effects, and (iii) preventive costs. The cost of IP theft on the internet is considered to be the most difficult to estimate (Home Office, 2018, p. 58), mainly because intellectual property theft can be easily conflated with other effects of IP theft, including customer information and funds. Although intellectual property or commercially sensitive information stolen during a cyber-attack may be estimated as the value of the intellectual property or commercially sensitive information if sold on the open market, it may also be estimated as the damage to a company's competitiveness because of the loss.

Table 4.1 shows that international costs of IP theft have increased considerably since 2008. It is noteworthy that IP theft considerably impacts employment, foreign direct investment (FDI) and economic growth. Millions of workers lose their jobs (2 to 2.6 million in 2013,

Table 4.1 Estimated international economic losses due to counterfeiting and piracy (US$b, unless otherwise stated)

Category	2008	2013	2015	2022 (forecast)
Internationally traded counterfeit and pirated products	285–360	461	770–960	991
Domestically produced and consumed counterfeit and pirated products	140–215	249–456	370–570	524–959
Digitally pirated products	30–75	213	80–240	384–856
Total	**455–650**	**923–1,130**	**1,220–1,770**	**1,900–2,810**
Wider economic and social costs				
• Displacement of legitimate economic activity	N/A	470–597	N/A	980–1244
• Estimated reduction in FDI	N/A	111	N/A	231
• Estimated fiscal losses	N/A	96–130	N/A	199–270
• Estimated costs of crime	N/A	60	N/A	125
Total wider economic and social costs	--	**737–898**	--	**1,540–1,870**
Estimated employment losses		2–2.6m		4.2–5.4m
Foregone economic growth in OECD 2017: $30 billion to $54 billion				

Sources: *Frontier Economics, Estimating the Global Economic and Social Impacts of Counterfeiting and Piracy*. A Report Commissioned by Business Action to Stop Counterfeiting and Piracy (BASCAP), February 2011; see also BASCAP and INTA (2016, p. 8).[19]
Notes:
BASCAP economic loss estimates are restricted to the G20 economies. The number for pirated digital product in 2013 has been aggregated; film = $160b, music = $29b and software = $24b.

which is projected to increase to about 4 million, on the lower tier, by 2022). The cost of foregone economic growth in the OECD was estimated to be about $30 billion to $54 billion; implicitly, the estimates indicate that a percentage point reduction in the intensity of counterfeiting and piracy could have led to a gain of about $30 billion to $54 billion for the 35 OECD countries in 2017. Counterfeit and pirated goods accounted for up to 5 percent of imports in the EU, or $116 billion, in 2013.[20] As far as the UK is concerned, the Home Office reports that in the most likely scenario, the cost of cybercrime, including IP could have amounted to a top-tier estimate of £27 billion in 2011 (Home Office, 2018, p. 12). IP theft estimate by Oxford Economics (2014), amounted to about £17.3 million (Home Office, 2018, p. 54). The value of technological theft is prospectively much greater than lost output. Surely, by utilizing all the levers of instructive morality, there is a compelling need to readjust the moral compass of the global community.

4.3 THE ECONOMIC CONSEQUENCES OF INNOVATION

Long ago, economists determined that there is a positive correlation between innovation and economic activity. The Schumpeterian theory of innovation and growth suggests that there is no boom without innovation and there is no slump without an exhaustion of innovation. Therefore, Schumpeter regarded theories that associated business cycles with monetary policies as misguided. He estimated cycles to be about nine to ten years long, but later added the concept of "long wave," which spans approximately 50 years.[21] Studying output, employment, and capital stock for the period through World War I, Schumpeter discovered three long waves of economic activities that were associated with technological breakthroughs.

Similarly, the Russian statistician, Kondratiev/Kondratieff (1892–1938) who studied European prices, wages, and interest rates, found long upward and downward trends in economic activity.

Kondratiev cycles can be linked to multiple innovations: (i) the steam engine (1787–1842), (ii) the railway (1843–1897), (iii) electrification (1897–c.1940), and (iv) autos and petrochemicals [c.1930–1970];[22] today we can add the Internet Revolution and the tech boom and bust.

Innovation is a cornerstone of the competitive economy and Schumpeter (1934) probably provided the most eloquent reminder of that fact. His "perennial gale of creative destruction" synthesized the essence of market-oriented economies, innovation, and the dynamism of capitalism at a time when some had misgivings about the vitality of the capitalist system; competition forces innovation for survival in the capitalist economy. Newer and better products will replace the old because they are more appealing to consumers. Therefore, companies that cannot innovate (produce useful inventions) will be outcompeted.

> Joseph Schumpeter (1934 [1912]): Innovators undertake research, experiments, tests, planning and other activities in order to generate "excess profit that hopefully, exceeds the up-front costs …. [I]nnovations such as engineering a better product, designing a more attractive product, or improving production methods to lower production costs, give innovators an advantage over the competition and permits them to charge prices above their marginal costs. Schumpeter described technological progress as a dynamic process of profit-driven **technological competition**, in which innovators continually apply costly resources to create new products, change production methods, reduce costly inputs, and change product characteristics to gain a competitive advantage over existing producers."
>
> (Van den Berg, 2017, p. 340)

The economic theory of innovation elicits some fundamental concepts that are worthy of restatement for the development of innovation models: (i) innovators undertake risks, (ii) they use a fraction of available societal resources to innovate, (iii) successful innovation reduces the cost of production (or investment), (iv) innovation increases output, (v) innovators expect to make profits, (vi) the amount of profits dissipate over time because of legal restrictions and prospects of improving on older innovations, and (vii) consumers and societies benefit from innovation. I will subsequently refer to all or most of these fundamental concepts as *ex ante* assumptions.

Consider Van den Berg's representations of the Schumpeterian theory with some subsequent notational readjustments:

$$\pi = \mu X \tau, \tag{4.1}$$

where π is for profits to be realized, μ is for the profit markup, X is for the level of production, τ is for the time it takes for the innovator to produce and enjoy the fruits of his/her labor before the monopoly power expires ($E(\tau)=1/q$ or β/N) (see Equation 4.1). The level of production must depend on the amount of resources that are devoted to the innovation apart from R&D activities, which is the sum of productive factors and resources, ΣR, a fraction of which (r) is devoted to innovation on a daily basis. The total amount of resources devoted to innovative activity (N) on a daily basis can then be defined as:

$$r\Sigma R = N. \tag{4.2}$$

The cost of resources for innovation, *ceteris paribus*, will be cheaper as the sum of productive factors and resources (ΣR) increases; but as innovative activity (N) increases, the cost of innovation, say wages (for simplicity, since other costs are involved), w, will increase. It will also take some amount of productive resources (β) to generate one unit of innovation (q):

$$q\beta = N \rightarrow q = N/\beta. \tag{4.3}$$

Figure 4.2 summarizes the key assumptions and results of the Schumpeterian model; where CoI is the cost of innovation and PVI is the present value of innovation (the future value of incremental profits, each of which is discounted to the present). Since entrepreneurs are far-sighted, they optimistically envision the potential for profits and evaluate that potential against various forms of risks before undertaking an investment; that is the considerations of risk do not stifle innovations; piracy increases perceptions of risk with deleterious effects.

The inverse and positive gradients show the relationships between pairs of variables (see Figure 4.2(a)). Notably, increases in innovation increase the PVI (see Figure 4.2(b)). Increase in the supply of productive factors decreases the cost of investment and increases the number of innovations per day and the present value of investment (see Figure 4.2(c)). Improvements in productivity reduce cost and increase units of innovation

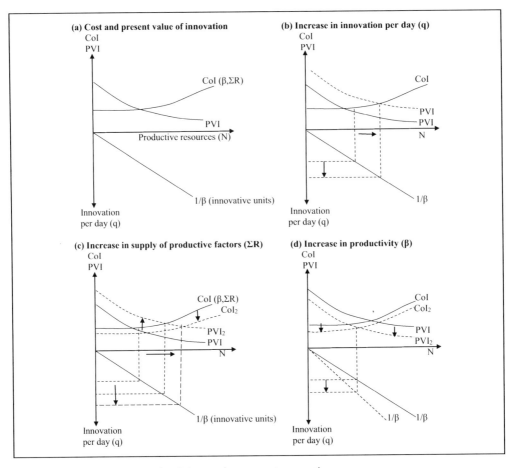

Figure 4.2 Innovation, productivity, and economic growth
Source: Van den Berg (2017, pp. 339–41).

without increasing the amount of resources for innovative activity (N). Present value of innovation falls as a result of the rapid creation of new ideas and the dissipation of returns to old ideas. The decline in beta, which increases the number of innovations per day, is an indicator of efficiency and the decline suggests that economies are generating new ideas at a rapid pace without the redundant use of resources. Intellectual property theft is paralyzing and it inefficiently diverts economic resources from productive to counterproductive uses (see Table 4.1). Accordingly, the legal use of knowledge encourages innovation, stimulates international trade, and creates pull factors that welcome FDI and technology transfer. In reality, the implications of innovation are far-reaching. Innovations fosters a positive interaction of the economic and natural spheres to facilitate sustainable development.[23]

IP cannot be considered irrelevant to economic growth; more so, dynamic comparative advantage emanating from innovation is essential to competitive international trade. As such, industries rely on IP protection. US Department of Commerce data for 2014

Table 4.2 Growth rate of patents and trademarks applications (2017–2018)

	Patents	**World share**	**Trademarks**	**World share**
China	11.6	46.4	28.3	51.4
US	-1.6	18	4.3	4.5
Japan	-1.5	9.4	-8.6	3.6

Source: WIPO's World Intellectual Property Indicators (2019).

reveal that a subset of the most IP-intensive industries were estimated to account for approximately 30 percent of US direct employment and 52 percent of US merchandise exports (Akhtar & Fergusson, 2019, p. 1). More than 3 million patents were in force in the US in 2018.[24] An estimated 14 million patents were in force across 125 jurisdictions in 2018, representing an increase of 6.7 percent on 2017 figures. In 2018, the largest number of patents in force was recorded in the US (3.1 million). China (2.4 million) and Japan (2.1 million) each had around 2 million patents and the Republic of Korea had 1 million; with 703,606 patents in force, Germany ranked fifth. Half of all patents in force in the US originated from non-resident applicants, while resident applicants accounted for around 70 percent of all patents in force in China. Non-resident applicants accounted for more than half of all patents in force in each of the top 20 offices, except for China, the Republic of Korea, and the Russian Federation (WIPO, 2019, p. 19). At the same time, it is noteworthy that the growth rate of global patents for the US and Japan declined (see Table 4.2).

WIPO (2019a, p. 74) reports that an estimated 10.9 million trademark applications were filed worldwide in 2018—about 1.7 million more than in 2017—corresponding to a growth of 19.2 percent. The increase marks a ninth consecutive year of growth but is almost 11 percentage points lower than the extraordinary increase of nearly 30 percent seen in 2017. There are now twice as many trademark applications filed than in 2014 due to the high annual growth rates recorded in recent years. WIPO reports that seven of the last 15 years have seen double-digit growth, with only two in which the number of applications decreased over this period. When differences in filing systems across national and regional offices are harmonized using the application class count, trademark filing activity in 2018 also saw a double-digit increase, up 15.5 percent on the previous year. The total number of classes specified in applications—known as the application class count— reached an estimated 14.3 million; excluding the high 2018 application class count for China, trademark filing activity grew by 4.5 percent in the rest of the world. Japan did not really show growth in this area (see Table 4.2).

Madrid international trademark registrations have reflected an increase in the demand for trademarks.

> To obtain trademark protection in multiple countries or jurisdictions, applicants can either file their applications directly at each individual office—known as the "Paris

route"—or file an application for international registration through the Madrid System—the "Madrid route." In 2018, the Madrid System offered trademark holders the ability to obtain protection for their branded products and services in an area covering a total of 119 countries. Combined, Madrid members represent about 60% of all countries, home to over 70% of the world's population, and in which just over 80% of global GDP occurs, with the potential to increase these shares as membership grows.

(WIPO, 2019a, p. 82)

WIPO (2019a, p. 83) finds that for the second year in a row, the EU attracted the highest number of designations (25,030) in Madrid applications in 2018, followed by China (24,289) and the US (22,827). Madrid applicants have sought to extend protection for their marks to the 28 EU member countries, as a whole, more than they did to any other Madrid member jurisdiction. Like China, half of the top 20 designated Madrid members were middle-income countries, notably the Russian Federation (15,627), India (12,254), Mexico (10,080), and Turkey (8,881). Among top destinations for international trademark registration via the Madrid System, the UK saw the largest surge in annual growth of 21.9 percent, albeit lower than its extraordinary increase of 60.6 percent from 2016 to 2017 (WIPO, 2019a, p. 83).[25]

Publishing constitutes a significant component of the creative economy. In 2017, the International Publishers Association (IPA) and the World Intellectual Property Organization (WIPO) launched a new survey to compile statistics on the creative economy.[26] In all, 35 national publishers' associations and copyright authorities shared their 2016 data covering the publishing industry. The following year, in 2017, 53 countries shared their data with WIPO (WIPO, 2019a, p. 188). The scope of the IPA-WIPO survey is limited to published materials (i.e., books monographs, and so on) that have been issued with an ISBN number, a Digital Object Identifier (DOI) or any other book identifier (WIPO, 2019a, p. 186). The IPA-WIPO survey resulted in publishing industry data from 58 countries (see Box 4.1 for creative activity).

Since IP law may impose restrictions on the duration of benefits that can be derived from creative activity, original knowledge becomes obsolete. Fresher knowledge replaces the old, and as returns to old ideas dissipate, the present value of innovation declines (see Figure 4.2(d)). The time limitation of creative benefits creates prospects for improvement on original ideas, or for others to replicate original ideas after protection has legally expired. International economists routinely allude to this phenomenon as a precondition for product cycles; a development in which newer ideas create new products and older ideas become more valuable to others. The cycle generates changing comparative advantage as formerly less efficient nations acquire new advantages.

The product cycle theory is largely credited to Raymond Vernon who argued that newly invented products are imperfectly produced on a relatively smaller scale for disproportionately larger consumption in high-income countries. Accordingly, additional R&D is required for producing and marketing new products by the producers. Over time,

BOX 4.1 CREATIVE RIGHTS 2017/2018

In total, 49 national publishers' associations and copyright authorities shared their 2018 data, while a further nine associations/authorities shared their 2016/2017 data. Moreover, a number of respondents indicated a willingness to share their 2018 data when available. U.S. publishing industry revenue reached over 23 billion USD in 2018. The 2018 total sales and licensing revenue generated by both the trade and the educational sectors are available for 14 countries. These 14 countries generated USD 42.5 billion revenue in 2018. The United States of America (U.S.) (USD 23.3 billion) reported the largest net revenue, followed by Germany (US6.1 billion), the U.K. (USD 5.4 billion) and France (USD 3 billion). Trade sector revenue accounted for 50% or more of total revenue in nine of the countries – ranging from 56.6% in Finland to 93.3% in the Czech Republic. Educational sector revenue accounted for over 50% of total revenue in Brazil (67.8%) and Turkey (50.5%). The total revenue generated from sales of "children's books", a subcategory of the trade sector, is available for five countries and amounted to USD 5.1 billion in 2018. The share of children's books revenue as a percentage of total trade sector revenue was largest for the U.S. (27.5%) and Sweden (21.5%).

The online sales channel generated 51.5% of trade sector revenue in the UK. The 2018 trade sector revenue is available for 14 countries. The U.S., with USD 16.2 billion, reported the largest revenue, followed by Japan (USD 8.4 billion), the U.K. (USD 3.2 billion) and France (USD 2.1 billion)… . Eight countries provided their 2018 trade sector revenue broken down by format, that is, printed, digital and other format categories. For each of these eight countries, print editions generated more than three-quarters of trade sector revenue, whereas digital editions accounted for the largest revenue share in Japan (24.5%), Sweden (23.2%) and the U.S. (19.4%)… .

The 2018 trade sector revenue broken down by destination market is available for 10 countries. Domestic sales accounted for the bulk of total revenue for all observed countries, ranging from 60.6% in Belgium to 99.9% in Japan. The share of revenue from foreign sales and licensing represents a relatively high proportion of trade revenue in Belgium (39.4%) and the U.K. (33%)… .

The online sales channel generated more than half of total trade sector revenue in the UK. The US (41.6%), Brazil (25.5%) and Sweden (23.5%) also had a large proportion of their total trade sector revenue generated by the online sales channel. However, the brick and mortar channel continues to generate the largest share of total trade sector revenue for all reported countries, except for Slovenia, the UK and the US…

> **BOX 4.1 CONTINUED**
>
> Foreign sales accounted for 55.9% of educational sector revenue in the UK. Revenue generated by the educational sector is available for 11 countries. The U.S. with USD 7.1 billion reported the largest total revenue, followed by the U.K. (USD 2.3 billion) and Brazil (USD 0.9 billion).... For all reported countries, print editions accounted for the bulk of total educational sector revenue, ranging from 67.4% in Denmark to 96.9% in France, while digital editions accounted for 32.6% in Denmark, 28.8% in Norway and 19.6% in the U.K. Breakdown of the total educational sector revenue by domestic and foreign markets shows that the U.K. (55.9%) and Belgium (24.9%) had the largest shares of total revenue generated from the foreign market. Revenue generated from the domestic market accounted for almost all the educational sector revenue in Denmark, Finland, Norway and the US.... In 2018, the UK published 188,000 titles covering the trade and educational sectors.
>
> Data on the total number of titles published in 2018 covering both the trade and educational sectors are available for 43 countries. The U.K. reported a combined total of 188,000 published titles in 2018, followed by the Russian Federation (116,915) and France (106,799).... The trade sector accounted for more than half of all titles published in most of those countries where a breakdown according to sector was available – ranging from 50.5% (Belarus and Brazil) to 97.7% (Estonia).
>
> Source: WIPO (2019, pp. 187–8).

as the production technology becomes more standardized, familiar (mature), and diffused, factor intensity in production tends to shift away from skilled labor to less skilled labor.

Empirical evidence suggests developments in many industries tend to follow the product cycle hypothesis; for example, computer firms in the US and Japan began R&D to design small, portable computers (laptops) in the 1970s and early 1980s. The firms had planned to meet the demand by businesspeople and researchers in the US and other high-income countries. Several early models were produced in the US and Japan, with continuing R&D. In the late 1980s and early 1990s, IBM, Toshiba, Texas Instruments, and other US and Japanese firms introduced improved models that were exported to other countries. As the components of the laptops became standardized, and as competition among sellers intensified in the 1990s, firms shifted much of the assembly production of laptops, first to Taiwan and later to China to reduce production costs. The innovating countries became importers (Pugel, 2016, p. 129).[27] Improvements in innovation can create displacements in alternative ways.

> In 1980, Hong Kong's garment and textile sectors employed almost 450,000 workers, close to 20% of total employment. The workers overwhelmingly made apparel—shirts,

trousers, dresses, and more—for export, especially to the US. Since then, however, the Hong Kong clothing industry has fallen sharply in size—in fact, it has almost disappeared. So, too, have Hong Kong's apparel exports. [Hong Kong] got better at other things. Apparel production is a labor-intensive, relatively low tech industry; comparative advantage in that industry has historically always rested with the poor, labor-abundant economies. Hong Kong no longer fits that description; Bangladesh does. Hong Kong's garment industry was a victim of the city's success [creative destruction].

(Krugman & Wells, p. 137)

Should thieves be deterred from stealing intellectual property? The economic evidence in support of deterrence is overwhelming.

4.4 INTELLECTUAL PROPERTY LAW

Intellectual property (IP) law confers exclusive rights to prevent unauthorized reproduction or use of certain intangible creations of the human mind. The US Constitution provides an IP clause that gives US Congress the authority to grant *"Authors and Inventors the exclusive Right to their respective Writings and Discoveries"* in order *"[t]o promote the Progress of Science and useful Arts"* (Hickey, 2018, p. 1). Invariably, the essence of IP law is to affirm the economic benefits that have been highlighted in the previous section. The US Patent and Trademark Office (PTO) have found that IP-intensive industries—such as computer technology, entertainment, and pharmaceuticals—account for 28 million American jobs and $6.6 trillion in economic value, representing 38 percent of US GDP.[28]

US federal law protects patents, copyrights, and trademarks, each of which has its own unique features that are recognized by US law. The patent law requires the invention or discovery of a useful process, machine, manufacture, or composition of matter, or any new and useful pertinent improvement. At a very fundamental level, natural phenomena cannot be patented. Therefore, patents require novel inventions that are useful and non-obvious, which should be filed by the inventor. The process for obtaining a patent before the PTO ("patent prosecution") is streamlined, including written specifications of claims to be ascertained. Table 4.3 lists three forms of IP protections with their stated constitutional and statutory provisions.

Patentees have the exclusive right to make and use their inventions for a particular period of time, which is usually 20 years from the date that the application was filed. Persons wishing to practice the inventions of patentees must be permitted to do so by the patent holder during the active period of protection. To enforce the patent, the patent holder may sue for alleged infringements in federal courts to seek an injunction, damages, and other remedies. Even when patents are valid, the US adversarial system offers defendants the right to defend themselves against lawsuits.[29]

Unlike patents, copyrights grant creators of "original works of authorship" exclusive rights to their creative works. Forms of expression that are copyrightable include literary works

Table 4.3 Forms of federal intellectual property protection

	Patent	**Copyright**	**Trademark**
Constitutional basis	IP clause (U.S. CONST. Art. I, § 8, cl. 8)	IP clause (U.S. CONST. Art. I, § 8, cl. 8)	Commerce clause (U.S. CONST. Art. I, § 8, cl. 3)
Statutory basis	1952 Patent Act, as amended, see 35 U.S.C. §§ 1–390	1976 Copyright Act, as amended, see 17 U.S.C. §§ 101–1332	1946 Lanham Act, as amended, see 15 U.S.C. §§ 1051–1141n
Initial rights-holder	Inventor	Author	Business or person using mark to identify goods or services
Duration	20 years	Life of author plus 70 years	Potentially indefinite
Selected legislative amendments	Leahy-Smith America Invents Act (2011); Hatch-Waxman Act (1984); Bayh-Dole Act (1980)	Digital Millennium Copyright Act (1998); Copyright Term Extension Act (1998); Berne Convention Implementation Act (1988)	Trademark Dilution Revision Act (2006); Anticybersquatting Consumer Protection Act (1999)

Sources: Hickey (2018, p. 2); www.crs.gov.

(such as books and computer code); musical works and sound recordings; pictorial, graphic, and sculptural works; audiovisual works (such as movies and television); and architectural works.[30]

Materials to be copyrighted must have been independently created, at least minimally creative, and fixed in some tangible form. Copyright does not extend to ideas, processes, systems, discoveries, or methods of operation.[31] Contrary to the requirements for patent and trademark rights, American copyright holders must register their copyrights with the US Copyright Office in order to have standing in American courts.

> Holders of copyrights generally have the exclusive right to reproduce their works, publicly perform and display it, distribute it, and prepare derivative works from it. For most works created today, the copyright does not expire until 70 years after the death of the author. Once the copyright is registered, copyright holders may sue infringers in court to seek injunctions and damages.
>
> (Hickey, 2018, p. 1)

The "fair use" of copyrighted materials circumscribes the rights of copyright holders. "Fair use" allows certain socially valuable uses that would otherwise be perceived as infringements. Hickey notes that the permissible use of copyrighted materials in the US must meet four legitimate criteria (four factor test): (i) a legal purpose and character,

(ii) the nature [standing] of the original work, (iii) the substantiality [amount] of what is copied, and (iv) the character [nature] of the use of copyrighted material. Courts may also consider whether the use of copyrighted material is "transformative"; that is, whether the use adds new expression, has a different purpose, and/or alters the original work with new expression or meaning.[32]

Although trademarks fall under the category of IP, trademarks are not a product of a constitutional IP clause in the US. The Congress' authority to regulate interstate commerce has been the source of authority for federal trademark law.[33] Trade secrets are also protected under the commerce clause law. The Copyright Act, Patent Act, and Lanham Act provide legal protection for intellectual property against unauthorized use, theft, and other violations of the rights granted by those statutes to the IP owner. Trademark law protects consumers from unfair competition because they are partly intended to prevent businesses from misrepresenting the origins of goods or services; especially when inferior and dangerous products can be issued to degrade the original and legal quality. Generally, any "word, name, symbol, or device" may be used as a trademark to identify the goods or services that are provided by firms. Generic or general expressions cannot be granted trademark protection. To be granted US federal trademark protection, businesses are required to register the mark with the PTO and each registration for a mark is limited to a particular type of good or service.[34] Owners of trademarks have the legal right to prevent other businesses or persons from using similar marks that already have trademark protection. In cases of abrogation, aggrieved parties may sue to obtain injunctions and damages in US courts of law. Copyrights and trademarks have longer spans of protection and different statutory bases. In fact, all the IP protections have different statutory foundations (see Table 4.3).

In the US, IP infringements are penalized and Table 4.4 provides a list of infringements against the corresponding statutes. Intellectual property disputes are typically litigated in the federal courts.[35] The federal courts have subject matter jurisdiction in cases that relate to federal issues, including intellectual property conflicts. In patent and copyright disputes, this subject matter jurisdiction excludes state courts. Though federal and state courts have concurrent jurisdiction over trademark matters, most trademark cases are heard by federal courts.[36] In addition to subject matter jurisdiction, the court must also be the appropriate venue to hear an IP dispute, with personal jurisdiction over defendants.

Federal courts have jurisdiction in matters involving foreigners and amounts in excess of $75,000. However, federal courts also do not possess automatic subject matter jurisdiction when the federal issues are considered to be tangential to what are essentially non-federal claims; for example, when the interpretation of a patent license or the ownership of a trademark or copyright may not arise under the federal patent, trademark, or copyright laws.[37] McNeely and others find that the costs and risks of litigation make it likely for cases to be either settled or decided in advance of trial. IP cases may also be decided on their merits prior to any trial by a motion for summary judgment. After reviewing affidavits, documents, depositions, and other discoverable evidence, courts may find that there is no

Table 4.4 US intellectual property protections and sanctions

US Statute	Infringement
• 17 U.S.C. § 501	Copyright infringement
• 17 U.S.C. § 506(a)(1)(A) and 18 U.S.C. § 2319(b)	Criminal copyright infringement for profit
• 17 U.S.C. § 506(1)(B) and 18 U.S.C. § 2319(c)	Criminal copyright infringement without a profit motive
• 17 U.S.C. § 506(a)(1)(c) and 18 U.S.C. § 2319(d)	Pre-release distribution of a copyrighted work over a computer network)
• 17 U.S.C. § 1309	Infringement of a vessel hull or deck design
• 17 U.S.C. § 1326	Falsely marking an unprotected vessel hull or deck design with a protected design notice
• 17 U.S.C. §§ 1203, 1204	Circumvention of copyright protection systems
• 18 U.S.C. § 2319A	Bootleg recordings of live musical performances
• 18 U.S.C. § 2319B	Unauthorized recording of films in movie theaters
• 15 U.S.C. § 1114(1)	Unauthorized use in commerce of a reproduction, counterfeit, or colorable imitation of a federally registered trademark
• 15 U.S.C. § 1125(a)	Trademark infringement due to false designation, origin, or sponsorship
• 15 U.S.C. § 1125(c)	Dilution of famous trademarks
• 15 U.S.C. §§ 1125(d) and 1129	Cybersquatting and cyberpiracy in connection with internet domain names
• 18 U.S.C. § 2318	Counterfeit/illicit labels and counterfeit documentation and packaging for copyrighted works
• 35 U.S.C. § 271	Patent infringement
• 35 U.S.C. § 289	Infringement of a design patent
• 35 U.S.C. § 292	False marking of patent-related information in connection with articles sold to the public
• 28 U.S.C. § 1498	Unauthorized use of a patented invention by or for the United States, or copyright infringement by the United States
• 18 U.S.C. § 2320	Trafficking in counterfeit trademarks
• 19 U.S.C. § 1526(e), 15 U.S.C. § 1124	Importing merchandise bearing counterfeit marks
• 18 U.S.C. § 2320(h)	Trans-shipment and exportation of counterfeit goods
• 18 U.S.C. § 1831	Trade secret theft to benefit a foreign entity
• 18 U.S.C. § 1832	Theft of trade secrets for commercial advantage

Source: Yeh (2016), CRS.

genuine issue of material fact on one or more issues and, therefore, render a judgment on such issues. "While a decision on a motion for summary judgment may not decide contested factual issues and thereby substitute for a trial of those issues, judges have been increasingly sympathetic to such motions."[38] Notably, summary judgments may be biased or unfair when judges substitute corruptive motives for the decisions of jurors. Therefore, summary judgments are usually presumed to be valid by inferring judicial rectitude. Of course, litigants may appeal perceived wrongful decisions.

At the time of this writing the US Supreme Court has granted six IP *cert petitions* for the upcoming term, two each in patents, trademarks, and copyrights. The cases are usually focused on narrow issues.[39] In the US, multiple forums are available to resolve IP disputes. Apart from federal courts, the International Trade Commission (ITC), the US Patent & Trademark Office and *ad hoc* alternative dispute settlement mechanisms (arbitration) provide avenues for the resolution of IP disputes. The administrative proceedings are generally expeditious and less costly, but not all mechanisms provide compensatory monetary awards; for example, ITC enforcement remedies are limited to injunctions and exclusion orders. Arbitrations are generally binding with limited procedural safeguards and improbable prospects of appeal. PTO proceedings may require further judicial action.

A patent infringement claim is an assertion by the patent holder that an alleged infringer's product or process practices the patent holder's patented invention without authorization (Kasdan & Rothstein, 2013, p. 2) In the US, there are two types of patent infringements: (i) direct infringement, and (ii) indirect infringement. In the case of direct infringement, the accused infringer is said to have practiced each element of the patent holder's patent claim.[40] In cases of indirect infringement, accused infringers can either contribute to an infringement via a third party or they can induce third parties to engage in infringements. Accordingly, the infringers do not have to practice all elements of the patent holders claim, but infringers can be liable on a contributory or inducement basis (another party is encouraged to be the direct infringer). To prevail in patent infringement cases, patent holders must show by a preponderance of the evidence that each asserted patent claim limitation can be found in the accused product or process.[41]

Parties are liable for direct infringement if they import a patented invention into the US, or if they make, use, offer to sell, or sell the patented invention within the US in violation of 35 U.S.C. § 271(a) (a *contributory* offense). Direct patent infringement is considered a strict liability offense, meaning that:

> [The] intent to infringe the patent is not needed for a finding of direct infringement. An alleged infringer does not have to copy a patented invention or even know about the patent to be held liable for infringement. The alleged infringer must only have performed one of the prohibited acts listed in Section 271(a) (making, selling, using, offering to sell or importing into the US) with respect to a product or process that is covered by the patent.
>
> (Kasdan & Rothstein, 2013, p. 2)

However, to be legally covered by the patent law, the allegedly infringing device or process must include each element of a patented claim either literally or under the "doctrine of equivalents."

In inducement cases (encouragement to take infringing actions), infringers must have knowledge that the induced acts comprise patent infringement; see *Global-Tech Appliances, Inc. v. SEB S.A.*, 131 S. Ct. 2060 (2011) (Global-Tech.).

In patent cases, *claim construction* is critical to ascertaining rights. A *claim construction* is the language defining the scope of the rights of a patent holder to exclude others from using his/her patented product. Accordingly, the meaning of the claim limitations involving infringement and validity of claims must be legally and judiciously established. In the US, the process of establishing patent infringements and validity of claims is usually referred to as the "Markman Process."[42]

The process derives its name from a US Supreme Court case, *Markman v. Westview Instruments, Inc.* (517 U.S. 370 (1996)) in which the Supreme Court ruled that the responsibility for *claim construction* determinations falls on a judge and not on a jury. After claims have been judiciously evaluated, judges must provide instructions to the jurors on the meaning of disputed patent claim terms, after which jurors should apply the claim construction of courts in making factual findings on the issues of infringement and invalidity (or validity of claims). Markman hearings enable judges to make informed decisions with the use of expert witnesses. Ever since the *Daubert Rule* in *Daubert v. Merrell Dow Pharmaceuticals* (509 U.S. 579 (1993)), expert testimony (scientific evidence) has played a critical role in US courts of law, with judges as gatekeepers. Notwithstanding, judges may limit testimony to the arguments of attorneys after which the judges will issue orders (rulings) on *claim construction*. The proper methodology for *claim construction* can be found in *Vitronics* and *Phillips* (*Vitronics Corp. v. Conceptronic, Inc.*, 90 F. 3d 1576 (Fed. Cir. 1996) and *Phillips v. AWH Corp.*, 415 F. 3d 1303 (Fed. Cir. 2005) (en banc)).[43]

Patent cases can be very costly and claims (spurious or scientific) can run up to billions of US dollars; for example, in *Viskase Corporation* (*Viskase Corporation v. American National Can Co.*, US District Court for the Northern District of Illinois—18 F. Supp. 2d 873 (N.D. Ill. 1998)), the court awarded $164 million for willful infringement. In *Applied Medical Resources Corp. v. United States Surgical Corp.* (US District Court for the Eastern District of Virginia—967 F. Supp. 861 (E.D.Va. 1997)), *Allied Medical* prevailed on a suit for infringement on a patented medical device that claimed up to $300 million. In *Rolls-Royce PLC v. United Technologies Corporation* (*No. 09–1307* (Fed. Cir. May 5, 2010)), Rolls-Royce brought a multi-million-dollar case against United Technologies. The technology at issue was related to the jet engines (particularly the fan blades) used on the world's largest airplane, the Airbus A380. Rolls-Royce sought almost $4 billion in damages and an injunction preventing further sales of the supposed infringed engines, which are sold by a joint venture between United Technologies and General Electric. The court granted summary judgment in United Technologies' favor finding that United Technologies' engine did not infringe the Rolls-Royce patent.[44] Unlike patents, trademark infringement cases involve marks.

Trademark infringement, unfair competition, and trademark dilution are the three main claims of trademark violations in the US that can be filed in federal and state courts. Trademark infringement occurs when a mark is unauthoritatively used to confuse consumers about the source of the goods or services to obtain illicit gains.

> To establish infringement, the owner must show that (1) it owns a valid and legally protectable mark (as previously defined), and (2) the alleged infringer's use of the mark in commerce causes a likelihood of confusion about the source of goods or services. The primary focus of an infringement claim is "likelihood of confusion." In deciding whether likelihood of confusion exists, courts typically consider the following factors: (1) the similarity of the marks in sound, meaning and appearance; (2) the proximity of the goods; (3) the strength of the owner's mark; (4) the similarity of marketing and advertising channels used; (5) how careful the typical consumer is likely to be before making a purchase; (6) evidence of actual confusion; and (7) the alleged infringer's intent in choosing the mark.
>
> (Smith et al.)[45]

All factors are deemed to be equally relevant to claims in US courts of law. However, if two marks are not similar in sound, meaning, and appearance, the other factors may be redundant. Actual confusion and the alleged infringer's intent are treated with great importance. Evidence of actual confusion is not necessary to prove infringement and when it exists, it is very difficult to overcome. Consequently, if the marks are similar in sound, meaning, and appearance, and the alleged infringers have intent to confuse consumers, the likelihood of confusion is most likely to be established in US courts of law. While it may be challenging to prove evidence of actual confusion and intent of infringers, business records indicating instances of confusion, purchases made by mistake, consumer complaints, misdirected deliveries or phone calls, and testimony of consumers can evince confusing intent. In the absence of evidence of actual confusion, trademark owners may use tools such as survey evidence to show that consumers are likely to be confused about the source of a good.[46]

Under federal dilution law, a claim for trademark dilution may only be brought if the mark is considered "famous." Smith et al. note that

> in evaluating whether a mark is famous, courts usually consider various factors, including the degree of distinctiveness and the level of recognition in trading areas. Under some state laws, a mark does not need to be famous to bring a dilution claim. Instead, a trademark owner can assert a dilution claim if its mark is distinctive.

Dilution may also occur through tarnishment that generates an unflattering light on a mark, because of affiliation with inferior or unbecoming products.

Howard, Avsec, and Fleming (2019) find that most states have enacted statutes that include prohibitions against trademark infringement and unfair competition. Several states also have trademark dilution laws. Further, the common law for those states often prohibits trademark infringement, passing off, and a variety of unfair and deceptive business practices. Common law trademark claims can be made without any federal or state trademark registration.[47] Trademark cases can be *estop* or contested and the majority of defenses to trademark case can be found in Section 1115(b) of the Lanham Act or common law.[48]

Appeals can be made to superior courts when decisions are deemed to be unfavorable in lower courts.

> In general, an appeal in a trademark case is taken from a US District Court to the US Court of Appeals for the circuit embracing that judicial district (28 USC Section 1294). However, in cases in which a trademark claim is joined with a patent claim, any appeal must be brought to the US Court of Appeals for the Federal Circuit, which has exclusive jurisdiction over patent appeals. 28 USC Section 1295(a)(1) vests the Federal Circuit with exclusive appellate jurisdiction in cases where the jurisdiction of the district court was based, in whole or in part, on a patent claim under 28 USC Section 1338. In such an appeal, the Federal Circuit would apply its own law in deciding the patent issues on appeal, but would apply the law of the regional circuit in which the district court sits in deciding the trademark issues.
>
> (Howard et al., 2019)[49]

In the UK, trademark law is governed by the Trademarks Act (1994), as amended, which implements the EU Trademarks Directive (2008/95/EC) to approximate the laws of the EU member states (Radivojevic, Reid, & Holman, 2019); further clarifications were made in 2017. It is probable that this law will be amended further now that the UK has exited the EU. All parties conducting civil litigation in the UK are expected to follow the Civil Procedure Rules, which stipulate the way and manner in which cases should be conducted before and after proceedings have been issued.

Litigation is usually seen as a last resort in Germany, the US, and the UK; therefore disputants are expected to explore settlements before using up the resources of courts. To achieve this objective in the UK, trademark owners will usually send infringers cease and desist (demand letters), incorporating appropriate undertakings for the infringer to sign, in an attempt to resolve the matter without the need for court proceedings.[50] However, a considerable amount of precaution must be undertaken before releasing cease and desist letters to traders and distributors. Strong evidentiary support must underlie the bases of such letters, because reckless demands can trigger actionable threats which may induce the recipients of such restraining letters to commence proceedings in courts to seek damages and injunction against further threats. It is recommended that potential claimants keep records of any infringing items or activities found online, carry out test purchases, and hire private investigators to conduct suitable investigations.

Radivojevic (2019) and others note that the English courts take a proactive approach to case management and can utilize costs awards to incentivize parties to conduct litigation proportionately. The protection of trademark rights can be found in Section 10 of the Trademark Act. Under Section 10, UK-registered marks are considered to be violated in the UK when infringers use UK-registered marks to: (i) trade goods or services that are identical to protected marks, (ii) cause public confusion, (iii) derive unfair advantage that is detrimental to the lawful holders of the marks. Safeguards against frivolous (spurious) trademark suits are provided in laws relating to unjustified threats. Frivolous suits, which are nearly always costly and reputationally damaging, may cause businesses to unfairly capitulate to prevent the erosion of their reputation even when their marks are legitimate. Extortionary threats are unjustified threats that are bad for innovation and the evolution of businesses.

The British common law protects unregistered rights like goodwill. A claim for passing off is often run in conjunction with a claim for registered trademark infringement; however, passing off may be the only cause of action available if no trademarks have been registered.[51]

In a claim for passing off, the claimant must prove that: (i) a trading name has been in existence for a number of years, (ii) a defendant has misrepresented goods and services to the public in order to create public confusion by using a mark, brand name, or license that was previously unaffiliated with the defendant, (iii) the actions (misrepresentations) of a defendant have caused reputational and financial damage.

Radivojevic and others (2019) find that it is generally difficult to succeed in a claim for passing off based on the get-up of products—the form in which brand owners choose to market their products—alone, as in such cases the "look and feel" or shape of a product must serve as an indication of origin in its own right.[52] The evidence required to support such a claim tends to be difficult to gather and surveys are not generally favored by the courts; see *Interflora Inc v. Marks & Spencer plc* ([2012] EWCA Civ 1501), which remains the leading UK authority governing requests for permissions to admit survey evidence.[53]

"Look and feel" is actually a challenging but surmountable problem in some jurisdictions of law; for example in the US *Mixed Chicks Case*, considered to be a proverbial and biblical case of David and Goliath, *Mixed Chicks LLC v. Sally Beauty Supply LLC* (879 F. Supp. 2d 1093—Dist. Court, CD California, (2012)), Mixed Chicks was awarded over $8 million for actual and punitive damages in a case for which the violation of property right was presumed to be incidental. The punitive cost in the vicinity of over $7 million actually outweighed the estimated damages.[54]

In early 2011, Sally Beauty LLC, considered to be the world's largest retailer of beauty supplies, rolled out what was supposed to be its own product line, Mixed Silk, for multiracial women, though Mixed Chicks was a forerunner of the hair line for mixed races. Consumers had to decide whether they should buy "Mixed Chicks" or "Mixed Silk." Everything about Sally's new product line, including the size and color of bottles, appeared to be a knock-off. Consumers were confused, partly because the color of the liquid was the same; also, the scent and texture of the products were almost identical.

In March 2011, Mixed Chicks filed a lawsuit alleging that Sally Beauty "intentionally, knowingly, and willfully" infringed the Mixed Chicks trademark and trade dress. The trial proceeded and the jury decided that Mixed Chicks had suffered actual damages as a result of the replication of products. The jury found that Sally Beauty had acted willfully and with malice, oppression, or fraud, for which actual and punitive damages must be awarded. Costs of infractions are usually managed, but in principle, monetary limits may not be placed on IP cases in the High Court of the UK.

Since civil trials are usually structured, they proceed in juridical tiers, phases, and jurisdictions. Liability and awards (quantum) are also bifurcated in the UK. The UK contains three separate judicial systems: England and Wales, Scotland, and Northern Ireland, and, like the US, all courts within the UK are bound by the decisions of the Supreme Court. Trademark infringement proceedings are typically brought before either the High Court or the Intellectual Property Enterprise Court (IPEC), but the High Court is considered to be the premier venue for large and complex litigation in the UK (Radivojevic et al., 2019).[55] Usual informal settlement mechanisms are available, including arbitration, with no formal regulatory requirement to engage in arbitration, barring (excluding) contractual obligations.[56]

Trademark damages may be calculated based on lost profits attributable to infringement or the notional license fee. While damages for infringement of a UK-registered trademark can be recovered from the date of the trademark application, owners of EU trademarks may recover damages only in relation to acts of infringement committed after the date of registration. Notwithstanding, reasonable compensation may be claimed in respect of acts occurring after the date of publication. "Damages may include damage to reputation and goodwill, which—although difficult to assess—may yield a figure significantly higher than can be gained by opting for an account of profits" (Radivojevic et al., 2019).[57]

According to Radivojevic et al. (2019), decisions of county courts or the High Court in the UK, which includes the IPEC, can be made to the Court of Appeal and ultimately the Supreme Court. In all cases, permission to appeal must be sought and granted. *In deciding whether to give permission to appeal, courts will consider whether: the appeal would have a real prospect of success; there is any other compelling reason for the appeal to be heard; and whether it raises an issue of general public importance. Appeals will usually only be allowed if the lower court erred in law or fact, or if the decision is unjust due to a serious procedural or other irregularity.*

CHAPTER SUMMARY

- Innovation fuels economic growth and prosperity. Consequently, when the benefits of innovation are expropriated, the incentives to innovate are endangered and economic growth and prosperity are threatened. It is a long-held principle in international law that humans are entitled to the fruits of their creativity as a matter of economic and human right.
- Intellectual property theft can take multiple forms, including: (i) piracy of books, films, and videos, (ii) dilution of trade marks by opening stores to market goods and services with a particular trade mark, and (iii) mass production of generic drugs with identical patented ingredients under different names.
- Duty is the disposition to honor obligations even without hope of reward or fear of punishment. One reveals himself [/herself] to be a moral person not merely by honoring obligations but by being disposed to honor them even when it is not in his [/her] interest to do so (Wilson, 1993, p. 100).
- *Intellectual property theft is costly to the global community.*
- IP law confers exclusive rights to prevent unauthorized reproduction or use of certain intangible creations of the human mind.

KEY WORDS

• Copyright	• *Estop*	• Trademark
• Claim construction	• Fair use	• Trade secret
• Cyber crime	• Get-up of products	• Product cycle
• Direct infringement	• Goodwill	• Patent
• Doctrine of equivalents	• Indirect infringement	• Present value of investment
• Exclusive right	• Look and feel	• Unjustified threats

CHAPTER QUESTIONS

1. What is the relationship between innovation and economic growth? With reference to specific examples, discuss the effects of intellectual property theft on national income.
2. Is intellectual property theft an ethical issue? Evaluate the concept of "duty" and its implications for the integrity of intellectual property rights.
3. Alluding to Schumpeter's model, show and explain why innovation can reduce the cost of production and enhance productivity.
4. What is the difference between all elements and inducement patent infringement? How have courts of law used the two types of infringement to punish violators?
5. Using *Vitronics Corp. v. Conceptronic, Inc* and *Phillips v. AWH Corp.*, identify and discuss the central elements of a claim construction in the cases.
6. Why are unjustified threats detrimental to the macroeconomic performance of a nation?

NOTES

1. Helfer maintains that during the decades following World War II, "the most pressing concern for the human rights community was elaborating and codifying legal norms and enhancing monitoring mechanisms. The evolutionary process resulted in a de facto separation of human rights into several categories, ranging from a core set of peremptory norms for the most egregious forms of state misconduct, to civil and political rights, to economic, social and cultural rights. Among these categories, economic, social, and cultural rights are the least well developed and the least prescriptive, having received significant jurisprudential attention only in the last decade. Advocates of intellectual property protection directed the focus of international lawmaking to the gradual expansion of subject matters and rights through periodic revisions to the Berne, Paris and other conventions, and later, the creation of a link between intellectual property and trade" (Helfer, 2003, p. 51).
2. Article 66 of the TRIPS convention provides least-developed countries with a longer timeframe to implement all the provisions of the TRIPS agreement and encourages technology transfer.
3. See Slomanson (2011, pp. 724–5).
4. See McNeely, Hare, and War, LLP: www.patentek.com.
5. See "Intellectual Property Rights and International Trade," Akhtar and Ferguson (2015, pp. 1–2).
6. Op. cit., p. 8.
7. McNeely et al., op. cit.
8. Ibid.
9. See "Intellectual Property Rights and International Trade," CRS (2015), p. 7.
10. Boatright (2014) pp. 27–28.
11. See Wilson (1993) p. 80.
12. Op. cit., p. 91.
13. Op. cit., p. 102.
14. See Velasquez (2002) p. 14.
15. Kohlberg assigns two subsidiary levels to each of his three stages. *Punishment and obedience orientation* (avoidance of punishment), and *instrument and relativity orientation* (sensitivity to the needs of others) are correlates of the first stage. *Interpersonal concordance orientation* (good behavior to appease family, friends, and authority figures) and *law and order orientation* (loyalty to larger community) are correlates of the second stage. *Social contract orientation* (awareness of competing interest and willingness to compromise), and *universal ethical principles orientation* (acknowledgements of universal principles that define the apogee of human moral development); see also Velasquez (2002) pp. 27–30.
16. It is noteworthy that some criminals may have a sense of morality as they grow older; see Wilson (1993) p. 11.
17. See Velasquez (2002) p. 25.
18. The ICC reports that it "works to promote a balanced and sustainable system for the protection of intellectual property. ICC launched BASCAP (Business Action to Stop Counterfeiting and Piracy) to connect and mobilize businesses across industries, sectors and national borders in the fight against counterfeiting and piracy;" www.iccwbo.org. The International Trademark Association (INTA) is a global organization of over 7,000 trademark owners and professionals from over 190 countries. It is

a non-profit association that is dedicated to supporting trademarks and related intellectual property to protect consumers and promote fair and effective commerce since 1878. TECXCIPIO is an IT company specialized in building scalable solutions to accurately track and analyze worldwide copyright infringements on the internet.

19 Frontier estimates based on OECD 2013 data on counterfeiting in international trade, and UN trade and GDP data to derive estimates for domestic production and consumption. Data for piracy based on latest industry sources (2015).
20 See BASCAP and INTA (2016) pp. 8 & 14.
21 See Kurz (2017) p. 117.
22 Loc. cit.
23 See Van den Berg (2017) pp. 280–3; see also Warburton (2018) for the contributions of innovation to sustainable development and intergenerational equity.
24 Patent rights generally last for up to 20 years from the date applications are filed.
25 For further information and statistics, see WIPO's Madrid Yearly Review 2019 (WIPO, 2019b).
26 The following data were used to cover the publishing industry: (a) IPA–WIPO survey data, (b) legal deposits data compiled by WIPO through a simple questionnaire, and (c) data provided by the Nielsen Company. Publishing industry data are not unified under a single authority. Therefore, WIPO compiles publishing data from different sources to provide a broader perspective on the publishing industry in any particular country. Readers should be aware that the IPA–WIPO survey data and the Nielsen Book data differ due to differences in methodology and market coverage (WIPO, 2019, p. 188). Based on additional feedback received by WIPO, WIPO's questionnaire was simplified and methodological guidance was refined. Moreover, WIPO started to collect additional data to validate and/or supplement the data compiled through the IPA–WIPO questionnaire; see the WIPO 2019 report for further discussions about methodology.
27 Notably, the lengths of cycles are unpredictable and transfers can be internalized within companies rather than externalized.
28 Loc. cit.
29 Kasdan and Rothstein (2013) provide a comprehensive legal framework for a defense against such suits; see "Patent infringement Claims and Defenses," www.practicallaw.com
30 See Hickey (2018) p. 1.
31 Loc. cit.
32 Ibid.
33 Op. cit., p. 2.
34 Limited common law rights are available without registration, loc. cit.
35 The US federal court system includes 13 federal circuit courts for the various US territories along with the Court of Appeals for the Federal Circuit, which has exclusive jurisdiction over patent and other intellectual property appeals. Except for the D.C. Circuit, there are several federal district courts covering sub-territories (McNeely et al.).
36 Loc. cit.
37 Ibid.
38 Ibid.
39 There are generally two ways in which a case comes before the US Supreme Court: by an appeal and by means of a writ of certiorari. Appeals from federal circuit courts

of appeals are limited to those cases where a circuit court has held a state statute unconstitutional or otherwise invalid under federal law. Review of the decisions of federal and state courts under the certiorari procedure is discretionary and in only a very few of the cases when petitions for certiorari are presented to the court does the court actually review the decision below. In the intellectual property area, the Supreme Court acts to enunciate the broad principles of law which must then be filled in by the lower courts (McNeely et al.).

40 Under the "all elements" of the infringement, a claim must be literally satisfied and the doctrine of equivalents is applied to individual elements of the claim and not to the invention as a whole. This rule acts to limit the doctrine of equivalents, which seeks to establish whether an element of an accused product or process "performs substantially the same function in substantially the same way to obtain the same result" as an element of the patented invention; see Kasdan and Rothstein (2013) p. 3; see also USlegal.com and *Siemens Med. Solutions USA, Inc. v. Saint-Gobain Ceramics & Plastics, Inc.*, 637 F. 3d 1269, 1279 (Fed. Cir. 2011).

41 Kasdan and Rothstein (2013), op. cit.

42 Loc. cit.

43 The *Markman Process* includes (i) competing claims to be construed by courts, (ii) competing proposals on *claim construction*, (iii) submission of briefs on *claim construction*, and (iv) the *Markman* hearing; see Kasdan and Rothstein (2013, p. 4) for methodology, including intrinsic (claims, patent specification, and prosecution history) and extrinsic (expert testimony, dictionaries, and learned treatises) claims, and defenses against patent claims. The words of claims are generally given their ordinary and customary meaning. "*Estop*" may prevent a person from bringing a legal claim; see the principle of estoppel.

44 See also Bartlit-beck.com for a variety of IP cases.

45 See Smith, Gambrell and Russel LLP, "Trademark Law." Retrieved from Sgrlaw.com.

46 Loc. cit.

47 See Howard, Avsec, and Fleming (2019), "Litigation Procedures and Strategies: United States." *World Trademark Review*.

48 Trademark infringement claims must meet standards of genericness, non-fraudulent registration, continuity of use (non-abandonment), and timely assertion of rights (no acquiescence or *estoppel by laches*). Licensee estoppel may also be used to prevent a plaintiff from claiming rights to a mark when a plaintiff had previously licensed a mark from a defendant. Fair use, which involves using a in a non-trademark manner to describe unique goods or services, or the geographic origin of products or services may be exculpatory. "Nominative fair use occurs when the defendant uses the plaintiff's mark to refer to the plaintiff's goods or services and often occurs in the context of comparative advertising" (Howard et al., 2019).

49 *A party that is dissatisfied with the final decision of the Trademark Trial and Appeal Board in an opposition proceeding, cancellation proceeding, concurrent use proceeding or ex parte case has two options for obtaining review of the board decision:*

> *A party can appeal a final decision of the Board to the Federal Circuit, the board's primary reviewing court (Section 21(a)(1) of the Lanham Act, 15 USC Section 1071(a)(1)). The Federal Circuit will review the decision from which the appeal is taken on the record that was developed before the board. No new evidence can be*

submitted and no new issues raised. A party can seek review of a board decision by filing a civil action in a US district court (Section 1(b)(1) of the Lanham Act, 15 USC Section 1071(b)(1)).

Unlike a Federal Circuit appeal, where the record is closed, the civil action path permits the parties to present to the court evidence that was not presented to the board during the course of the proceeding. Further, the parties in the civil action can expand the case beyond the issues that were before the board by raising new claims and seeking additional relief (loc. cit).

50 See Radivojevic et al. (2019). Until Brexit is finalized, the UK courts will continue to serve as EU trademark courts; also see *World Trademark Review*, at www.worldtrademarkreview.com, for authoritative and comparative analyses of international trademark laws.
51 Goodwill (G) is the difference between the purchase or acquisition price (P) of one company and the sum of the fair market value of all purchased assets (A) (identifiable tangible and intangible) and liabilities (L) incurred or assumed in the process; $G = P - \Sigma(A+L)$, for $P > \Sigma(A+L)$.
52 The get-up and "look and feel" of products includes labeling and packaging, arrangements, graphics, color combinations, and other design elements (the framework within which a good is marketed).
53 Courts may consider: the method by which the survey participants are selected; the size of the survey; the questions asked (these must be non-leading questions); the exact answers provided by the participants (abbreviations or digests will not be accepted); the instructions given to participants; and the costs of carrying out the survey (Radivojevic et al., 2019). Expert witnesses may be permitted by a trademark court, but evidence is restricted to that which is reasonably necessary to resolve disputes; expert testimony on issues like the likelihood of confusion is generally not admissible.
54 "Mixed Chicks LLC introduced a unique range of hair care products under the trade mark MIXED CHICKS®. The design of the bottles of the MIXED CHICKS® line of products was very unique in that the bottles [were] translucent, the color of the content of the products varied depending on the type of product and prominent orange lettering features on the bottles. A much larger competitor, Sally Beauty Products, introduced the exact same range of products under the name MIXED SILK using bottles that were exactly the same shape as the MIXED CHICKS® bottles carried the same orange lettering and contained product contents of the same color. The court found that Sally Beauty Products' conduct amounted to trade mark and trade dress infringement and punitive damages in the amount of USD7.3 million and actual damages in the amount of USD840 000 were awarded to Mixed Chicks LLC" (Castleman, 2014, pp. 1–2).
55 The IPEC provides a mechanism for reducing the cost of trademark litigation. Trials in the court are expeditious (limited to one or two days), claims brought to the court must not exceed £500,000, and claims are capped at £50,000. Claims that do not exceed £10,000 are presented in the small claims track of the court.
56 The growth in global commerce and the concomitant increase in international IP disputes have made mechanisms for alternative dispute resolution (ADR) very attractive. Block (2016–2017) provides an overview of the benefits of ADR to

international intellectual property and commercial disputes. He argues that ADR and the support of World Intellectual Property Organizations (WIPO) offers a proper medium to address the unique substantive and procedural issues of international litigation.

57 Account of profit is defined as an equitable remedy, which requires the infringing party to surrender the profits made from its infringing activity in a non-punitive manner. Section 11 of the Trademarks Act provides provisions for statutory defenses in the UK, including invalid trademarks, use of personal names, and continuous usage. Article 16 of the EU Trademark Regulation (2017/1001) provides for (intervening) defense to EU trademarks.

FURTHER READING

Akhtar, S. I., & Fergusson, I. F. (2015, April). Intellectual property rights (IPR) and international trade. *In Focus*, 7.–5700, 1–2. Congressional Research Service.

BASCAP & INTA. (2016). *The economic impacts of counterfeiting and piracy*. Brussels: Frontier Economics.

Block, M. J. (2016–17). The benefits of alternate dispute resolution for international commercial and intellectual property. *Rutgers Law Record*, 44, 1–20.

Boatright, J. R. (2014). *Ethics in finance* (3rd ed.). West Sussex, UK: John Wiley & Sons.

Castleman, A. (2014). *Protecting the get-up of a product and the benefits associated with it*. Adams & Adams. Retrieved from lexology.com.

Hickey, K. J. (2018). *Intellectual property law: A brief introduction*. Congressional Research Service. Retrieved from www.fas.org.

Helfer, L. R. (2003). Human rights and intellectual property: Conflict or coexistence? *Minnesota Intellectual Property Review*, 5(1), 47–61.

Home Office. (2018). *Understanding the cost of cyber crime: A report of key findings from the Costs of Cyber Crime Working Group*.

Howard, M., Avsec, A. J., & Fleming, D. S. (2019). Litigation procedures and strategies: United States. *World Trademark Review*. Retrieved from www.worldtrademarkreview.com.

Kasdan, M. J., & Rothstein, A. (2013). *Patent infringement claims and defenses*. Thomson Reuters.

Krugman, P., & Wells, R. (2018). *Macroeconomics* (5th ed.). New York: Worth Publishers.

Kurz, H. D. (2017). *Economic thought: A brief history*. New York: Columbia University Press.

Pugel, T. A. (2016). *International economics*. New York: McGraw-Hill.

Radivojevic, A., Reid, A., & Holman, T. (2019). Litigation procedures and strategies: United Kingdom. *World Trademark Review*. Retrieved from www.worldtrademarkreview.com.

Schumpeter, J. (1934). *The theory of economic development*. Cambridge, MA: Harvard University Press.

Slomanson, W. (2011). *Fundamental perspectives on international law* (6th ed.). Boston, MA: Wadsworth, Cengage Learning.

Trebilcock, M., Howse, R., & Eliason, A. (2013). *The regulation of international trade* (4th ed.). New York: Routledge.

Van den Berg, H. (2017). *Economic growth and development* (3rd ed.). Hackensack, NJ: World Scientific.

Velasquez, M. G. (2002). *Business ethics: Concepts and cases* (5th ed.). Upper Saddle River, NJ: Prentice Hall.
Warburton, C. E. S. (2018). Positive time preference and environmental degradation: The effects of world population growth and economic activity on intergenerational equity, 1970–2015. *Applied Econometrics and International Development, 18*(2), 5–24.
Wilson, J. Q. (1993). *The moral sense.* New York: Free Press.
World Intellectual Property Organization. (2015). Intellectual property rights and international trade. Congressional Research Service. Retrieved from www.fas.org.
World Intellectual Property Organization. (2019a). *World intellectual property indicators 2019.* Geneva, Switzerland: WIPO.
World Intellectual Property Organization. (2019b). *Madrid Yearly Review 2019: International Registration of Marks.* Geneva, Switzerland: WIPO.
Yeh, B. T. (2016). Intellectual property rights violations: Federal civil remedies and criminal penalties related to copyrights, trademarks, patents, and trade secrets. Congressional Research Service. www.copyrightalliance.org.

CHAPTER 5
ECONOMETRICS FOR THE COURTROOM

LEARNING OBJECTIVES

LO 1   To understand the econometric tools that are used to estimate the value of damages in courts of law. Econometrics is broadly defined to encompass all the relevant disciplines of economics.
LO 2   To present the *Daubert Rule* (scientific standards) that are required in courts of law.
LO 3   Discuss the structure of data and sampling strategies.
LO 4   Explain divergent forecasting methodologies.
LO 5   The use of Excel and financial calculator to facilitate data estimation and calculation of the time value of money.
LO 6   Discuss the advantages and challenges of regression analysis.
LO 7   Illustrate the use of econometrics in the court room.
LO 8   Present the economic and legal views of discounting and the discount rate.
LO 9   Explain the importance of Chi Square in scientific analysis.
LO 10 Describe the procedures for valuing public companies.

Econometrics is the economic methodology for estimating economic variables and models to arrive at scientific econometric conclusions. The scope of economics is very broad. It includes money and banking, finance, labor market, macroeconomics, microeconomics, healthcare, forecasting, international trade, and economic growth and sustainable development. Forensic economics is the application of economic theories and laws to contending positions of economic value in courts of law. As such, the discipline of economics is broadly defined here to include the subcategory of finance.

Perhaps the most contentious set of issues deals with the amount of damages awarded in medical malpractice cases. The most straightforward part of the damage calculation would seem to be adding up the actual out-of-pocket losses that resulted from a negligent injury. These would include lost wages, medical care expenses, and other actual economic losses. Although it is simple in theory to measure economic losses, in reality it can become somewhat complicated when trying to estimate how much a person would have earned far into the future, or what medical or long-term care they might need and how much it would cost many years after their injury. As difficult as calculating economic losses are, the more controversial part of calculating damages is estimating the dollar value of non-economic losses. In particular, there is substantial disagreement over the way to measure the "pain and suffering" that resulted from the injury.

Awards can vary substantially, reinforcing the idea that non-economic damage awards can be too arbitrary to be fair. Medical accidents and malpractices have heightened the need for scientific evidence in litigation. The damages for medical malpractices have varied considerably and some states have enacted statutes to reduce variability and cap liability. However, these caps and awards show wide variability as well.[1]

In the 1990s, the US Supreme Court opened the door for expert testimony and scientific evidence to be used in courts of law in order to properly evaluate professional facts for dispute resolution. Incidentally the case that heightened the need for scientific evidence in the courtroom was a medical case, *Daubert v. Merrell Dow Pharmaceuticals Inc.*, 509 U.S. 579 (1993). Notwithstanding, judges perform gatekeeping roles to ensure that those with the required expertise from education, practice, or teaching, perform the role of experts on technical matters. The *Daubert Standard* is now a widely accepted principle of American jurisprudence and lawyers who are not skilled in the quantitative requirements of economics can be at a considerable disadvantage.[2] This chapter is designed to fill a quantitative void in legal issues that appertain to economics.

5.1 FEDERAL RULES OF EVIDENCE AND SCIENTIFIC REQUIREMENTS (THE *DAUBERT STANDARD*)

The *Daubert Standard*, which emerged from *Daubert v. Merrill Dow Pharmaceuticals* (1993), affirmed and elevated the need for scientific evidence in the court room. In this regard, expert witnesses who may be accountants, financial experts, psychologists, economists, etc., can help the courts to understand technical concepts in their field in order to arrive at reasonable estimates for compensation and punishment. Rule 702 of the Federal Rules of Evidence makes provision for expert witnesses to use scientific, technical, and specialized knowledge to help courts to understand disputed technical issues.

A witness who is qualified as an expert by knowledge, skill, experience, training, or education, can testify to: (i) the use of data or quantitative fact; (ii) reliable principles and methods; and (iii) reliable application of methodology to the facts of a case; based on sound theories that are generally accepted and measurable. In effect, forensic analysis has more to do with valuation in court rooms based on scientific evidence. In this regard, a fundamental understanding of quantitative concepts in accounting, finance, and economics are crucially important for any undertaking in forensic analysis.[3]

Weil, Frank, Hughes, and Wagner (2007) and others identify the following gatekeeping criteria:

- Is the theory or technique testable? Has it been tested?
- Has it been subjected to peer review or publication?
- Is the potential rate of error known?
- Is it generally accepted within the relevant community of experts?

In their analysis of the gatekeeping function of a judge, Brookshire, Slesnick, and Ward (2007) note that the absence of one of the criteria listed above may not be sufficient to bar the testimony of an expert when the emphasis of the inquiry focuses on an expert's principles and methodology and not on the conclusion that is generated.[4] It is therefore not entirely surprising that forensic economics plays a significant role in finance whenever there is a dispute over lost value or asset and who is culpable for the loss of value. Of course, the dangers of aberrant conduct or testimony can be mitigated by vigilant judges who act as gatekeepers to determine what will be admissible, based on the federal rules of evidence and qualifications of experts.[5]

The *Daubert* decision also contained a number of preconditions for determining the scientific validity and relevance of an expert's testimony—the most intrinsic being testing, peer review, common (standard) error rates, and external validity (the general acceptability of a methodology). The most serious challenges to forensic economists under *Daubert* are related to personal injury and wrongful death cases where the calculation of hedonic damages, costs associated with the foregone pleasures of life, are critical and significant. Recent changes in the Federal Rules of Evidence have resulted in fuller disclosures of experts' opinions, data sources, litigation experience and academic credentials. Over time, such disclosures have the potential of improving the ethical quality of economic analysis in litigation.[6] All empirical and scientific analyses start with data (information).

5.2 THE STRUCTURE OF DATA

Data provide information about variables, conditions and, in the context of this book, economic circumstances that generate information. Economists refer to the actual underlying circumstances that generate valuable information as the "data generating process." An understanding of the data generating process is important because it is not just enough to obtain economic information without knowing the underlying circumstances that generate the information upon which economic and legal arguments are based. For example, economic shocks, seasonal variations, and number of respondents to a survey are actual underlying factors that will affect the final value of economic information. In effect, data are generated by processes. After understanding the data generating process, data can be arranged in a very structured (organized) form known as data set (structure, see Table 5.1).

The variables in good data sets are conceptualized (clearly defined) and operationalized (measured). Measurement may take different forms: percentage changes, levels, or qualitative indicators (dummies) for non-numeric attributes like race, gender, religion, and region.[7] More often than not, economists strive to obtain data from reputable sources, and courts will generally prefer data from reputable sources that are incontrovertible. Academic institutions, US Government agencies, and world organizations generally provide reliable and unbiased information. Table 5.1 presents four major types of data sets: time series, cross-sectional, panel, and pooled.

Table 5.1 US educational attainment of the population 18 years and over (thousands of civilian non-institutionalized population, 1st Grade through Ph.D.)

	Time series 18–24 years	Age (years)	Cross-sectional (2012)	Age (years)		Panel
2012	30,140	18–24	30,140	18–24	2012	30,140
2013	30,030	25–29	20,893		2013	30,030
2014	30,054	30–40	20,326		2014	30,054
2015	30,116	35–39	19,140	25–29	2012	20,893
2016	29,791	40–44	20,787		2013	21,138
2017	29,404	45–49	21,583		2014	21,486

Source: US Census Bureau, Current Population Survey, 2012. Annual and Social Economic Supplement.

Pooled data (2016–2017 respectively)

	Age cohort (years)	Educational attainment	Educational attainment	No attainment	No attainment
1	18–24	29,791	29,404	51	53
2	25–29	22,434	22,745	28	18
3	30–40	21,329	21,505	29	51
4	35–39	20,387	20,773	57	53
5	40–44	19,618	19,273	49	53
6	45–49	20,679	20,662	71	46

The time series data show a chronological sequence of observations on a single variable or unit; people who fall between the ages of 18 and 24 with educational attainment. The data are in annualized form from 2012 to 2017, thereby accounting for six observations. Other forms of chronological sequences include weekly, bi-weekly, monthly, bi-monthly, quarterly, annual, and bi-annual series. Time series may exhibit trends (non-stationarity), seasonality, cyclicality, and volatility or irregular patterns. Data with trends and cyclicality are refractory for analytical purposes. Therefore, they have to be differenced for stability in order to make econometric decisions. Differencing means that the data should have zero mean and a constant variance. These concepts will be further discussed at a rudimentary level in the forecasting section of this chapter. For advanced analyses see Gujarati and Porter (2009, pp. 737–68), and Hill, Griffiths, and Lim (2011, pp. 474–92).

Cross-sectional data are different from time series data because they take cross-sectional units and time into consideration. Cross-sectional data have information on cross-sectional units at the same point in time. Table 5.1 shows six cross-sectional units for an age interval, ranging from 18 to 49. It must be noted that the educational attainment for all the units were collected for 2012. Cross-sectional units or categories may take various forms: public corporations, states or countries, institutions, and variables.

The panel data, also known as "micropanel" or "longitudinal data," have repeated observations on each cross-sectional unit as time progresses. Panel data may have an equal number of observations for each cross-sectional unit (balanced panel), or they may have variations in the number of observations for each cross-sectional unit (unbalanced panel). Table 5.1 shows three observations for each cross-sectional unit; three for people between the ages of 18 and 24, and three for people between the ages of 25 and 29.

Pooled data combine attributes of time series and cross-sectional data. However, pooled data are based on samples that are presumed to be independent of each other. Table 5.1 shows pooled data for educational and no educational attainment in 2016 and 2017, giving a combined pool of 12 observations. The choice of data structure will ultimately be dependent on the research objective or objectives.

Researchers who are interested in parametric estimates of the true population value (the elusive value that cannot be precisely obtained) will increase their sample size or number of observations so that the sample size will approximate the population. The successful parameter is usually a proximate estimate of the population, because of a low margin of error. Smaller samples, which are usually less than 30 observations, may also be used on occasions of less ambitious objectives and successful small sample tests like the t-test. For a shorter time period, monthly data, panel data, and pooled data are capable of increasing sample sizes. Data must be reliable, because findings will be spurious and generally unacceptable when they are not. Litigants will routinely test and defend the validity of their data in courts of law.

After conceptualizing the type of data that will be required, and operationalizing the issues of measurement for a case, an economist must determine the acceptable sampling procedure. There are certain samples that are empirically repugnant; especially samples that are based on convenience (low-hanging fruit), rather than samples that are randomized and representative of a population. Some surveyors inadvertently utilize haphazard and convenient samples as valid information for empirical inquiry. However, these samples should be avoided at all costs.

5.3 SAMPLING STRATEGIES

There are certain types of sampling strategies that are widely acceptable when they are randomized: systematic samples, stratified samples, and cluster samples. The common denominator of the systematic and cluster sampling strategies is that randomness is subsumed. That is, every member of a population has an equal probability of being selected for an empirical inquiry, and all selections are independent.

The systematic sample is a probability sample that is not randomized. The units are selected in a uniform interval of a systematic order; for example, after every 5, 10, or 15 observations. If the sampling units are selected after every 5 observations, 20 percent of the population will be selected, which makes the sampling procedure probabilistic. This sampling strategy is generally good for a very large population.

A cluster sample is a sample that is derived from subgroups of a population. Sampling can also be multistage. For example, a researcher might want a sample of crime statistics from townships, after which he/she can collect samples from counties. However, different clusters increase the margin of errors. Units of the population can only be assigned to a specific cluster.

Unlike cluster sampling, stratified sampling controls for different attributes of a population by generating subpopulations with nominal attributes, say males, females, whites, and Hispanics. The rationale of the sampling strategy is that the subgroups might respond differently to a research objective. It is usually advisable for the researcher to have equitable proportions of the subpopulation; for example, 30 percent of males and females respectively. Of the various forms of data identified earlier, time series data are particularly useful for making economic forecasts or projections. The algorithms and relevance of forecasting to economic and legal decisions will be discussed next.

5.4 FORECASTING ECONOMIC VALUE

Good forecasts start with an understanding of the characteristics of time series data and how the attributes can be managed or processed to arrive at scientific conclusions that minimize errors, because all forecasts will have some amount of errors. Forecasting is not an exact science, but forensic economists routinely make projections about economic variables in courts of law. In effect, economists make conditional forecasts.

Recall that the problematic issue of non-stationarity arises from trends, seasonality, cyclicality, and irregularity of a series. Revealing representations of the concepts should be rather instructive. Despite the presence of intermediate variability along the way, trends show a general upward or downward direction. Realistically, not all trends are created equal. Trends may be linear or deterministic, exponential (constant growth and declining trends), and stochastic. Examples of these trends have been provided in Figure 5.1 as an ocular exposition of the concepts.

The deterministic trend is just a virtual straight line with slight variations. It can be associated with the formula for a straight line:

$$Y = a + \alpha t; \tag{5.1}$$

where a is for the intercept value, α is for the slope that tells the amount by which Y is going to change when time (or an independent variable) changes incrementally (by one unit), and the trend can be estimated by ordinary least squares (OLS) regression by minimizing errors:

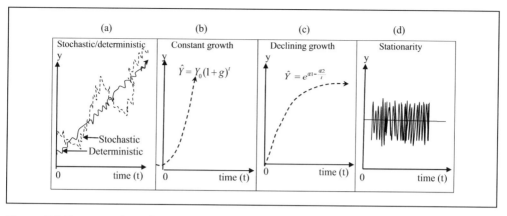

Figure 5.1 Data trends and stationarity

$$\hat{Y} = a + \alpha t; \tag{5.2}$$

where y hat is the forecast or predicted value for time t. Regression models may add an e (a catchall expression) at the end of Equation 5.1 to denote errors and omissions that are presumed to be normally distributed with zero mean and constant variance. Regression analysis will be discussed more fully in the next section.

In addition to the deterministic trend, Figure 5.1(a) also shows a stochastic trend, which is volatile and inclusive of downward and upward trends in the series. Stock market returns usually show similar patterns of gyrations. In the case of stochastic seasonality, the forecast value will be determined by past seasonality and unpredictable occurrences known as noises (errors).

The constant growth function (Figure 5.1(b)) is suitable for modeling proportional percentage changes. This can be envisioned by taking the log of both sides and estimating the rate of change, which is akin to the elasticity concept in economics. Exponential functions generally take the form, $f(x) = X^b$ $((\forall X \neq 0 > 1))$, with b as the coefficient. When the average annual percentage change (growth rate) of a variable is fairly constant, say population for example, exponential functions can be used to estimate or fit the data. The dividend payments of some stocks may also be expected to grow at a constant rate unlike some variable ones. Implicitly, the earnings of some corporations also exhibit a similar pattern. The declining growth function (Figure 5.1(c)) is the opposite of Figure 5.1(b). In many respects, it can be conceptualized in terms of Schumpeter's creative destruction model. Innovation generates an intense enthusiasm (fad), sales soar, but utility eventually declines. New products, market saturation, and consumer responses to product quality and prices are good indicators of the performance of this model as time progresses. These models have underlying theories that are important for making economic and legal projections. That is, the forecaster must be able to reasonably ascertain the data generating process and the nature of economic variables that he/she is dealing with for forensic evaluation and acceptance.

Figure 5.1(d) depicts the characteristics of a stationary data. It is evidently trendless. In effect, the trends that are associated with the expositions in the previous Panels (a) to (c) have been removed. The picture presupposes that the mean and variance of the series are constant over time and that the covariance between any two periods will be the same regardless of the time periods in the series. The stationary series show a mean-reverting tendency (a constant tendency to get back to the mean). The characteristics of stationarity can be mathematically formulated as follows:

$$E(Y_t) = \mu \text{ (Mean)}, \tag{5.3}$$

$$\text{Var}(Y_t) = E(Y_t - \mu)^2 \text{ (Variance)}, \tag{5.4}$$

$$E[(Y_t - \mu)(Y_t + k - \mu)] = \gamma_k \text{ (Covariance)}; \tag{5.5}$$

where μ is for the average value of the Y series, and E is an expectation operator. These days, a lot of statistical software packages have the capability to test for stationarity or random walk (unit root tests) so that a researcher can obtain a reliable scientific forecast.[8] The moving average capability of Excel can facilitate smoothing. Excel is also suitable for exponential smoothing. Eviews has built-in stationarity tests, for example the Augmented Dickey-Fuller and Phillips-Perron tests. Accordingly, the patterns of series must be studied.

Cycles are major expansions and contractions that occur every several years. As a result, when sales rise and fall over the course of a week, such a pattern should not be counted as a cycle. It might take five to ten years or more to complete cycles. Unlike cycles, a seasonal pattern is one that repeats itself every year. The performances of some businesses are sensitive to seasonal changes in demand. For example, circumstances or values remaining unchanged (*ceteris paribus*), sales in the US can be expected to be high in the third quarter. This is the quarter in which a substantial amount of people celebrate Thanksgiving and Christmas, and fairly predictable patterns provide valuable information about the data generating process (DGP) and the forecasting model.

When aggregate expenditure is relatively higher, some firms rundown their inventories, which may be in summer or in winter. The seasonal component of a forecasting model allows the forecaster to adjust for seasonal variations. The seasonal variations are not considered to be irregular patterns. Irregularity has no predetermined pattern. Shocks, unforeseen disturbances, and windfall profits could generate fluctuations in data. Snowstorms are likely to increase the sale of snow blowers. Wars, hurricanes, and windfall wealth will affect consumption, investment, and saving. Figure 5.2 shows a trend, cycles, seasonal variations, and random influences.

When time series exhibit increasing and decreasing seasonal components, they can be modeled by what is called the multiplicative decomposition model. It is presumed that the parameters describing the series are not changing overtime. The four component parts of the multiplicative decomposition model are: (i) trend component (T_t), (ii) seasonal component (S_t), (iii) the cyclical component (C_t), and (iv) the irregular or stochastic component (I_t). That is,

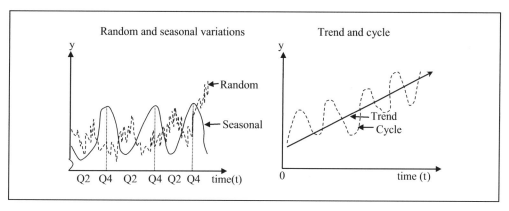

Figure 5.2 Components of time series data

$$Y_t = Tt^{\star}St^{\star}C_t^{\star}I_t \text{ or } Y_t = f(T_t, S_t, C_t, E_t). \tag{5.6}$$

It must be noted that in the decomposition model, the seasonal factor is multiplicative. In effect, the seasonal factor is multiplied by a trend. To remove the irregular and seasonal variations from the data, the trend and cyclical patterns must first be removed by estimating the centered moving average (CMA_t), which is the product of the trend and cycle ($T_t^{\star}C_t$) or:

$$C_t \star T_t = \frac{Y_t}{S_t \star I_t} = CMA_t = c_t \star t_t \tag{5.7}$$

The CMA can be derived from the simple moving average (MA). By removing the cyclical and irregular components (factors), we are left with the seasonal and irregular components, which can also be eliminated from the data:

$$S_t \star I_t = \frac{Y_t}{C_t \star T_t} = s_t \star i_t \tag{5.8}$$

The subscript t means that there is a separate value of information for each time period. Grouping the values of the seasonal and irregular components by month will facilitate the deseasonalization of the data (Y_t/sn) to estimate a trend forecast by OLS. In effect, to obtain the trend value, the deseasonalized data are regressed on the progression of time:

$$d_t = Y_t/sn = f(t) \text{ and } t_t = a + bt; \tag{5.9}$$

where a is the average value of the detrended data and b is the slope of the detrended regression.

For any given value of the intercept (100) and the slope (10), the trend value can be estimated.

In period one, the trend value is just going to be 110 [$t_t = 100 + 10(1)$] and so on. Additionally, the trend and seasonal value, say 0.5, can be estimated for each time period:

$$t_t * sn = [100+10(1)]*.05 = 100.5 \tag{5.10}$$

It must be noted that the seasonal factor and time will vary. The product of trend and seasonality gives the estimated forecast for each unit of time, say month, quarter, or year:

$$\hat{y} = t_t * sn_t \tag{5.11}$$

It must be recalled that each forecast is a scientific projection with some amount of error. The root mean squared error (RMSE) is variously utilized to estimate the amount of error that is associated with a forecast:

$$\text{RMSE} = \sqrt{\frac{(Y-\hat{Y})_t^2}{n_{FE}}} = \sqrt{ASoSD}; \tag{5.12}$$

where n_{FE} is the number of forecast errors, and $ASoSD$ is for the average sum of squared deviation. RMSE is an indicator of the number of standard deviation units above the expected value. Other forms of forecast error estimates include the mean squared error (MSE), the mean absolute error (MAE), and the mean absolute percentage error (MAPE).[9]

We are now ready to conduct a forecast of monthly sales by motor vehicle and parts dealers, using monthly data from 2014 to 2016. The essence of the ensuing exercise is purely didactic. The data for the industry has been obtained from the Census Bureau and the North American Industry Classification System (NAICS) (code is 441). Procedures for accessing the moving average function in Excel have been provided in Figure 5.3.

The fundamental idea is to access Excel's Moving Average function via the "Data" and "Data Analysis" tabs on the Excel ribbon (Panel 5.3(d)). Data Analysis may not readily be available, but it can be installed or added in. First, click on the Microsoft button and then select "Excel Options" (Panel 5.3(a)). After the "Excel Options" button has been selected, click on "Add-ins," highlight "Analysis ToolPak," (not Analysis ToolPak – VBA"), click on "Go" and "OK" (not shown) (Panel 5.3(b)). In the ensuing dialogue box (Panel 5.3(c)), check the "Analysis ToolPak" box and click "OK." Notice that in Panel (d), several important tools are displayed and accessible, including: "Descriptive Statistics," "Exponential Smoothing," and "Regression."

After the "Add-in" procedures have been completed, click on the "Data" tab on the Excel ribbon to select the "Data Analysis" tab on the far right. The moving average of a series can then be estimated by highlighting the "Moving Average" function and clicking "OK." The data to be estimated must already be in the Excel spreadsheet before going through the procedures. Excel will require a range of cells to report the results of the moving average computation. It is important to center the results, since the CMA must be computed first (see Table 5.2). The same "Add-in" procedures can be followed for estimating a regression model, bearing in mind that Excel is not very well suited for advanced econometric analysis of endogenous and simultaneous models. Eviews, RATS, SPSS, and R provide better alternatives.

The results for the multiplicative decomposition experiment have been reported in Table 5.2. Eight steps have been outlined, starting with the twelve-month moving average (12MMA). There might be slight notational variations with forecast results elsewhere. The notations in this chapter have been selected for brevity and ease of reference. Column 3 removes the trend (t_t) and cyclical (c_t) factors (the CMA). Dividing sales (Y) by the CMA accounts for the seasonal (s_t) and irregular components (i_t). The seasonal factors (s_t or sn_t) are just the monthly averages derived from column 4. The division of sales by the seasonal factors detrends the data for regression analysis or estimates of the monthly trend.

Following the "Add-in" procedures discussed earlier on, Figure 5.4 shows how to run a trend regression. Regression procedures will be fully discussed in the next section, but you must note the important arrows for labels (since Excel will not ordinarily recognize non-numeric values), entry of the dependent variable (Input Y Range) and entry of independent variable(s) (Input X Range).

The simple moving average assigns equal weight to the values in the series. In real life the most recent information can be more valuable when making projections. Exponential smoothing technique is usually adopted to deal with the problem of invariable weight. However, smoothing techniques have been discovered to work very well when data series change sluggishly. Core inflation goods—other than food and energy—are good candidates for smoothing. Once weights have been established, the forecasting procedure becomes mechanical.

$$\hat{F}_{t+1} = wA_{t-1} + w(1-w)F_{t-1} + \ldots wA_{t-N} + (1-w)F_{t-N}; \tag{5.13}$$

where A_{t-1} is for the actual values in the previous period, and F_{t-1} is for the previous forecasted value. Recall that Excel's Data Analysis function can be used to generate exponential smoothing forecasts (see Figure 5.3(d)). However, it must be noted that a damping factor (1-w) will be required, where the weight is alpha (α). A damping factor of 0.8 and the 2015 data can be utilized to generate the 2016 forecast as follows:

$$\hat{F}_{t+1} = wA_{t-1} + w(1-w)F_{t-1} + \ldots wA_{t-N} + (1-w)F_{t-N}$$

Feb 2015 = (0.2)69.28 + (0.8)69.28 = $69.28b

Mar 2015 = (0.2)73.008 + (0.8)69.238 = $70.028b

. . . . .
. . . . .
. . . . .

Jan 2016 = (0.2)78.19 + 0.8(79.0083) = $78.84b (5.14)

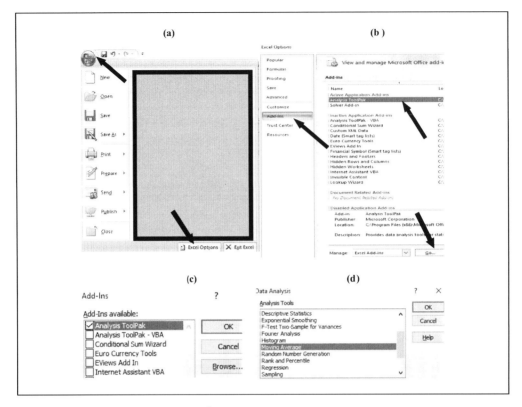

Figure 5.3 Excel's moving average function

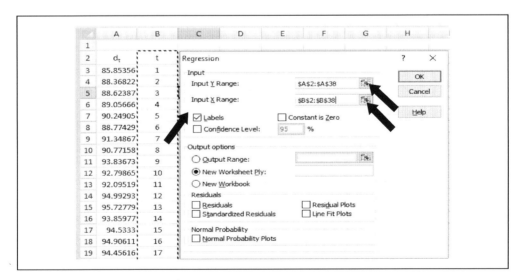

Figure 5.4 Regression in Excel

Table 5.2 Monthly sales of US motor vehicle and parts dealers (2013–2015, $b)*

Month	Sales, Y (1)	12MMA (2)	CMA (3)	$s_t * i_t$ (4)	s_t (5)	d_t (1/5) (6)	t_t (7)	$\dfrac{DY}{DG} = \left(\dfrac{1}{1-MPC}\right)$ (8)	$\dfrac{DY}{-DT} = \left(\dfrac{-MPC}{1-MPC}\right)$ (9)
Jan	69.28		$t_t * c_t$	(1/3) 0.82	85.85	88.05	72.18		8.37
Feb	73.01			0.85	88.37	88.53	75.08		4.28
Mar	83.63			1.02	88.62	89.01	90.90		52.93
Apr	81.49			0.99	89.06	89.49	88.41		47.89
May	86.71			1.03	90.25	89.97	92.96		39.06
Jun	82.59			0.98	88.77	90.45	88.35		33.17
Jul	86.03	85.07	85.41	1.01	1.00	91.35	90.93	90.86	23.30
Aug	88.68	85.75	85.94	1.03	1.02	90.77	91.41	93.27	21.04
Sep	75.51	86.13	86.38	0.87	0.89	93.84	91.89	81.62	37.40
Oct	78.80	86.64	86.88	0.91	0.91	92.80	92.37	83.94	26.40
Nov	75.38	87.12	87.30	0.86	0.86	92.10	92.85	79.61	17.88
Dec	78.19	87.48	87.82	0.89	0.91	94.99	93.33	85.04	46.93
Jan	70.38	88.15	88.43	0.80	0.82	95.73	93.81	76.90	42.54
Feb	74.94	88.70	88.93	0.84	0.85	93.86	94.29	79.96	25.22
Mar	90.51	89.15	89.47	1.01	1.02	94.53	94.77	96.78	39.40
Apr	87.98	89.78	90.04	0.98	0.99	94.91	95.25	94.10	37.44
May	93.25	90.29	90.51	1.03	1.03	94.46	95.73	98.91	32.07
Jun	86.71	90.72	91.00	0.95	0.98	97.04	96.21	93.97	52.75
Jul	91.28	91.28	91.35	1.00	1.00	97.96	96.69	96.62	28.49
Aug	92.62	91.41	91.81	1.01	1.02	96.06	97.17	99.15	42.62
Sep	83.35	92.21	92.36	0.90	0.89	102.34	97.65	86.74	11.47
Oct	84.33	92.51	92.63	0.91	0.91	99.52	98.13	89.17	23.47
Nov	78.96	92.74	92.75	0.85	0.86	98.10	98.61	84.54	31.20
Dec	86.56	92.76	92.87	0.93	0.91	102.42	99.09	90.29	13.94
Jan	78.47	92.98	93.02	0.84	0.82	97.61	99.57	81.62	9.92
Feb	79.60	93.06	93.27	0.85	0.85	105.20	100.05	84.85	27.56
Mar	96.54	93.49	93.65	1.03	1.02	97.97	100.53	102.67	37.50
Apr	93.76	93.81	93.88	1.00	0.99	97.79	101.01	99.79	36.37
May	97.60	93.96	94.19	1.04	1.03	94.66	101.49	104.86	52.82
Jun	94.78	94.42	94.72	1.00	0.98	99.76	101.97	99.60	23.23
Jul	97.89	95.01			1.00	98.84	102.45	102.37	20.09
Aug	98.01				1.02	101.15	102.93	105.02	49.15
Sep	90.91				0.89	106.69	103.41	91.85	0.90
Oct	90.43				0.91	101.44	103.89	94.40	15.77
Nov	84.11				0.86	104.60	104.37	89.48	28.90
Dec.	93.32				0.91	110.20	104.85	95.54	4.92
	RMSE= 0.90					d_t =f(t)	$t_t * s_t$		**Σ 29.07**

Note:
*12 MMA= Twelve-month moving average.

Table 5.3 Evaluating forecasts ($b)

	Actual 2016	**Multiplicative decomposition**	**Exponential smoothing**
Jan 2016	80.013	88.05	78.84
Feb	89.217	88.53	69.283
Mar	100.052	89.01	70.028
Apr	96.61	89.49	72.4496
May	97.804	89.97	74.25808
Jun	97.437	90.45	76.74886
Jul	98.76	90.93	77.91649
Aug	103.208	91.41	79.53979
Sep	94.771	91.89	81.36863
Oct	92.18	92.37	80.19591
Nov	89.676	92.85	79.91613
Dec	100.414	93.33	79.0083
		RMSE=0.9	RMSE=9.0

Overall, the exponential smoothing model produces a value that closely approximates the January 2016 sales, but the model is not superior to the multiplicative decomposition model. With a lower RMSE of 0.90, the multiplicative decomposition model outperformed the exponential smoothing model. In effect, the decompositional model does not show a very large deviation from the expected value of sales. It accounts for very low deviation from the expected value of sales. The error of the model is less than one standard deviation above the mean. The decomposition model also provides reasonably excellent forecasts for sales in February and October of 2016. However, the forecasting horizon of 12 months is rather ambitious; the longer the forecasting horizon, the greater the probability of larger errors. Macro variables can change, and disturbances (shocks or innovations) can interrupt seemingly predictable patterns of economic transactions.

It should also be noteworthy that the number of observations for the decompositional model far exceeds that of the exponential smoothing algorithm. Implicitly, forecasting models need adequate and essential information to increase their reliability. Annual estimates of sales that do not account for seasonality can also pose problems of their own. Accordingly, univariate (one-variable) and bivariate (two-variable) models must be used with a great amount of precaution. Such models have high exposure to omitted variable bias that exponentially increases the RMSE.

Notably, high frequency data have drawbacks. Serial correlation, the persistence of past disturbances into subsequent periods, is particularly relevant. However, such a problem may not necessarily be inimical to the objectives of forecasting models. Regression limitations will be discussed in the next section.

The industry data are instructive for assessing individual company performance. Litigants might want to compare the performance of a particular company to that of an industry to which the company belongs. Therefore, industry performance can be said to be barometric. The aggregate information is also an indication of why trends are not very conspicuous in the data, even when the series are decomposed into annual denominations. The cumulative information tends to smooth out some amount of volatility and trends.

So far, we have dealt with stationarity for a single variable (sales). There are times when the combination of two or more series or variables can generate a stationary outcome when one of the series or variables is not stationary. Under such circumstances, the series are said to be collectively stationary or cointegrated. The concept of cointegration is beyond the scope of this work, but discussions of the concept can be found in Warburton (2018b) and, more extensively, in the work of Hill et al. (2011, pp. 488–94). Cointegration is a routine occurrence in economic activity; especially when economic variables are greatly interdependent. For example, consumption and income, and inventories and sales cointegrate easily. That is, they tend to show a long-run relationship. Stationary linear combinations imply that the cointegrated series should not be differenced for stationarity.[10] The next section will discuss regression analysis, otherwise known as the ordinary least squares (OLS) estimator.

5.5 ORDINARY LEAST SQUARES (OLS)

Regression is an estimating method that is used to evaluate the relationship between independent variable(s) and dependent variable by minimizing the error sum of squares (ERSS)—ordinary least squares (OLS). The unit of analysis is usually on the right-hand side (RHS) of a model specification, and it is generally known as the dependent variable; generically, the Y variable. OLS is generally intended to be a linear estimator, but nonlinear data can be linearized for estimation by OLS. The overarching objective is to estimate the line of best fit; the line that minimizes the sum of errors in a data set:

$$Y = \alpha + \beta^1 X + \varepsilon \tag{5.15}$$

Therefore, the concept of linearity is central to OLS estimation. The concept of linearity is more meaningful when it is applied to the coefficients (βs) of regressors or independent variables (Xs). Invariably, not all variables can be included in a regression model. As such, less important variables are omitted (ε) since parsimony is treasured (Ockham's razor). It is presumed that the omitted variables have a normal distribution with zero mean and constant variance.

Regressors are the most important variables that can help to explain the behavior or response of the dependent variables to incremental changes of the independent variable(s) on the left-hand side of a regression model, excluding endogenous models (models for which independent variables can also be considered dependent variables).[11]

When nonlinear data requires the use of OLS, the data can be transformed to obtain linearity:

$$Y = \alpha X^\beta. \tag{5.16}$$

Taking the log transformation:

$$\ln Y = \ln \alpha + \beta \ln X \tag{5.17}$$

Taking the derivative of 5.17 gives:

$$\frac{1}{Y}dY = \beta \frac{1}{X}dX \tag{5.18}$$

Equation 5.18 shows that the double log estimate of y is just an elasticity estimation (see also Equation 1.5 in Chapter 1). As such, double log models estimate percentage changes in dependent variables when independent variable(s) change by 1 percent (see the ANCOVA result of Table 5.4).

OLS imposes some regularity conditions for better estimates. There must be no undesirable: multicollinearity, serial correlation, heteroskedasticity (large variances among regressors), and misspecification. Consequently, no independent variable must be a perfect linear function of another independent variable in a model. The variances of the errors from the mean must be constant for the independent variables (homoskedasticity). Past shocks or disturbances should not affect current errors or shocks (no serial correlation), and errors must be normally distributed with zero mean and constant variance. When the regularity conditions are satisfied OLS is said to be the best (B) linear (L) and unbiased (U) estimator (E). That is, OLS is BLUE. Errors can be minimized by standardizing measures, using log estimates, avoiding collinear variables like income and wealth, acquiring data from reputable sources, and not including variable and total costs in the same regression. OLS specification requires theoretical foundations and, sometimes, foreknowledge of the expected signs of the coefficients (based on theories or laws).

OLS is also suitable for dealing with some legal controversies appertaining to nominal variables, race, religion, and gender. Nominal variables can be granted numerical codes to generate dummy or binary variables. However, less experienced researchers can easily fall into the dummy variable trap. Using the same amount of dummy variables as the categories to be estimated will create a dummy trap. For example, an analyst who is interested in investigating wage discrimination between males and females should not have two dummy variables, one for males and another for females. He/she must have one less dummy than categories (D =k-1). In this chapter, the pay data provided in Chapter 1 will be evaluated as an example of dummy variable regression.

There are certain objectionable regression results. Regression coefficients must not have the wrong theoretical signs; except of course, if a novel theory without bad data and omitted variables can be presented. Courts of law are not likely to accept such theories that lack foundation in the discipline of economics. Regression results showing high R^2 but very few significant t-statistics are usually suspect; they espouse multicollinear tendencies. Results with negative R^2 or very low F-statistic are usually symptoms of bad data or model misspecification.

Results showing very high R^2 and very high t-statistic might be symptoms of autocorrelation. Heteroskedasticity is likely to be present when regression results show very high t-statistics and very low R^2. Contemporary statistical packages provide capabilities to conduct various diagnostic tests. For example, Breusch-Godfrey (1978) and Durbin-Watson's (1950, 1951) Serial Correlation Test, and White's (1980) heteroskedasticity test.

Some researchers pay extravagant attention to R^2 for very bad reasons. Occasionally, there is an impulse to force data to produce compliant or premeditated outcomes. Torturing data for confession at all cost can produce counterintuitive rather than persuasive results. In reality, there is no need to maximize the value of R^2. The R^2 barely indicates the amount of variation in the dependent variable that is explained by the regressors. Depending on the theory that is being proposed, it might make sense for the R^2 to be manifestly low; especially when few regressors are utilized. As noted earlier, excessively high R^2 can be a symptom of multicollinearity or autocorrelation. Multicollinear models will surprisingly report variables that have insignificant t-statistics though the variables are normally expected to be theoretically significant (a multicollinearity problem). This is because the individual effects of the variables on the dependent variable cannot be cleanly separated. Figure 5.5 summarizes some of the main arguments of the OLS theory.

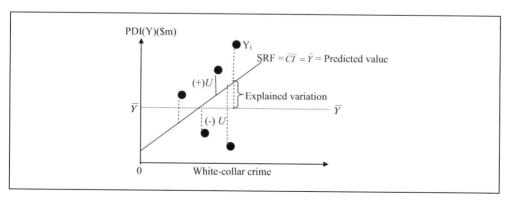

Figure 5.5 Personal disposable income (PDI) and white-collar crime (WCC)

A model is a formal statement of a theory, usually in mathematical form. Models can be expressed in words, equations, and graphs. Figure 5.5 is a graph with a simple theory. It shows that as white-collar crime (WCC) increases, personal disposable income increases in tandem. The sample regression function (SRF) is an estimate of the data, and it provides the best estimate that can minimize the error sum of squares:

$$Min \sum u^2 = \sum (Y - \hat{Y})^2 \tag{5.19}$$

The Us, which are positive and negative deviations (error) from the regression line, can be minimized by the OLS estimator to produce the best linear estimate. The slope of the line (β) is the regression coefficient, which estimates the change in PDI to the change in WCC. That is, the amount by which incremental changes in WCC will increase PDI (the rise over the run).

Pointedly, regression specifications must be based on convincing theories. By engaging in white-collar crimes, people can increase their personal disposable income (PDI) without performing duties that require the arduous and legitimate use of their physical and mental capacities. The PDI of white-collar criminals will increase as the criminals engage in criminal activities that produce pecuniary rewards with impunity. That is, there is a positive relationship between unrestrained WCC and the PDI of those who successfully engage in white-collar criminal activities.

A sociologist, Edward Sutherland, is generally credited for the use and empirical application of the concept of WCC, though the expression, "white collar," had earlier usage. Sutherland noted that a white-collar crime is a "crime committed by a person of respectability and high social status in the course of his occupation" (Podgor & Israel, 2009, p. 1). While some are yet to be caught, some highly respected individuals, including judges, chief executive officers, accountants, and politicians have been convicted of white-collar crimes. The jurisdictional basis for prosecuting white-collar crimes is generally based on various federal statutes of the commerce clause.[12]

The amount of variation that is explained is the difference between $\hat{Y}_i$ and the mean of Yi ($\bar{Y}_i$), and the total variation is the sum of explained and unexplained (portion above explained) variation. Analysis of variance studies the decomposition or distribution of variation. Essentially, the total sum of squares (TSS) must be equal to the explained (E) and unexplained (error, ER) sum of squares (SS):

$$TSS = ESS + ERSS. \tag{5.20}$$

Some mathematical representations might be helpful. The variation that is explained is:

$$\hat{Y}_i = Y_i - \varepsilon. \tag{5.21}$$

Therefore, the variation that is unexplained (error) must be:

$$\varepsilon = Y_i - \hat{Y}_i. \tag{5.22}$$

From Figure 5.5, the explained variation is:

$$\hat{Y}_i - \bar{Y}_i, \text{ and} \tag{5.23}$$

The total variation is:

$$Y_i - \bar{Y}_i. \tag{5.24}$$

Taking the total sum of variation, squaring the components and decomposing the variation gives

$$(Y_i - \bar{Y}_i)^2 = (\hat{Y}_i - \bar{Y}_i)^2 + (= Y_i - \hat{Y}_i)^2$$

$$R^2 = 1 - \frac{(\hat{Y}_i - \bar{Y}_i)^2}{(Y_i - \bar{Y}_i)^2}; \tag{5.25}$$

See Gujarati and Porter (2009; also Chapter 3) for a detailed exposition of the analysis of variance that has been presented here.

I will now proceed to estimate the pay data, which was introduced to you in Chapter 1, by OLS. It is important to note that regression models can be univariate, bivariate or multivariate. Univariate models are less robust, and they must be used with precaution. They generally lack complete theoretical support. Therefore, it is generally advisable to use bivariate and multivariate models; except there are precise reasons for not doing so. Recall that 30 occupations were considered to determine if the wages of men are significantly different from females in those occupations.[13] The occupations require levels of education across the academic spectrum, and two regression results are reported in Table 5.4, one by Excel and another by Eviews 10.

The first regression, Regression (1), shows that the pay for women is significantly less than that of men for the 30 occupations that have been considered in the sample. The model is an analysis of variance (ANOVA) model, because it does not include any covariate or regressor. As expected, the R^2 and F-statistic are very low. Accordingly, analysts should use ANOVA models only for very limited empirical objective, because they do not have theoretical foundations; they barely test for significant differences or the lack thereof. The coefficient for *male pay* is a differential intercept coefficient. The coefficient is expected to show the amount by which male pay is greater or less than female pay. The positive

Table 5.4 ANOVA and ANCOVA results (p-value in parenthesis)

Dependent variable: full-time earnings of male and female employees (30 occupations)

	Regression (1)	Regression (2)$^\Phi$
Observations	60	60
R^2	0.04	0.14
F-stat	2.2	4.8
	(0.14)	(0.01)
Variable	Coefficient (1)	Coefficient (2)
Female pay	$61,228.3	11.8
	(1.6 E-17)**	(0.0)**
Male pay	$10,611.2	0.18
	(0.14)	(0.08)*
Log (number of employees)	N/A	-0.08
		(0.0)**

Note:
Φ A double log specification.

coefficient reveals that, for the occupations that have been considered, males make about $10,611.2 more than females.

The second regression model, Regression (2), is an analysis of covariance (ANCOVA) model. It incorporates an economic theory to explain pay disparity. The model presupposes (hypothesizes) that non-gender-neutral employment will have an impact on pay disparities. It should be recalled from Chapter 1 that there are approximately five million more female employees than their male counterpart in the sampled occupations. The model is specified as a double log model, which means that the objective is to capture the effect of an incremental percentage increase in the number of employees while controlling for gender disparity.[14]

The results are rather revealing. First, by adding the number of employees, the explanatory power of the model goes up by about ten percentage points. The explained variation in pay increased from 0.04 to 0.14, suggesting that the theoretical model provides a better performance. An incremental percentage increase in the number of workers significantly increases the pay of males by 0.18 percent but significantly reduces the overall pay of the workers in the occupations by 0.08 percent. The finding suggests that some kind of transfer effect might be taking place in the occupations considered.

The employment theory is by no means exhaustive, because the model has omitted other exogenous or explanatory variables such as experience, productivity, gender disutility

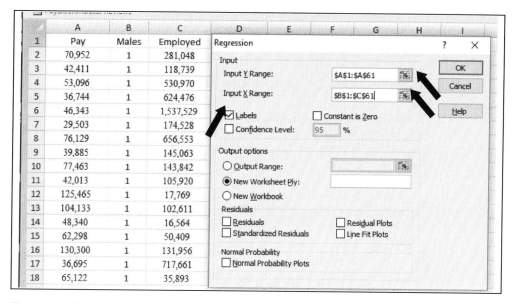

Figure 5.6 Dummy variable regression (ANOVA and ANCOVA) models

(discrimination), and levels of education. These are issues that will have to be addressed in courts of law with admissible evidence.

If "Data Analysis" is unavailable, follow the "Add-in" procedures that were discussed earlier on to run the ANOVA regression. Figure 5.6 provides additional insights. Highlight "Regression" from the menu and click "OK." The "Input Y Range" text box must be used to enter the dependent variable. The independent variable is a dummy for males and females (1 for males and 0 for females). The "Input X Range" should be used for independent variables, in this case, the male dummy. The box is capable of holding multiple independent variables. The number of employed must not be included in the ANOVA model (recall the dummy variable trap discussion). In the next regression you can include "Employed" with the dummy to get two independent variables. However, you must note that I estimated a double log model, so your result will be in levels. You can transform both pay and employed into percentages before running the second regression. It is important to check labels so that Excel can identify your independent variables. Unchecking the box will make it impossible for you to identify your independent variables. Excel will return default labels (X Variable 1, X Variable 2).

In the US, discrimination models must be sensitive to both economic theory and the Civil Rights Act of 1964. Title VII of the Civil Rights Act of 1964 forbids employers to make employment decisions that favor a particular group because of race, color, religion, sex, or national origin. Plaintiffs in Title VII suits can prove liability under either of two theories: disparate treatment or adverse impact.

In disparate treatment cases, plaintiffs are required to prove intentional discrimination as shown by sufficient evidence of the disparate treatment of employees with comparable qualifications. In adverse impact cases, plaintiffs must prove that a facially neutral employment practice that is not justified by business necessity has a disproportionate impact on members of a particular group.[15]

In 1971, more than 50 employees of the North Carolina Agricultural Extension Service sued their employer in Federal District Court for intentional discrimination in employment practices related to salary determinations, job assignments, promotions, and the provision of services.[16]

Prior to 1965, the Extension Service had segregated its employees into black and white branches, intentionally setting the salaries of black professionals lower than those of their white counterparts. When the two branches merged, shortly after the effective date of the Civil Rights Act of 1964, these pay disparities were allowed to continue. As a result, plaintiff-employees who had been hired before the merger continued to receive salaries based on a racially discriminatory wage differential.

To show that discrimination occurred, the plaintiffs used multiple regression analysis. They controlled for tenure, education, job title, and race. The plaintiffs' experts concluded that statistically significant salary differentials occurring for the years 1974 and 1975 were attributable to race and that their regressions show that in 1974 the average black employee earned $331 less per year than a white employee with the same job title, education, and tenure. In 1975 the disparity in wages rose to $395. The regression for 1981 showed a smaller disparity, which lacked statistical significance.

The district court employed disparate treatment analysis and found that the plaintiffs' evidence established salary disparities. However, the court concluded that the defendants successfully repudiated the payment disparities by using "explanatory evidence [variables]" other than race that might have accounted for the salary variations. The court found that an appropriate regression model of salary disparities should include all measurable variables that can affect salary levels.[17]

The court also criticized the plaintiffs' analysis for overparametrization (the inclusion of irrelevant variables in the regression specification), which included data on the salaries of employees hired before the enactment of Title VII. In the court's estimation, discrimination before the civil rights law was non-actionable discrimination and a redundant parameter. In effect, the Fourth Circuit interpreted Title VII as a law that did not require an employer to eliminate salary disparities that stem from a discriminatory wage scale before the Civil Rights Act of 1964.

A divided panel of the Appellate Court for the Fourth Circuit upheld the ruling of the lower court. The panel found support for this holding in two Supreme Court opinions, *Hazelwood School District v. United States* and *United Air Lines v. Evans*. *Hazelwood* protected an employer from liability for its pre-Act discrimination. However, the Supreme Court later countered by stating that these cases do not extend to the maintenance of a discriminatory salary structure that originated prior to the effective date of Title VII.

However, in dealing with the case, the US Supreme Court found merit in the regression model of the plaintiffs. The court ruled that: The Court of Appeals erred in stating that petitioners' regression analyses were "unacceptable as evidence of discrimination," because they did not include "all measurable variables thought to have an effect on salary level." The court's view of the evidentiary value of the regression analyses was plainly incorrect.

> While the omission of variables from a regression analysis may render the analysis less probative than it otherwise might be, it can hardly be said, absent some other infirmity, that an analysis which accounts for the major factors must be considered unacceptable as evidence of discrimination. Normally, failure to include variables will affect the analysis' probativeness, not its admissibility...

> A plaintiff in a Title VII suit need not prove discrimination with scientific certainty; rather, his or her burden is to prove discrimination by a preponderance of the evidence. *Texas Dept. of Community Affairs v Burdine*, 450 U.S. 248, 252 (1981). Whether, in fact, such a regression analysis does carry the plaintiffs' ultimate burden will depend in a given case on the factual context of each case in light of all the evidence presented by both the plaintiff and the defendant. However, as long as the court may fairly conclude, in light of all the evidence, that it is more likely [478 U.S. 385, 401] than not that impermissible discrimination exists, the plaintiff is entitled to prevail.[18]

In *Ted Smith et al v. Virginia Commonwealth University*, which was decided on August 24, 1995, the appellants, five male professors at Virginia Commonwealth University (VCU), were very successful in using omitted variable bias to support their claims filed under the Equal Pay Act and Title VII of the Civil Rights Act of 1964 in the Eastern District of Virginia. The appellants objected to pay raises that VCU gave to its female faculty in response to a salary equity study conducted at the university. The Study Committee chose to employ a multiple regression analysis, which compares many characteristics within a particular set of data and enables the determination of how one set of factors is related to another, single factor. The VCU study controlled for such differences as doctoral degree, academic rank, tenure status, number of years of VCU experience, and number of years of prior academic experience.

After controlling for the multiple factors, difference in salary was attributed to gender disparity. The multiple regression analysis did not control for the performance factors because of perceptible difficulties associated with the quantification of performance, since performance variables were confounding and presumed to have been included in the categories of academic rank, status, and experience.

Two regression estimates for the summer of 1989 and 1991, coinciding with a merit system of teaching, publications, and community service (performance factors), showed disparities in the range of $1,354 to $1,982. Other variables, like administrative experience which commanded higher retained earnings, were also excluded. After the studies, a Salary Equity Implementation Committee made up of three women implemented increases for female faculty members.

The defendants used eight independent variables: (i) national salary average (same discipline and rank), (ii) doctorate or otherwise, (iii) tenure status, (iv) quick tenure (within four years of appointment) or not, (v) years of experience at VCU, (vi) academic experience before VCU, (vii) service, if any, as department chair, and (viii) gender. The selection of variables however failed to control for the amount of time actually spent on teaching and other performance factors.

The appellants' expert noted that the study was not valid without adding the performance factors, and that studies performed by disinterested outside researchers have regularly included productivity measures such as teaching loads and publications that have shown that productivity has a positive effect on the level of faculty compensation. Further, the appellants complained that the multiple regression study was flawed because of the inclusion of an inflated pool of faculty members, and that the failure to account for significant variables that could have a bearing on wage disparities between the male and female faculty members tainted the results of the regression estimates, citing manifest imbalance.

The appellants directed attention not only to omitted variable bias, but sampling bias—the preponderant representation of male faculty members returned from higher paying positions in the administration and retained their administrative level pay. The salary differential was not accounted for. Of the 82 faculty members considered in the pool who were paid more because they had held administrative positions, 71 were male. It was argued that the inflated pool discredited the validity of the statistical results.

The Appellate Court concluded that because the institution's pay system is based on merit, and the factors on which faculty pay scales are decided, the performance-based factors were left out of the regression analysis. Therefore, the court found that the omitted variable bias is material, because the inclusion of the performance factors could very well alter the results of the multiple regression analysis.

Omitted variable bias has also been used to question the probative value of cross-sectional analysis and pricing policy. In the *Federal Trade Commission (FTC) v. Staples* (1997), the expert witness for Staples argued that the regression analysis of the FTC was fraught with omitted variable bias. The case involved a proposed merger of Staples and Office Depot, two superstore chains, for which the FTC successfully sought preliminary injunction from Federal District Court in Washington, DC.[19]

In unusual cases of civil immunities, regression models and evidence are worthless. Obviously, experts cannot counter civil immunities, if and when civil immunities are legal to begin with, even with a mountain of evidence. Further, the categories of immunity must be properly and lawfully defined, and defendants must provide incontrovertible evidence that they executed their duties in good faith (without intentional discrimination); failing which, the basis of civil immunity is prejudicial. The next section deals with the time value of money and the relevance of the concept to valuation and damages. The concept of regression will be revisited after an evaluation of the economic and legal issues that are associated with the discount rate.

5.5 (A) TIME VALUE OF MONEY

Directions of cash flows: present value (PV), payments, for annuities (PMT), and future value (FV) are indicative of cash flows. Outflows are payments to others, or payments that others have to make. The +/- button on the HP 10bII+ financial calculator must be used to indicate the direction of cash flow, mindful that when there are two or more nonzero amounts of cash flows, the calculator will return no solution. This issue will subsequently be discussed fully. As an investor, it is usually a good idea to think in terms of cash outflows. As an investor, use negative PV to get positive FV with interest payments and a definite time horizon. Simple interest is interest payment on principal only:

$$FV = PV(1 + r \star t). \tag{5.26}$$

Compound interest is interest on principal and interest on an annual basis:

$$FV = PV\left(1 + \frac{r}{n}\right)^{r \star n}; \tag{5.27}$$

It is generally misleading to think that the annual percentage rate (APR), a cost of credit, is a controlling rate of payment. On occasions of compounding, the effective annual rate (EAR) is what consumers are actually going to pay. The effective annual rate is the rate that annualizes payments after controlling for compounding. That is, it is the rate that adjusts for compounding.

Consider the following example: Solomon has been given a credit of $1000 with an APR of 18 percent. Solomon may think that his annual payment will be $1000(1+.18) = $1180.00. In actual fact, if compounding takes place during the year, say for late payments, Solomon will be paying an amount that is associated with the EAR:

$$EAR = \left(1 + \frac{APR}{N}\right)^N - 1 \rightarrow \left(1 + \frac{.18}{12}\right)^{12} - 1 = 0.1956 \tag{5.28}$$

Solomon will pay approximately $1200, $1000(1.20).

5.5 (B) FUTURE VALUE OF MONEY

$$FV = PV(1+i)^N = FVIF_{i,N} \tag{5.29}$$

Suppose $8,000 that is deposited in a bank today can earn a 5 percent interest rate or rate of return for 15 years, what is the value of the $8000 in 15 years (assuming that interest is compounded annually)?

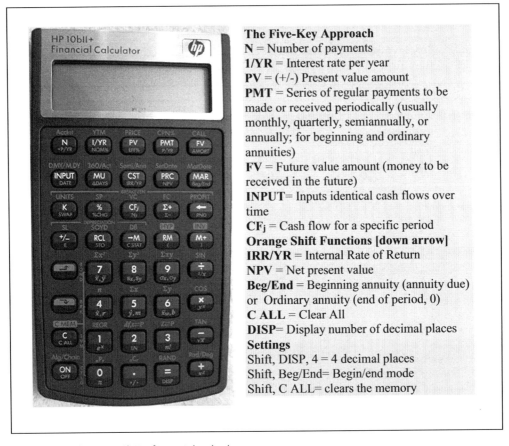

Figure 5.7 The HP 10bII+ financial calculator

Enter   15   5   8000±   0   ?   1

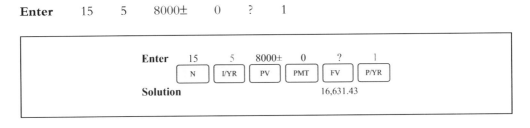

Solution   16,631.43

Multiple compounding occurs when payments are made on interest and principal on two or more occasions within a year:

$$FV = PV\left(1 + \frac{r}{n}\right)^{r*n};$$

(5.30)

The I/YR and P/YR functions are interrelated. Dividing 1/YR by 12 or N and setting P/YR equal to 12 or N will produce misleading results. It is better to set P/YR equal to 1 when dividing I/YR by 12 or any number of payments within a year. A number of issues are noteworthy: you have a present value amount of $1000 and you want to save it for five years. A bank promises to make two interest payments, but you are illegally deprived of the money before you make the deposit. How much money will you lose? You must note that the money will be discounted to the present in a court of law. Notice that cash outflows must be recognized by using the +/– button and not the button with a negative sign:

Enter   10   2.5   1000±   0   ?   1

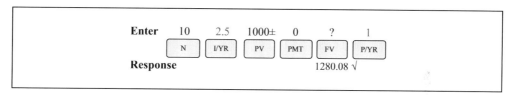

Response   1280.08 √

A wrong approach will be to set P/YR=2 while dividing I/YR by 2 at the same time.

Enter   10   2.5   1000±   0   ?   2

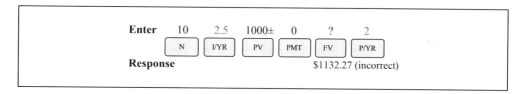

Response $1132.27 (incorrect)

Alternatively, it is better to leave the interest rate alone if P/YR is set to 2. It should be noted that unlike Excel, the HP 10bII+ financial calculator does not require unnecessary use of decimals to enter interest rates (see the illustration below).

Enter   10   5   1000±   0   ?   2

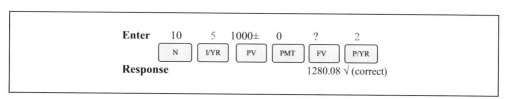

Response   1280.08 √ (correct)

On occasions when an investment is compounded continuously into the future, the value of the investment can be estimated by using the following formula:

$$FV = CF_0 \star e^{rN} \qquad (5.31)$$

where CF_0 is for the initial cash flow, N is for the amount of payments, r is the annual rate of interest (in decimal form), and e is a base for the year-end value to which the principal will grow even if interest at a rate of 100 percent per annum is compounded continuously. The future value function becomes a natural exponential function, otherwise known as a "natural logarithmic function." The log of the base e is just the value of the exponent of e. Therefore, the natural logarithmic function has some very attractive properties. Unlike the EAR, continuous compounding is not limited to a specific year.

Consider the following example. A cash flow of $10,000 with an interest of 10 percent that is compounded continuously for 12 years will have the following value:

$$FV = \$10000 e^{(0.1 \star 12)}.$$

By multiplying 0.1 by 12 and using the orange shift button to access e^x (3.32), the future value can be computed as $10000\star 3.32 = 33,201.17$. This is powerful information to check if the rate of return or time corresponds to the amount by re-specifying the problem.

$$\frac{33,201.17}{\$10,000} = e^{r\star 12} \rightarrow 3.32 = e^{r\star 12}$$

$\ln 3.32 = r \star 12$

$1.20/12 = r = 10\%$

5.5 (C) PRESENT VALUE OF MONEY

Since money today has more value than money to be received in the future, money that is expected to be received in the future must be discounted to know what it is worth today. This is a very important principle in litigation. For example, if you are wrongfully terminated or permanently injured in such a way that you cannot earn the natural amount of money you could have otherwise received into the distant future, courts would have to determine your work life expectancy and the money that you could have received. The courts will not give you the future value amount, because that will overestimate the value of your work life. You can invest the money and actually double the reasonable amount that you should have otherwise received. Therefore, the courts will have to discount the future value amount to the present.

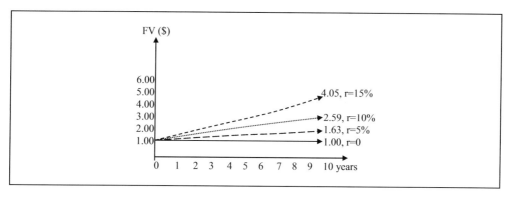

Figure 5.8 The future value of a dollar

The discount rate is obviously contentious. The higher the discount rate, the lower the present value of money (see Equation 5.32, see also Figure 5.9). Therefore, plaintiffs will generally seek a lower discount rate, while defendants will prefer a higher discount rate to limit their liabilities or damages. Courts must ultimately determine what the discount rate should be, and with legitimate or good economic reasons. The present value of an amount of money to be received in the future is just the product of the future value amount and its present discounted factor (PVIF), which consists of the discount rate and number of projected payments to be received (see Equation 5.32).

$$PV = \frac{FV}{(1+i)^n} \tag{5.32}$$

What is the present value of $1,000 to be received in 12 years from today, discounted back to the present at 8 percent?

Enter   15   8   ?   0   1000   1

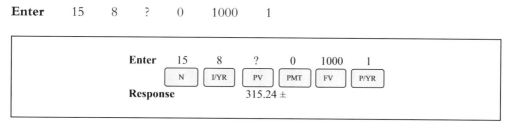

Response   315.24 ±

The negative sign indicates the direction of cash flow. If you are setting aside that amount of money (on an annual basis) to receive $1,000, then it should be considered a cash outflow (−). On the contrary, if you are on the receiving end, then it should be a cash outflow for whomsoever will be making the payment. It is noteworthy that double negatives (a negative future value and present value) will not yield a solution.

There are times when a forensic economist might be required to estimate interest rates or yields. For example, he/she might want to know the rate that will increase $1,000 to $2,000 in 15 years:

Enter   15   ?   1000 ±   0   2000   1

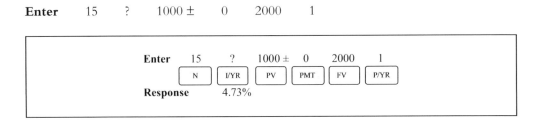

Response   4.73%

The forensic economist will need a return of 4.73 percent to increase $1,000 to $2,000 in 15 years. You must note the negative and positive signs of the present and future values of money. To get $2,000 in 15 years the investor must be willing to give up (-) $1,000 today for an annual return of 4.73 percent.

The concept of present value (PV) and discount rates can be more revealing than intuitive. Consider Figure 5.9 and the discounted value of a dollar over a ten-year period. It can be seen that as the discount rate increases from 0 to 15 percent, the present value of the dollar decreases.

The present value concept annualizes all costs and benefits, and the discount rate, which is imprecise, has to be convincingly estimated and accepted.

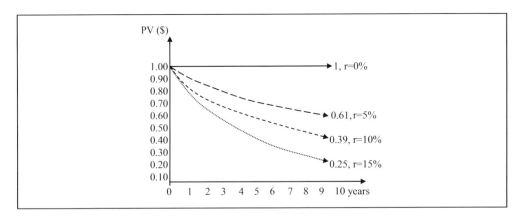

Figure 5.9 The present value of a dollar

5.5 (D) LITIGATING THE DISCOUNT RATE

The discount rate is a natural source of conflicts. Higher discount rates reduce the present value of money. While defendants will like very high discount rates if they are paying money into the future, plaintiffs will object. Equation 5.32 shows that future awards that are due to unlawful behavior and injury must be discounted. While the idea of discounting is much more apparent to economists, there was a time when some courts did not give the concept due attention because of some underlying assumptions.

In 1967, the Alaskan Supreme Court ruled that the discount rate must be set to zero (see *Beaulieu v. Elliot*). The zero-discount rate approach became known as the total offset method or the *Alaskan Rule*. The rationale behind the ruling was based on the idea that returns on investment should offset the rate of inflation. Implicitly, the growth rate of earnings (g) must correspond to the discount rate (i). Therefore, the present value interest factor (PVIF) or adjustment factor (AF) was presumed to be:

$$PV = \frac{(1+g)}{(1+i)} = 1 \text{ for } \forall g = i. \tag{5.33}$$

The value of a future stream of income (V_0) was calculated to be the base year earnings (B_1) multiplied by the terminal year of the award (t), or:

$$V_0 = B_1 * t \tag{5.34}$$

The *Alaskan Rule* is very straightforward, and it was intended to minimize wild speculation about the discount rate at the time the case was decided. The offset approach was also adopted in Pennsylvania. In 1980, the Pennsylvania Supreme Court decided that future inflation shall be presumed equal to future interest rates with the two factors offsetting each other; see *Kaczkowski v. Bolubusz* (491 Pa 561, 421 A 2d 1027, 1980). Some scholars have argued that at the time of the Alaskan and Pennsylvanian decisions, the offset method was not entirely implausible. Feldman (1990) reports that at the time the Alaska and Pennsylvania decisions were made, the offsetting assumptions were not implausible.[20] In *Havens v. Tonner* (243 Pa Super 371, 365 A 2nd 1271, 1976), the court ruled that inflation (π) and productivity (P) were speculative and inadmissible.

Decisions on the nominal rate have been based on: (i) weighted average cost of equity with varying maturities, (ii) high quality corporate bonds, (iii) the risk-free rate (based on 10- or 30 year-treasury securities),[21] and (iv) the capital asset pricing model (CAPM).

The total offset method has a chequered and uncertain history. In *Pfeifer*, the district court miscalculated the plaintiff's damages by using a total offset method. While it was assumed that return on present day award would offset the growth of the plaintiff's wage, the court did not include cost of living adjustments to be received on wages. Future lost income stream was not discounted.

However, the Supreme Court held that the total offset method was not required. "In all cases where it is reasonable to suppose that interest may safely be earned upon the amount that is awarded, the ascertained future benefits ought to be discounted in the making up of the award" (*Chesapeake & Ohio Ry. Co. v. Kelly* (241 U.S. 485, 1916)). The Supreme Court, however, tempered this assertion by explaining this method was necessary as a duty to mitigate damages. *Pfeifer* elaborated by providing "the best and safest investments." However, *Pfeifer's* applicability is limited as the case deals with an injured employee under the Longshoremen's and Harbor Workers' Compensation Act ("LSHWA") and does not apply generally to all discount rate calculations.[22]

Theoretically, and if applicable, the discount rate is normally expected to be greater than the rate of inflation. The Fisher Equation is illustrative:

$$i = r + \pi^e; \tag{5.35}$$

where i is for the nominal rate, r is for the real rate, and π^e is for the expected inflation rate. The use of the risk-free rate has slight complications for business valuation, which will be discussed later. The discount rate has not always been applied in all states and circumstances. Although the Supreme Court has addressed discount rate in several cases, such as *Jones & Laughlin Steel Corp. v. Pfeifer*, 462 U.S. 523 (1983); *Monessen Southwestern Ry. Co. v. Morgan*, 486 U.S. 330 (1988); and *Chesapeake & Ohio Ry. Co. v. Kelly*, 241 U.S. 485 (1916), a general approach to calculating a proper discount rate has not been established.[23] Some states have legislated rates to reduce controversies and frictions over the appropriate discount rate.

Invariably, judges, jurors, and experts have influential roles to play when the rates are not legislated. The underlying objective is to ensure the stability of rates. Consumption rates are less reliable because of their volatility. Yet, these rates are sometimes quoted in research. Core inflation generally provides more stability, because it excludes volatile food and energy prices; for example Table 5.5 shows that the 10-year risk-free rate is much more stable than that of consumer prices, while the implicit deflator shows the most stability, and zero inflation growth over the past ten years.

In projecting future earnings, the forensic economists make assumptions about inflation (π), productivity growth (P), and nominal interest rate (i). Some assume that inflation and productivity grows at a constant rate, and that the interest rate is flat regardless of the time horizon. Assumptions about the risk-free rate are usually plausible (see Table 5.5). Productivity in the nonfarm business sector does not grow at a remarkably rapid pace, but it tends to have slight variations from one year to the next. Total factor (multifactor) productivity, productivity not associated with labor and capital, has been constant for the period under review. Therefore, the change is zero. The interaction of productivity and inflation is used for the so-called "inflate-discount" approach.

When historical data are not relied upon, an expert may seek opinions about expected inflation by polling investment managers or other appropriate personnel to determine what the future inflation might be. However, the impartiality of opinions sought for

Table 5.5 US inflation rates*

	10 year inflation—index bond (π)	Consumer prices	Growth rate of the implicit deflator	Productivity (P)	π*P
2008	2.063	3.839	0.004	-0.2	-0.41
2009	1.66	-0.356	0.001	6.1	10.13
2010	1.15	1.640	0.003	1.6	1.84
2011	0.55	3.157	0.006	-0.2	-0.11
2012	-0.48	2.069	0.004	0.3	-0.14
2013	0.08	1.465	0.004	1.5	0.12
2014	0.44	1.622	0.004	0.4	0.18
2015	0.45	0.119	0.000	0.7	0.32
2016	0.27	1.262	0.003	1.0	0.27
2017	0.46	2.130	0.0048	1.0	0.46
2018	0.83	N/A	0.0055	1.9	1.58
Avg.	**0.68**	**1.69**	**0.0036**	**1.3**	1.29

Data Source: Federal Reserve Bank of St. Louis: https://fred.stlouisfed.org/.
Note:
* Ten year inflation indexed bond is computed from daily averages up to December 20; consumer prices are annual percentages and not seasonally adjusted; the implicit deflator shows average growth rates; and productivity (nonfarm labor until December 7, 2018).

litigation purposes may not be credibly established. As such, data provided by reliable government agencies tend to be more credible. Though experts are entitled to make informed judgment about expected inflation (π^e) and productivity, such a judgment can be challenged by triers of fact.

Although the Supreme Court came to the conclusion that the appropriate discount rate should be determined by considering the "safest available investment" in the *Pfeifer Case*, it did not make a general rule for the discount rate. Essentially, the court gave deference to the idea that governments are better equipped to perform a comprehensive economic analysis for a general rule.

Absent the legislative requirement, a consistent theme has evolved that jurors, with the assistance of expert witnesses, can play a critical role in deciding what the appropriate discount rate should be. In *Monessen Southwestern Ry. Co.*, the Supreme Court examined whether it was proper for a state court judge to instruct a jury to apply a zero-discount rate to future damages as a matter of law. The court held that failure to instruct the jury to consider the discount rate, improperly took away from the jury the essentially factual question of the appropriate rate at which to discount the Federal Employers' Liability Act (FELA) award to present value.

In the post-*Pfeifer* era, there has been disagreement on whether jurors should have absolute authority to determine when the total offset method should be applied. It is apparent however, that although controversies remain as to which method must be used to determine present value, the estimation of awards cannot easily avoid discounting the value of future awards to the present. Additionally, present value of awards should take into account inflation and other sources of wage increases as well as the rate of interest. In the *Monessen Case,* it also became apparent that failure to instruct a jury that present value is the proper measure of damages to award is erroneous.

Since the discount rate selection requires a finding of fact, the choice of the appropriate discount rate has been left to the wisdom of fact finders. In practice, jurors have arrived at inconsistent conclusions, and judges have ruled in favor of rates based on competing rationales. In contract discount rate cases the range of discretion is much greater than cases involving lost future wages in tort adjudications, where courts simply choose an interest rate that would be earned on "the best and safest investments."

Courts have treated the choice of discount rate as case specific, allowing complex calculations and vital assumptions to vary based on the nature of a given dispute; what Bowers (1996) alludes to as "discretion without guidance." He notes that the selection of a discount rate is generally considered a finding of fact and not a matter of law. Thus, the ultimate choice of the appropriate discount rate is the domain of the fact finder, be it judge or jury.

In jury trials, judges may instruct jurors in broad terms on how to choose the discount rate based on expert testimony and other evidence. The Fifth Circuit's description of the Texas jury instruction for discounting damages in breach of contract cases reveals that fact finders have broad discretion. The Texas cases are not ambiguous.[24] In *Budge v. Post*, 643 F. 2d 372, 375–76 (5th Cir. 1981), it was revealed that discounting of future damage awards should be adequately handled by the trial judge if he/she simply instructs the jury that damages are equal to the sum of money, if any, that would compensate the plaintiff if paid contemporaneously in cash.

Texas courts refuse to amplify this simple instruction because of the belief that further explanation can confuse the jury. The instruction in *Budge v. Post* informs fact finders only "to compensate," leaving them to decide how with few constraints and no specific definition of the appropriate discount rate. Given this combination of broad discretion and little guidance, Bowers contends that "it is not surprising that jurors regularly fail to understand the need to discount to present value, let alone the mechanics of finding the proper discount rate."[25] In the *Budge Case*, in which the Fifth Circuit affirmed Texas's simple jury instruction, the Circuit Court found that although the instruction was correct, the jury evidently did not follow it.

The Circuit Court then remanded the case, without definition of the discount rate, so that the trial judge could determine an appropriate discount rate and compute the present value of the award for contract earnings. A similar development occurred in *Sierra Blanca Sales*

Co. v. Newco Industries, Inc., 88 NM 472, 542 P. 2d 52, 54 (NM App 1975) after the jury had failed to follow the lower court's discount instruction for a contract damage award.

A few jurisdictions have tried to eliminate jury discretion in discounting, expressly leaving the choice of discount rates in tort cases up to the discretion of judges or even defining that rate by statute. When confronted with the task of selecting an appropriate discount rate in contract disputes, courts may routinely select from assorted possibilities, including the United States Treasury bill, note, or bond rate, as well as the AAA or high-yield corporate bond rate. Though courts have been reluctant to provide a definitive solution to the discount rate problem, in *CHR Equipment Financing, Inc. v. C&K Transport Inc.*, 448 NW 2d 693, 695 (Iowa App 1989), there is evidence of some form of agreement that a commercial interest rate must be determined to compute the present value of damages. This is consistent with the US Supreme Court's position that some amount of discounting is essential for damages award.

Recall our discussion of Rule 702 earlier in the chapter. Expert economic testimony is a powerful tool in litigation, but expert testimony can be excluded from evidence by a trial judge if the testimony does not meet the elements of an expert as outlined in Rule 702 of the Federal Rules of Evidence. Litigants routinely rely on expert witnesses to persuade fact finders. Fact finders may defer to experts for clarity. As such, litigants who fail to present opposing views of an undesirable rate can be at a disadvantage.[26] Fact finders can arbitrate competing proposals or methodologies to find a happy mean.

Courts are aware that the value of the actual "discount rate" is elusive and have accepted discount rates proposed by economists at trial. For example, in *LLECO Holdings, Inc. v. Otto Candies, Inc.*, (E D La 1994) the court discounted lost future profits of an oil and gas lease at a rate of 25 percent after accepting an expert's testimony that the rate was a fair return on investment for plaintiffs. In *Westman Commission Co. v. Hobart Corp.*, (D Colo 1982), the court accepted an expert's use of a 16.8 percent rate to discount lost sales. Obviously, the rates are excessively at variance with risk-free rates. Some decisions merely state agreement with an expert's conclusion without clarifying economic explanations.[27]

By deferring to experts, judges and jurors shift the decisional challenges to litigants and encourage the contending parties to use experts during a trial. "Battered by financial formulae and confused by conflicting expert testimony, fact finders operate a perverse legal lottery that commercial parties are obliged to play. Uncertainty and unnecessary expense thus prevail in a system without a clear default rule."[28] Without sound econometric explanations, there are three problematic issues with expert testimony: (i) use of unsettled theories, (ii) the potential of bias, and (iii) exorbitant costs.

Experts can manipulate assumptions and numbers so that their findings can reflect the theories of their cases. Estimating results that are based on prejudices are obviously biased, unreliable, and unethical, but the less discerning jurors may not be able to arrive at a judicious conclusion. A review of the professional ethics chapter (Chapter 4) in this book should be instructive. In actual fact, some economists estimate the net discount rate.

That is, the difference between the discount rate and the rate associated with increase in earnings, since this differential is perceived as very important.[29] Inevitably, experts and expert testimony can be costly to the parties involved in a legal dispute. Evidently, when all is said and done, the *Daubert Standard* provides a guidepost to the admissibility of evidence, including the appropriate discount rate. A looming question is whether the courts, under the *Daubert Standard*, will allow economists to testify about new economic methodologies.[30]

5.5 (E) ANNUITIES AND AMORTIZATION

Annuities are series of equal payments to be made or received over time. Such payments include mortgages, car loans, awards, and promises to pay. Financial calculators are equally useful to compute annuities. Later, I will use an Excel alternative in this chapter. Suppose you have won an award of $120,000 at an interest rate of 1.5 percent, which a court has decided to be the risk-free rate, what will be the payment amount if the court decides that the money should be paid on a monthly basis (rather than a lump sum) over a period of five years?

First, you should be thinking about 60 payments (12 payments for each year); second, the award should be considered a future value award since the money is not in the plaintiff's possession; had the money been in his/her possession, like the receipt of a bank loan, then it should be considered a present value amount without the negative sign. Additionally, the full amount of the money should be received in five years' time. The plaintiff must also determine whether the money should be paid at the start of the month (beginning annuity) or by the end of the month (ordinary annuity).

We can make the assumption that because of the plaintiff's attorney, economic conditions or circumstances of the defendant, and the decision of the court, the defendant is required to make reparations at the end of each month. The calculator must be adjusted accordingly for the annuity calculation. You must use the shift key to select "End" from the "MAR" button, since you are dealing with an ordinary annuity problem, and ensure that you do not have "BEG" on the screen of the calculator:

Enter   MAR   60   1.5   0   120000   12

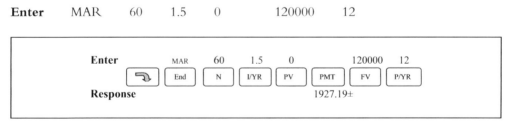

Response   1927.19±

Table 5.6 Amortization schedule

Begin	Year	Loan	Principal	Interest	Total	Balance
1 to 12	1	$50000	8601.97	3760.31	12362.28	41398.03
13 to 24	2		9001.76	3360.52	12362.28	32396.27
25 to 36	3		9846.18	2516.10	12362.28	22550.09
37 to 48	4		10769.83	1592.45	12362.28	11780.26
49 to 60	5		11780.11	582.17	12362.28	0.15
		Σ	$49,999.85	$118,11.55	$618,11.4	

Note:
Type =1 [Beginning Annuity].

As a plaintiff, you should be receiving $1,927.19 by the end of each month. Though the amount has a negative sign next to it, you should note that the defendant will be paying the money; a cash outflow from elsewhere. The money can be amortized, and you can generate an amortization table (see Table 5.6).

Amortization decomposes a series of payments into the principal and interest paid, and the remaining balance that has to be paid. Consider a $50,000 loan that is supposed to be paid over a five-year period with a 9 percent rate of return (APR). Since amortized loans are generally scheduled to be paid on a monthly basis, essentially at the start of each month, the interest rate and number of payment periods must be defined accordingly. Use the begin function on your financial calculator. A table is generally helpful. By setting the calculator to the begin mode, you should see "BEG" on the screen this time. Also, notice that only the payment is a cash outflow (-). The present value is not a cash outflow, because it is a loan:

| Enter | MAR | 60 | 0.75 | 50000 | | 0 | 1 |

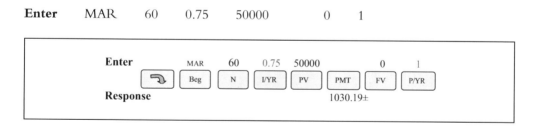

Response   1030.19±

The illustration below shows the relationship between P/YR and I/YR that was alluded to earlier on. This time P/YR is set to 12. It is highly recommended that you use the shift and "C ALL" (clear all) buttons to check for the correct Beg/End mode.

Enter   MAR   60   9   50000   0   12

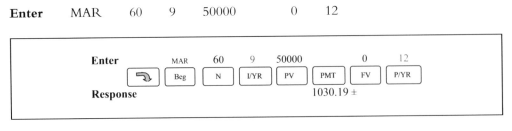

Response   1030.19 ±

It is critically important to compute the periodic payments before proceeding to decomposing principal and interest payments. The illustration below typifies the protocol for amortizing the first year of the loan with the HP 10bII+ calculator:

Enter

Responses $8601.97 $3760.31 $41398.03

The principal, interest payments, and balance are reported by reiteratively using the equal to sign (=) on the calculator. The first response gives the principal (p), the second response gives the interest payments (r), and the third response gives the balance (Bal) on the loan. It should be noted that the forensic economist can use any timeframe or window to get the principal, interest payment, and balance. For example, the second year should be 13, INPUT, and 24 to clearly delineate starting and ending periods in order to avoid overlaps. Beginning amortization schedule can be constructed for the previous example (see Table 5.6).

Time value calculations can also be done with Excel and financial tables in the appendix. For the sake of brevity, limited examples will be illustrated in this chapter, but the procedures are very mechanical when using the formula bar of Excel (as illustrated in Figure 5.10). The equal to (=) must be utilized to trigger any calculation in Excel. Once that has been done, the function to be estimated can then be selected, such as future value (FV), present value (PV), payments (PMT, for annuities), number of payment periods (nper), and in the case of annuities, the type of annuity (1 for beginning annuity, and 0 for ending annuity). Other functions include net present value (NPV) and internal rate of return (IRR). NPV and IRR will be discussed in the next section. The Excel protocol uses abbreviations, an open bracket (followed by prompts for additional information), commas (to separate arguments), and a closed bracket.

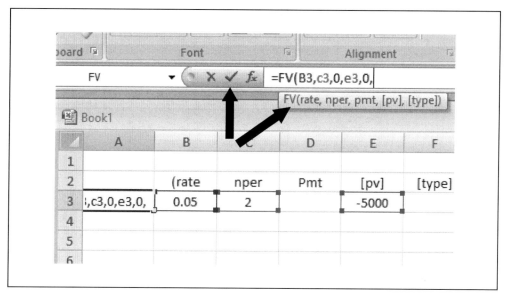

Figure 5.10 Future value with Excel

In the example above, we can assume that Jane Booker has $5,000 today (PV) and that she is looking for a 5 percent return over two years or two payment periods. By typing FV and an open bracket in the formula bar, Excel provides guidance for entering the required information in a predetermined sequence. When dealing with multiple payments in a year, it is important to make an adjustment to the number of payments and time. For example, two payments in a year over a two-year period should give 4 *nper* and not 2. Similarly, the interest rate must be divided by 2.

In the illustration above, Excel is asking for the rate, number of payment periods, payments, present value, and type of annuity). It should be noted that not all the requested information is necessary for the computation of Jane Booker's future value amount. Therefore, the zeros indicate redundant information. It is recommended that you enter interest rates as decimals in Excel. There is no payment in the case, because the problem is not an annuity problem that requires a stream of payments to be made or received at regular intervals.

The present value amount is negative because it is a cash outflow in search of return at a later date and the problem is not a beginning or ending annuity issue. Invariably, when payment is zero, the type of annuity must also be zero. If the type of annuity is not selected, Excel will default to an ordinary annuity. Cell references have been used to appropriately identify the arguments in the formula bar. To complete the calculation, close the open bracket and click on the check button as shown on Figure 5.10. Excel should return a solution of $5,512.50. Jane Booker should receive $5,512.50 in nominal terms. An alternative but laborious way to compute time value problems in Excel is to use the

Table 5.7 Future value interest factors

n	1%	2%	3%	4%	5%	6%	7%	8%	9%	10%
1	1.01	1.02	1.03	1.04	1.05	1.06	1.07	1.08	1.09	1.1
2	1.0201	1.0404	1.0609	1.0816	1.1025	1.1236	1.1449	1.1664	1.1881	1.21

dropdown arrow after selecting a cell for the solution, choose more functions, and select the financial category.

To use the financial tables, the appropriate table must first be identified, because the tables provide interest factor values for different financial calculations. For example, Future Value Interest Factors (FVIF$_{i,n}$) with the corresponding interest rate and number of payment periods, the Future Value Interest Factors for Annuities (FVIFA$_{i,n}$), also with the relevant interest rate and number of payment periods, and the present value equivalents (PVIF$_{i,n}$ and PVIFA$_{i,n}$). Annuity tables must be used with precaution, because it might be important to separate beginning annuities from ordinary annuities. Analogously, FVIF$_{i,n}$ must not be confused with FVIFA$_{i,n}$. As with all procedures, adjustments must be made for multiple payments within a year. In our Jane Booker example, we need the Future Value Interest Factor for 5 percent and 2 years. That is:

FV = $5000 (FVIF$_{5,2}$) → 5000(1.1025) = $5512.5. The solution is consistent with that of Excel.

Financial calculators, Excel, and financial tables can be used to solve most of the problems in economics, and virtually all problems that are associated with the time value of money. The next section will discuss the net present value of money as a foundation for its application later on in the chapter.

5.5 (F) THE NET PRESENT VALUE (NPV) OF MONEY

There are times when money spent today (cash outflow) should be evaluated against prospective cash inflows to make a determination as to whether the spending is wise or profitable. On such occasions, the net present value of spending or an investment (PV-outlay) must be estimated. Investments that do not have a positive net present value must be rejected because the present value of the anticipated cash flows will be less than the initial outlay. Equation 5.36 defines the net present value of an investment, which is simply the difference between the discounted cash flows to be received and the initial investment, cash outflow, or current cost.

$$NPV = +\sum_{t=1}^{N} \frac{C_1}{(1+r)^2} + \frac{C_2}{(1+r)^2} + \cdots \frac{C_N}{(1+r)^N} - Co \qquad (5.36)$$

Intuitively, a project is only viable when the net present value is positive. That is, the sum of discounted cash flows to be received in the future must be greater than the current cost. A project should never be accepted when its NPV is negative. The NPV can be easily estimated by using an Excel spreadsheet. The procedures for estimating the net present value with a calculation and Excel spreadsheet is provided below (see Table 5.8 and Figure 5.11).

Table 5.8 Net present value with financial calculator and Excel (cells in parenthesis)

Financial calculator	INPUT function	Excel	Excel
10000 (±)Cf_0		=NPV(A1,A2:A6)+A7	=IRR (D1:D6)
2000 CF 1		(A1) = r = 0.1	(D1) -10000
2000 CF 2	2000 INPUT 2 CF	(A2) 2000	(D2) 2000
4000 CF 3		(A3) 2000	(D3) 2000
4000 CF 4	4000 INPUT 2 CF	(A4) 4000	(D4) 4000
5000 CF 5		(A5) 4000	(D5) 4000
10, I/YR		(A6) 5000	(D6) 5000
		(A7) -10000	
NPV	$2,312.99	=NPV(r,A2:A6)+A7	=IRR (D1:D6)
IRR	17.30%		17%

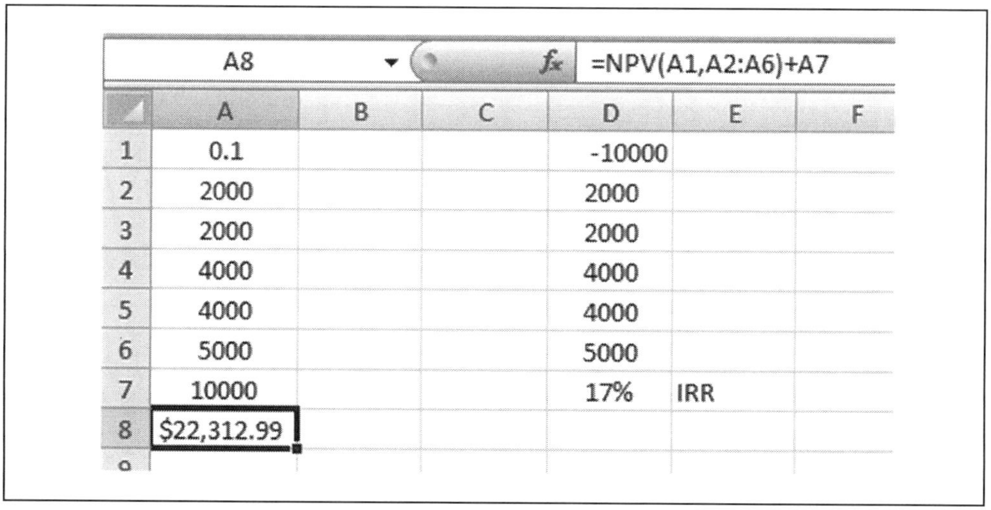

	A	B	C	D	E	F
1	0.1			-10000		
2	2000			2000		
3	2000			2000		
4	4000			4000		
5	4000			4000		
6	5000			5000		
7	10000			17%	IRR	
8	$22,312.99					

A8 f_x =NPV(A1,A2:A6)+A7

Figure 5.11 Net present value and IRR with Excel

The financial calculator is a bit tedious, because the series of prospective cash inflows have to be entered systematically. The initial cost $10,000 must be entered first as an outflow. All discounted flows must be entered orderly and not in a randomized form. On occasions when adjacent amounts are identical, the INPUT button can be used to minimize repetitive entries. The example above shows that $2,000 and $4,000 are expected to sequentially occur twice. After all entries have been made, the shift button can be used to determine the NPV and IRR. Obviously, the calculator will be less suitable for a very large number of cash flows. The Excel protocol barely requires referencing the cells of initial cost and projected flows in the formula bar to compute the NPV and IRR. It must be noted that the initial cost must be entered last for NPV computation and first for IRR computation in Excel. The example shows that for a current cost of $10,000, the subsequent anticipated flows, and a discount rate of 10 percent, the NPV is $2,312.99. The project can be accepted, because the NPV is positive.

The IRR is critical for evaluating a range of acceptable discount rates for an investment. It is occasionally referred to as the "hurdle rate." In this context, the "hurdle rate" simply means that the discount rate cannot exceed 17 percent for the project to be acceptable. It is called an IRR because its value is contingent on the cash flows that are associated with specific projects or investments, and it is the discount rate for which the net present value of an investment is zero. That is, the discounted cash flows minus initial cost is zero:

$$IRR \rightarrow \sum_{t=1}^{N} \frac{C_1}{(1+r)^{t-1}} + \frac{C_2}{(1+r)^2} + \cdots \frac{C_N}{(1+r)^N} - C_0 = 0 \qquad (5.37)$$

The IRR is not dependent on the Fed funds rate, discount rate, or macroeconomic performance. Rather, it is dependent on projected cash flows. A variant of the concept, net asset value (NAV), will be introduced in Chapter 7 (in the context of antitrust damages).

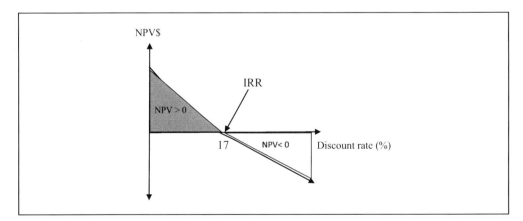

Figure 5.12 The internal rate of return

5.6 PUTTING IT ALL TOGETHER: THE *MOORESVILLE HONDA CASE* AND WORK LIFE EXPECTANCY

The interface of regression analysis and the time value of money can be found in the *Mooresville Honda Case*, which was a case about bribery, kickbacks, corruption, diverted cars, lost revenue, and damages. Throughout the 1980s, Honda cars were in short supply, and consumers were willing to pay a premium in excess of sticker/market prices. Dealers who had enough Hondas to sell, particularly the most popular models, were guaranteed robust sales and wealth. Many Honda dealers who wanted to be assured that they would receive adequate supply of the best cars from the factory were more than willing to shower Honda executives with gifts.

About one-third of the nation's 1,000 Honda dealers, the so-called "dirty dealers," participated in the bribery scheme by offering corrupt cash payments (of as much as $800,000), Rolex watches, home improvements, shopping sprees in Hong Kong, golf memberships, college tuition, and luxurious vacations. As the bribery became more widespread, the Honda executives became increasingly greedy. Some chief executives lived like millionaires though they were not paid a million dollars. "At American Honda, they don't pay you a million dollars, but you can live like a millionaire" (Lynch, 1997, p. 2).

Mooresville Honda Company, one of the "clean dealers," suffered losses because it did not participate in the bribery scheme. Cars were diverted from the company, and the diversion had multiple effects. Sales of used cars declined, revenue from parts and services also declined, and the company lost revenue. Mooresville sued American Honda Motor Co., Inc. to recover lost profits (damages) from 1980 to 1992. The company had to estimate losses associated with new car sales, used car sales, and parts and services. Honda was found guilty of racketeering, conspiracy, fraud, and obstruction of justice.

Regression was used for multiple estimates, including: (i) sales-related income and each expense category associated with new car sales, (ii) units of used car sales on units of new car sales, (iii) historical amounts for sales-related income and cost categories on used car sales, and (iv) number of service orders written on total new and used car sales. After the estimates were derived, the present value of damages was then determined. The regression models were helpful, but they were not without challenges.

The data points of 13 observations are rather limited. It would have been interesting to analyze monthly data with seasonal sales. It was also presumed that the errors were not correlated. The case also underscored the importance of discounting. Unlike some of the other cases that had been previously discussed, the discount rate was legislated to be 8 percent at the time of the trial in New York.

One of the specification issues, which is also an operationalization issue, is whether new car sales could have been denominated in units rather than cash to determine lost sales. If dollars of cost are regressed against dollars of sales, possible biases could have resulted in the regression results, because of price variations over a thirteen-year period during which the illegal act was conducted. Serial correlations are likely to be greater when dollars are used. Consequently, the experts used unit sales of new cars as an independent variable when necessary.

Although parameter estimates are unbiased in the presence of serial correlation, diagnostic tests are more likely to indicate that a coefficient is statistically significant when it is not. In their regressions, the experts used a low cut-off metric to determine statistical significance (0.025 one-tail), so that it is less likely that they will assume that a relationship is present when there is not.

It was extremely difficult to estimate the cost of equity (CoE), because Mooresville Honda was not a publicly traded company. Market prices per share could not be established to determine the expectations of stockholders. In this imperfect setting, the average long-run accounting rate of return generated by total assets provides a proxy for automobile dealers. Others have suggested a defendant's debt rate, the opportunity cost of an investment in assets with comparable risk.[31] When one party incurs costs (losses) due to the actions of another party, the relevant alternative investment of comparable risk is a loan to the responsible party for which interest must be paid. The risk-free rate could also be applied as a conservative lower bound for award of damages.[32]

A discussion of earning capacity and work life expectancy is essential to complete a discussion of the relevance of present value to forensic economics. The concept of work life must be separated from the natural lifespan of an individual. Work life is the active span of employment of an individual and earning capacity is what an individual is capable of earning absent any form of illegal impediment. In terms of earning capacity, some experts have looked at the market forces of supply and demand.[33]

The supply side takes into consideration what a member of the labor force is able and willing to do for a given wage rate, where ability is a function of the member's capacities. What the member is willing to do for a given wage rate is a function of his/her preferences, which are difficult to measure directly. The determination of preference is a fundamental problem with the measurement of earning capacity based on observation of past earnings.

The demand side is contingent on the probabilities of a person actually finding work at given wage rates, and the probabilities are relevant to the question of whether an economic projection of future earnings has a reliable foundation that is not speculative. Actual earnings are more discernible but difficult to forecast. The stream of actual earnings, it is argued, is a series of outcomes of complex stochastic processes involving the interaction of a person's abilities and preferences with employers' needs (a random variable). Some courts have held that loss of actual earnings is the standard that applies to past losses, while earning capacity is the standard that applies to future earnings.

Earning capacity has some interesting properties. It is not usually affected by voluntary or non-binding choices. Consequently, a preference for leisure over work may not necessarily be a probative issue when the latent or unused ability is still available.[34] This is because the higher paying job (maximum option) is a distinct option that can be exercised. On the contrary, the estimation of expected earnings warrants consideration of latent capabilities. When maximum possible earnings is used as a standard for earning capacity, nebulous concepts can be used to inflate earnings potential of individuals based on pure speculation. This is normally driven by a preference-capacity dichotomy.

The law recognizes earning capacity as "the ability to earn money" and "impairment of earning capacity" is "a diminution or loss of the ability to earn money."[35] Since earning capacity cannot be calculated with mathematical precision, judges and jurors are afforded discretion in the determination of earning capacity within reasonable bounds.[36] Although some courts may not rely on the historical past as a basis for earning capacity, some may require actual earnings or earning capacity prior to injury (see *Crown Plumbing Inc. v. Petrozak* (Tex. Ct. App., 1988)).

Vocational experts, like rehabilitation counselors, and forensic economists have become relevant to earnings cases when historical references are inadequate and when prospective employment is contingent on mental and physical abilities. Education, health, psychological condition, and age are believed to be supply-side indicators that must be considered against the state of an industry and potential for employment.

However, even when the loss of actual earnings is the standard applied to past earnings, courts may hear arguments about a post-injury latent capacity—a situation where an injured person decides not to work to enhance the value of a lawsuit. Attempts to divide actual past losses into the part caused by choice and the part caused by the injury, suggests that the true standard was loss of earning capacity, even in the past.[37] Brookshire and others (2007) find that many economists will simply use past earnings as a proxy for earning capacity in order to avoid wild speculation.

Clearly stated intentions in cases of frictional unemployment, recent improvements in qualification, and work history are mitigating considerations for the determination of earning capacity. As such, baseline income may only be a reasonable starting point. In cases of injury or death, the expected life span of a victim is extremely important. Yet a distinction must be made between the time that a victim is supposed to live and the time that he/she is expected to work before leaving the labor force.

The US labor force consists of those who are working and those who are actively looking for work. Discouraged workers are not usually factored into consideration. To estimate the work life of victims, work life tables are routinely used to compute the probability of someone staying in the workforce for a specific period of time and work life tables may not be summarily dismissed (see *Marcel v. Placid Oil*, 11 F. 3d 563, United States Court of Appeals (5th Cir. 1994)).

The Horner-Slesnick paradigm for earning capacity (before present value estimation) suggests two broad principles: (i) identification of jobs to match pre- and post-injury capacity, and (ii) providing usable information about available jobs. These broad principles have intrinsic concepts: a workable definition of earning capacity—the expected earnings of a worker who chooses to maximize the expectation of actual earnings to minimize ambiguous mathematical calculations (with unknown probabilities of achieving a particular job), consistency of measurement applicable to pre- and post-injury calculations, functional capacity (mental and physical ability), vocational capacity (training and/or length of training), history, maximum earning capacity, probability of earning or job acquisition, minimum capacity (minimum wage floor), age-earnings cycle (probability of deviation from others with similar characteristics), and work life expectancy.[38]

The Bureau of Labor Statistics (BLS) has provided estimates of work life over periods of time, with periodic variations. However, current socioeconomic conditions are complicating the stability of the data. Current trends in suicides, opioid use, and homicides are currently affecting labor force participation rates, employment, earnings capacity, and work life expectancy. The BLS estimates incorporates labor force attachments over time that are affected by attributes such as age, sex, race, education, children, marital status, health, and occupation.

5.7 CHI SQUARE ANALYSIS

Unlike regression analysis, chi square is a nonparametric test. That is, it is not designed to estimate the true value of a population attribute. It is therefore suitable for analyzing small samples and relationships of nominal or categorical variables. However, if a random variable x is normally distributed, then that variable can form a chi square distribution for samples of any size:

$$X^2 = \frac{(n-1)s^2}{\sigma^2};$$

(5.38)

where n is for the number of observations, s^2 is for the sample variance, and β is for the population variance.

The chi square distribution is a family of curves that are defined by degrees of freedom. The larger the degrees of freedom, the more dispersed is the chi square distribution. Chi square values are equal to zero or always positive and the confidence interval for variance have degrees of freedom of one less the number of categories, $(k-1)$, for single-variable experiments, or $(r-1)(c-1)$ for test of independence between two variables; where r is for the number of rows, and c is for the number of columns. The chi square distribution is positively skewed, but like the normal distribution, the area under each curve of the chi square distribution is equal to one.

Beyond categorical or nominal attributes, the chi square test may also be used for interval and ratio data. Notwithstanding the actual scaling, the raw data must be of mutually exclusive categories and the frequencies must be in well-defined units before X^2 can be used. The researcher or analyst must first calculate a chi square test statistic, which must be evaluated against a critical value and an alpha level (the level of hypothesis test) provided in the chi square table in the appendix, before a chi square test can be conducted.

The objective of a properly constituted hypothesis test is to reject the hypothesis—the hypothesis of independence that the attributes or values are **not** significantly related or different. This can be done by evaluating the chi square statistic that has been computed against the critical chi square in the chi square table. Traditionally, the level of confidence is 95 percent, which means that researchers are willing to tolerate no more than 5 percent error (0.05). Of course, the level of confidence is not sacrosanct and individual researchers might use the much less stringent measure of 90 percent. In fact, it is not uncommon to use the 90 percent level of confidence, in which case a ten percent error (0.10) is accommodated.

An investigator can reject a hypothesis, or "fail to reject" a hypothesis, depending on the results of his/her test statistic and the level on which hypothesis tests are conducted. A common mistake is to claim that a hypothesis is "accepted." Although failure to reject can inadvertently be misconstrued as "accepting" a hypothesis, it must be remembered that hypotheses are tests defined by statistical probabilities and not facts. Of course, the difference is a technicality. Rejecting a hypothesis when in fact the researcher should fail to reject causes a Type I error

(α) and failing to reject a null hypothesis when it should be rejected leads to a Type II error (β). The correct decisions about the averages are $(1-\alpha,)$ and $(1-\beta)$ respectively. The obtained chi square statistic from the raw data takes the following form:

$$X^2_{ob} = \sum \left[\frac{(f_o - f_e)^2}{f_e} \right];$$

(5.39)

where f_o is the actual or reported frequency, f_e is the expected frequency that has to be calculated from row and column marginals, and sigma is the summation operator that informs the researcher that the summation of the ratio must be computed.

It must be immediately noted that the expected frequencies for a single-variable experiment is identical for each cell. This is because the average of all values is evenly distributed as expected frequency for a single-variable experiment. This will be made clearer in the ensuing illustration.

The first step to calculating the test statistic is to create a contingency table, which divides the variables into mutually exclusive categories with their actual frequencies in each cell. This makes it easy to add up the rows and columns to get the marginals. Once the test statistic has been calculated, the null of independence must be rejected if the calculated or obtained chi square is greater than or equal to the critical chi square on a chi square table. That is, the null must be rejected if and only if (iff):

$$X^2_{ob} \geq X^2_{crit} \quad [\text{Reject Ho}] \tag{5.40}$$

The chi square algorithm was once applied to a case of vanishing female jurors. In a case that made its way to the US Court of Appeals for the First Circuit in the 1960s, the defendant used chi square to challenge the proposition that there was no bias in jury selection. This case is illustrative, and it has data for further practice. The defendant was acquitted on the basis of First Amendment rights and not necessarily on the basis of the statistical evidence. However, the statistical evidence in the case provides a valuable insight into the litigation of bias and discrimination under any circumstance.

As the Vietnam War loomed in the 1960s, a number of academic, clerical, and professional persons discussed the need for more vigorous opposition to governmental policies in August 1967. A document titled "A Call to Resist Illegitimate Authority" came from the consolidated effort of vigorous opposition with a cover letter requesting signatures and support. The letter was signed by defendants Dr. Benjamin Spock and defendant Rev. William Sloane Coffin, Jr.

Dr. Benjamin Spock, a well-known pediatrician and child development author, and his associates were charged with conspiring to violate the Military Service Act of 1967 and put on trial in 1968, but in Dr. Spock's trial, there was no female juror, though the jury pool was supposed to have been constituted by random draws during preliminary processes.

In the Boston District Court of his time, jurors were selected in three stages. The police of the court's district compile a list of eligible jurors. The clerk of the court then selected 300 names at random from the city directory and put a slip with each of these names into a box.[39] From this box, the clerk then drew a venire of jurors who were then ordered to appear in court on the day of the trial (the process by which jurors are summoned, or a jury pool).

In Dr. Spock's trial, this sample included only 102 women, although 53 percent of the eligible jurors in the district were female. At the next stage, the judge selected 30 or more names from those in the box, which constituted the venire The trial judge drew

100 potential jurors out of these 300 people, but his choices included only nine women. In the final analysis, only 12 actual jurors were selected after interrogation by both the prosecutor and the defense counsel, and only one potential female juror came before the court.

Apparently, the female was dismissed by the prosecution; meaning that there was no female juror for Dr. Spock's trial. In actual fact, the 1960 census compiled by the US Department of Commerce showed that there were roughly 1,721,000 women over the age of 21 and 1,524,000 men over the age of 21 in the district.[40] Dr. Spock was convicted on charges of conspiracy to violate the Selective Service Act by encouraging young men to avoid the draft. Was Dr. Spock denied the right to be tried by females (jury of his peers) who were well acquainted with his work?

His lawyers filed an appeal and argued that the trial judge had a history of venires in which women were systematically underrepresented. They compared the gender breakdown of the judge's venires with the venires of six other judges in the same Boston court from a then recent sample of court cases shown in Table 5.9. The table reports the frequency obtained (f_o) for the venires of seven judges over a two-year period in the Boston court, including that of the trial judge. It should be recalled that the ultimate challenge was to use the data to show by statistical analysis that the venires of the trial judge differed significantly from those of his colleagues in terms of the representation of women. The chi square test became a very valuable tool for evaluating bias.

The case is an evident reminder of the role of statistics and econometrics in forensic analysis. Writing in the late 1960s, Zeisel (1969) states:

> Proof by statistical inference is not unknown to our courts. As a rule it comes up in the simple form of sampling operations from which inferences are urged about the populations from which the sample was drawn: sample surveys from which to estimate market shares in anti-trust litigation; quality samples from produce, or from mineral fields from which to estimate the quality of the whole. This type of inference is now fairly well established in the law, although at times it runs into the barrier of the hearsay rule if the sample properties have been obtained by personal interviews. There is also another, more complicated, type of statistical inference that occasionally reaches the courts. It may be based on sampling operations, but it need not be. Its ultimate aim is not the measurement of a population, but proof of an individual event.[41]

In this example we will compare the male representation with the female representation in the suspect venires of the trial judge. The objective is to test the hypothesis that the male representation in the venires of the trial judge is not significantly different from the female representation. This test will be conducted with the probability of 5 percent error. It must be noted that this is a single-variable experiment. Refer to the data in Table 5.9.

Table 5.9 Venires of district judges in Boston (1966–1968)*

Date	Judge A Male	Judge A Female	Venires	Date	Judge B Male	Judge B Female	Venires
May-67	27	18	45	May-66	35	20	55
Sep-67	35	15	50	Oct-66	41	19	60
Feb-68	38	7	45	Jan-67	45	21	66
Apr-68	26	14	40	Aug-67	40	15	55
Sep-68	23	23	46	Apr-68	40	16	56
Total	149	77	226	Oct-68	34	28	62
				Total	235	119	354

Date	Judge C Male	Judge C Female	Venires	Date	Judge D Male	Judge D Female	Venires
Oct-66	33	17	50	Apr-66	38	12	50
Jan-67	35	15	50	May-66	43	18	61
Feb-67	34	16	50	Total	81	30	111
Apr-67	25	10	35				
Sep-67	38	12	50				
Nov-67	36	14	50				
Sep-68	44	11	55				
Oct-68	42	23	65				
Total	287	118	405				

Date	Judge E Male	Judge E Female	Venires	Date	Judge F Male	Judge F Female	Venires
Sep-66	47	23	70	May-66	55	15	70
Nov-66	35	20	55	Sep-66	63	17	80
Jan-67	51	20	71	Nov-66	48	22	70
Mar-67	41	10	51	Mar-67	51	19	70
Sep-67	37	8	45	May-67	58	12	70
Nov-67	136	44	200	Oct-67	50	20	70
Sep-68	36	24	60	Jun-68	59	21	80
Total	383	149	552	Jun-68	67	28	95
				Sep-68	82	43	125
				Total	533	197	730

(continued)

Table 5.9 Cont.

Date	Trial judge Male	Trial judge Female	Venires
May-66	42	8	50
Sep-66	42	8	50
Jan-67	43	7	50
May-67	50	3	53
Oct-67	41	9	50
Mar-68	110	19	129
Mar-68	59	11	70
May-68	91	9	100
Oct-68	34	11	45
Total	512	85	597

Source: *The University of Chicago Law Review* (1969), 39(1), 4–5.
Note:
*Author's calculation of gender count from female percentages.

Step 1: Load the data (frequency obtained) into Excel in mutually exclusive categories (other software programs may be used, but Excel is the preferred program here).

Trial Judge		
Males	Females	Total
512	85	597

Step 2: Calculate the expected frequencies as (597/2) and distribute them evenly between males and females (2 categories).

Trial Judge		
Males	Females	Total
f_o 512	f_o 85	597
f_e (298.5)	f_e (298.5)	(597)

Step 3: Find the difference between the frequencies obtained and the expected frequencies for males and females. Square the differences and divide by the expected frequencies for each category.

Males

f_o	f_e	$f_o - f_e$	$(f_o - f_e)^2$	$\dfrac{(f_o - f_e)^2}{f_e}$
512	298.5	213.5	45582.25	152.7044

Females

f_o	f_e	$f_o - f_e$	$(f_o - f_e)^2$	$\dfrac{(f_o - f_e)^2}{f_e}$
85	298.5	-213.5	45582.25	152.7044

$$X^2_{ob} = \sum \left[\frac{(f_o - f_e)^2}{f_e} \right] = \text{males} \frac{(f_o - f_e)^2}{f_e} + \text{females} \frac{(f_o - f_e)^2}{f_e} = 305.4087 > X^2_c \; 3.841.$$

We reject H_o for df = 2 categories minus 1, $(K - 1) = 1$ and α level = 0.05 (see chi square table A5.6 at the back of the text to check that the critical chi square = 3.841). The hypothesis that the venires are not significantly different is rejected because the obtained X^2_{ob} is greater than the critical X^2_c. As a result, there is statistical evidence at the 95 percent level of confidence to show that females were underrepresented in the venires of the trial judge.

Actually, a cursory examination of the data will reveal that it was not entirely unusual for females to be underrepresented in the venires of all the judges. Critically estimate the data to arrive at an independent conclusion. We will close this chapter of econometrics in the courtroom by taking a look at the valuation of public companies.

5.8 THE INTRINSIC VALUE OF PUBLIC COMPANIES

Valuation of businesses is a challenging proposition; especially when companies are not classified as publicly traded companies. Information about publicly traded companies is usually available because securities law mandate transparency when companies deal with the public to raise funds and invest. Intrinsic valuation is based on the present value of the discounted cash flows of a company. Therefore, intrinsic valuation of a company is based on its own performance, including its exposure to risk, and not the performance of markets or comparable companies.

Evaluators may focus on the value of a firm (enterprise valuation) or the amount of equity that a firm commands. When the objective is to value a company, existing investments and growth potential (assets) are considered. On the contrary, when the objective is to value the equity of a business, then debt is subtracted from the value of the business. The value of a business is:

$$V_F = A_t + A_{t+1} \tag{5.41}$$

where V_F is for the value of a firm, A_t is for the assets today, and A_{t+1} are for the assets that will generate returns tomorrow (growth assets). Value must be discounted if the equity option is not the desired outcome. Alternatively, the value of equity (V_E) is:

$$V_E = A_t + A_{t+1} - D; \tag{5.42}$$

where D is for the debt of the firm. That is, V_E gives the value of the shares of the company. Since cash is king, knowing the value of cash flow is critical to valuing a company. Therefore, net cash flow from assets must be determined. Net cash flow (NCF) is cash flow minus reinvestment needs (IR) and tax liability (T):

$$NCF = CF - (I_R + T) \tag{5.43}$$

In addition to NCF, it is also important to know the growth rate of the cash flow into the future (ΔCF), the cost of financing assets that generate the cash flow (CoA), and the value of the firm at a terminal period (FV_F).

$$V_F = NCF + \Delta CF + CoA + FV_F \tag{5.44}$$

A very good proxy of the cash flow of a public company is its dividend payments. However, as Damodaran (2011) noted, many companies are using stock buybacks for returning cash to stockholders rather than dividends.[42] An augmentation approach, whereby stock buybacks should be combined with dividend payments while controlling (averaging) for volatility of buybacks can be considered. It is not very evident that by buying back shares, public companies are meeting their operating and reinvestment needs. Share purchases are psychologically consoling, and they reduce the tax exposure of shareholders. Share repurchases are considered signaling effects. Share repurchases suggest that shares are undervalued, and that management does not have to pay down outstanding debts. The repurchases also signal that a company's management is reasonably confident about future cash inflows and that the management will not spend cash on value-destroying investments. In the final analysis, the repurchases reduce the tax liability of investors but do not create intrinsic value, since the PE ratio drops by the same percentage. In effect, the repurchases do not clearly express long-term commitments.[43]

The amount of cash left over after taxes, reinvestment, and debt cash flows can be estimated by the free cash flow to equity (FCFE):

$$FCFE = NI + Dep - KE - \Delta NCWC - ND; \tag{5.45}$$

where NI is net income, Dep is depreciation (capital consumption allowance), KE is capital expenditure (a cash outflow), $\Delta NCWC$ is change in non-cash working capital, and ND is the difference between principal repayments (cash outflows and new debt issues (cash inflows).

Equation 5.45 estimates excess cash after all expenditures are met. A positive FCFE is indicative of potential dividend payment; when negative, the FCFE suggests that there is a cash fall that might require the infusion of new equity.

Equation 5.45 can alternatively be rewritten as:

$$FCFE = NI - NKE - \Delta NCWC + D, \tag{5.46}$$

where NKE is for net capital expenditure, and D is for new debt, an indicator of investment in long-term assets.[44] Reinvestment is the difference between capital expenditure and depreciation (KE-Dep), while total reinvestment (TRI) is:

$$TRI = NKE + \Delta NCWC. \tag{5.47}$$

Non-cash working capital (NCWC) excludes cash from the computation of working capital. It is the difference between the sum of all current assets and all current liabilities (excluding cash). The change is compared to a reference period. The $\Delta NCWC$ is important to understand how much working capital a business will require to support ongoing operations. The cash flow to a company is the cash flow before interest and debt payments. That is, after taxes and reinvestment allotments.[45]

The desired starting point for estimating cash flow to a public company is operating earnings rather than net income. Therefore, FCFE and free cash flow to the firm (FCFF) are different because of the underlying financial statements that are used in their computations.

$$FCFF = OIAT - (NKE + \Delta NCWC); \tag{5.48}$$

where OIAT is operating income after taxes. The Reinvestment rate (R_r) becomes:

$$R_r = \frac{NKE + \Delta NCWC}{OIAT} \tag{5.49}$$

Combining Equation 5.48 and Equation 5.49 it can be seen that the FCFF = $1 - R_r$. When firms reinvest more than they earn, the reinvestment rate can exceed 100 percent, or it could be less than zero when firms divest themselves of capital.[46]

All valuations consider the risk exposures of businesses. A firm's risk is measured by the risk of its operations. On the other hand, equity valuation is highly contingent on the nature of a firm's investment exposure and how much debt is required to manage the business. The indebtedness of a firm is an attribute of risk. Equity exposure is usually estimated by the cost of equity, while the exposure of a business is normally measured by the cost of capital. In this case, cost is a measurement of enticement, because it is contingent on the price that will entice investors to buy the debt or equity of a firm (the required return).

The cost of equity can be estimated by three factors: (i) a risk-free rate (alluded to earlier on), (ii) a price of risk (occasionally measured as a spread between the market rate of return and the risk-free rate or equity risk premium (ERP)), and (iii) a relative risk or beta. The CAPM is usually utilized as a measure of relative risk, but it is based on historical data and an assumption that errors are normally distributed with zero mean and constant variance. Some scholars propose using the average of beta that is industry specific as opposed to the regression beta.[47] Hence the cost of equity can be estimated as:

$$CoE = R_f + \beta \star ERP. \tag{5.50}$$

To cover default risk, lenders may include a default spread (ds) (the difference between risky and riskless returns on bonds with similar maturity) to the riskless rate, the size of which will vary with the probability of default. Rating agencies like Moody's and Standard and Poor (S&P) provide quotes for default spread based on bond rating. Bond ratings or interest coverage ratios (operating income to interest expense) can provide helpful information about default spread. The after-tax cost of debt (ATCoD) is then computed as:

$$ATCoD = R_f + ds \star (1 - MRT); \tag{5.51}$$

where MRT is for the marginal tax rate and CoK is for the cost of capital:

$$CoK = CoE\left(\frac{MVE}{MVE + D}\right) + ATCoD\left(\frac{MVE}{MVE + D}\right); \tag{5.52}$$

where MVE is for the market value of equity, and D is for the value of debt.

Will the weights remain constant? The question is rather tricky because time horizon is important, delineating the variables of interests is important, and the velocity of change is equally important. Growth rates can be volatile when they are not constant as time progresses. Some analysts might want to use geometric mean rather than arithmetic mean.[48] Additionally, the quality and type of earnings to be evaluated are also important. Should net income, EPS, or operating income be used to measure growth of earnings?

In making a decision, the choice between equity and the operations of the firm is still relevant, and the quality and type of investment will have to be related to that choice. If equity is preferred, the return on equity (ROE) is generally a very good indicator of the quality of equity. It should also be noted that the ROE can be defined as a product of a profitability ratio, asset turnover ratio, and equity multiplier when it is decomposed accordingly (see the DuPont identity). The product of the ROE and retention ratio gives a reasonable indicator of the growth of net income, which can also be defined as stable growth.[49] Stable growth indicates the maximum rate at which revenues can grow without a firm issuing new equity or debt. In which case, retained earnings will suffice to facilitate growth. New debts and retained earnings will stabilize the debt-to-equity ratio. Growth efficiency is an indicator of cost minimization.

When the earnings of a firm are pertinent to valuation, the reinvestment rate, operating income, and return on capital are critical indicators of the growth potential of a firm. The product of reinvestment rate and return on capital will give the growth of operating income. Essentially, the growth in earnings is the product of the proportion that is invested and the return on investment. The growth of operating income can then be used to project actual sales for a given time horizon. For example, suppose the growth of operating income is 5 percent, the value of a firm's FCFF that is worth $5 can be projected over a period of four years.

ATOI is after-tax operating income, R_r is the reinvestment rate, and FCFF is the free cash flow to the firm. It must be noted that R_r is not the stable reinvestment rate that is required to estimate terminal value (TV). This is because it is assumed that there will be no excess return in the terminal period.

The stable reinvestment rate (sR$_r$) is the growth of the nth year FCFF (which is different from the growth estimate of operating income) divided by the cost of capital CoK. Consider the hypothetical illustration:

$$sR_r = \frac{g_T}{CoK} = \frac{2\%}{6\%} = 33\%$$

Stable reinvestment growth is usually less ambitious and consistent with the nominal growth rate of an economy. Therefore, the product of the retention ratio and the ROE, which can by definition be considered stable, may not necessarily be good enough to measure the terminal growth rate. Since no firm can grow faster than the economy in which it operates, it is generally suggested that the sustainable rate should not exceed the risk-free rate that is used in valuation.

The risk-free rate consists of expected inflation and the real rate (see the Fisher Equation that was discussed earlier), and it is expected that the nominal rate should correspond to the growth of an economy in the long run.[50] Koller, Goedhart, and Wessels (2010) vividly capture the limitations of growth in terms of the *S-curve* (natural life cycles of products). Initially, a successful product appeals to early adopters. After the initial appeal, sales accelerate to a point of maximum penetration. Immediately thereafter, and depending on the nature of the product, the growth of sales can either decelerate to the growth rate of the population of an economy, or sales might start to shrink.[51]

Therefore, the risk-free rate can be a proxy of terminal growth. Suppose cost of capital is 6 percent, and terminal growth is 2 percent, ABC's terminal value as a going concern can be estimated as follows:

$$TV = \frac{AToIyr5(1-sR_r)}{CoK - g_T}, \tag{5.53}$$

$$TV = \frac{3.94(1-.33)}{0.06-0.02} = \$66.$$

The terminal value should then be discounted together with the FCFF in Table 5.10.

Table 5.10 Expected free cash flow of ABC

	Actual ($m)	Year 1	Year 2	Year 3	Year 4	Growth
ATOI	5	5.25	5.51	5.788125	6.0775	5%
R$_r$ (35%)		1.8375	1.9285	2.02615	2.1273	
FCFF		3.4125	3.5815	3.76285	3.9507	

$$PV = \frac{CF_1}{1+CoK} + \frac{CF_2}{(1+CoK)^2} + \frac{CF_3}{(1+coK)^3} + \frac{(CF_4 + TV)}{(1+CoK)^4}$$

$$PV = \frac{4.13}{1+.06} + \frac{4.34}{(1.06)^2} + \frac{4.56}{(1.06)^3} + \frac{(3.93 + 66)}{(1.06)^4} = \$67$$

Discounting FCFE on a per share basis at cost of equity should yield value per share (see Damodaran, 2011, p. 55).

The terminal value of the assets of a firm can be computed as if the firm is either going out of business (liquidated value) or continuing to stay in business (going concern). When the liquidation option is preferred, the market values of the real estate and estimates can be used to appraise the assets. If the assets of a firm can be utilized into the distant future (going concern), then it is assumed that the cash flow of the firm will grow at a constant rate in the distant future.

Valuation with the going concern methodology as outlined above has gained juridical appeal. In *Weinberger v. UOP, Inc.*, (457 A. 2d 701, 713 (Del. 1983)),[52] the Delaware Supreme Court ruled that a more liberal approach must include proof of value by a methodology that is generally valid in the financial community and admissible in the court. Implicitly, the court applied the *Daubert Standard*. The court explained that:

> market value, asset value, dividends, earnings prospects, the nature of the enterprise and any other facts which were known or which could be ascertained as of the date of the merger and which throw any light on future prospects of the merged corporation are not only pertinent to an inquiry as to the value of the dissenting stockholders' interest, but must be considered … .
>
> (Bainbridge, p. 106)

In the years following *Weinberger*, the Delaware Chancery Court has recognized the discounted cash flow valuation method. The steps of the discounted cash flow for valuing a public company as outlined above include: projection of cash flows, the determination of a terminal value, capitalized earnings, a discount rate for discounting cash flows and terminal value, and discounting the projected cash flows and terminal value to the present. Further discussions of firm value and the challenges of valuation across international boundaries will be provided in Chapter 8. The next chapter will look at taxation.

CHAPTER SUMMARY

- Econometrics is the economic methodology for estimating economic variables and models to arrive at scientific econometric conclusions.
- In the 1990s, the US Supreme Court opened the door for expert testimony and scientific evidence to be used in courts of law in order to properly ascertain facts for

dispute resolution. The elevated role of experts arose out of a medical case, *Daubert v. Merrell Dow Pharmaceuticals Inc.*, 509 U.S. 579 (1993).
- A witness who is qualified as an expert by knowledge, skill, experience, training, or education, can testify to: (i) the use of data or quantitative fact, (ii) reliable principles and methods, and (iii) reliable application of methodology to the facts of a case, based on sound theories that are generally accepted and measurable.
- Data provide information about variables, conditions, and the economic circumstances that generate information. Economists refer to the actual underlying circumstances that generate valuable information as the "data generating process."
- Data may take the following forms: (i) time series, (ii) cross-sectional, (iii) panel, and (iv) pooled. Credible data must be collected by random sampling, which may take various forms: (i) cluster, (ii) systematic, and (iii) stratified. Qualitative variables may be given numerical values to become dummy variables.
- Unless a determination is made that variables are cointegrated, reliable forecasts can only be made when data are stationary.
- Cycles are major expansions and contractions that occur every several years. As a result, when sales rise and fall over the course of a week, such a pattern should not be counted as a cycle. A trend shows the general direction of a variable over time even when there are variations in a series.
- Root mean squared error (RMSE) is a measurement of error that gives the number of standard deviation units above the expected value. Other forms of forecast error estimates include the mean squared error (MSE), the mean absolute error (MAE), and the mean absolute percentage error (MAPE).
- Regression is an estimating method that is used to evaluate the relationship between independent variable(s) and dependent variable by minimizing the error sum of squares (ERSS)—ordinary least squares (OLS). It provides the best linear and unbiased estimates when the coefficients of models are linear, variances of the regressors are constant, the errors of the regressors are not correlated, and the most relevant variables are not omitted.
- Money today has more value than money to be received in the future. Therefore, money to be received in the future must be discounted to the present. A stream of payment to be made or received is known as annuity. Annuities may be due or paid at the end of a payment period (ordinary annuity). Amortization schedule breaks down annuity payment into principal and interest components to determine what has been paid and what is owed.
- The net present value is the difference between an initial outlay or investment and the discounted stream of cash flows to be received. Net present value must be positive for worthwhile investments.
- Intrinsic valuation is based on the present value of the discounted cash flows of a company. Therefore, intrinsic valuation of a company is based on its own performance, including its exposure to risk, and not the performance of markets or comparable companies.

KEY WORDS

• Amortization	• FCFE	• Reinvestment rate
• Annuity	• F-stat	• RMSE
• ANCOVA	• Future value	• R-squared
• ANOVA	• Hypothesis	• Seasonality
• Cluster sampling	• Intrinsic value	• Standard deviation
• Cost of capital	• Moving average	• Stationarity
• Cross-sectional data	• Net cash flow	• Stratified sampling
• Cycle	• Net present value	• Stochastic trend
• Daubert Rule	• OLS	• Systematic sampling
• Deterministic trend	• Panel data	• Terminal value
• Dummy variable	• Present value	• Time series
• F-test	• Random sampling	• t-stat

CHAPTER QUESTIONS

1. Critically review and discuss the scientific evidence in the *Daubert v. Merrell Dow Pharmaceuticals Inc.* Is expert testimony important? Why? How do judges perform the role of gatekeepers?
2. Collect monthly data for five years and explain whether there is a deterministic or stochastic trend in the data. Does the data show seasonal patterns? Why? Use your data to generate a univariate forecast. What is the RMSE?
3. Adding two more variables and a time trend to your original data, specify and estimate a regression model. What is the proportion of variation in the independent variable that has been explained (hint: see the R^2)? Are the variables significant? Why? What is the projected one-year forecast of your dependent variable?
4. Suppose you are expecting to receive $600,000 in damages today. Further, imagine that you should have received the money in ten years (your work life expectancy). How much money should a court award you today if the discount rate in your state is 8 percent? Is the discount rate fair? Why?
5. You are planning on making a $100,000 investment today from a trust fund, with the expectation of receiving the following cash flows: $20,000, $30,000, $50,000, $40,000, and $10,000. If your cash flows are discounted to the present at 5 percent, explain why you may or may not invest the money from the trust fund. What is the internal rate of return?
6. Refer to Table 5.9; were the venires of Judge F statistically different from those of the trial judge? Why? [Use the chi square algorithm.]
7. The free cash flow to a public company is $8 million, the growth of operating income is 4 percent for the next five years, and the stable investment rate is 21 percent. If the

firm is projected to grow at a stable rate of 4 percent for the next five years, with a cost of capital of 5 percent and terminal growth of 1.5 percent, estimate the present value of the firm for a law firm. What are the potential problems with your estimate? Is the terminal growth rate modest? Why?

NOTES

1. See Warburton (2019). However, punitive damages are not usually awarded in such cases. Liabilities can be "joint and several;" meaning that the financially sound defendant can be financially responsible for an indigent or financially incapable defendant; see also Budetti and Waters (2005) for state legislation.
2. The case, which started in trial courts, was centered on the issue of whether experts can provide scientific testimony in a case for which children suffered birth defects after their mothers consumed Benedictin (an anti-nausea medication)—a product of Merrell Dow Pharmaceuticals—during pregnancies.
3. Some states have specific standards for medical experts, requiring that they be of the same specialty as the physician being sued, or that the experts must actually be practicing physicians. Experts may be required to have training in diagnosing or treating conditions similar to those of the patient, and they must devote at least 60 percent of their professional time to clinical practice or teaching in their field or specialty (see Budetti & Waters, 2005).
4. See Weil et al. (2007) in *Litigation Services Handbook*, 1.2–1.3; see also Brookshire et al. (2007, 1.12–1.13).
5. See *Daubert v. Merrell Dow Pharmaceuticals* (1993). In this case the Supreme Court provided guidance to federal trial court judges as to how expert testimony can be admitted. Trial judges are granted discretionary power to determine the admissibility of expert testimony; see also Weil et al. (2007), 1.3–1.4.
6. See Thornton and Ward (1999, p. 109).
7. Measurements may take different forms: ratio scale (2/4 or 2 >1.8), interval scale (18–24 years), ordinal scale (upper, middle, and lower income groups), and nominal/attributes (gender, race, and religion). The nominal category is unique, but attributes can be coded numerically for estimation.
8. A unit root process simply means that the current value of a series is a reflection of current disturbances (innovations or errors) the its past value: $Y_t = \rho Y_{t-1} + u_t$, where $\rho=1$. Therefore, the value of a cointegration (unit root) test is to ascertain that ρ is not equal to 1. The cointegration tests by Engle-Granger (1987) and Phillips-Ouliaris (1990) can be utilized to diagnose nonstationarity.
9. $MSE = \dfrac{\sum(Y-\hat{Y})^2_t}{n_{FE}}$, $MAE = \dfrac{\sum|Y_t-\hat{Y}_t|}{n_{FE}}$, and $MAPE = \dfrac{\sum\left|\dfrac{Y_t-\hat{Y}t}{Y_t}\right|}{n_{FE}}$; see Bowerman, O'Connell, and Koehler (2005) for further reading on the multiplicative and additive—constant seasonal—decompositions.
10. Suppose $Y = \alpha_1 + \alpha_2 X + u_t$ and Y_t and X_t are individual I(I) (nonstationary); it can be shown that the linear combination of Y_t and X_t can be said to be stationary if unit root tests can validate $Y_t - \alpha_1 - \alpha_2 X_t = u_t = I(0)$. The stochastic trends will be cancelled and a regression of Y_t on X_t cannot be judged to be spurious.

11 The independent variables are variously referred to as predictor, stimulus, exogenous, and control variables or covariates.
12 The US Constitution gives Congress the power to regulate commerce with foreign nations and among states and Indian Tribes. For example, mail fraud (18 U.S.C. § 1341), wire fraud (18 U.S.C. § 1343), conspiracy (18 U.S.C. § 371), racketeering (18 U.S.C. §§ 1961–1963), bribery (18 U.S.C. § 201), false statements (18 U.S.C. § 1001), obstruction of justice (18 U.S.C. §§ 1501–1521), and tax crimes (26 U.S.C. §§ 7201–7217); see Podgor and Israel (2009, pp. 2–3). Ever since the bifurcated classification of crimes for empirical work in the 1930s, some sociologists and criminologists have focused on polemics (nuanced definitions and controversy), typology, and operations of white-collar criminals.
13 Registered nurses, secretarial and administrative assistants, elementary and middle school teachers, customer service representatives, first-line supervisors of retail sales workers, nursing, psychiatric, and home workers, accountants and editors, office clerks, human resources managers, book-keeping/accounting, actuaries, aerospace engineers, agricultural and food science technicians, appraisers and assessors of real estate, architectural and engineering managers, automotive service technicians and managers, biological Scientists, biological technicians, budget analysts, chemical engineers, chemists and material scientists, chief executives, civil engineers, computer programmers, credit analysts, designers, economists, electricians, financial analysts, and insurance underwriters.
14 Log models should be interpreted in terms of percentage changes. Of course, they may be specified as semi-log models when the dependent variables are in logs or levels relative to the independent variables. Recall that double log models are also known as elasticity models (%Δy/%Δx).
15 See *Harvard Law Review*, 1986, 99(3), 655.
16 The purpose of North Carolina's agricultural extension program, administered through the North Carolina Agricultural Extension Service, was to aid the dissemination of useful and practical information on subjects relating to agriculture and home economics. The Extension Service operated in four major areas: home economics, agriculture, youth, and community resource development.
17 Although researchers are obsessed with omitted variable bias, research by Clarke suggests that there is nothing in the mathematics of regression analysis to suggest that the inclusion of a large number of omitted variables in a regression model can ameliorate the danger of omission. Clark argues that for both OLS and generalized linear models, the inclusion of additional control variables may increase or decrease the bias, and we cannot know for sure which case applies in any particular situation. See Clarke's "Return of the Phantom Menace," *Conflict Management and Peace Science,* 26(1), 46–66.
18 See *Bazemore v. Friday*, 478 U.S. 385 (1986) 478 U.S. 385, by US Supreme Court.
19 The FTC presented econometric study to show that Staples historically passed through reduced cost (savings) to consumers in the form of lower prices where it was in competition with Home Depot. The merging firms countered by arguing that omitted costs were higher in other areas because of exogenous costs associated with the effects of zoning laws and congestion. The FTC argued that the superstore chains engaged in price discrimination by charging lower prices for office supplies in cities where they directly compete, and higher prices in cities where they do not face each other in direct competition. These higher costs, Staples argued, simultaneously

caused prices to be above what it charged elsewhere, which discouraged Office Depot from entering the market in higher-priced areas. The merging firms' economic expert sought to test the omitted variable bias hypothesis statistically and proposed a comparison of the cross-section estimates [random effects] with those derived from the fixed effects model, which controlled for individual stores by dummy variables to capture cross-sectional-unit peculiarities (omitted effect). It was argued that if the fixed effects model gives similar estimates to the random effects model, then the relationship observed in the cross-market comparisons is not likely to have been biased by the omitted unobservable effects across stores; see Wooldridge (2002) Chapter 10 for Fixed and Random effects estimation of cross-sectional data; see also the prepared remarks of Jonathan Baker (Director Bureau of Economics, Federal Trade Commission), before the American Bar Association Antitrust Section Economics Committee, March 31, 1998.

20 See Feldman (1990, p. 69).
21 The risk-free rate is based on the idea that only entities that are not likely to default on debt obligations can issue risk-free securities. The US Government has an exorbitant privilege in that regard.
22 See Cleveland and Dawson III (2008).
23 Some see the case law on the discount rate as a law in disarray and a source of great fortune. See Cleveland and Dawson III (2008) for case law and commentary.
24 See Bowers (1996, pp. 1107–8).
25 Bowers (1996, op. cit., p. 1108).
26 See Bowers (1996) for a comprehensive discussion of the adversarial system and the prospects of good fortune based on the accepted discount rate. He argues that courts should dismantle the discretionary discount rate and thereby eliminate many of the costs and uncertainties of the legal lottery. He proposes that courts adopt an easily identifiable, fixed market peg, such as the Dow Jones Industrial Average, a corporate-bond index, or the Treasury bill rate, when discounting lost future profits in breach of contract cases. By fixing the discount rate to such a market peg on the day of the breach, neither judge, jury, nor expert determines the discount rate and many of the private and social costs of the discretionary approach can be eliminated without causing unreasonable disruptions.
27 Bowers (1996, op. cit., p. 1111).
28 Bowers (1996), ibid; see also the critique of expert testimony, pp. 1112–25.
29 See Brookshire et al. (2007, p. 32).
30 See Spitzman and Kane (1998).
31 See Coller, Harrison, and Spiller (2004), Patel et al. (1982).
32 See Fisher and Romaine (1990).
33 See Horner and Slesnick (1999).
34 Ibid.
35 See *Landry v. Melancon* (La. Ct. App. 1989); see also Horner and Slesnick (1999, p. 16).
36 See *Walker v. Bankston* (1990).
37 Horner and Slesnick (1999), op. cit.
38 For detailed discussion of the earnings paradigm see Horner and Slesnick (1999, op. cit., pp. 26–9).
39 The City Directory was renewed annually by a census of households visited by the police, and it listed all adult individuals in the Boston area.
40 See Zeisel (1969, p. 1).

41 See Zeisel (1969, op. cit, pp. 11–12).
42 Buybacks occur when companies repurchase their shares to return wealth to their shareholders, thereby reducing the number of shares in the market and increasing the value of shareholders, because of the reduction in outstanding shares. Earnings per share (EPS) increases as the number of outstanding shares dwindle. Therefore, companies can look very profitable.
43 See Koller et al. (2010, pp. 510–11).
44 A capital expenditure is expenditure on plant, machines, and long-term assets that is not immediately featured (expensed or capitalized) in the income statement of a company. If the benefit accruing to the expenditure can be realized in one year, the expenditure must be reflected in the income statement. If the benefit will be realized over a longer time horizon it should be expensed in the balance sheet. The direct measure of NKE subtracts value received from assets sold from the sum of spending on assets. The indirect method subtracts the value of property plant and equipment (PPE) in the current period from PPE from a previous period and adds current depreciation to the difference.
45 See Damodaran (2011, p. 38).
46 See Damodaran (2011, p. 41).
47 Op. cit., p. 44.
48 The geometric mean, $\sqrt[n]{x_1 * x_2 * x_3 ... x_n}$, which is the nth root of the product of n numbers, is not excessively skewed by larger values. More so, it provides a better result for values that increase over time.
49 Usually, retained earnings for a given reporting period is found by subtracting the dividends a company has paid to stockholders from its net income. Since net income is dividends plus addition to retained earnings, addition to retained earnings is net income less dividends. The retention or *plowback* ratio is addition to retained earnings divided by net income. Retained earnings constitute a portion of a company's net income that is used for reinvestment to foster growth or pay off debts. It is a portion of earnings that is not paid to shareholders.
50 See Damodaran (2011, p. 52).
51 See Koller et al. (2010, p. 89).
52 Weinberger and other minority shareholders sued UOP because they were not given material information prior to a merger with Signal Companies, Inc.; accordingly, the dissenting shareholders challenged the merger to obtain a fair value for their shares. The Court found that the shareholders were entitled to material information and that widely accepted principles must be used to value public companies.

FURTHER READING

Bainbridge, S. M. (2012). *Mergers and acquisitions* (3rd ed.). New York: Foundation Press.
Bowerman, B. L., O'Connell, R.T., & Koehler, A. B. (2005). *Forecasting and time series, and regression: An applied approach* (4th ed.) Pacific Grove, CA: Brooks/Cole.
Bowers, C. P. (1996). Courts, contracts, and the appropriate discount rate: A quick fix for the legal lottery. *University of Chicago Law Review, 63,* 1099–1100.
Brookshire, M. L., Slesnick, L., & Ward, J. O. (2007). *The plaintiff and defense attorney's guide to understanding economic damages.* Tuscon, AZ: Lawyers and Judges Publishing Company.

Budetti, P. P., & Waters, T. M. (2005). *Medical malpractice law in the United States.* San Francisco, CA: Kaiser Foundation.

Ciecka, J. E., & Skoog, G. R. (2017). Expected labor force activity and retirement behavior by age, gender, and labor force history. *Statistics and Public Policy, 4*(1), 1–8.

Cleveland, C. W., & Dawson III, W. T. (2008). Applying the appropriate discount rate in commercial litigation. *Practical Litigator, 19*(4), 37–39.

Coller, M., Harrison, G. W., & Spiller, E. A. (2004). Mooresville Honda Company: A case in forensic accounting. *Journal of Accounting Education, 22,* 69–94.

Damodaran, A. (2011). *The little book of valuation: How to value a company, pick a stock, and profit.* Hoboken, NJ: Wiley.

Depperschmidt, T. (1997). The impact of the *Daubert* decision on forensic economists. *Journal of Forensic Economics, 10*(2), 127–138.

Feldman, A. M. (1990). Discounting in forensic economics. *Journal of Forensic Economics, 3*(2), 65–71.

Financial Crisis Inquiry Commission. (2011). *The financial crisis inquiry report.* New York: Public Affairs.

Fisher, F., & Romaine, R. C. (1990). Janis Joplin's yearbook and the theory of damages. *Journal of Accounting, Auditing & Finance, 5,* 145–157.

Groppelli, A. A., & Nikbakht, E. (2012). *Finance.* Hauppauge, NY: Barron's Educational Series.

Gujarati, D. M., & Porter, D. C. (2009). *Basic econometrics* (5th ed.). New York: McGraw-Hill.

Hill, R. C., Griffiths W. E., & Lim, G. C. (2011). *Principles of econometrics* (4th ed.). Hoboken, NJ: John Wiley and Sons.

Horner, S. M., & Slesnick, F. (1999). The valuation of earning capacity definition, measurement and evidence. *Journal of Forensic Economics, 12,* 12–32.

Ireland, T. R. (2010). Why Markov process worklife expectancy tables are usually superior to the LPE method. *Journal of Forensic Economics, 16*(2), 95–110.

Koller, T., Goedhart, M., & Wessels, D. (2010). *Valuation: Measuring and managing the value of companies* (5th ed.). Hoboken, NJ: John Wiley.

Krueger, K.V., & Slesnick, F. (2014). Total worklife expectancy. *Journal of Forensic Economics, 25*(1), 51–70.

Label, W. A. (2013). *Accounting for non-accountants* (3rd ed.). Naperville, IL: Sourcebooks.

Lloyd, T. (2000). Calculating lost profits damages to new businesses (Chapter 31A). In R. L. Weil, M. J. Wagner, & P. B. Frank (Eds), *Litigation services handbook: The role of the accountant as expert* (2nd ed., Cumulative Supplement). New York: John Wiley & Sons.

Lynch, S. (1997). *Arrogance and accords: The inside story of the Honda scandal.* Irving, Texas: Pecos Press.

McGuigan, J. R., Moyer, C. R., & Harris, F. H. (2016). *Managerial economics: Applications, strategy, and tactics* (14th ed.). Boston, MA: Cengage Learning.

McBurney, D. H., & White, T. L. (2007). *Research methods* (7th ed.). Belmont, CA: Thomson Learning.

Millimet, D. L, Nieswiadomy, M., Ryu, H., & Slottje, D. (2003). Estimating worklife expectancy: An econometric approach. *Journal of Econometrics, 113*(1), 83–113.

Moyer, C. R., McGuigan, J. R., & Rao, R. P. (2015). *Contemporary financial management* (13th ed.). Stamford, CT: Cengage Learning.

Pagano, R. R. (2007). *Understanding statistics in the behavioral sciences.* Belmont, CA: Thomson Wadsworth.

Parrino, R., Gillan, S. L., Bates, W. T., & Kidwell, D. S. (2018). *Fundamentals of corporate finance.* Hoboken, NJ: Wiley.

Pelaez, R. F. (1989). The total offset method. *Journal of Forensic Economics, 2*(2), 45–60.

Podgor, E. S., & Israel, J. H. (2009). *White collar crime* (4th ed.). St, Paul, MN: Thomson-West.

Rosenhouse, M. A. (1983). Effect of anticipated inflation on damages for future loss: Modern cases. *American Law Report, 21*(4).

Ross, S. A., Westerfield, R. W., & Jordan, B. D. (2014). *Essentials of corporate finance* (7th ed.). New York: McGraw-Hill.

Rubenfeld, D. L. (1985). Econometrics in the courtroom. *Columbia Law Review, 85*(5), 1048–1097.

Schilit, H. M., & Perler, J. (2010). *Financial shenanigans: How to detect accounting gimmicks and fraud in financial reports*. New York: McGraw-Hill.

Schmidt, S. J. (2005). *Econometrics*. New York: McGraw-Hill.

Skoog, G. R., Ciecka, J. E., and Krueger, K. V. (2011). The Markov process model of labor force activity: Extended tables of central tendency, shape, percentile points, and bootstrap standard errors. *Journal of Forensic Economics, 22*(2), 165–229.

Smith, S. (1986). *Worklife estimates: Effects of race and education*. US Department of Labor, Bureau of Labor Statistics Bulletin 2254.

Spitzman, L. M., & Kane, J. (1998). Defending against a Daubert challenge: An application in projecting the lost earnings of a minor child. *Litigation Economics Digest, 1*, 43–49.

Sykes, A. O. (1993). *An introduction to regression analysis*. Coase-Sandor Institute for Law & Economics. Working Paper No. 20, University of Chicago Law School.

Thornton, R., & Ward, J. (1999). The economist in tort litigation. *Journal of Economic Perspectives, 13*(2), 101–112.

Trentacosta, J. R. (1997, October). Damages in breach of contract cases. *Michigan Bar Journal, 76*, 1068–1070.

Warburton, C. E. S. (2018a). Covered interest parity and frictions in currency and money markets: Analysis of British Pound and Dollar for the period 1999–2006. *Applied Econometrics and International Development, 18*(1), 55–73.

Warburton, C. E. S. (2018b). *The development of international monetary policy*. Oxon, UK: Routledge.

Warburton, C. E. S. (2019). Uneasy coexistence: Profit maximization and affordable healthcare in the US. *Applied Econometrics and International Development, 19*(1), 55–80.

Weil, R. L., Frank, P. B., Hughes, C. W., & Wagner, M. J. (2007). *Litigation services handbook: The role of the financial expert* (4th ed.). Hoboken, NJ: John Wiley & Sons.

Wooldridge, J. M. (2002). *Econometric analysis of cross section and panel data*. Cambridge, MA: MIT Press.

Zeisel, H. (1969). Dr. Spock and the case of the vanishing women jurors. *University of Chicago Law Review, 37*(1), 1–18.

Appendices

Table A5.1 Future Value Interest Factors for a dollar (from 1% to 10% for 26–50 years)

n	1%	2%	3%	4%	5%	6%	7%	8%	9%	10%
26	1.2953	1.6734	2.1566	2.7725	3.5557	4.5494	5.8074	7.3964	9.3992	11.9182
27	1.3082	1.7069	2.2213	2.8834	3.7335	4.8223	6.2139	7.9881	10.2451	13.11
28	1.3213	1.741	2.2879	2.9987	3.9201	5.1117	6.6488	8.6271	11.1671	14.421
29	1.3345	1.7758	2.3566	3.1187	4.1161	5.4184	7.1143	9.3173	12.1722	15.8631
30	**1.3478**	**1.8114**	**2.4273**	**3.2434**	**4.3219**	**5.7435**	**7.6123**	**10.0627**	**13.2677**	**17.4494**
31	1.3613	1.8476	2.5001	3.3731	4.538	6.0881	8.1451	10.8677	14.4618	19.1943
32	1.3749	1.8845	2.5751	3.5081	4.7649	6.4534	8.7153	11.7371	15.7633	21.1138
33	1.3887	1.9222	2.6523	3.6484	5.0032	6.8406	9.3253	12.676	17.182	23.2252
34	1.4026	1.9607	2.7319	3.7943	5.2533	7.251	9.9781	13.6901	18.7284	25.5477
35	**1.4166**	**1.9999**	**2.8139**	**3.9461**	**5.516**	**7.6861**	**10.6766**	**14.7853**	**20.414**	**28.1024**
36	1.4308	2.0399	2.8983	4.1039	5.7918	8.1473	11.4239	15.9682	22.2512	30.9127
37	1.4451	2.0807	2.9852	4.2681	6.0814	8.6361	12.2236	17.2456	24.2538	34.0039
38	1.4595	2.1223	3.0748	4.4388	6.3855	9.1543	13.0793	18.6253	26.4367	37.4043
39	1.4741	2.1647	3.167	4.6164	6.7048	9.7035	13.9948	20.1153	28.816	41.1448
40	**1.4889**	**2.208**	**3.262**	**4.801**	**7.04**	**10.2857**	**14.9745**	**21.7245**	**31.4094**	**45.2593**
41	1.5038	2.2522	3.3599	4.9931	7.392	10.9029	16.0227	23.4625	34.2363	49.7852
42	1.5188	2.2972	3.4607	5.1928	7.7616	11.557	17.1443	25.3395	37.3175	54.7637
43	1.534	2.3432	3.5645	5.4005	8.1497	12.2505	18.3444	27.3666	40.6761	60.2401
44	1.5493	2.3901	3.6715	5.6165	8.5572	12.9855	19.6285	29.556	44.337	66.2641
45	**1.5648**	**2.4379**	**3.7816**	**5.8412**	**8.985**	**13.7646**	**21.0025**	**31.9204**	**48.3273**	**72.8905**
46	1.5805	2.4866	3.895	6.0748	9.4343	14.5905	22.4726	34.4741	52.6767	80.1795
47	1.5963	2.5363	4.0119	6.3178	9.906	15.4659	24.0457	37.232	57.4176	88.1975
48	1.6122	2.5871	4.1323	6.5705	10.4013	16.3939	25.7289	40.2106	62.5852	97.0172
49	1.6283	2.6388	4.2562	6.8333	10.9213	17.3775	27.5299	43.4274	68.2179	106.719
50	**1.6446**	**2.6916**	**4.3839**	**7.1067**	**11.4674**	**18.4202**	**29.457**	**46.9016**	**74.3575**	**117.3909**

Future Value Interest Factors for a dollar at a specific interest rate, i, which is compounded for a stated period of time or number of payments n:

$$FVIF_{i,n} = (1+i)^n$$

Table A5.2 Present Value Interest Factors for a dollar (from 1% to 10% for 31–40 years)

n	1%	2%	3%	4%	5%	6%	7%	8%	9%	10%
1	0.9901	0.9804	0.9709	0.9615	0.9524	0.9434	0.9346	0.9259	0.9174	0.9091
2	0.9803	0.9612	0.9426	0.9246	0.907	0.89	0.8734	0.8573	0.8417	0.8264
3	0.9706	0.9423	0.9151	0.889	0.8638	0.8396	0.8163	0.7938	0.7722	0.7513
4	0.961	0.9238	0.8885	0.8548	0.8227	0.7921	0.7629	0.735	0.7084	0.683
5	**0.9515**	**0.9057**	**0.8626**	**0.8219**	**0.7835**	**0.7473**	**0.713**	**0.6806**	**0.6499**	**0.6209**
6	0.942	0.888	0.8375	0.7903	0.7462	0.705	0.6663	0.6302	0.5963	0.5645
7	0.9327	0.8706	0.8131	0.7599	0.7107	0.6651	0.6227	0.5835	0.547	0.5132
8	0.9235	0.8535	0.7894	0.7307	0.6768	0.6274	0.582	0.5403	0.5019	0.4665
9	0.9143	0.8368	0.7664	0.7026	0.6446	0.5919	0.5439	0.5002	0.4604	0.4241
10	**0.9053**	**0.8203**	**0.7441**	**0.6756**	**0.6139**	**0.5584**	**0.5083**	**0.4632**	**0.4224**	**0.3855**
11	0.8963	0.8043	0.7224	0.6496	0.5847	0.5268	0.4751	0.4289	0.3875	0.3505
12	0.8874	0.7885	0.7014	0.6246	0.5568	0.497	0.444	0.3971	0.3555	0.3186
13	0.8787	0.773	0.681	0.6006	0.5303	0.4688	0.415	0.3677	0.3262	0.2897
14	0.87	0.7579	0.6611	0.5775	0.5051	0.4423	0.3878	0.3405	0.2992	0.2633
15	**0.8613**	**0.743**	**0.6419**	**0.5553**	**0.481**	**0.4173**	**0.3624**	**0.3152**	**0.2745**	**0.2394**
16	0.8528	0.7284	0.6232	0.5339	0.4581	0.3936	0.3387	0.2919	0.2519	0.2176
17	0.8444	0.7142	0.605	0.5134	0.4363	0.3714	0.3166	0.2703	0.2311	0.1978
18	0.836	0.7002	0.5874	0.4936	0.4155	0.3503	0.2959	0.2502	0.212	0.1799

(continued)

Table A5.2 Cont.

n	1%	2%	3%	4%	5%	6%	7%	8%	9%	10%
19	0.8277	0.6864	0.5703	0.4746	0.3957	0.3305	0.2765	0.2317	0.1945	0.1635
20	0.8195	0.673	0.5537	0.4564	0.3769	0.3118	0.2584	0.2145	0.1784	0.1486
21	0.8114	0.6598	0.5375	0.4388	0.3589	0.2942	0.2415	0.1987	0.1637	0.1351
22	0.8034	0.6468	0.5219	0.422	0.3418	0.2775	0.2257	0.1839	0.1502	0.1228
23	0.7954	0.6342	0.5067	0.4057	0.3256	0.2618	0.2109	0.1703	0.1378	0.1117
24	0.7876	0.6217	0.4919	0.3901	0.3101	0.247	0.1971	0.1577	0.1264	0.1015
25	0.7798	0.6095	0.4776	0.3751	0.2953	0.233	0.1842	0.146	0.116	0.0923
26	0.772	0.5976	0.4637	0.3607	0.2812	0.2198	0.1722	0.1352	0.1064	0.0839
27	0.7644	0.5859	0.4502	0.3468	0.2678	0.2074	0.1609	0.1252	0.0976	0.0763
28	0.7568	0.5744	0.4371	0.3335	0.2551	0.1956	0.1504	0.1159	0.0895	0.0693
29	0.7493	0.5631	0.4243	0.3207	0.2429	0.1846	0.1406	0.1073	0.0822	0.063
30	0.7419	0.5521	0.412	0.3083	0.2314	0.1741	0.1314	0.0994	0.0754	0.0573
31	0.7346	0.5412	0.4	0.2965	0.2204	0.1643	0.1228	0.092	0.0691	0.0521
32	0.7273	0.5306	0.3883	0.2851	0.2099	0.155	0.1147	0.0852	0.0634	0.0474
33	0.7201	0.5202	0.377	0.2741	0.1999	0.1462	0.1072	0.0789	0.0582	0.0431
34	0.713	0.51	0.366	0.2636	0.1904	0.1379	0.1002	0.073	0.0534	0.0391
35	0.7059	0.5	0.3554	0.2534	0.1813	0.1301	0.0937	0.0676	0.049	0.0356
36	0.6989	0.4902	0.345	0.2437	0.1727	0.1227	0.0875	0.0626	0.0449	0.0323
37	0.692	0.4806	0.335	0.2343	0.1644	0.1158	0.0818	0.058	0.0412	0.0294
38	0.6852	0.4712	0.3252	0.2253	0.1566	0.1092	0.0765	0.0537	0.0378	0.0267
39	0.6784	0.4619	0.3158	0.2166	0.1491	0.1031	0.0715	0.0497	0.0347	0.0243
40	0.6717	0.4529	0.3066	0.2083	0.142	0.0972	0.0668	0.046	0.0318	0.0221

Present Value Interest Factors for a dollar discounted at interest rate i for a certain number of payments, n, to be received or made over time:

$$PVIF_{i,n} = \frac{1}{(1+i)^n}$$

Table A5.3 Future Value Interest Factors for a dollar ordinary annuity (from 1% to 9% for 31–40 years)

n	1%	2%	3%	4%	5%	6%	7%	8%	9%
1	1	1	1	1	1	1	1	1	1
2	2.01	2.02	2.03	2.04	2.05	2.06	2.07	2.08	2.09
3	3.0301	3.0604	3.0909	3.1216	3.1525	3.1836	3.2149	3.2464	3.2781
4	4.0604	4.1216	4.1836	4.2465	4.3101	4.3746	4.4399	4.5061	4.5731
5	**5.101**	**5.204**	**5.3091**	**5.4163**	**5.5256**	**5.6371**	**5.7507**	**5.8666**	**5.9847**
6	6.152	6.3081	6.4684	6.633	6.8019	6.9753	7.1533	7.3359	7.5233
7	7.2135	7.4343	7.6625	7.8983	8.142	8.3938	8.654	8.9228	9.2004
8	8.2857	8.583	8.8923	9.2142	9.5491	9.8975	10.2598	10.6366	11.0285
9	9.3685	9.7546	10.1591	10.5828	11.0266	11.4913	11.978	12.4876	13.021
10	**10.4622**	**10.9497**	**11.4639**	**12.0061**	**12.5779**	**13.1808**	**13.8164**	**14.4866**	**15.1929**
11	11.5668	12.1687	12.8078	13.4864	14.2068	14.9716	15.7836	16.6455	17.5603
12	12.6825	13.4121	14.192	15.0258	15.9171	16.8699	17.8885	18.9771	20.1407
13	13.8093	14.6803	15.6178	16.6268	17.713	18.8821	20.1406	21.4953	22.9534
14	14.9474	15.9739	17.0863	18.2919	19.5986	21.0151	22.5505	24.2149	26.0192
15	**16.0969**	**17.2934**	**18.5989**	**20.0236**	**21.5786**	**23.276**	**25.129**	**27.1521**	**29.3609**
16	17.2579	18.6393	20.1569	21.8245	23.6575	25.6725	27.8881	30.3243	33.0034
17	18.4304	20.0121	21.7616	23.6975	25.8404	28.2129	30.8402	33.7502	36.9737
18	19.6147	21.4123	23.4144	25.6454	28.1324	30.9057	33.999	37.4502	41.3013

(continued)

Table A5.3 Cont.

n	1%	2%	3%	4%	5%	6%	7%	8%	9%
19	20.8109	22.8406	25.1169	27.6712	30.539	33.76	37.379	41.4463	46.0185
20	**22.019**	**24.2974**	**26.8704**	**29.7781**	**33.066**	**36.7856**	**40.9955**	**45.762**	**51.1601**
21	23.2392	25.7833	28.6765	31.9692	35.7193	39.9927	44.8652	50.4229	56.7645
22	24.4716	27.299	30.5368	34.248	38.5052	43.3923	49.0057	55.4568	62.8733
23	25.7163	28.845	32.4529	36.6179	41.4305	46.9958	53.4361	60.8933	69.5319
24	26.9735	30.4219	34.4265	39.0826	44.502	50.8156	58.1767	66.7648	76.7898
25	**28.2432**	**32.0303**	**36.4593**	**41.6459**	**47.7271**	**54.8645**	**63.249**	**73.1059**	**84.7009**
26	29.5256	33.6709	38.553	44.3117	51.1135	59.1564	68.6765	79.9544	93.324
27	30.8209	35.3443	40.7096	47.0842	54.6691	63.7058	74.4838	87.3508	102.7231
28	32.1291	37.0512	42.9309	49.9676	58.4026	68.5281	80.6977	95.3388	112.9682
29	33.4504	38.7922	45.2189	52.9663	62.3227	73.6398	87.3465	103.9659	124.1354
30	**34.7849**	**40.5681**	**47.5754**	**56.0849**	**66.4388**	**79.0582**	**94.4608**	**113.2832**	**136.3075**
31	36.1327	42.3794	50.0027	59.3283	70.7608	84.8017	102.073	123.3459	149.5752
32	37.4941	44.227	52.5028	62.7015	75.2988	90.8898	110.2182	134.2135	164.037
33	38.869	46.1116	55.0778	66.2095	80.0638	97.3432	118.9334	145.9506	179.8003
34	40.2577	48.0338	57.7302	69.8579	85.067	104.1838	128.2588	158.6267	196.9823
35	**41.6603**	**49.9945**	**60.4621**	**73.6522**	**90.3203**	**111.4348**	**138.2369**	**172.3168**	**215.7108**
36	43.0769	51.9944	63.2759	77.5983	95.8363	119.1209	148.9135	187.1021	236.1247
37	44.5076	54.0343	66.1742	81.7022	101.6281	127.2681	160.3374	203.0703	258.3759
38	45.9527	56.1149	69.1594	85.9703	107.7095	135.9042	172.561	220.3159	282.6298
39	47.4123	58.2372	72.2342	90.4091	114.095	145.0585	185.6403	238.9412	309.0665
40	**48.8864**	**60.402**	**75.4013**	**95.0255**	**120.7998**	**154.762**	**199.6351**	**259.0565**	**337.8824**

Future Value Interest Factors for a dollar ordinary annuity with interest, i, compounded for n periods over time, t:

$$\text{FVIFA}_{i,n} = \left[\frac{(1+r)^n - 1}{r}\right]$$

Table A5.4 Present Value Interest Factors for a dollar annuity (from 1% to 9% for 31–40 years)

n	1%	2%	3%	4%	5%	6%	7%	8%	9%
31	26.5423	22.9377	20.0004	17.5885	15.5928	13.929	12.5318	11.3498	10.3428
32	27.2696	23.4683	20.3888	17.8736	15.8027	14.084	12.6466	11.435	10.4062
33	27.9897	23.9886	20.7658	18.1476	16.0025	14.23	12.7538	11.5139	10.4644
34	28.7027	24.4986	21.1318	18.4112	16.1929	14.368	12.854	11.5869	10.5178
35	**29.4086**	**24.9986**	**21.4872**	**18.6646**	**16.3742**	**14.498**	**12.9477**	**11.6546**	**10.5668**
36	30.1075	25.4888	21.8323	18.9083	16.5469	14.621	13.0352	11.7172	10.6118
37	30.7995	25.9695	22.1672	19.1426	16.7113	14.737	13.117	11.7752	10.653
38	31.4847	26.4406	22.4925	19.3679	16.8679	14.846	13.1935	11.8289	10.6908
39	32.163	26.9026	22.8082	19.5845	17.017	14.949	13.2649	11.8786	10.7255
40	**32.8347**	**27.3555**	**23.1148**	**19.7928**	**17.1591**	**15.046**	**13.3317**	**11.9246**	**10.7574**

Present Value Interest Factors for a dollar annuity discounted at i percent for n periods over time, t:

$$PVIFA_{i,n} = \left[\frac{1 - \left(\frac{1}{(1+i)^n}\right)}{i}\right]$$

Table A5.4 Present Value Interest Factors for a dollar annuity (from 1% to 9% for 1–30 years)

n	1%	2%	3%	4%	5%	6%	7%	8%	9%
1	0.9901	0.9804	0.9709	0.9615	0.9524	0.9434	0.9346	0.9259	0.9174
2	1.9704	1.9416	1.9135	1.8861	1.8594	1.8334	1.808	1.7833	1.7591
3	2.941	2.8839	2.8286	2.7751	2.7232	2.673	2.6243	2.5771	2.5313
4	3.902	3.8077	3.7171	3.6299	3.546	3.4651	3.3872	3.3121	3.2397
5	**4.8534**	**4.7135**	**4.5797**	**4.4518**	**4.3295**	**4.2124**	**4.1002**	**3.9927**	**3.8897**
6	5.7955	5.6014	5.4172	5.2421	5.0757	4.9173	4.7665	4.6229	4.4859
7	6.7282	6.472	6.2303	6.0021	5.7864	5.5824	5.3893	5.2064	5.033
8	7.6517	7.3255	7.0197	6.7327	6.4632	6.2098	5.9713	5.7466	5.5348
9	8.566	8.1622	7.7861	7.4353	7.1078	6.8017	6.5152	6.2469	5.9952
10	**9.4713**	**8.9826**	**8.5302**	**8.1109**	**7.7217**	**7.3601**	**7.0236**	**6.7101**	**6.4177**
11	10.3676	9.7868	9.2526	8.7605	8.3064	7.8869	7.4987	7.139	6.8052
12	11.2551	10.5753	9.954	9.3851	8.8633	8.3838	7.9427	7.5361	7.1607
13	12.1337	11.3484	10.635	9.9856	9.3936	8.8527	8.3577	7.9038	7.4869
14	13.0037	12.1062	11.2961	10.5631	9.8986	9.295	8.7455	8.2442	7.7862
15	**13.8651**	**12.8493**	**11.9379**	**11.1184**	**10.3797**	**9.7122**	**9.1079**	**8.5595**	**8.0607**

16	14.7179	13.5777	12.5611	11.6523	10.8378	10.106	9.4466	8.8514	8.3126
17	15.5623	14.2919	13.1661	12.1657	11.2741	10.477	9.7632	9.1216	8.5436
18	16.3983	14.992	13.7535	12.6593	11.6896	10.828	10.0591	9.3719	8.7556
19	17.226	15.6785	14.3238	13.1339	12.0853	11.158	10.3356	9.6036	8.9501
20	**18.0456**	**16.3514**	**14.8775**	**13.5903**	**12.4622**	**11.47**	**10.594**	**9.8181**	**9.1285**
21	18.857	17.0112	15.415	14.0292	12.8212	11.764	10.8355	10.0168	9.2922
22	19.6604	17.658	15.9369	14.4511	13.163	12.042	11.0612	10.2007	9.4424
23	20.4558	18.2922	16.4436	14.8568	13.4886	12.303	11.2722	10.3711	9.5802
24	21.2434	18.9139	16.9355	15.247	13.7986	12.55	11.4693	10.5288	9.7066
25	**22.0232**	**19.5235**	**17.4131**	**15.6221**	**14.0939**	**12.783**	**11.6536**	**10.6748**	**9.8226**
26	22.7952	20.121	17.8768	15.9828	14.3752	13.003	11.8258	10.81	9.929
27	23.5596	20.7069	18.327	16.3296	14.643	13.211	11.9867	10.9352	10.0266
28	24.3164	21.2813	18.7641	16.6631	14.8981	13.406	12.1371	11.0511	10.1161
29	25.0658	21.8444	19.1885	16.9837	15.1411	13.591	12.2777	11.1584	10.1983
30	**25.8077**	**22.3965**	**19.6004**	**17.292**	**15.3725**	**13.765**	**12.409**	**11.2578**	**10.2737**

Table A5.5 Normal distribution table (z-distribution)

Probability of areas to the right of a positive Z-score

Z	0	0.01	0.02	0.03	0.04	0.05	0.06	0.07	0.08	0.09
0	0.5	0.496	0.492	0.488	0.484	0.4801	0.4761	0.4721	0.4681	0.4641
0.1	0.4602	0.4562	0.4522	0.4483	0.4443	0.4404	0.4364	0.4325	0.4286	0.4247
0.2	0.4207	0.4168	0.4129	0.409	0.4052	0.4013	0.3974	0.3936	0.3897	0.3859
0.3	0.3821	0.3783	0.3745	0.3707	0.3669	0.3632	0.3594	0.3557	0.352	0.3483
0.4	0.3446	0.3409	0.3372	0.3336	0.33	0.3264	0.3228	0.3192	0.3156	0.3121
0.5	0.3085	0.305	0.3015	0.2981	0.2946	0.2912	0.2877	0.2843	0.281	0.2776
0.6	0.2743	0.2709	0.2676	0.2643	0.2611	0.2578	0.2546	0.2514	0.2483	0.2451
0.7	0.242	0.2389	0.2358	0.2327	0.2296	0.2266	0.2236	0.2206	0.2177	0.2148
0.8	0.2119	0.209	0.2061	0.2033	0.2005	0.1977	0.1949	0.1922	0.1894	0.1867
0.9	0.1841	0.1814	0.1788	0.1762	0.1736	0.1711	0.1685	0.166	0.1635	0.1611
1	0.1587	0.1562	0.1539	0.1515	0.1492	0.1469	0.1446	0.1423	0.1401	0.1379
1.1	0.1357	0.1335	0.1314	0.1292	0.1271	0.1251	0.123	0.121	0.119	0.117
1.2	0.1151	0.1131	0.1112	0.1093	0.1075	0.1056	0.1038	0.102	0.1003	0.0985
1.3	0.0968	0.0951	0.0934	0.0918	0.0901	0.0885	0.0869	0.0853	0.0838	0.0823
1.4	0.0808	0.0793	0.0778	0.0764	0.0749	0.0735	0.0721	0.0708	0.0694	0.0681
1.5	0.0668	0.0655	0.0643	0.063	0.0618	0.0606	0.0594	0.0582	0.0571	0.0559
1.6	0.0548	0.0537	0.0526	0.0516	0.0505	0.0495	0.0485	0.0475	0.0465	0.0455
1.7	0.0446	0.0436	0.0427	0.0418	0.0409	0.0401	0.0392	0.0384	0.0375	0.0367
1.8	0.0359	0.0351	0.0344	0.0336	0.0329	0.0322	0.0314	0.0307	0.0301	0.0294
1.9	0.0287	0.0281	0.0274	0.0268	0.0262	0.0256	0.025	0.0244	0.0239	0.0233
2	0.0228	0.0222	0.0217	0.0212	0.0207	0.0202	0.0197	0.0192	0.0188	0.0183

	0	1	2	3	4	5	6	7	8	9
2.1	0.0179	0.0174	0.017	0.0166	0.0162	0.0158	0.0154	0.015	0.0146	0.0143
2.2	0.0139	0.0136	0.0132	0.0129	0.0125	0.0122	0.0119	0.0116	0.0113	0.011
2.3	0.0107	0.0104	0.0102	0.0099	0.0096	0.0094	0.0091	0.0089	0.0087	0.0084
2.4	0.0082	0.008	0.0078	0.0075	0.0073	0.0071	0.0069	0.0068	0.0066	0.0064
2.5	**0.0062**	**0.006**	**0.0059**	**0.0057**	**0.0055**	**0.0054**	**0.0052**	**0.0051**	**0.0049**	**0.0048**
2.6	0.0047	0.0045	0.0044	0.0043	0.0041	0.004	0.0039	0.0038	0.0037	0.0036
2.7	0.0035	0.0034	0.0033	0.0032	0.0031	0.003	0.0029	0.0028	0.0027	0.0026
2.8	0.0026	0.0025	0.0024	0.0023	0.0023	0.0022	0.0021	0.0021	0.002	0.0019
2.9	0.0019	0.0018	0.0018	0.0017	0.0016	0.0016	0.0015	0.0015	0.0014	0.0014
3	**0.0013**	**0.0013**	**0.0013**	**0.0012**	**0.0012**	**0.0011**	**0.0011**	**0.0011**	**0.001**	**0.001**
3.1	0.001	0.0009	0.0009	0.0009	0.0008	0.0008	0.0008	0.0008	0.0007	0.0007
3.2	0.0007	0.0007	0.0006	0.0006	0.0006	0.0006	0.0006	0.0005	0.0005	0.0005
3.3	0.0005	0.0005	0.0005	0.0004	0.0004	0.0004	0.0004	0.0004	0.0004	0.0003
3.4	0.0003	0.0003	0.0003	0.0003	0.0003	0.0003	0.0003	0.0003	0.0003	0.0002
3.5	**0.0002**	**0.0002**	**0.0002**	**0.0002**	**0.0002**	**0.0002**	**0.0002**	**0.0002**	**0.0002**	**0.0002**
3.6	0.0002	0.0002	0.0001	0.0001	0.0001	0.0001	0.0001	0.0001	0.0001	0.0001
3.7	0.0001	0.0001	0.0001	0.0001	0.0001	0.0001	0.0001	0.0001	0.0001	0.0001
3.8	0.0001	0.0001	0.0001	0.0001	0.0001	0.0001	0.0001	0.0001	0.0001	0.0001
3.9	0	0	0	0	0	0	0	0	0	0
4	**0**	**0**	**0**	**0**	**0**	**0**	**0**	**0**	**0**	**0**

Table A5.6 The chi square (X^2) distribution

Probabilities that obtained $X^2 \geq$ critical X_c^2 (α Level of 0.005 to 0.995)

df	0.995	0.99	0.975	0.95	0.90	0.10	0.05	0.025	0.01	0.005
1	---	---	0.001	0.004	0.016	2.706	3.841	5.024	6.635	7.879
2	0.010	0.020	0.051	0.103	0.211	4.605	5.991	7.378	9.210	10.597
3	0.072	0.115	0.216	0.352	0.584	6.251	7.815	9.348	11.345	12.838
4	0.207	0.297	0.484	0.711	1.064	7.779	9.488	11.143	13.277	14.860
5	**0.412**	**0.554**	**0.831**	**1.145**	**1.610**	**9.236**	**11.070**	**12.833**	**15.086**	**16.750**
6	0.676	0.872	1.237	1.635	2.204	10.645	12.592	14.449	16.812	18.548
7	0.989	1.239	1.690	2.167	2.833	12.017	14.067	16.013	18.475	20.278
8	1.344	1.646	2.180	2.733	3.490	13.362	15.507	17.535	20.090	21.955
9	1.735	2.088	2.700	3.325	4.168	14.684	16.919	19.023	21.666	23.589
10	**2.156**	**2.558**	**3.247**	**3.940**	**4.865**	**15.987**	**18.307**	**20.483**	**23.209**	**25.188**
11	2.603	3.053	3.816	4.575	5.578	17.275	19.675	21.920	24.725	26.757
12	3.074	3.571	4.404	5.226	6.304	18.549	21.026	23.337	26.217	28.300
13	3.565	4.107	5.009	5.892	7.042	19.812	22.362	24.736	27.688	29.819
14	4.075	4.660	5.629	6.571	7.790	21.064	23.685	26.119	29.141	31.319
15	**4.601**	**5.229**	**6.262**	**7.261**	**8.547**	**22.307**	**24.996**	**27.488**	**30.578**	**32.801**
16	5.142	5.812	6.908	7.962	9.312	23.542	26.296	28.845	32.000	34.267
17	5.697	6.408	7.564	8.672	10.085	24.769	27.587	30.191	33.409	35.718
18	6.265	7.015	8.231	9.390	10.865	25.989	28.869	31.526	34.805	37.156
19	6.844	7.633	8.907	10.117	11.651	27.204	30.144	32.852	36.191	38.582
20	**7.434**	**8.260**	**9.591**	**10.851**	**12.443**	**28.412**	**31.410**	**34.170**	**37.566**	**39.997**
21	8.034	8.897	10.283	11.591	13.240	29.615	32.671	35.479	38.932	41.401
22	8.643	9.542	10.982	12.338	14.041	30.813	33.924	36.781	40.289	42.796

23	9.260	10.196	11.689	13.091	14.848	32.007	35.172	38.076	41.638	44.181
24	9.886	10.856	12.401	13.848	15.659	33.196	36.415	39.364	42.980	45.559
25	**10.520**	**11.524**	**13.120**	**14.611**	**16.473**	**34.382**	**37.652**	**40.646**	**44.314**	**46.928**
26	11.160	12.198	13.844	15.379	17.292	35.563	38.885	41.923	45.642	48.290
27	11.808	12.879	14.573	16.151	18.114	36.741	40.113	43.195	46.963	49.645
28	12.461	13.565	15.308	16.928	18.939	37.916	41.337	44.461	48.278	50.993
29	13.121	14.256	16.047	17.708	19.768	39.087	42.557	45.722	49.588	52.336
30	**13.787**	**14.953**	**16.791**	**18.493**	**20.599**	**40.256**	**43.773**	**46.979**	**50.892**	**53.672**
40	20.707	22.164	24.433	26.509	29.051	51.805	55.758	59.342	63.691	66.766
50	27.991	29.707	32.357	34.764	37.689	63.167	67.505	71.420	76.154	79.490
60	**35.534**	**37.485**	**40.482**	**43.188**	**46.459**	**74.397**	**79.082**	**83.298**	**88.379**	**91.952**
70	43.275	45.442	48.758	51.739	55.329	85.527	90.531	95.023	100.425	104.215
80	51.172	53.540	57.153	60.391	64.278	96.578	101.879	106.629	112.329	116.321
90	59.196	61.754	65.647	69.126	73.291	107.565	113.145	118.136	124.116	128.299
100	**67.328**	**70.065**	**74.222**	**77.929**	**82.358**	**118.498**	**124.342**	**129.561**	**135.807**	**140.169**

Table A5.7 Regression data

	Male ($)	M Dummy	M Employees
Registered nurses	70,952	1	281,048
Secretarial and administrative assistant	42,411	1	118,739
Elementary and middle school teachers	53,096	1	530,970
Customer service representatives	36,744	1	624,476
First-line supervisors of retail sales workers	46,343	1	1,537,529
Nursing, psychiatric, and homehealth aides	29,503	1	174,528
Accountants and auditors	76,129	1	656,553
Office clerks general	39,885	1	145,063
Human resources managers	77,463	1	143,842
Bookkeeping accounting and auditing clerk	42,013	1	105,920
Actuaries	125,465	1	17,769
Aerospace engineers	104,133	1	102,611
Agricultural and food science technicians	48,340	1	16,564
Appraisers and assessors of real estate	62,298	1	50,409
Architectural and engineering managers	130,300	1	131,956
Automotive service technicians and managers	36,695	1	717,661
Biological scientists	65,122	1	35,893
Biological technicians	50,495	1	8,401
Budget analysts	75,399	1	16,123
Chemical engineers	101,626	1	46,688
Chemists and material scientists	75,433	1	49,013
Chief executives	141,108	1	813,898
Civil engineers	89,218	1	271,698
Computer programmers	87,064	1	293,334
Credit analysts	58,520	1	12,589
Designers	60,035	1	328,481
Economists	111,514	1	15,164
Electricians	51,289	1	635,090
Financial analysts	93,203	1	117,808
Insurance underwriters	73,389	1	36,949
Registered nurses	64,413	0	2,036,445
Secretarial and administrative assistant	36,929	0	210,7852
Elementary and middle school teachers	50,021	0	1,867,475
Customer service representatives	32,893	0	1,158,158

Table A5.7 Cont.

	Male ($)	M Dummy	M Employees
First-line supervisors of retail sales workers	33,778	0	1,140,049
Nursing, psychiatric, and homehealth aides	25,706	0	1,081,522
Accountants and auditors	57,370	0	972,271
Office clerks general	33,492	0	696,284
Human resources managers	70,342	0	225,676
Bookkeeping accounting and auditing clerk	38,665	0	723,611
Actuaries	92,500	0	7,428
Aerospace engineers	91,982	0	12,345
Agricultural and food science technicians	40,927	0	11,104
Appraisers and assessors of real estate	50,291	0	23,281
Architectural and engineering managers	130,255	0	12,856
Automotive service technicians and managers	28,342	0	8,776
Biological scientists	56,853	0	29,218
Biological technicians	44,796	0	7,815
Budget analysts	68,955	0	26,287
Chemical engineers	84,137	0	11,124
Chemists and material scientists	63,426	0	28,010
Chief executives	103,564	0	254,360
Civil engineers	75,052	0	39,309
Computer programmers	80,528	0	77,178
Credit analysts	51,419	0	13,793
Designers	46,516	0	300,384
Economists	103,723	0	6,583
Electricians	50,082	0	12,832
Financial analysts	73,427	0	77,124
Insurance underwriters	56,465	0	61,245

Source: US Department of Labor; https://dol.gov/wb/occupations_interactive.htm.

CHAPTER 6
TAX AVOIDANCE AND EVASION

LEARNING OBJECTIVES

LO 1 To understand the importance of tax revenue and public spending obligations.
LO 2 To realize the economic and legal consequences of tax avoidance and evasion.
LO 3 To be familiar with national tax laws and cases.
LO 4 To evaluate the theories of tax avoidance and evasion.
LO 5 To know how to determine tax liability.

Taxes are an integral part of fiscal policy; the policy that deals with government revenue and spending. All responsible governments have spending priorities that must be met, but the obligations to meet spending priorities cannot be met without adequate revenue. Therefore, governments must decide the mechanisms through which they can raise funds in order to meet their spending obligations. In the US, public spending can be discretionary or mandatory. Discretionary spending refers to spending allocations that are decided by Congress on an annual basis through the annual appropriation process. Mandatory spending is federal spending that is contingent on existing laws rather than the budgetary process. As such, mandatory spending is *not* part of the annual appropriations process. Some governments get revenue from individuals, businesses, profits that are derived from investments, and bequests. In the modern economy, not all transactions are considered taxable. Some economic transactions or investments are tax-free or tax deductible to a limited extent, based on evolving tax laws.

6.1 TYPES OF TAXPAYERS

Taxes are sources of government revenue all over the world and they may be imposed on individuals (natural persons), business entities, estates, trusts, or other forms of organization. Taxes may be based on property, income, transactions, transfers, importations of goods, business activities, or a variety of factors, and are generally imposed on assets for which taxpayers have tax liability; for example, property taxes are imposed on property owners who are required to pay taxes on property. Similarly, US citizens with assets in foreign territories may be expected to pay taxes on assets that are not exempt from taxation, just as publicly traded companies are expected to pay taxes on profits.

Income may take several forms, but it can be classified under three broad headings: (i) earnings, (ii) return on investment, and (iii) passive (income that is unrelated to one's active pursuit of revenue). Taxes may be progressive or regressive. Taxes are progressive when marginal tax rates increase in tandem with taxable income. On the contrary, regressive taxes extract a higher percentage of income from low income earners relative to high-income earners.

Gross income is the sum of income earned by an individual or business in a year that is unrelated to expenditures and taxes. It may include wages, dividends, alimony, capital gains, interest income, royalties, rental income, and retirement distributions (or premature withdrawals from retirement savings). Adjusted gross income (AGI) is gross income after certain deductions have been made from gross income. Further reductions (itemized deductions) may then be made to determine taxable income. Taxpayers may opt for standard instead of itemized deductions.[1] AGI factors are permissible or allowable deductions that are separated from exemptions for military service and number of dependents.

AGI factors include retirement plan contributions, such as Individual Retirement Accounts (IRAs, individual retirement arrangements encompassing diverse financial instruments like stocks, bonds, exchange traded funds, and mutual funds), SIMPLE IRA (retirement plans provided by small businesses with fewer employees), simplified employee pension (SEP, self-employed Keogh plans), Roth IRA (plans with tax-free growth and early withdrawal (after five years of ownership at 59+ years) without tax penalty), and medical expenses.[2]

The global income of US citizens and residents is taxed, but there are accommodations for permissible credits, including foreign taxes, education, and charitable contributions. Sales taxes are rather inconspicuous and usually taken for granted. They vary from state to state and may even vary within certain jurisdictions. Traditionally, those who are selling taxable products collect the taxes from consumers at the time or point of purchase. Other forms of taxes include estate tax on inheritance, tariffs, which will be dealt with in Chapter 8, and wealth taxes on personal financial assets. Some people pay taxes as law-abiding citizens, but others find ways to evade or avoid paying taxes while relying on governments to provide essential social services.

When some people think about tax shelters, they instinctively think about foreign jurisdictions in which taxable income could be concealed; but tax shelters may also be innocuous and legitimate venues to reduce tax exposures. Pointedly, a tax shelter could also be a financial vehicle that is used by investors and taxpayers to minimize their tax liabilities. Tax shelters also range from investments that provide tax-free returns to activities that lower tax liabilities. The most common types of tax shelters include: employer-sponsored 401(k) plans, charitable contributions, student loan interest deductions, and mortgage interest deductions. Of course, for the purposes of this book, the distinction between evasion and avoidance is not technical. Evasion alludes to deliberately violating tax laws and the accompanying exposure to legal culpability, while avoidance means schemes to defeat the purposes of taxes that are not directly illegal. The dichotomy is rather blurry when there is no divergence of intent. In this chapter, tax flight is also considered to be a form of avoidance when tax laws are not violated. This chapter will explore a range of tax-related issues that include the essence of taxation, tax liabilities, theories that explain predispositions to evade and avoid taxes, tax laws and violations, and forums for dealing with tax violations in the US.

6.2 THE ECONOMICS AND LAWS OF TAXATION

Taxation has been a historical necessity. The Revenue Act of 1861, which was signed into law by Abraham Lincoln, is traditionally regarded as the first US federal income tax. Like all taxes that are paid to governments, the essence of the tax emanated from a financial necessity to finance the Civil War (1861–1865). The tax was levied on the annual income of every individual residing in the US, regardless of the source of income. The 1861 Act imposed a 3 percent tax on income exceeding $800,[3] suggesting that the individuals making less than $800 a year would have been considered poor in the 1860s.

The flat tax of 3 percent is very much unlike the tax brackets and marginal tax rates that are contemporaneously apportioned for various categories of income. Interestingly, some have treated the flat tax with a nostalgic appeal to simplify the contemporary US tax code. A fundamental problem with such an argument is that though the flat tax has a proportional basis that is associated with income volatility, deductions and exemptions (or implementations) can make such a tax policy quickly regressive. The old Revenue Act of 1861, which was repealed by the Revenue Act of 1862, laid the foundation of the modern progressive tax system of variable marginal tax rates and income brackets though it was expected to be temporary until 1866. Table 6.1 suggests that the marginal tax rate (MTR) for $800 in 1862 corresponds to the average tax rate (the ratio of the tax liability to taxable income). In effect, the tax wedge (the difference between the marginal tax rate and the average tax rate) is zero.[4] The 1862 MTR concept can be compared to that of the MTR concept of the Tax Cuts and Jobs Act of 2018 (Table 6.2), which reduced marginal tax rates from the previous tax law, including those of public corporations and small businesses.

The legality of taxes on investments has constantly been challenged going all the way back to the 1890s. For example, in 1895, the US Supreme Court ruled that US federal income tax on interest income, dividend income, and rental income was unconstitutional. In a case, *Pollock v. Farmers' Loan & Trust Company* (157 U.S. 429), which made its way to the US Supreme Court, Pollock complained that a federal tax on income derived from property was unconstitutional when the tax was not levied among the states according to representation of the states in the United States House of Representatives. The court decided in a 5-to-4 decision that the Wilson-Gorman Tariff Act was unconstitutional.[5]

However, the Sixteenth Amendment to the US Constitution eventually gave the US Congress the authority to impose income taxes without apportionment among states on the basis of population.[6]

Income may take multiple forms that can be classified under three broad headings: (i) earnings, (ii) return on investment, and (iii) passive (income that is unrelated to one's active pursuit of revenue). Earned income includes wages, salaries, commissions, fees, tips, and bonuses. Investment income includes dividends, interests, and rent from investments. Passive income is derived from rental property, limited partnership, or other enterprise in which a person is not actively involved. Gross income is a non-discriminatory concept, since it is insensitive to the source of income, which is somewhat analogous to the Revenue Act of 1861.

In the US, corporations and shareholders independently pay taxes on their taxable income; this form of taxation is generally considered to be "double taxation." Shareholders pay tax on dividends that they receive from corporations. Partnerships and S-Corporations, limited liability companies that distribute their tax liabilities, are not typically subjected to double taxation. The 2018 tax law reduced marginal tax rates for C-Corporations (corporations that are taxed separately from their owners) from 35 percent to 21 percent and there is no longer a 15 percent tax on the first $50,000 of the corporate income of such corporations.

There are special rules for certain types of capital gains. Gains on art and collectibles are taxed at ordinary income tax rates up to a maximum rate of 28 percent. Up to $250,000 ($500,000 for married couples) of capital gains from the sale of principal residences is tax-free if taxpayers meet certain conditions including having lived in the house for at least two of the previous five years. Up to the greater of $10 million of capital gains or ten times the basis on stock held for more than five years in a qualified domestic C-corporation with gross assets under $50 million on the date of the stock's issuance are excluded from taxation. Also excluded from taxation are capital gains from investments held for at least ten years in designated Opportunity Funds. Gains on Opportunity Fund investments held between five and ten years are eligible for a partial exclusion. Capital losses may be used to offset capital gains, along with up to $3,000 of other taxable income. The unused portion of a capital loss may be carried over to future years.

The tax basis for an asset received as a gift equals the donor's basis. However, the basis of an inherited asset is "stepped up" to the value of the asset on the date of the donor's death. The step-up provision effectively exempts from income tax any gains on assets held until death. C-corporations pay the regular corporation tax rates on the full amount of their capital gains and may use capital losses only to offset capital gains, not other kinds of income. For most of the history of the income tax, long-term capital gains have been taxed at lower rates than ordinary income (see Figure 6.1). The maximum long-term capital gains and ordinary income tax rates were equal in 1988–2000. Since 2003, qualified dividends have also been taxed at the lower rates (Tax Policy Center).

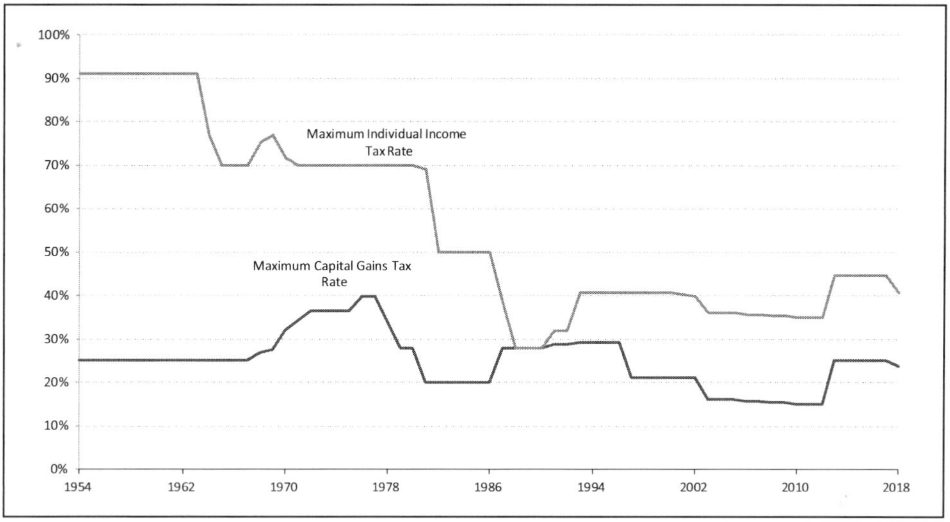

Figure 6.1 Maximum capital gains and individual income tax rate; tax years 1954–2018
Sources: US Department of the Treasury, Office of Tax Analysis (2016); Urban-Brookings Tax Policy Center calculations.
Note: The maximum rates include 3.8 percent tax on net investment income (2013–) and adjusts for the phaseout of itemized deductions (1991–2009, 2013–2017). https://taxpolicycenter.org/.

US tax law permits gross income to be adjusted for tax purposes. Deductions from gross income are generally considered to be adjusted gross income (AGI) for direct taxes (taxes on labor or property that are not necessarily based on transactions). The deductions are technically separated from exemptions that are based on tax status or circumstances like geographic location and religious preconditions. Deductions may be itemized or standardized. Itemized deductions are permissible expenses that can be deducted from AGI while standardized deductions are predetermined amounts on which no taxes may be paid, based on filing status, age, and health conditions. AGI factors include retirement plans, education expenditures, income related to jury duty, and business-related expenditures. Tax credits reduce income tax liability at the federal and state levels. Some credits are available to individuals or businesses. Individuals can obtain child tax credit, credit for educational expenses, and earned income tax credit for low levels of income.[7] Businesses may get Work Opportunity Tax Credit.

Superfluous itemized deductions may trigger an alternative minimum tax (AMT), which is a mandatory alternative to the standardized federal income tax. Hence, in addition to baseline income tax for certain individuals, corporations, estates, and trusts that have exemptions (rather than exclusions) or special circumstances that lower tax liabilities of standard income, the AMT can be utilized to supplement the revenue received by the US Government from some tax payers with exemptions.[8] State and local taxes are deducted from federal tax liability.

According to the Organization for Economic Cooperation and Development (OECD), over an eighteen-year period, an average single worker in the US faced the lowest tax wedge (TW) in 2018. The labor tax wedge (TW) is a measure of the tax on labor income, which includes the tax paid by both the employee and the employer:

$$TW = \frac{PIT + SSC_{Em+EP} - FB}{GW + SSC_{EP}}; \qquad (6.1)$$

where PIT is for personal income tax, SSC_{Em+EP} is for employee (Em) and employer (EP) social security contributions, FB is for family benefits, and GW is for gross wages (total labor costs are equal to GW and SSC_{EP} (employer social contributions)).

Australia had the 24th lowest tax wedge in the OECD for an average married worker with two children at 21.5 percent in 2018, which compares with the OECD average of 26.6 percent. The country occupied the 26th lowest position in 2017. In 2018, the UK had the 27th lowest tax wedge. In 2018 the United States had the 29th lowest tax wedge among the 36 OECD member countries, compared with the 27th in 2017. The 2018 tax wedge is the lowest an average single worker in the United States has faced over the 2000–2018 period; see Table 6.1 for a comparative analysis of the tax-to-GDP ratio for the US and the rest of the OECD countries.[9]

Though the OECD tax-to-GDP ratio is systematically higher relative to the US, corporate tax receipt as a percentage of GDP has been comparatively higher as well (see Figures 6.2 and 6.3). The juxtaposition of tax assessment and receipt is interesting for a variety of theoretical reasons. For quite some time, it has been fashionable to argue that higher tax rates discourage payment of taxes and increase the propensity to avoid or evade taxes; the Tax Laffer Curve, which has been somewhat discredited, is a case in point. Apart from the US, the OECD countries have higher tax rates (in relation to GDP) that also coincide with higher tax receipts as a percentage of GDP. Theories of avoidance and evasion will be subsequently explored in this chapter.

Long-term assets—assets that last longer than a year—depreciate (recall discussions of financial statements and depreciation in Chapter 3) and for accounting and tax purposes, expenditures on such assets are decomposed over the useful lifespan of long-term assets. The straight line method equally depreciates the expenditure on long-term assets over

Table 6.1 Marginal tax rates (MTR) and tax brackets for $800 (Revenue Act of 1862)

MTR	Income bracket ($)	Taxable income	Tax liability	Average tax rate
3%	601–10,000	800	24	3% [24/800]
5%	>10,001			

TAX AVOIDANCE AND EVASION

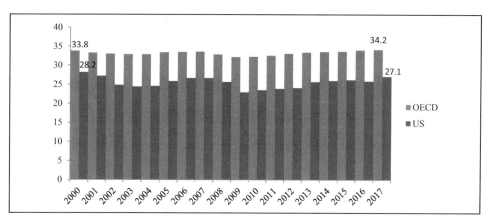

Figure 6.2 OECD and US tax-to-GDP ratio (2000–2017)
Source: OECD.

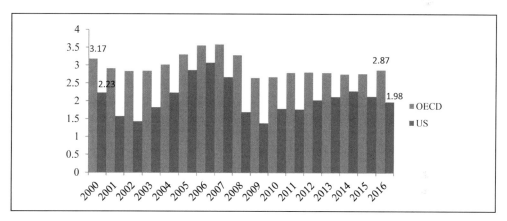

Figure 6.3 OECD and US corporate tax receipt as a percentage of GDP (2000–2016)
Source: OECD.
Note: Taxes on income, profits, and capital gains of corporations. A capital gain is realized when an asset is sold or exchanged at a higher price relative to its *basis*; where *basis* is considered to be an asset's purchase price, plus commissions and the cost of improvements less depreciation.

its useful years. Alternative methods exhibit variations and variability in the rules of depreciation. Depreciation rules for accounting purposes are generally based on Generally Accepted Accounting Principles (GAAP), which are unidentical to those required by the Internal Revenue Service (IRS). When it comes to depreciation, accountants are given latitudes of reasonable discretion under GAAP rules. They can predict the longevity of assets in ways that can reduce capital consumption expenditures. In the US, an accelerated method of depreciation known as the Modified Accelerated Cost Recovery System (MACRS) was enacted for federal tax calculations by the Tax Reform Act of 1986 (see Table 6.3).

Table 6.2 Marginal tax rates (MTR) and tax brackets (Tax Cuts and Jobs Act of 2018)

Marginal tax rate	Individual	Married filing jointly
10%	Up to $9,525	Up to $19,050
12%	$9,526–$38,700	$19,051–$77,400
22%	$38,701–$82,500	$77,401–$165,000
24%	$82,501–$157,500	$165,001–$315,000
32%	$157,501–$200,000	$315,001–$400,000
35%	$200,001–$500,000	$400,001–$600,000
37%	Over $500,000	Over $600,000

Unlike the reliance on reasonable professional discretion for depreciating long-term assets, MACRS stipulates tax charges on an accelerated manner to increase expedited tax savings; though the straight-line method is not followed in its traditional form in Table 6.3, all classes convert to the straight-line depreciation in optimal years (denoted by asterisks). The table shows the percentage of long-term expenditures that can be depreciated for stipulated years, ranging from three to 20 years. It is noteworthy that the depreciation schedules or years are extended incrementally; for example, depreciation for a three-year-schedule goes into the 4th year. The overlap compensates for assets that are introduced into operations in the middle of a year. The categories of specific assets have legally defined stipulated life span (see Table 6.4).

Invariably, taxes are good for essential social spending and investments. Not all goods and services can be provided by the private sector, because they generate positive and social external effects that are too costly. Additionally, it may be undesirable for the private sector to unduly profit from such essential goods and services when poorer people are priced out of the markets for essential goods like healthcare and education (national investment in human capital). That is, the exorbitant profits to be realized will not necessarily be in the national interest of a nation. Accordingly, taxes must be wisely levied, and revenues must be utilized to facilitate long-term economic growth and improvement on national welfare. Inadequate revenue or mismanagement cannot attain long-term economic growth and improvement in national welfare. Further, theories that prospectively rely on contingent revenue are not likely to attain the twin objectives of economic growth and development; they lean against the wind or are founded on "hope against hope."

In Chapter 4, I alluded to innovation and economic growth. Government revenue is not neutral to the process of economic growth. Therefore, it is critical for governments to be able to collect all the revenue that is essential for social spending obligations, including investment in human capital that is so critical to innovation and stabilization of aggregate economies and unemployment insurance. Before the Great Depression of the 1930s, the stabilizing role of government spending and taxes did not attract much attention.

Table 6.3 MACRS depreciation schedules by allowable recovery period

Recovery year	3-year	5-year	7-year	10-year	15-year	20-year
1	33.33	20.00	14.29	10.00	5.00	3.750
2	44.45	32.00	24.49	18.00	9.50	7.219
3	14.81 *	19.20	17.49	14.40	8.55	6.677
4	7.41	11.52 *	12.49	11.52	7.70	6.177
5		11.52	8.93 *	9.22	6.93	5.713
6		5.76	8.92	7.37	6.23	5.285
7			8.93	6.55 *	5.90 *	4.888
8			4.46	6.55	5.90	4.522
9				6.56	5.91	4.462 *
10				6.55	5.90	4.461
11				3.28	5.91	4.462
12					5.90	4.461
13					5.91	4.462
14					5.90	4.461
15					5.91	4.462
16					2.95	4.461
17						4.462
18						4.461
19						4.462
20						4.461
21						2.231

Notes:
The 3-, 5-, 7-, and 10-year classes use 200% and the 15- and 20-year classes use 150% declining balance depreciation. All classes convert to straight-line depreciation in the optimal year, shown with an asterisk (*). Half-year depreciation is allowed in the first and last recovery years. If more than 40% of the year's MACRS property is placed in service in the last three months, then a mid-quarter convention must be used with depreciation tables that are not shown here. Various schedules can be found in IRS publication 946 (2018).

The prevalent orthodoxy was reliance on free market operations and market efficiency. As the Depression worsened, it became apparent that government spending could play a stabilizing role during and after the Depression of the 1930s. Some people fell into a period of forgetfulness in periods of prosperity and the oil shocks of the 1970s and stagflation prefaced notions about the natural death of Keynesian policies. It took another recession or mild depression (2007/2008) to reaffirm the importance of deficit financing.

In the morass of the mortgage-backed crisis (MBS), the US Congress passed the American Recovery and Reinvestment Act (2009 stimulus bill). The law provided for an estimated

Table 6.4 MACRS depreciation schedules and asset description*

Class	Depreciation period	Description
3-year property	3 years	Tractor units for over-the-road use, racehorses over 2 years old when placed in service, any other horse over 12 years old when placed in service, qualified rent-to-own property
5-year property	5 years	Automobiles, taxis, buses, trucks, computers and peripheral equipment, office equipment, any property used in research and experimentation, breeding cattle and dairy cattle, appliances etc., used in residential rental real estate activity, certain green energy property
7-year property	7 years	Office furniture and fixtures, agricultural machinery and equipment, any property not designated as being in another class, natural gas gathering lines
10-year property	10 years	Vessels, barges, tugs, single-purpose agricultural or horticultural structures, trees/vines bearing fruits or nuts, qualified small electric meter and smart electric grid systems
15-year property	15 years	Certain land improvements (such as shrubbery, fences, roads, sidewalks, and bridges), retail motor fuels outlets, municipal wastewater treatment plants, clearing and grading land improvements for gas utility property, electric transmission property, natural gas distribution lines
20-year property	20 years	Farm buildings (other than those noted under 10-year property), municipal sewers not categorized as 25-year property, the initial clearing and grading of land for electric utility transmission and distribution plants

Source: Accountingtools.com and IRS (2018).
Notes:
* Description and schedules for 3 to 20- year property on December 15, 2018.
Some types of business expenses are deductible over a period of years rather than when incurred. These include the cost of long-lived assets such as buildings and equipment. The cost of such assets is recovered through deductions for depreciation or amortization (see Chapter 5).

$800 billion in lopsided government spending and tax cuts to resuscitate a moribund economy. Spending on infrastructure was conspicuous, but unemployment insurance was probably the most redeeming aspect of the stimulus levers. Unemployment insurance spending contributed about $54 billion a year to the recovery of the US economy. It is estimated that the fiscal stimulus reduced the unemployment rolls by as much as three million and kept the economy from contracting by around 2 percent (Blinder & Zandi, 2010). The effects of government spending on national output are obviously derived from the ability of governments to collect revenue and spend it wisely. Economists have traditionally appraised these effects in conjunction with contingent Keynesian multipliers: (i) spending multiplier, and (ii) tax (cut) multiplier:

$$\frac{\Delta Y}{\Delta G} = \left(\frac{1}{1-MPC}\right);\qquad(6.2)$$

where ΔY is for the change in national output, ΔG is for the change in government spending, and MPC is for the marginal propensity to consume (MPC); Equation 6.2 defines the contingent spending multiplier, which is dependent on the intensity of leakage (saving, imports, and taxes) that could attenuate the real effect of autonomous government spending on output. In macroeconomics, a corollary of the spending multiplier is the tax multiplier:

$$\frac{\Delta Y}{-\Delta T} = \left(\frac{-MPC}{1-MPC}\right);\qquad(6.3)$$

In this case, the reduction in taxes—not avoidance and evasion, but the contribution to spending—is what is driving economic activity. By definition, it could be seen that the spending effect is greater than the tax effect for any comparable measure of propensity

Table 6.5a Narrative approach: first year tax multipliers*

Study	Country	T	Notes
Cloyne (2013)	United Kingdom	0.6	Maximum multiplier reached after 10 quarters (about 2.5)
Favero and Giavazzi (2012)	United States	0.7	Maximum multiplier reached after 9 quarters (just below 1)
Guajardo and others (2014)	Panel of OECD countries	1	After two years, multiplier reaches about 3
Hayo and Uhl (2014)	Germany	1	Maximum multiplier after 8 quarters (about 2.4)
Mertens and Ravn (2013)	United States	1	Maximum multiplier reached after 8 quarters (about 2)
Romer and Romer (2010)	United States	1.2	Maximum multiplier reached after 10 quarters (around 3)

Source: Batini, Eyraud, Foni, and Weber (2014, p. 4).
Notes:
* Response of output in percent following an exogenous tax shock of 1 percent of GDP.
The narrative approach seeks to identify exogenous fiscal shocks directly, since structural VARs that use output elasticities and revenue may not completely filter out automatic stabilizers; changes in output may also be due to asset and commodity price movements. The tax method uses estimates of fiscal measures from budget documents (Romer & Romer, 2010), while excluding the subset of tax measures in response to short-term macroeconomic fluctuations (such fluctuations are not considered to be exogenous).

Table 6.5b Narrative approach: first year spending multipliers*

Study	G	Notes
Barro and Redlick (2011)	0.4–0.6	Based on US defense spending news; 1917–2006; lower multiplier for temporary spending changes, higher end of range for permanent spending changes
Guajardo and others (2014)	0.3	Overall spending shock. After two years, multiplier reaches about 1
Hall (2009)	0.6	Based on US defense spending news; 1930–2008
Owyang, Ramey, Zubairy (2013)	United States: 0.8. Canada: 0.4–1.6	Based on US defense spending news; 1890–2010 for the United States, 1921–2011 for Canada. Two-year multipliers; in Canada range of multipliers reflects low unemployment (low multiplier) and high unemployment (high multiplier) regimes. In the United States, multipliers do not differ significantly across regimes
Ramey (2011)	1.1–1.2	Based on US defense spending news; 1939–2008 "defense-news" reflect changes in the expected present value of government spending in response to military events; peak multiplier after 6 quarters

Source: Batini et al. (2014, p. 5).
Notes:
* Reported estimates correspond to the response of output in percent following an exogenous spending shock of 1 percent of GDP. First year multiplier unless otherwise noted.

On the spending side, some studies have used news about future military spending as a measure of *exogenous shocks* (e.g., Ramey, 2011). "The idea is that military spending is determined by wars and foreign policy developments and not by concerns about the state of the economy" (Romer, 2011).

to consume and choice of stimulus amount. Over the years, some economists have spent time studying the sizes of the multipliers from which the propensities to consume can be derived by mathematical manipulation or simple cross-multiplication.

The size of the multipliers are generally determined by the structural characteristics—factors that are indispensable to the way an economy operates over a longer period of time—which impact an economy's response to fiscal disturbances in normal times, and the conjunctural (temporary, cyclical, or policy related) phenomena, which cause the effects of multipliers to deviate from normal levels. The incremental effect of structural factors on multipliers is unknown. Structural characteristics are defined by trade regime, labor market rigidity or flexibility, the size of automatic stabilizers, exchange rate regimes, and levels of indebtedness.

Empirical evidence shows that large economies with lower propensities to import and partial openness to trade tend to have higher fiscal multipliers; demand leakage through imports is less pronounced in these countries.[10] Countries with more rigid labor markets (with stronger unions, and/or with stronger labor market regulation) and wage inflexibility tend to have larger fiscal multipliers, since rigid wages amplify the response of output to demand shocks (Cole & Ohanian, 2004).

As far as automatic stabilizers and exchange rates are concerned, Dolls, Fuest, and Peichl (2012) show that larger automatic stabilizers reduce fiscal multipliers, since mechanically, the automatic response of transfers and taxes offsets part of the initial fiscal shock, thus lowering its effect on GDP. Highly indebted countries generally have lower multipliers since fiscal consolidation (simultaneous reduction of deficits and debts) is likely to have positive credibility and confidence effects on private demand and the interest rate risk premium.[11] Multipliers are expected to be smaller when evasion and avoidance (difficulties to collect taxes) limit the impact of fiscal policy on output. Countries with flexible exchange rate regimes have been discovered to have smaller multipliers, because exchange rate movements can counteract the effect of discretionary fiscal policy on the economy.[12]

The conjunctural or temporary factors have been linked to the state of the business cycle. Fiscal multipliers tend to be larger in downturns than in expansions; a finding that seems to hold both for fiscal consolidation and stimulus. Notably, expansionary monetary policy and a lowering of interest rates can dilute the impact of fiscal contraction on demand. By contrast, Erceg and Lindé (2010) and Woodford (2011) multipliers can potentially be larger, when the use and/or the transmission of monetary policy is impaired—as is the case at the zero interest lower bound (ZLB).

Since taxes must fund discretionary and non-discretionary spending, taxes must be collected and spent prudently. Discretionary spending is the portion of the US federal budget that is decided by the US Congress through the annual appropriations process; such spending is set each year by the US Congress. Figure 6.4 shows the proposed discretionary spending for 2020. By far, the biggest category of proposed spending is defense, which shows the philosophical preference of the government when it comes to spending revenue. Investment-enhancing categories like education and health are given residual considerations.

Unlike discretionary spending, mandatory spending is spending that has been legislated and is unrelated to the annual appropriations process. It is dominated by benefit programs like Social Security and Medicare. It also includes welfare- or life-supporting spending like Supplemental Nutrition Assistance Program (SNAP, formerly food stamps), and federal spending on transportation, among other things for those who are poorer and generally priced out of goods and financial markets. Figure 6.5 shows proposed mandatory spending for 2020.

Many mandatory programs have predetermined eligibility rules and spending levels are determined by eligibility rules. Recipients of Social Security and Medicaid must meet age

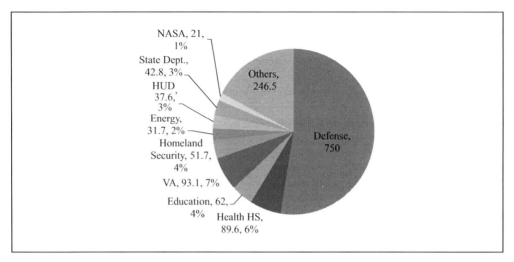

Figure 6.4 US proposed discretionary spending in 2020 ($1.43 trillion)
Source: Amadeo, Kimberly (www.thebalance.com).
Note: Annual spending appropriation ($1.43 trillion).

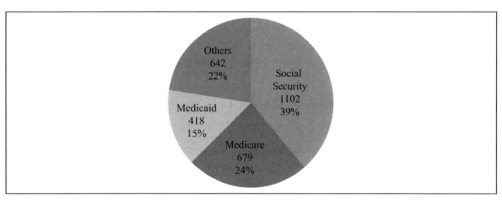

Figure 6.5 US total proposed mandatory spending in 2020 ($2.84 trillion)
Data Source: Amadeo, Kimberly (www.thebalance.com).

and/or medical and income requirements. The amount of money spent on Social Security each year is then determined by how many people are eligible and apply for benefits; for example, at the time of this writing, there are age requirements to get old age insurance benefits (Social Security): (i) 65 years for those who were born in 1937 or earlier, (ii) 66 years for those who were born between 1943 and 1954, and (iii) 67 years for those who were born in 1960 or thereafter. Medicaid is tied to relative poverty lines. Instead of increasing or decreasing the spending limits for mandatory spending, the US Congress periodically revisits the eligibility requirements. Figure 6.5 shows that Social Security is the most pressing component of mandatory spending and it has been a very financially demanding component for a very long time. Can the governments collect enough revenue to meet their spending obligations? Government policies, tax evasion and avoidance, and economic conditions (shocks) are ultimate revenue determinants. While policy makers do not necessarily have control over exogenous shocks, they can impact the intensity of tax evasion and avoidance.

6.3 THE US TAX GAP

The gross tax gap is the difference between true tax liability for a given tax year and the amount that is paid on time. It is comprised of the nonfiling gap, the underreporting gap, and the underpayment (or remittance) gap. The net tax gap is the portion of the gross tax gap that will never be recovered through enforcement or other late payments. Table 6.6 provides information about tax gaps for tax years 2006 and 2008 to 2010. Overall voluntary compliance rate actually fell for the period under consideration, but this drop is not considered to be significant. The gaps for tax years 2008–2010 are estimated averages.[13]

Table 6.6 Tax gap estimates for tax years 2006 and 2008–2010 and decomposition of change (money amounts are in billions of US$)

Tax gap component	TY 2006	TY2008–2010[1]	Total change	Change due to: Updated methods[2]	Change due to: Other factors
Estimated total true liability	2,660	2,496	-164	14	-178
Gross tax gap	450	458	8[3]	22	-14
Nonfiling tax gap	28	32	4	4	[5]
Underreporting gap	376	387	11	24	-13
Underpayment gap	46	39	-7	-6	-1
Overall voluntary compliance rate	83.1%	81.7%	-1.4%	-0.8%	-0.7%
Enforced and other late payments	65	52	-13	-12	-1
Net tax gap[4]	385	406	21	34	-13
Overall net compliance rate	85.5%	83.7%	-1.8%	-1.2%	-0.6%

Source: IRS, *Research Analysis and Statistics* (2016, p. 8).
Notes:
1 The estimates are the annual averages for the Tax Year 2008–2010 timeframe.
2 Difference between the TY 2006 and TY2008–2010 tax gap estimates accounted for by updated methods and new tax gap components.
3 Difference between the TY2006 and TY 2008–2010 tax gap estimates accounted for by changes in economic activity, changes in compliance behavior and statistical variability.
4 The net tax gap is the gross tax gap reduced by the amount of enforced and other late payments that will eventually be collected. Compliance rate is net tax gap as a percent of gross.
5 Less than 0.5 billion. Detail may not add to total due to rounding.

The gross tax gap for nonfiling, underreporting, and underpayment increased from $450 billion to $458 billion for the period under review with a declining compliance rate of about 1.4 percent. The nonfiling tax gap is the tax gap associated with tax returns that were filed after the filing deadline or valid extension date—or were not filed at all. Underreporting is deliberately reporting less income or revenue than what is actually received. Underpayment occurs when taxpayers do not pay the required tax liability for a given tax year.

The new estimates suggest that compliance is substantially unchanged, mainly as a result of the methodological improvements in estimates. The estimated Voluntary Compliance Resolution (VCR) is lower than the previous TY 2006 estimate. The IRS maintains that about half of the 1.4 percentage point difference in overall compliance rate is attributable to the updated methods. The challenges in estimating the tax gap and the many factors that contribute to differences of 0.7 percent over time do not necessarily infer that noncompliance has increased.

Many factors have been identified as contributory to the differences over time in both the gross tax gap and the VCR:

> These include factors such as the overall level of economic activity, changes in the composition of economic activity with shifts toward those with higher or lower compliance rates, changes in tax law and administration, updated data and improved methodologies, and changes in underlying compliance behavior on the part of taxpayers and preparers. Since the tax gap typically moves with the economy, the December 2007 through June 2009 recession and the weak recovery that followed contributed to the gross tax gap remaining substantially unchanged from the previously released TY 2006 estimate.
>
> (IRS, 2016, p. 8)

The estimated net compliance rate (NCR) is 83.7 percent, which is 1.8 percentage points lower than the 85.5 percent NCR for TY 2006. According to the IRS,

> there is no single approach for estimating all the components of the tax gap. Each approach is subject to nonsampling error; the component estimates that are based on samples are further subject to sampling error. The uncertainty of the estimates is therefore not readily captured by standard errors that typically accompany estimates based on sample data. For that reason, standard errors, confidence intervals, and statistical comparisons across years are not reported.
>
> (IRS, 2016, p. 1)

The reasons and sources for the gross tax gap as outlined by the IRS show expected variations. The individual income tax nonfiling tax gap is estimated to be $26 billion, or about 81 percent of the total estimated nonfiling tax gap. The self-employment tax nonfiling tax gap is estimated to be $4 billion, or about 13 percent of the total estimated nonfiling tax gap. The estate tax nonfiling tax gap is estimated to be $2 billion. The individual income tax underreporting tax gap estimate is $264 billion, or 68 percent of the overall gross underreporting tax gap. The corporation income tax underreporting tax gap estimate is $41 billion, or about 11 percent of the overall underreporting tax gap. The employment tax underreporting tax gap estimate is $81 billion, and the estate tax estimate is $1 billion, representing 21 percent and less than one-half of one percent of the overall underreporting tax gap, respectively.[14]

The IRS tax data reveal that about 9 percent of the gross tax gap results from taxpayers not paying taxes in full at the time when reports are filed on a timely basis. The estimated underpayment tax gap is $39 billion (2000–2010). About $29 billion (4 percent) of the underpayment tax gap is attributed to underpayment of individual income tax. Underpayment of employment taxes (Federal Insurance Contributions Act, FICA, and Federal Unemployment Tax Act, FUTA) and the railroad retirement tax is estimated to account for 15 percent of the underpayment tax gap. Underpayment of corporation income taxes accounts for 8 percent of the underpayment tax gap. These shares correspond to $6 billion and $3 billion respectively. Excise tax and estate tax account for the remaining $1 billion.[15]

Some of the gross tax gap is collected through IRS enforcement and administrative efforts and some is paid late without any IRS action taken. The total amount of enforced and other late payments is $52 billion. About 54 percent of the total, or $28 billion, is associated with individual income tax. About 17 percent of the total is the $9 billion in corporation income tax enforced and other late payments. Employment tax enforced and other late payments are 23 percent of the total or $12 billion. Estate tax enforced and other late payments are $3 billion or about 6 percent of the total. Excise taxes enforced and other late payments account for less than one-half of one percent of all enforced and late payments.[16]

Figure 6.6 captures time dynamics of the tax gap since the 1980s, recognizing an obvious methodological shift in the computation of the gap. The illustration shows a steep climb in the gap after the 1990s, with incremental ascent thereafter. Reasons for the ascent are rather imprecise, but general methodological change, economic conditions, tax laws, and enforcement can be good candidates; invariably, tax avoidance and evasion cannot be discounted.

6.4 THEORIES OF TAX AVOIDANCE AND EVASION

Tax analysts or theorists have developed diverse theories to explain why some taxpayers, including financial institutions, are predisposed to reduce their tax liability. Less altruistic humans can hardly envision why they should pay their "fair" share to society. Of course, "fair" is subjective and ambivalent when it is not legally defined, and its subjective attribute implies that it is permissible to avoid paying taxes whenever illegal intent cannot be ascertained. Not

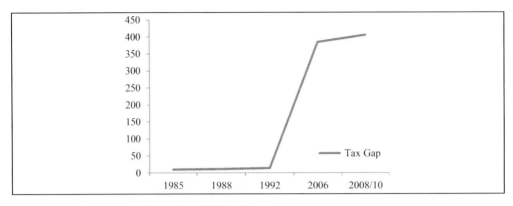

Figure 6.6 US tax gap (1985–2010) (US$ billion)
Sources: IRS' *Research Analysis and Statistics* (1996, p. 5) and *Research Analysis and Statistics* (2016, p. 8).
Notes: The gaps for TY1985, TY1988 and TY1992 are the high end numbers for the gross tax gap. The numbers for TY2006 to TY 2008/10 are net numbers. The methodology of tax gap measures changed after the 1990s (see footnote number 4 of Table 6.6). The magnitude of the net tax gap from 2006 to 2010 obscures the gross tax gap for TY1985 ($9.8b), TY 1988 ($11.2b) and TY1992 ($13.8b). It is probable that the gaps of the 1980s were underestimated.

surprisingly, there is a general perception that it is always best to pay the least amount of taxes possible whenever a tax law is not violated; a lot of personal finance texts and financial analysts make such an argument. The analysts and texts are not entirely wrong, because deficient tax laws permit conjectures about "fairness" and quizzical notions of (in)adequate tax revenue for investment, provision of essential services, and economic growth.

Accordingly, the distinction between avoidance and evasion is a legal issue. While tax evasion is outright illegal, tax avoidance is nuanced and strenuously contingent on willful intent. Inevitably, those with the financial and intellectual wherewithal will exploit tax loopholes to pay less, which calls into question the actual progressivity of a tax structure beyond the theoretical insinuations and stipulations of progressivity. Notably, humans are instinctively predisposed to acquire money for transaction, investment, precaution, and consumption. For quite some time in the 1930s and 1940s, corporations paid more in taxes (as a percentage of total federal revenue) in the US than individuals (see Figure 6.7).

However, from the mid-1940s to 1984, the share of corporate taxes as a percentage of federal revenue plummeted precipitously; suggesting that the incidence or burden of federal taxes fell heavily on individuals and, to varying degrees of intensity, individuals have carried such a burden. While this book is less suited for the diagnoses of entrepreneurial reward, the literature on the performance of corporations and fairness of entrepreneurial reward is abundantly controversial and disturbing, which raises the question—as some have pointed out— of whether the US can also be seen as a corporate tax haven.

TAX AVOIDANCE AND EVASION

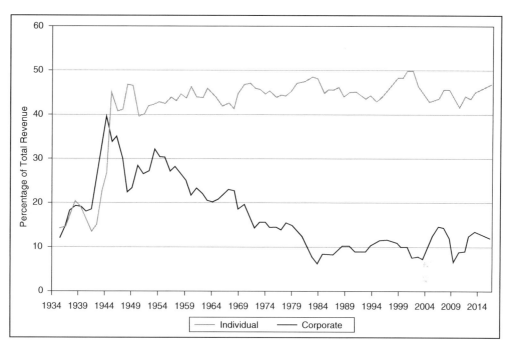

Figure 6.7 Individual and corporate income taxes, 1934–2015 (as percentage of total federal revenue)
Source: National Priorities Project (2011).

The reluctance to raise sufficient tax revenue is usually grounded on the theory that taxes compromise the ability of nations to grow; the argument does not pay very close attention to the growth-enhancing prospects of investments. It presupposes that taxes are for consumption purposes. Consequently, the argument can only be plausible if and only if (iff) taxes are collected to finance unproductive consumption (consumption that does not promote investment and enhance human welfare). For a randomly selected geographic cluster of countries, albeit a small number of countries, the evidence does not unequivocally support the theory that higher levels of taxes impede economic growth. Consider Figure 6.8 and Table 6.6.

In Figure 6.8, South Africa, UK, Australia, and France form a cohort of countries for which the tax revenue as a percentage of GDP is relatively higher than that of the other countries in the simple clustered sampling; yet, the record of economic growth over the ten-year period does not negatively correlate with the contribution of tax revenue as a percentage of GDP. Australia and South Africa recorded relatively higher levels of economic growth than countries with lower levels of tax revenue as a percentage of GDP; both countries grew at an average rate of 2.78 and 2.08 percent respectively. Further, countries in the lower tax cohort like Brazil, Mexico, and Canada outperformed the US during the decade under review. Of all the countries in the higher tax cohort, only France was outcompeted by the others for the period under consideration.

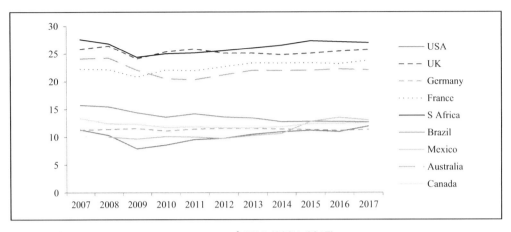

Figure 6.8 Tax revenue as a percentage of GDP (2007–2017)
Data Source: World Development Indicators (2019).

Table 6.7 Average annual GDP growth (2007–2017)*

Rank	Country	GDP growth	Rank	Country	GDP growth
(i)	Australia	2.78	(v)	US	1.5
(ii)	Mexico	2.09	(vi)	Germany	1.43
(iii)	South Africa	2.08	(vii)	UK	1.25
(iv)	Brazil	2.02	(viii)	France	0.93

Data Source: World Development Indicators (2019).
Note:
*Annual percentage growth rate of GDP at market prices based on constant local currency. Aggregates are based on constant 2010 US dollars. GDP is the sum of gross value added by all resident producers in the economy plus any product taxes and minus any subsidies not included in the value of the products. It is calculated without making deductions for depreciation of fabricated assets or for depletion and degradation of natural resources.

Apart from the much more routine argument that relates taxes to economic growth, one of the earliest theories that focused on avoidance and evasion—a human psychological response to taxes—made its debut in the 1970s. The Tax Laffer Curve, which crystallized the main arguments for instinctive human behavior, was greeted with acclaim by all those who were interested in keeping a large portion of income, which has been classified under three broad headings: (i) earnings, (ii) return on investment, and (iii) passive (income that is unrelated to one's active pursuit of revenue).

Actually, Laffer's theory, which was widely perceived as a supply-side theory, is a hybrid rendition of human psychological behavior and economic performance. The tax theory holds that humans who are prone to hide their money from governments will be discouraged from paying taxes as their tax liabilities increase, which will result in a loss in revenue for governments. On the contrary, lower taxes will stimulate economic growth. Supply-side theories have always presumed that what is produced will be consumed via

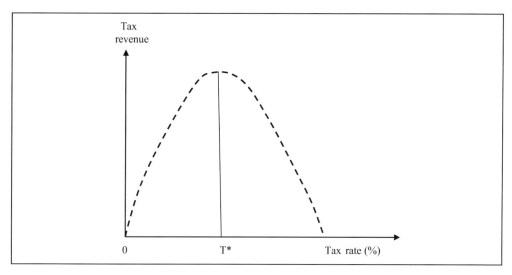

Figure 6.9 The Tax Laffer curve

the employment channel (Say's eighteenth-century theory relied on derived demand and a phobia of saving, because of inflation). By so doing, supply siders have always inadvertently discounted the role of aggregate consumption in a macroeconomy. In reality, consumption is the engine of economic growth; it is what drives production. Consumption facilitates increased revenues, taxes, and innovation. Therefore, income must be adequate to finance consumption. Alternatively, businesses will have to warehouse and accumulate inventories without adequate consumption. Figure 6.9 shows the precarious and embattled relationship between tax revenue and marginal tax rate as it was conceived by the provocative Laffer theory. The positive relationship between marginal tax rate, which is implicitly based on levels of income and tax revenue, is positive only to a certain point of tax rate (T★); thereafter, increases in tax rates will lead to falling tax revenues. Alternatively, on the negative side of the relationship, reducing higher tax rates has the potential of increasing tax revenue. The real shape of the curve is a shifting target that is dynamically and empirically imprecise; a rather refractory phenomenon for policy analysis. Tax policy is inherently dynamic.

The prohibitive tax rate (T)★, say 100 percent (on the scale of 0 to 100 percent) is generally impractical; since not tax policy nor structure can be so confiscatory and odious on a systematic basis. Rates that are higher than 100 percent are untenable. The incentive to work and the employment channel have provided ample fodder for supply siders.

A positive correlation between business tax cuts and employment is somewhat presumptive. When people are employed, they will purchase goods and services. However, the employment channel must be unclogged for the theory to work nicely. There is an *ex ante* assumption that business will hire to increase their costs of doing business without reducing their short- and long-term liabilities or paying their shareholders handsome dividends. The unintended paradox is that wealth will circulate within the mercantile class with little revenue for government as the tax rate remains statically low and delinked from economic realities; public investment is sacrificed as businesses instinctively find ways to further reduce their tax liabilities by legally avoiding tax payments. What if the businesses want to save instead of spend money (a leakage)? What if it is too costly to provide healthcare benefits for new employees? What if it is better to employ unskilled labor or maintain an underemployed army of workers? Wealthier folks may even take a vacation to Utopia without stimulating aggregate consumption. These salient questions underscore the concept that poorly targeted tax policies may not necessarily create an economic environment for robust public investment and aggregate consumption.

Historically, economic theories have revealed that there is hardly a school of economic thought with a monopoly of correctness. The regularity conditions of some economic models might just be too restrictive for the models to gain practical effect and universal appeal. Modern economies have become more complex and relatively wealthy consumers are also investors. Accordingly, it has become a laborious proposition to separate the interests of some investors from those of consumers. Rich investors are also consumers. Yet, there are consumers who are not investors; such consumers are usually priced out of essential markets and unmoored from the fortunes of financial markets. Therefore, taxes must neither be too prohibitively high nor too ridiculously low to prevent governments from fulfilling their financial obligations. This means that tax policies must be targeted to achieve balanced budgets and economic growth without incapacitating the ability of businesses to generate wealth and innovate. That is, tax policy must be based on economic necessity rather than political expedience for re-election. Pointedly, the stringency of taxes must be based on economic necessity rather than political conjecture. Of course, history has shown that tax rates have never been sacrosanct; meaning that the outcome of general prosperity will inevitably lower taxes in a market-oriented economy. Questions abound as to whether policymakers can accomplish their targeted objectives even before they get to the midpoint of the rising segment of the Laffer Curve.

Some of the most intriguing assessments of the Laffer Curve can be found in the work of Goolsbee (1999). The literature on tax rates and labor supply has shown that there is very little impact of changes in tax rates on labor supply for most people, especially for prime age working men. That is, tax cuts and economic growth via the employment channel is very tenuous. Some of the studies have not pointedly addressed the relationship between tax cuts and economic growth, or the channels of economic growth and equity, which are implicit outcomes of the Laffer theory. Rather, a lot of intellectual capital has been spent on evaluating the income effect of tax cuts on specific groups *ex post facto* (the elasticity approach), a rather pointed response to the theoretical prognostications of the theory in relation to labor and leisure. Over the years, data quality has posed additional empirical pitfalls. Goolsbee's paper provides a comprehensive analysis of the elasticity approach, dating all the way back to the 1920s and the various ways in which the Laffer theorem has fallen short.

The basic framework for appraising the theory has been an optimization algorithm, in which individuals maximize utility with respect to a budget (income) constraint that is sensitive to tax changes.[17] Additionally, an individual can also make choices about shifting income and consumption out of taxable forms to tax-free forms when tax changes conduce people to make such adjustments, thereby justifying the Laffer prognosis.[18] Feldstein's model adds nontaxable income (E) and nontaxable consumption (D) to a prototypical model with consumption, C, and leisure (L). An individual could then maximize utility over consumption, leisure, nontaxable income, and nontaxable consumption, U(C, L, E, D), subject to the income constraint:

$$C = (1 - \tau)[w(1 - L) - E - D], \tag{6.4}$$

where w is the wage rate and τ is the marginal tax rate. The term in square brackets on the right-hand side of Equation 6.4 is defined as taxable income. It is total compensation minus deductions and tax-exempt income. Rearranging the budget constraint makes obvious the dependence of the deadweight loss on factors that transcend the labor supply. If 1 + z can be defined to be $1/(1 - \tau)$, the Feldstein budget constraint can be redefined as:

$$C(1 + z) = w(1 - L) - E - D. \tag{6.5}$$

In this model a rise in the standard income tax (τ) raises the price of taxable consumption, but it does not change the relative price of L, E, or D. In other words, all of the nontaxed factors make up a "composite outside good." The deadweight loss of the income tax is stipulated to be equivalent to the deadweight loss from a sales tax at rate z on taxable consumption. The magnitude of the deadweight loss is contingent on the size of the reduction of taxable consumption.

In models like Equation 6.5, the idea of whether lower consumption increases leisure, nontaxable income, or consumption is presumed to be irrelevant. If the utility maximizer is not in a corner solution (unable to make a trade-off, because the quantity of one of the maximizing arguments is zero), it is unnecessary to know the elasticity of substitution in the utility function of the untaxed goods. Feldstein estimates the deadweight loss will be:

$$\frac{1}{2}\left(\frac{z}{1+z}\right)e_C zC, \tag{6.6}$$

where eC is the elasticity of taxable consumption with respect to 1 + z, and compensated changes is equal to:

$$\frac{1}{2}\tau^2\left(\frac{z}{1+z}\right)e\pi TI; \tag{6.7}$$

where TI is taxable income and eTI is the elasticity of taxable income with respect to the net-of-tax share $(1 - \tau)$.

Allusions to some efficiency costs and normative issues of tax avoidance and evasion can be found in the work of Slemrod and Yitzhaki (2002). They present a general theory of optimal tax systems, in which tax rates and bases are chosen simultaneously with the administrative and enforcement regimes. A marginal efficiency cost of funds, which is expanded to include administrative costs, avoidance, and evasion, is utilized to summarize the normative issues.

The study finds that though most economic analysis of taxation presumes that tax liability can be ascertained and collected costlessly, tax liabilities may not be paid (see also discussions of the tax gap in the previous section). The resource cost of collecting taxes can be substantial and the costs of tax administration need to be incorporated into the positive and normative assessments of taxation. Tax models in this tradition, dating back to the 1970s, presume that taxpayers know their tax liabilities (A-S model, see Allingham & Sandmo, 1972) but are also aware that the collection of taxes by collecting agencies is not a costless endeavor. This precondition incentivizes a taxpayer to understate his/her tax obligation. Therefore, in the A-S model, it is assumed that all real decisions, and implicitly taxable income (y), are constant; the taxpayer chooses what to report. The risk-averse taxpayer chooses to report (x), and thus an amount of unreported income is y-x. The taxpayer must then maximize the following tax utility function:

$$EU = (1-p)U(v + \tau(y-x)) + pU(v - \theta(y-x)) \qquad (6.8)$$

where v is true after-tax income, $y(1-t)$, τ being the rate of (proportional) income tax. The von Neumann-Morgenstern utility function $U(.)$ represents the individual's preferences toward risk. In this model, it is argued that the choice of whether and how much to evade is akin to a choice of whether and how much to gamble. Each dollar of taxable income understatement offers a payoff of τ with probability $(1-p)$, along with a penalty of θ with probability, p. If and only if the expected payoff to this gamble, $(1-p)\tau - p\theta$, is positive, every risk-averse taxpayer will embrace some tolerable level of evasion by deliberating tying the evading amount to the taxpayer's expected payoff and risk preferences.[19]

The expected payoff per dollar of evaded income becomes $(1-p)\tau - p\theta\tau$. The expected payoff suggests that the tax rate has no effect on the terms of the tax evasion gamble; as τ rises, the reward from a successful understatement of a dollar rises, but the cost of a detected understatement rises proportionately. The first order condition for optimal evasion becomes:

$$\frac{U'(y_A)}{U'(y_U)} = \frac{(1-p)}{p\theta}; \qquad (6.9)$$

where y_A and y_U refer to net income in the audited and unaudited states respectively. Equation 6.9 does not present the tax rate (τ) as a multiplicative factor, where increases in the tax rate will incentivize the understatement of income. Equation 6.9 shows that individuals with higher income will evade more when absolute risk aversion is decreasing; whether higher-income individuals will evade more, as a fraction of income, is contingent on relative risk aversion. It

TAX AVOIDANCE AND EVASION

is argued that evasion relative to income will decrease, increase, or stay unchanged as a fraction of income depending on whether relative risk aversion is an increasing, decreasing, or constant function of income. Increases in either p or θ will decrease evasion.

Increasing τ has both an income effect and, possibly, a substitution effect. If the taxpayer has decreasing absolute risk aversion, the income decline makes a less risky position optimal. An increase in τ has a substitution effect, increasing the relative price of consumption in the audited state, and thereby encouraging evasion, if the penalty is related to income, rather than tax avoided. In the latter case, if the penalty is related to the tax evaded, a tax increase has no substitution effect, so that an increase in τ *reduces* evasion as long as there is decreasing relative risk aversion. The modified version of the A–S model has been criticized for its probabilistic allotments of audited returns (p) and statutory penalty for avoidance (θ). It is presumed that in reality, people should avoid the payment of taxes a lot more based on the degree of risk aversion in some situations where people pay more. Probabilistic model imperfections and assumptions have bedeviled the issue of why people pay more taxes than evade them. The intriguing question becomes why people *pay* taxes rather than why people *evade*. Much subsequent research, some of it surveyed below, has been addressed to reconciling the facts with the theory.[20]

In 1991, Mayshar posed the taxpayer's problem as a general model:

$$\max_{X,S,L,Y} U(Y,L) \text{ subject to } X = w[L - S - m(E)], Y = X - T(X,S,E); \qquad (6.10)$$

where X is output, S is sheltering effort, L is total labor effort, and Y is consumption. Mayshar labels $T()$ the "tax technology"; it specifies the maximal taxes, T, collectible from a base X, when the tax authority selects a vector E of policy instruments, while the taxpayer devotes S in labor units to sheltering activity. It is reasonable to assume that $T_X > 0$ and $T_S < 0$ and, by construction $T_E > 0$. The function $m(E)$ represents unavoidable compliance costs associated with taxpaying, measured in labor units.[21]

From the perspective of an A–S evasion model, $T_S < 0$ means that more evasion can lower expected tax payments, at a cost of more uncertainty. Consider Mayshar's first order conditions with respect to L and S, respectively, where asterisks indicate an optimal value:

$$\frac{-U_L(Y^\star, L^\star)}{U_Y(Y^\star, L^\star)} = w[1 - T_X(X^\star, S^\star, E)], \qquad (6.11)$$

$$w[1 - T_X(X^\star, S^\star, E)] \geq -T_S(X^\star, S^\star, E); \qquad (6.12)$$

where Equation 6.12 holds as an equality if $S^\star > 0$.

Equation 6.11 shows that the marginal rate of substitution between consumption and leisure is equal to the net wage and the effective marginal tax rate, $Tx(X\star,S\star,E)$, allows for more complex marginal tax rates than the standard linear tax model, where $T(X\star,S\star,E)$ would equal $tX\star$, suggesting that T_x would equal τ. Equation 6.11 is specified to show that the effective marginal tax rate may depend on the sheltering activity of the taxpayer and/or the policy instruments of the government, beyond a stipulated or announced tax schedule. Equation 6.12 shows that, because sheltering is accomplished by using labor, the sheltering opportunity cost, $w(1 - Tx())$, will be equal to the marginal private gain, which is the marginal tax saving, $-Ts$; similarly related models can be found in the work of Slemrod and Yitzhaki (2002).

Tax avoidance can be minimized by promulgating clearly defined laws that stipulate the tax obligations of avoiders and the rates at which payments must be made. The concept of avoidance may well be redundant when tax laws provide no compelling stipulation or obligation to pay taxes but rely on the intent of law makers and tax avoiders; in such situations societies inadvertently rely on the generosity or willingness of people to pay taxes for a common good that requires the evaluation of private interests or arbitration of interests.

The international understanding of tax evasion has evolved over time. In British jurisprudence, a landmark case of *Bullivant v. AG* (1900) provides a reference point. In the 1900s, the concept of tax evasion was seen to be rather nebulous or ambiguous in Britain (Xuereb, 2015, p. 218). A solicitor could help a person to better understand an Act of Parliament in order to avoid paying taxes. Deliberately avoiding an Act of Parliament constituted a different problem with manifest intent to evade a tax. In 1997, tax avoidance was defined to mean a course of action designed to conflict with or defeat the evident intention of the British parliament (see *IRC v. Willoughby* (1997)). Tax avoidance is an issue that is related to imprecise legislative intent. Clarification of legislative intent is usually warranted in cases of avoidance to reduce tax liability or gain a tax advantage.

In 1955, the Radcliffe Commission of the UK provided some resolution to the tax conundrum. It noted that:

> It is usual to draw a distinction between tax avoidance and tax evasion. The latter denotes all those activities, which are responsible for a person not paying tax that the existing law charges upon. Ex hypothesis he is in the wrong … By tax avoidance, on the other hand, is understood some act by which a person so arranges his affairs that he is liable to pay less tax than he would have paid for the arrangement.[22]

To clarify legislative intent and minimize tax avoidance, Britain enacted specific and general anti-avoidance tax laws to close tax loopholes. The Income Tax Act (ITA), (CAP 123 of the Laws of Malta) contains specific provisions that are inserted in articles throughout the Act. Thus specific anti-avoidance provisions may be found, for instance in the exemptions contained in Article 12(1)(c), the group provisions (Articles 16–22), and the flat-rate foreign tax credit provisions wherein the legislator is ensuring that the particular benefits are reaped by specific beneficiaries without benefiting unintended beneficiaries and structures (Xuereb, 2015, p. 222). The tax provisions are accompanied by general provisions with a clearance procedure, such as the general anti-avoidance provision contained in Article 51 of the ITA.

Specific anti-avoidance provisions are stipulated to deal with specific abuse and resolve disputes in specific areas. Nevertheless, tax laws are hardly comprehensive enough to eliminate all loopholes; they deliberately minimize loopholes, but general principles of tax law can have far-reaching consequences even when tax laws are targeted at specific areas. In effect, general anti-avoidance provisions are general expressions of principles that are directed to a particular category of tax-related transactions that inveigh against widespread tax avoidance. As Xuereb noted:

> Statutory anti-avoidance provisions of a general nature are often expressed and intended to impose a general overlay upon either the whole or specified parts of tax legislation. Furthermore, Arnold is of the opinion that any tax system requires some general anti-avoidance rule to ensure that taxpayers cannot avoid obligations that the law seeks to impose by engaging in transactions designed to avoid those obligations.
>
> (Xuereb, 2015, p. 222)[23]

Since remediating tax laws have inclusionary and exclusionary provisions, the elimination of all controversies is a tenuous proposition. In the UK, general anti-avoidance provisions have been present in the ITA since its enactment in 1948, but the evolution of the tax law suggests that tension continues to exist between the rights of taxpayers and the needs of the state. The ITA includes a general anti-avoidance clause that empowers the commissioner to disregard artificial or fictitious transactions or schemes detailed simply to reduce the tax liability of a tax avoider, even if such schemes are not consummated. Since a general tax rule is intended to deny all undue tax advantages that can be associated with the intent of law, the rule can be seen as a deterrent that does not necessarily give effect to law. "It is therefore critical that any anti-avoidance rule must contain a targeting mechanism that operates to permit or deny taxation advantages by reference to legislative policy."[24]

Foundational and interesting cases of tax avoidance in Britain include: the sale of land for profit without intention to pay taxes (*WT Ramsay Ltd v. CIR* (1981)); a similar case to create material loss in order to avoid paying taxes (*Eilbeck v. Rawling* (1981)); and *Furniss v. Dawson* (1984), a case in which shareholders of two related companies tried to hide their capital gains by using an intermediary company to sell their shares. British courts have traditionally looked at preordained series of transactions and whether steps were inserted without any valid commercial justification to defeat the purpose of a tax by reducing tax liability or avoiding a tax. The judicial procedure was widely recognized as a so-called "Ramsay principle."[25] A 1988 case, *Craven v. White*, which was decided in the House of Lords indicated that, for the Ramsay principle to apply, all transactions have to be preordained with such a degree of certainty that at the time of the earlier transactions, there is no practical likelihood that the transaction would not have taken place.[26] In *Furniss*, which extended the "Ramsay principle," the Inland Revenue issued an assessment as if shares had been disposed of directly to the company before the insertion of an intermediary company; noting that the intermediating activity was an insertion that was designed to defeat the purpose of a tax by exploiting the law of company reconstructions.

However, the legal nuances of tax evasion and avoidance present common macroeconometric and macro problems beyond bifurcated characterizations of efforts to defeat a tax; countries lose essential revenue to finance social obligations and various economists have focused on the aggregate loss of revenue. That is, while the legal characterizations have to be sought out in courts of law, the budgetary effects, including the economic and social costs that are associated with loss of revenue are non-discriminatory. Comparatively, newer econometric and economic discussions, including tax flights (foreign shelters or offshore havens), tend to focus or emphasize the budgetary effects of lost revenue without meticulous attention to the infrastructure that is utilized to defeat the purpose of tax laws. Accordingly, the joint effect of the loss of revenue rather than multiple methods to defeat the purpose of tax laws is being accentuated. The loss theory is nothing new, because it had coexisted with the embattled theories of separating evasion from avoidance; for example, in 1982, Cross and Shaw suggested that the joint effects of revenue loss be evaluated. However, other behavioral scientists have not been persuaded to overlook the costs of dichotomous behavioral motives. It is likely that individuals perceive the fairness of different methods of reducing tax liability differently (Kirchler, Maciejovsky, & Schneider, 2001).[27] The US tax court system and some notable cases of avoidance are discussed in the next section.

6.5 THE TAX COURT SYSTEM OF THE US

The US Congress and Constitution determine the types of cases that federal courts may hear. The federal judicial system is divided into 12 judicial circuits and each of the 12 circuits is further divided into districts. The US federal court system has three levels: the trial courts, the appellate courts, and the US Supreme Court. At the very preliminary level, the trial (district) courts are courts of original jurisdiction in federal criminal and civil cases. Accordingly, criminal and civil cases must first be heard in the trial courts. Criminal cases are cases involving violations of the US Penal Code. Cases between or among private parties are considered "civil." In civil cases, the US Government may act in a non-prosecutorial capacity, especially on occasions when the constitutional rights of a private party have been violated. The appellate courts have no original jurisdiction, meaning that cases in front of the appellate (circuit) judges are the results of unsatisfactory rulings in the district courts. Unlike the district and circuit courts, the US Supreme Court has original jurisdiction in matters affecting US states and foreign nationals.

The US tax system is well structured, and taxes are paid to the federal, state, and local governments. Taxes amounted to slightly more than 10 percent of GDP in 2017 (see

Figure 6.8). While there are various sources of taxable income, income derived from labor and capital constitutes the largest sources of revenue in the US, and state rules for ascertaining tax liability and marginal tax rates may not necessarily be identical to federal stipulations. State taxes are generally considered to be deductible expenses for federal tax purposes, with the caveat that the deductions may be capped. In the US, disputes involving taxes are resolved in a tax tribunal.

Unlike the district courts, the competence of the US Tax Court is very limited. The Tax Court is a specialized adjudicatory tribunal that was established by Congress for tax purposes. The court, which is located in Washington DC, conducts hearings in various cities of the US that are presided over by a single judge. The court consists of 19 judges who are appointed by a US President for a 15-year term and it has original jurisdiction over tax disputes between taxpayers and the Internal Revenue Service (IRS). If and when the Commissioner of the IRS determines a tax deficiency, a taxpayer may contest the deficiency in the Tax Court to determine if there are outstanding tax arrears. Additionally, the court facilitates a uniform interpretation of the Internal Revenue Code (IRC).

After hearing a case, the assigned judge submits the findings of fact and an opinion, in writing, to the Chief Judge who then decides whether the case should be reviewed en banc. If sufficient facts are stipulated, the assigned judge may render an opinion without a formal trial. Unlike district courts, juries are not used in the Tax Court. In most cases, the Chief Judge will decide against a full review by all 19 judges; in which case the opinion will stand and be issued as either a "regular" or "memorandum" decision of the Tax Court.[28]

Each state has at least one district court in which both tax and nontax litigation is heard. Taxpayers may sue in a federal district court only if they first pay the tax deficiency assessed by the IRS and then sue for a refund. In addition, the District Court for the District of Columbia along with the Tax Court and the Claims Court handles IRC 7428 declaratory judgment cases for taxpayers nationwide (see Box 6.1). A taxpayer can only request a jury trial in a district court.

Taxpayers may individually appeal decisions of the Tax Court and the district courts to the US Circuit Court of Appeals of Jurisdiction. Jurisdiction is based on the location of the taxpayer's residence. Each circuit court must follow the decisions of the Supreme Court but not those of the other circuits. However, the IRS notes that the Eleventh Circuit has announced that it will follow the case precedent of the Fifth Circuit for those cases decided prior to its creation on October 1, 1981.[29]

The US Supreme Court is the final arbiter of tax cases. Appeals to the court are made via the "Writ of Certiorari" (request for an order to a lower court requiring the certification and release of record of a particular case for review), which may not be granted. Refusal to grant the writ, which is reported as "cert. den.," simply means that the Supreme Court does not wish to hear the case without necessarily approving or disapproving of the

BOX 6.1 INTERNAL REVENUE CODE

IRC 7428 grants declaratory judgment rights to organizations on four issues: (1) exempt status under IRC 501(c)(3); (2) qualification as an organization to which contributions are deductible by reason of being described in IRC 170(c)(2); (3) IRC 509 foundation classification; and, (4) IRC 4942(j)(3) private operating foundation status. IRC 509 foundation classification is the sole area where a controversy has arisen. It is evident that IRC 7428 grants declaratory judgment rights to an organization that is a private foundation. The Service initially administered the IRC 7428 provisions on the basis that no declaratory judgment rights existed on foundation classification so long as the organization was not classified to be a private foundation. This approach was initially acceptable to the courts. See Ohio County and Independent Agriculture Societies, Delaware County Fair v. Commissioner (6th Cir.) 610 F. 2d 448 (1979), affirming an unreported Tax Court Case. However, the Tax Court thought otherwise in Friends of the Society of Servants of God v. Commissioner, 75 T.C. 209 (1980). The key element triggering the difference in result apparently was produced by the difference in reasons given for seeking a preferred foundation classification. In Ohio, the organization baldly stated that it was seeking a benefit under IRC 511–514 in asking for IRC 170(b)(1)(A)(v) status. In Friends, the organization persuasively argued that it only marginally qualified under IRC 170(b)(1)(A)(vi) and thus should be able to contest an adverse 170(b)(1)(A)(i) ruling. Friends can be argued to stand for the proposition that declaratory judgment rights should only exist where a final foundation status is sought and only an advance ruling is given. However, the decision seems to go further than that. Furthermore, the appellate court decision, Create, Inc. v. Commissioner, 634 F. 2d 803 (1981), clearly states otherwise. Although declaratory judgment rights were for other reasons found not to be present, the Create opinion clearly states that declaratory judgment rights exist where a favorable, definitive public charity status has been given but it is not the public charity status that the organization prefers.

Source: Internal Revenue Service.

decisions of circuit courts. The IRS reports that most tax cases heard by the Supreme Court involve conflicts of law among the circuit courts. However, certiorari may also be granted in cases involving constitutional issues or when the government can demonstrate unusual administrative significance.

In Britain or the US, it is not unusual for tax cases to involve capital gains, since labor and capital constitute robust sources of government income. Somewhat analogous to the capital gains cases in Britain that were discussed earlier, is the *Conner v. Commissioner* case in the US (T.C. Memo 2018-6). The case addressed whether the sale of real estate generated ordinary income or capital gain.[30] In another scheme to defeat a tax, *Meruelo v. Commissioner* (TC Memo 2018-16), shareholders in an S-Corporation tried to reduce their tax liability via a "debt basis."

Tax avoidance may be encouraged by religious obfuscations; especially when compensation for services is not considered to be income but a gift. *Felton v. Commissioner* (T.C. Memo 2018–168) is a case that underscored a case of religious obfuscation.[31] Though Section 61(a) provides the overarching rule of income taxation that unless specifically excluded, gross income means income from all derived sources, including "compensation for services," Felton construed donations to his church that were used as compensation rather than gifts to be tax-free. The IRS disagreed, audited Felton, and estimated a tax deficiency of $250,000.

Section 102 of the Tax Code removes from the income category "the value of property acquired by gift." Specifically excluded from the definition of a gift, however, is "any amount transferred by or for an employer to, or for the benefit of, an employee."[32] In *Duberstein*, the Supreme Court defined a gift as proceeding "from a detached and disinterested generosity ... out of affection, respect, admiration, charity, or like impulses." Accordingly, the transferor's *intention* is integral to the definition of a gift. Implicitly, intent has to be adjudicated, but precedents of decisions involving transfers in the religious tradition are rather substantial.

In the case of *Felton*, the Tax Court distinguished compensation from gifts by identifying four distinguishing parameters: (i) an ascertainment of whether donations were provided in exchange for services, (ii) the extent to which personal donations may or may not have been requested, (iii) the regularity or irregularity of the donations to the church by individual members or the congregation for structured programs, and (iv) whether the pastor received a salary from the church and the extent to which the salary differed from personal donations.

The Tax Court reached some precise decisions. Since the pastor was not retiring, donations were made to sustain his leadership of the church.[33] To the extent that the pastor parsimoniously mentioned the blue envelopes, the Tax Court concluded that the donations were objective provisions of gifts rather than income. The donations to the church that were assigned to the blue envelopes as "pastoral gifts" represented contributions to a structured program, but they were unusually and consistently large; implying undue transfer to the pastor that qualifies as compensation. Did the congregants know that the pastor was benefiting from contributions to the blue envelopes? The lopsided difference between "gifts" in the blue envelope, $250,000, and taxable income in the white envelope, $40,000—a ratio of approximately $6.3:$1—raised a judicious specter that the pastor was financially induced to shepherd the sheep. Consequently, the donations were imploring and not based on "detached and disinterested generosity."[34]

Another avenue of tax avoidance is the acquisition of fungible debt. Since cancellation of debt income (COD) imposes tax liability under certain circumstances, cancellations can be problematic when they impose tax liability. However, Section 108 of the tax code provides some mitigating conditions for tax deferrals. Section 108 provides exceptions to the general rule that COD generates taxable income, *inter alia*: (i) Chapter 11 bankruptcy (Section 108(a)(1)(A)), (ii) on occasions of insolvency before forgiveness (also when debt exceeds the fair market value of assets) (Section 108(a)(1)(B)), (iii) forgiveness of "qualified real property business indebtedness" (Section 108(a)(1)(D)), and (iv) forgiveness of "qualified farm indebtedness" (Section 108(a)(1)(C)). The deferrals provide scope for financial resuscitation so that taxes can be subsequently paid when the financial conditions of a taxpayer are reasonably good.

Some tax cases like *Simonsen v. Commissioner* (150 T.C. 2018-8) are multidimensional and instructive. In the case of *Simonsen*, Simonsen borrowed $556,000 from a bank in 2005 to purchase a $695,000 house, which he subsequently rented. The mortgage was considered a "nonrecourse" debt, which means that the lender carried the risk of the loss of asset value. The lender's only recourse is foreclosure and absorption of the loss of value. Inherently, risk is not shared. In 2010, the fair market value (FMV) of the house dropped to $495,000. During the following year, 2011, the house was sold for $336,000 (a "short-sale").[35]

The Simonsens claimed a loss in their tax return of 2011, amounting to $159,000 (the difference between the sale price, $336,000, and FMV, $495,000) and a debt cancellation of $220,000, which was not considered to be income (under Section 108(a)(1)(E)) after the cancellation. The IRS dissented because the mortgage was a nonrecourse debt. Realizing that the loan was $556,000 and that the basis (market value) of the home was $495,000 (after the conversion to rental property), the IRS assessed a deficiency of $61,000. "Under the Section 1001 regulations, the amount realized on a sale includes any liability from which a taxpayer is relieved upon the disposition of the property" (Nitti, 2019). The basis changes when a residence is converted to a rental property. Reg. Section 1.165–9(b)(2) provides that the new basis is the *lower of* the original basis of the home, or the FMV at the time of the conversion. The Simonsens maintained that two transactions occurred: (i) the sale price, and (ii) the contracted nonrecourse debt, even if the debt was recourse. The court concluded that only one transaction took place for which there was no gain or loss: a sale of the property for a realized amount equal to the entire balance of the nonrecourse debt. The bank reconveyed the deed of trust for the sale to close and the debt forgiveness occurred at that time. The sale price was set equal to the loan, $556,000, and no COD could be assessed; that is, all the debt was included in the sale price and debt was not forgiven.

The issue of whether the Simonsens could have availed themselves of Section 108(a)(1)(E) remained moot since there was no COD.[36] Notably, tax flight is another peculiar "avoidance" mechanism.

6.6 TAX FLIGHT AND THE FOREIGN ACCOUNT TAX COMPLIANCE ACT (FATCA)

Tax flight—the flight of money to foreign havens to avoid taxes—is a very costly macroeconomic leakage. It is estimated that tax havens collectively cost governments between $500 billion and $600 billion of annual loss of corporate revenue (Crivelli, de Mooji, & Keen, 2015; Cobham & Janský, 2018). Shaxson (2019) reveals that American Fortune 500 companies held an estimated $2.6 trillion offshore in 2017, though a small portion was repatriated in 2018 as a result of US tax reform law.[37] In addition to corporations, individuals concealed about $8.7 trillion in tax havens. It is estimated that for US multinationals, corporate profit shifting into tax havens has increased from 5 percent to 10 percent of gross profits in the 1990s to a range of about 25 percent to 30 percent by 2017 (Cobham & Janský, 2017). Multinationals can use transfer pricing (the prices at which unitary companies exchange goods and services) techniques to reduce their tax liabilities by reporting profits in low tax jurisdictions rather than high tax jurisdictions.[38]

The Foreign Account Tax Compliance Act (FATCA) of 2010 (26 U.S.C. § 6038D) requires certain US taxpayers holding financial assets outside of the US to report those assets to the IRS, using Form 8938, Statement of Specified Foreign Financial Assets.[39] The Act also requires certain foreign financial institutions to directly report information about financial accounts held by US taxpayers or by foreign entities in which US taxpayers hold a substantial ownership interest to the IRS. The reporting institutions are required to include the names of banks and other financial institutions, such as investment entities, brokers, and certain insurance companies. Some non-financial foreign entities will also have to report certain of their US owners.

Specified foreign financial assets include foreign financial accounts and foreign non-account assets held for investment (as opposed to those held for use in a trade or business), such as foreign stock and securities, foreign financial instruments, contracts with non-US persons, and interests in foreign entities. There are some exceptions to the reporting requirement.[40] Valuation metric is based on the highest fair market value. However, periodic financial accounts, especially for publicly traded companies, may be used to establish value of assets during a tax year and the corresponding tax liability thresholds. Fair market value may also be based on publicly available information from reliable financial information sources or from other verifiable sources. For assets denominated in foreign currencies, exchange rates provided by the US Department of the Treasury's Bureau of the Fiscal Service must be used for conversion rates.

Failure to declare foreign assets is subject to penalties: a $10,000 failure to file penalty, an additional penalty of up to $50,000 for continued failure to file after IRS notification, and a 40 percent penalty on an understatement of tax attributable to non-disclosed assets (irs. gov). The statute of limitations is extended to six years for omission from gross income in excess of $5,000 that is attributable to a specified foreign financial asset, without regard to the reporting threshold or any reporting exceptions. The statute of limitations for a tax year is extended to three years after required information of asset disclosure is not properly provided on Form 8938. Omission that can be attributable to reasonable cause (on a case by case basis) may not be penalized.

The IRS is extensively involved with international investigations to deter tax avoidance. The IRS Criminal Investigation (IRS-CI) coordinates its efforts with other countries to counteract tax schemes, money laundering, and the flow of narcotics and terrorist funding. These crimes are generically considered to be financial crimes and many countries have agreed to adopt international tax standards on exchanging information. In the post-crisis period of 2008, the OECD launched the Common Reporting Standards (CRS), whereby financial information can be automatically exchanged across international boundaries to minimize tax flights. Foreign financial institutions (FFIs) may register with the IRS and report to the IRS certain information about their US accounts, including accounts of certain foreign entities with substantial US owners.[41]

The CRS mechanism seems to have retarded tax flight. The OECD estimated that 90 countries had shared information on 47 million accounts worth €4.9 trillion in July 2019 (Shaxson, 2019, p. 9). It is becoming increasingly apparent that the arm's-length orthodoxy is a flawed procedure for estimating income and tax liability. Alternative proposals, including a unitary tax system for transnational corporations are being now being considered.[42] Controversy exists over where transnationals should pay taxes and on what basis.

CHAPTER SUMMARY

- Taxes are an integral part of fiscal policy; the policy that deals with government revenue and spending. All responsible governments have spending priorities that must be met, but the obligations to meet spending priorities cannot be met without adequate revenue.
- Taxes are sources of government revenue all over the world and they may be imposed on individuals (natural persons), business entities, estates, trusts, or other forms of organization. Taxes may be based on property, income, transactions, transfers, importations of goods, business activities, or a variety of factors, and are generally imposed on assets for which taxpayers have tax liability.
- The effects of government spending on national output are obviously derived from the ability of governments to collect revenue and spend it wisely. Economists have traditionally appraised these effects in conjunction with contingent Keynesian multipliers.
- The size of the multipliers are generally determined by the structural characteristics—factors that are indispensable to the way an economy operates over a longer period of time—which impact an economy's response to fiscal disturbances in normal times,

and the conjunctural (temporary, cyclical, or policy related) phenomena, which cause the effects of multipliers to deviate from normal levels.
- The distinction between tax avoidance and tax evasion is a legal issue. While tax evasion is outright illegal, tax avoidance is nuanced and strenuously contingent on willful intent.
- Tax analysts or theorists have developed diverse theories to explain why some taxpayers, including financial institutions, are predisposed to reduce their tax liability. Less altruistic humans can hardly envision why they should pay their "fair" share to society.
- The Foreign Account Tax Compliance Act (FATCA) of 2010 (26 U.S.C. § 6038D) requires certain US taxpayers holding financial assets outside of the US to report those assets to the IRS, using Form 8938, Statement of Specified Foreign Financial Assets.

KEY WORDS

• Adjusted gross income	• Tax evasion	• Tax gap
• Capital gains	• Tax flight	• Tax liability
• MACRS	• Tax haven	• Tax multiplier
• Marginal tax rate	• Taxable income	• Tax wedge
• Tariffs	• Tax Laffer Curve	
• Tax avoidance	• Tax shelters	

CHAPTER QUESTIONS

1. What is the difference between tax avoidance and tax evasion? Why do individuals and businesses try to avoid or evade taxes?
2. Are tax shelters illegal? Why? Explain why tax shelters are different from tax havens.
3. Suppose a US public company made $200,000 in the previous year, what will be its marginal tax rate and tax liability? Assuming the company paid out dividends, are the shareholders of the company expected to pay taxes on their dividends? Why?
4. Under what circumstances are private entities exempted from tax payments?
5. Using any of the estimated tax multipliers in the text, explain how a tax reduction amounting to $700 billion or £600 billion could impact a national economy if there is no leakage.
6. Can policymakers minimize tax avoidance? How?
7. Refer to the *Simonsen* case; can debt forgiveness always trigger a tax liability? Why?
8. Refer to the Foreign Account Tax Compliance Act (FATCA); when is foreign income taxable?
9. Why was the investment of Professor Willoughby taxed (see *IRC v. Willoughby* (1997))? Could his investment have been taxed under the FATCA (assuming he was a US citizen in 2011)? Why?

NOTES

1. Standard deductions are sensitive to filing status, age, and legal ability to see. The threshold is periodically adjusted for inflation. Spouses who are filing separately must opt for the same procedure.
2. Some category of moving expenses may apply, especially for military personnel and income from jury duty. These AGI factors are usually considered to be "above the line" deductions.
3. $800 has been estimated to be approximately $12,742 in 2009, which corresponds to about a 5 percent rate of inflation (an underestimation in the view of the author); see wiki.org.
4. Tax wedges are usually due to the progressivity of taxes; tax rates increase as taxable income increases. Alternatively, marginal tax rates are lower at lower levels of taxable income and higher levels. The concept is efficacious when taxes are efficiently administered without evasion or avoidance. Measurements of a tax wedge may vary from country to country.
5. The Wilson-Gorman Tariff of 1894, which was a Revenue Act, slightly reduced US tariff rates from the numbers set in the McKinley tariff (1890) and imposed a 2 percent tax on income over $4,000.
6. The Sixteenth Amendment (Amendment XVI) to the United States Constitution was passed by Congress in 1909 in response to the 1895 Supreme Court case of *Pollock v. Farmers' Loan & Trust Co.* It was ratified by the required number of states on February 3, 1913, thereby superseding the Supreme Court's ruling in the *Pollock Case* of 1895.
7. Based on the 2018 tax law, a child is defined as someone who is 16 years of age or younger on the last day of the year who is a US citizen, US national, or a resident alien. The tax beneficiary must claim the child as a dependent who is related to the child by blood, step-relationship, or legal adoption. The child must have resided with the tax beneficiary for more than half of the year (special rules apply for special circumstances such as divorce) and the beneficiary must have provided the child with more than half of his/her support.
8. Citizens and residents of the US living and working out of the US may be entitled to a foreign earned income exclusion that reduces taxable income. In 2019, the maximum exclusion is $105,900 per taxpayer (future years indexed for inflation). Exclusion is partly based on the idea that foreign income may have been taxed anyway. Foreign tax credit is provided to tax payers of all classifications.
9. The convention of the Organization for Economic Cooperation and Development (OECD) went into force on September 30, 1961 and the organization is currently made up of 36 members (at the time of this writing.) In alphabetical order, the countries and years of accession are as follows: Australia (1971), Austria (1961), Belgium (1961), Canada (1961), Chile (2010), Czech Republic (1995), Denmark (1961), Estonia (2010), Finland (1969), France (1961), Germany (1961), Greece (1961), Hungary (1996), Iceland (1961), Ireland (1961), Israel (2010), Italy (1962), Japan (1964), Korea (1996), Latvia (2016), Lithuania (2018), Luxembourg (1961), Mexico (1994), Netherlands (1961), New Zealand (1973), Norway (1961), Poland (1996), Portugal (1961), Slovak Republic (2000), Slovenia (2010), Spain (1961), Sweden (1961), Switzerland (1961), Turkey (1961), UK (1961), and US (1961).
10. See Batini et al. (2014, pp. 6–8) for additional references.
11. See Ilzetzki, Mendoza, & Vegh (2013).

12 See Born, Juessen, & Mueller (2013); Ilzetzki and others (2013); see also Batini et al. (2014), op. cit.
13 The IRS prefers to combine multiple years of annual National Program Research (NRP) data of individual income tax compliance to increase the reliability of the resulting estimates. Also, starting with TY2006, the NRP individual income tax sample design moved from larger periodic samples to smaller annual samples. The sample design allocated evenly over three tax years the total number of returns that previously would have formed a single larger periodic sample (IRS, 2016, p. 6).
14 See IRS (2016, p. 9). "Federal Tax Compliance Research: Tax Gap Estimates for Tax Years 2008–2010."
15 Loc. cit.
16 Ibid.
17 An individual who is maximizing utility can be subjected to a budget constraint; who has forms of income or consumption that are not taxable (such as fringe benefits, nontaxed perquisites, or tax deductions). In the standard model, the individual will make choices between labor and leisure when taxes change.
18 The work of Martin Feldstein (1995) is very influential in this regard.
19 The penalty can be for understatement of income or understatement of taxes, the maximand for the latter has been estimated to be: $EU = (1-p)U(v + \tau(y-x)) + pU(v - \theta t(y-x))$; see Slemrod and Yitzhaki (2002, p. 1430).
20 One problem with this argument is that, for many types of evasion, the effective probability of detection is much higher than the fraction of returns audited would suggest. For example, the p for non-reporting of wage and salary income subject to information reporting by employers is probably close to 1.0. Moreover, as long as several years of returns may be audited at once, the effective p may be several times higher than a one-year probability of audit would indicate, op. cit., p. 1431. See Slemrod and Yitzhaki (2002) for discussions of the labor model, pp. 1432–4. The decision about how much income to report is simultaneously made with the decision of how much to work; this poses a problem for adjusting the labor supply based on revelations and punishments for avoidance.
21 Although evasion as a gamble is not explicitly treated in this model, Mayshar (1991) argues that it can be presented in this framework; to do so S is defined as that certain payment which causes the same expected utility loss as the extra risk an evader takes on, for given expected tax payments; this forms the link between the A-S models of tax evasion and the models discussed in this section.
22 Cited in Xuereb (2015, pp. 218–9).
23 See also Arnold (1995), "The Canadian general anti-avoidance rule", *British Tax Review*.
24 Ibid.
25 In 2001, Lord Nicholls noted that rather than establishing a principle, the House of Lords merely highlighted the legal nature of a transaction in question and related it to fiscal legislation when the House was confronted with the duty to determine the nature of new and sophisticated tax avoidance devices.
26 See Xuereb (2015, p. 227).
27 Utilizing a sample of about 252 fiscal officers, business students, business lawyers, and entrepreneurs to provide perspectives about methods of reducing tax liability, it was found that as a matter of spontaneous perception, tax evasion was perceived rather negatively, tax flight neutrally, and tax avoidance positively.

28 "Memorandum opinions involve well established principles of law that, in the opinion of the Chief Judge, require only a delineation of the facts" and they have precedent; see "Review of Tax Research Materials," www.irs.gov. Regular decisions are presumed to have value as precedents, involving issues that have not been previously considered. Actions on Decisions (AODs) are legal memoranda prepared by Chief Counsel when a Service loses a case in the Tax Court, the US District Court, or a US Court of Appeals.
29 The Eleventh Circuit is composed of three states (Alabama, Georgia, and Florida) previously included in the Fifth Circuit. When conflicts develop between the circuits, district courts of each individual circuit are required to follow precedents set by the appellate court of their own circuit. Also, the Tax Court follows the policy of observing precedent set by the appellate court of the circuit in which the taxpayer resides (www.irs.gov).
30 In 2013, Conner placed land in a conservation program to lower property taxes. However, he was required to certify that no business would be conducted on the land. Later in 2013, without ever having advertised the land for sale, Conner sold the land for $1.5 million to an unrelated party. Conner deducted the $1.8 million loss as an ordinary loss on his tax return; see Nitti (2019).
31 Felton was a pastor of a church that routinely collected offerings and provided therapeutic services. Contributions to the church were for different purposes that were color-coded. White envelopes were for the pastor's taxable income, blue envelopes were less transparent for donations that were not taxed as charitable deductions but considered to be "gifts," and gold envelopes were set aside for special programs like retreats, which would not constitute part of the pastor's taxable income. Somehow, and at some point, the intent of the blue and white envelopes were conflated to the tune of $250,000; see Nitti (2019).
32 Cited in Nitti (2019).
33 Nitti (2019) notes that the tax law recognizes returns on a faithful person's donation as "intangible religious benefits" under Section 170(f)(8)(B)(iii). Consequently, the donations do not count as an item of value received by the donor in exchange for the donation.
34 Op. cit.
35 Since the loan was a nonrecourse loan, the bank is required to consent to the loss of value and the forgiveness of debt that will be associated with the loss of value that will otherwise be assessed on the borrower if the loan was a "recourse" debt. Additionally, the home was not a principal residence at the date of sale.
36 See Nitti (2019) for a comprehensive review of tax cases and law.
37 See Shaxson (2019, p. 7); estimates are contingent on methods of estimation. Ironically, low income economies account for about $200 billion, which is also a larger percentage of GDP than advanced economies, and more than the amount ($150 billion) that they receive each year in foreign development assistance.
38 Companies may charge higher intra-corporate costs (above fair market value) to pay lower taxes in low-tax jurisdictions. In such situations, arm's length principle is disregarded. Additionally, patents can be held in low tax jurisdictions to extract exorbitant brand royalties from affiliates in high tax jurisdictions; implicitly, reducing tax liabilities in high tax jurisdictions.
39 Reporting thresholds are set with some filing status and jurisdictional (locational) variations. The basic reporting threshold at the time of this writing is $50,000. A taxpayer who is single or filing separately must submit a Form 8938 if he/she has more than $200,000 of specified foreign financial assets at the end of the year and is

living abroad; or more than $50,000, if he/she lives in the US. The thresholds double for those who are filing jointly. Taxpayers are considered to live abroad if they are US citizens whose tax homes are in a foreign country and must have been present in a foreign country or countries for at least 330 days out of a consecutive 12-month period. There are some exceptions to filing Form 8938; those who do not have to file a US income tax return for a corresponding year do not have to file Form 8938, regardless of the value of foreign financial assets. However, it may be necessary to complete and file other reports about foreign assets, such as FinCEN Form 114, Report of Foreign Bank and Financial Accounts (FBAR) (formerly TD F 90-22.1), in addition to Form 8938.

40 A financial account maintained by a US branch (payor), beneficial interest in a foreign trust or estate, and interest on a social security, social insurance, or other similar program of a foreign government. Additional exemptions include: trusts and foreign gifts reported on Form 3520 or Form 3520-A (filed by the trust); foreign corporations reported on Form 5471; passive foreign investment companies reported on Form 8621; foreign partnerships reported on Form 8865; and registered Canadian retirement savings plans reported on Form 8891 (irs.gov).

41 FFIs include, but are not limited to: depository institutions (banks), custodial institutions (for example, mutual funds), investment entities (for example, hedge funds or private equity funds), certain types of insurance companies that have cash value products or annuities. Unless otherwise exempt, FFIs that do not both register and agree to report face a 30 percent withholding tax on certain US-source payments made to them. Registered FFIs receive Global Intermediary Identification Number (GIIN) from the IRS, unless the FFI is treated as a Limited FFI.

42 Under a unitary tax system, the profits of the various branches of an enterprise or the various corporations of a group are calculated as if the entire group is a unity. A formula is (then) used to apportion the net income of the whole group to the various parts of the group. Usually a combination of property, payroll, turnover, capital invested, manufacturing costs, etc., are formula factors (USlegal.com).

FURTHER READING

Allingham, M. G., & Sandmo, A. (1972). Income tax evasion: A theoretical analysis. *Journal of Public Economics*, *1*(3–4), 323–338.

Arnold, J. B. (1995). The Canadian general anti-avoidance rule. *British Tax Review*, 6, 541–556.

Batini, N., Eyraud, L., Foni, L., & Weber, A. (2014). *Fiscal multipliers: Size, determinants, and use in macroeconomic projections*. Washington, DC: International Monetary Fund.

Baumohl, B. (2013). *The secrets of economic indicators* (3rd ed.). Upper Saddle River, NJ: Pearson Education.

Blinder, A. S., & Zandi, M. (2010). How the Great Recession was brought to an end. Retrieved from economy.com.

Born, B., Juessen, F., & Mueller, G. J. (2013). Exchange rate regimes and fiscal multipliers. *Journal of Economic Dynamics and Control*, *37*(2), 446–465.

Cobham, A., & Janský, P. (2017). Measuring misalignment: The location of US multinationals' economic activity versus the location of their profits. *Development Policy Review*, *37*(1), 91–110.

Cobham, A., & Janský, P. (2018). Global distribution of revenue loss from corporate tax avoidance; re-estimation and country results. *Journal of International Development*, *30*(2), 206–232.

Cole, H. L., & Ohanian, L. E. (2004). New Deal policies and the persistence of the Great Depression: A general equilibrium analysis. *Journal of Political Economy*, *112*(4), 779–816.

Crivelli, E., de Mooji, R.A., & Keen, M. (2015). *Base erosion, profit shifting, and developing countries*. IMF Working Paper 15/118. Washington, DC: International Monetary Fund.

Cross, R.B., & Shaw, G. K. (1982). The evasion-avoidance choice: A suggested approach. *National Tax Journal*, *34*, 489–491.

Department of Treasury IRS. (2018). How to depreciate property. Publication 946 Cat. No. 13081F. Retrieved from https://irs.gov/pub/irs-pdf/p946.pdf.

Dolls, M., Fuest, C., & Peichl, A. (2012). Automatic stabilizers and economic crisis: US vs. Europe. *Journal of Public Economics*, *96*, 279–294.

Erceg, C. J., & Lindé, J. (2010). Is there a free lunch in a liquidity trap? International Finance Discussion Papers 1003. Washington: US Federal Reserve System.

Feldstein, M. (1995). The effect of marginal tax rates on taxable income: A panel study of the 1986 Tax Reform Act. *Journal of Political Economy*, *103*(3), 551–572.

Goolsbee, A. (1999). Evidence on the high-income Laffer Curve from six decades of tax reform. *Brookings Papers on Economic Activity*, *2*, 1–64.

Grewal, A. S. (2016). The un-precedented tax court. *Iowa Law Review*, *101*, 2065–2104.

Ilzetzki, E., Mendoza, G., & Vegh, C. A. (2013). How big (small?) are fiscal multipliers? *Journal of Monetary Economics*, *60*, 239–254.

Internal Revenue Service. (1996, April). Federal tax compliance research: Individual income tax gap estimates for 1985, 1988, and 1992. *Research Analysis and Statistics*, Publication 1415 (Rev. 4–96) Washington, DC.

Internal Revenue Service. (2016, May). Federal tax compliance research: Tax gap estimates for tax years 2008–2010. *Research Analysis and Statistics*, Publication 1415 (Rev. 5–2016) Washington, DC.

International Monetary Fund. (2010, October). Will it hurt? Macroeconomic effects of fiscal consolidation (Ch. 3). World economic outlook. Washington, DC.

Kirchler, E., Maciejovsky, B., & Schneider, F. (2001). *Social representations on tax avoidance, tax evasion, and tax flight: Do legal differences matter?* Working Paper No. 0104.

Mayshar, J. (1991). Taxation with costly administration. *Scandinavian Journal of Economics*, *93*(1), 75–88.

Nitti, T. (2019). Top tax court cases of 2018: Where is your tax home? Retrieved from www.forbes.com.

Parrino, R., Bates, T., Gillan, S. L., & Kidwell, D. (2018). *Fundamentals of corporate finance* (4th ed.). Hoboken, NJ: John Wiley & Sons.

Ramey, V. (2011). Identifying government spending shocks: It's all in the timing. *Quarterly Journal of Economics*, *126*(1), 1–50.

Reuter, P., & Truman, E. M. (2004). *Chasing dirty money: The fight against money laundering*. Washington, DC: Institute for International Economics.

Romer, C. D. (2011, November 7). What do we know about the effects of fiscal policy? Separating evidence from ideology. Hamilton College. Retrieved from https://eml.berkeley.edu/~

Romer, C. D., & Romer, D. H. (2010). The macroeconomic effects of tax changes: Estimates based on a new measure of fiscal shocks. *American Economic Review, 100*, 763–801.

Ruccio, D. (2011, April 9). Real world economics review. Retrieved from https://rwer.wordpress.com/2011/04/09/the-u-s-corporate-tax-haven/.

Shaxson, N. (2019). The billions attracted by tax havens do harm to sending and receiving nations alike. *Finance & Development*. International Monetary Fund.

Slemrod, J. (1996). Which is the simplest tax system of them all? In H. Aaron & W. Gale (Eds.), *Economic effects of fundamental tax reform* (pp. 355–391). Washington, DC: Brookings Institution.

Slemrod, J., & Yitzhaki, S. (2002). Tax avoidance, evasion, and administration. In A. J. Auerbach & M. Feldstein (Eds.), *Handbook of public economics* (Vol. 3, pp. 1425–1442). Atlanta, GA: Elsevier.

Woodford, M. (2011). Simple analytics of the government expenditure multiplier. *American Economic Journal: Macroeconomics, 3*(1), 1–35.

Xuereb, A. (2015). Tax avoidance or tax evasion? *Symposia Melitensia, 10*, 217–229.

Yitzhaki, S. (1974). A note on income tax evasion: A theoretical analysis. *Journal of Public Economics, 3*(2), 201–202.

CHAPTER 7
US ANTITRUST LAW AND ENFORCEMENT

LEARNING OBJECTIVES

LO 1 To present the economic conditions that gave rise to US antitrust law.
LO 2 To discuss the key provisions of US antitrust statutes.
LO 3 Describe the nature and waves of mergers.
LO 4 Present the economic and legal rationales behind the enforcement of merger laws.
LO 5 Discuss the economic and legal problems associated with measuring concentration.
LO 6 Revisit arguments about rule of reason and per se rule.
LO 7 Examine the pros and cons of combinations.
LO 8 Evaluate the problems that are associated with antitrust damages.

7.1 THE EVOLUTION OF US ANTITRUST LAW

In the 1870s and 1880s, there were various trusts and combinations in several industries, including petroleum, meat packing, railroads, sugar, lead, coal, whisky, and tobacco. The trusts generally limited production and charged consumers high prices for poor quality products. The relationship between monopoly and perfect competition can be posited.

Combinations (mergers or trusts) were pervasive in the nineteenth century, and they were not peculiar to the US. However, Nevins and Commager (1992) note that they were more pronounced in the US than anywhere else except Germany. The extensive presence of combinations in the US was based on resource availability and excess capacity.

Improvements in transportation and patent rights facilitated the practice of combinations in the US. The completion of the railroads ensured the creation of markets for manufactured products, and patent laws gave monopolies on crucially important processes.[1] Additionally, generous land grants and interpretation of land laws were favorable to large companies with the capacity to exploit the extraction of natural resources on a large scale. Timber, copper, coal, iron ore, and oil became attractive resources for exploitation by large companies. The railroads linked the world of rational management to the world of finance capital and did more than anything else to create the New York Stock Exchange, though the Exchange had been established in 1817.[2]

The regulatory environment also favored the emergence of large corporations. Companies could incorporate in states where the laws were very lenient for doing business, and the laws before the 1940s generally prevented foreign competition. The Standard Oil Company pioneered the way for interstate operations on a large scale. For a while, fierce competition persisted in western Pennsylvania, but Rockefeller was able to buy a substantial amount of independent refineries in the 1870s. He also obtained successes in Cleveland, New York, Philadelphia, and Pittsburgh.

In 1882, the Standard Oil Company emerged as the first great trust, and it continued to thrive even after it was dissolved by the Ohio courts by reconstituting itself into a holding company under the more lenient laws of New Jersey. Nevins and Commager (1992) report that before 1900, Rockefeller had eliminated a considerable amount of competition, amassed fabulous profits by reducing prices, and created the greatest monopoly in the US.

As Rockefeller prospered, other trusts emerged in quick succession: the cotton seed oil (1884), the linseed oil (1885), the lead, whisky, and sugar trusts (1887), the match trust (1889), the tobacco trust (1890), and the rubber trust (1892). The protagonists of the trusts were equally aggressive in controlling markets and profits.[3] A survey in 1904 showed that 319 industrial trusts, capitalized at over $7 billion, had gobbled up 5,300 previously independent concerns, and that 127 utilities (including railroads), capitalized at over $13 billion, had absorbed 2,400 smaller enterprises (Nevins & Commager, 1992, p. 270). Invariably, the mergers were driven by quest for size.

The most powerful of the trusts was regarded as "the money trust" by J.P. Morgan. As Greenspan and Wooldridge noted:

> Morgan succeeded in transforming the face of corporate America. He created new companies such as General Electric, American Telegraph and Telephone (AT&T), the Pullman Company, National Biscuit (Nabisco), International Harvester, and of course, US Steel. He increased the total amount of capital in publicly traded manufacturing companies from $33 million in 1890 to more than $7 billion in 1903.
> (Greenspan & Wooldridge, 2018, p. 144)

Nevins and Commager (1992) provide a dramatic and poetic rendition of the socioeconomic consequences of the trust-oriented economy:

> The life of the average man, especially if he was a city dweller, was profoundly changed by this development. Almost everything he ate and wore, the furnishings of the house, the tools he used, the transportation he employed, were made and controlled by trusts. When he sat down to breakfast he ate bacon packed by the beef trust, seasoned his eggs with salt made by the Michigan salt trust, sweetened his coffee with sugar refined by the American sugar trust, lit his American Tobacco Company cigar with a Diamond Match Company match. The he rode to work on a bicycle built by the bicycle trust or on a trolley car operating under a monopolistic franchise and running on steel rails made by the United States Steel. Yet it is probable that his food was better, his transportation more efficient than a generation earlier. What the average

man noticed most was the effect of trusts on the business life of his community. Local industry dried up, factories went out of business or were absorbed, mortgages were placed with Eastern banks or insurance companies, and neighbors who worked not for themselves but for distant corporations were exposed to the vicissitudes of policy over which they had no control.

(Nevins & Commager, 1992, p. 270)

According to Greenspan and Wooldridge (2018), before the mid-nineteenth century, companies came in two distinct forms: partnership and chartered companies. Partnerships are relatively easy to establish but they are susceptible to impermanence and limited liability (recall the forms of business organization in Chapter 3). In many respects, the characteristics of the chartered companies were very much unlike the attributes of contemporary companies. For example, Carnegie disliked public ownership; essentially because "where stock is held by a great number, what is everybody's business is nobody's business" (Greenspan & Wooldridge, 2018, p. 136).

Most of the earlier mergers took the form of vertical integration. That is, companies purchased their suppliers and distributors. Vertical mergers involve the complementary combination of firms at different stages of manufacturing or production that limits competition. But the early merger boom between 1895 and 1904, witnessed a combination of vertical and horizontal (competitive) combinations, with Rockefeller and J.P. Morgan as the major actors. Mergers that do not cleanly fall into either of the two categories are considered conglomerate mergers. The waves of combinations will be discussed later in the chapter.

In response to the euphoria for combinations (trusts) and the visible effect of the trusts on the lives of Americans, the US Congress passed the Sherman Antitrust Act (1890). However, the concept of combinations had taken a strong hold on American society and some states were sympathetic to the practice of combinations. For example, New Jersey passed legislation that made it possible to circumvent the intent of the Sherman Act via the creation of holding companies that could hold shares in subsidiary companies. Analogously, Delaware created an amicable business environment to incorporate disgruntled companies. By 1930, Delaware became the host of more than a third of the industrial corporations (Greenspan & Wooldridge, 2018, p. 143).

The effects of antitrust laws and their limitations will be presented in the next section. Antitrust laws are intended to prevent unlawful mergers (combinations or monopolies) in order to foster competition that will spur innovation, generate fair prices, and enhance consumer welfare.

7.1 (A) THE SHERMAN ACT (1890)

The intent of the Sherman Act was to prevent unlawful monopolies. However, though the intent of the law was clear, the language of the law was not without ambiguities.

> Every person who shall monopolize, or attempt to monopolize, or combine or conspire with any other person or persons, to monopolize any part of the trade or commerce among the several States, or with foreign nations, shall be deemed guilty of a felony, and, on conviction thereof, shall be punished by fine not exceeding $10,000,000 if a corporation, or, if any other person, $350,000, or by imprisonment not exceeding three years, or by both said punishments, in the discretion of the court …
>
> Every contract, combination in form of trust or otherwise, or conspiracy, in restraint of trade or commerce in any Territory of the United States or of the District of Columbia, or in restraint of trade or commerce between any such Territory and another, or between any such Territory or Territories and any State or States or the District of Columbia, or with foreign nations, or between the District of Columbia and any State or States or foreign nations, is declared illegal. Every person who shall make any such contract or engage in any such combination or conspiracy, shall be deemed guilty of a felony, and, on conviction thereof, shall be punished by fine not exceeding $10,000,000 if a corporation, or, if any other person, $350,000, or by imprisonment not exceeding three years, or both said punishments, in the discretion of the court.
>
> (15 U.S.C. §§ 2–3)

Courts interpreted the ambiguities in the law to enjoin labor unions that engaged in collective action to disrupt the smooth operations of business. In effect, the law was initially used to outlaw labor unrest more than it was used to control the power of monopolies. The concept that contracts, combinations, and conspiracies could restrain trade, made it possible for collective action to be considered a disruption of trade. Trade has both domestic and international dimensions.

For more than a decade after its passage, the Sherman Act was rarely invoked and less successfully against industrial monopolies. Narrow judicial interpretations of the law paved the way for an age of injunctions. The injunctions became the principal mechanism for judicial action in railway-labor conflicts; as the number of strikes escalated, so did the number of injunctions.[4]

The first application of the Sherman Act to industrial dispute occurred in New Orleans (*US v. Working Men's Amalgamated Council* (5th Circuit 1893)). The longshoremen went on strike, but the US attorney secured an injunction under the theory that the unions were "a gigantic combination for the effect of restraining the commerce among several states and with foreign countries" (Forbath, 1991, p. 71). The case became a precedent to show that when workers "conspired" to disrupt or quit a railroad's service, they could be held to be in violation of the Sherman Antitrust law. Other cases followed suit, including the famous *US v. Debs* (1894) that subsequently engulfed 27 states. On July 4, 1894, President Grover Cleveland, on the advice of the US Attorney General, Richard Olney, ordered 2,500 federal troops to Chicago. The strike ended within a week and the troops were recalled on July 20. Debs was convicted of contempt of court and conspiring against interstate commerce. It became very apparent that the Sherman Act could be enforced against labor unions that conspired to disrupt interstate commerce.

The concept of conspiracy was inchoate and nebulous, but Judge Denman provided a judicial and functional interpretation of conspiracy:

> [A conspiracy is] a combination of two or more persons by concerted action, to accomplish a criminal or unlawful purpose, or some purpose not in itself criminal or unlawful, by criminal or unlawful means.
>
> (Forbath, 1991, p. 71)

Unlike labor unions, corporations had some surprising successes under the Sherman Act. In *US v. E.C. Knight* (1894), the Supreme Court was asked to decide whether American Sugar Company's purchase of four refineries in Philadelphia was a conspiracy to restrain trade, and whether the purchase gave the company control over 98 percent of the nation's sugar refining capacity. With one dissenting opinion, the court ruled that:

> The fact that an article is manufactured for export to another state does not of itself make it an article of interstate commerce.
>
> (Landenburg, 2007, p. 34)[5]

The Attorney General, Richard Olney (who lacked confidence in the Sherman Act), and the pro-business Supreme Court, produced only 18 cases against businesses under the administrations of three Presidents: Harrison, Cleveland, and McKinley. The government lost seven of its first eight cases. The prosecutorial failures invigorated the impulses of businesses to form combinations. Between 1880 and 1902, approximately 5,000 small businesses were gobbled up into 300 large combinations. Two-thirds of the combinations were formed between 1898 and 1902, well after the Sherman Act was passed.[6] However, by 1906, the Knight decision was reversed. The reversal paved the way for a successful prosecution of Standard Oil (*US v. Standard Oil*). Evidently, the courts were ill-prepared for the turmoil that ensued after the Sherman Act, and they were equally incapable of mitigating the disastrous consequences of an ambiguous antitrust law. Congress was left with no alternative but to clean up the Sherman Act for the emancipation of workers; the result was the Clayton Act of 1914.

7.1 (B) THE CLAYTON ACT (1914)

The Clayton Act is multidimensional. It not only outlaws labor action as a restraint of trade, it incorporates price discrimination and the acquisition of stocks that is intended to stifle competition. In addition, the law prohibits tying contracts (Section 3),[7] and interlocking directorates (Section 8). *Clayton* outlaws discrimination in price, services, or facilities (§ 2 of the Clayton Act) (15 U.S.C. § 13):

> It shall be unlawful for any person engaged in commerce, in the course of such commerce, either directly or indirectly, to discriminate in price between different purchasers of commodities of like grade and quality, where either or any of the purchases involved in such discrimination are in commerce, where such commodities

are sold for use, consumption, or resale within the United States or any Territory thereof or the District of Columbia or any insular possession or other place under the jurisdiction of the United States, and where the effect of such discrimination may be substantially to lessen competition or tend to create a monopoly in any line of commerce, or to injure, destroy, or prevent competition with any person who either grants or knowingly receives the benefit of such discrimination, or with customers of either of them …

(15 U.S.C. §§ 13:2(a))

The law also forbids unlawful acquisition by one corporation of stock of another (§ 7 of the Clayton Act) (15 U.S.C. § 18):

No person engaged in commerce or in any activity affecting commerce shall acquire, directly or indirectly, the whole or any part of the stock or other share capital and no person subject to the jurisdiction of the Federal Trade Commission shall acquire the whole or any part of the assets of another person engaged also in commerce or in any activity affecting commerce, where in any line of commerce or in any activity affecting commerce in any section of the country, the effect of such acquisition may be substantially to lessen competition, or to tend to create a monopoly. No person shall acquire, directly or indirectly, the whole or any part of the stock or other share capital and no person subject to the jurisdiction of the Federal Trade Commission shall acquire the whole or any part of the assets of one or more persons engaged in commerce or in any activity affecting commerce, where in any line of commerce or in any activity affecting commerce in any section of the country, the effect of such acquisition, of such stocks or assets, or of the use of such stock by the voting or granting of proxies or otherwise, may be substantially to lessen competition, or to tend to create a monopoly. This section shall not apply to persons purchasing such stock solely for investment and not using the same by voting or otherwise to bring about, or in attempting to bring about, the substantial lessening of competition. Nor shall anything contained in this section prevent a corporation engaged in commerce or in any activity affecting commerce from causing the formation of subsidiary corporations for the actual carrying on of their immediate lawful business, or the natural and legitimate branches or extensions thereof, or from owning and holding all or a part of the stock of such subsidiary corporations, when the effect of such formation is not to substantially lessen competition ….

Clayton clearly shows that antitrust laws are not applicable to labor organizations (§ 6 of the Clayton Act):

The labor of a human being is not a commodity or article of commerce. Nothing contained in the antitrust laws shall be construed to forbid the existence and operation of labor, agricultural, or horticultural organizations, instituted for the purposes of mutual help, and not having capital stock or conducted for profit, or to forbid or restrain individual members of such organizations from lawfully carrying out the legitimate objects thereof; nor shall such organizations, or the members thereof, be held or construed to be illegal combinations or conspiracies in restraint of trade, under the antitrust laws.

(15 U.S.C. § 17)

Laws are merely symbolic when they do not have appropriate enforcement provisions. Therefore, the Federal Trade Commission (FTC) Act was passed to ensure the enforcement of US antitrust laws *inter alia*.

7.1 (C) THE FEDERAL TRADE COMMISSION (FTC) ACT (1914)

The FTC Act is a proactive law to forewarn against undesirable mergers and enforce antitrust laws. It is composed of five Commissioners who are appointed by the US President, with the advice and consent of the US Senate. Not more than three of the Commissioners can be members of the same political party. The Commissioners are appointed to have staggered terms in order to ensure some amount of continuity and stability. The first Commissioners that were appointed on September 26, 1914, were expected to continue in office for terms of three, four, five, six, and seven years, respectively, and the term of each is designated by the President. The successors of the Commissioners have been appointed for terms of seven years, except that any person chosen to fill a vacancy will be appointed only for the unexpired term of the Commissioner whom he will succeed. Explicitly, a Commissioner's departure is contingent on the availability of his/her successor. The President shall choose a chairman from the Commission's membership, and no Commissioner can engage in any other business, vocation, or employment. Commissioners may be removed by the President for inefficiency, negligence, or malfeasance in his/her official capacity, but a vacancy in the Commission should not impair the ability of the remaining Commissioners to exercise all the powers of the Commission (15 U.S.C. § 41).

The Commission is empowered to prevent unfair methods of competition in or affecting commerce, and unfair or deceptive acts or practices in or affecting commerce, which are declared to be unlawful. The Commission is also given authority to prevent persons, partnerships, or corporations, except banks and savings and loan institutions described in Section 57a(f)(3) of the FTC Act, to regulate commerce, air carriers, and foreign air carriers subject to Part A of Subtitle VII of Title 49, so that they cannot use unfair methods or deceptive acts or practices to unduly and illegally affect commerce (15 U.S.C. § 41(a)(1)(2)).

The Commission is granted extensive investigative authority under Section 46. Accordingly, the Commission may investigate persons, partnerships and corporations:

> To gather and compile information concerning, and to investigate from time to time the organization, business, conduct, practices, and management of any person, partnership, or corporation engaged in or whose business affects commerce, excepting banks, savings and loan institutions described in section 57a(f)(3) of this

title, Federal credit unions described in section 57a(f)(4) of this title, and common carriers subject to the Act to regulate commerce, and its relation to other persons, partnerships, and corporations.

(15 U.S.C. § 46(a))

The Commission may also investigate compliance with antitrust decrees:

Whenever a final decree has been entered against any defendant corporation in any suit brought by the United States to prevent and restrain any violation of the antitrust Acts, to make investigation, upon its own initiative, of the manner in which the decree has been or is being carried out, and upon the application of the Attorney General it shall be its duty to make such investigation. It shall transmit to the Attorney General a report embodying its findings and recommendations as a result of any such investigation, and the report shall be made public in the discretion of the Commission.

(15 U.S.C. § 46(c))

Upon the direction of the President or either House of Congress, the Commission may investigate and report the facts relating to any alleged violations of the antitrust acts by any corporation (15 U.S.C. § 46(d)), and it may "investigate, from time to time, trade conditions in and with foreign countries where associations, combinations, or practices of manufacturers, merchants, or traders, or other conditions, may affect the foreign trade of the United States"; after which it may present a report to Congress with such advisable recommendations (15 U.S.C. § 46(h)).[8] In the final analysis, courts, and not the FTC, have peremptory authority in interpreting the antitrust laws of the US.

7.1 (D) THE ROBINSON-PATMAN ACT (1936)

The Robinson–Patman Act (15 U.S.C. § 13(a–f)) amended Section 2 of the Clayton Act. With limited exceptions, the law prohibits a seller of commodities from engaging in price discrimination when dealing with different purchasers, especially when the grade or quality of a good is comparable. However, businesses routinely engage in price discrimination when elasticities (sensitivities to price changes) are different and when they can feasibly separate one market from another to prevent the resale of goods for arbitrage profits. Price discrimination may also prevent competition, especially when the intent of price discrimination is predatory. Firms with higher per unit cost of production will be outcompeted.

For quite some time, federal courts could not clearly apply the Clayton Act to incidents of price discrimination based on pricing and quantity. With some exceptions, Robinson-Patman prohibits discounts based on quantity, and the law inveighs against discriminatory pricing schemes:

It shall be unlawful for any person engaged in commerce, in the course of such commerce, either directly or indirectly, to discriminate in price between different purchasers of commodities of like grade and quality, where either or any of the purchases involved in such discrimination are in commerce, where such commodities are sold for use, consumption, or resale within the United States or any Territory thereof or the District of Columbia or any insular possession or other place under the jurisdiction of the United States, and where the effect of such discrimination may be substantially to lessen competition or tend to create a monopoly in any line of commerce, or to injure, destroy, or prevent competition with any person who either grants or knowingly receives the benefit of such discrimination, or with customers of either of them: *Provided*, That nothing herein contained shall prevent differentials which make only due allowance for differences in the cost of manufacture, sale, or delivery resulting from the differing methods or quantities in which such commodities are to such purchasers sold or delivered: *Provided, however*, That the Federal Trade Commission may, after due investigation and hearing to all interested parties, fix and establish quantity limits, and revise the same as it finds necessary, as to particular commodities or classes of commodities, where it finds that available purchasers in greater quantities are so few as to render differentials on account thereof unjustly discriminatory or promotive of monopoly in any line of commerce …

(15 U.S.C. § 13(a))

By outlawing the receipt of anything of value as a compensation or allowance to transact business, Robinson-Patman also outlaws bribery or corrupt intent in the conduct of commerce, even when the unlawful act is perpetrated by intermediaries:

It shall be unlawful for any person engaged in commerce, in the course of such commerce, to pay or grant, or to receive or accept, anything of value as a commission, brokerage, or other compensation, or any allowance or discount in lieu thereof, except for services rendered in connection with the sale or purchase of goods, wares, or merchandise, either to the other party to such transaction or to an agent, representative, or other intermediary therein where such intermediary is acting in fact for or in behalf, or is subject to the direct or indirect control, of any party to such transaction other than the person by whom such compensation is so granted or paid.

(15 U.S.C. § 13(c))

Corrupt payments also include payments for services or facilities for processing or transacting a business or sale:

It shall be unlawful for any person engaged in commerce to pay or contact for the payment of anything of value to or for the benefit of a customer of such person in the course of such commerce as compensation or in consideration for any services or facilities furnished by or through such customer in connection with the processing, handling, sale, or offering for sale of any products or commodities manufactured, sold, or offered for sale by such person, unless such payment or consideration is available on proportionally equal terms to all other customers competing in the distribution of such products or commodities.

(15 U.S.C. § 13(d))

Discriminatory pricing schemes (prices not accorded to all purchasers on proportionally equal terms) via the use of facilities for processing and handling are also outlawed when it comes to the resale of goods:

> It shall be unlawful for any person to discriminate in favor of one purchaser against another purchaser or purchasers of a commodity bought for resale, with or without processing, by contracting to furnish or furnishing, or by contributing to the furnishing of, any services or facilities connected with the processing, handling, sale, or offering for sale of such commodity so purchased upon terms not accorded to all purchasers on proportionally equal terms.
>
> (15 U.S.C. § 13(e))

Like virtually all laws, Robinson-Patman puts a premium on guilty intent (*mens rea*) in the furtherance of a crime that is associated with discriminatory pricing:

> It shall be unlawful for any person engaged in commerce, in the course of such commerce, knowingly to induce or receive a discrimination in price which is prohibited by this section.
>
> (15 U.S.C. § 13(f))

Robinson-Patman has encountered criticisms that are reminiscent of the ambiguities of the Sherman Act, but also because of some omissions. Courts have wrestled with the clarity of its language. For example, see *FTC v. Ruberoid Co.* 343 US 470, 72 S, Ct. 800, 96L.Ed.1081 (1952). Transfers and leases are not clearly classified under the Act. While bilateral transactions are considered to evaluate price discrimination, there seems to be a necessity for an interstate transaction in one of the sales under the commerce clause. The law is equally deficient when it comes to services (for example, banking, insurance, and photography), since it is preoccupied with trade in goods or commodities.

The timing of the passage of the Act is important. The service industry became prominent in the late 1980s, and it was not until 1995 that it was fully integrated into international trade convention (see the World Trade Organization). In effect, service industries were not "dominant features" in the 1930s—a central precondition for standing in courts of law. Services feature prominently as an accessorial element of a crime in the conduct of tangible business.

7.1 (E) THE WHELLER-LEA ACT (1938)

The Wheller-Lea Act amended Section 5 of the FTC Act to define unfair or deceptive acts, unfair methods of competition, and the penalties that are associated with false advertising, especially in matters that are related to food, drugs, and cosmetics. Two interrelated concepts underpin the legislation: (i) the minimization of the deleterious effects of asymmetric information (and its corresponding adverse selection) on the free market economy, and (ii) the consumption of safe products to ensure the welfare of consumers. There are some definitional issues in the law, which run afoul of its original and general intent.

In large measure, Wheller-Lea repudiates if not augments the ancient doctrine *caveat emptor*, the doctrine that shifted the culpability of adverse consumption to consumers when they are negligent or not vigilant. Contemporary law requires sellers to be forthright when they are dealing with consumers, meaning that sellers are culpable for fraudulently peddling hazardous or unwanted products by deceptive practices.

The law, which was enacted after the request or recommendation of the FTC, was introduced as a bill to amend Section 5 of the FTC Act by Senator Wheller on January 14, 1935. In an effort to prohibit unfair and deceptive practices, the bill did not get prompt support and it died on the Senate Calendar. After the original bill died, a successor bill was introduced (S. 3744). The successor bill was less successful and it died prematurely in the House Committee.[9] The bill was resuscitated in the 75th Congress and was eventually passed as the Wheller-Lea Act of 1938 after revisions involving food, drugs, and cosmetics were made in the House. Though the Food and Drug Act of 1906 made no explicit allusion to advertising, its misbranding provisions were not conspicuously different from false advertising, at least in terms of the impact on consumers.

A major challenge of the Wheller-Lea Act was to distinguish its verbiage from the 1906 Drug Act.

A market economy cannot function properly when information is not evenly distributed in the marketplace. As such, false advertising endangers the stability and vitality of a competitive economy. Relatively even distribution of information means that all participants (buyers and sellers) must be privy to factual information even when they are unsophisticated. By "market economy," economists generally mean all sectors of an economy (micro- and macroeconomics). The interaction of buyers and sellers generate signals that are critical for long-term investment, innovation, production, investment, and the smooth operations of real and financial markets. Material deception distorts prices and availability of goods and services. Therefore, the quality of advertising is an intrinsic component of the free market system. Transaction law generally emphasizes materiality, because materiality alters perception and decisions in the marketplace. It is broadly defined to mean relevant information that will otherwise determine a decision to engage or disengage in an (economic) transaction. Therefore, it cannot be comprehensively defined without a reliance or persuasive component.

The Act defines false advertising as:

> an advertisement, other than labeling, which is misleading in a material respect; and in determining whether any advertisement is misleading, there shall be taken into account (among other things) not only representations made or suggested by statement, word, design, device, sound, or any combination thereof, but also the extent to which the advertisement fails to reveal facts material in the light of such

representations or material with respect to consequences which may result from the use of the commodity to which the advertisement relates under the conditions prescribed in said advertisement, or under such conditions as are customary or usual. No advertisement of a drug shall be deemed to be false if it is disseminated only to members of the medical profession, contains no false representation of a material fact, and includes, or is accompanied in each instance by truthful disclosure of, the formula showing quantitatively each ingredient of such drug ...

(15 U.S.C. § 55(1))[10]

(b) ... The term "food" means (1) articles used for food or drink for man or other animals, (2) chewing gum, and (3) articles used for components of any such article. (c) ... The term "drug" means (1) articles recognized in the official United States Pharmacopoeia, official Homoeopathic Pharmacopoeia of the United States, or official National Formulary, or any supplement to any of them; and (2) articles intended for use in the diagnosis, cure, mitigation, treatment, or prevention of disease in man or other animals; and (3) articles (other than food) intended to affect the structure or any function of the body of man or other animals; and (4) articles intended for use as a component of any article specified in clause (1), (2), or (3); but does not include devices or their components, parts, or accessories (15 U.S.C. § 55(2)(b-c)).

The FTC is granted authority to take enforcement measures against individuals, partnerships, and corporations engaging in, or about to engage in the dissemination of false advertising that is in violation of the law. Several enforcement mechanisms and procedures are also provided in the statute. Some of the most instructive criticisms or deficiencies of the law can be found in the work of Handler (1939). He identified five areas of definitional difficulties concerning the following elements: (i) *scienter* (guilty intent), (ii) reliance, (iii) nature of the representation, (iv) materiality, and (v) injury.[11]

The original representation placed no emphasis on reliance, which is a critical element of a fraudulent crime. That is, consumers must rely on the false information for the information to have injurious effect, and the seller of false information must knowingly peddle the misinformation. The concept of reliance was undefined; especially when misinformation can generate persistent memory that is adversarial.

However, Handler suggests that although the Wheeler-Lea Act omits the element of reliance from its definition of false advertising, it is possible for the requirement to be imported into the statute in the guise of judicial construction (interpretation) of the word "material."[12] The statute is violated only when an advertisement is misleading in a "material respect," but it did not provide the metric for the measurements of falsity and materiality. Some amount of evidence beyond opinion is required to show falsity and materiality. An unsettling issue is whether a consumer could rely on immaterial information.

The connection between misrepresentation and reasonability poses an additional problem. Tort law shows that a misrepresentation becomes material when its willful articulation conveys believability and action on the part of the victim. Are all consumers reasonable and sophisticated? Therefore, false advertising can only be eliminated by the prohibition of all falsity, material or immaterial.[13] Accuracy can be ascertained by scientific affirmations in a profession rather than exaggerated opinions (see the *Daubert Standard*).

The advertising requirement to disclose consequences of the consumption of a product gives the law an unfortunate scope of conjecture that may be right or wrong. The law does not create provisions to ascertain the types of tests that should be applied to the curative effects of advertising, and the statute does not clearly demand proof of injury to consumers and competitors under the regular order of antitrust provisions. Advertising by the medical profession is deemed to be false only if it does not correctly disclose the quantitative component of each ingredient in a drug.

The penalties for injury have not been found to be entirely swift and palliative.

> Whenever the Commission has reason to believe that any person is disseminating or causing to be disseminated any false advertising of food, drugs, devices or cosmetics, and it appears to the Commission that the institution of a proceeding would be in the public interest, it may issue a complaint setting forth the charges against the advertiser. A hearing may be had any time after the expiration of a period of thirty days from the date of service of the complaint. Hearings are generally held before trial examiners who render an intermediate report … .
>
> Will the modified procedure deter the dissemination of false advertising? The Commission must undertake a preliminary investigation before issuing a complaint in order to satisfy itself that grounds exist for the institution of proceedings. This naturally takes time. Hearings cannot be held sooner than thirty days after service of the complaint. Various jurisdictional requirements, such as proof of interstate commerce, tend to prolong the trial. The examiner must take the matter under advisement and prepare his report. The case is then put on the Commission's calendar for argument.
> (Handler, 1939, p. 105)

7.1 (F) THE CELLAR-KEFAUVER ACT (1950)

The Cellar-Kefauver Act is a law against the anticompetitive acquisition of assets. It amends the Clayton's provision of stock acquisition, which omitted asset acquisition, especially when firms are not direct competitors. The omission permitted entrepreneurs to purchase the assets of competitors without necessarily purchasing their shares. Eventually, the Cellar-Kefauver Act was passed to deal with asset acquisition and mergers of firms that were not in direct competition (vertical and conglomerate mergers).[14]

It should be recalled that Congress enacted the Clayton Act in 1914, and that Section 7 of the Act generally prohibited the acquisition of the stock of a corporation by another corporation where the effect of the acquisition could lessen competition. Cellar-Kefauver proscribes anticompetitive acquisition of assets:

No person engaged in commerce or in any activity affecting commerce shall acquire, directly or indirectly, the whole or any part of the stock or other share capital and no person subject to the jurisdiction of the Federal Trade Commission shall acquire the whole or any part of the assets of another person engaged also in commerce or in any activity affecting commerce, where in any line of commerce or in any activity affecting commerce in any section of the country, the effect of such acquisition may be substantially to lessen competition, or to tend to create a monopoly. No person shall acquire, directly or indirectly, the whole or any part of the stock or other share capital and no person subject to the jurisdiction of the Federal Trade Commission shall acquire the whole or any part of the assets of one or more persons engaged in commerce or in any activity affecting commerce, where in any line of commerce or in any activity affecting commerce in any section of the country, the effect of such acquisition, of such stocks or assets, or of the use of such stock by the voting or granting of proxies or otherwise, may be substantially to lessen competition, or to tend to create a monopoly. This section shall not apply to persons purchasing such stock solely for investment and not using the same by voting or otherwise to bring about, or in attempting to bring about, the substantial lessening of competition. Nor shall anything contained in this section prevent a corporation engaged in commerce or in any activity affecting commerce from causing the formation of subsidiary corporations for the actual carrying on of their immediate lawful business, or the natural and legitimate branches or extensions thereof, or from owning and holding all or a part of the stock of such subsidiary corporations, when the effect of such formation is not to substantially lessen competition.

(15 U.S.C. § 18)

The language of the statute was broad enough to generate apprehension about prospective mergers. Two major issues created difficulties for the enforcement of the law: (i) the concept of commerce and (ii) the probabilistic metric that was used to measure market concentration and restraint of trade (commerce). By every indicator, the law was proactive and anticipatory, without any specific measure of market concentration, of the problems that might arise from mergers. This issue will be dealt with in the next section.

Commerce is defined as "trade or commerce among the several States and with foreign nations ..." which provides a basis for federal jurisdiction. As far back as 1948, the concept of interstate commerce was resolved by judicial decision (*Mandeville Island Farms v. Am. Crystal Sugar Co.*, 334 U.S. 219 (1948)). However, it is subsumed that all corporations will carry out interstate accounts. "For this reason, the parameters of the statute's operation are critical to a corporation contemplating a merger. The scope of Section 7 can best be analyzed by discussion of judicial interpretation regarding each of its component parts" (Blackwell, 1972, p. 624).

The probabilistic dimension meant that the government did not need to establish certainty that a restraint of trade would result from a given acquisition. The government merely needed to show a "reasonable probability," which was largely based on the type of merger involved, that a merger would have a restraining effect on commerce (*United States v. Bethlehem Steel* Corp, 168 F. Supp. 576 (S.D.N.Y. 1958)). While the legality of the horizontal merger was contingent on the resultant increase in market power under Clayton, the extent to which potential competitors would be foreclosed by an acquirer became a new metric for vertical and conglomerate mergers.

It became rather difficult to index diversification mergers on a straightforward percentage basis. In the case of a horizontal merger, the Supreme Court had ruled that the merger of two brewery companies supplying an aggregate of 4.49 percent of the national beer market was violative of antitrust law (*United States v. Pabst Brewing Co.*, 384 U.S. 546 (1966)). A trend toward increased concentration was considered an exposure of the market to further restraining horizontal amalgamation. However, the court held that a vertical merger which would foreclose one percent of the acquired firm's market would substantially lessen competition in a market characterized by vertical integration (*Brown Shoe Co. v. United States*, 370 U.S. 294 (1962)). Therefore, according to Blackwell, "to lessen" commerce "would require proof of probable *diminution* of *existing* competition in order to establish a Section 7 violation."[15] Cellar–Kefauver obtained some successes (see Table 7.1).

What happens when a firm grows too big in a post-acquisition period? Cellar–Kefauver was originally seen as a preemptive law. However, the notion that it was merely applicable to pre-merger arrangements became nugatory in 1957 (*United States v. E. I. du Pont de Nemours and Co*, 353 U.S. 586 (1957)). The Supreme Court held that the acquisition of 23 percent of General Motors' stock by du Pont blossomed into a Section 7 violation after 40 years. The court further directed that du Pont be ordered to divest itself of the shares (Blackwell, 1972, p. 625). Hence, it became possible for acquisitions to be reversed under Section 7, regardless of the elapsed time and the resulting hardship of a divestiture.[16]

The definition of assets within the statute is very broad. It is sufficiently broad to include "property or property rights, real or personal, tangible or intangible, which are subject to transfer and which have been used by the seller and could be used by the buyer competitively." Thus, customer lists, exclusive licenses, trademarks, and patents have been found to be assets within the purview of Section 7 (Blackwell, 1972, p. 627; see also *United States v. Columbia Pictures Corp.*, 1960 TRADE CASES 69–766 (S.D.N.Y. 1960)). Additionally, the law does not clearly delineate the relevant markets in terms of product or line of commerce and geography. Sampling seven decisions, Blackwell (1972) found that relevant geographic markets can be as large as the entire country, or as small as a single metropolis (*United States v. Philadelphia Nat'l Bank*, 374 U.S. 321 (1963)). Alluding to the product market, the Supreme Court observed:

> The District Court properly found that the predominantly medium-priced shoes which appellant manufactures do not occupy a product market different from the predominantly low-priced shoes which the other corporation sells … .
>
> Insofar as the vertical aspect of this merger is concerned, the relevant geographic market is the entire Nation, and the anticompetitive effects of the merger are to be measured within that range of distribution.
> (Chief Justice Warren, *Brown Shoe Co. v. United States* (370 U.S. 294 (1962)))[17]

Table 7.1 Antitrust enforcement 1952 to March 1961

Year	Justice Department	FTC	Total
1952	---	1	1
1953	---	---	---
1954	---	2	2
1955	5	3	8
1956	6	12	18
1957	1	6	7
1958	5	3	8
1959	10	11	13
1960			24
1961 (March)	7	1	8
Σ	**45**	**44**	**89**

Source: Handler and Robinson (1961).

The product market itself had a complicating mixture of product variety that can provide competitive dimensions in end-use markets; for example, bottles and cans are not identical products, but they can be used as containers for beer by a brewery company or alcohol industry. However, the government was able to successfully define products and geographic limits by what Blackwell (1972) called "economic legerdemain" to score substantial victories beyond the 1961 record of Table 7.1 (see *United States v. Von's Grocery Co.*, 384 U.S. 270 at 301 (1966)).

Conglomerate mergers do not instinctively suggest anticompetitive effects. Notwithstanding, the law does not suggest a decisive evaluation of a pending conglomerate acquisition. Successful prosecution of such cases depends on the full discovery of intent that the acquired firm would otherwise have competed in the acquirers market as a result of internal expansion (see *United States v. El Paso Natural Gas Co.* 376 U.S. 651 (1964)). Two propositions circumscribe the thought: (i) the acquisition is seen as a removal of a competitive threat, especially in an oligopolistic market structure, and (ii) subsequent competition is diminished by the foreclosure of internal expansion.

When it comes to conglomerate mergers, additional problems can be associated with reciprocal trading arrangements when firms exploit their diversities to promote reciprocal trade, tying arrangements, or exclusive intra-firm agreements (Whitney). Conglomerates also have the potential of offsetting losses by relying on the income of profitable divisions (the Deep Pocket Doctrine), which will enable them to set price below per unit cost (predatory pricing); see *Smith-Victor Corp. v. Sylvania Elec. Prods., Inc.*, 242 F. Supp. 315 (D.C. Ill. 1965). However, Turner maintains that such intra-firm advantages are subject to review under Section 5 of the FTC Act. The following table provides an overview of the antitrust laws:

Table 7.2 US antitrust laws

Law	Year	Objective
Sherman Act	1890	Antitrust
Clayton Act	1914	To prohibit: (i) the purchase of competitors' stocks in order to monopolize financial markets; (ii) conflict of interests in the corporate organizations by Board of Directors, and (iii) the criminalization of organized [labor] action
FTC Act	1914	To establish an agency, Federal Trade Commission (FTC), to administer antitrust law
Robinson-Patman Act	1936	To prohibit price discrimination that reduces competition
Wheller-Lea Act	1938	Modified the focus of the FTC
Cellar-Kefauver Act	1950	To prohibit mergers that will reduce competition
Williams Act	1968	Regulates tender offer practices
Hart-Scott-Rodino	1976	Authority for the FTC and Justice Department to evaluate pre-merger attempts

7.1 (G) THE WILLIAMS ACT (1968)

In cases of hostile takeovers and raids, board members and a preponderant amount of shareholders are usually opposed to a takeover bid or acquisition by a bidder. When a bidder seeks a target company under normal and amicable circumstances, the bidder and target sign a merger agreement. If a board is opposed to a takeover, the takeover bid becomes very contentious or hostile. A bidder will first try to pressure management to accept an offer with an implied intent to contact the stockholders directly (bear hug).[18] In a hostile takeover, the acquirer usually makes an offer to the shareholders of a target company (tender offer) that exceeds the prevailing share price. The shareholders are presented with an enticing opportunity to sell their shares at a premium for cash and renunciation of voting rights (greenmail). Alternatively, non-voting investments (bond-like equity) can be offered. A successful bid will give the bidder control (voting) rights over the target to restructure the target company. Restructuring may take different forms, divestitures, equity carve-outs, spin-offs, split-offs, exchange offer, and split-ups (Gaughan, 2015, p. 391).

In the aftermath of a takeover, the former management of the target is typically replaced, its assets divested, and employment is adjusted to achieve efficiency. The combined market value of the bidder and target usually increases when synergies are created. Over the years, companies have developed various defense mechanisms to thwart takeover bids.[19]

The Williams Act was a response to financial irregularities and a series of coercive hostile takeover attempts. The Act, which covers disclosure requirements, tender offers, shareholder rights, fiduciary duties and defensive tactics, and much more, is a multifaceted response to prevent financial shenanigans and protect investors (sophisticated and unsophisticated).

At the time the Williams Act was passed, the vast majority of shareholders were not institutional investors but individual shareholders who were usually fragmented, ill-informed, and unprepared to exert their rights as shareholders though they held about 80 percent of equity.[20] The wealth of shareholders and market value were diminished by the infusion of cash for shares within a very limited time. Accordingly, the Williams Act was designed to protect these investors against raiders and financial hostility in the marketplace. The economic reasoning or value behind acquisition is not destructive, but an orderly process was essential to promote synergy and efficiency when companies are underperforming and exposing the financial and real sectors to inevitable danger.

The laws on the books were not entirely bereft of orderly requirements but offers of cash for equity posed a destabilizing problem in financial markets. Consequently, the Act was a delicate balancing act to safeguard the interests of all stakeholders, including the interests of financial managers, potential acquirers, and shareholders. The Williams Act, which amended portions of the Security and Exchange Act of 1934, requires investors to file a disclosure statement within ten days of acquiring "beneficial ownership" of more than five percent of the equity of a public company.[21] Filing procedures are stipulated in Schedule 13D.

Persons or groups acquiring beneficial ownership exceeding five percent of a voting class of a registered company's equity must file a Schedule 13D with the SEC, disclosing their name and address, the number of shares actually owned, and the source of the funds used to acquire the target *inter alia*. The Act requires tender offer to be kept open for a minimum of 20 business days, during which the bidder or acquiring firm must accept all shares that have been tendered. Actually, it may not buy any of the shares until the end of the offer period so that undecided or reluctant shareholders will not be pressured into tendering their shares. If there is a perceived violation of Schedule 13D, shareholders or the target company may sue for damages.[22]

Hostile bidders must first submit a registration statement to the Securities and Exchange Commission (SEC) and wait for the registration to be declared effective before they can proceed with the submission of tender offers to shareholders. Section 13(d) of the Act requires shareholders and management to be alerted to the possibility that a threat of control is pending.

In various ways, the Williams Act inveighs against deceptive and fraudulent practices in the acquisition of equity:

> It shall be unlawful for any person to make any untrue statement of a material fact or omit to state any material fact necessary in order to make the statements made, in the

light of the circumstances under which they are made, not misleading, or to engage in any fraudulent, deceptive, or manipulative acts or practices, in connection with any tender offer or request or invitation for tenders, or any solicitation of security holders in opposition to or in favor of any such offer, request, or invitation. The Commission shall, for the purposes of this subsection, by rules and regulations define, and prescribe means reasonably designed to prevent, such acts and practices as are fraudulent, deceptive, or manipulative.

(15 U.S.C. § 78n (8)(e))

7.1 (H) THE HART-SCOTT-RODINO (HSR) ACT (1976)

In 1976 the Clayton Act was amended one more time. Section 201 of the HSR Act amended the Clayton Act by adding a new Section 7A, 15 U.S.C. § 18(a). According to the statute, various types of pre-merger activities are required to be reported to the FTC. The pre-merger activities will generally include proposed acquisitions of voting securities, non-corporate interests, or assets be reported to the Commission and the Antitrust Division prior to consummation.

After reporting their intent, the parties must then wait a specified period of time, usually 30 days (or 15 days in the case of a cash tender offer or bankruptcy sale), before they may complete the transaction.[23] The applicability of the general requirements is contingent on the value of the acquisition and, in certain acquisitions, the size of the sales and assets. Acquisitions valued below a certain threshold, acquisitions involving parties with assets and sales below a certain threshold, and certain classes of acquisitions that are less likely to raise antitrust concerns are excluded from the Act's coverage.[24]

On July 31, 1978, the Commission in conjunction with the Assistant Attorney General for the Antitrust Division of the Justice Department, promulgated final rules for implementing the pre-merger notification program. A Statement of Basis and Purpose was also published at the same time together with the rules for filing a pre-merger notification request. The program eventually became effective on September 5, 1978. The rules and filing forms have since been amended periodically to improve compliance and enforcement effectiveness of the program as mandated by the statutory scheme.

The pre-merger notification program and the filing and waiting requirements provide the agencies and pre-merger applicants with the time and information that is necessary to conduct the antitrust review. Much of the information for a preliminary antitrust evaluation is included in the notification that is filed with the agencies by the aspiring merger parties.[25] If either of the reviewing agencies determines that further inquiry is necessary during the waiting period, additional information may be requested under Section 7A(e) of the Clayton Act.

> The Second Request extends the waiting period for a specified period of time (usually 30 days, but 10 days in the case of a cash tender offer or bankruptcy sale) after all

parties have complied with the Second Request (or, in the case of a tender offer or bankruptcy sale, after the acquiring person complies). This additional time provides the reviewing agency with the opportunity to analyze the information and to take appropriate action before the transaction is consummated.[26]

A reviewing agency may then seek an injunction in a federal district court before consummation if it believes that a proposed transaction may substantially lessen competition. The Commission may also challenge the transaction in administrative litigation. The applicable provisions of the law can be found in 15 U.S.C. § 18(a) (Box 7.1).

BOX 7.1 15 U.S.C. § 18(A)

(c), no person shall acquire, directly or indirectly, any voting securities or assets of any other person, unless both persons (or in the case of a tender offer, the acquiring person) file notification pursuant to rules under subsection (d)(1) and the waiting period described in subsection (b)(1) has expired ….

[T]he acquiring person, or the person whose voting securities or assets are being acquired, is engaged in commerce or in any activity affecting commerce; and

(2) as a result of such acquisition, the acquiring person would hold an aggregate total amount of the voting securities and assets of the acquired person—

(A) in excess of $200,000,000 (as adjusted and published for each fiscal year beginning after September 30, 2004, in the same manner as provided in section 19(a)(5) of this title to reflect the percentage change in the gross national product for such fiscal year compared to the gross national product for the year ending September 30, 2003); or

(B)(i) in excess of $50,000,000 (as so adjusted and published) but not in excess of $200,000,000 (as so adjusted and published); and

(ii)(I) any voting securities or assets of a person engaged in manufacturing which has annual net sales or total assets of $10,000,000 (as so adjusted and published) or more are being acquired by any person which has total assets or annual net sales of $100,000,000 (as so adjusted and published) or more;

(b) Waiting period; publication; voting securities

(1) The waiting period required under subsection (a) shall—

US ANTITRUST LAW AND ENFORCEMENT

> **BOX 7.1 CONTINUED**
>
> **(A)** begin on the date of the receipt by the Federal Trade Commission and the Assistant Attorney General in charge of the Antitrust Division of the Department of Justice (hereinafter referred to in this section as the "Assistant Attorney General") of—
>
> **(i)** the completed notification required under subsection (a), or
>
> **(ii)** if such notification is not completed, the notification to the extent completed and a statement of the reasons for such noncompliance, from both persons, or, in the case of a tender offer, the acquiring person; and
>
> **(B)** end on the thirtieth day after the date of such receipt (or in the case of a cash tender offer, the fifteenth day), or on such later date as may be set under subsection (e)(2) or (g)(2).
>
> **(2)** The Federal Trade Commission and the Assistant Attorney General may, in individual cases, terminate the waiting period specified in paragraph (1) and allow any person to proceed with any acquisition subject to this section, and promptly shall cause to be published in the Federal Register a notice that neither intends to take any action within such period with respect to such acquisition …
> (15 U.S.C. § 18(a)).

The law imposes some controlling requirements for pre-merger considerations, considered to be tests (hurdles): (i) the Commerce Test, which requires the participants to be engaged in the appropriate commerce, (ii) the Size-of-the-Person Test, as measured by total assets and net sales, and (iii) the Size-of-the-Transaction Test, which is based on the amount or percentage of assets to be acquired. The Commission and the Antitrust Division have continued their efforts to promote competition by identifying and investigating mergers and acquisitions that potentially threaten the competitive criterion of commerce. Figure 7.1 is indicative of the efforts of the enforcement agencies.

Ohlhausen and Delrahim (2017) report that in fiscal year 2017, 2,052 transactions were reported under the HSR Act, representing about a 12.0 percent increase from the 1,832 transactions reported in fiscal year 2016.

> Over the past five years, the number of HSR reportable transactions has increased significantly—in FY2013, 1,326 HSR transactions were reported and in FY2017, 2,052 HSR transactions were reported, an increase of over 50%. This is in the face of flat, or effectively decreasing, budgets and restrictions on hiring.

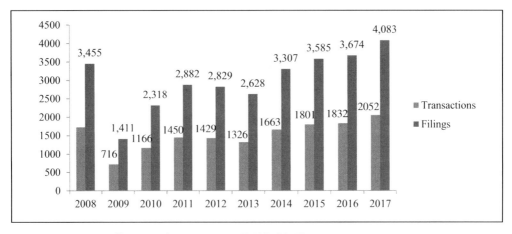

Figure 7.1 Merger filings and transactions (2008–2017)
Source: Hart-Scot-Rodino Annual Report: Fiscal Year 2017, Appendix A.
Notes: Usually, two filings are received, one from the acquiring person and one from the acquired person when a transaction is reported. Only one application is received when an acquiring party files for an exemption under Section 7A(c)(6) or (c)(8) of the Clayton Act.

Additionally,

> during fiscal year 2017, the Commission brought 21 merger enforcement challenges, including 14 in which it accepted consent orders for public comment, all of which resulted in final orders; six in which the transaction was abandoned or restructured as a result of antitrust concerns raised during the investigation; and one in which the Commission initiated administrative or federal court litigation. These enforcement actions preserved competition in numerous sectors of the economy, including consumer goods and services, pharmaceuticals, healthcare, high-tech and industrial goods, and energy.
>
> (Ohlhausen & Delrahim, 2017, pp. 1–2)[27]

The US antitrust laws arose out of economic circumstances or conditions with accompanying penalties. The issue of damages will be discussed at the end of the chapter. I have already alluded to some of the circumstances that gave rise to the laws without fully conveying the circumstances that underpin the enactment of each law, except perhaps for the Sherman Act. The next section examines the waves of consolidations and the industry-specific changes that gave rise to the legal responses.

7.2 THE DEVELOPMENT OF MERGERS AND ACQUISITIONS (MERGER WAVES)

There has not been a monolithic theory of merger waves. Merger waves have been driven by economic conditions, imprecise market valuations, economic shocks, and managerial challenges or inefficiencies. Harford (2004) provides a range of possibilities and some of the empirical work that has been conducted on the subject matter. The neoclassical theory directs attention to various types of shocks to an industry; specifically, economic, technological, regulatory, and environmental. It is noteworthy that antitrust laws circumscribed the lack of continuity of some of the waves.

When capital liquidity and reduction in financing constraints are correlated with high asset values, there is a tendency for shocks to propagate a wave; supporting the neoclassical theory that merger waves respond to specific industry shocks that require large scale asset reallocation.[28] Neoclassical explanations of rational merger waves are based on an economic disturbance that leads to industry reorganization (Harford, 2004, pp. 530–2). The neoclassical hypothesis contends that once a technological, regulatory, or economic shock to an industry's environment occurs, the collective reaction of firms inside and outside the industry causes industry assets to be reallocated through mergers and partial-firm acquisitions.

> This activity clusters in time as managers simultaneously react and then compete for the best combinations of assets. The capital liquidity argument modifies the neoclassical hypothesis of waves to predict that only when sufficient capital liquidity exists to accommodate the reallocation of assets, will an industry shock generate a merger wave. Thus, even if industry shocks do not cluster in time, the importance of capital liquidity means that industry merger waves as reactions to shocks will cluster in time to create aggregate merger waves.
> (Harford, 2004, p. 533)

An alternative view for merger waves is associated with stock valuations (behavioral hypothesis). Bull markets encourage groups of bidders with overvalued stocks to use their stocks to buy real assets of undervalued targets through mergers. These mergers may also be influenced by misperceived synergies and target managers may rashly accept the overvalued equity of bidders. The behavioral hypothesis projects some predetermined expectations.[29] Merger historians have characterized merger waves by some specific developments.

The first wave, which is estimated to be between 1897 and 1904, was dominated by horizontal mergers (firms that compete with one another in proximate geographic environments).

The industries affected were mostly primary metals, food products, petroleum products, chemicals, transportation equipment, and fabricated metals. It is estimated that the industries accounted for about two-thirds of all mergers during the period. The mergers occurred at an accelerated pace, and approximately 50 significant manufacturing and mining mergers were consummated yearly during the period from 1898 to 1902, each absorbing 10 or 11 firms.[30] Advances in communication and transportation, which expanded geographic markets, coincided with a bullish stock market (see also Greenspan & Wooldridge, 2018, pp. 142–4). The Sherman Act retarded the progress of the wave.

The second merger movement (in the late 1920s), affected a number of new industries (such as automobiles and parts, various branches of food manufacturing, and food retailing). The wave accounted for the elimination of approximately 1,000 manufacturing and mining corporations annually. The wave was disrupted by stock market crashes, but the cumulative effect of the two waves materially transformed the structure of the American economy.[31] Though the collapse of financial markets disrupted the propagation of the second wave, the Sherman and Clayton Acts made the legal environment less conciliatory for the growth of mergers. After the enactment of Section 7 in 1914, major horizontal and vertical mergers could be blocked. In 1957, the du Pont-GM decision foreshadowed the intolerance for sizable vertical mergers (Blackwell, 1972).

The third wave (1965–1969) occurred at a time of economic prosperity. The period witnessed the growth of conglomerate mergers and smaller firms targeted larger firms for acquisition. The conglomerates were diversified because they had subsidiaries in other industries, but production was highly concentrated in the telecommunications industry. The Cellar-Kefauver Act of 1950 strengthened the antitrust environment during this period. The conglomerates did not significantly affect competition, but accounting irregularities assisted acquirers to inflate their gains on paper. Several conglomerate acquisitions were consummated by exchanging common stock for convertible debentures. However, in the late 1960s, the use of convertible debt was largely seen as having an anticompetitive effect on the market, and the synergistic attributes of the mergers became questionable. Managers were not very knowledgeable about the operations of some of the firms under their control or some of the industries that they were entering.

The fourth merger wave (1984–1989) was unique in its own respect. Although the number of hostile takeovers was not exceedingly high, the phenomenon of hostile takeover created a footprint for merger activities during the period. Large firms became targets of acquisitions during the 1980s, and the total value of acquisitions increased sharply. There was noticeable evidence of corporate raider activities.[32] For example, the successive raids of Singer Corporation were intended to sell the shares of Singer at higher prices than the raider actually paid before its acquisition in the 1980s. In an era of deregulation, mergers increased in deregulated industries, air transportation, entertainment, broadcasting, natural gas, trucking, and banking. Interstate banking became widespread in the mid-1980s. Bank holding companies were permitted to acquire out-of-state banks on a reciprocal basis with other states. Interstate banking gave rise to regional and national banking chains. The fourth wave ended in 1989 with a less prosperous economic condition.[33]

The fifth merger wave (1990–2001) occurred at a time of economic expansion. Banking, finance, communication, and broadcasting (of the service sector) accounted for 26.5 percent of all US deals between 1993 and 2004. The period also witnessed a lot of international mergers in Europe, Asia, and Central and South America, ended by the 2001 recession.[34] The fifth merger wave coincided with the longest post-war expansion, increase in aggregate output, and fewer hostile deals in financial markets.

During the sixth wave (post-2001), and prior to the Great Recession, the US economy was highly liquid. The high liquidity increased equity prices and equity financing was robust. The real and financial sector thrived, and the housing market thrived dangerously. Some attributed the subprime bubble to excessive liquidity. However, Greenspan and Wooldridge (2018) argue that the housing boom arguably started in 1998, well before the Federal Reserve's 2001 rate cut. "For another, the housing boom was a global problem: Britain saw a sharp increase in house prices at about the same time as the United States, despite running a much more restrictive monetary policy" (Greenspan & Wooldridge, 2018, p. 384). There have been three distinctive types of mergers during this period: (i) the pre-financial crisis mergers, (ii) the post-financial crisis mergers that involved financial intermediaries during and immediately after the Great Recession, and (iii) mergers that cannot be associated with the Great Recession.

In the pre-recession period, the FTC prohibited a product extension merger between Procter & Gamble Co, and Clorox, a large soap manufacturer (see *Federal Trade Commission v. The Procter & Gamble Co.*, 386 U.S. 568 (1967)) on the basis that Procter's marketing and advertising power would solidify Clorox's already dominant position in the household bleach market. The decision revealed that large mergers that could foreclose new entrants can be challenged under Section 7. The decision also indicates that smaller firms could be intimidated and prevented from engaging in price competition for fear of retaliation and predatory pricing schemes. The prospects of probability of foreclosure were not very apparent.[35]

The financial crisis and recession caused a steep increase in the number of commercial bank and savings institution failures in the United States. Mergers of non-failed commercial banks and savings institutions eliminated some banks, and in total, the number of US banks fell by 12 percent between December 31, 2006, and December 31, 2010. Typically, federal law prohibits any bank from obtaining more than 10 percent of total US deposits or more than 30 percent of a single state's total deposits by acquiring other non-failed banks, and some states have imposed even lower deposit share limits. Bank regulators also use Department of Justice (DoJ) guidelines for market concentration to evaluate the competitive effects of proposed bank mergers and acquisitions (Wheelock, 2011, pp. 419–21). A noteworthy effect of the financial crisis and the accompanying recession is that it led to a wave of bank failures and mergers that exacerbated the ongoing consolidation of the US banking industry.

> Although Wachovia Bank NA merged with Wells Fargo Bank NA in March 2010, the Board of Governors of the Federal Reserve System approved the application of Wells Fargo & Company to acquire Wachovia Corporation and its subsidiaries, including Wachovia Bank NA, on October 12, 2008 … In evaluating the competitive implications

of an acquisition of Wachovia Corporation by Wells Fargo, the Board of Governors used deposit and market share data for June 30, 2007.

(Wheelock, 2011, p. 431)

Merger activities and court challenges have continued in the US. The combined actions by the FTC and the US DoJ increased from 34 cases in 2015 to 39 cases in 2016, and the court challenges increased from 8 to 12 for the same period; see Figures 7.2(a) and 7.2(b). Notable challenges and wins include the cases against *Aetna and Humana* (2015), *Advocate and NorthShore* (2016), *Hershey and PinnacleHealth* (2015), *Staples and Office Depot* (2016), and *Tribune publishing and Freedom Communications* (2016). Some merger attempts were abandoned in the face of enforcement opposition.[36]

Some of the relatively recent cases involve Aetna, Advocate, Hershey, and Staples. In the *Aetna Case*, the DoJ alleged that the merger would reduce competition in the Medicare Advantage market, arguing that Humana is the second largest and Aetna is the fourth largest insurer in the Medicare Advantage market. The DoJ also alleged that the merger would reduce competition on the public healthcare exchanges in at least a hundred counties. In the *Advocate Case*, the FTC alleged that the transaction would allow Advocate to control more than half of the general acute care inpatient hospital services in northern Cook County and southern Lake County, Illinois.

In December 2015, the FTC filed an administrative complaint and a motion for preliminary injunction in the Middle District of Pennsylvania to prevent the merger of two Harrisburg, Pennsylvania health systems, Hershey and PinnacleHealth. The FTC characterized the companies as "the two largest health systems in the greater Harrisburg, Pennsylvania area," and alleged that the post-merger entity would own all but one small community hospital in the area.

In the *Staples Case*, the FTC alleged that the parties were the only two nationwide companies capable of providing office supplies, services, and logistics to other large, national companies. Figures 7.2a and 7.2b show the formal actions brought by US antitrust

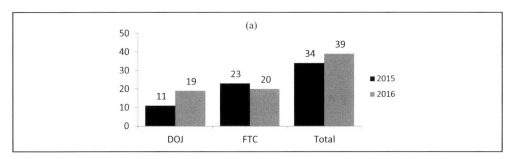

Figure 7.2a Formal actions by US antitrust authorities (2015–2016)
Source: US Competition Law-Merger Enforcement, 2016 Year in Review, p. 4.

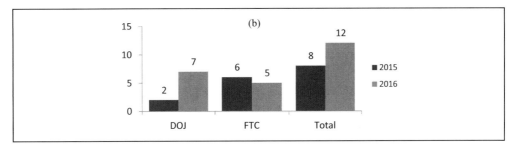

Figure 7.2b Court challenges (2015–2016)
Source: US Competition Law-Merger Enforcement, 2016 Year in Review, p. 4.

authorities and the court challenges between 2015 and 2016. In both instances the cumulative effects have increased, with formal actions increasing from 34 to 39, and court challenges increasing from 8 to 12.

7.3 MEASURING MARKET CONCENTRATION: THE HERFINDAHL-HIRSCHMAN AND LERNER INDICES

The establishment of a reliable measurement of the market share is a challenge for enjoining anticompetitive behavior in courts of law. Accordingly, in 1968, the Justice Department issued merger guidelines that set forth the parameters that the government will use to oppose or challenge mergers that are considered to be anticompetitive. The guidelines provided an efficient mechanism to target specific cases rather than all cases of combinations. Conglomerate mergers provided an additional challenge to the pervasively known and rather well defined horizontal and vertical mergers that have already been alluded to.

The central issue is whether merging firms will have undue size advantage and leverage that will stifle competition and prevent other firms from entering a market. Proof of potential entry is tricky but estimating the sizes of markets in an industry is not necessarily a herculean task. The earlier guidelines used concentration ratios in an industry. As such, under the 1968 guidelines, an industry was considered concentrated if the four largest firms held at least 75 percent of the total market.[37]

The measures that determined antitrust activities in the late 1960s and 1970s were less precise and confounding. However, more streamlined quantitative methods for measuring market concentration started to gain attention in the 1980s.[38] One of the measures that is instrumental in quantifying market share is the Herfindahl–Hirschman Index (HHI). The index measures market concentration in a specific industry by squaring the market share of each firm in an industry. The index is a rather expedient

Table 7.3 The HHI and size of market concentration*

Number of firms in an industry	Market share (MS)	HHI value (MS)²
1	(100/1)	10,000
2	(100/2)= (50)+(50)	5,000
3	(100/3)= (33.33)+(33.33)+(33.33)	3,300
4	(100/4)= 25 each	2,500
5	(100/5)= 20 each	2,000

Note:
*Assuming that horizontal market share is equally distributed.

and straightforward metric for measuring concentration in horizontal merger cases (see Equation 7.1 and Table 7.3).

$$HHI = \sum_{i=1}^{n}(MS_i)^2;\qquad(7.1)$$

where sigma is a summation operator, and MS is for the market share of each company (i) in an industry.[39] Table 7.3 shows the value of the HHI as we move from monopoly to competition. The assumption here is that each firm has an equal share of the markets in an industry. It is evident that as we move from monopoly to competition, the value of the index declines from 10,000 to 2,000; suggesting that higher values of the index are more likely to reflect a less competitive and stringent pre-merger environment.

Should firms decide to combine, the market share of aspiring mergers will be combined and squared to evaluate the impact of the merger on competitiveness in an industry, and the extent to which the merger will increase or alter the pre-existing value of the index. For example, suppose an industry has 4 firms with an equally distributed 25 percent market share; if two of the firms decide to merge then the index will be altered:

$$HHI = (25+25)^2 + (25)^2 + (25)^2 = 3,750$$

The index has increased by 1,250 points (from 2,500 to 3,750) and the combined market share of the firms now has an HHI of 2,500. A determination will have to be made as to whether the merger should be consummated. *Prima facie* evidence suggests that the merger will be in legal jeopardy, since the firms will have an inordinate size advantage to enhance market power. Apparently, the current structure of the market is not anywhere close to the competitive market structure we reviewed in Chapter 1. The firms operate in an oligopolistic industry in which there are only four firms with market shares that are equally distributed. In fact, in this type of market structure, variations in ownership are redundant because of the attributes of the oligopolistic structure (few producers).

US ANTITRUST LAW AND ENFORCEMENT 343

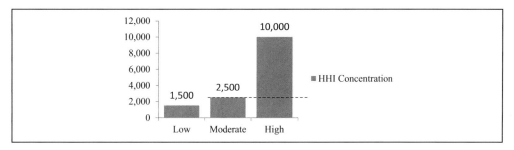

Figure 7.3 The HHI and levels of concentration

The HHI has preliminary implications. When one firm has 100 percent market share, the firm is a monopoly (the only one producing a product) with an HHI of 10,000. Two firms with equal share in a duopolistic environment will have an HHI of 5,000. An HHI of 1,500 suggests low concentration, while values of 2,500 and 10,000 suggest moderate and high concentrations respectively (see Figure 7.3).

Post-merger results of less than 1,000 are considered to have unconcentrated effects. Post-merger values that lie between 1,000 and 1,800 are considered moderately concentrated, and post-merger values exceeding 1,800 are considered highly concentrated. Mergers that increase HHI by less than 50 will not be challenged, mergers that increase HHI by 50–100 may be challenged, and increases by 100 will be challenged.

The merger guidelines were further revised in June 1984. The quantitative mechanisms had made the reviews rather deterministic and inflexible. As a result, some qualitative variables were subsequently factored into consideration. Additional information includes: the efficiency effects arising from synergies, the financial viability (insolvency) or the lack thereof of the firms, and the propensity to compete in international markets. Contemporary guidelines provide an admixture of the quantitative and qualitative components. The five percent (elasticity) test was also included during this period (see Chapter 1). The five percent elasticity test was used to determine the effects of a five percent increase in price on consumers and competitors (Gaughan, 2015, p. 120).

Recall that elasticity is a responsiveness indicator. In this context, it measures the responsiveness of consumers to price changes (review the log representation in Chapter 5):

$$|e_d| = \frac{dQ}{dP} \star \frac{P}{Q} \begin{cases} > 1, \ elastic \\ = 1, \ Unitary\ elastic \\ < 1, \ inelastic \end{cases}$$

where e_d is the price elasticity of demand coefficient with continuous data, dQ is for the change in quantity, dP is for the change in price, P is for the price of a good and Q is for the quantity or units. Coefficients that are greater than one suggest that consumers are very sensitive to price changes because they have options *inter alia*. The market environment is most likely to be competitive. Coefficients that are less than one (in absolute terms), suggest that consumers are very sensitive to price changes because they lack options *inter alia*. The market structure is more likely to be less competitive and restrictive. Accordingly, if market demand is inelastic over a five percent price range of price change, then the merged firms are more likely to have greater market power and vice versa.

Apart from the consumption effects, other indicators are considered: (i) comparison based on experience (historical events that impinge on a merger—recent mergers, expansions, exits, and geographic presence), (ii) the unlikelihood of enhancing market power, (iii) likely status without the merger, and (iv) the propensity of a merger to exacerbate disruption in a market (endangering firms that enhance consumer welfare).[40] Some merger proposals have pitched the case for efficiency and positive external effects on consumers (see the case of *Pfizer and Wyeth*, 2010).

Synergistic alliances occur when combinations perform better as a team, or become more efficient and profitable, rather than operating as individual units. Therefore, the combination produces a positive net acquisition value (NAV):

$$NAV = \Sigma V - [v_1 + v_2] - P - E, \text{ or}$$

$$NAV = [\Sigma V - (v_1 + v_2)] - (P + E); \tag{7.2}$$

where ΣV is the sum of values for the two units or companies $(v_1 + v_2)$, P is the premium paid for acquisition, and E is for the total expense of acquisition. Equation 7.2 suggests that the value to be derived must be greater than the cost (P+E) of acquisition. The definition of the NAV is conventional and does not include the external benefits of replacing inefficient management with a more competent management of the acquirer.[41] Synergy is associated with the operations and finance of the merging companies. Operating synergies occur when revenue is enhanced and the internal cost of operations is reduced. Financial synergies reduce the cost of raising capital.

Synergistic benefits are not indefinite, and they may not apply to all types of mergers. As firms expand or acquire other interests, they may encounter economies of scale, constant returns to scale, or diseconomies of scale as they continue to produce output. When there are economies of scale to be derived, the acquisition of firms will reduce the long-run average total cost (LRATC) of the acquirer. The benefits that accrue to the acquirer will also include managerial competencies as outlined by Asquith (1983), and Jensen and Ruback (1983). However, these competencies may not be easily quantifiable. The LRAC in Figure 7.4 shows that it is profitable for firms to merge rather than operate in the increasing cost (diseconomies) segments of their short-run per unit costs (review the cost concepts in Chapter 1).

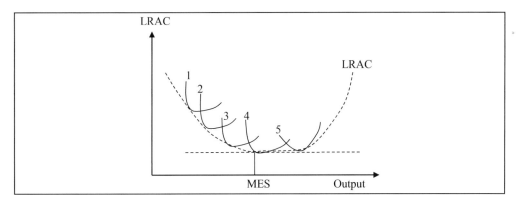

Figure 7.4 Output and per unit cost in the long run

Rather than operating on the increasing cost (upward sloping) segments of firms 1, 2, 3, and 4, it might be beneficial for firms to merge. Falling per unit costs should be beneficial to consumers as the firms enjoy economies of scale. Obviously, firms may not continue to expand forever, because they will encounter diseconomies of scale when they encounter managerial problems, worker alienation, and lack of access to sufficient and efficient resources. Figure 7.4 shows that it is inefficient for the enterprise to expand beyond the fifth acquisition. In fact, economies of scale are exhausted after the acquisition of the fourth firm, which produces the minimum efficient scale (MES) of production.

While considerable attention has been directed to the HHI and efficiency, a less consequential index that can be used to study pricing behavior is the Lerner Index, which tracks the relationship between the price of a good and its marginal cost:

$$L = 1 - \frac{MC}{P}; \tag{7.3}$$

where L is for the Lerner Index, P is for price, and MC is for the marginal or incremental cost of production that was discussed in Chapter 1. Equation 7.3 shows that the index measures the marginal cost as a percentage of the price of a product. When price is equal to the value of the marginal cost of production, then the Lerner Index is just zero. That is, consumers are paying a price that corresponds to the incremental cost. As price increases relative to the MC, the value of the index falls; this means that a falling index value is an indication of increasing market power.[42] Higher values of L denote greater market power. However, the index is more useful for evaluation pricing behavior rather than direct assessments of combinations and market share. As such, it can only provide complementary information about market power. What happens when firms innovate, reduce prices, and tie their products to get competitive advantage?

7.4 INNOVATION, TYING, AND MONOPOLIZATION: ANTITRUST LAW AND THE *MICROSOFT CASE*

Until the *Microsoft Case* of 1994, the interface of innovation, tying, and market share attracted very little attention. The case subsequently went to a Circuit Court. On May 18, 1998, the United States Department of Justice, and the Attorneys General of 19 States and the District of Columbia sued Microsoft (a technology company) for violation of antitrust provisions under the Sherman Act. Law and economics collided on several frontiers, especially in the areas of technological innovation, the preservation of intellectual property rights, and the desire to increase market share. Additionally, beyond apparently restrictive behavior or commercial restraint, the law was inadequate to deal with the benefits and measurements of network externalities. To what extent was antitrust law lagging behind technological progress and the requirements for competition in the industry? Economides (2001) and Weinstein (2002) provide an interesting summary of the changing technological landscape and the ramifications for law and economics in the literature. Ahlborn, Evans, and Padilla (2004) provide a comprehensive analysis of tying and per se illegality.

By the 1990s high-technology industries became notable for their distinguishing knowledge-intensive attribute that was in contradistinction to the labor-intensive underpinnings of antitrust laws. Apparently, the knowledge that is needed to develop software, biotechnology, and other types of high-tech products, is generally expensive to develop. However, after the products have been developed, the incremental or marginal cost of producing subsequent units is generally low. As such, the technology products are characterized by comparatively higher fixed costs. These preconditions generate economies of scale on the supply side for high-technology companies.

The knowledge-based requirements for using high-tech products, consumer psychology, affinity, first- or prime-user advantage, and familiarity with the products usually make it difficult for consumers to switch from one high-tech product to a similarly related product when they do not have a compelling reason to do so. Consequently, the products, say computers, generate strong network externalities. Under such circumstances, as more consumers become fond of a high-tech product, the value of the product increases because more consumers are using the product. It becomes relatively difficult to measure this network externality in courts of law. Closely aligned with knowledge acquisition, the network effect, and affinity effect (knowledge and consumer psychology), is the lock-in effect, which makes it less likely for consumers to switch to other related products, especially substitutes.

The characteristics of the high-tech products create boundless opportunities for tying high-tech products to reduce per unit cost, reinforce network externalities, and maintain hegemony in a competitive environment in which innovation and product attraction are indispensable to success.

Inasmuch as tying generates economies of scale and cost savings when high-tech products are created and marketed, it also produces undesirable welfare effects when its coercive intent is deliberative. It has the appearance and probable effects of stifling innovation and reduces consumer freedom. Accordingly, companies in the technology industry must maintain a delicate balance between innovation and competition that cleanly avoids the appearance of impropriety and violation of antitrust law, even though the innovation rate in the software industry might be much higher. Product differentiation or character of demand (in law) and functionality (in economics) must be clearly delineated to determine whether products are separable or inseparable.[43]

The *Microsoft Case* reveals that Microsoft was a large diversified computer software manufacturer in the 1990s, and that it produced the Windows family of operating systems for personal computers and servers. Additionally, it also produced applications software that runs on the Windows family of operating systems, most notably the MS-Office Suite, which consisted of Word (word processor), Excel (spreadsheet), PowerPoint (presentations), Outlook (e-mail and news), and Access (database) (Economides, 2001).

Almost all Microsoft products were complementary to a member of the Windows family of operating systems for personal computers and servers. Microsoft produced software, including operating systems for PC (Windows 95, 98, NT, 2000), operating systems for local network and Internet servers (Windows NT, 2000), "back-office" products for network and internet servers, internet clients, internet and network servers, desktop applications (Office, Word, Excel, Access, Outlook, PowerPoint, MS Money, etc.), games, and programming languages (Visual Basic, Java). Microsoft also produced services, including internet service (MSN, WebTV), Internet content (MSN), and product support, and some hardware such as branded mice and keyboards, etc. (Economides, 2001).

The FTC and the US DoJ investigated Microsoft on various antitrust allegations in the 1990s. The 1991–1993 and 1993–1994 investigations by the FTC ended with no lawsuits, but the 1994 investigation by the DoJ was terminated with a consent decree in 1995. The 1995 agreement reflects that Microsoft agreed to end its "per-processor" agreement (contract) with original equipment manufacturers (OEMs); for example, free additions like Internet Explorer contracts with computer manufacturers. The company also agreed to enter into contracts in which licensing agreements are not implicitly or expressly (explicitly) conditioned upon the licensing of any other Covered Product. The company was not enjoined from producing integrated product, and OEMs were not prevented from licensing, purchasing, using, or distributing any non-Microsoft product.[44]

On July 15, 1994, the DoJ sued Microsoft under Section 2 of the Sherman Act, complaining that Microsoft entered into licensing agreements with OEMs that prevented other operating system vendors from gaining widespread distribution of their products. At the center of the complaint were the company's efforts to maintain a monopoly over its operating system by destroying threats posed by Netscape Navigator, a web browser, and Sun Java, a cross-platform programming language. Both Navigator and Java were considered to be species of "middleware," software programs[45] that can serve as platforms for other software applications (Weinstein, 2002).

According to the plaintiffs' theory, middleware posed two distinct threats to the Windows monopoly. The middleware applications could be used as software platforms that competed directly with Windows, but they were also designed to run on more than one operating system that would allow software developers to write programs that worked on any number of these operating systems. The plaintiffs alleged that Microsoft engaged in a number of anticompetitive acts to destroy the threats posed by Navigator and Java, including arrangements to secure exclusive dealing contracts with OEMs and Internet Access Providers (IAPs).

The agreement foreclosed the OEMs and IAPs from using Navigator and Internet Explorer (IE), and pressured Apple Computer to drop its use of Navigator. In addition, the plaintiffs alleged that Microsoft had illegally tied IE to Windows in an effort to destroy competition in the browser market.[46] A number of areas in the US antitrust law were implicated. The charges against the company included monopolization and attempted monopolization under Section 2 of the Sherman Act,[47] and tying under Section 1 of the Sherman Act.[48] According to Weinstein (2002), liability under Section 2 of the Sherman Act (monopolization), requires: "(1) the possession of monopoly power in the relevant market and (2) the willful acquisition or maintenance of that power" not based on "a superior product, business acumen, or historic accident."[49] In applying the initial prong of the test, a court will first define the relevant antitrust market. In general, the market will encompass all products "reasonably interchangeable by consumers for the same purposes."[50]

Once the market is defined, the court will decide whether the defendant has monopoly power in that market, with monopoly power defined as "the power to control prices or exclude competition."[51] Direct proof of monopoly power is rarely available, so courts typically rely on circumstantial evidence, such as market share combined with barriers to entry. There are also criteria for attempted monopolization and tying.

In order to establish liability for attempted monopolization under Section 2 of the Sherman Act, the evidence must prove that (1) the defendant engaged in "predatory or anticompetitive conduct" with (2) "a specific intent to monopolize" and (3) "a dangerous probability of achieving monopoly power." Just as in a monopolization analysis, a court must define the relevant antitrust market in order to rule on the third prong (Weinstein, 2002; see also Ahlborn et al., 2004). The *Eastman Kodak Case* provides some parameters for evaluating the tying criteria.

For a tying violation to occur, the products must be differentiated, customers must not have been allowed to purchase the tied product without tying the product in the first place, the tying arrangement must have significant interstate footprint, and the defendant must have market power in the tying product.[52] If all the outlined elements are satisfied, then a per se criterion (test) can be established without redeeming features; suggesting that extraneous evidentiary support to prove the existence of an infraction is redundant.[53] Weinstein notes that most tying litigation cases focus on the first and fourth elements and that in technological innovation cases the question of whether one product or two is involved has become a very difficult doctrinal issue.

The Supreme Court laid out the standard test for determining whether a combination of goods or services represents one product or two in *Jefferson Parish Hospital District No. 2 v. Hyde*.[54] The court held that the question of whether there are two products involved turns "not on the functional relation between them, but rather on the character of the demand for the two items." In other words, if there is "sufficient demand" for the purchase of one product, which is "separate from" the second product, then there are two products for the purpose of tying analysis.[55]

The DC. Circuit could not find evidence that Microsoft tied IE with Windows. Consequently it overturned the district court's holding that Microsoft's bundling of IE and Windows was per se unlawful. By so doing, some legal scholars argue that the court announced a new tying rule for situations "involving platform software products." Rather than judging tying arrangements under the per se rule, as was the case in *Northern Pacific and Jefferson Parish*, the court held that the rule of reason is the appropriate test and remanded the case to the district court for judgment under this standard.[56]

However, the circuit judge found anticompetitive practices and the presence of monopoly power in some areas of the operating system market; for example, in the market for Intel-compatible PC operating systems, attempts to convince Netscape to release its version of a browser at a later date, exclusive contracts with OEMs, and contracts with Independent Software Vendors (ISVs) to use this version of Java Virtual Machine (JVM). After finding both monopoly power and anticompetitive behavior, the judge held that Microsoft violated Section 2 by illegally maintaining its monopoly in the operating system market.

In the case of attempted monopolization, Microsoft was found liable for tying but not exclusive dealing. The judge found that IE and Windows were separate products (separate demand test). Therefore, by conditioning the licensing of Windows on the purchase of IE, the judge found that Microsoft illegally tied the products. The judge failed to find exclusive dealing because Microsoft had not foreclosed a significant share of the market for the sale of its browser.

When it comes to monopolization, the circuit court upheld the lower court's ruling that Microsoft possessed monopoly power in the market for Intel-compatible PC operating systems in addition to alterations and programming algorithms by OEMs to give Microsoft a competitive advantage.[57]

7.5 ESTIMATING ANTITRUST DAMAGES

US Antitrust laws have provisions for nonmonetary and pecuniary damages that should be construed as instruments of deterrence. Yet there exist unusual situations in which all those who are injured in one form or another by anticompetitive practices may not possibly be compensated for anticompetitive violations. Only those who can show material injury can be awarded damages in courts of law. That is, in antitrust cases only the market participants are generally considered to have standing in courts of law. Non-market participants must be able to prove otherwise. External effects are not successfully litigated and victims of external effects are not directly compensated.

The original applications of US antitrust laws were limited to the domestic environment and the laws initially developed with a municipal dimension. Antitrust laws were eventually expanded to have an international effect or extraterritorial dimension. The consequential impact of offshore (international) merger activities on the US domestic market and financial shenanigans has led American courts to develop the "effects doctrine." The extraterritoriality of US and interpretations will be discussed in the next chapter. The laws enumerate several penalties for violations.

Section 2 of the Sherman Act makes monopolization of trade or conspiracy to restrain a felony with some clearly defined penalties:

> Every person who shall monopolize, or attempt to monopolize, or combine or conspire with any other person or persons, to monopolize any part of the trade or commerce among the several States, or with foreign nations, shall be deemed guilty of a felony, and, on conviction thereof, shall be punished by fine not exceeding $10,000,000 if a corporation, or, if any other person, $350,000, or by imprisonment not exceeding three years, or by both said punishments, in the discretion of the court.
>
> (Sherman Act)

Further, 15 U.S.C. § 15 makes provisions for recovery and prejudgment interest:

(a) Except as provided in subsection (b), any person who shall be injured in his business or property by reason of anything forbidden in the antitrust laws may sue therefore in any district court of the United States in the district in which the defendant resides or is found or has an agent, without respect to the amount in controversy, and shall recover threefold the damages by him sustained, and the cost of suit, including a reasonable attorney's fee. The court may award under this section, pursuant to a motion by such person promptly made, simple interest on actual damages for the period beginning on the date of service of such person's pleading setting forth a claim under the antitrust laws and ending on the date of judgment, or for any shorter period therein, if the court finds that the award of such interest for such period is just in the circumstances. In determining whether an award of interest under this section for any period is just in the circumstances, the court shall consider only—

   (1) whether such person or the opposing party, or either party's representative, made motions or asserted claims or defenses so lacking in merit as to show that such party or representative acted intentionally for delay, or otherwise acted in bad faith;

(2) whether, in the course of the action involved, such person or the opposing party, or either party's representative, violated any applicable rule, statute, or court order providing for sanctions for dilatory behavior or otherwise providing for expeditious proceedings; and

(3) whether such person or the opposing party, or either party's representative, engaged in conduct primarily for the purpose of delaying the litigation or increasing the cost thereof.

Payments are also elucidated for foreign entities. A critical element of the law is the trebling provision for antitrust cases. The literature on trebling will be dealt with shortly. As an extension of the Act, the Clayton Act penalizes price-fixing schemes (§ 15d):

> In any action under section 15c(a)(1) of this title, in which there has been a determination that a defendant agreed to fix prices in violation of sections 1 to 7 of this title, damages may be proved and assessed in the aggregate by statistical or sampling methods, by the computation of illegal overcharges, or by such other reasonable system of estimating aggregate damages as the court in its discretion may permit without the necessity of separately proving the individual claim of, or amount of damage to, persons on whose behalf the suit was brought.

In the case of the FTC Act, there are penalties for violations of FTC order and injunctive relief:

> (l) Any person, partnership, or corporation who violates an order of the Commission after it has become final, and while such order is in effect, shall forfeit and pay to the United States a civil penalty of not more than $10,000 for each violation, which shall accrue to the United States and may be recovered in a civil action brought by the Attorney General of the United States. Each separate violation of such an order shall be a separate offense, except that in a case of a violation through continuing failure to obey or neglect to obey a final order of the Commission, each day of continuance of such failure or neglect shall be deemed a separate offense. In such actions, the United States district courts are empowered to grant mandatory injunctions and such other and further equitable relief as they deem appropriate in the enforcement of such final orders of the Commission …
>
> (15 U.S.C. § 45(e)(1))

Wheller-Lea imposes penalties for false advertising:

> (a) Any person, partnership, or corporation who violates any provision of section 52(a) of this title shall, if the use of the commodity advertised may be injurious to health because of results from such use under the conditions prescribed in the advertisement thereof, or under such conditions as are customary or usual, or if such violation is with intent to defraud or mislead, be guilty of a misdemeanor, and upon conviction shall be punished by a fine of not more than $5,000 or by imprisonment

for not more than six months, or by both such fine and imprisonment; except that if the conviction is for a violation committed after a first conviction of such person, partnership, or corporation, for any violation of such section, punishment shall be by a fine of not more than $10,000 or by imprisonment for not more than one year, or by both such fine and imprisonment: Provided, That for the purposes of this section meats and meat food products duly inspected, marked, and labeled in accordance with rules and regulations issued under the Meat Inspection Act [21 U.S.C.A. § 601 et seq.] shall be conclusively presumed not injurious to health at the time the same leave official "establishments."

(15 U.S.C § 54)[58]

Civil penalties for Hart–Scott–Rodino violations can be found in (15 U.S.C. § 18(a))

Any person, or any officer, director, or partner thereof, who fails to comply with any provision of this section shall be liable to the United States for a civil penalty of not more than $10,000 for each day during which such person is in violation of this section. Such penalty may be recovered in a civil action brought by the United States.

Damages that result from monopolistic infringements emerge from markups above the competitive price. Recall from Chapter 1 that in competitive markets prices eventually correspond to the marginal costs of production, and that consumer surpluses are greater in such markets. There are natural efficiency losses in monopolistic markets, which become pronounced in cases of illegal monopolies or violation of antitrust laws. Consider the competitive industry in contradistinction to the monopolistic in Figure 7.5.

There is no deadweight loss (the shaded triangles) in the competitive model. This is because price (P_C) corresponds to the marginal revenue (MR_{PC}) and marginal cost (MR_{PC}). In the long run, allocative and productive efficiencies are expected in the competitive industries, because the competitive price will move towards the incremental and per unit costs (MC and ATC). Monopolists will charge higher prices, because they are "price makers" and not "price takers." As a result, consumers lose surplus and there is

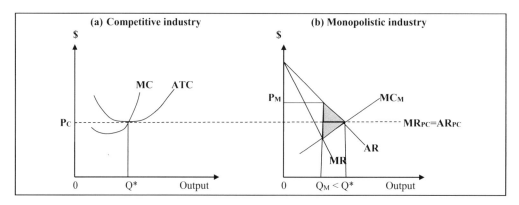

Figure 7.5 Efficient allocations versus efficiency loss

an efficiency loss to society, which is represented by the grey triangles. Deadweight losses (DWLs) can emanate from contrivances by firms to increase market power by various mechanisms, including collusion and price-fixing schemes. Such contrivances generate higher prices like P_M for lower quantities like Q_M.

The appropriate compensation for efficiency loss has generated a considerable amount of controversy in antitrust litigation cases. More so, identifying the victims for societal loss has become an elusive matter. Litigants who are the beneficiaries of compensation in antitrust litigation cases cannot be representative of the societies that are affected by the violation of antitrust laws.

Surprisingly, some theorists think that the DWL is efficiency-neutral and need not be relevant to antitrust litigation. On the contrary, theorists who see the spirit of antitrust laws to be protective of consumers, argue that the loss of consumer surplus ought to be worthy of legitimate consideration. However, the DWL has not been an element of liability in antitrust cases. Even when courts recognize the theoretical existence of the DWL in antitrust cases, plaintiffs are not generally accorded standing for DWL claims. The argument has also been made that plaintiffs could exploit the law by accumulating damages over a protracted period of time.[59]

There is an econometric issue that is associated with the DWL problem. How should the DWL be measured? What is the slope of the market demand curve or the elasticity of price changes for non-purchasers of the product that is monopolized? A speculative element involves verifying how people could have been able to purchase the product without the monopoly price. Plaintiffs or antitrust violators can be made better off or worse off because of inadequate information that compensates or inflates compensation without making society better off.[60]

Since damages cannot be unduly speculative under such circumstances, and since plaintiffs are expected to prove the infliction of injuries that antitrust laws are supposed to prevent, the DWL concept has not been fully granted legal recognition; though it is very prominent in economics. It is rather precarious that victims of antitrust violations are adequately compensated; even with trebling (Wheeler, 1973, p. 1337). Additionally, judges are not given much discretion in issues appertaining to trebling. The vagaries of the marketplace deny courts the ability to know with a reasonable amount of certainty, definite knowledge of what a plaintiff's situation would have been without antitrust violation; see *J. Truett Payne Co., Inc v. Chrysler Motors Corporation* (US 557, 566; 1981).

However, some courts have recognized that antitrust violations can result in DWL; see *Ball Memorial Hosp. v. Mutual Hosp. Ins.* (7th Cir. 1986); *Brown v. Pro Football Inc.* (D.C. Cir. 1995); and *Telecor Communications Inc. v. Sw. Bell Tel. Co.* (10th Cir. 2002). The aggregate harm to consumers is not only the exorbitant prices that are charged, but the costs that are associated with finding substitute goods as a result of price-fixing. Yet, even courts that recognize DWL in theory do not necessarily grant standing to plaintiffs who attempt to recover damages based on DWL.[61]

The Sherman Act requires that after the jury has determined the amount of the plaintiff's actual damages, the court must award three times that amount. Other statutes make similar provisions; see, *Cohen v. De La Cruz*, 523 U.S. 213 (1998). The US Supreme Court has recognized the concept of trebling as a mechanism to protect consumers against the effects of excessive prices that are violative of antitrust law. External costs that are associated with responses by other suppliers in reaction to price-fixing are not normally factored into consideration; see *Warner Mgmt. Consultants, Inc. v. Data Gen. Corp.* (N.D. III. 1982).

Is trebling a proxy for DWL compensations? Some scholars have suggested that firms that are liable for illegal monopolization or cartelization might be paying for the DWL that is associated with price-fixing (Cavanagh, 1987). But the stated goals of trebling do not necessarily purport to provide a proxy for DWL. However, trebling may serve some interdependent purposes: (i) the perception that it is a form of remedy for their antitrust suffering; and (ii) acknowledgment of culpability to prevent the application of the trebling law. Yet most antitrust awards, even after trebling, do not include the claims of all affected consumers.[62]

The evidence for adequate deterrence is imprecise, but in *Blue Shield of Va. v. McCready* (US 465, 1982), the Supreme Court recognized that: "Only by requiring violators to disgorge the fruits of their illegality can the deterrent objectives of the antitrust laws be fully served." Notwithstanding, disgorgement is not a means of calculating DWL; it ensures the return of gains from illegal activities to victims.[63] A proposal for estimating the DWL includes five elements (a review of Figure 7.5 Panel (b) should be instructive): (i) the market output that results from violation (Q_M); (ii) the amount of the overcharge (that is the difference between P_M and P_C); (iii) the competitive output (Q_C); (iv) the competitive price (PC); and (v) the shape of the demand between Q_M and Q_C (knowledge of the elasticity of demand can be helpful in this regard).[64] The next and final chapter of this book will examine the international law of money, investment, and strategic trade.

CHAPTER SUMMARY

- In the 1870s and 1880s, there were various trusts and combinations in several industries, including petroleum, meat packing, railroads, sugar, lead, coal, whisky, and tobacco. The trusts generally limited production and charged consumers high prices for poor quality products. The relationship between monopoly and perfect competition can be posited.
- The regulatory environment also favored the emergence of large corporations. Companies could incorporate in states where the laws were very lenient for doing business, and the laws before the 1940s generally prevented foreign competition.
- The life of the average man, especially if he was a city dweller, was profoundly changed by this development. Almost everything he ate and wore, the furnishings of the house, the tools he used, the transportation he employed, were made and controlled by trusts ... (Nevins & Commager, 1992, p. 270).

- The intent of the Sherman Act was to prevent unlawful monopolies. However, though the intent of the law was clear, the language of the law was not without ambiguities. Subsequent merger laws clarified the intent and included financial transactions.
- There has not been a monolithic theory of merger waves. Merger waves have been driven by economic conditions, imprecise market valuations, economic shocks, and managerial challenges or inefficiencies.
- The establishment of a reliable measurement of the market share is a challenge for enjoining anticompetitive behavior in courts of law. The central issue is whether merging firms will have undue size advantage and leverage that will stifle competition and prevent other firms from entering a market. Proof of potential entry is tricky, but estimating the sizes of markets in an industry is not necessarily a herculean task.
- US Antitrust laws have provisions for nonmonetary and pecuniary damages that should be construed as instruments of deterrence. Yet there exists unusual situations in which all those who are injured in one form or another by anticompetitive practices may not possibly be compensated for anticompetitive violations.
- The appropriate compensation for efficiency loss has generated a considerable amount of controversy in antitrust litigation cases. More so, identifying the victims for societal loss has become an elusive matter. Litigants who are the beneficiaries of compensation in antitrust litigation cases cannot be representative of the societies that are affected by the violation of antitrust laws.

KEY WORDS

• Antitrust	• FTC Act	• Robinson-Patman Act
• Cellar-Kefauver Act	• HHI	• Rule of reason
• Clayton Act	• HSR Act	• Sherman Act
• Conglomerate merger	• Horizontal merger	• Trebling
• Damages	• Lerner Index	• Tying
• DWL	• Mergers	• Vertical merger
• Economies of scale	• Net asset value	• Wheller-Lea Act
• Elasticity	• Per se rule	• Williams Act

CHAPTER QUESTIONS

1. What are the circumstances that gave rise to the laws of the nineteenth and twentieth centuries? How did the concept of financial stability shape the dimensions of US antitrust laws?
2. Why do firms merge? With reference to specific examples, explain the differences between horizontal and vertical mergers, and vertical mergers and conglomerate mergers. Is the Herfindahl-Hirschman Index an adequate measure of market

concentration and basis for challenging mergers? Why? Explain why the Lerner Index can help to ascertain market power.
3. With reference to some specific cases, explain why the rule of reason is different from the per se rule. What was the reasoning for using the rule of reason in the *Microsoft Case*? How does the use of the rule compare to some previous cases?
4. Discuss the legal and economic importance of the FTC and the US DoJ.
5. Should estimation of the deadweight loss (DWL) be included in antitrust cases? Explain why the language of the Sherman Act is not necessarily an economic measurement of the deadweight loss. Is the concept of DWL legally refractory? Why? How have the courts dealt with the issue of DWL?

NOTES

1 See Nevins and Commager (1992, p. 269).
2 See Greenspan and Wooldridge (2018, p. 138).
3 Philip D. Armour and Gustavus F. Swift established a beef trust, the McCormicks established pre-eminence in the reaper business, and the Duke family built a great tobacco trust (see Nevins & Commager, 1992, p. 270).
4 See Warburton (1998, p. 63).
5 See http://digitalhistory.uh.edu/.
6 Ibid. The government claimed that Standard Oil Company obtained its monopoly not by superior efficiency, but by unfair and immoral acts—rebate taking, and local price-cutting *inter alia*, in defiance of local and federal laws.
7 Tying contracts are agreements that coerce buyers to purchase different or distinctive types of products other than the ones that they are primarily interested in. Section 8 of the Clayton Act prevents a person from serving as a director or officer of two or more competing corporations when the combined income of the corporations exceeds a certain amount (about $25 million or more after January 29, 2008).
8 For a concise presentation of some of the antitrust laws see http://stern.nyu.edu/ and https://law.cornell.edu/.
9 One of the motives for recommending the legislation was to ensure the binding effect of FTC enforcement procedures if they are not appealed in 60 days.
10 In the case of oleomargarine or margarine an advertisement shall be deemed misleading in a material respect if in such advertisement representations are made or suggested by statement, word, grade designation, design, device, symbol, sound, or any combination thereof, that such oleomargarine or margarine is a dairy product, except that nothing contained herein shall prevent a truthful, accurate, and full statement in any such advertisement of all the ingredients contained in such oleomargarine or margarine (15 U.S.C. § 55(2)). See the law for other definitions.
11 See Handler (1939, p. 96).
12 Op. cit., p. 97.
13 Op. cit., p. 99.
14 While horizontal and vertical mergers can be characterized easily, conglomerate mergers require more intricate analysis. They can be classified as any merger other than the linear horizontal or vertical mergers. Three defining characteristics are instructive for the conglomerate classification: (i) product extension, (ii) market

extension or geographic separation, and (iii) pure conglomerate (product disparities). Merging firms may produce related products when they are not necessarily in direct competition (product extension), or they can produce identical products and market them in different territorial delineations (geographic extension). Alternatively, firms could merge when they produce products that are totally unrelated in all aspects; see also Reilly (1968, p. 294).

15 See Blackwell (1972, p. 629). Acquisition of non-voting preferred stock for investment purposes are not considered to restrain trade. Cellar-Kefauver did not outrightly prohibit the purchase of corporate stock by a partnership and vice versa. Such mergers are not generally considered to be a cynosure of antitrust enforcement because of their relatively small size.

16 The *du Pont* ruling brought conglomerate mergers into the orbit of Section 7 (du Pont was a supplier of automobile seat cover fabric). The extension was premised on the argument that the 1950 extension was to reach all mergers, whether by stock or asset acquisition.

17 The government had argued that a merger of two corporations that produce, distribute, and sell shoes is violative of Section 7 and will reduce competition across the country. It enjoined the appellant from having or acquiring any further interest in the business, stock, or assets of the other corporation, called for full divestiture by appellant of the other corporation's stock and assets, and ordered appellant to propose in the immediate future a plan for carrying into effect the Court's order of divestiture (see https://supremejustia.com).

18 There are two types of bear hugs: (i) a *teddy bear hug*, which does not include a price tag or precise deal terms, and (ii) a price-specific bear hug, which establishes a cost for damages if dissenting shareholders are to be compensated in situations of litigation. The latter type is public and coercive.

19 These mechanisms include: poison pills (see *Moran v. Household International, Inc.*, 500 A. 2d 1346 (Del. 1985), shark repellents, staggered (classified) board amendments, Pac-man defense (counter offer to bidders), white knight (solicitation of a friendly bidder), and white square (finding a custodian investor to hold the shares or assets of the target). Of course, litigation is always an option. With a poison pill, the shareholders of targets are given the opportunity to purchase additional shares of the target or bidder at a discount. This increases the cost of acquisition. The poison pill has undergone metamorphosis (see Gaughan, 2015, Chapter 5). Shark repellents are deterrent measures adopted via the targets charter or byelaws. In classified board amendments, bidders will have to win more than one proxy fight after obtaining majority control, because the staggered board might prevent the bidders from electing managers (see Verizon, and Hewlett-Packard; see also Gaughan, 2015, pp. 204–13).

20 Source: https://corpgov.law.harvard.edu.

21 Source: https://corpgov.law.harvard.edu; when the law was originally passed, the threshold was ten percent. For a fuller discussion of the Williams Act, see Gaughan (2015, pp. 77–88).

22 Oversubscribed offers and partial bids are accepted on a pro-rata (proportional) or weight-oriented basis. Shareholders may withdraw their shares at any time prior to the end of the 20th day or a later date if the offer is extended. Under Rule 14e-2, targets must respond within ten business days from the dissemination of the bidder's offer. Targets have an option to: (i) accept, (ii) reject, (iii) maintain a position of neutrality,

and (iv) take no position. Targets respond by filing states that target must respond by filing a Schedule 14D-9, under the requirements of Rule 14d-9.
23 See Ohlhausen and Delrahim (2017, pp. 5–6).
24 Ibid.
25 Ibid.
26 Ibid.
27 See the 2017 report for actions by the Justice Department. To avoid double-counting, this report includes only those merger enforcement actions in which the Commission or the Antitrust Division took its first public action during fiscal year 2017. The Antitrust Division challenged 18 merger transactions, including 11 with filed complaints in US district court. In nine of these 11, the Division simultaneously filed a proposed settlement (Ibid).
28 Capital liquidity is cyclical and it affects industries, households, and workers.
29 Merger waves will occur following periods of abnormally high stock returns or market-to-book ratios, especially when variations in returns are large. Industries affected by waves will experience poor returns after the peak of the waves. Identifiable economic and regulatory shocks will not systematically precede waves, since they are not facilitators. Cash mergers should not increase in frequency during the waves (stock payments will be more attractive); see Harford (2004, p. 534).
30 See Reilly (1968, pp. 292–3).
31 Ibid.
32 Corporate raiders are bidders who do not acquire target companies but who use tender offers to make profits by greenmail (selling the stocks of targets to other bidders).
33 See Gaughan (2015, p. 66).
34 Op. cit., p. 69
35 See Blackwell (1972, p. 634).
36 For complete details see the work of Bernstein, Schultz, Pisano, and Young (2016).
37 See Gaughan (2015, p. 118).
38 William Baxter, who became head of the Antitrust Division of the Justice Department in the 1980s, has been credited for the elevation of economics into antitrust law enforcement measures; see Gaughan (2015), ibid.
39 The index has been around since the 1940s. It was originally used to show the extent to which the trade of the large trading nations was directed by preference toward the smaller trading countries. In Chapter VI, Hirschman (1945) provided index numbers for the degree of concentration of foreign trade on one or a few big markets or sources of supply. Rhoades (1993, p. 188), notes that Herfindahl's doctoral dissertation, "Concentration in the US Steel Industry," similarly alluded to an index of concentration.
40 Though firms may be encouraged to achieve internal efficiencies within the competitive structure, mergers can be beneficial to an economy when they generate significant efficiencies to compete, reduce prices, improve quality, enhance service, or create new products.
41 See Gaughan (2015, p. 136); see also Asquith (1983), and Jensen and Ruback (1983).
42 By rewriting Equation 7.3 as $L = (P-MC)/P$, the markup can be estimated as $1/(1-L)$.
43 A legal threshold for tying requires a robust market for the products involved so that they can establish distinctive characteristics in the marketplace.
44 See Economides (2001) for discounted pricing arrangements.

45 *United States v. Microsoft Corp.*, 84 F. Supp. 2d 9, 22–23 (1999).
46 See Economides (2001) and Weinstein (2002).
47 15 U.S.C. § 2 (1994).
48 15 U.S.C. § 1 (1994).
49 *United States v. Grinnell Corp.*, 384 U.S. 563, 570–71 (1996); see Weinstein (2002, p. 274).
50 *United States v. E.I. DuPont de Nemours & Co.*, 351 U.S. 377, 395 (1956).
51 Ibid.
52 *Eastman Kodak Co. v. Image Technical Servs., Inc.*, 504 U.S. 451, 461–62 (1992); *Jefferson Parish Hosp. Dist. No. 2 v. Hyde*, 466 U.S. 2, 12–18 (1984).
53 In 1911, the Supreme Court used a Rule of Reason criterion to show that antitrust law must be applied to cases of unreasonable restraint of trade or anti-competitive behavior. The applicability of the Rule of Reason is more often juxtaposed against the per se rule, but largely inapplicable to cases of price fixing.
54 466 U.S. 2, 19 (1984).
55 See Weinstein (2002, p. 276); see also Ahlborn et al. (2004).
56 See Weinstein (2002, p. 284). Evidence was not presented to show that tying is a logical extension of Section 2 of the Sherman Act: "Every person who shall monopolize, or attempt to monopolize, or combine or conspire with any other person or persons, to monopolize any part of the trade or commerce among the several States, or with foreign nations, shall be deemed guilty of a felony, and, on conviction thereof, shall be punished by fine not exceeding $10,000,000 if a corporation, or, if any other person, $350,000, or by imprisonment not exceeding three years, or by both said punishments, in the discretion of the court." What was the market? Can a browser market be monopolized under the statute? The Circuit judge also found that agreement by Microsoft and Netscape to split the browser market was speculative, but that proof of network effect could have demonstrated monopoly power.
57 See Weinstein (2002) for additional violations, exculpations, and commentary on the case.
58 The statute provides some exceptions for radio broadcast, publishers, and agencies.
59 See Leslie in *The Economics of Antitrust Injury and Firm-Specific Damages*, pp. 48–49; see the concept of consumer surplus in Chapter 1; see also mitchellhamline.com, and Wheeler (1973).
60 Price-fixing is injurious to society because of resource misallocation. Consumers are likely to consume alternative or replacement goods when they are priced out of markets, causing a diversion of resources to alternative products at higher costs.
61 Ibid.
62 See Leslie, op. cit.; see also *Andrx Pharm., Inc. v. Biovail Corp. Int'l* (D.C. Cir. 2001) and *Montreal Trading Ltd. v. Amax Inc.* (10th Cir. 1981).
63 See Leslie, op. cit., p. 77. Also research shows that antitrust damages are often too low to completely disgorge ill-gotten gains.
64 Elasticity of demand measures the responsiveness of consumers to price change and this measurement gives an indication of the slope of the demand curve (see Chapters 1 and 5). It also indicates the substitutability of products. The elasticity coefficient is usually calculated by the ratio of percentage change of quantity demanded to the percentage change in price. Demand is said to be price elastic if the elasticity coefficient is greater than 1, and inelastic when the elasticity of demand is less than 1. An elastic demand suggests that consumers are highly responsive to

price changes, and this is usually the case when substitutes are available or when a large percentage of income is required to be spent on a good or service. The elasticity of supply is irrelevant to consumers but not society because defendants are not responsible for paying damages for lost producer surplus (the shaded lower triangle of Figure 7.5 Panel (b)). However, courts have found problems with the use of elasticity (see Leslie, op. cit., 55).

FURTHER READING

Adelman, M. A. (1961). The Antimerger Act, 1950–1960. *American Economic Review*, 51(2), 236–244.

Ahlborn, C., Evans, D. S., & Padilla, A. J. (2004). The antitrust economics of tying: A farewell to per se illegality. *Antitrust Bulletin*, 49(1–2), 287–341.

Asquith, P. (1983, April). Merger bids, uncertainty and stockholder returns. *Journal of Financial Economics*, 11(1–4), 51–83.

Bainbridge, S. E. (2012). *Mergers and acquisitions* (3rd ed.). New York: Foundation Press.

Barnes, I. R. (1962). The law of trade practices-II false advertising. *Ohio State Law Journal*, 23(4), 597–664.

Baye, M. R., & Prince, J. T. (2017). *Managerial economics and business strategy*. New York: McGraw-Hill.

Bernstein, M. B., Schultz, M. M., Pisano, F. M., & Young, D. S. (2016). US competition law-merger enforcement: 2016 year in review. Arnold & Porter. Retrieved from https://arnoldandporter.com.

Blackwell, R. B. (1972). Section 7 of the Clayton Act: Its application to the conglomerate merger. *William & Mary Law Review*, 13(3), 623–637.

Carney, W. J. (2009). *Essentials: Mergers and acquisitions*. Frederick, MD: Aspen Publishers.

Cavanagh, E. D. (1987). Detrebling antitrust damages: An idea whose time has come? *Tulane Law Review*, 61(4), 777–848.

Coase, R. H. (1988). *The firm, the market, and the law*. Chicago, IL: University of Chicago Press.

Coffee, J. C., Seligman, J., & Sale, H. A. (2007). *Securities regulation* (10th ed.). New York: Foundation Press.

Economides, N. (2001). The Microsoft antitrust case. *Journal of Industry, Competition and Trade: From Theory to Policy*, 1(1), 71–79.

Forbath, W. E. (1991). *Law and the shaping of the American labor movement*. Cambridge, MA: Harvard University Press.

Gaughan, P. A. (2015). *Mergers, acquisitions, and corporate restructurings*. Hoboken, NJ: Wiley.

Greenspan, A., & Wooldridge, A. D. (2018). *Capitalism in America: A history*. New York: Penguin Press.

Handler, M. (1939). The control of false advertising under the Wheeler-Lea Act. *Law and Contemporary Problems*, 6(1), 91–110.

Handler, M., & Robinson, S. D. (1961). A decade of administration of the Cellar-Kefauver Antimerger Act. *Columbia Law Review*, 61(4), 629–679.

Harford, J. (2004). What drives merger waves? *Journal of Financial Economics*, 77, 529–560.

Hirschman, A. O. (1945). *National power and the structure of foreign trade.* Berkeley, CA: University of California Press.

Hirschman, A. O. (1964). The paternity of an index. *American Economic Review, 54*(6), 761–762.

Jensen, M., & Ruback, R. (1983, April). The market for corporate control: The scientific evidence. *Journal of Financial Economics, 11*(1–4), 5–50.

Landenburg, T. (2007). The Sherman Anti-Trust Act and Standard Oil. *Digital History.* Retrieved from http://digitalhistory.uh.edu.

Leslie, C. R. (2008). Antitrust damages and deadweight loss. In K. S. Marshal (Ed.), *The economics of antitrust injury and firm-specific damages.* Tucson, AZ: Lawyers and Judges Publishing Co.

McConnell, C. R., Brue, S. L., & Flynn, S. M. (2012). *Economics.* New York: McGraw-Hill.

Marshall, K. S. (Ed.) (2008). *The economics of antitrust injury and firm specific damages.* Tuscon, AZ: Lawyers and Judges Publishing Company.

Nevins, A., & Commager, H. E. (1992). *A pocket history of the United States.* New York: Pocket Books.

Oesterle, D. A. (2006). *Mergers and acquisitions in a nutshell.* St. Paul, MN: Thomson-West.

Ohlhausen, M. K., & Delrahim, M. (2017). *Hart-Scot-Rodino annual report: Fiscal year 2017.* Washington, DC: Federal Trade Commission and Justice Department.

Ramirez, E., & Baer, W. J. (2014). *Hart-Scot-Rodino annual report: Fiscal year 2014.* Washington, DC: Federal Trade Commission and Justice Department.

Reilly, J. R. (1968). The conglomerate merger: A need for clarity. *Ohio State Law, 29*, 290–313.

Rhoades, S. A. (1983). The antitrust treble damages remedy. *William Mitchell Law Review, 9*(2), Article 9. Available at: http://open.mitchellhamline.edu/wmlr/vol9/iss2/9.

Rhoades, S. A. (1993, March). The Herfindahl-Hirschman Index. *Federal Reserve Bulletin,* 188–189.

Rhoades, S. A. (2011). The Williams Act: A truly "modern" assessment. *Harvard Law.* Retrieved from https://corpgov.law.harvard.edu.

Turner, D. F. (1965). Conglomerate mergers and Section 7 of the Clayton Act. *Harvard Law Review, 78*(7), 1313–1395.

Warburton, C. E. S. (1998). *Slaves, serfs, and workers labor under the law.* Pittsburgh: PA Dorrance.

Weinstein, S. N. (2002). United States v. Microsoft Corp. *Berkeley Technology Law Journal, 17*(1), 273–294.

Wheeler, M. E. (1973). Antitrust treble-damage actions: Do they work. *California Law Review, 61*(6), 1319–1352.

Wheelock, D. C. (2011). Banking industry consolidation and market structure: Impact of the financial crisis and recession. *Federal Reserve Bank of St. Louis Review,* 419–438.

Whitney, S. N. (1967). Mergers, conglomerates, and oligopolies: A widening of antitrust target. *Rutgers Law Review, 21*, 187.

8

CHAPTER 8
INTERNATIONAL ECONOMICS IN INTERNATIONAL COURTS OF LAW

LEARNING OBJECTIVES

LO 1 To understand the relevance of international economic theories to international economic law and judicial decisions.
LO 2 To be familiar with the sources of international economic law.
LO 3 To envision the problems and benefits of foreign investment.
LO 4 To be aware of international dispute resolution processes.
LO 5 To be familiar with international conventions and judicial precedents.

This chapter presents the study of international economic issues and dispute resolutions in international courts. In this chapter, the concept of "international courts" is specifically related to judicial authority that emanates from multilateral arrangements. As such, the reference to "international courts" must neither be perceived as courts of national jurisdiction nor a comparative study of the interpretation of national laws by courts of law. Invariably, the laws that are proactively applied to international economic disputes are not necessarily estranged from the multiplicity of state laws and economic practices that have shaped the perceptions and determinations of acceptable international (economic) behaviors. That is, a coalescence of state laws and practices can be used to authoritatively resolve economic disputes in a single forum (a global tribunal) rather than multiple forums (national courts) with different and distinguishing (variegated) interpretations of law that lend themselves to comparative analysis of internal law and adjudication.

8.1 THE SOURCES OF INTERNATIONAL LAW

International law is a body of laws and practices that is used to regulate the international political, economic, and social interaction of states, individuals, and businesses across international boundaries in order to ensure the orderly conduct of international relations for global peace and stability. The word "source" may have very imprecise meanings. It can be used to: (i) indicate the basis of international law, (ii) show the social origin of international law, (iii) identify the formal law-making agency, and (iv) indicate the intellectual instrument by which law is made.[1] The relevance of international law is based on mutual agreement and general willingness or preference to have order and stability in the conduct of international relations. Therefore, adherence to international law is antithetical to anarchical situations in which states presume that "sovereignty" is tantamount to the pursuit of national self-interest that injures others and threatens global peace and stability.

By "sources" of international law, I allude to the types of law that are specified in the Statute of the International Court of Justice (SICJ) for the resolution of international disputes:

1. The Court, whose function is to decide in accordance with international law such disputes as are submitted to it, shall apply:
   a. international conventions, whether general or particular, establishing rules expressly recognized by the contesting states;
   b. international custom, as evidence of a general practice accepted as law;
   c. the general principles of law recognized by civilized nations;
   d. subject to the provisions of Article 59, judicial decisions and the teachings of the most highly qualified publicists of the various nations, as subsidiary means for the determination of rules of law.
2. This provision shall not prejudice the power of the Court to decide a case *ex aequo et bono*, if the parties agree thereto. (SICJ, Article 38).

Five sources are identifiable: (i) customs, (ii) general principles of law recognized by "civilized nations," (iii) judicial decisions (*stare decisis* or precedents), (iv) what is fair, right, and reasonable (*ex aequo et bono*), and (v) international conventions (treaties). There has been controversy over which genre of law should be granted primacy. This book is not very well suited for that debate. However, it is reasonable to state that various forms of law have evolved from customary practices that are timeless and reflective of judicial necessity.

Customary law reflects a compelling desire to engage in widespread practices with unquestionable normative attributes. As a result, there is a compulsive urge to engage in the practices for human development and preservation. Customary law has been associated with four basic elements: (i) a generalized repetition of similar acts by competent state authorities, (ii) juridical necessities of the customary acts to develop and maintain international relations. It is believed that identical situations of fact should lead to reciprocal and similar behavioral patterns, and (iii) general acquiescence in the practice by other states; meaning that the practices do not excite the ire of other nations because they are not considered to be offensive. Invariably, the elements have to be ascertained by competent judicial authorities.[2] A conduct is customarily lawful when there is a legal compulsion or obligation to engage in it during the conduct of international relations (*opinio juris sive necessitates*).

> International law is part of our [US] law, and must be ascertained and administered by the courts of justice of appropriate jurisdiction as often as questions of right depending upon it are duly presented for determination. For this purpose, where there is no treaty and no controlling executive or legislative act or judicial decision,

resort must be had to the customs and usages of civilized nations, and as evidence of these, to the works of jurists and commentators who by years of labor, research, and experience have made themselves peculiarly well acquainted with the subjects of which they treat ...

(Justice Gray, in Brierly, (The Lola, 175 U.S. 677 (1900)) p. 65)

Treaties, charters, conventions, or protocols form another category of law with somewhat precise procedures. Treaties generally consist of three parts: (i) a preamble or introductory text (chapeau) delineating the overall principles, objectives, and background of the treaties, (ii) the body, and (iii) the final clauses, including signatures. Signatures indicate formal agreement with the treaty. Ratification may be required to go beyond expressions of agreement. For example, treaties must be ratified by the Senate before they can have binding effect on the US.[3] Though treaties may be objectionably regarded as a source of law, the SICJ recognizes treaties (contracts) as a source of law with binding effect when they are ratified. Objection usually stems from the fact that treaties are based on rules that are already in existence; specifically, the rules of customary law by which the binding effect of treaties can be evaluated. In effect, treaties importantly validate customary rule or they can provide a stimulus to one.[4]

[T]he more States subscribe to a treaty, and the more its provisions reflect the juridical conscience of mankind, the more will it be a stimulus to the creation of law. Once treaty provisions have become law even repudiation of the treaty will not disengage the parties from liability thereunder.

(O'Connell, 1956, p. 25)

The Vienna Law of Treaties specifies the evaluative criteria of treaties, the obligations of Members, circumstances for derogations, and procedures for suspension, termination, reservations, and material breaches.[5]

Treaties are agreements that nations are obligated to fulfill until sudden and exceptional conditions inhibit their ability to do so.[6] Fundamental changes are unanticipated or inconceivable changes that alter the conditions for the treaty to be effective or operable.[7] Treaties are usually not based on arbitrary constructions or principles, but customary practices and some general principles of law with peremptory axioms.

Judges play a very important role in the development of international law. They not only interpret laws, they contribute to the formulation of general principles of law by reference to contingent circumstances and deductions from accepted hypothesis.[8] Therefore Article 38 of the SICJ recognizes municipal judicial decisions as a subsidiary means for the determination of rules of international law. However, the patchwork of municipal decisions must conform with well-settled rules that international tribunals (permanent or temporary) sitting in judgment between independent states, must not treat the judgments of the courts in one state as binding on other states, except when they have been determined to be the law common to all countries (in harmony with international law).[9]

> The law of nations is the great source from which we derive those rules, respecting belligerent and neutral rights, which are recognized by all the civilized and commercial states throughout Europe and America. This law is in part unwritten, and in part conventional. To ascertain that which is unwritten, we resort to the great principles of reason and justice; but as these principles will be differently understood by different nations under different circumstances, we consider them as being, in some degree, fixed and rendered stable by a series of judicial decisions …
> (Chief Justice Marshall; see *Thirty Hogsheads of Sugar v. Boyle* (US, 1815))

The concept of general principles of law is one of the legal plugs that were adopted to deal with the inadequacy of sources of law based on the perceived preferences of different nations; the others being equity and publicists. Customary international law might be inadequate when some nations don't actively participate in a practice (see *Columbia v. Peru* (ICJ, 1950)). There could be similar limitations when judicial precedents and statutes could not be convincingly applied to some states. Therefore, the founding fathers of the Permanent Court of International Justice (PCIJ) (a committee of jurists in the 1920s), had to wrestle with perceived and real limitations of the sources of law. The debate started with mapping out the legal conscience of civilized nations and international jurisprudence (court decisions) (a proposal by the Chairman Baron Descamps of Belgium). But judicial decisions had already been identified and Mr. Root from the US expressed concern about the language. Mr. Root believed that compulsory decision of the court would be accepted if it was deemed to be the conscience of civilized peoples. Mr. Loder (Netherlands) felt that the court's duty included the development of law, the "ripening" of customs, and the crystallization of customs and rules into positive rules. Lord Phillimore (Great Britain) had difficulties believing that international law could be limited to treaties and customary law. M. De Lapradelle (France) believed that a judge should not act as a legislator and that the judgment should be contingent on law, justice, and equity. Mr. Hagerup (Norway) argued that instead of the court declaring itself incompetent (due to lack of rules of law), it must fill up the gaps in law. Mr. Root expressed further concerns about applying rules under compulsory jurisdiction that would be understood differently in different countries. He subsequently proposed "the general principles of law recognized by civilized nations."[10]

Subsequently, scholarly interpretations have considered natural law and obvious maxims of jurisprudence that have a general and fundamental character;[11] for example, a man cannot be a judge in his/her own cause, justice delayed is justice denied, legal obligation must be exercised in good faith, and breach of a contractual obligation requires reparation. Lord Phillimore makes the case for maxims that can be separated from those in cognate disciplines like religion but recognized and accepted by all nations. The phrase, "civilized nations," was generally intended to preempt subjectivity and arbitrariness on the part of a judge.[12] In the *Chorzów Factory Case* it was determined that it is a principle of international law that the breach of an engagement involves an obligation to make reparation.

Laws can be overzealous or perverse. In such situations triers of fact (judges) can be expected to apply fairness—what O'Connell (1965) considers to be natural law—to fill in the gaps. Though the concept has prompted debates between naturalists (those who believe in natural law when written law is inadequate) and positivists (those who believe in written law and are hesitant to give judges a wide latitude of discretionary power), it can be applied when a tribunal or court is authorized to apply it without deference to the rules of law (in a manner that is not arbitrary).[13]

The teachings of the most highly qualified publicists of various nations are a subsidiary means for the determination of the rules of international law. Writers are also considered to be an important source of law when they pointedly allude to treaties and usage that receive assent. As such, publicists cannot make laws, but can create avenues for the making of laws. For example, see the writings of the Dutch jurist, Hugo Grotius (1583–1645). His philosophy of international law combined natural law and state practice. He extensively wrote about war and peace, and is generally regarded as the father of modern international law. Additionally, see the writings and works of Pufendorf (1632–1694), Wolff (1679–1754), Vattel (1714–1767), and Judge Hersch Lauterpacht (1897–1960); see also *Flores v. Southern Peru Corporation 343 F. 3d 140 (2d. Cir. 2003)*.

What compelled the free nations of the world to regulate trade among themselves in the 1940s? Why was it so urgent for the free nations of the world to promote trade liberalization on a very large (multilateral) scale in the 1940s? Trade agreements between and among nations were nothing new in the 1940s. The agreements espoused some amount of reciprocity and fairness. For example, during the latter part of the nineteenth century, extensive economic development, spurred by industrialization and technological change, complemented trade liberalization that was supported by a network of bilateral trade treaties.

The 2007 World Trade Report (WTR) by the World Trade Organization (WTO) explains that the network started with the Anglo-French (Cobden-Chevalier) treaty of 1860, which triggered a series of other treaties among European countries (WTO, 2007, p. 35). Bilateral reciprocal tariff reductions, together with the application of the unconditional most favored nation (MFN) treaties, led to historically low tariff levels in agricultural and other products. This period of liberalized trade across Europe lasted for nearly two decades up to 1879 before its slow degeneration and ultimate collapse after World War I.

However, the spirit of liberalization was not eviscerated. For example, prior to the 1940s, nations engaged in reciprocal trade agreements. A lot of goods from Canada, Latin America, and other countries entered the US duty-free, and many countries had MFN agreements with the US.[14] However, when there is a breach of fairness, which causes undue hardship on other nations, they will retaliate and trade wars will drive the global economy into a tailspin; so it was in the 1940s.

MFN agreements make it somewhat difficult for countries to directly retaliate against other countries. However, countries can use alternative trade policies like quotas, product quality, and other forms of non-tariff barriers (NTBs) to indirectly retaliate against the imposition of an odious tariff. For example, France used import quotas to tacitly retaliate against the Smoot-Hawley tariff. Quite apart from imposing a tariff of its own, as a result of the Smoot-Hawley tariff, Spain withdrew MFN treatment from the US (Irwin, 2011, pp. 167–8).[15]

The combination of unregulated monetary policy and the contractionary effects of restrictive trade policies during the interregnum created conditions for a structured environment to regulate trade and international monetary policy. The deficiencies in the global system of the 1930s and 1940s led to the institutionalization of the International Monetary Fund (IMF) and General Agreements on Tariffs and Trade (GATT, now the WTO). Today, the IMF responds to sudden and temporary disruptions (shocks) that are capable of destabilizing the global economy.

The Great Depression and the World War II created the conditions for GATT. The causes of the Great Depression were multifarious, but one can safely postulate that a combination of contractionary monetary policy and international trade caused and prolonged the Great Depression. Simply put, trade did not generate enough income for nations (falling exports) and monetary policy was not properly implemented to prevent unemployment, bankruptcies, and panics. Obviously, one would be remiss to disregard the shenanigans that infected the financial markets, which also paved the way for financial regulation and reforms.

A concise explanation of the monetary quagmire can be found in the work of Crabbe (1989), Irwin (2011), and Bernanke (2013). Fixed exchange rates among countries tend to deprive them of the ability to make independent monetary policy and favorable and unfavorable policies that are being made in one or more countries are easily transmitted to others; especially through trade and interest rate mechanisms. For example, when Britain came off the Gold Standard in 1931, the US started to deplete its stock of gold rapidly, and the Fed had to increase the interest rate to staunch the bleeding. The shared contractionary effects of trade cannot be easily reversed when nations engage in competitive devaluation.

The predicament of the US after Smoot-Hawley is particularly noteworthy and paradoxical. Although the imports of the US increased relative to its exports, sufficient income was not generated for other nations to engage in robust trade. "While the volume of imports fell by 12 percent between 1930 and 1931, the volume of exports fell 19 percent." (Irwin, 2011, p. 125). The dramatic fall in US export is not inconsequential because it was symptomatic of a broader problem in the global economy. Irwin identifies four notable reasons for the decline: (i) obstacles confronted by foreign nations to derive income from the US, (ii) declining foreign incomes due to the Great Depression abroad, (iii) higher tariffs and other trade restrictions that were explicitly directed at the US [as retaliatory measures], and (iv) the appreciation of the dollar relative to flexible rates after other countries left the gold standard (Irwin, 2011, p. 126).

After Smoot-Hawley, the US lost income from its major trading partner, Canada. While US imports from Britain fell 16 percent, Canada's imports from the US fell 27 percent in 1930 from the previous year. Cuba lost about one-third to one-half of its earnings from the US after 1930. Recall that US export to Spain dropped by 94 percent in three years pursuant to Smoot-Hawley. The share of US import to Italy fell from 18 percent in 1929 to 11 percent in 1935.[16]

The combination of a US drought in 1930, ill-advised monetary policy, and the Smoot-Hawley tariff sealed the fate of the southern farmers. Agricultural prices plummeted, farmers lost income, mortgages went unpaid, rural banks failed, and unemployment soared in the US. It is impracticable to see how the US could have absorbed foreign imports to any substantial degree at a time when its global partners could not have been mollified after the Smoot-Hawley debacle.

The prevailing attitude to international trade and the global fiasco could not have been normalized by any stretch of the imagination. The global economy was paralyzed and international trade restrictions had somehow contributed to the paralysis. It became unavoidable to have a structure for international trade with well-established legal principles; that structure became GATT, initially known as the International Trade Organization (ITO).

However, as the WTO Director, Pascal Lamy, noted in 2007:

> As far as the trade rules are concerned, the GATT/WTO has made a valuable contribution over the years to greater stability, certainty and fairness in trade. But the rules are not perfect and there is always room for improvement. This is one reason why governments continue to negotiate and to seek out further mutually advantageous accommodation. Like trade liberalization, crafting better rules remains a work in progress.
> (WTR, 2007, p. iv)

8.2 TRADE THEORIES AS FOUNDATIONS OF INTERNATIONAL TRADE LAW

International economic laws are intricately related to the liberal exchange of goods and assets across international boundaries. That is, goods and financial assets are expected to be exchanged across international boundaries without undue or unfair restrictions that will imperil the welfare of business and consumers. Consequently, international economic laws must be evaluated against welfare effects and economic theories that articulate collective improvements on the welfare of nations. The bases and effects of international trade are probably the most important foundational concepts to understand the spirit and intent of international economic laws.

The initial impulses suggested that international trade must be done to the peril of other nations. Essentially, the early proponents of international exchange believed that trade was a zero-sum game. Pointedly, nations can only gain at the expense of others, meaning that nations must impose restrictions on international exchange that will only be beneficial to their self-interests. The problem is that no nation will benefit if each and every nation behaves as such.

The mercantilists were the first to experiment with the idea of restrictive exchange in order to amass national wealth for proprietary access to international markets and international dominance. The primitive trade theory, which was well received and propagated for many reasons, became fashionable in an era of aggression to acquire bullion (commodity money) and power.[17] The obvious intent of mercantilism, which was to acquire bullion and surpluses, was eloquently expressed by Mun in England, and Colbert in France:

> The ordinary means therefore to encrease [sic] our wealth and treasure is by Forraign [sic] Trade, wherein wee [sic] must ever observe this rule; to sell more to strangers yearly than wee [sic] consume of theirs in value.
>
> (Mun, 1630, p. 3)[18]

The German equivalent of mercantilism was known as "Cameralism." It was essentially designed to restore fiscal soundness to Germany after the Thirty Years War (1618–1648).

Nations subsequently realized that the mercantilist theory was self-destructive, inflationary, and unsustainable. In fact, as far back as the seventeenth and eighteenth centuries, some mercantilists like John Locke (1632–1704) and Charles Davenant (1656–1714), were already questioning the wisdom of collecting and hoarding money. It was apparent to the critics that economic activity can be stifled when money is withdrawn from circulation and hoarded (saving or leakage). Additionally, it was also apparent that the circulation of a growing money supply would eventually generate inflationary pressures (Kurz, 2017, p. 13).

When other nations are sufficiently impoverished as a result of beggar-thy-neighbor policies, they cannot possibly have enough national income to continuously absorb goods from nations that are unwilling to reciprocate. This asymmetric relationship surely portends that the volume of trade will decline and that a substantial amount of people can easily become poorer (a decline in the national welfare of other nations).

As far as the price effect is concerned, David Hume (1711–1776) was able to use the price specie flow identity to convincingly articulate the long-run futility of mercantilism:

$$m + v = p + t; \tag{8.1}$$

where m is for the stock of money supply, v is for velocity of money (the speed at which money circulates in an economy), p is for the general price level, and t is for the number of transactions. Today, the transaction velocity of money (in the logarithmic form) has been replaced by its macroeconomic variant, which substitutes national output (y) for t. The relationship between m and p can be easily conceptualized when v and t/y are invariant. That is, the two variables (m and p) can be expected to move in the same direction. As Hume (1752) noted:

> Suppose four-fifths of all the money in GREAT BRITAIN to be annihilated in one night, and the nation reduced to the same condition, with regard to specie, as in the reigns of the HARRYS and EDWARDS, what would be the consequence? Must not the price of all

labour and commodities sink in proportion, and everything be sold as cheap as they were in those ages? What nation could then dispute with us in any foreign market, or pretend to navigate or to sell manufactures at the same price, which to us would afford sufficient profit? In how little time, therefore, must this bring back the money which we had lost, and raise us to the level of all the neighbouring nations? Where, after we have arrived, we immediately lose the advantage of the cheapness of labour and commodities; and the farther flowing in of money is stopped by our fulness and repletion.

(www.la.utaxas.edu)

Implicitly, if prices are flexible (not distorted or regulated), gold inflows cannot be sustained over a longer period of time when the excess supply of bullion coincides with inadequate foreign demand and loss of competitiveness. Accordingly, beggar-thy-neighbor policies can only be transient. Implicitly, Equation 8.1 suggests a constant state of flexible prices and full employment in the short-run. The theory is imprecise when prices are sticky at less than full employment.

While economists of the sixteenth and seventeenth centuries did not spend a lot of time talking about innovation and productivity in the age of buccaneering mercantilism, they gradually discovered that innovation and productivity are the best antidotes to some of the undesirable effects of international trade and competition. By advancing the theory of *laissez-faire*, which was later popularized by Adam Smith (1723–1790), the French Physiocrats (philosophers) made a compelling case for the acquisition of wealth and welfare enhancement through freer trade as an alternative to restrictive trade. Adam Smith subsequently popularized and validated the thoughts of the French Physiocrats by discrediting mercantilism and arguing, in his *Wealth of Nations* (1776), that nations can actually become wealthier and prosperous by engaging in international trade and expanding it rather than restricting it.

The benefits from freer trade, as envisioned by Smith, are far-reaching. Freedom and ethical behavior in the marketplace are capable of improving human welfare without the unnecessary intrusions of public policy.[19] Human institutions are configured to ensure that self-interest works in the direction of the common good. By pursuing rational self-interest, which is not devoid of ethical behavior, the interests of societies can be well served because exchange or trade is the logical outgrowth of interdependent wants. As Smith noted:

> It is not from the benevolence of the butcher, the brewer, or the baker, that we expect our dinner, but from their regard to their own interest. We address ourselves, not to their humanity but to their self-love, and never talk to them of our own necessities but of their advantages.
>
> (Fusfeld, 2002, p. 29)

Analogously,

> actions of a beneficent tendency, which proceed from proper motives, seem alone to require reward; because such alone are the approved objects of gratitude, or excite the sympathetic gratitude of the spectator....

Actions of a hurtful tendency, which proceed from improper motives, seem alone to deserve punishment; because such alone are the approved objects of resentment, or excite the sympathetic resentment of the spectator.

(Smith, 1759 [2000], p. 112)

When the happiness or misery of others depends in any respect upon our conduct, we dare not as self-love might suggest to us, prefer the interest of one to that of many ... One individual must never prefer himself so much even to any other individual as to hurt or injure that other in order to benefit himself, though the benefit to the one should be much greater than the hurt or injury to the other.

(Smith, 1759 [2000], pp. 194–5)

Smith based his theory of trade on the cost of inputs that are necessary to produce outputs and the theory became known as absolute advantage. According to Smith, the abundant and cheap use of inputs (factors of production) must ultimately determine the goods that nations should utilize for production and exchange. So why, for example, should the US trade with Mexico, Canada, Peru, Vietnam, Japan, and Australia? The foregoing discussion provides a rudimentary insight. It is in the interest of all nations to trade, given their natural advantages. This precondition will be extended later. Second, geographic or regional proximity provides additional advantages. Third, there are static and dynamic gains that can be realized from international trade. No nation will engage in international trade if trade is not beneficial. Figure 8.1 reveals some of the basic propositions for international trade.

Alluding to Figure 8.1, it can be seen that the US has a natural advantage in the production of manufacturing goods relative to Mexico. Since the US is contiguous to Mexico and more efficient in the production of manufacturing goods, the US should specialize in the production of manufacturing goods because it enjoys productive efficiency or natural advantage. The per unit manufacturing production cost in Mexico

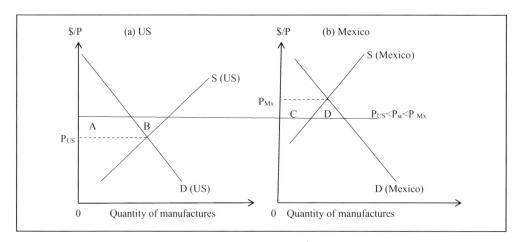

Figure 8.1 Cost of producing and consuming manufacturing goods

(P_{Mx}) is much higher than that of the US (P_{US}). Therefore, the US can devote more time and resources to the production of manufacturing goods while Mexico can produce something else for which it has a natural advantage. Smith propounded this theory in the eighteenth century. It is probably obvious by now that natural advantage is an insufficient international trade theory, because the US may well be capable of producing several goods more than Mexico. Therefore, the theory of comparative cost should be more appealing.

Figure 8.1 is also revealing of some of the rancorous discussions that have polarized and stymied international trade negotiations. By producing and supplying more manufacturing goods to Mexico at a higher price (P_w) relative to the US "autarkic price" (P_{US}), US consumers are going to lose consumer surplus (area A) but consumers in Mexico are going to gain areas C and D. It should be noted that the benefit to US producers is captured by areas A and B.[20] Lobbyists and opponents of international trade are hardly interested in the net benefits of international trade. Rather, acrimonious opposition of international trade is sometimes centered on narrow interests that impinge on immediate job losses and prospects of losing an election. But the relevance of Smith must not be limited to factor endowment and cost of production. The legal ramifications of trade are based on the benefits that freer trade can confer on international producers and consumers.

International trade brings about socioeconomic benefits that have been historically and pervasively recorded. The gains from freer trade can be classified under two broad headings: (i) static, and (ii) dynamic. Static gains from trade arise from specialization and an increase in the welfare (utility) of a nation relative to autarkic levels of consumption. These gains are clearly presented in Figure 8.2, which will be discussed later as part of a comparative advantage theory. Specialization brings about new gains from trade as individuals, firms, and national economies exploit the external benefits that are associated with economies of scale; as a result of institutional changes, transportation or improvement on human capital. Consider Smith's pin factory with division of labor and production in a large production facility:

> [O]ne man draws out the wire, another straights it, a third cuts it a fourth points it, a fifth grinds it at the top for receiving the head; to make the head requires two or three distinct operations … but if they had all wrought separately and independently, and without any of them have been educated to this particular business, they certainly could not each of them have made twenty, perhaps not one pin a day …
> (Smith, 1776 [1994], p. 4)

Smith also noted that nations are more likely to discover easier and readier methods of production as they intensify or increase their levels of specialization. But the benefits of trade cannot be realized without a maximum or reasonable amount of freedom.

One of the benefits of specialization and freer trade is that consumers benefit from competitive prices as businesses are incentivized or forced to innovate. Schumpeter's creative destruction provides instructive insight into the concept of the drive to innovate and outcompete others. Trade and innovation create newer products that replace outdated ones and only firms that are capable of providing useful or marketable inventions will withstand the ferocity of competition in the free and open marketplace.

As a result, even though Smith based his theory of trade on absolute (natural) advantage, he quickly reached the conclusion that the basis of trade is intuitive and mutually beneficial:

> The natural advantages which one country has over another in producing particular commodities are sometimes so great that it is acknowledged by all the world to be in vain to struggle with them ....
>
> As long as the one country has those advantages, and the other wants them, it will always be more advantageous for the latter rather to buy of the former than to make. It is an acquired advantage only, which one artificer has over his neighbor, who exercises another trade; and yet they both find it more advantageous to buy of one another than to make what does not belong to their particular trades.
>
> (Smith, 1776 [1994], p. 487)

> What is prudence in the conduct of every private family can scarce be folly in that of a great kingdom. If a foreign country can supply us with a commodity cheaper than we ourselves can make it, better buy it of them with some part of the produce of our own industry employed in a way in which we have some advantage. The general industry of the country, being always in proportion to the capital which employs it, will not thereby be diminished, no more than that of the above-mentioned artificers; but only left to find out the way in which it can be employed with the greatest advantage.
>
> (Smith, 1776 [1994], p. 486)

Smith was not oblivious of the limits of freer trade. International trade must be conducted without undue restrictions; implying that freer trade does not preclude reasonable considerations of defense:

> But if foreigners, either by prohibitions or high duties, are hindered from coming to sell, they cannot always afford to come to buy; because coming without a cargo, they must lose the freight from their own country to Great Britain. By diminishing the number of sellers, therefore, we necessarily diminish that of buyers, and are thus likely not only to buy foreign goods dearer, but to sell our own cheaper, than if there was a more perfect freedom of trade. As defence, however, is of much more importance than opulence, the act of navigation is, perhaps, the wisest of all the commercial regulations of England.
>
> (Smith, 1776 [1994], p. 494)

However, nations that do not play by the rules of the game should be punished. Today, dispute settlement mechanisms and countervailing duties are included in trade negotiations and treaties to deal with trade inequities. Of course, trade inequities have also been historical infractions:

> The case in which it may sometimes be a matter of deliberation how far it is proper to continue the free importation of certain foreign goods is, when some foreign nation restrains by high duties or prohibitions the importation of some of our manufactures into their country. Revenge in this case naturally dictates retaliation, and that we should impose the like duties and prohibitions upon the importation of some or all of their manufactures into ours. Nations, accordingly, seldom fail to retaliate in this manner. The French have been particularly forward to favour their own manufactures by restraining the importation of such foreign goods as could come into competition with them. In this consisted a great part of the policy of Mr. Colbert, who, notwithstanding his great abilities, seems in this case to have been imposed upon by the sophistry of merchants and manufacturers, who are always demanding a monopoly against their countrymen. It is at present the opinion of the most intelligent men in France that his operations of this kind have not been beneficial to his country.
>
> (Smith, 1776 [1994], p. 497)[21]

More so, the benefits from trade among nations need not be symmetric:

> First, though it were certain that in the case of a free trade between France and England, for example, the balance would be in favour of France, it would by no means follow that such a trade would be disadvantageous to England, or that the general balance of its whole trade would thereby be turned more against it. If the wines of France are better and cheaper than those of Portugal, or its linens than those of Germany, it would be more advantageous for Great Britain to purchase both the wine and the foreign linen which it had occasion for of France than of Portugal and Germany. Though the value of the annual importations from France would thereby be greatly augmented, the value of the whole annual importations would be diminished, in proportion as the French goods of the same quality were cheaper than those of the other two countries. This would be the case, even upon the supposition that the whole French goods imported were to be consumed in Great Britain.
>
> (Smith, 1776 [1994], p. 505)

Above all, Smith aptly noted that geographic proximity (gravity) can spur gains from trade even in times of adversity (war) and peace:

> The wealth of a neighbouring nation, however, though dangerous in war and politics, is certainly advantageous in trade. In a state of hostility it may enable our enemies to maintain fleets and armies superior to our own; but in a state of peace and commerce it must likewise enable them to exchange with us to a greater value, and to afford a better market, either for the immediate produce of our own industry, or for whatever is purchased with that produce. As a rich man is likely to be a better customer to the industrious people in his neighbourhood than a poor, so is likewise a rich nation. A rich man, indeed, who is himself a manufacturer, is a very dangerous neighbour to all those who deal in the same way. All the rest of the neighbourhood, however, by far the greatest number, profit by the good market which his expence affords them. They even

profit by his underselling the poorer workmen who deal in the same way with him. The manufacturers of a rich nation, in the same manner, may no doubt be very dangerous rivals to those of their neighbours. This very competition, however, is advantageous to the great body of the people, who profit greatly besides by the good market which the great expence of such a nation affords them in every other way.

(Smith, 1776 [1994], p. 527)

It is in consequence of these maxims that the commerce between France and England has in both countries been subjected to so many discouragements and restraints. If those two countries, however, were to consider their real interest, without either mercantile jealousy or national animosity, the commerce of France might be more advantageous to Great Britain than that of any other country, and for the same reason that of Great Britain to France. France is the nearest neighbour to Great Britain. In the trade between the southern coast of England and the northern and north-western coasts of France, the returns might be expected, in the same manner as in the inland trade, four, five, or six times in the year. The capital, therefore, employed in this trade could in each of the two countries keep in motion four, five, or six times the quantity of industry, and afford employment and subsistence to four, five, or six times the number of people, which an equal capital could do in the greater part of the other branches of foreign trade.

(Smith, 1776 [1994], pp. 528–9)

Pointedly, there is nothing wrong with preferential trade agreements (PTAs). Dynamic gains occur over a period of time as nations expand their participation in international trade. Nations are able to produce and/or acquire a variety of goods as a result of trade, innovation, and dynamic comparative advantage. Nations can therefore acquire income beyond their autarkic levels, benefit from technological transfers, and develop new skills, including entrepreneurial abilities from their neighbors. Therefore, while trade is an engine of economic growth, it also provides scope for development.[22]

The theory of comparative advantage by David Ricardo (1772–1823) provided an alternative and improved theory of international trade in terms of resource allocation and comparative cost (*Principles of Political Economy and Taxation*, 1817). Unlike Smith, he argued that even if a nation is comparatively less efficient in the production of multiple goods, there is still a basis for mutually beneficial trade if the nation specializes in the production of the good for which its comparative disadvantage is less. The earlier trade theories gave capital very scanty consideration and defined international trade mostly in terms of labor requirements. More so, they provided no explanation for differences in levels of productivity and consumer preferences.

Consider a representation of Ricardo's theory (see Figure 8.2). The illustration shows that the US has an advantage in the production of both manufactures and farm products. Both nations, the US and Mexico, can produce and consume at autarkic levels (A) on the demand diagonal (DD) line. However, the autarkic levels are suboptimal, because both nations have an opportunity to consume at levels that are superior (C) to the autarkic levels (A) if they can specialize in the production of the goods in which their relative advantages are greater. The relative price lines, which are the opportunity (relative) costs are given by relative prices; where the opportunity cost of producing manufactures is the cost of producing farm product relative to manufactures (P_F/P_M). Since the cost of producing farm product in lieu of manufactures is greater in the US, the US is better off producing manufactures. The opposite must be true for Mexico. Evidently, the illustration shows that by specialization and consumption both nations are better off than not trading at all. The welfare effect must be noteworthy even with trade that is based on comparative advantage.

In theory and practice, comparative cost does not mean that the US should give up farming altogether in order to produce manufacturing goods. It simply means that the US should devote more of its efficient resources to manufacturing goods rather than misallocating more of its productively scarce resources to agricultural products. Similarly, the theory does not suggest that Mexico should give up manufacturing and focus on agriculture; it simply suggests that the two nations can engage in mutually beneficial trade by devoting more time and resources to agriculture. Therefore, it should not be surprising that the US can export and import agricultural and manufacturing products (engage in intra-industry trade; see Figure 8.3).

According to the US Department of Agriculture, Mexico is a major participant in international agricultural trade and Mexico's agricultural imports (from all countries) in 2016 totaled about $26.0 billion. The United States is Mexico's largest agricultural trading partner, buying 79 percent of Mexican exports and supplying 70 percent of the country's imports in this category.

Agricultural trade between the US and Mexico has increased considerably since 1975 (see Figure 8.3); for example, exports and imports have ranged from about $1 billion in 1975 to about $26 billion in 2016.

A turning point in agricultural trade between Mexico and the United States came in the late 1980s, when Mexico emerged from a period of economic difficulties and adopted a series of trade reforms. In 1986, Mexico signed the GATT, the predecessor to the WTO. In the early 1990s, Mexico lowered a number of agricultural trade barriers, and in 1994, it joined Canada and the United States in implementing the North American Free Trade Agreement (NAFTA). Mexico also has free trade agreements with about 40 other countries (USDA, Economic Research Service (ERS), 2018).

Further, the agriculture department notes that "with a growing population, an expanding economy, and a more market-oriented agricultural sector, Mexico has become the United States' second-largest agricultural trading partner, trailing only Canada in combined exports and imports." (USDA (ERS), 2018).

Evidently, despite its manufacturing comparative advantage the US has expanded its agricultural exports to Mexico. In 2016, Mexico accounted for 13.1 percent of

US agricultural exports and 17.8 percent of US agricultural imports, as defined and categorized by USDA.

> Between 1993 (the year before NAFTA's implementation) and 2016, US agricultural exports to Mexico expanded at a compound annual rate of 7.2 percent, while agricultural imports from Mexico grew at a rate of 9.7 percent. [However,] lower prices for many bulk agricultural commodities have caused the total value of US agricultural exports to Mexico to experience little to no growth between 2012 and 2016.
>
> (USDA (ERS), 2018)

Lower prices mean that surplus was transferred from farmers to US consumers.

For the limited time horizon that is considered in Figure 8.2, the two nations acquire static gains from trade. Mexico specializes in the production of agricultural goods by moving from A_{Mexico} to S_{Mexico} to increase its national welfare by consuming at C_{Mexico}, which is superior to A_{Mexico}. Similarly, the US increases its national welfare by specializing in the production of manufactures and moving from A_{US} to S_{US} and consuming at $C_{US} > A_{US}$ along the demand diagonal (DD). The demand diagonal (a 45-degree line) presupposes that in the autarkic state, consumption of the two goods is proportional (see Reinert, 2012, p. 35 for further discussion of the concept). The opportunity cost concept of the theory was further refined in the twentieth century by a Swedish economist, Eli Heckscher,

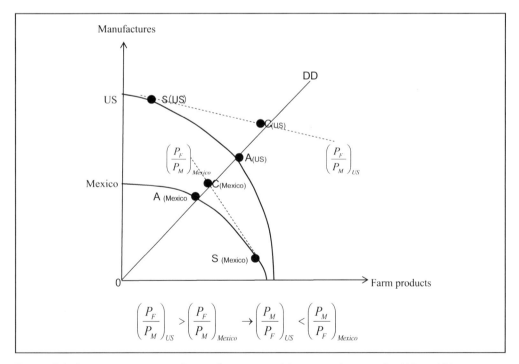

Figure 8.2 Comparative cost of manufactures and farm products in the US and Mexico

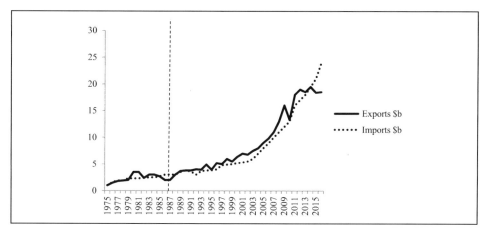

Figure 8.3 US–Mexico agricultural exports and imports (US$b, 1975–2016 estimates)
Source: USDA, Economic Research Service using data from US Census Bureau, Foreign Trade Statistics, as compiled by USDA, Foreign Agricultural Service, Global Agricultural Trade System.
Note: US-Mexico agricultural trade has generally experienced strong growth since the late 1980s.

and one of his students, Bertil Ohlin, in 1924 (the H-O Theorem), and subsequently by Gottfried Haberler (1936). The H-O Theorem has defined the pattern of North-South trade for several generations.[23] A major advantage of the relative cost theory is its adaptability to other trade theories like intra-industry trade and strategic trade.

8.3 TRADE RESTRICTIONS WITH PARTIAL EQUILIBRIUM ANALYSIS (SUBSIDIES AND TARIFFS)

There are times when nations will argue that it is important to protect infant industries before they are decimated by international competition. Indeed, many developing countries have made such an argument. International trade restrictions take multiple forms and international trade negotiations are generally intended to limit trade restrictions and provide a structure for equitable evaluation of trade restrictions. The next section will be devoted to international trade negotiations and law. The multiple forms of trade restrictions are generally classified under two broad headings: (i) tariffs/taxes, and (ii) non-tariff barriers (NTBs). NTBs constitute everything else that cannot be classified as direct taxation. They include subsidies, quotas, voluntary export restraints (VERs), product quality, sanitary and phytosanitary requirements, government procurement policies, and domestic content requirements.

Trade restrictions may be unfair policies with discriminatory intentions and effects. As such, they prevent certain businesses and countries from doing business in foreign countries on an even playing field. Taxes and subsidies reduce imports and, in some cases, exports because in some countries taxes can be imposed on imports and exports. The objective of this section is to cursorily take a look at the effects on tariffs and subsidies on international trade and why it is important to have trade negotiations that effectively deal with issues surrounding tariffs and trade. Domestic subsidies enhance domestic production by providing savings and research assistance to companies that would otherwise not be able to compete in the global economy. Some aspects of NTBs will be subsequently discussed in the remaining chapter of the book.

Figure 8.4 provides a framework for understanding the consequences of tariffs and subsidies. Tariffs prolong inefficiencies (such as the type that affected the US Rust Belt and the auto and steel industries), generate revenues for governments, increase the cost of consumption, and transfer surplus from consumers to producers. Ironically, it is very easy to confuse the long-term effects of a tariff with trade negotiations or agreements (an economic misdiagnosis). The US Rust Belt and the Boeing-Airbus dispute will be used to present very reasonable economic expositions of trade restrictions in the areas of tariff and subsidies. In Figure 8.4, I start with a very simple economic model for a small open economy without loss of generality.

Assuming that A is an initial point of equilibrium without trade, the per unit autarkic price of the good in question will be P_A. The nation can open up to international trade, which will cause price to fall to P_W (see Figure 8.4). At P_W, consumers can consume 4,000 units of the good, but domestic production will fall to 1,000 units. Then, 3,000 units will have to be imported (the difference between 4,000 and 1,000). Suppose the nation imposes a ten percent tariff (t); the tariff will encourage domestic producers to increase production by 1,000 units, but consumers will now reduce consumption by 1,000 units (reducing consumption from 4,000 to 3,000) and the nation will import 1,000 units (the difference between 3,000 and 2,000). The government will collect revenue of $1,100 (area c), assuming that other nations are willing to pay the tariff and that there is no tax evasion or avoidance. The protection of infant industry argument is occasional adopted to protect young industries.

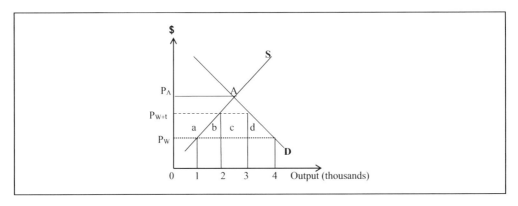

Figure 8.4 Tariff (without loss of generality)

The imposition of the tax reveals that there are at least four outcomes: (i) a transfer effect from consumer to producers (area a), (ii) a production effect (an increase in domestic production and probably employment), (iii) a revenue effect (area c), and (iv) a consumption effect (area d). It is evident that consumers are not going to be better off as a result of the tariff. It is very common for this type of tariff to be supported in order to protect infant industries. While the argument is somewhat appealing and reasonable, it should be pertinent to note that the policy might not necessarily create a basis for innovation if its implementation is infinite.

Obviously, no nation would like to see the decimation of its domestic industries before the industries have a fighting chance to survive in the global economy. Conversely, no nation would like to indulge its entrepreneurs in inefficient production. Therefore, sensible trade policy must consider or respond to two critical issues in trade negotiations: (i) are the industries viable over a longer period of time? (ii) what should be the reasonable time horizon for the protection of the industries? Implicitly, industries must not be perpetually protected in a competitive global economy.

In a similar manner, industries must not be subsidized indefinitely. When it comes to subsidizing the production of pharmaceutical products, a production subsidy may not necessarily increase the cost of consuming pharmaceutical drugs.

However, subsidies that are outlawed by the WTO and other trade agreements are illegal by definition. The issues with subsidized production are significant; some of which trade negotiations have not successfully resolved since the 1940s. They may include interrelated issues of research cost, dumping, market access, the duration of tolerable subsidy, and the role of governments. On many levels, the epic subsidy dispute between Boeing and Airbus is very instructive to show deficiencies in modern trade law and negotiations.

A concise history of the companies can be found in the work of Heyman (2007). The history of the evolution of the companies is important because, *inter alia*, it provides theoretical bases for understanding the concepts of first-mover advantage, dominant strategy, and non-dominant strategy in game theory. Boeing was founded in 1916, long before Airbus came into existence in 1970. There are very big differences between the histories of the two companies. Since civil aviation was not very dominant, war time orders helped to ensure the success of Boeing. In effect, it can be incontrovertibly stated that Boeing had a first-mover advantage or monopoly.

In the 1950s, the first commercially successful jet airplane was developed for civilian and military purposes, the Boeing 707 (Heyman, 2007, p. 4). Other versions like the 737, and 747 jumbo jet created very good opportunities for Boeing to be profitable without threatening competition. The dominance of Boeing became much more secured after it purchased its competitor, McDonnell Douglas, in 1997. However, throughout its history, Boeing has derived considerable financial and technological benefits from orders placed by the Pentagon and National Aeronautics and Space Administration (NASA) (Heyman, 2007, p. 4).

The first-mover advantage of Boeing was challenged by the creation of Airbus as a Franco-German joint venture in 1970. However, Figure 8.9 shows that the presence of Airbus was not felt until much later. Airbus orders were insignificant in the 1970s relative to the 1990s and 2000s. According to Heyman, the creation of Airbus was originally intended to reduce Europe's dependence on US civil aviation while bolstering the fragmented European aircraft industry (Heyman, 2007, p.4).

It was not until the 1980s that Airbus made a commercial breakthrough with the A320 family, which was first delivered in 1988. The successful launch of the A320 facilitated increased orders, superseding those of Boeing in 2001. The preference for Airbus planes was not without research support, technological innovation, and duopolistic competition. Airbus became so successful and threatening, that the US signed an agreement on trade in large civil aircraft with the EU in 1992.

Though Adam Smith was preoccupied with transaction costs and geographic proximity in his promotion of freer trade, contemporary international trade law focuses on the welfare effects of the geographic proximity of states and regional trade agreements. Viner (1950) is generally credited for the introduction of the concepts of "trade creation" and "trade diversion" to the economic analysis of the static effects of preferential trade arrangements (PTAs). However, contemporary analyses of the concepts are much more nuanced.

Viner focused solely on the production effects of the customs union. He defined trade creation as the displacement of domestic production by imports from other customs union members, implying that this was economically desirable since production shifts from costly domestic producers to lower cost customs union partners. Trade diversion was the shift in the source of imports from a cheaper non-member to a higher-cost custom union member, which for Viner was undesirable because production shifted from low-cost to higher-cost countries (WTO, 2007, p. 138).

Contemporary theories that first emerged in the 1950s (Lipsey, 1957), tend to focus on welfare analysis (depicted in Figure 8.5, Panels (a) and (b)). The welfare implication of unionization redirects focus from the cost of production to consumption effects of unionization. Partial equilibrium analysis Figure 8.5 Panel (c) presents a fuller representation of the comparative cost benefit consideration.

Figure 8.5, Panels (a), (b), and (c) summarize the main welfare arguments of trade creating and diverting unions. As usual, triangles b and e are indicative of the welfare gains or benefits (see Chapters 1 and 7), Rectangles c are indicative of the costs that are associated with unionization. Nations must conduct their cost-benefit analysis to decide on the viability of unionization, and economic law also takes the welfare benefits into consideration. In the case of trade creation the benefit outsizes the national cost (b>c; net gain). On the contrary, national cost outsizes benefits (c>b; net loss) in the case of trade diversion.[24] The welfare effects will be revisited as part of the discussion of regional trade agreements (RTAs).

INTERNATIONAL ECONOMIC LAW

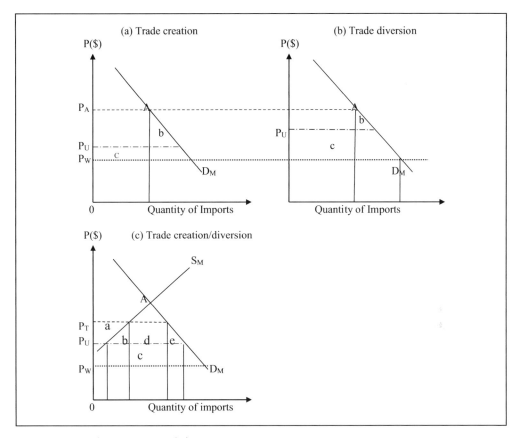

Figure 8.5 Trade creation and diversion

As nations trade to increase their welfare, they can also engage in unfair trade practices. They can dump their goods, discriminate, and subsidize the production costs of domestic firms to create artificial comparative advantages. Dumping occurs when identical or similar goods are sold for cheaper prices in foreign markets relative to domestic markets. Dumping may occur for various reasons, but the effects of dumping cannot necessarily be differentiated. Sporadic (seasonal) dumping usually occurs when sellers want to dispose of excess inventories as a result of bad planning, ill-luck, or shocks (sudden and temporary disruptions). Persistent dumping is a prolific form of dumping that exploits differences in price sensitivities (elasticities) as depicted in Figure 8.7 (to be discussed later). The sellers tend to have more monopoly power at home than abroad. Cyclical dumping is usually associated with the business cycle in the home country. In recessionary periods, business can accumulate inventory and they might want outlets to dispose of their inventory. Predatory dumping is a form of dumping that is deliberately intended to eliminate competition in foreign markets. It is rather temporary than persistent.

The problem with the economic classifications of dumping is that they do not cleanly delineate their individual economic effects on foreign import-competing industries and the specter of unemployment. Additionally, dumping is one of those cases in which the

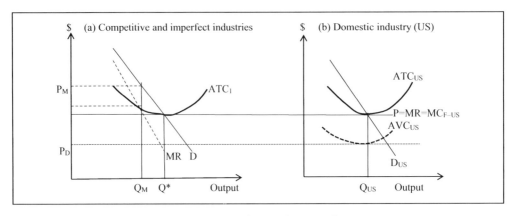

Figure 8.6 Dumping under competitive and imperfect conditions

intent is not necessarily material. The act itself is sufficient to cause injury to foreign firms. We can now consider the relevant economic arguments that underpin the dumping law. International law generally considers the differences in per unit cost (average total cost, ATC) rather than average variable cost (AVC) of production (see Figure 8.6).

Economists use the AVC to determine the survivability of a firm. Firms cover part of their AFC when the price of their product is less than ATC but greater than AVC, because ATC-AVC=AFC. Firms can no longer be viable when the prices of their products fall below the AVC of production. However, the distinction can be problematic when production costs vary across countries and firms. A domestic firm with a higher AVC will be unable to compete without subsidy when a foreign firm uses a lower AVC as an indicator of dumping. While intent (*mens rea*) is usually considered to be a culpable state of mind and element of criminal offense, economic cycles and bad planning are not mitigating conditions for dumping in international markets.

In effect, apart from the predatory intent to stifle or prevent competition, bad planning, shocks (exogenous and temporary circumstances) can also influence the desire of firms to dispose of inventories and finished goods in economies that are performing reasonably well. However, international trade law rarely accommodates such economic circumstances under contingency provisions to ensure the survivability of foreign firms in unfortunate situations; partly because of cost differences and export of unemployment that can be detrimental to domestic firms. Consider Figure 8.6, Panels (a) and (b). Without any predatory pricing activity, the market price (P) corresponds to the marginal revenue (MR), marginal cost (MC), minimum per unit cost (ATC), and market quantity $Q^*=Q_{US}$. If foreign competitors can dump at a price below P_D, they can destabilize the US market in which P_D is the equivalent of AVC. The US firms cannot possibly drop their price below P_D.

Additionally, by accommodating foreign dumping, foreign firms can destabilize the competitive market and transform it into an imperfect one; they will become price makers with tremendous market power to set a higher price (P_M) and reduce industrial quantity from $Q\star$ to Q_M. In keeping with the freer trade theory, the competitive price will no longer be attainable and consumers will lose surplus (a welfare loss). In the competitive market structure, firms can absorb some amount of losses when price falls below per unit cost of production (Figure 8.6 Panel (b)) but not below AVC. Evidently, economics and law diverge on the issue of a tolerable amount of dumping, because of international cost differentials and unpredictable macroeconomic circumstances. Dumping provides an opportunity for nations to export their unemployment, but no nation will willingly accept the unemployment of other nations. This reality makes the economic classifications of international dumping a philosophical exercise rather than differences with significant legal connotations in the interpretation of international law.

Firms have a tendency to discriminate when it is propitious and profitable for them to do so over extended periods. The tendency to persistently discriminate is largely based on differences in taste and economic conditions that cause consumers to be sensitive or insensitive to price differences. Of course, the ability of sellers to engage in discriminatory practice is also contingent on the successful separation of the markets in which they operate and their ability to prevent the successful retailing of products across international boundaries at competitive or lower prices. The problem of price discrimination is mostly associated with PTAs (or RTAs) in international trade. A cohort of countries within an agreement can have privileged access to markets at favorable prices. On the other hand, non-members may not have such access at lower or comparative prices (special and differential treatment).

Figure 8.7 summarizes the key arguments of discriminatory pricing. The countries that operate as a bloc with an optional pricing scheme can charge each other a lower price. The countries are highly sensitive to price changes because they have options within a trade agreement. They can trade with each other at lower contractual prices that cannot be summarily abrogated (Figure 8.7 Panel (b)). Countries that are not within the regional

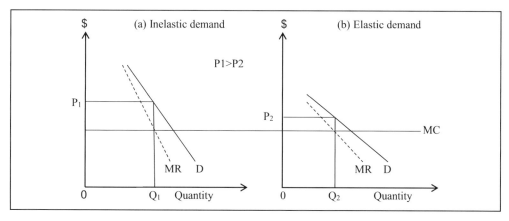

Figure 8.7 The discriminating price-maker

arrangement (treaty) are exposed to higher prices and are normally insensitive to the price differential, especially when they want essential goods. The regularity condition presupposes that the member countries cannot illicitly sell the goods to non-member countries at the preferential prices that are reserved for members.

The trade theories that have been presented in this chapter have significantly shaped the theoretical positions of international trade law over the years. Notably, there are other forms of restrictions, which will be discussed subsequently, but they all tend to have deleterious welfare effects as those that have been presented by the trade theories. Implicitly, all forms of undesirable (illegitimate) trade restrictions reduce the volume of trade and decrease consumer welfare. Contemporary trade law has been shaped by World War experiences, technological innovation, and changing economic conditions. As such, the law has evolved over time to include customary practices and international treaties (conventions). Some of the most significant developments that ultimately laid the foundations of contemporary international trade law were restrictive trade practices between the World Wars (the interregnum). Actually, the restrictive practices created abundant opportunities to test the viability of international trade theories that advocate for freer trade.

World War I forced nations to embrace mercantilist policies of restrictive policies to gain wealth and reduce their current account deficits. Trade restrictions were accompanied by exchange rate policies as nations tried to improve their current account situation and minimize the loss of reserves (gold). Trade policies between the two World Wars (the interregnum) put the economic theories to the test and shaped international trade law thereafter. Trade policies during the interregnum were largely antithetical to liberalization theories. The reversion to mercantilist policies during the war reduced the volume of trade, depressed prices, and contributed to a depression. The trade and exchange rate adjustments were largely in response to falling income and loss of reserves. The war caused a drop in GDP across most of the Western European countries, with the greatest drop in Belgium, France, and Austria. Surprisingly, over the objections of many, the US Congress passed the Smoot-Hawley tariff in 1930. The tariff produced devastating results and arguably contributed to the longevity of the Great Depression.

The Smoot-Hawley Act raised tariff to about 53 percent on protected imports, partly as an effort to protect domestic industries. Predictably, other trading partners of the US, including Spain, Cuba, Canada, Switzerland, New Zealand, Mexico, and Australia, imposed retaliatory tariffs of their own across a spectrum of goods. By 1932, US trade with other nations failed so badly that Congress passed the Reciprocal Trade Agreement Act (1934) as a reversal of the protectionist policy.

On September 19, 1931, Britain abandoned the gold standard and allowed sterling to depreciate. This move sent shockwaves through the world economy. Other countries either followed Britain in coming off the gold standard or imposed restrictions on trade and payments as a defensive measure to reduce imports and strengthen the balance of payments. Within days, other countries with close trade and financial ties

Table 8.1 Applied tariff rates of major traders in 1913 and 1925: all products (percentage)

Country	1913	1925	Country	1913	1925
Argentina	26	26	France	18	12
Australia	17	25	Germany[b]	12	12
Austria-Hungary	18	--	India	4	14
Austria	(18)	12	Italy	17	17
Czechoslovakia	(18)	19	Netherlands	3	4
Hungary	(18)	23	Spain	33	44
Poland[a]	(12–18)	23	Sweden	16	13
Belgium	6	8	Switzerland	7	11
Canada	18	16	United Kingdom	--	4
Denmark	9	6	United States	33, 16[c]	29

Source: World Trade Organization (2007, p. 41).
Notes:
Unweighted arithmetic average.
a Germany and Austria for 1913.
b Average of old and new tariff (from October 1925) for 1925.
c Referring to Underwood Tariff applied in 1914.

to Britain—Denmark, Finland, Norway, and Sweden among them—allowed their currencies to depreciate relative to gold. Japan, concluding that its recent resumption of gold convertibility had been a mistake, followed in December (Eichengreen & Irwin, 2010, pp. 876–7). Between 1913 and 1925 tariffs had already gone up in some European countries (see Table 8.1). Import taxes were stable in very few European countries like Italy and Germany. They went down in Denmark and France.

After the British devaluation, several countries found ways to minimize the adverse effects of the devaluation.

> A large number of countries ratcheted up their tariffs to block cheap imports. France imposed a 15 percent surcharge on British goods to offset the depreciation of sterling and adopted more restrictive import quotas. Canada and South Africa, which did not delink from gold along with Britain, adopted antidumping duties aimed at imports from Britain. In January 1932 the German government was empowered to raise "equalizing" tariffs on goods coming from countries with depreciated currencies. The Netherlands also broke from its traditional policy of free trade, raising its duties by 25 percent to offset currency depreciation abroad.
> (Eichengreen & Irwin, 2010, p. 877)

It is estimated that the volume of world trade fell by 16 percent from the third quarter of 1931 to the third quarter of 1932. Between 1929 and 1932 it fell 25 percent, and nearly half of this reduction was due to higher tariff and non-tariff barriers. In November 1931, Britain also enacted an Abnormal Importation Duties Act, which gave the authorities discretion to impose higher duties on selected types of goods. The trade war was amplified. The level of protection was also very high within the Japanese empire. The hopeless economic situation in most European countries and the unstable political situation in Europe made it extremely difficult to liberalize international trade. Yet it was equally apparent that the chaotic and precarious interwar situation was unsustainable for robust international trade and financial stability when international trade and finance are mutually inclusive. By the end of World War II, the US started to make proposals for an international system that would provide a structure for orderly international trade.

Negotiations to establish such a framework started in Geneva, Switzerland, in 1947, with a draft charter for an International Trade Organization (ITO) that was completed in Havana, Cuba. The Charter fell into disfavor in the US Congress and was momentarily abandoned. The ITO relapsed in 1954, but the contracting parties used the GATT framework to discuss the long-term situation of the GATT. The GATT was established as a default organization of the ITO—with "Contracting Parties"—since it was supposed to serve as a temporary agreement until the ITO Charter was ratified. Part of the provisions of the ITO was subsequently resuscitated and co-opted into the GATT. On October 30, 1947, the GATT was signed by 23 countries and entered into force on January 1, 1948. Originally, most of the trade and development-related provisions of the ITO were not included in GATT, but some were subsequently included as the membership of GATT increased with decolonization.

The overall objective of the GATT was to reduce barriers to trade, especially tariffs, and to limit the use of certain trade barriers, such as quotas. The negotiating parties agreed that substantial tariff cuts could only be achieved if certain exceptions were included in the structure of trade rules (WTO, 2007, p. 180).

However, the interests and goals are diverse and convergent in multilateral organizations. The newly independent countries first sought exemptions, which are numerous in contemporary trade law, but eventually pursued the goal of market penetration into the markets of advanced economies. Developing countries have been able to secure a revision of GATT Article XVIII to protect infant industries.[25]

8.4 INTERNATIONAL TRADE LAW

The scope of international trade law is very broad and evolving, but this section will provide sufficient coverage. The following aspects will be covered: (i) exemptions, including infant industry and most favored nation (MFN) provision, (ii) tariffs, (iii) dumping, (iv) RTAs, (v) price discrimination, (vi) subsidies, (vii) product quality, and (viii) the dispute settlement mechanism of the WTO. GATT was reconstituted as the WTO during the Uruguay Round of talks. Despite the assorted categories of laws, the WTO has three basic or fundamental principles: (i) liberalization (reduction in tariffs and removal of undesirable trade barriers, including quantitative restrictions), (ii) principle of non-discrimination (MFN principle), and (iii) trade fairness.

The GATT agreement contains multiple contingent provisions (escape clauses) to reflect historical (previous) arrangements and the development and economic status of certain groups of countries; initially in the context of post-war reconstruction and decolonization. Today, these clauses can be more readily understood as exemptions based on economic circumstances or conditions. Ironically, such clauses can benefit all the participants in a convention. They generally manifest good faith efforts that should enable economic growth and development. Evidently, courts have routinely favored agreements or contracts with good faith intentions. Among the contingency clauses are those relating to dumping and subsidies (Article VI), balance-of-payment exceptions (Article XII), and safeguards against import surges (Article XIX). Countervailing (retaliatory) provisions of the WTO are also relevant to contingencies. In effect, the contingent provisions make some adjustments to the three central principles of liberalization, non-discrimination, and fairness that have been identified above.

Exemptions must comply with certain conditions that: (i) are general, (ii) are conducive to global security, (iii) promote the improvement of regional welfare, (iv) enhance the stability of international payments, and (v) are exceptional and unanticipated (*rebus sic stantibus*, a fundamental change in circumstance). General exceptions take into consideration the protection of lives (human, animal, and plant) that can limit the volume of trade, but which must not be contrived by arbitrary, discriminatory, and unjustifiable or surreptitious measures. The general exceptions also apply to trade in goods and services (see the General Agreement on Trade in Services, GATS, 1995; see also Arts. XX-XXIV https://wto.org/).

Security exceptions are generally designed to protect national interests, which might decrease the volume of trade. Intellectual property rights have national security implications (see Trade Related Aspects of Intellectual Property Rights (TRIPS, 1994, https://wto.org/). Similarly, the provision of services in the banking, insurance, finance, and communication sectors also have vested national security interests (see GATS).

Plurilateral RTAs are also granted exceptions from the MFN non-discrimination clause. The exception makes it possible for some countries to get preferential treatment for their articles of trade and provision of services. Countries in diverse forms of trade integration, customs union, free trade area, and common market enjoy privileges that are not extended to all WTO members. Members are also granted the authority to maintain balance of payments stability that might reduce the volume of trade. Invariably, such programs are usually suggested or administered by the IMF. As is the case with all treaties or conventions (see the Vienna Law of Treaties), political and economic circumstances may change in a fundamental way that can incapacitate a country from fulfilling its treaty obligations. Countries are granted waivers to derogate (contract out) from their obligations under such verifiable circumstances. One of the earliest issues that called for accommodation or derogation from stringent or uncompromising treaty provisions was the protection of infant industries in some developing economies.

8.4 (A) INFANT INDUSTRY PROTECTION (ART. XIII)

Developmental issues have shaped the philosophy of multilateral trade agreements since the 1940s. Article XVIII of GATT is a case in point. When the Article was originally considered under the ITO, infant industry protection was derogatory. It was subsequently rephrased as a contingent clause within the meaning of the GATT rather than derogation from it.

The contracting parties recognize that the attainment of the objectives of this Agreement will be facilitated by the progressive development of their economies, particularly of those contracting parties the economies of which can only support low standards of living and are in the early stages of development (Article XVIII (1): *Governmental Assistance to Economic Development*).

The Article created provisions for members to take protective measures that will enable them to improve the development and welfare of their nations. Consequently, the members agreed to extend tariff relief to some countries to protect their burgeoning industries *inter alia*, but also to maintain quantitative restrictions that would enable them to manage their capital accounts for balance of payments stability and economic development (see Figure 8.4).

8.4 (B) DUMPING (ART. VI, ANTI-DUMPING AGREEMENT, AND AGREEMENT TO IMPLEMENT)

Dumping is outlawed by Article VI and provisions are created for retaliatory measures:

> The contracting parties recognize that dumping, by which products of one country are introduced into the commerce of another country at less than the normal [fair] value of the products, is to be condemned if it causes or threatens material injury to an established industry in the territory of a contracting party or materially retards the establishment of a domestic industry. For the purposes of this Article, a product is to be considered as being introduced into the commerce of an importing country at less than its normal value, if the price of the product exported from one country to another (a) is less than the comparable price, in the ordinary course of trade, for the like product when destined for consumption in the exporting country, or, (b) in the absence of such domestic price, is less than either (i) the highest comparable price for the like product for export to any third country in the ordinary course of trade, or (ii) the cost of production of the product in the country of origin plus a reasonable addition for selling cost and profit. Due allowance shall be made in each case for differences in conditions and terms of sale, for differences in taxation, and for other differences affecting price comparability.
>
> (Art. VI)

However, the effects of dumping must be materially injurious:

> No contracting party shall levy any anti-dumping or countervailing duty on the importation of any product of the territory of another contracting party unless it determines that the effect of the dumping or subsidization, as the case may be, is such as to cause or threaten material injury to an established domestic industry, or is such as to retard materially the establishment of a domestic industry.
>
> (Art. VI(6)(a))

Subsection b of the Article provides for waivers:

> The CONTRACTING PARTIES may waive the requirement of subparagraph (a) of this paragraph so as to permit a contracting party to levy an anti-dumping or countervailing duty on the importation of any product for the purpose of offsetting dumping or subsidization which causes or threatens material injury to an industry in the territory of another contracting party exporting the product concerned to the territory of the importing contracting party. The CONTRACTING PARTIES shall waive the requirements of subparagraph (a) of this paragraph, so as to permit the levying of a countervailing duty, in cases in which they find that a subsidy is causing or threatening material injury to an industry in the territory of another contracting party exporting the product concerned to the territory of the importing contracting party.
>
> (Art. VI(6)(b))

Additionally, in highly regulated economies of some source countries, government regulation creates monopolies that distort prices. Price setting mechanisms are contrary to those of the competitive model (see Figures 8.6 and 8.7):

> It is recognized that, in the case of imports from a country which has a complete or substantially complete monopoly of its trade and where all domestic prices are fixed by the State, special difficulties may exist in determining price comparability for the purposes of paragraph 1, and in such cases importing contracting parties may find it necessary to take into account the possibility that a strict comparison with domestic prices in such a country may not always be appropriate.
>
> (Ad Art. VI para.(1)(2))

The concept of material injury has notable exceptions in cases of stabilization or regulatory policies that depress prices for reasons that are unrelated to free market operations or the normal course of business transactions that reflect the movements of prices (see Art.VI(7)). On the contrary, hidden (proxy) dumping by associated (domestic) houses (that is, the sale by an importer at a price below that corresponding to the price invoiced by an exporter with whom the importer is associated, and also below the price in the exporting country) constitutes a form of price dumping with respect to which the margin of dumping may be calculated on the basis of the price at which the goods are resold by the importer (Ad Art.VI para.(1)(1)) (see Figure 8.6, Panels (a) and (b)). Similarly, the use of multiple currency practices (exchange rates) can in certain circumstances constitute dumping by means of a partial depreciation of a country's currency, which may be met by countervailing duties or can constitute a form of subsidy. By "multiple currency practices," are practices by governments or practices sanctioned by governments (Ad Art. VI paras.(2/3)(2)). The effects of competitive devaluation and currency manipulation will be discussed more fully in Sections 8.4 and 8.5.

A product is to be considered as being dumped, i.e. introduced into the commerce of another country at less than its normal value, if the export price of the product exported from one country to another is less than the comparable price, in the ordinary course of trade, for the like product when destined for consumption in the exporting country (Art. 2(1)). When there are no sales of the like product in the ordinary course of trade in the domestic market of the exporting country or when, because of the particular market situation or the low volume of the sales in the domestic market of the exporting country,[26] such sales do not permit a proper comparison, the margin of dumping shall be determined by comparison with a comparable price of the like product when exported to an appropriate third country, provided that this price is representative, or with the cost of production in the country of origin plus a reasonable amount for administrative, selling and general costs and for profits (Art. 2(2)).

Sales of the like product in the domestic market of the exporting country or sales to a third country at prices below per unit (fixed and variable) costs of production plus administrative, selling, and general costs may be treated as not being in the ordinary course of trade by reason of price and may be disregarded in determining normal value only if the authorities determine that such sales are made within an extended period of time in substantial quantities and are at prices which do not provide for the recovery of all costs within a reasonable period of time.[27] If prices which are below per unit costs at the time of sale are above weighted average per unit costs for the period of investigation, such prices shall be considered to provide for recovery of costs within a reasonable period of time (Art. 2(2)(1)).

In cases where there is no export price or where it appears to the authorities concerned that the export price is unreliable because of association or a compensatory arrangement between the exporter and the importer or a third party, the export price may be constructed on the basis of the price at which the imported products are first resold to an independent buyer, or if the products are not resold to an independent buyer, or not resold in the condition as imported, on such reasonable basis as the authorities may determine (Art. 2(3)).

A fair comparison shall be made between the export price and the normal value. This comparison shall be made at the same level of trade, normally at the ex-factory level, and in respect of sales made at as nearly as possible the same time. Due allowance shall be made in each case, on its merits, for differences which affect price comparability, including differences in conditions and terms of sale, taxation, levels of trade, quantities, physical characteristics, and any other differences which are also demonstrated to affect price comparability (Art. 2(4)).

When the comparison under paragraph 4 requires a conversion of currencies, such conversion should be made using the rate of exchange on the date of sale,[28] provided that when a sale of foreign currency on forward markets is directly linked to the export sale involved, the rate of exchange in the forward sale shall be used. Fluctuations in exchange rates shall be ignored and in an investigation the authorities shall allow exporters at least 60 days to have adjusted their export prices to reflect sustained movements in exchange rates during the period of investigation (Art. 2(4)(1)).

In the case where products are not imported directly from the country of origin but are exported to the importing member from an intermediate country, the price at which the products are sold from the country of export to the importing member shall normally be compared with the comparable price in the country of export. However, comparison may be made with the price in the country of origin, if, for example, the products are merely transshipped through the country of export, or such products are not produced in the country of export, or there is no comparable price for them in the country of export (Art. 2(5)).[29]

The Agreement on Implementing Article VI of GATT stipulates the criteria for the determination of injury:

> A determination of injury for purposes of Article VI of GATT 1994 shall be based on positive evidence and involve an objective examination of both *(a)* the volume of the dumped imports and the effect of the dumped imports on prices in the domestic market for like products, and *(b)* the consequent impact of these imports on domestic producers of such products.
>
> (Art. 3(1))

With regard to the volume of the dumped imports, the investigating authorities are expected to consider whether there has been a significant increase in dumped imports, either in absolute terms or relative to production or consumption in the importing country. With regard to the price effect on the importing (receiving) country, the investigating authorities must consider whether there has been a significant price undercutting by the dumped imports as compared with the price of a like product of the importing member, or whether the effect of such imports is otherwise to depress prices to a significant degree or prevent price increases, which otherwise would have occurred, to a significant degree. No one or several of these factors can necessarily give decisive guidance (Art. 3(2)).

Dumping of a product can be done simultaneously. Where imports of a product from more than one country are simultaneously subject to antidumping investigations, the investigating authorities may cumulatively assess the effects of such imports only if they determine that *(a)* the margin of dumping established in relation to the imports from each country is more than *de minimis* [minor and insignificant] as defined in paragraph 8 of Article 5 and the volume of imports from each country is not negligible and *(b)* a cumulative assessment of the effects of the imports is appropriate in light of the conditions of competition between the imported products and the conditions of competition between the imported products and the like domestic product[30] (Art. 3(3)).

The examination of the impact of the dumped imports on the domestic industry concerned shall include an evaluation of all relevant economic factors and indices having a bearing on the state of the industry, including actual and potential decline in sales, profits, output, market share, productivity, return on investments, or utilization of capacity; factors affecting domestic prices; the magnitude of the margin of dumping; actual and potential negative effects on cash flow, inventories, employment, wages, growth, ability to raise capital or investments. This list is not exhaustive, nor can one or several of these factors necessarily give decisive guidance (Art. 3(4)).

Material injury that is attributable to dumping can only be based on the criteria provided in paragraphs 2 and 4 of the Implementation Agreement. The demonstration of a causal relationship between the dumped imports and the injury to the domestic industry shall be based on an examination of all relevant evidence before the authorities. The authorities shall also examine any known factors other than the dumped imports which at the same time are injuring the domestic industry, and the injuries caused by these other factors must not be attributed to the dumped imports. Factors which may be relevant in this respect include, *inter alia*, the volume and prices of imports not sold at dumping prices, contraction in demand or changes in the patterns of consumption, trade restrictive practices of and competition between the foreign and domestic producers, developments in technology and the export performance and productivity of the domestic industry (Art. 3(5)).

The effect of the dumped imports shall be assessed in relation to the domestic production of the like product when available data permit the separate identification of that production on the basis of such criteria as the production process, producers' sales and profits. If such separate identification of that production is not possible, the effects of the dumped imports shall be assessed by the examination of the production of the narrowest group or range of products, which includes the like product, for which the necessary information can be provided (Art. 3(6)).

A determination of a threat of material injury shall be based on facts and not merely on allegation, conjecture or remote possibility. The change in circumstances which would create a situation in which the dumping would cause injury must be clearly foreseen and imminent.[31] In making a determination regarding the existence of a threat of material injury, the authorities should consider, *inter alia*, such factors as:

(i) a significant rate of increase of dumped imports into the domestic market indicating the likelihood of substantially increased importation;
(ii) sufficient freely disposable, or an imminent, substantial increase in, capacity of the exporter indicating the likelihood of substantially increased dumped exports to

the importing Member's market, taking into account the availability of other export markets to absorb any additional exports;
(iii) whether imports are entering at prices that will have a significant depressing or suppressing effect on domestic prices, and would likely increase demand for further imports; and
(iv) inventories of the product being investigated.

No one of these factors by itself can necessarily give decisive guidance but the totality of the factors considered must lead to the conclusion that further dumped exports are imminent and that, unless protective action is taken, material injury would occur (Art. 3(7)).

8.4 (C) BALANCE OF PAYMENTS STABILITY AND QUANTITATIVE RESTRICTIONS (ART. XII)

International trade, currency valuation, and national income are interrelated concepts that impact the net exports of a nation; the ability of a nation to import or export more or less. With limiting regularity conditions, countries may restrict trade to safeguard their external financing or their balance of payments position. Import restrictions must not be exaggerated beyond the limits that are essential to maintain sustainable balance of payments position. Sustainability is essential to prevent destabilizing or disruptive stop-go policies. Therefore, the availability and access to foreign reserves are also taken into consideration in the interest of increasing global trade.

Contracting parties undertake, in carrying out their domestic policies, to pay due regard to the need for maintaining or restoring equilibrium in their balance of payments on a sound and lasting basis and to the desirability of avoiding an uneconomic employment of productive resources. They recognize that, in order to achieve these ends, it is desirable so far as possible to adopt measures which expand rather than contract international trade (Art. XII (3)(a): *Restrictions to Safeguard the Balance of Payments*).

The exemptions are not sweeping. They are measured in consideration of the economic circumstances of other members. Accordingly, members are expected to apply restrictions in such a way that the restrictions do not unreasonably impede the progress of trade and commerce, prevent the importations of commercial samples, and prevent compliance with patent, trade mark, copyright, or similar procedures. Therefore, even though contracting parties might face demand pressures that threaten the availability of monetary reserves and adjustments to balance of payments positions, they must not impose unnecessary restrictions that defeat the principle of freer trade. In cases where escalation of restrictions is warranted to maintain balance of payments stability, such restrictions must not be escalated without consultations, which is part of the dispute settlement mechanisms. More so, alternative measures must be explored to correct chronic or persistent balance of payments problems (see Art. XII).

8.4 (D) NON-DISCRIMINATION, QUOTAS, AND EXEMPTIONS (ARTS. I, XIII AND XIV)

Countries may not discriminate against trading partners:

With respect to customs duties and charges of any kind imposed on or in connection with importation or exportation or imposed on the international transfer of payments for imports or exports, and with respect to the method of levying such duties and charges, and with respect to all rules and formalities in connection with importation and exportation, and with respect to all matters referred to in paragraphs 2 and 4 of Art. III, any advantage, favour, privilege or immunity granted by any contracting party to any product originating in or destined for any other country shall be accorded immediately and unconditionally to the like product originating in or destined for the territories of all other contracting parties (Art. I: *General Most Favoured Nation Treatment*).

No prohibition or restriction shall be applied by any contracting party on the importation of any product of the territory of any other contracting party or on the exportation of any product destined for the territory of any other contracting party, unless the importation of the like product of all third countries or the exportation of the like product to all third countries is similarly prohibited or restricted (Art. XIII(1)).

Nondiscriminating procedures require transparency. Wherever practicable, quotas (the total amount of permitted imports, whether allocated among supplying countries or not) must be fixed with public notice in accordance with public notice of: (i) the total quantity or value of the product or products which will be permitted to be imported during a specified future period of time, including changes in the quantity or value of the quantitative restriction; (ii) the excluded quantity in transit before public notice of the required imported quantities; (iii) a thirty-day notice to parties that are traditionally exempted from the restrictions.

In cases in which import licences are issued in connection with import restrictions, the contracting party applying the restrictions shall provide, upon the request of any contracting party having an interest in the trade in the product concerned, all relevant information concerning the administration of the restrictions, the import licences granted over a recent period and the distribution of such licences among supplying countries; Provided that there shall be no obligation to supply information as to the names of importing or supplying enterprises (Art. XIII (3)(a)). The provisions of the Article are made applicable to tariff quota instituted or maintained by any contracting party and, in so far as applicable, to export restrictions.

Exemptions from the non-discrimination law are provided in Article XIV:

> A contracting party which applies restrictions under Article XII or under Section B [preferential trade arrangements] of Article XVIII may, in the application of such

restrictions, deviate from the provisions of Article XIII in a manner having equivalent effect to restrictions on payments and transfers for current international transactions which that contracting party may at that time apply under Article VIII or XIV of the Articles of Agreement of the International Monetary Fund, or under analogous provisions of a special exchange agreement entered into pursuant to paragraph 6 of Article XV.

(Art. XIV: Exceptions to the Rule of Nondiscrimination)

8.4 (E) REGIONAL TRADE AGREEMENTS (RTAS) (ARTS. XXIV AND I)

Since the GATT convention did not prevent regional trade agreements, it could not nullify the provisions or the welfare benefits emanating from such agreements. The contracting parties agreed that there are economic advantages accruing to the frontier traffic of trade—contiguous trade in goods and services by adjacent (frontier) countries—especially when the arrangements enhance human welfare and promote peace and security.[32] The contracting parties recognize the desirability of increasing freedom of trade by the development, through voluntary agreements, of closer integration between the economies of the countries parties to such agreements. They also recognize that the purpose of a customs union or of a free trade area should be to facilitate trade between the constituent territories and not to raise barriers to the trade of other contracting parties with such territories (Art. XXIV(4)).

Therefore the Agreement does not impugn benefits that are derived from plurilateral agreements.

Accordingly, the provisions of the Agreement encourage territories of contracting parties to form customs unions and free-trade areas, or the adoption of interim agreements that are necessary for the formation of a customs union or of a free trade area, provided that discriminatory charges are not exorbitantly set above the general incidence of the duties and regulations of commerce that was applicable in the constituent territories prior to the formation of customs unions or the adoption of interim agreements. Similar provisions apply to free-trade areas.[33]

The provisions of paragraph 1 of this Article shall not require the elimination of any preferences in respect of import duties or charges which do not exceed the levels provided for in paragraph 4 of this Article and which fall within the following descriptions: (a) Preferences in force exclusively between two or more of the territories listed in Annex A, subject to the conditions set forth therein; (b) Preferences in force exclusively between two or more territories which on July 1, 1939, were connected by common sovereignty or relations of protection or suzerainty and which are listed in Annexes B, C and D, subject to the conditions set forth therein; (c) Preferences in force exclusively between the United States of America and the Republic of Cuba; (d) Preferences in force exclusively between neighbouring countries listed in Annexes E and F (Art. 1(2)(a)-(d)).

8.4 (F) AGREEMENT ON SUBSIDIES AND COUNTERVAILING MEASURES (SCM) (ART. XVI AND SCM)

When the GATT was constituted, it contained very general provisions on subsidy that were not far-reaching enough. Members were merely encouraged to notify one another and conduct consultations on the use of subsidies. As such, the law did not directly and broadly address countervailing duty laws that are related to subsidies.

If any contracting party grants or maintains any subsidy, including any form of income or price support, which operates directly or indirectly to increase exports of any product from, or to reduce imports of any product into, its territory, it shall notify the CONTRACTING PARTIES in writing of the extent and nature of the subsidization, of the estimated effect of the subsidization on the quantity of the affected product or products imported into or exported from its territory and of the circumstances making the subsidization necessary. In any case in which it is determined that serious prejudice to the interests of any other contracting party is caused or threatened by any such subsidization, the contracting party granting the subsidy shall, upon request, discuss with the other contracting party or parties concerned, or with the CONTRACTING PARTIES, the possibility of limiting the subsidization (Art. XVI(1)(A)).

The contracting parties recognized that export subsidies have harmful effects on other contracting members. Both importing and exporting subsidies can cause undue disturbances to the normal course of commerce and the commercial interests, and the subsidies can impede the achievement of the objectives of the trade Agreement. Consider the effects of import and export subsidies on a country that cannot significantly alter the world supply as depicted by Figure 8.8.

In Panel (a) of Figure 8.8, the target policy is to increase the quantity supplied while holding the domestic price comparable to the world price (P_w). However, the quantity of imports can be expected to fall from MP_1 to MP_2. The relative price stability can be

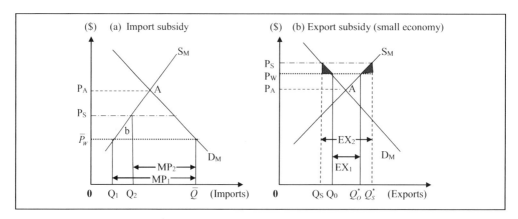

Figure 8.8 Import and export subsidies (Good M)

compared to the tariff (tax) effect depicted in Figure 8.4. Domestic producers can now produce more but, barring competition, the subsidy can cause detrimental inefficiencies in domestic production. Clearly, the law is intended to increase the volume of trade and market access.

Unlike Panel (a), Panel (b) shows the probable results of an export subsidy. It is noteworthy that the country is trading above its autarkic price (P_A) at P_W without a subsidy to exporters. Recall that the subsidy will not increase world supply in the case of small economies. The subsidy increases exports from EX_1 to EX_2, pushes the price of Good M from P_W to P_S, and reduces the domestic quantity consumed from Q_0 to Q_S. That is, the subsidy creates detrimental welfare effects. Producers gain and consumers lose (review consumer and producer surpluses in Chapter 1), resulting in a net loss that is equivalent to the shaded triangles.[34]

It is noteworthy that subsidies may take several forms, including direct and indirect formats of price support (price floors). Though the original Agreement alludes to "products," primary products were granted specific attention. More so, the maintenance of equitable market share was required on occasions of the unilateral application of export subsidies: accordingly, contracting parties should seek to avoid the use of export subsidies on the export of primary products. If, however, a contracting party grants directly or indirectly any form of subsidy which operates to increase the export of any primary product from its territory, such subsidy shall not be applied in a manner which results in that contracting party having more than an equitable share of world export trade in that product, account being taken of the shares of the contracting parties in such trade in the product during a previous representative period, and any special factors which may have affected or may be affecting such trade in the product (Art. XVI(3)).

In the 1940s, the multilateral Agreement neither incorporated the service sector nor the concept of intellectual property rights in the provision of subsidies. The Agreement on subsidies and countervailing measures (SCM) that emanated from the Uruguay Round of talks (1986–1994) was much more comprehensive and consequential. It imposes tighter constraints and binds all members. The decision to tighten restrictions on subsidization has been partly attributed to recessionary conditions and rising government deficits during the negotiating period (Trebilcock, Howse, & Eliason, 2013, p. 367).

The definition and types of subsidies are precisely stipulated: grants, loans, equity infusions, loan guarantees, tax credits, purchase of goods, and the use of proxies to provide material benefits.

For the purpose of this Agreement, a subsidy shall be deemed to exist if: (a)(1) there is a financial contribution by a government or any public body within the territory of a Member (referred to in this Agreement as "government"), i.e. where: (i) a government practice involves a direct transfer of funds (e.g. grants, loans, and equity infusion), potential direct transfers of funds or liabilities (e.g. loan guarantees); (ii) government revenue that is otherwise due is foregone or not collected (e.g. fiscal incentives such as tax credits); (iii) a government provides goods or services other than general infrastructure, or purchases goods; (iv) a government makes payments to a funding mechanism, or entrusts or directs a private body to carry out one or more of the type of functions illustrated in (i) to (iii) above which would normally be vested in the government and the practice, in no real sense, differs from practices normally followed by governments; or (a)(2) there is any form of income or price support in the sense of Article XVI of GATT 1994; and (b) a benefit is thereby conferred (Art. 1.1(a)(1)-(a)(2)(b)).

The application of the subsidy law requires specificity that appertains to an enterprise, enterprises, industry, or group of industries that are generically referred to as "certain enterprises" within the jurisdiction of the granting authority. The controlling principles are applicable to specificity:

> (b) Where the granting authority, or the legislation pursuant to which the granting authority operates, establishes objective criteria or conditions[35] governing the eligibility for, and the amount of, a subsidy, specificity shall not exist, provided that the eligibility is automatic and that such criteria and conditions are strictly adhered to. The criteria or conditions must be clearly spelled out in law, regulation, or other official document, so as to be capable of verification.
>
> (c) If, notwithstanding any appearance of non-specificity resulting from the application of the principles laid down in subparagraphs (a) and (b), there are reasons to believe that the subsidy may in fact be specific, other factors may be considered. Such factors are: use of a subsidy programme by a limited number of certain enterprises, predominant use by certain enterprises, the granting of disproportionately large amounts of subsidy to certain enterprises, and the manner in which discretion has been exercised by the granting authority in the decision to grant a subsidy. In applying this subparagraph, account shall be taken of the extent of diversification of economic activities within the jurisdiction of the granting authority, as well as of the length of time during which the subsidy programme has been in operation.
>
> (Art. 2.1(a)-(c))

To lawfully evaluate material benefits and injury, contemporary subsidies can be classified under three broad headings: (i) Nonactionable subsidies, (ii) Prohibited subsidies, and (iii) Actionable subsidies. Research-oriented subsidies may be nonactionable when they are not specific within the meaning of Article 2, but also when they are contracted by firms even within the meaning of Article 2. The research assistance must cover no more than 75 percent of the cost of industrial research or 50 percent of the cost of pre-competitive development activity. Additionally, the assistance must be limited exclusively to: (i) costs of personnel—researchers, technicians, and other supporting staff—employed exclusively in the research activity; (ii) costs of instruments, equipment, land and buildings used exclusively and permanently (except when disposed of on a commercial basis) for the research activity; (iii) costs of consultancy and equivalent services used exclusively for the research activity, including bought-in research, technical knowledge, patents, etc.;

(iv) additional overhead costs incurred directly as a result of the research activity; (v) other running costs (such as those of materials, supplies and the like), incurred directly as a result of the research activity (Art. 8(2)(a)(i)-(v)). The allowable levels of non-actionable assistance allude to the total eligible costs incurred over the duration of an individual project.[36]

Exemptions also apply to disadvantaged regions of a Member state when the disadvantaged region is: (i) clearly designated to be a contiguous geographical area with a definable economic and administrative identity; (ii) considered as disadvantaged on the basis of neutral and objective criteria, indicating that the region's difficulties arise out of more than temporary circumstances, which must be clearly spelled out in law, regulation, or other official document, for verification; and (iii) considered to be in want of development based on income per capita, or household income per capita, or GDP per capita, which must not be above 85 percent of the average for the territory concerned.

With the exception of Agreement on Agriculture, prohibited subsidies meet the specificity criterion and are contingent on law or fact (Art. 3(1)).

The prohibition standard is met when the facts demonstrate that the granting of a subsidy, without having been made legally contingent upon export performance, is in fact tied to actual or anticipated exportation or export earnings. Actionable subsidies are injurious subsidies. As such, the adverse subsidies generate damaging effects on the domestic industries of other Member, cause a nullification or impairment of the benefits accruing directly or indirectly to other Members, and are the results of serious prejudice to the interests of other Members (Art. 5).

Serious prejudice exists when a subsidy is intended to cover: (a) the total *ad valorem* of a product exceeding 5 percent (which does not apply to the civil aircraft industry); (b) operating losses incurred by an industry; (c) operating losses sustained by an enterprise, other than one-time measures which are non-recurrent and cannot be repeated for that enterprise, but which are also given merely to provide time for the development of long-term solutions to avoid acute social problems and (d) government-held debt, including grants to cover debt repayment (direct forgiveness of debt) (Art. 6.1(a)-(d)).[37]

Serious prejudice may also arise in any case where one or several of the following apply:

(a) the effect of the subsidy is to displace or impede the imports of a like product of another Member into the market of the subsidizing Member;
(b) the effect of the subsidy is to displace or impede the exports of a like product of another Member from a third country market;
(c) the effect of the subsidy is a significant price undercutting by the subsidized product as compared with the price of a like product of another Member in the same market or significant price suppression, price depression or lost sales in the same market;
(d) the effect of the subsidy is an increase in the world market share of the subsidizing Member in a particular subsidized primary product or commodity as compared to

the average share it had during the previous period of three years and this increase follows a consistent trend over a period when subsidies have been granted (Art. 6.3(a)-(d)).

8.5 THE WTO'S DISPUTE SETTLEMENT UNDERSTANDING (DSU)

Trade disputes are inevitable occurrences of international trade as some nations overzealously try to pursue their national interests. Although dispute among nations is a timeless occurrence, it was not until the 1920s that the Permanent Court of International Justice (PCIJ) provided a functional and legal definition. "A dispute is a disagreement on a point of law or fact, a conflict of legal views or of interests between two persons" *Mavrommatis Palestine Concessions Case (Jurisdiction)*, (1924) PCIJ, Ser. A, No. 2 at 11. In the process of deriving maximum benefits from trade, they deliberately or inadvertently deviate from reasonable expectations and agreements or rules of international trade. While earlier agreements were less successful in resolving international trade disputes equitably, the WTO's Dispute Settlement Understanding (DSU) has provided a structured and consequential framework for peacefully resolving bilateral and plurilateral international trade disputes. The rules and procedures of the DSU apply to the use of consultations, mediation, good offices, and trade tribunals, including an appellate provision.

The dispute settlement system of the WTO is a central element in providing security and predictability to the multilateral trading system. The Members recognize that it serves to preserve the rights and obligations of Members under the covered agreements, and to clarify the existing provisions of those agreements in accordance with customary rules of interpretation of public international law. Recommendations and rulings of the DSB cannot add to or diminish the rights and obligations provided in the covered agreements (Art. 3(2)).

Before initiating a case, a Member country is expected to exercise proactive judgment as to whether its case is viable under the dispute settlement procedures. The fundamental objective of the dispute settlement mechanism is to secure a mutually acceptable solution that is positive and consistent with the covered agreements. In the absence of a mutually agreed solution, the first objective of the dispute settlement mechanism is usually to secure the withdrawal of the measures concerned if these are found to be inconsistent with the provisions of any of the covered agreements (Art. 3(7)).

To resolve international disputes and implement trade laws, the Dispute Settlement Body (DSB) was established, except as otherwise provided in a covered agreement. As such, the DSB has the authority to establish panels, adopt panel and Appellate Body (AB) reports, maintain surveillance of implementation of rulings and recommendations, and authorize suspension of concessions and other obligations under the covered agreements. With respect to disputes arising under a covered agreement which is a Plurilateral

Trade Agreement, only those Members that are parties to the relevant Plurilateral Trade Agreement will have standing in the dispute resolution process. Accordingly, when the DSB administers the dispute settlement provisions of a Plurilateral Trade Agreement, only those Members that are parties to that Agreement may participate in decisions or actions taken by the DSB with respect to that dispute (Art. 2(1)).

At a very fundamental level, the dispute resolution process starts with consultations. Consultations are not expected to be contentious and they should not be perceived as such. All Members are required to engage in consultations with one another in good faith to bring about the resolution of disputes and counter-complaints should be considered distinct (Art. 3(10)).

Except when there is a mutual agreement to initiate consultations after 10 days, a Member that has received a request for consultations must reply to the request within 10 days from the receipt of the request, and must enter into consultations no later than 30 days after the date of the request. If the Member does not respond within ten days after the date of receipt of the request, or does not enter into consultations within a period of no more than 30 days, or a period otherwise mutually agreed, after the date of receipt of the request, then the Member that requested the holding of consultations may proceed directly to request the establishment of a panel (Art. 4(3)).

A Member requesting consultations must notify the DSB and the relevant Councils and Committees that are facilitating the resolution of the dispute (Art. 4(4)). Consultations must be confidential and Members are expected to resolve trade disputes during the consultation process to avoid nonprejudicial escalation. During consultations Members are expected to give special attention to specific problems and interests of developing country Members (Art. 4(10)). If the consultations fail to settle a dispute within 60 days after the date of receipt of the request for consultations, the complaining party may request the establishment of a panel. The complaining party may request a panel during the 60-day period if the consulting parties jointly consider that consultations have failed to settle the dispute (Art. 4(7)).[38]

Cases involving perishable goods are considered to be urgent and Members must enter into consultations no later than 10 days after the receipt of a request for consultations. If the consultations have failed to settle the dispute within a period of 20 days after the date of receipt of the request, the complaining party may request the establishment of a panel (Art. 4(8)). Panels and the AB are also expected to expedite dispute proceedings.

Apart from consultations, Members may voluntarily also use good offices, conciliation and mediation to resolve their trade disputes (Art. 5(1)). The proceedings involving the lower level channels of resolution are confidential and they do not prejudice the rights of the disputing parties to escalate the mechanisms of resolution. Good offices, conciliation or mediation may be requested at any time by any party to a dispute and the Director-General may, acting in an ex officio capacity, offer good offices, conciliation or mediation with the view to assisting Members to resolve their disputes (Art. 5(6)). The resolution procedures may begin and be terminated at any time. Once procedures for good offices, conciliation or mediation are terminated, a complaining party may then proceed with a request for the establishment of a panel (Art. 5(3)). Subject to the mutual agreement of the disputing parties, conciliation or mediation may continue even when the panel process is in progress (Art. 5(5)).

If necessary, the DSB may decide by consensus not to establish a panel. If the DSB decides to establish a panel, the panel will be established during the first meeting for which the issue is on the agenda after the receipt of request for a panel in writing (Art. 6(1)-(2)).[39] The panels are made up of well-qualified governmental and/or non-governmental individuals, including persons who have served on or presented a case to a panel, served as a representative of a Member or of a contracting party to GATT 1947 or as a representative to the Council or Committee of any covered agreement or its predecessor agreement, or in the Secretariat, taught or published on international trade law or policy, or served as a senior trade policy official of a Member (Art. 8(1)).

The Secretariat will propose nominations for panels to the disputing parties, keeping in mind that the panel members should be selected to ensure the independence of highly qualified members, a sufficiently diverse background, and a wide spectrum of experience (Arts. 8(2) and (6)). Notably, the parties to the dispute cannot oppose nominations except for compelling reasons (Art. 8(6)). Unless the parties to a dispute request five panelists within ten days from the establishment of a panel, the panels will be composed of three panelists (Art. 8(5)).

If there is no agreement on the panelists within 20 days after the date of the establishment of a panel, at the request of either party, the Director-General, in consultation with the Chairman of the DSB and the Chairman of the relevant Council or Committee, shall determine the composition of the panel by appointing the panelists whom the Director-General considers most appropriate in accordance with any relevant special or additional rules or procedures of the covered agreement or covered agreements which are at issue in the dispute, after consulting with the parties to the dispute. The Chairman of the DSB shall inform the Members of the composition of the panel thus formed no later than 10 days after the date the Chairman receives such a request (Art. 8(7)).

On occasions when more than one Member requests the establishment of a panel for the same matter, a single panel may be established to examine these complaints taking into account the rights of all Members concerned. A single panel should be established to examine such complaints whenever feasible (Art. 9(1)). The single panel will organize its examination and present its findings to the DSB in such a manner that is protective of the rights of the disputants and consistent with the results of a multiplicity of panels. However, if more than one panel is established to examine the complaints related to multiple members and the same matter, to the greatest extent possible the same persons shall serve as panelists on each of the separate panels and the timetable for the panel process in such disputes shall be harmonized (Art. 9(3)). Any Member having a substantial interest in a matter before a panel [third party] and having notified its interest to the DSB will have an opportunity to be heard by the panel and to make written submissions to the panel. These submissions shall also be given to the parties to the dispute and shall be reflected in the panel report (Art. 10(2)).

Each party to the dispute shall deposit its written submissions with the Secretariat for immediate transmission to the panel and to the other party or parties to the dispute. The complaining party shall submit its first submission in advance of the responding party's first submission unless the panel decides, in fixing the timetable referred to in paragraph 3 and after consultations with the parties to the dispute, that the parties should submit their first submissions simultaneously. When there are sequential arrangements for the deposit of first submissions, the panel shall establish a firm time-period for receipt of the responding party's submission. Any subsequent written submissions shall be submitted simultaneously (Art. 12(6)).

If the disputants fail to resolve their disputes and a panel is established, the panel will confidentially deliberate and submit its findings in the form of a written report to the DSB. In such cases, the report of a panel shall set out the findings of fact, the applicability of relevant provisions and the basic rationale behind any findings and recommendations that it makes. Where a settlement of the matter among the parties to the dispute has been found, the report of the panel shall be confined to a brief description of the case and to reporting that a solution has been reached (Art. 12(7)).[40] The reports of panels shall be drafted without the presence of the parties to the dispute in the light of the information provided and the statements made (Art. 14(2)) and opinions expressed in the panel report by individual panelists will be anonymous (Art. 14(3)).

Following the findings of the panels, the panels will produce a draft report for review, to which the disputing parties may provide written responses within a specified period to be determined by the panels. At the expiration of such a period, the panel will issue an interim report to the parties, including both the descriptive sections and the panel's findings and conclusions. Within a period of time set by the panel, a party may submit a written request for the panel to review precise aspects of the interim report prior to circulation of the final report to the Members (Art. 15(2)). The panel reports will be distributed by the DSB, but Members will have 20 days after distribution before they can consider the reports for consideration. Members who have objections to a panel report shall give written reasons to explain their objections for circulation at least ten days prior to the DSB meeting at which the panel report will be considered (Art. 16(2)).

Within 60 days after the date of circulation of a panel report to the Members, the report shall be adopted at a DSB meeting unless a party to the dispute formally notifies the DSB of its decision to appeal or the DSB decides by consensus not to adopt the report. If a party has notified its decision to appeal, the report by the panel shall not be considered for adoption by the DSB until after completion of the appeal. This adoption procedure is without prejudice to the right of Members to express their views on a panel report (Art. 16(4)).

The DSB appoints persons to serve on the Appellate Body (AB) for a four-year term, and each person may be reappointed once. The Appellate Body hears appeals from panel cases and it is composed of seven persons, three of whom are expected to serve on any one case. To prevent conflict of interests and preserve the integrity of the resolution procedures, disputants and parties with vested interest will not be considered (Art. 17(3)). Vacancies are filled as they arise and a person who has been appointed to replace someone whose term of office has not expired shall hold office for the remainder of the predecessor's term (Art. 17(2)). Only parties to the dispute, not third parties, may appeal a panel report.[41] An appeal shall be limited to issues of law covered in the panel report and legal interpretations developed by the panel (Art. 17(6)). Third parties which have notified the DSB of a substantial interest in the matter may make written submissions to, and be given an opportunity to be heard by, the Appellate Body (Art. 17(4)).

As a general rule, the proceedings shall not exceed 60 days from the date a party to the dispute formally notifies its decision to appeal to the date the Appellate Body circulates its report. In fixing its timetable the Appellate Body shall take into account the provisions of paragraph 9 of Article 4, if relevant. When the Appellate Body considers that it cannot provide its report within 60 days, it shall inform the DSB in writing of the reasons for the delay together with an estimate of the period within which it will submit its report. In no case shall the proceedings exceed 90 days (Art. 17(5)).

An Appellate Body report shall be adopted by the DSB and unconditionally accepted by the parties to the dispute unless the DSB decides by consensus not to adopt the Appellate Body report within 30 days following its circulation to the Members. This adoption procedure is without prejudice to the right of Members to express their views on an Appellate Body report (Art. 17(14)). When a panel or AB concludes that a measure is inconsistent with a covered agreement, it shall recommend that the Member concerned bring the measure into conformity with that agreement. In addition to its findings and recommendations, the panel or Appellate Body may suggest ways in which the Member concerned could implement the recommendations (Art. 19(1)) without adding to or diminishing the rights and obligations of Members provided in the covered agreements (Art. 19(2)).

Unless otherwise agreed to by the parties to the dispute, the period from the date of establishment of the panel by the DSB until the date the DSB considers the panel or appellate report for adoption shall as a general rule not exceed nine months where the panel report is not appealed or 12 months where the report is appealed. Where either the panel or the Appellate Body has acted, pursuant to paragraph 9 of Article 12 or paragraph 5 of Article 17, to extend the time for providing its report, the additional time taken shall be added to the above periods (Art. 20).[42] Members are expected to promptly comply with the recommendations or rulings of the DSB in order to ensure effective resolution of disputes to the benefit of all Members (Art. 21(1)). However, particular attention should be paid to matters affecting the interest of developing country members in dispute settlements.

At a DSB meeting held within 30 days after the date of adoption of the panel or Appellate Body report, the Member concerned shall inform the DSB of its intentions in respect of implementation of the recommendations and rulings of the DSB. If it is impracticable to comply immediately with the recommendations and rulings, the Member concerned shall have a reasonable period of time in which to do so. The reasonable period of time shall be: (a) the period of time proposed by the Member concerned, provided that such period is approved by the DSB; or, in the absence of such approval, (b) a period of time mutually agreed by the parties to the dispute within 45 days after the date of adoption of the recommendations and rulings; or, in the absence of such agreement, (c) a period of time determined through binding arbitration within 90 days after the date of adoption of the recommendations and rulings). In such arbitration, a guideline for the arbitrator should be that the reasonable period of time to implement panel or Appellate Body recommendations should not exceed 15 months from the date of adoption of a panel or Appellate Body report. However, that time may be shorter or longer, depending upon the particular circumstances (Art. 21(3)).[43]

The DSB shall keep under surveillance the implementation of adopted recommendations or rulings. The issue of implementation of the recommendations or rulings may be raised at the DSB by any Member at any time following their adoption. Unless the DSB decides otherwise, the issue of implementation of the recommendations or rulings shall be placed on the agenda of the DSB meeting after six months following the date of establishment of the reasonable period of time pursuant to paragraph 3 and shall remain on the DSB's agenda until the issue is resolved. At least 10 days prior to each such DSB meeting, the Member concerned shall provide the DSB with a status report in writing of its progress in the implementation of the recommendations or rulings (Art. 21(6)). If the matter is one which has been raised by a developing country Member, the DSB shall consider what further action it might take which would be appropriate to the circumstances (Art. 21(7)).

As a temporary outcome of the trade resolution process, Members may be compensated (when they have been wronged) or have their preferential benefits (concessions) suspended (when they are in violation of the terms of an agreement). If the Member concerned fails to bring the measure found to be inconsistent with a covered agreement into compliance therewith or otherwise comply with the recommendations and rulings within the reasonable period of time determined pursuant to paragraph 3 of Article 21 [below], such Member shall, if so requested, and no later than the expiry of the reasonable period of time, enter into negotiations with any party having invoked the dispute settlement procedures, with a view to developing mutually acceptable compensation. If no satisfactory compensation has been agreed within 20 days after the date of expiry of the reasonable period of time, any party having invoked the dispute settlement procedures may request authorization from the DSB to suspend the application to the Member concerned of concessions or other obligations under the covered agreements (Art. 22(2)).

In considering what concessions or other obligations to suspend, the complaining party shall apply the following principles and procedures:

(a) the general principle is that the complaining party should first seek to suspend concessions or other obligations with respect to the same sector(s) as that in which the panel or Appellate Body has found a violation or other nullification or impairment; (b) if that party considers that it is not practicable or effective to suspend concessions or other obligations with respect to the same sector(s), it may seek to suspend concessions or other obligations in other sectors under the same agreement; (c) if that party considers that it is not practicable or effective to suspend concessions or other obligations with respect to other sectors under the same agreement, and that the circumstances are serious enough, it may seek to suspend concessions or other obligations under another covered agreement; (d) in applying the above principles, that party shall take into account: (i) the trade in the sector or under the agreement under which the panel or Appellate Body has found a violation or other nullification or impairment, and the importance of such trade to that party; (ii) the broader economic elements related to the nullification or impairment and the broader economic consequences of the suspension of concessions or other obligations;

(e) if that party decides to request authorization to suspend concessions or other obligations pursuant to subparagraphs (b) or (c), it shall state the reasons therefor in its request. At the same time as the request is forwarded to the DSB, it also shall be forwarded to the relevant Councils and also, in the case of a request pursuant to subparagraph (b), the relevant sectoral bodies.

(Art. 22(3))

In disputes involving rules and procedures under more than one covered agreement, if there is a conflict between special or additional rules and procedures of such agreements under review, and where the parties to the dispute cannot agree on rules and procedures within 20 days of the establishment of the panel, the Chairman of the Dispute Settlement Body provided for in paragraph 1 of Article 2 … in consultation with the parties to the dispute, shall determine the rules and procedures to be followed within 10 days after a request by either Member. The Chairman shall be guided by the principle that special or additional rules and procedures should be used where possible, and the rules and procedures set out in this Understanding should be used to the extent necessary to avoid conflict (Art. 1(2)).

8.6 APPLICATIONS OF ECONOMIC LAW TO TRADE DISPUTES

International trade disputes have covered a wide range of issues, including subsidy, dumping, illegal tariffs, trade discrimination, retaliatory measures, policies that are based

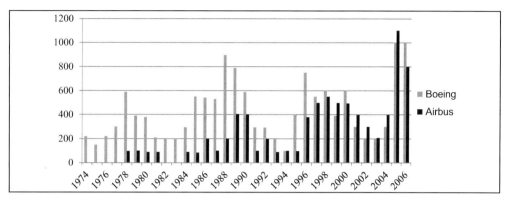

Figure 8.9 Boeing v. Airbus commercial aircraft orders (1974–2006)
Source: Heyman (2007) (deliveries have been excluded).

on contingent revenues, the limits of investigating authorities, similar products, the cost of production, material injury, and exemptions. Since this section cannot possibly cover the scope of international trade disputes, it will only present a limited but significant amount of cases that have gone through the DSU or dispute settlement mechanism (DSM). The cases have been selected because they have been considered to be pertinent to economic theory and international law.

8.6 (A) EXPORT SUBSIDY

On several fronts the *Boeing v. Airbus Case* presents a variety of interesting concepts. At a very fundamental level, it is a case in which the prime-mover advantage of Boeing (an American company) that was unchallenged for several years was all of a sudden challenged by a consortium of European states. Figure 8.9 mirrors the advantage of Boeing from the 1970s to the start of the 1990s. Therefore, until the late 1990s, Airbus was not very competitive in the duopolistic market structure. However, by the start of the twenty-first century the company started to make significant inroads into the commercial aircraft market. Why? According to the US, the European Community provided launch aid to Airbus that detrimentally affected the operations and profitability of Boeing. Actually, some researchers believe that the response to the American dominance (monopoly) started in the late 1960s when the European nations created a European organization that could rival the American aircraft industry (Kienstra, 2012, p. 75).

As competition between the two companies intensified and as Airbus continued to receive subsidy for competitive advantage, the companies decided to engage in negotiations about the support for the production of large commercial aircraft. In 1979, the Tokyo Round of talks provided a code for subsidizing civil aircraft. It also generated a plurilateral Agreement on Trade in Civil Aircraft (ATCA) and the US started negotiations with the EC in the 1980s. An overarching objective of the Tokyo Round was to achieve freer trade or competitiveness, and a reasonable amount of fairer trade, including elimination of governmental support for the development, production, and marketing of civil aircraft that generates injurious effects or material injury.

In 1992, a supplemental bilateral treaty on trade in Large Civil Aircraft (LCA) between the US and the EC extended agreements that were reached in the 1970s. The Uruguay Round of talks, which ran from 1986 to 1994, ultimately created a subsidy and countervailing measures agreement and the dispute settlement mechanism that was presented in the previous section; the GATT was not very successful in dealing with trade disputes and aircraft negotiations often ended in a stalemate without much resolution. The Bilateral Agreement on Trade in Large Civil Aircraft (1992) banned future production subsidies and limited development subsidies to 33 percent of a new plane's total development costs. However, the agreement provided no remedy for breach and the only recourse for noncompliance was abrogation of the agreement.[44] Although A GATT disputes panel found in favor of the United States in January 1992, the EC blocked adoption of the ruling in the GATT council, thereby precluding any remedy (Kienstra, 2012, p. 580).[45]

While multiple negotiations between the US and the EC were conducted in the 1990s, the concept of subsidy was multilaterally imprecise until one was provided by the SCM Agreement during the Uruguay Round of talks:

> A subsidy exists where—there is a financial contribution by a government, and—a benefit is thereby conferred. Financial contribution is broadly construed as meaning—money or anything else of value provided to a manufacturer or exporter at a cost less than would have been charged in a commercial transaction. This includes measures such as exchange rate guarantees, debt forgiveness, export credits, and equity infusions, and any capital or development supports provided on terms more favorable than terms available from commercial lenders. In addition, this can also include indirect support such as benefits from government or defense contracts.
> (Kienstra, 2012, p. 583)

Newer agreements meant newer negotiating framework and contending reference points, which further complicated negotiations. While the Uruguay Round, as it was signed on December 15, 1994, did not include a new agreement on civil aircraft, the SCM Agreement and the DSU included the LCA industry.

In the SCM Agreement, subsidies fall into three broad classifications: (i) permissible, (ii) actionable, and (iii) prohibited; the so-called "green, yellow, and red lights." Contingent subsidies (in law or fact) are prohibited subsidies. Prohibited subsidies are based on prospective export performance and are intended to give firms a competitive edge while also increasing their revenue base. Actionable (specific) subsidies cause adverse effects on free trade (see Figure 8.8 Panel (b)). Specific subsidies are injurious; they cause nullification and create serious prejudice to the interests of other Members. Serious prejudice occurs when a subsidy displaces or impedes imports into the subsidizing country or a third country market. The subsidy must also cause significant price undercutting, suppression, depression, or increase the world market share of the subsidizing country that causes loss to others.[46]

The subsidy criteria have been variously adjudicated by WTO panels and the Appellate Body (AB). The AB in *Canada – Aircraft* (July 2000) identified three elements for subsidy contingency: (i) the granting of a subsidy, (ii) tying the subsidy to something of value, and (iii) anticipated benefits.[47] The initial inquiry is premised on whether the granting authority imposed a condition based on export performance when providing the subsidy. The AB finds that the treaty obligation is imposed on the granting Member, and not on the recipient.

The second element is the linkage of contingency with conditionality, which means that a relationship of conditionality or dependence must be demonstrated. "In any given case, the facts must 'demonstrate' that the granting of a subsidy is tied to or contingent upon actual or anticipated exports."[48] The court noted that the third substantive element is anticipated or expected export. Yet the element of expectation must be gleaned from an examination of objective evidence and not mere conjecture. The objective evidence is tied to the expectation of exports.

The elements are used to distinguish lawful subsidy from unlawful subsidy. In *Canada – Aircraft* (Article 21.5 – Brazil), the AB noted:

> [It is] worth recalling that the granting of a subsidy is not, in and of itself, prohibited under the SCM Agreement. Nor does granting a "subsidy", without more, constitute an inconsistency with that Agreement. The universe of subsidies is vast. Not all subsidies are inconsistent with the SCM Agreement. The only "prohibited" subsidies are those identified in Article 3 of the SCM Agreement.
> (Appellate Body Report, Canada – Aircraft (Article 21.5 – Brazil), para. 47)

Without successful negotiations with the EC, the US unilaterally renounced its trade agreement with the EC and started a dispute resolution within the structure of the WTO's dispute settlement mechanism. The US complained that the EC violated treaty obligations by providing launch aid to Airbus. On the same day, EC counter-filed a separate complaint in the WTO against the United States, alleging that Boeing received prohibited government subsidies in the form of tax breaks and preferential government contracts (Kienstra, 2012, p. 570). The US complaint, which was centered on launch aid, alleged that the loans to Airbus were provided at no-interest or below-market interest rates. Further, the repayment arrangement was contingent on the success of the aircraft being funded, which enhanced the prospects of projects that would not have been commercially feasible. The United States alleged that this financing accounted for one hundred percent of the development costs of the A300 family, up to 90 percent for the A320, 60 to 90 percent for the A330 and A340, and one-third of the development costs for the A380 (Kienstra, 2012, p. 588).

The US estimated the subsidies for the A380 alone, which included government grants, goods, and services to develop, expand, and upgrade manufacturing sites, and preferential terms for research and development (R&D), to be about $6.5 billion. The US alleged that Airbus received $22 billion in illegal subsidies. US officials estimated the economic benefit of those subsidies (in 2006 dollars) to be more than $200 billion.[49]

The EC's counter-complaint alleged that Boeing received just under $5 billion in benefits from the states of Washington and Kansas relating to the 787 Dreamliner and $25 million from the State of Illinois and City of Chicago for the relocation of its headquarters. In addition, the complaint alleged Boeing received over $16 billion in indirect subsidies in the form of R&D and procurement contracts with NASA, the Department of Defense, and the National Institute of Standards and Technology, an agency of the US Department of Commerce; all of which amounted to subsidies to LCA, because of undue benefits from intellectual property rights, data access, trade secrets, and benefits from government-funded research. Finally, the complaint alleged that Boeing benefited in the amount of over $2 billion from special tax treatment for Foreign Sales Corporations under the Internal Revenue Code. These alleged subsidies totaled $23.7 billion (Kienstra, 2012, p. 589).

The complaints subsequently went through the DSU process with some specific rulings on points of law, facts, and economic losses. On July 20, 2005, the DSB established separate panels for the two proceedings, designated as DS316 for the complaint by the United States and DS317 for the complaint by the EC. On October 17, 2005, the Director-General determined the composition of the panels since the disputants could not arrive at a consensus (see Art. 8.7 of the DSU). As a result of the objection of the US over the scope of inquiry, a third panel, DS353, was established.[50]

As far as the case (DS316) against Airbus was concerned, the panel found substantial amounts of subsidies to Airbus. The launch aid measures were considered to be subsidies. The Panel also found that 14 of the 17 challenged provisions of infrastructure and infrastructure-related grants were specific subsidies, including the provision of manufacturing sites in Hamburg and Toulouse, a runway extension at the Bremen Airport in Germany, and grants from Germany and Spain for manufacturing and assembly facilities (Kienstra, 2012, p. 594). French equity infusion and various forms of technological transfer were also considered to be specific subsidies. The Panel found that the subsidies had caused adverse effects of serious prejudice to the United States' interests under Article 6.3 of the SCM Agreement by displacing imports and exports and causing significant loss of revenue.

The subsidies enabled Airbus to launch, sell, and deliver aircraft to the EC and third country markets (see Figure 8.9). However, while the adverse effects were sufficient to make the subsidies actionable, the Panel did not find that the subsidies caused adverse effects of price undercutting, suppression, or depression under Article 6.3(c) of the SCM Agreement, or injury to the US domestic industry under Article 5(a) of the SCM Agreement. Accordingly, the panel concluded and recommended for adoption that the subsidies must be withdrawn without delay.

The case found its way to the AB as both parties filed appeals. The EC disagreed with various conclusions that the launch aid, infrastructure measures, and equity infusions constituted specific subsidies with prejudicial effects. The US disagreed with the finding that no launch aid program existed that would bring future launch aid to the A350 into the scope of the complaint, and that the launch aid did not constitute prohibited export subsidies except for the A380 (Kienstra, 2012, p. 596).

The AB panel upheld the Panel's conclusion that the launch aid measures were specific subsidies, but reversed the conclusion that the launch aid for the A380 constituted an export subsidy. The AB also reversed some of the Panel conclusions about infrastructure and R&D measures. Some capital investments and R&D programs were considered to be specific subsidies. The AB concluded and recommended that the EC bring its measures in to conformity with its obligations under the SCM Agreement, based on the findings of the Panel and the modification by the AB. On December 1, 2011, the EC notified the DSB that it had taken appropriate steps to conform with the DSB recommendations and its WTO obligations. The US disagreed and requested compliance measures, including countermeasures to the tune of about $10 billion.[51]

In the case against the US, the Panel found that some of the measures from Washington, Kansas, and Illinois, and municipalities therein constituted specific subsidies, including tax breaks from Washington and Kansas, and a headquarters relocation incentive package from Illinois and the City of Chicago.[52] Further, the Panel found that various NASA aeronautics R&D programs constituted specific subsidies to Boeing in the amount of $2.6 billion.[53]

The Panel also found that Boeing received prohibited export subsidies in the form of foreign sales corporation (FSC) tax benefits in the amount of $2.199 billion. Additionally

Table 8.2 Rulings of the panels and appellate body

EC Specific Subsidies (DS316)	US Specific Subsidies (DS353)
Launch aid*	FSC tax breaks**
Infrastructure-related grants	Research and development
Equity infusion	
Research and development	

Notes:
* Of each of these measures that the Panel found to be specific subsidies, the Panel found only the launch aid provisions by three of the four Airbus nations to the A380 to be in the category of prohibited subsidies as export subsidies. The remaining launch aid subsidies were not held to be contingent on either law or fact upon anticipated export performance, so they were not held to be prohibited subsidies. The remaining launch aid subsidies and the rest of the specific subsidies required a showing of adverse effects to be actionable (Kienstra, 2012, p. 594).
** The Panel also found that Boeing received prohibited export subsidies under foreign sales corporation (FSC) tax benefits in the amount of $2.199 billion, but declined to make a recommendation as to those because they were subject to a previous WTO adjudication. FSC, which allowed for a reduction in taxes on income derived from sales of exported goods, is now a defunct provision in the US federal income tax code.

the Panel found that some subsidies caused the adverse effects of serious prejudice to the interests of another member by displacement, significant price suppression, and significant lost sales. The Panel also concluded and recommended that the US take appropriate steps to remove the adverse effects by withdrawing the subsidies. The EC and the US appealed the findings.

The US disagreed that certain state and local tax benefits and aspects of Boeing's NASA and Department of Defense contracts constituted subsidies, and therefore appealed the conclusions of adverse effects that were premised on the measures. The EC disagreed that certain transfers of intellectual property rights and purchases of services did not constitute subsidies, and that the Panel should have considered the total effect of the subsidies when making a determination of adverse effects. With minor modifications, the AB upheld most of the Panel's determinations of subsidies and adverse effects. Accordingly, the AB concluded and recommended that the US must remove the adverse effects by withdrawing the subsidies. On March 23, 2012, the US reported that it had fully complied with the recommendations and rulings of the DSU. However, the EC disagreed and on September 27, 2012, it requested authorization to impose countermeasures against the US amounting to $12 billion annually to offset continuing adverse effects of the subsidies. Such requests are consistent with the initiation of DSU process; in this instance, as a matter of enforcement.

The Boeing-Airbus dispute has become an epic trade issue. In February 2015, the EU brought a tax break case to the WTO, because Washington State enacted a tax break law to attract new investment in aerospace companies. While the WTO dismissed most of the claims, the EU temporarily prevailed on a "claw back" provision, considered to be a prohibited subsidy. However, the AB reversed the decision since the tax incentives were not considered to be prohibited subsidy. Nevertheless, in 2019, the AB upheld a decision that the US had not enforced a subsidy order to stop Washington State tax breaks. In May 2018, the AB had upheld a 2016 ruling that the EU had failed to eliminate billions in illegal aid to Airbus on two aircraft, the A380 superjumbo and the A350 twin aisle jet. It seems unlikely that the subsidy dispute will taper anytime soon as two companies in a duopolistic industry fight for competitive edge. Can trade law be consequential in this case? How?

8.6 (B) DUMPING

A somewhat clearer interpretation of salient aspects of international dumping law was provided by the *US–Hot-Rolled Steel Case*. The case is significant because it alludes to the definition of dumping, provides a mechanism for the estimation of the margins of dumping, and defines the meaning of the "ordinary course of trade."

On October 15, 1998, the United States Department of Commerce ("USDOC") initiated an anti-dumping investigation into imports of hot-rolled steel from, among others, Japan. Since it was impractical to examine all known Japanese producers and exporters, the US conducted a sample of the activities of Japanese producers.[54] The

USDOC calculated an individual dumping margin for each of these companies by establishing a single rate of anti-dumping duty that was made applicable to all Japanese producers and exporters, including those that were not individually investigated ("all others," et al.). Based on Panel Report, the "et al." rate was calculated as the weighted average of the individual dumping margins calculated for KSC, NSC, and NKK.[55] On May 6, 1999, USDOC published its final affirmative dumping determination.[56] On June 23, 1999, the United States International Trade Commission (the "USITC") published its final affirmative determination of injury to the United States hot-rolled steel industry.[57] On June 29, 1999, USDOC published an anti-dumping duty order imposing anti-dumping duties on imports of hot-rolled steel from Japan.[58] Japan complained that the US actions were inconsistent with several provisions of the anti-dumping measures that could be found in Articles 2, 3, 6, 9, and 10, and a Panel ultimately considered the claims of the disputing parties.

There were tricky provisions of law; one of which was the meaning of "the ordinary course of trade," which was not defined by the Anti-Dumping Agreement (ADA). However, the disputing parties accepted a definition that had been provided by the US and the AB subsequently agreed:

> Generally, sales are in the ordinary course of trade if made under conditions and practices that, for a reasonable period of time prior to the date of sale of the subject merchandise, have been normal for sales of the foreign like product.

The expression was intimately connected with price determination, since competitive prices must be determined above or below the ordinary course of trading prices. In *US–Hot-Rolled Steel*, the AB stipulated that the text of Article 2.1 expressly imposes four conditions on sales transactions in order that they may be used to calculate normal value: first, the sale must be "in the ordinary course of trade"; second, it must be of the "like product"; third, the product must be "destined for consumption in the exporting country"; and, fourth, the price must be "comparable."[59]

On February 28, 2001, the panel circulated its report. The Panel rejected most of Japan's claims, but found that, *inter alia*, particular aspects of the anti-dumping duty calculation, as well as one aspect of the US anti-dumping duty law (deficient provisions of the US Anti-Dumping Act (1921) and US Tariff Act of 1930) were inconsistent with the WTO Anti-Dumping Agreement. The Panel found that the US acted inconsistently with its obligations with Article 2.1 of the ADA in excluding certain home-market sales to affiliated parties from the calculation of normal value on the basis of the "arm's length" test and concluded that the replacement of those sales with sales to unaffiliated downstream purchasers was inconsistent with Article 2.1 of the ADA.

The US did not act inconsistently with its obligations under Articles 3.1, 3.2, 3.4, 3.5, 3.6, and 4.1 of the ADA (when determining injury to the US industry), or Articles 10.1, 10.6, and 10.7 relating to critical circumstances. Additionally, a causal connection between dumped imports and injury to the domestic industry were not considered to be inconsistent under Articles 3.1, 3.4, and 3.5 of the ADA. On April 25, 2001, the United States filed a notice of appeal on certain issues in the panel report.

The AB report, which was issued on July 24, 2001, provided mixed results. It partly affirmed some of the Panel's decisions. The reports were adopted on August 23, 2001 and, following a February 19, 2002, arbitral award, the United States was given 15 months or until November 23, 2002, to implement the DSB's recommendations and rulings. On November 22, 2002, Commerce issued a new final determination in the hot-rolled steel anti-dumping duty investigation, which complied with the recommendations and rulings of the DSB concerning the calculation of anti-dumping margins.

Relying on Article 2.1 of the ADA, the AB provided a basis for establishing whether "sales below cost" are "in the ordinary course of trade." Yet the Article does not purport to exhaust the methods of price determination.

The AB noted that Article 2.2.1 of the ADA itself provides for a method for determining whether sales below cost are "in the ordinary course of trade." However, that provision does not purport to exhaust the range of methods for determining whether sales are "in the ordinary course of trade," nor even the range of possible methods for determining whether low-priced sales are "in the ordinary course of trade." Article 2.2.1 sets forth a method for determining whether sales between any two parties are "in the ordinary course of trade"; it does not address the more specific issue of transactions between affiliated parties. In transactions between such parties, the affiliation itself may signal that sales above cost, but below the usual market price, might not be in the ordinary course of trade. Such transactions may, therefore, be the subject of special scrutiny by the investigating authorities.[60] The AB recognized that as between affiliates, a sales transaction might not be "in the ordinary course of trade," either because the sales price is higher than the "ordinary course" price, or because it is lower than that price.

In determining whether a sales price is higher or lower than the "ordinary course" price, the AB reached the conclusion that the decision on fair price is not merely a matter of comparing prices, but one of the terms and conditions of a transaction. Therefore, other terms and conditions must be taken into consideration to determine whether a price is high or low in the ordinary course of trade. For example, the volume of trade (supply) will affect prices and the liabilities that are undertaken by sellers—say cost, insurance, and freight—are also expected to affect prices in the normal course of trade. Cost estimates are extensive. They include obligations to compute costs based on records (a narrower estimate of costs, Art. 2.2.1.1) and the cost of production in the country of origin (Art. 2.2). When the records methodology does not (adequately) apply, an investigating authority may have recourse to alternative bases to calculate costs. Accordingly, the investigating authority is not prohibited from relying on information other than what is contained in the records kept by the exporter or producer, including in-country and out-of-country evidence.[61]

The AB found that differences impinging on price comparability cannot be excluded from investigation. That is, when there are differences between export price and normal value, which affect the comparability of prices, due consideration must be given to the disparities. Notably, the text provides examples of factors which may affect the comparability of prices: "differences in conditions and terms of sale, taxation, levels of trade, quantities, physical characteristics, and any other differences." Yet, it found that Article 2.4 expressly requires that "allowances" be made for "any other differences which are also demonstrated to affect price comparability." In effect, differences (factors) affecting price comparability cannot be disregarded. The AB reversed the Panel's finding that the United States acted inconsistently with Article 2.1 of the ADA by using, in its calculation of normal value, certain downstream sales made by an investigated exporter's affiliates to independent purchasers.

When it comes to the cost of production, Article 2.2 of the ADA and Article VI 1(b)(ii) of the GATT 1994 makes clear that the determination is of the "cost of production … in the country of origin." Thus, whatever the information that it uses, an investigating authority has to ensure that such information is used to arrive at the "cost of production in the country of origin." Compliance with this obligation may require the investigating authority to adapt the information that it collects.[62] In *US–Softwood Lumber V*, the AB concluded that the requirement to consider all available evidence on the proper allocation of costs may in certain circumstances require the authorities to compare advantages and disadvantages of alternative cost allocation methodologies.

Legal punishments for dumping are particularly instructive. They present appropriate criteria for countervailing measures. For quite some time, the US and some European states considered the issue of zeroing to be an appropriate remedy for perceived or actual dumping violations. That is, they did not allow lower export prices abroad (under-pricing) to be offset by higher prices abroad (over-pricing).[63] In *US–Zeroing* (Japan), the Panel identified two concepts of zeroing: (i) model zeroing, and (ii) simple zeroing. Japan alluded to the former as average-to-average comparisons of export price and normal value within individual "averaging groups," which is based on physical attributes that disregard any amount by which average export prices for particular cohort exceed normal value in aggregating the results of the cohorts to compute the weighted average margin of dumping. Therefore, the numerator of the margin of dumping will only include the results of models for which the average export price is less than the normal value. The variant of model zeroing, simple zeroing, considers transaction-to-transaction comparisons in which export prices of individual transactions for which the export or traded value is in excess of the normal value. In *US–Softwood Lumber V* (Article 21.5)–Canada, the AB found that:

> [T]he use of zeroing under the transaction-to-transaction comparison methodology artificially inflates the magnitude of dumping, resulting in higher margins of dumping and making a positive determination of dumping more likely. This way of calculating cannot be described as impartial, even-handed, or unbiased. For this reason, we do not consider that the calculation of "margins of dumping", on the basis of a transaction-to-transaction comparison that uses zeroing, satisfies the "fair comparison" requirement within the meaning of Article 2.4 of the Anti-Dumping Agreement.[64]

Zeroing under the transaction-to-transaction (T-T) comparison methodology inflates the margin of dumping to a greater extent when compared to model zeroing under the weight to weight (W-W) model zeroing framework. The AB notes that zeroing under the T-T comparison methodology disregards the result of each comparison involving a transaction in which the export price exceeds the normal value, whereas under the W-W comparison zeroing occurs only across the subgroups in the process of aggregation.

> Furthermore, the W-W comparison methodology involves the calculation of a weighted average export price. By contrast, under the T-T comparison methodology, all export transactions are taken into account on an individual basis and matched with the most appropriate transactions in the domestic market. Therefore, the phrase "all comparable export transactions" is not pertinent to the T-T comparison methodology. Consequently, no inference may be drawn from the fact that these words do not appear in relation to this methodology.[65]

The W-T comparison methodology in the second sentence of Article 2.4.2 is considered to be an exception to the comparison methodologies that are set out in the first sentence and are normally to be used.[66] Although the W-W and T-T comparison methodologies have been determined to likely yield substantially equivalent results, the AB has not discounted the possibility that, in a particular case, they might yield different material results that might impact differently the possible use of the W-T comparison methodology.

In EC—Bed Linen the AB examined the first method under Article 2.4.2 for establishing the existence of margins of dumping and concluded that the EC's practice discounts negative dumping margins. In effect, the EC had not taken fully into account all the prices of export transactions. Similarly, in *US–Washing Machines*, the AB struck down the zeroing procedure:

> We have concluded above that, under the second sentence of Article 2.4.2, dumping and margins of dumping pertaining to all export transactions of an exporter or foreign producer and to the product under investigation are limited to "pattern transactions". The exceptional W-T comparison methodology in the second sentence of Article 2.4.2 requires a comparison between a weighted average normal value and the entire universe of export transactions that fall within the pattern as properly identified under that provision, irrespective of whether the export price of individual "pattern transactions" is above or below normal value.[67]

However, in *US–Zeroing* (Japan), the AB did not support the view that there can be a general prohibition against zeroing:

> [A] general prohibition of zeroing would undermine the effectiveness of provisions in Article 9 that in our view clearly permit Members to assess anti-dumping duties on a transaction-specific basis. There is nothing in the second sentence of Article 2.4.2 or in Article 9 that indicates that these provisions establish exceptions to the

"fair comparison" requirement of Article 2.4. Therefore, if the "fair comparison" requirement operates to prohibit zeroing, it necessarily also applies in the context of these provisions. Consequently, it is impossible, in our view, to reconcile the proposition that the "fair comparison" requirement must be interpreted to create a general prohibition of zeroing with the second sentence of Article 2.4.2 and the provisions on duty assessment in Article 9 in a manner consistent with the requirement of effective treaty interpretation.[68]

8.6 (C) DISCRIMINATORY MARKET ACCESS

An integral concept of contemporary international trade law is the principle of non-discrimination, otherwise known as the most favored nation (MFN) principle. The principle is a rather simple concept, which states that trade benefits that are extended to any member of a treaty must be extended to all others of the same convention. However, the MFN principle has been complicated by the coexistence of plurilateral and multilateral treaties as well as the varying levels of development of the countries of the world. As such, even though discriminatory market access is a conceptually forbidden theory, economic arrangements and developmental circumstances have created specified exceptions to the rule of non-discrimination.

There are various reasons why nations have historically embraced freer trade. An aggregation of the welfare effects can best summarize the bases for international trade (see Figure 8.2). Intra-regional trade arrangements can serve as launching pads for multilateral arrangements and increase the global volume of trade; especially when trade creation is generated (see Figure 8.5, Panels (a), (b) and (c)). Consequently, nations have engaged in international treaties to enhance their welfare even before the contemporary system of international trade that has been designed for the furtherance of free trade. The collapse of mercantilism, which was discussed earlier in this chapter, prefaced the appreciation of a newer trade theory in favor of liberalization. Accordingly, freer trade treaties became more prominent in the nineteenth century. The Cobden-Chevalier Treaty of 1860, signed by Britain and France, promoted the concept of freer trade, which was eventually enhanced by the 1862 treaty between France and Germany, and subsequently included other European countries by the end of the decade.[69] Actually, MFN clauses have been traced back to the seventeenth century.[70] The principle of non-discrimination is so important that it is referred to in the preamble of GATT Article I and further amplified in GATT Article III. Countries in a trade convention must equally and unconditionally enjoy any advantage, favor, privilege, or immunity that is granted to any particular member; except that conditionality applies when they form regional or PTAs, which is permitted by Article XXIV, or when they fall into a particular category of development. Of course, pre-existing treaties were not to be nullified by GATT.

However, the efficacy of preferential arrangement (frontier traffic) is contingent on legal discrimination and fairness. In *Canada—Autos*, Canada invoked an Article XXIV exception with respect to a certain import duty exemption which had been found to be inconsistent with GATT Article I. The Panel rejected this defense, partly because Canada was not granting the import duty exemption to all NAFTA manufacturers. Additionally, manufacturers from countries other than the United States and Mexico were being provided with duty-free treatment. Since Canada did not appeal this finding of the Panel, the AB did not address the issue. The AB reviewed the Panel's finding that the Canadian import duty exemptions granted to motor vehicles originating in certain countries were inconsistent with Article I.1. The AB found the prohibition of discrimination under Article I.1 to include both *de jure* and *de facto* discrimination.[71] Accordingly, by granting an advantage to some products from some Members and not to others, the measure in question was inconsistent with Article I.1.

Today, legal and illegal trade discrimination is an encompassing concept of international trade law. Trade discrimination encircles other aspects of international trade law. Trade discrimination involves discriminatory access to foreign markets in which the deprivation of fair access can take various forms and arrangements beyond PTAs. Levels of development, product quality, environmental considerations, harassment, and denial of import licenses are mechanisms that can be exploited to create discriminatory access to international markets. The WTO Agreements contain special provisions that accommodate the levels of development of members. Developed countries are permitted to treat developing countries more favorably because of their level of development. The special provision is known as the "Enabling Clause" or more formally as "Decision on Differential and More Favourable Treatment, Reciprocity and Fuller Participation of Developing Countries," which was adopted under GATT in 1979. In effect, in 1979, the GATT contracting parties permitted derogations to the most favored nation (non-discrimination) clause in favor of developing countries.

Non-discriminatory market access also means that domestic (national) producers must not be given undue advantage over their foreign counterparts when domestic policies are being crafted or implemented. Once imported goods have made their way into domestic markets, they should not be treated differently from domestic goods. External goods need not be identical. They can be similar or substitutable goods.

The Enabling Clause is the WTO legal basis for the Generalized System of Preferences (GSP). Under the GSP, developed countries offer preferential treatment (such as zero or low duties on imports) to products originating in developing countries without seeking reciprocal trade concessions. The preference-granting countries can unilaterally determine which countries and which products are to be included in their concessions. The special concessions provide longer time periods for implementing Agreements and commitments or measures to increase trading opportunities for developing countries. The derogations, which are generally referred to as "special and differential treatment" (S&D), provide for: (i) longer time periods for implementing Agreements and commitments, (ii) measures to increase trading opportunities for developing countries, (iii) provisions requiring all WTO members to safeguard the trade interests of developing countries, (iv) support to help developing countries build the capacity to carry out WTO work, handle disputes, and implement technical standards, and (v) concessions to least-developed country (LDC) Members.[72]

In *EC—Tariff Preferences*, the AB addressed the relationship between Article I.1 of the GATT 1994 and the Enabling Clause and upheld the Panel's characterization of the Enabling Clause as an exception to Article I.1 based on the ordinary meaning of paragraph 1 of the Enabling Clause. It also stated that such a characterization does not affect the importance of the policy objectives of the Enabling Clause: "By using the word 'notwithstanding', paragraph 1 of the Enabling Clause permits Members to provide 'differential and more favourable treatment' to developing countries 'in spite of' the MFN obligation of Article I.1. Such treatment would otherwise be inconsistent with Article I.1 because that treatment is not extended to all Members of the WTO 'immediately and unconditionally'. Paragraph 1 thus excepts Members from complying with the obligation contained in Article I.1 for the purpose of providing differential and more favourable treatment to developing countries, provided that such treatment is in accordance with the conditions set out in the Enabling Clause. As such, the Enabling Clause operates as an 'exception' to Article I.1. ...."[73] However, the AB stated (in *EC—Tariff Preferences*) that the ultimate burden of proof under the Enabling Clause falls on the respondent. Discriminating practices can also involved methods of production or harvesting methodologies.

In 1991, Mexico brought a case against the US because the US banned imports of tuna from Mexico. By using purse seine fishing nets (netting deployed around an entire fishing area or school of fish) dolphins were endangered in the process of catching tuna. The US Marine Mammal Protection Act requires US tuna fishermen to use nets and by Article XX(g) of GATT, the US believed that the same principle should be extended to Mexico. GATT XX(g) provides exceptions to rules against ostensible inhibitions against trade when the prohibitive measures are made effective in conjunction with restrictions on domestic production or consumption.

The Panel decided that the US could not embargo imports of tuna products from Mexico simply because Mexican regulations concerning the way tuna was produced (the methodology used to produce tuna) did not satisfy US regulations. However, the US could apply its regulations on *the quality or content* of the tuna imported. The ruling indicates that "process" must be separated from the phytosanitary requirements of law. Pointedly, GATT rules can limit extraterritoriality. A country is not allowed to adopt trade action for the purpose of enforcing its own domestic laws in another country even when environmental degradation is at stake. However, the panel report was not adopted since Mexico decided to withdraw the case and the case did not provide finality. An obvious implication of the case is that permitting a country to ban a product from another country merely because of process of production or health considerations of his own may not be permissible. Extraterritoriality can create retaliatory measures that drastically reduce the volume of trade.

The *Shrimp-Turtle Case* of the 1990s provides some amount of clarity for environmental protection. In the *Shrimp-Turtle Case*, India, Malaysia, Pakistan, and Thailand appealed to the WTO against US ban on shrimp imports. The case is somewhat similar to the *Tuna-Dolphin Case*, because the US complained that sea turtles were not protected in the process of harvesting shrimps. The harvesting processes were inconsistent with the US Endangered Species Act of 1987, which is also consistent with Article XX(g) of the GATT. The US reasoned that the provisions of the laws should be extended to the Asian countries.

Though the AB ruled against the US, it did not uphold the prior ruling on production processes that favor environmental degradation. In effect, it did not rule against the principle that one country could restrict import based on production processes or methods used by another country that deplete environmental resources. Therefore, the ruling recognized the conservation of exhaustible natural resources referred to in Article XX(g). However, the recognition is not without a discriminatory caveat. Though the AB found that sea turtles constitute an exhaustible natural resource that should be protected by the language of Article XX(g), it recalled the chapeau of Article XX to find "unjustifiable discrimination" that is legally impermissible.[74]

Thus, the AB concluded that US law (16 U.S.C. § 609) "is a measure 'relating to' the conservation of an exhaustible natural resource within the meaning of Article XX(g)."

The law, which has formed a basis for prohibiting imports of shrimp and tuna that have been harvested by indiscriminate and wild methods, prohibits the use of fishing technology that endangers marine life of sea turtles (endangered species). The law requires US trawlers to use turtle excluder devices (TEDs) to prevent the unwarranted capture or harvest of sea turtles. Nevertheless, the AB found problems with the application of the law rather than its spirit and intent. It ruled that the law was applied "in a manner which would constitute a means of arbitrary or unjustifiable discrimination between countries," which violates the requirements set forth in the preamble, or "chapeau," of Article XX.[75]

The AB found discriminatory treatment on the following grounds: (i) the US did not take into account other policies and measures that the country may have adopted under different conditions that may exist in foreign countries, thereby causing an "arbitrary discrimination" that violates the chapeau of Article XX, (ii) while the US negotiated with some countries to bring about the Inter-American Convention for the Protection and Conservation of Sea Turtles that was concluded in 1996, it did not do so with other countries, (iii) although the United States gave 14 countries a three-year phase-in period (1991–1994) to develop conformable practices, the US did not impose an import ban on others until 1996; moreover, it did so with only four-months' notice, which created a burdensome and unreasonable time constraint for others to develop conformable standards. Additionally, the AB concluded that insufficient efforts were made to transfer TED technology to the exporting countries, and (iv) there was no formal and transparent process to debate the merits of a certification process, including reasons for denial of certification and a structure to appeal the denial. Were the Asian exporters of shrimps treated differently from exporters of shrimps in the western hemisphere?

The case presented a superior legal and economic outcome to the *Tuna-Dolphin Case*. As Chang observed:

> [T]he Appellate Body avoided the use of any general per se rules against environmental trade measures like the sweeping rules announced by panels in the past. Instead, the Appellate Body endorsed a case-by-case analysis that relies on the requirements explicit in the chapeau of Article XX to guard against the abuse of the Article XX exceptions ....
>
> (Chang, 2005, p. 30)

Should national products be preferred to foreign products in domestic markets, or should national companies be given more generous extensions to satisfy product quality and conformability requirements? This was an issue that was presented to the WTO for resolution in *Venezuela and Brazil v. US* in 1994. The US restricted imports of gasoline from Venezuela and Brazil because the gas did not meet the requirements of the US Clean Air Act (which mandates a maximum amount of certain smog-causing chemicals). Like the *Shrimp-Turtle Case*, the AB found, *inter alia*, that trade discrimination can be premised on dichotomous temporal extensions for conformability with standards. While a three-year grace period was extended to US refineries for compliance with the Act, the AB found that a similar extension was not extended to oil refineries in Venezuela and Brazil. Additionally, the Panel found that, in violation of Article III.4, the measure treated imported gasoline less favorably than domestic gasoline. The imported gasoline effectively experienced less favorable sales conditions than those afforded to domestic gasoline, especially because importers had to adapt to an average statutory baseline (standard) while refiners of domestic gasoline had only to meet individual refinery baseline (standard) linked to their own product in 1990. The AB report was adopted on May 20, 1996. The banana trade between the EU and some developing countries has also generated legal issues about discriminatory market access.

The EU and the African, Caribbean, and Pacific (ACP) countries arranged preferential market access in December 1989 known as Lomé IV (Lomé waiver). The arrangement gave the ACP countries preference to the EU market. The preference for the sale of bananas, which was formalized by EEC Council Reg. No. 404/93, disadvantaged some countries that were not part of the Lomé accord, and countries that were not traditional suppliers of the EU market. The EU allocated tariff quota shares to some Members that did not have a substantial interest in supplying bananas, but not others. Arrangements were also made for tariff quotas to be exclusively reallocated to other Members of the Framework Agreement on Bananas (BFA) when quotas were not exhausted by individual Members. As part of implementation rules, import licenses were distributed among the EU Members for the importation of bananas from non-traditional ACP suppliers.

The Banana trouble (case) had three notable phases. The first set of complaints against the EU was brought by Ecuador, Guatemala, Honduras, and Mexico. The AB upheld the Panel's finding that the allocation of tariff quota shares to some Members not having a substantial interest in supplying bananas, but not to others, was inconsistent with Art. XIII.1. The AB also agreed with the Panel, which was established on May 8, 1996, that the (BFA) tariff quota reallocation rules, under which a portion of a tariff quota share not used by one BFA country could be reallocated exclusively to other BFA countries, were inconsistent with Arts. XIII.1 and XIII.2, chapeau. Further, reversing the Panel's findings, the AB found that waivers must be narrowly interpreted and subjected to strict disciplines. Accordingly, the AB failed to see why the waiver could be exempted from Art. XIII when it actually referred to Art. I.1.

The AB considered the activity function rules, which applied only to license allocation rules for imports from other than traditional ACP countries, to be inconsistent with Art. I.1. The Panel and the AB agreed that the EC procedures and requirements for the distribution of licences for importing bananas from non-traditional ACP suppliers were inconsistent with Art. III.4. The Panel and the AB also agreed that the aim and effect of a measure are irrelevant to Arts. II and XVII (MFN) and that the EC measures were discriminatory under the Articles. The AB considered Art. X.3(a) and Art. I.3 to be applicable to administrative procedures for rules and not rules per se, and the AB report was adopted on September 25, 1997.

The second phase of the banana dispute over access to the EU market involved adverse effects of amendments (Reg. No. 1637/98) to Reg. No. 404/93 and regulations for implementation of the amended rules (Reg. No. 2362/98). The complaint, which was brought by Ecuador, was pertinent to three categories of bananas. The issue was referred to the original panel on January 12, 1999. The Panel found that the new Regulation was inconsistent with Art. XIII.1. It provided disparate treatment between the traditional ACP suppliers and other non-substantial suppliers and third countries because of varying restrictions to the trading partners.

The Panel found a violation of Art. XIII.2 because the EC banana regime provided for a large quota to ACP countries with excess capacity. The ACP countries collectively used only 80 percent over a two-year period. The MFN quota had always been filled and even some out-of-quota imports had been made. "Therefore, the Panel found that the regime did not aim at a distribution of trade that would represent as closely as possible the market share that countries would have had in the absence of restrictions."[76] In the case of Ecuador, the new Regulation generated a base period for future quota allocations that was inconsistent with GATT Art. XIII:2(d) (non-discriminatory administration of quantitative restrictions—quota allocation).[77]

GATT Art. I:1 (most favored nation treatment): The Panel found that a quota level more favourable for ACP countries was a requirement under the Lomé Convention. However, it found a violation of Art. I:1 in the collective allocation of the quota to the ACP countries, calculated on the basis of individual countries' pre-1991 best-ever export volume as it could have resulted in some countries exporting more than their pre-1991 best-ever export volume, which would not have been justified under the Lomé Waiver. The Panel further found that licensing rules disadvantaged Ecuador in violation of Arts. II and XVII. The Report of the Panel was adopted on May 6, 1999.

In the third phase of the banana dispute, the US and Ecuador continued to complain about deprivation of access to the EU banana market and it was a Second Recourse to Article 21.5 of the DSU by Ecuador. The US also invoked Article 21.5 of the DSU, but only Ecuador invoked Art. II. The dispute was over the EC Regulation No. 1964/2005 of November 24, 2005, which consisted of a duty-free quota of 775,000 mt (metric tons) for bananas from ACP countries and a tariff rate of €176/mt for all other imported bananas. The AB upheld the Panel's finding that the EC bananas import regime, in particular its duty-free tariff quota reserved for ACP countries, was inconsistent with Arts. XIII:1 and XIII:2. The AB upheld the Panel's finding that the tariff applied by the EC to MFN imports of bananas, set at €176/mt, without consideration of the tariff quota of 2.2 million mt bound at an in-quota tariff rate of €75/mt, was an ordinary customs duty in excess of what was provided for in the EC's Schedule of Concessions. The tariff was therefore inconsistent with Art. II:1(b).[78] The AB Panel Report for Ecuador was adopted on December 11, 2008, and that of the US, on December 22, 2008.

> Most disputes concerning the effect of domestic policies on market access have been based on GATT Article III (national treatment) and/or Article XX (general exceptions), or on WTO Agreements concerning specific domestic measures like the Agreement on Subsidies and Countervailing Measures, the Agreement on Technical Barriers to Trade or the Agreement on Sanitary and Phytosanitary Measures …[79]

The next section takes a look at the functions of money and monetary disputes in international law.

8.7 MONETARY ECONOMICS AND INTERNATIONAL LAW: THE CONFISCATORY EFFECTS OF CURRENCY DEVALUATION OR MANIPULATION OF VALUE

What is money? Money is anything that is generally accepted as a medium of exchange, unit of account, store of value, and standard of deferred payment (payment of debts). Therefore, the central attribute of money is its widespread acceptability. The attributes of money also define the functionality of money. That is, money can be kept to store value and used to measure value and make contractual debt repayments. Anything that is not generally acceptable cannot be considered to be money, though it might have limited value within a community in which it is circulated as a complement of money.

Money has a long history dating back to the days of the barter system when various physical objects were used as money. The objects included salt, tobacco, boulders, shells, and cattle. Some of the items are bulky, indivisible, and perishable. Some were considered to have intrinsic value or a transcendental transactional value (the objects may have value beyond their transactional purpose). Issues of portability and double coincidence of wants made the barter system a clumsy monetary system, since exchange can only take place when market participants have wants that coincide. For example, someone with salt who is in search of cattle must find someone with cattle who also needed salt. But how many units of the cattle must be exchanged for salt? Will the cattle have any further value if it is destroyed for salt? What will it take to transport the cattle from one market to the next?

The troubling questions made it essential to develop alternative and superior forms of money that were scarce, portable, divisible, durable, and generally acceptable. As a result, metal rings were used in Egypt c.2500 BC. In the 600s BC, the government of Lydia (Western Turkey) introduced the combination of silver and gold (electrum) as currency. The Greek city-states started to use their own coinage of currency (electrum) known as "staters" within the next hundred years, and the Romans issued their silver denarius c.150 BC.[80] Gold and silver continued to play a dominant role in the international monetary system until the nineteenth century and, in the case of gold, until the twentieth century.

The regulation of international monetary value (exchange rates) is highly related to the purpose of using money in international transactions. Individuals, businesses, and governments use money to facilitate exchange, make investments, and pay debts. Consequently, all three aspects of international transactions are adversely affected when the value of money changes in arbitrary, adverse, and capricious ways. In effect, such changes can cause international financial instability and chaos when there is no framework or rules for the orderly use of money in the conduct of commerce or international transactions. Exchange rates are the basic unit of analysis.

An exchange rate is a ratio of the value of currencies; usually, the ratio of the value of the domestic currency to that of the foreign currency. For example, if the USD/£ exchange rate is $1.25/£1, it means that an American businessman will need $1.25 to buy £1. Therefore, the American businessman will need $1.25★ £2,000, $2,500, to fetch a British commodity that costs £2,000. Analogously, $2,500 will be required to pay a debt of £2,000 in one year. However, if the value of the USD falls to $1.30 (since the American businessman will now need more dollars to buy the same unit of pounds), the value of the debt increases to $2,600 if there is no agreement (forward contract) to ensure that the exchange rate remains unchanged. Debt repayments become costly when the values of currencies change in undesirable ways that violate contractual arrangements (breach of monetary or financial contracts). As a result, there is a confiscatory effect that can be attributed to deliberate and illegal changes in the value of money. It is noteworthy that there might be circumstances under which a change in the value of a currency is warranted. These circumstances will be discussed later.

Table 8.3 Determinants of exchange rates

Factor	Change	Effect on domestic currency
Foreign demand of goods and services (absorption)	Increase	**Appreciation:** supply of foreign currency increases.
Expected appreciation of domestic currency	Exchange rate falls	**Appreciation:** supply of foreign currency increases. Speculative attack on a domestic currency will have an opposite effect.
Restrictive trade policy*	Exchange rate falls	**Appreciates:** reduction in domestic absorption of foreign goods.
Relative increase in domestic interest rate	Exchange rate falls	**Appreciation:** increase in domestic and foreign capital flows (contractionary domestic monetary policy without a trap).
Relative decrease in the general price level	Exchange rate falls	**Appreciation:** Increase in the absorption of domestic relative to foreign goods.

Note:
* Restrictive trade policy is not a panacea, because the effects of trade policy are contingent on reciprocation and elasticities. Relative price changes affect both demand and supply of foreign currencies. Further, when the conventional ratio (domestic-to-foreign value) is maintained (in this case), it should be noteworthy that inverse changes will lead to a depreciation of the domestic currency rather than an appreciation; see also the various forms of exchange rates in Chapter 2.

Various factors can affect the value of exchange rates (currencies). Some of the most important factors have been identified in Table 8.3 and, by extension, Figure 8.10, Panels (a) and (b).

In Figure 8.10 Panel (a), the increase in foreign demand shifts the supply curve to the right. Implicitly, the supply curve is representative of foreign demand. The exchange rate falls (appreciates) as a result of the increase in foreign demand for American goods. In Figure 8.10 Panel (b) the relative increase in interest rate causes an increase in capital inflows and domestic investment. While the effect of the interest rate change on the foreign money supply is rather ambiguous, the value of the US dollar appreciates as a result of the direction of capital flows.

Over the years, nations have experimented with a variety of exchange rate regimes to facilitate international trade, investments, and sovereign debt repayments. The nations have done so within the framework of an international monetary system.

> The international monetary system can be defined as the institutional framework within which international payments are made, movements of capital are accommodated, and exchange rates among currencies are determined.
> (Resnick & Eun, 2015, p. 27)

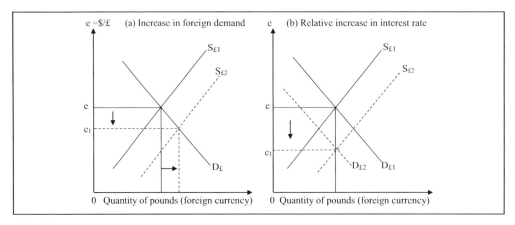

Figure 8.10 Influential determinants of exchange rate

The contemporary international monetary system evolved through various phases: (i) The bimetallic standard predating 1875, (ii) the classical gold standard (1875–1914), (iii) the interregnum (1918–1939), (iv) the Bretton Woods system (1945–1972), and the contemporary system (1973–present). Each phase had its own challenges, but older phases were replaced because they could no longer provide effective mechanisms for international cooperation or stability. Not all the phases will be discussed in this book, but suffice it to say that the classical gold standard, the Bretton Woods system and the post-Bretton Woods international architecture have provided valuable experiences for the appreciation of a lawful international monetary environment.[81]

An advantage of the bi-metallistic system is that it minimized price volatility. When gold became expensive, cheaper silver could be used because of the substitutability of the metals (an increase in the supply of silver). Since the value of the metals were clearly defined without debasement (devaluation) in a fixed exchange rate regime, the cheaper or more abundant metal ("bad money") was used extensively, while the more expensive one ("good money") was hoarded. The practice of hoarding precious metal gave rise to a phenomenon known as Gresham's Law; a situation in which "bad money" chases out the "good."

The classical gold standard is instructive for understanding the fixed exchange rate regime, balance of payments stability, problems that are associated with the supply of gold, and the impracticality of the limited (finite) supply of gold—and transaction costs—to keep pace with expanding national output and employment. Wars and other man-made catastrophe made the impracticality more apparent.[82] Once nations defined their money supply in terms of gold, and therefore exchange rates, they were forced to limit their absorption of foreign goods. Additionally, they could not engage in expansionary monetary policies during periods of adverse economic shocks without suspending convertibility or devaluing the gold content of exchange rates. Instability and insecurity created problems for the preservation of the gold standard even though exchange rates were predictably fixed. Consider Figures 8.11 Panels (a) and (b).

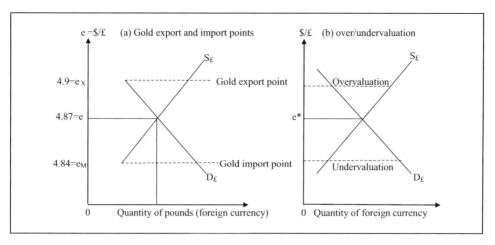

Figure 8.11 The fixed exchange rate under the classical gold standard

During the classical gold standard the gold contents in currencies were fixed and the grain content of gold defined exchange rates. For example, a £1 coin contained 113.0016 grains of pure gold in 1879. The gold content of the US was 23.22. The gold contents defined a \$/£ exchange rate of \$4.87. Since the cost of shipping £1 worth of gold between New York and London was three cents, the dollar exchange rate was not expected to rise above \$4.90 (a depreciation) or fall below \$4.84 (an appreciation). The band means that an American investor will not be willing to pay more than \$4.90 or accept \$4.84 in a currency market since he/she could just export or import gold and exchange the gold for the appropriate rates including the transaction cost of three cents per £1. Nations that wanted to increase their money supply must also credibly increase their gold supply, failing which there will be a run on their gold supply under the convertibility arrangement. That is, when nations defined their currencies in terms of gold, they demonstrated a willingness and ability to redeem their currencies for gold. As a result of the outbreak of World War I in 1914, the classical gold standard subsequently collapsed; partly because warring countries could not increase their supply of gold rapidly enough to meet wartime expenditures.

The interregnum (1918–1939) revealed the importance of exchange rates for international transactions and the volume of trade *inter alia*. The link between the value of a currency and the capacity to export goods and services became very important for the post-war architecture and the regulation of the value of currencies to promote international trade. Prior judicial decisions on monetary conflicts in the nineteenth century had been mostly focused on the confiscatory effect of contractual breaches. The interregnum was turbulent and the preference to store gold ensured the turbulence.

In 1928, France required payments for its current account surpluses to be made in gold, but some countries had abandoned the gold standard. The UK had set the price of the pound at pre-war parity although it had lost a considerable amount of gold and liquidated some of its assets to compensate for the loss of gold. In effect the pound was realistically overvalued (see Figure 8.11 Panel (b)); the exchange rate then rises to an extent that it is above its market value.[83] During the interregnum, countries engaged in competitive devaluations to push their exports or export their unemployment. The supply of gold was simply inadequate to meet the post-war challenges as some countries aspired to be financial capitals of the world. More so, the supply could not have been expeditiously increased to deal with the immediate post-war dislocation. The juxtaposition of a depleted supply of gold and increasing demand for gold forced the UK to suspend convertibility in 1931; the US suspended convertibility in 1934. To address the post-war paucity of gold, the gold standard was reconstructed as a gold exchange standard; meaning that an accommodative policy was adopted so that convertible currencies like sterling and the dollar (foreign exchange reserves) could be used to augment the supply of gold.

Various economic models can be used to show the relationship between exchange rates and prospective aggregate macroeconomic performance. Nations periodically intervene in foreign exchange markets to influence (stabilize) the value of their currencies. Obviously, the intervention can be clean or dirty. Dirty interventions in currency markets are deliberately intended to make it difficult for other countries to make adjustments in order to gain undue competitive trade advantage. Even under conditions of fixed exchange rates, countries have found ways to sterilize the effects of current account imbalances on their money supply. For example, Nurkse and Bloomfield found that some monetary authorities sterilized the effects of current account imbalances on their money supply during the gold standard.[84] As Eichengreen and Irwin noted:

> Some countries remained on the gold standard in the hope that sufficient wage and price deflation could restore internal and external balance. But the difficulties of wage deflation were considerable, and the burden of long-term debts denominated in nominal terms became progressively heavier. Rising unemployment also had political costs; more than a few governments fell as a result. Therefore, some countries banned capital outflows and imposed direct controls on payments for imports to conserve gold and foreign exchange reserves.
>
> (Eichengreen & Irwin, 2010, p. 874)

Sterilized intervention does not alter the monetary base (currency in circulation and reserves), of the liabilities side of a central bank's balance sheet. Essentially, a central bank offsettingly trades government bonds for international reserves. In an unsterilized intervention, a central bank tries to alter the monetary base (liability side of the ledger) by increasing (+) or decreasing (-) foreign assets (international reserves) to increase (+) or decrease (-) local deposits with a central bank.[85] In close proximity of sterilization is the concept of currency manipulation; a situation in which countries aggressively intervene in currency markets to make their currencies weaker even when they have trade surpluses.

Bergsten and Gagnon (2012) have identified some indicators of manipulation: (i) foreign exchange reserves are usually in excess of what is required to make payments for six months' worth of goods and services. The IMF has used a three-month benchmark (a traditional rule of thumb is for reserves to be equivalent to three months' worth of imports)[86], (ii) foreign exchange reserves tend to grow faster than GDP, (iii) on average, the current account as a percentage of GDP is in a surplus for a given period of review, and (iv) gross national income per capita of at least $3,000, roughly the median income of 215 countries covered by the World Bank's Atlas method of rankings. The issue of currency manipulation poses a threat to international economic stability, but the juridical structure for its litigation is less apparent. Most of the issues involving currency manipulation are channeled through international trade advantages. The WTO is well suited for trade disputes but not currency manipulation, which is in the purview of the IMF. The IMF's Articles of Agreement inveigh against currency manipulation and the relevant contents of the Articles will be addressed in short order.

The illustrations in Figures 8.12 and 8.13 provide visual expositions of the relationship between money, interest rates, and national economic performance, and why the values of exchange rates have to be regulated; especially in the aftermath of the interregnum. Figure 8.12 shows that changes in the money supply can impact nominal interest rates in the absence of a liquidity trap (see Table 8.3 for the determinants of exchange rates, see also Table 2.3). A liquidity trap exists when increases in the money supply have no noticeable impact on short-term rates in the zero-bound territory. Decreases in interest rates depress the value of currencies, which can generate advantages for the sale of some products in international markets. The pass-through occurs when there are no adverse restrictions on international trade like some of the impediments that have been discussed in the previous section. Interest rates, in conjunction with the type of exchange rate regime, can also affect capital inflows and outflows and domestic monetary and fiscal policies.

The illustrations in Figure 8.13 Panel (a) show the various combinations of interest rate and national output for which there are internal and external equilibria. The goods market is defined by the investment and saving (IS) curve, the money market is defined by the

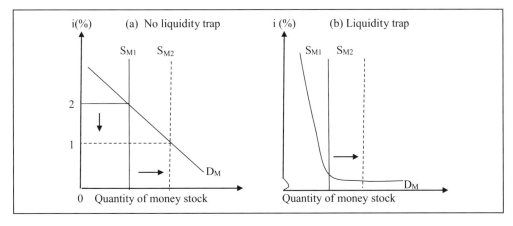

Figure 8.12 The relationship between money supply and interest rate

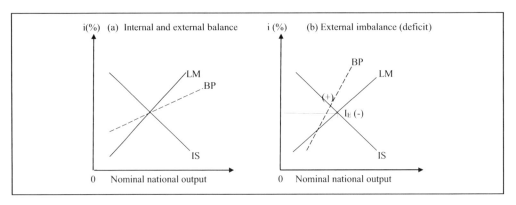

Figure 8.13 Money supply, exchange rate, interest rate, and national income

liquidity and money (LM), and the external balance is defined by the balance of payments (BP or BoP) curve. The shifts (or the lack thereof) of the BP curve and its slope are contingent on the type of exchange rate regime, the sensitivity of capital flows to interest rates, and foreign income. The flatter the BP curve, the more sensitive are capital flows to interest rate changes. Other than interest rate changes, exogenous disturbances will cause a shift of the IS and LM accordingly. That is, the curves will shift depending on the sources of disturbances.

In Figure 8.13 Panel (b), using the Mundell–Fleming model, I show the situation of a deficit nation, such as those of the interregnum. The combination of interest rate and output shows that interest rate is lower than what is required to achieve the net financial account balance necessary to offset the current account deficit (note that the intersection of the IS and LM, internal equilibrium, is to the right of the BP). If aggregate demand is equal to aggregate supply, money demand is equal to money supply, and exports are equal to imports for the various combinations of interest rate and output, then the IS curve can be exogenously impacted by fiscal policy, household consumption, and exchange rate (appreciation or depreciation). The LM curve can be exogenously impacted by monetary policy or sterilization. This means that the use of monetary policy to stabilize an economy will be dependent on whether the exchange rate is fixed or flexible, since the BP curve cannot shift with a fixed exchange rate regime.

Figure 8.13 Panel (a) shows that contractionary monetary policy can be used to correct the deficit without altering the exchange rate. However, without adequate funds, most of the nations used exchange rate policy to correct the balance of payments problem. Some countries abandoned the peg while others devalued their currencies; hence the shift from BP_1 to BP_2 in Figure 8.14. It is also revealing that national output increased in Figure 8.14 Panel (b), which is not the case in Figure 8.14 Panel(a). Varieties of the Mundell–Fleming models can be used to simulate various macro challenges with combinations of exchange rate regimes and fiscal and monetary policies. It is important to note that shifts of the IS curves cause depreciation or appreciation, which must be corrected by monetary policy when the exchange rate is fixed and resistant to adjustment. On occasions when

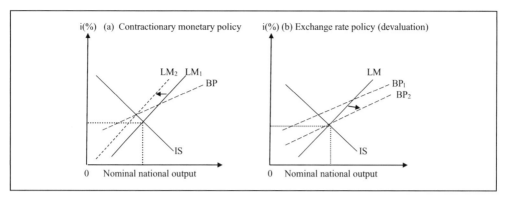

Figure 8.14 Monetary policy and exchange rate adjustment

the exchange rate is permitted to float, the exchange rate (BP curve) can bet adjusted accordingly to maintain internal and external equilibria.[87]

The proliferation of restrictions on international trade and payments in the aftermath of Britain's devaluation detrimentally impacted global commerce. World trade volume fell 16 percent from the third quarter of 1931 to the third quarter of 1932. Between 1929 and 1932 it fell 25 percent, and nearly half of this reduction was due to higher tariff and non-tariff barriers. As many as 20 other countries abandoned gold following the Bank of England's announcement (Eichengreen & Irwin, 2010, p. 877). In the midst of the global depression, countries that remained loyal to the gold standard sought to improve their balance of payments position and preserve their gold and foreign exchange reserves. This was achieved either by limiting capital exports through exchange controls (Germany) or by limiting spending on imports through trade restrictions (France), or both.[88]

Accordingly, the most pressing international monetary regulations were based on the occurrences of the interregnum and the financial disturbances that showed up after World War II. The theoretical background that has been provided should suffice to understand the philosophy of the Bretton Woods system and international economic law. Theoretically, Bretton Woods was a creature of the interregnum and the Great Depression, and a necessity to prevent the deleterious consequences of both occurrences.

Representatives of 44 countries met in Bretton Woods, New Hampshire, in July of 1944 to determine what the international monetary system should look like after World War II. The representatives called for an International Monetary Fund (IMF). The policies that were instituted until 1972 were generally known as the "Bretton Woods system." Two principles were integral to the mission of the new institution: (i) to set rules for financing of international trade, and (ii) to provide borrowing facilities for nations in temporary balance-of-payments difficulties. Under Bretton Woods, the US dollar was pegged to gold at $35 an ounce and each country established a fixed rate (par value) in relation to the US dollar (similar to the mint parity of $4.87/£1 under the gold standard). The countries were then permitted to maintain parity at one percent above or below par (a band). However, a member with a "fundamental disequilibrium" was permitted to make a change in the par value of its currency under the concept of monetary sovereignty. The concept of "fundamental disequilibrium" was not clearly defined, but it was subsequently understood to mean destabilizing large, persistent, and unsustainable current account deficits. Essentially, the inadequacy of gold supply made the system a continuation of the gold exchange standard that was experimented with during the interregnum, with the US dollar acting as a numeraire.

The US started to experience deficits in the late 1950s and 1960s, partly as a result of the Korean and Vietnam Wars, which made it less tenable to defend the US dollar at $35 an ounce. Uncertainty was built into the system and the inadequacy of reserve assets led to the creation of a new reserve asset known as "special drawing rights" (SDRs) or ("paper gold").[89] The excessive expenditures created a Triffin Paradox in which the holder of the reserve currency cannot guarantee confidence in the reserve currency. In August 1971, President Nixon suspended convertibility, thereby effectively bringing the Bretton Woods system to an end. The Jamaican Accord, which was formally ratified in January 1976, formally ushered in a new era of flexible exchange rate regimes and the demonetization of gold in the international payment system. Gold was no longer an international reserve asset.

International monetary conflicts can be dichotomized into two broad categories: (i) conflicts preceding Bretton Woods that were largely dependent on customary monetary law and grounded on some of the confiscatory issues that have already been discussed, and (ii) the stability of the value of currencies in the Bretton Woods and post-Bretton Woods era. The latter has not been litigated in courts of law because of the pass-through effects and the absence of a clear juridical environment to address the issue. Pointedly, the IMF does not have a dispute settlement mechanism (DSU) like the WTO and the monetary sovereignty of states is circumscribed by treaty provisions (the Articles of Agreement).

8.8 CUSTOMARY AND CONVENTIONAL MONETARY LAW

Are conventional monetary laws (like the Articles of Agreement) really laws or contracts? Does it make a difference if monetary agreements are laws or contracts?

> It is quite incorrect to speak of treaties as "sources" of international law. They are no more than contracts between the parties, and their significance as legal acts derives from the existence of rules of customary law by which their validity and their binding quality is determined, and according to which they are interpreted. In discussing the formation of international law, however, treaties are not without significance. They might be either evidence of a customary rule or the stimulus to one.
>
> (O'Connell, 1965, p. 22)

8.8 (A) THE LIMITS OF MONETARY "SOVEREIGNTY": CONTRACTUAL MONETARY ARRANGEMENTS

The concept of "sovereignty" is somewhat inchoate in international law. It has a long history of imprecision when its medieval connotation is granted omnipresent application. That is, some might think that the absolutism of Bodin and Hobbes are applicable to contemporary political and economic relations. Invariably, there is a tendency to conflate the theory of medieval political sovereignty (in its unlimited form) with the desire to attain economic interdependence by contemporary states. Simply put, political autonomy is not tantamount to economic autonomy.

In the contemporary global economy, the concept of "sovereignty" is not an unbounded or absolute construct. Contracts that are freely negotiated and ratified by states limit the authority of states to engage in arbitrary and unilateral malfeasance that is deliberately injurious to others (a preference for lawlessness). In reality, freedom has never attained absolute rights and medieval absolutism never attained perfection. When kings were perceived to have divine rights and authority, the divinity of their authority was linked to their ability to act as benign Gods on earth. That is, kings were expected to act with restraint in a manner befitting Gods on earth and consistent with the precepts of religious dogma that are respectful of inalienable rights. When kings became reckless, citizens decided to codify inalienable liberties even by revolutionary fervor that disregarded tranquility. Notably, authority and freedom have ethical limitations. Today, authoritarianism is a political aberration that is confined to the territorial geography of states for as long as it is not injurious to the international community. Pointedly, the excesses of authoritarianism or disruptive behaviors (political, economic, and social) are monitored by the UN Security Council. "Sovereign" states can be punished for threats to international peace and stability:

> The Security Council may investigate any dispute, or any situation which might lead to international friction or give rise to a dispute, in order to determine whether the continuance of the dispute or situation is likely to endanger the maintenance of international peace and security.
>
> (UNC Article 34)

The Security Council shall determine the existence of any threat to the peace, breach of the peace, or act of aggression and shall make recommendations, or decide what measures shall be taken in accordance with Articles 41 and 42, to maintain or restore international peace and security (UNC Article 39).[90]

In relative terms, there are certain things that states can do without foreign interference or constraint; in which case the states must be considered "sovereign." For example, states have the sovereign right to determine the value of their currencies. A state can no longer claim unlimited authority to determine the value of its currency once it renounces its "sovereign" authority to establish the value of its currency by acceding to a contractual arrangement that limits its ability to unilaterally determine the value of its currency without injury to others.

International contract law is pretty elementary, straightforward, and numerously illustrated in the Vienna Law of Treaties. "Every treaty in force is binding upon the parties and must be performed by them in good faith," *pacta sunt servanda*. Of course, contracting parties are not naïve about unforeseen circumstances that can render treaties inoperable. Therefore, members usually make accommodative provisions to deal with sudden and inhibitive changes; the fundamental and unanticipated circumstances that compromise the ability of states to fulfill their treaty obligations (*rebus sic stantibus*). Accordingly, the IMF's Articles of Agreement make provisions for those changes. The Articles require members to construct with the Fund before altering the par value of their currencies when circumstances change. That is, it is illegal and unacceptable to make arbitrary and capricious changes to the value of a currency after freely entering into a contractual arrangement with other members.

Notably, the Bretton Woods system was set up with the intent of liberalizing global trade in order to restrict capricious national policies appertaining to currency valuation. The system was a response to the dislocation of global trade during the interregnum and the post-World War II economy. Therefore, though a state has uninhibited capacity to determine the value of its currency in municipal law, the unrestrained use of monetary authority is susceptible to discrimination, defalcation, and injury to others. Judge Lauterpacht notes:

> Currency legislation is not necessarily within the reserved domain of domestic jurisdiction. Moreover, if a State contracts with respect to a standard of payment other than that afforded by its currency at any given moment it remains bound by it, and cannot alter that standard by monetary manipulation, or by reference to the monetary manipulation of other countries.
>
> (O'Connell, 1965, p. 1098)

8.8 (A) (I) OBLIGATIONS REGARDING EXCHANGE ARRANGEMENTS (ART. IV)

Recognizing that the essential purpose of the international monetary system is to provide a framework that facilitates the exchange of goods, services, and capital among countries, and that sustains sound economic growth, and that a principal objective is the continuing development of the orderly underlying conditions that are necessary for financial and economic stability, each member undertakes to collaborate with the Fund and other members to assure orderly exchange arrangements and to promote a stable system of exchange rates. In particular, each member shall: (i) endeavor to direct its economic and financial policies toward the objective of fostering orderly economic growth with reasonable price stability, with due regard to its circumstances; (ii) seek to promote stability by fostering orderly underlying economic and financial conditions and a monetary system that does not tend to produce erratic disruptions; (iii) avoid manipulating exchange rates or the international monetary system in order to prevent effective balance of payments adjustment or to gain an unfair competitive advantage over other members; and (iv) follow exchange policies compatible with the undertakings under this Section.

8.8 (A) (II) SURVEILLANCE OVER EXCHANGE ARRANGEMENTS (ART. IV § 3)

(a) The Fund shall oversee the international monetary system in order to ensure its effective operation, and shall oversee the compliance of each member with its obligations under Section 1 of this Article. (b) In order to fulfill its functions under (a) above, the Fund shall exercise firm surveillance over the exchange rate policies of members, and shall adopt specific principles for the guidance of all members with respect to those policies. Each member shall provide the Fund with the information necessary for such surveillance, and, when requested by the Fund, shall consult with it on the member's exchange rate policies. The principles adopted by the Fund shall be consistent with cooperative arrangements by which members maintain the value of their currencies in relation to the value of the currency or currencies of other members, as well as with other exchange arrangements of a member's choice consistent with the purposes of the Fund and Section 1 of this Article. These principles shall respect the domestic social and political policies of members, and in applying these principles the Fund shall pay due regard to the circumstances of members.

8.8 (A) (III) WAIVER CONDITIONS (ART. V § 4)

The Fund may in its discretion, and on terms which safeguard its interests, waive any of the conditions prescribed in Section 3(b)(iii) and (iv) of this Article, especially in the case of members with a record of avoiding large or continuous use of the Fund's general resources. In making a waiver it shall take into consideration periodic or exceptional requirements of the member requesting the waiver. The Fund shall also take into consideration a member's willingness to pledge as collateral security acceptable assets having a value sufficient in the opinion of the Fund to protect its interests and may require as a condition of waiver the pledge of such collateral security.[91]

8.8 (A) (IV) INELIGIBILITY TO USE THE FUND'S GENERAL RESOURCES (ART. V § 5)

Whenever the Fund is of the opinion that any member is using the general resources of the Fund in a manner contrary to the purposes of the Fund, it shall present to the member a report setting forth the views of the Fund and prescribing a suitable time for reply. After presenting such a report to a member, the Fund may limit the use of its general resources by the member. If no reply to the report is received from the member within the prescribed time, or if the reply received is unsatisfactory, the Fund may continue to limit the member's use of the general resources of the Fund or may, after giving reasonable notice to the member, declare it ineligible to use the general resources of the Fund.

8.8 (A) (V) INTERPRETATION OF THE ARTICLES OF AGREEMENT (ART. XXIX)

(a) Any question of interpretation of the provisions of this Agreement arising between any member and the Fund or between any members of the Fund shall be submitted to the Executive Board for its decision. If the question particularly affects any member, it shall be entitled to representation in accordance with Article XII, Section 3(j).[92] (b) In any case where the Executive Board has given a decision under (a) above, any member may require, within three months from the date of the decision, that the question be referred to the Board of Governors, whose decision shall be final.

Evidently, Art. XXIX of the current Articles unequivocally gives the Executive Board of the Fund supranational and superseding authority to act as the final arbiter of currency dispute within the framework of the monetary treaty (contract).[93] The dispute resolution mechanism and abandonment of convertibility, quite apart from the demonetization of gold in the international payment system, has reduced the culpability or liability of international agents under currency valuation. Since convertible currencies are considered to be just as good as gold for international transactions, currency disputes have become a much more subdued economic phenomenon with less pervasive agitation. Monetary treaty has made it far more unlikely for courts to be the final arbiter of currency disputes among Member States; meaning that currency dispute resolutions and enforcement measures, appertaining to the Articles of Agreement, must be authoritatively resolved within the structure of the IMF. Though the pass-through effects of currency devaluations or revaluations are channeled through international trade, the DSU of the WTO was never designed to resolve currency disputes as a specialized agency of the UN.

8.9 APPLICATIONS OF MONETARY LAW: NO CONTRIVED CONFISCATION

In the past, it was usual for states to include gold clause obligations in treaties (bilateral and multilateral). The practice provided for a standard of value that affected private transactions between private persons and guaranteed protection by international law through the rules of treaty and diplomatic protection.[94] Most of the currency cases that have been settled in international courts involve loan payments or the arbitrary alteration of the value of currencies that are injurious. The cases generally generate fundamental principles that are essential to understanding the injurious effects of devaluative practice when states are involved.

In the 1920s, Serbian loans (bonds) were issued in France. French holders of the bonds claimed the right to have interest (coupon) payments and redemption of the bonds in gold currency. Countering, the Serb-Croat-Slovene Government claimed that it was barely obligated to make payments in French Paper currency. Based on a special agreement of April 19, 1928, the French and the Serb governments submitted the dispute to the Permanent Court of International Justice (PCIJ). By submitting the disputes to the court, the governments exercised their rights to act in the interest of the court (see also Chapter II of the Statute of the International Court of Justice (SICJ)). "Only states may be parties in cases before the Court" (SICJ Art. 34). The court ruled (in a 9 to 3 decision) that although French law stipulated that gold payments were null and void for domestic transactions, the stipulation did not apply to international transactions that were governed by the law of the borrowing state. More so, the loan contracts required payments that were based on the gold standard. Consequently, the Serbian Government breached contractual currency arrangement under the gold standard (see *France v. Serb-Croat-Slovene State* (1929) (PCIJ)).

A similar case, *Brazil v. France*, was also decided by the PCIJ in 1929. The borrower, Brazil, had issued some pre-World War I loans and was interested in making repayments in French francs that had badly depreciated. Should the "gold clause" apply to the repayment of interest and principal? By special agreement of August 27, 1927, the Brazilian and French Governments submitted the dispute to the PCIJ. In a 9 to 2 decision the court held that the relevant contract, "gold clause," and law of the borrower (Brazil), rather than French law, require Brazil (the borrower) to make payments in equivalent gold.

8.10 LONG-TERM FOREIGN INVESTMENT AND FOREIGN INVESTMENT LAWS

Nations that plan to grow in the future rely on long-term investment. Long-term investment is particularly significant for developing economies where the paucity of national saving and high levels of public debt inhibit or retard economic growth and development. Consequently, foreign direct investment (FDI) is a critical source of developmental asset for poorer countries with untapped resources and insufficient saving and capital (human and physical). FDI is a category of long-term investment in which the direct investor in a foreign country acquires lasting interest in an enterprise residing in another country (the recipient country). Since direct investment requires a long-term relationship between the direct investor and the direct investment, the direct investor exercises a significant amount of influence over the investment enterprise for a long period of time. Therefore, FDI is made up of initial transaction, establishing the enterprise between the contracting parties, and all subsequent transactions between the entities and other affiliated enterprises that may or may not be incorporated.[95] A firm is generally classified as a foreign entity if a foreign investor or entity (considered to be the parent) holds at least ten percent of the equity of a local firm (or the affiliate).

FDIs are normally undertaken on a contractual basis through bilateral investment agreements (BITs) or international investment agreements (IIAs) between international investors and resident governments. Of course, in all contracts, contracting parties have obligations that must be fulfilled. In this case, investors are making contracts with sovereign governments that have considerable power over the longevity and prosperity of long-term investments. Accordingly, cross-border investments are very risky propositions that require very attractive and assuaging conditions in recipient countries (pull factors) rather than push factors. Transnational companies (TNCs) or multinational companies (MNCs) that transport FDI to needy areas can generate multiple benefits in recipient countries. The external benefits include technological transfer, increase in innovation, learning by doing, and economic growth and development. In the process of conveying these benefits it must not be lost that TNCs can also create undesirable problems when they operate in an unethical manner. Residents might complain about environmental degradation, employment discrimination, transfer pricing, tax evasion, bribery or corruption, and surreptitious usurpation of political authority. Invariably, the negatives are generally undesirable and more likely to be in violation of contractual and ethical obligations.

Though economic theories favorably and incontrovertibly support the link between FDI and economic growth, the empirical inquiry into such a link has been mixed and controversial. The paradox surrounding the empirical findings can be attributed to multiple factors; for example, variable selection, quality of data, model specification, country characteristics, trade policy, type of FDI, and the extent to which contractual obligations are violated. Violations of contractual obligations will obviously impinge on the efficacy of FDI in the short and long run, and such violations can further deter the inflow of long-term capital when the violations push investment to other countries or regions. In effect, it should not be surprising that FDI flows to both developed and developing countries can be beneficial only in some circumstances.[96] Notwithstanding, some empirical studies have validated the stylized facts of economic theories.

Hansen and Rand (2006) report strong causality from FDI to growth, notwithstanding levels of economic development. Choe (2003) and Chowdhury and Mavrotas (2006) find bidirectional Granger causality between FDI and growth. Zhang (2001) affirms that country-specific conditions impinge on the impact of FDI on economic growth.

The United Nations Conference on Trade and Development (UNCTAD) closely tracks long-term investments and it has attributed the direction of FDI flows to policy and economic and business factors. In the last few years, restrictions on foreign ownership, based on national security considerations or strategic technologies, have again been front of mind for policymakers.[97] Rates of return on FDI equally affect the direction of FDI flows.[98] For the developing regions of the world, FDI rates of return have progressively declined (see Table 8.4). In Africa, for example, return on investment dropped from 11.9 per cent in 2010 to 6.5 per cent in 2018.

In general, from 2016 to 2018, Europe, North America, and transitional economies have seen a decline in FDI inflows (see Figure 8.15).[99] FDI flows can be tricky because of ebb and flow and political factors or changes. Longer periods are required to show a trend. The European slump, which is believed to be temporary, can be associated with uncertainties in the European Union, repatriating earnings of US transnationals, and a substantial amount of mergers and acquisitions that have been taking place. Greenfield projections show prospects of increased FDI flows.

Table 8.4 Inward FDI rates of return, 2010–2018 (%)

Region	2010	2011	2012	2013	2014	2015	2016	2017	2018
Developed	6.4	6.7	6.1	5.9	6.4	6.0	5.9	5.9	6.0
Developing	11.0	11.5	10.1	9.9	9.5	8.4	8.2	8.1	7.8
Africa	11.9	12.0	11.7	11.4	9.6	6.5	5.0	6.0	6.5
LAC	9.7	9.8	8.5	7.0	6.3	4.5	5.4	6.2	6.2
Asia	11.4	12.2	10.6	10.8	10.7	10.0	9.6	9.0	8.5
E & S-E Asia	12.5	13.4	11.6	11.9	11.8	11.1	10.4	9.9	9.4
South Asia	8.9	7.6	7.2	6.7	6.1	5.5	6.4	5.6	5.3

Source: UNCTAD (2019, p. 15).
Notes: Annual rates of return are measured as annual FDI income for year t divided by the average of the end-of-year FDI positions for years t and t – 1 at book values. Inward flows represent transactions that increase the investment that foreign investors have in businesses that exist in the resident (reporting) economy less transactions that decrease the investment of foreign investors in resident businesses. FDI flows are measured in US$ and as a share of GDP. FDI creates stable and long-lasting links between economies.

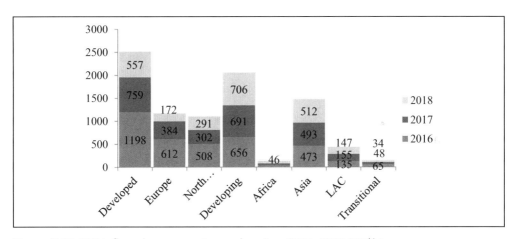

Figure 8.15 FDI inflows by economies and region, 2016–2018 (US$b)
Source: UNCTAD (2019b, p. 14). Projections and percentages have been excluded here. Values for Africa are $46b (2016), $41b (2017), $46b (2018).
Note: Unlike other regions of the world, Africa has not been very successful in attracting a comparatively larger amount of FDI. Between 2016 and 2018, FDI flows have hovered around $41b to $46b. However, in 2018, it escaped the global decline in FDI as it witnessed an 11 percent increase in FDI. FDI flows contracted in some countries but increased in others. For example, Nigeria and Egypt witnessed a decline but South Africa and Morocco experienced an increase.

8.10 (A) THE INTERNATIONAL LAW OF FOREIGN DIRECT INVESTMENT (FDI)

The investment laws governing FDI are largely bilateral, based on what foreign investors can ethically offer and legally adhere to, and the obligations of states to protect the property and returns of foreign investors. Although the treaties are generally considered to be bilateral, there are multilateral obligations of states that are willing to abide by the international laws of investment. The provisions of these international conventions must be appropriately reflected in municipal laws. Additionally, though foreign investors are not signatories of multilateral treaties, states can represent the interests of their nationals (also refer to the sources of international law in this chapter).[100] In the 1990s attempts were made to strike a Multilateral Agreement on Investment, but they officially failed in 1998.

International organizations create an environment for developing general principles of law and norms for international investment. The Organization of Economic Cooperation and Development (OECD) provides a forum for establishing international norms of investment. Treaty negotiators and experts (from OECD and non-OECD countries) work together to enhance the common understanding of core treaty provisions and emerging legal issues. The collaboration is intended to improve the results of international investment treaties between governments and investors. Therefore, together with governments, policy makers, and citizens, the OECD is committed to establishing international norms for investment, economic growth, and sustainable development *inter alia*.

Additionally, the United Nations Conference on Trade and Development (UNCTAD) creates a multilateral framework for nations to deal with trade, investment, and development issues. The organization was established in 1964 by the UN as a permanent intergovernmental body. At the time of this writing there are 195 members of the organization. The 2011 OECD Guidelines for Multilateral [Transnational] Enterprises provide a detailed outline of the obligations of transnational enterprises. The Guidelines are recommendations by governments to transnational enterprises. "They provide non-binding principles and standards for responsible business conduct in a global context consistent with applicable laws and internationally recognised standards. The *Guidelines* are the only multilaterally agreed and comprehensive code of responsible business conduct that governments have committed to promoting."[101] The *Guidelines* express the shared values of the sending governments with a large share of international direct investment whose laws are not necessarily applicable to the operations of transnationals in foreign lands (the home countries are sending countries but not the *situs* of large transnational enterprises). Adhering governments set up National Contact Points (NCPs) (agencies) to assist transnationals and their stakeholders (all those with vested interest in the successful operation of foreign enterprises, including shareholders) to further the implementation of the *Guidelines*.

Governments of 42 OECD and non-OECD countries started to work on an update for the Declaration on International Investment and Multilateral Enterprises on May 4, 2010 to reflect changes in the environment for international investment and multinational enterprises. The previous review occurred in 2000. The OECD Guidelines have been the "leading international instrument for the promotion of responsible business conduct" (OECD). The Declaration is based on four principal considerations: (i) that international investment is of major importance to the world economy, and has considerably contributed to the development of their countries, (ii) that multinational enterprises play an important role in this investment process, (iii) that international cooperation can improve the foreign investment climate, encourage the positive contribution which multinational enterprises can make to economic, social, and environmental progress, and minimize and resolve difficulties which may arise from their operations, and (iv) that the benefits of international cooperation are enhanced by addressing issues relating to international investment and multinational enterprises through a balanced framework of interrelated instruments. A Declaration usually declares existing law, with or without modification, and it may even create a new law; for example, the Universal Declaration of Human Rights. Declarations may also be made on principle of international law concerning friendly relations and cooperation among nations in accordance with the Charter of the UN; see also discussions of innovation and creative rights in Chapter 4.[102]

8.10 (B) NATIONAL TREATMENT (OECD GUIDELINES: DECLARATION II. 4)

1. That adhering governments should, consistent with their needs to maintain public order, to protect their essential security interests and to fulfil commitments relating to international peace and security, accord to enterprises operating in their territories and owned or controlled directly or indirectly by nationals of another adhering government (hereinafter referred to as "Foreign-Controlled Enterprises") treatment under their laws, regulations and administrative practices, consistent with international law and no less favourable than that accorded in like situations to domestic enterprises (hereinafter referred to as "National Treatment");[103]
2. That adhering governments will consider applying "National Treatment" in respect of countries other than adhering governments;
3. That adhering governments will endeavour to ensure that their territorial subdivisions apply "National Treatment";
4. That this Declaration does not deal with the right of adhering governments to regulate the entry of foreign investment or the conditions of establishment of foreign enterprises.

8.10 (C) INTERNATIONAL INVESTMENT INCENTIVES AND DISINCENTIVES (OECD GUIDELINES: DECLARATION IV. 1–3)

1. That they recognise the need to strengthen their co-operation in the field of international direct investment;
2. That they thus recognise the need to give due weight to the interests of adhering governments affected by specific laws, regulations and administrative practices in this

field (hereinafter called "measures") providing official incentives and disincentives to international direct investment; [and]
3. That adhering governments will endeavour to make such measures as transparent as possible, so that their importance and purpose can be ascertained and that information on them can be readily available.

8.10 (D) CONCEPTS AND PRINCIPLES[104]

Obeying domestic laws is the first obligation of enterprises. The *Guidelines* are neither a substitute for municipal laws nor should they be considered to override domestic law and regulation. While the *Guidelines* extend beyond the law in many cases, they should not be construed as instruments that are intended to place an enterprise in situations where it faces conflicting requirements or economic danger. However, in countries where domestic laws and regulations conflict with the principles and standards of the *Guidelines*, enterprises should seek ways to honour such principles and standards to the fullest extent which does not place them in violation of domestic law (OECD *Guidelines* 1.2).

Governments wish to encourage the widest possible observance of the *Guidelines*. While it is acknowledged that small- and medium-sized enterprises may not have the same capacities as larger enterprises, governments adhering to the *Guidelines* nevertheless encourage them to observe the *Guidelines'* recommendations to the fullest extent possible (OECD *Guidelines* 1.6).

Governments have the right to prescribe the conditions under which multinational enterprises operate within their jurisdictions, subject to international law. The entities of a multinational enterprise located in various countries are subject to the laws applicable in these countries. When multinational enterprises are subject to conflicting requirements by adhering countries or third countries, the governments concerned are encouraged to co-operate in good faith with a view to resolving problems that may arise (OECD *Guidelines* 1.8).

Governments adhering to the *Guidelines* set them forth with the understanding that they will fulfil their responsibilities to treat enterprises equitably and in accordance with international law and with their contractual obligations (OECD *Guidelines* 1.9).

The use of appropriate international dispute settlement mechanisms, including arbitration, is encouraged as a means of facilitating the resolution of legal problems arising between enterprises and host country governments (OECD *Guidelines* 1.10).

Governments adhering to the *Guidelines* will implement them and encourage their use. They will establish National Contact Points that promote the *Guidelines* and act as a forum for discussion of all matters relating to the *Guidelines*. The adhering Governments will also participate in appropriate review and consultation procedures to address issues concerning interpretation of the *Guidelines* in a changing world (OECD *Guidelines* 1.11).

8.10 (E) GENERAL POLICIES (OECD GUIDELINES II)

Enterprises should take fully into account established policies in the countries in which they operate, and consider the views of other stakeholders. In this regard:

A. Enterprises should:
   1. Contribute to economic, environmental and social progress with a view to achieving sustainable development.
   2. Respect the internationally recognised human rights of those affected by their activities.
   3. Encourage local capacity building through close co-operation with the local community, including business interests, as well as developing the enterprise's activities in domestic and foreign markets, consistent with the need for sound commercial practice.
   4. Encourage human capital formation, in particular by creating employment opportunities and facilitating training opportunities for employees.
   5. Refrain from seeking or accepting exemptions not contemplated in the statutory or regulatory framework related to human rights, environmental, health, safety, labour, taxation, financial incentives, or other issues.
   6. Support and uphold good corporate governance principles and develop and apply good corporate governance practices, including throughout enterprise groups.
   7. Develop and apply effective self-regulatory practices and management systems that foster a relationship of confidence and mutual trust between enterprises and the societies in which they operate.
   8. Promote awareness of and compliance by workers employed by multinational enterprises with respect to company policies through appropriate dissemination of these policies, including through training programmes.
   9. Refrain from discriminatory or disciplinary action against workers who make bona fide reports to management or, as appropriate, to the competent public authorities, on practices that contravene the law, the *Guidelines* or the enterprise's policies.
   10. Carry out risk-based due diligence, for example by incorporating it into their enterprise risk management systems, to identify, prevent and mitigate actual and potential adverse impacts as described in paragraphs 11 and 12, and account for how these impacts are addressed. The nature and extent of due diligence depend on the circumstances of a particular situation.
   11. Avoid causing or contributing to adverse impacts on matters covered by the *Guidelines*, through their own activities, and address such impacts when they occur.
   12. Seek to prevent or mitigate an adverse impact where they have not contributed to that impact, when the impact is nevertheless directly linked to their operations, products or services by a business relationship. This is not intended to shift responsibility from the entity causing an adverse impact to the enterprise with which it has a business relationship.

13. In addition to addressing adverse impacts in relation to matters covered by the *Guidelines*, encourage, where practicable, business partners, including suppliers and subcontractors, to apply principles of responsible business conduct compatible with the *Guidelines*.
14. Engage with relevant stakeholders in order to provide meaningful opportunities for their views to be taken into account in relation to planning and decision making for projects or other activities that may significantly impact local communities.
15. Abstain from any improper involvement in local political activities.

B. Enterprises are encouraged to:
 1. Support, as appropriate to their circumstances, cooperative efforts in the appropriate fora to promote Internet Freedom through respect of freedom of expression, assembly and association online.
 2. Engage in or support, where appropriate, private or multi-stakeholder initiatives and social dialogue on responsible supply chain management while ensuring that these initiatives take due account of their social and economic effects on developing countries and of existing internationally recognised standards.

8.10 (F) DISCLOSURE (OECD GUIDELINES III)

1. Enterprises should ensure that timely and accurate information is disclosed on all material matters regarding their activities, structure, financial situation, performance, ownership and governance. This information should be disclosed for the enterprise as a whole, and, where appropriate, along business lines or geographic areas. Disclosure policies of enterprises should be tailored to the nature, size and location of the enterprise, with due regard taken of costs, business confidentiality and other competitive concerns ….

8.10 (G) HUMAN RIGHTS (OECD GUIDELINES IV)

States have the duty to protect human rights. Enterprises should, within the framework of internationally recognised human rights, the international human rights obligations of the countries in which they operate as well as relevant domestic laws and regulations:

1. Respect human rights, which means they should avoid infringing on the human rights of others and should address adverse human rights impacts with which they are involved.
2. Within the context of their own activities, avoid causing or contributing to adverse human rights impacts and address such impacts when they occur ….

8.10 (H) ENVIRONMENT (OECD GUIDELINES V)

Enterprises should, within the framework of laws, regulations and administrative practices in the countries in which they operate, and in consideration of relevant international agreements, principles, objectives, and standards, take due account of the need to protect the environment, public health and safety, and generally to conduct their activities in a manner contributing to the wider goal of sustainable development. In particular, enterprises should:

1. Establish and maintain a system of environmental management appropriate to the enterprise, including:
    a) Collection and evaluation of adequate and timely information regarding the environmental, health, and safety impacts of their activities;
    b) Establishment of measurable objectives and, where appropriate, targets for improved environmental performance and resource utilisation, including periodically reviewing the continuing relevance of these objectives; where appropriate, targets should be consistent with relevant national policies and international environmental commitments; and
    c) Regular monitoring and verification of progress toward environmental, health, and safety objectives or targets ….

8.10 (I) COMBATING BRIBERY, BRIBE SOLICITATION AND EXTORTION (OECD GUIDELINES VII)

Enterprises should not, directly or indirectly, offer, promise, give, or demand a bribe or other undue advantage to obtain or retain business or other improper advantage. Enterprises should also resist the solicitation of bribes and extortion. In particular, enterprises should:

1. Not offer, promise or give undue pecuniary or other advantage to public officials or the employees of business partners. Likewise, enterprises should not request, agree to or accept undue pecuniary or other advantage from public officials or the employees of business partners. Enterprises should not use third parties such as agents and other intermediaries, consultants, representatives, distributors, consortia, contractors and suppliers and joint venture partners for channelling undue pecuniary or other advantages to public officials, or to employees of their business partners or to their relatives or business associates ….

8.10 (J) CONSUMER INTERESTS (OECD GUIDELINES VIII)

When dealing with consumers, enterprises should act in accordance with fair business, marketing and advertising practices and should take all reasonable steps to ensure the quality and reliability of the goods and services that they provide. In particular, they should:

1. Ensure that the goods and services they provide meet all agreed or legally required standards for consumer health and safety, including those pertaining to health warnings and safety information.

2. Provide accurate, verifiable and clear information that is sufficient to enable consumers to make informed decisions, including information on the prices and, where appropriate, content, safe use, environmental attributes, maintenance, storage and disposal of goods and services. Where feasible this information should be provided in a manner that facilitates consumers' ability to compare products.
3. Provide consumers with access to fair, easy to use, timely and effective non-judicial dispute resolution and redress mechanisms, without unnecessary cost or burden.
4. Not make representations or omissions, nor engage in any other practices, that are deceptive, misleading, fraudulent or unfair ....[105]

Public needs (purposes) and violations of BITs may usually result in expropriation or, more perversely, confiscation of foreign property. Case law and rules of expropriation now delineate the circumstances under which a state can expropriate foreign investment with and without compensation. In most if not all normal cases, expropriation requires compensation in a commensurate and timely manner.

8.10 (K) THE TAKING OF FOREIGN PROPERTY (INTERNATIONAL LAW OF EXPROPRIATION AND CONFISCATION)

Reckless seizure of foreign property is a disincentive to the inflow of foreign investment; especially when know-how and domestic national saving is inadequate to finance long-term growth. There are times when non-discriminatory taking might be necessary but for which commensurate and timely compensation must be made. There are generally two types of international takings: (i) direct, and (ii) indirect (*de facto*). UNCTAD's Expropriation Series on International Investment Agreements II (2012) together with Collins' *An Introduction to International Investment Law* (2017) provide a very comprehensive analysis of expropriation law. Direct takings involve the transfer of title and/or outright physical seizure of property. Some measures that are short of physical takings may also amount to takings in that they permanently destroy the economic value of the investment or deprive the owner of its ability to manage, use, or control its property in a meaningful way. Investors may bring expropriation claims with respect to any conduct that is attributable to the host State and in which the latter engaged in its sovereign capacity.[106]

States have a sovereign right under international law to take property held by nationals or aliens through nationalization or expropriation for economic, political, social, or other reasons. In order to be lawful, the exercise of this sovereign right requires, under international law, that the following conditions be met:

(a) Property has to be taken for a public purpose;
(b) On a non-discriminatory basis;
(c) In accordance with due process of law;
(d) Accompanied by compensation (UNCTAD, 2012, p. 1).

Therefore, a bona fide regulatory act, which is consistent with the doctrine of the police powers of states and the stipulated fairness parameters, may not be designated as expropriatory, despite an adverse economic impact. Risks arising from bona fide regulation are effectively placed on economic actors (UNCTAD, 2012, p. xiii).[107]

The principle of proportionality may be used to evaluate a public purpose. That is, counterbalancing the means that is deployed to accomplish an expropriation against the public purpose that is pursued. For example, compensation may be required as in the case of indirect expropriation when land is disproportionately expropriated for public use.[108] The ascertainment of intent is relevant to proportionality and expropriation can be unlawful when mere whimsical political consideration becomes the basis for ostensible abrogation of a BIT.

While it is relatively straightforward to ascertain when seizure without compensation is unlawful, it is quite nebulous to determine illegality under indirect (*de facto*) expropriation, partly because of the issues of intent and timeframe. Indirect expropriation is variously considered to be severe interferences with the use of foreign property. Interference may be in the form of excessive regulation that inhibits the smooth operation and profitability of companies or the replacement of authority to make managerial decisions. Indirect expropriations may be a long, drawn-out process (creeping or incremental expropriation).[109] The incremental nature of the expropriation raises questions about the sufficiency of each step or procedure in the expropriation process. However, some tribunals have recognized the effects of the incremental procedures. In *Siemens v. Argentina*, the tribunal found that each step taken by the government must have created an adverse impact.[110] In effect, a timeframe must be considered to determine whether a consequential creeping expropriation has occurred.

When unlawful abrogations of BITs are established by triers of facts, compensations are generally required. International law requires compensation to be prompt, adequate, and effective.[111] "Prompt" is considered to mean as soon as feasibly possible after an expropriation has occurred, failing which interest will be accrued. "Adequate" alludes to the amount of compensation that must be made, which is usually eclipsed by controversy and based on market valuation. Though the Hull Formula has gained widespread academic appreciation, tribunals may adopt flexible compensatory procedures when they are afforded the authority to do so (see the *Aminoil Case*). Market valuation, at least in developed countries, is considered to be the relevant measure of the value of an expropriated asset. A sticky point has been the point of reference to the diminution of value. In *Santa Elena v. Costa Rica* the tribunal observed: "[T]he expropriated property is to be evaluated as of the date on which the governmental 'interference' has deprived the owner of his rights or has made those rights practically worthless."[112] "Effective" means payments in convertible currency that is not undergoing devaluation.[113]

A distinctive characteristic of multiple BITs is that they allow for an alternative dispute resolution mechanism. Investors whose rights have been abridged could seek recourse in international tribunals under the auspices of the International Center for the Settlement of Investment Disputes (ICSID) rather than host country courts. The ICSID prides itself as "the world's leading institution devoted to international investment dispute settlement." It has administered the majority of all international investment cases and states have accepted the ICSID as a forum for investor-state dispute settlement in most international investment treaties and in numerous investment laws and contracts.

8.11 THE AMINOIL CASE (*GOVERNMENT OF KUWAIT V. AMERICAN INDEPENDENT OIL COMPANY, 1982*)

The American Independent Oil (Aminoil) Company case is a foreign investment case that is instructive for a variety of reasons. It involves: (i) a change of circumstances, (ii) sustainable development and business practices (ethical/unethical), (iii) fair and equitable treatment (FET), (iv) the parameters of lawful and unlawful expropriation, (v) the interface of municipal and public international law that can shape the competence of tribunals, (vi) valuation and compensation, (vii) the law of state succession and autonomous use of national resources, and (viii) the stability of exchange rate (currency valuation).

The first major oil discoveries in the Middle East were made in Iran in 1908. About three years later, an Anglo-Persian Oil Company, which later became British Petroleum, expressed interest in securing an oil concession from Sheikh Mubarak of Kuwait.[114] Companies sought concessions for several years, but it was not until December 23, 1934, that Kuwait offered the first concession to Kuwait Oil Company (KOC) (a joint venture comprising the Anglo-Persian Oil Company and Gulf Oil Corporation).

On June 28, 1948, Sheikh Ahmed Al Jabir al Sabah, Ruler of Kuwait (1921–1950) granted Aminoil a concession to exploit oil reserves in the "Neutral Zone," which was a buffer strip between Kuwait and the Kingdom of Saudi Arabia, that was designated as a neutral area by an agreement of 1922. Aminoil was incorporated in Delaware in 1947 on the initiative of a former executive of Standard Oil. Three small oil companies, Phillips Petroleum Company, Signal Oil and Gas Company, and Ashland Oil and Refining Company became its major shareholders. Aminoil posted a down payment of US$625,000 and started drilling in December 1949 after making an additional payment of US$.7.25 million to the Sheikh.[115]

Modeled on the KOC template, the Aminoil concession had annual financial obligations: (i) a royalty of US$2.50 for every ton of oil recovered subject to a minimum annual royalty of US$625,000, (ii) one-eighth of Aminoil's gross proceeds from the sale of natural gas, (iii) 15 percent of the shares in a subsidiary to be established to explore and exploit the Divided Zone, and (iv) 15 per cent of the shares in any subsidiary to be established to operate an oil refinery.[116] The concession also contained operational obligations (good business practices) within it. Aminoil was expected to engage in good oilfield practices though it had control over the quantities of production and the prices at which products were sold. The company was originally granted 60 years of exclusive right to exploit oil resources for a fixed payment per ton.

The concession contained provisions that were collectively considered to be a "stabilization clause." The stabilization clause was understood to be a bulwark against arbitrary abrogation of the concession. Kuwait undertook not to annul the concession or modify its terms. Article 17 of the 1948 Agreement stated that:

> The Shaikh shall not by general or special legislation or by administrative measures or by any other act whatever annul this Agreement except as provided in Article 11. No alteration shall be made in the terms of this Agreement by either the Shaikh or the Company except in the event of the Shaikh and the Company jointly agreeing that it is desirable in the interest of both parties to make certain alterations, deletions or additions to this Agreement.[117]

The clause was eventually amended in 1961. Yet Article 11(B) provided assurances against premature abrogation of the concession except by surrender, defined in Article 12 or default under the arbitration provisions of Article 18.

However, British colonial influence in Kuwait continued until 1961 when Kuwait and the United Kingdom entered into a Treaty of Independence. Kuwait declared sovereignty that was recognized by the British, thereby creating a change of circumstance. A new constitution was promulgated on November 11, 1962, proclaiming the independence and sovereignty of Kuwait, and on May 14, 1963 Kuwait became a member of the UN. Invariably, Kuwait gained (autonomy) control of its natural resources.

In 1961 Kuwait and Aminoil entered into a Supplemental Concession Agreement (the "1961 Agreement"). The Supplemental Concession coincided with an emerging practice of 50/50 profit sharing in oil concessions and 50 percent business taxes in the Arab Middle East. After some negotiations in the 1970s, a Draft Agreement was signed in 1973 to reflect changes that were taking place in the global oil market. However, the 1973 Draft Agreement was never ratified by the Kuwaiti parliament. The most notable developments were successive decisions by the Organization of the Petroleum Exporting Countries (OPEC) in Tehran (1971) and Geneva (1972 and 1973) to take control of posted oil prices and to increase their participation in oil ventures to 25 percent.[118] Accordingly, in October 1973 OPEC established posted prices that reflected a 70 percent markup above those set by oil companies. Kuwait gave Aminoil an ultimatum to comply or cease production immediately. Aminoil complied.

In November 1974 three Gulf States met at Abu Dhabi and resolved to increase royalties to 20 percent and income tax to 85 percent of posted prices with immediate effect. The resolution, which was adopted by OPEC in December 1974, became known as the "Abu Dhabi formula." The Gulf States had considered the returns on the foreign investment of the oil companies, emanating from dramatic increase in oil prices, to be "windfall profits." The Abu Dhabi formula reduced revenues to the companies. Revenues were predetermined on a fixed (package) basis of 22 cents per barrel, thereby transforming the concessions into *de facto* service contracts. Aminoil requested negotiations to mitigate the adverse terms and proposed a number of compromises. Negotiations between the two parties broke down in 1977 and Aminoil initiated arbitration proceedings.

On September 19, 1977, the Kuwaiti Government issued Decree Law No. 124, effectively terminating the agreement between the Kuwaiti Government and Aminoil. By invoking Article 1 of the concession, which terminated the concession, Article 2 became effective:

> All the interests, funds, assets, facilities and operations of the Company, including the refinery and other installations relating to the aforementioned Concession, shall revert to the State. Article 3 established a "Compensation Committee" to assess the amount of "fair compensation" due to Aminoil, and the extent of Aminoil's "outstanding obligations to the State or other parties." However, Aminoil had already commenced arbitration proceedings and declined to participate in the Committee's deliberations.[119]

To legitimize the nationalization, Kuwait issued Decree Law No. 174 in 1977, establishing a Compensation Committee to determine the amount of fair compensation. Nationalization is widespread takings of private property in all economic sectors, a sector, or an industry. The usual intent (ostensible or otherwise) is to effect complete state control of an economy by taking over all privately-owned means of production.[120]

Hunter and Sinclair (2005) report that Aminoil commenced arbitration proceedings in London, relying on Article 18 of the 1948 Concession which contained an arbitration agreement, but Kuwait refused to participate in the arbitration on the ground that the 1948 Concession had effectively been superseded by the subsequent 1961 and 1973 Agreements. Additionally, the appointing authority specified in Article 18, the "British Political Resident in the Persian Gulf," had long since ceased to exist with the demise of British colonial influence in the region. By denying the force of the 1973 Agreement, Aminoil refused to invoke the arbitration agreement contained therein. The disputants were deadlocked for a while, but *ad hoc* arbitration proceedings commenced in Paris after consensus on the submission to arbitration (the "Arbitration Agreement") on July 23, 1979. The London arbitration was discontinued.

8.11 (A) THE LAWS GOVERNING THE ARBITRATION

The parties agreed to mandatory procedural provisions and the tribunal was allowed to determine the procedural law in the *situs* of the court. The procedures to be used were to be based on natural justice and applicable principles of transnational arbitration procedure deemed necessary. The court was left to regulate all unspecified matters relating to the conduct of the arbitration. Much of the character of the proceedings came from public international law dispute settlement procedures, with each party appointing an agent with plenipotentiary powers; neither party was classified as claimant or respondent, and memorials were concomitantly exchanged.

Article 111(2) of the Arbitration Agreement calls on the tribunal to recognize the law governing the substantive issues between the parties while also considering the quality of the parties, the transnational character of their relations, and the principles of law and practice prevailing in the modern world. The Tribunal referred to the law of Kuwait as the "law most directly involved" in accordance with the traditional respect due to the state party to a state contract, subject to the proviso that "this conclusion does not carry any all-embracing consequences with it" because, as the Government had stressed, public international law formed a constituent part of Kuwaiti law. The pragmatic blend of municipal and international law thereby proposed echoed the solution found in Article 42 of the ICSID Convention. However, the tribunal did not expand on the relationship between Kuwaiti and international law and arguably obscured the "role of international law as the ultimate controlling standard." In practice, the applicable law presented the tribunal with few difficulties because it held that these sources were not in conflict with each other so, and on most issues, it could rely on the principals of customary international law.[121]

8.11 (B) SOVEREIGNTY OVER NATIONAL RESOURCES AND NATIONALIZATION

The tribunal had no difficulty establishing that a nation has autonomy over its natural resources. It therefore turned to the issues of coercion, expropriation, and restitution. Sovereignty was closely tied to decolonization (a supervening change of circumstances) (*rebus sic stantibus*), which conferred autonomous right on the state of Kuwait. General changes in the regime ran parallel to profound and general transformation in the terms of oil concessions in the Middle East. The tribunal held that the Concession had become a contract governed by changed circumstances. It noted that in most legal systems, while a state is bound to respect contracts, a state enjoys special advantages, including the right to terminate concessions and that stabilization clauses may not prohibit nonconfiscatory takings. In effect, the tribunal also relied on international conventions.[122]

The judges allude to UN General Assembly Resolutions as a source of customary international law; for example, UN Commission on Permanent Sovereignty over Natural Resources and the UN Economic and Social Council embodied in UN General Assembly ("GA") Resolution 1803 of December 14, 1962. The latter declared the "inalienable right of all States freely to dispose of their natural wealth and resources in accordance with their national interests."[123] GA Resolution 1803 was considered an accurate reflection of customary international law. But even assuming that the Resolutions do not carry legal weight, the tribunal could not find a rule of international law that prohibits a state from nationalizing a company during a limited period of time. However, the court was not very well disposed to the abusive use of state coercion.

One of the judges, Sir Gerald Fitzmaurice (a dissenting judge), found the change in circumstance to be plausible, but concluded that changes should have been made within the framework of the continuing concession. In his dissent of "considerable persuasive force," Fitzmaurice concluded that it was an "illusion" that monetary compensation alone could alter the clearly confiscatory character of a forced nationalization. Ultimately Fitzmaurice's disagreement was "over the principle of interpretation of the stabilization clauses." Article 17 was not confined to only confiscatory measures: "What they are concerned with is any measure *terminating the Concession* before its time." In his opinion the nationalization was "irreconcilable with the stabilization clauses" and therefore unlawful.[124]

The concept of sovereignty over natural resources ultimately superseded the stabilization clause. Kuwait unsuccessfully argued that the stabilization clauses should not remain binding after Kuwait was no longer under its protected colonial status, because the provisions of the clause had been imposed at a time when Kuwait had not been an independent sovereign state. The argument was considered to be spurious but inconsequential. Kuwait had confirmed the provisions in two separate amendments after gaining full independence. More so, there was nothing in the new constitution of 1961 that prohibited the state from entering into such commitments. Hence, the argument that Kuwait's act of nationalization was in violation of the fealty to international investment treaty (*pacta sunt servanda*), and therefore a manifestation of unlawful expropriation, did not gain much appeal. Nationalization is lawful when it is accompanied by a mechanism for fair compensation in a reasonable amount of time. Contemporary scholars embrace the Hull Formula of prompt, adequate, and effective compensation.

Was the nationalization unlawful? While Judge Fitzmaurice concluded that the nationalization was confiscatory because of the premature and coercive termination of the concession, the compensatory provisions of Decree Law No. 174 *ex post facto* persuaded the other judges otherwise. To be characterized as a "lawful taking" in international law, the tribunal held that a nationalization measure must be accompanied by a mechanism for assessing "fair compensation" payable to the party whose assets have been taken.[125] The independence of a body appointed by a government for the purpose of compensation was considered legally moot. Therefore, the tribunal accepted in principle that though a stabilization clause could be effective in public international law to fetter a state from unlawfully nationalizing foreign property, the clause must expressly and specifically be to that effect for a limited time.

Given that the Concession had already been in existence for 30 years, however, the tribunal failed to accept that the intended effect of the Concession was to exclude nationalization for the "especially long" full 60 years of the Concession. Further, the tribunal could not see why the nationalization was confiscatory when the government had provided mechanisms for fair compensation to be paid. By adopting a distinction between lawful and unlawful nationalization to guide its determination of the applicable standards of compensation, the majority held that the taking was lawful on the basis that the nationalization had been undertaken for a legitimate public purpose consistent with

Kuwait's overall policy for the development of its vital petroleum industry, designed to culminate in its complete nationalization.[126]

8.11 (C) FAIR AND EQUITABLE TREATMENT (FET)

Among the most comprehensive definitions of FET in any IIA is that contained in the negotiated text of the TTIP.[127] The list of actions that will constitute FET violations include: (a) denial of justice in criminal, civil or administrative proceedings; or (b) fundamental breach of due process, including a fundamental breach of transparency and obstacles to effective access to justice, in judicial and administrative proceedings; or (c) manifest arbitrariness; or (d) targeted discrimination on manifestly wrongful grounds, such as gender, race, or religious belief; or (e) harassment, coercion, abuse of power or similar bad faith conduct, or (f) a breach of any further elements of the fair and equitable treatment obligation adopted by the Parties in accordance with paragraph 3 of [Chapter II Art. 3].[128] Therefore, FET can be used to address a wide variety of governmental abuses that are adversarial to foreign investment when the rules are specific and unlawfully inhibitive. Collins (2017) notes that the essential purpose of FET clause as used in an investment treaty may indeed be to fill the gaps that have been left out by the more specific standards.[129]

Did the Kuwaiti Government engage in an unfair and discriminatory treatment to foster an illegal expropriation of the assets of Aminoil? Aminoil claimed that the nationalization of its company was discriminatory and unfair. The seizure or nationalization was not extended to the assets of the Arabian Oil Company (AOC), a Japanese company with an offshore concession. Kuwait argued that the AOC concession had different features and was not similarly situated. AOC concerned an offshore operation, which required special and uncommon expertise that was not readily available in Kuwait at the time. Further, the concession was jointly held with the Government of Saudi Arabia.

The tribunal dismissed Aminoil's argument that the taking was discriminatory because it did not include the assets of AOC who were operating an offshore concession in the Divided Zone, arguing further that nationalization should not necessarily be a sweeping and immediate undertaking. Apart from the compensatory provisions that influenced its decision, the tribunal concluded that a government that is pursuing a coherent policy of nationalization should be entitled to do so progressively (incrementally), in keeping with the development of necessary administrative and technical availabilities.

8.11 (D) GOOD BUSINESS (OILFIELD) PRACTICES

The government's case concerning Aminoil's management of the oilfield was substantially circumstantial and conflicting expert testimonies by the parties (disputants) provided no conclusive evidence for judicial clarity (adjudication). It was therefore difficult for Kuwait to satisfy the burden of proof that was required by the tribunal to demonstrate that Aminoil breached its contractual obligation to make the investment that was needed in compliance with the requirements of good oilfield practice (sustainable development). Accordingly, the tribunal failed to accept Kuwait's argument that Aminoil's oilfield practices were violative of the terms of the concession. "Nevertheless, in the aftermath of the award, there was a widely-held view within Government circles that the overall result of the arbitration must have reflected a certain feeling within the Tribunal that RJ Reynolds' adventure in Kuwait was aimed at extracting the maximum amount of money from the country without investing more than the minimum amount of capital to keep the operations running profitably. The Tribunal might have been even more sympathetic to Kuwait if it had known that, a mere two years after the award was issued, RJ Reynolds would apparently be able to sell Aminoil for US$1.7 billion."[130]

8.11 (E) THE GOLD CLAUSE AND ASSET (CURRENCY) PRICE STABILITY OR CONVERTIBILITY

The Kuwaiti Government wanted to maintain a steady stream of revenue (cash flow), unimpaired by currency devaluation or depreciation, from Aminoil's investment. Therefore, since Aminoil's payments to the government were to be made in US dollars, the government included a gold clause in the concession to protect itself against the depreciation or devaluation of the US dollar. As already noted in this chapter, gold clauses are also instrumental in making compensation judgments. On the day the concession was signed, Article 3(h) provided for future dollar payments to be based on the parity (benchmark) value of the dollar relative to an ounce of gold (analogously, see Figure 8.11). At the time, US$35 was "sufficient to purchase" one fine ounce of gold "at the official United States Government price then in force." However, in 1971 President Nixon suspended the convertibility of dollars to gold. The dollar price of gold significantly appreciated in the ensuing months after the suspension of convertibility.

By February 1972, the Ministry of Finance and Oil of the Government of Kuwait complained to Aminoil that royalties paid in US dollars were not adjusted for the depreciating value of the US dollar relative to the value of gold as required by the gold clause. As Aminoil equivocated and based its response on ongoing negotiations between the US Treasury and the IMF to establish a new dollar price for gold, Kuwait insisted on its right to maintain the gold value of its royalties by invoking the gold clause. In 1973, Aminoil asked for the gold clause to be expunged. Both parties subsequently agreed to accept the OPEC "Geneva" proposal of January 1972 to calculate oil prices based on an index that tracked changes in the exchange rates between the dollar and a basket of nine other currencies.[131] A 1973 Agreement confirmed the deletion of gold clause, but Aminoil disavowed the 1973 agreement in its case before the tribunal. The application of the gold clause would have required a significant re-evaluation of the financial relationship between the government and Aminoil.[132] Aminoil's indebtedness to the government was estimated by the government to be approximately $1,868 million in unpaid royalties and taxes by the date the concession was revoked. Any claim for lost future profits by the company would have been neutralized by the required financial commitments under the 1948 Concession.

The Tribunal could not determine a "virtual" official US gold price in the absence of a real one. Aminoil's 1973 letter and the 1973 Agreement had rendered the gold clause moot. However, the renunciation of the gold clause did not negate the effects of inflation. Both parties had showed intent to mitigate the effects of inflation.

8.11 (F) BUSINESS VALUATION AND COMPENSATION

Under Article III of the Arbitration Agreement, the parties called on an *ad hoc* tribunal to rule on (i) the amount of compensation payable by the government to Aminoil as a result of the nationalization, (ii) the amount of damages payable by the government to Aminoil as a result of the termination of the Concession, and (iii) the amount payable to the government by Aminoil, or by the government to Aminoil, in respect of outstanding royalties, taxes, or other obligations arising out of the parties' legal relationship.[133]

The *Aminoil Case* considered different methods of business valuation for expropriated assets. Kuwait favored the net book value of the assets in question, but Aminoil sought the monetary equivalent of the replacement value (*restitutio in integrum*) for its assets, also implying that its business must be evaluated as a going concern incorporating all relevant elements of lost profits.

In effect, Aminoil invoked the fundamental principle governing the duty to make reparation for an internationally wrongful act. The principle of *restitutio in integrum* was applied by the PCIJ (1927) in the *Chorzów Factory Case*:

> Reparation must, as far as possible wipe out all the consequences of the illegal act and reestablish the situation which would in all probability, have existed if that act had not been committed.[134]

The application of the principle is predicated on an illegal act, which is in direct conflict with state sovereignty and nonconfiscatory taking. Surprisingly, controversy surrounds the conditions under which it could be applied against a state in favor of a private party, especially when taking is nonconfiscatory for a public purpose.

The Tribunal rejected the net book value proposed by Kuwait and accepted the depreciated replacement value method. It stated that the net book value approach can only be appropriate when investment is recent and the original cost is not far removed from the present replacement cost. Net space book value may have provided the basis for a number of compensation settlements between Gulf States and oil companies, but there was a general absence of *opinion juris sive necessitates* (*opinio juris*). That is, the practice by the Gulf States could not have been considered to be a general practice accepted as law. It is insufficient to show that states habitually follow a certain course of conduct, either by action or acquiescence. To prove the existence of a rule of international customary law, it is necessary to establish that states engage in a conduct because of a compulsory legal obligation.[135]

The tribunal considered the company to be a going concern because its undertaking (investment) was a source of profit. "The value of Aminoil as a going concern was made up of the values of the various components of the undertaking separately considered, and of the undertaking itself considered as an organic totality—or going concern—therefore as a unified whole, the value of which is greater than that of its component parts."[136]

The disputing parties filed for staggering amounts of money (compensation). Aminoil sought to recover over US$423 million in overpaid royalties and taxes under the contested 1973 Agreement, and compensation and damages for the allegedly unlawful termination of its Concession totaling US$2,587 million. The government's claims were not as substantial but they were significantly eye-popping: US$32 million of unpaid money under the financial provisions of the 1973 Agreement, US$90 million under the Abu Dhabi formula, and US$18 million in respect of Aminoil's liabilities to third parties that the government had met after the nationalization.[137] There were also unqualified claims for damages arising out of Aminoil's alleged failure to meet its good oilfield practice obligations. On March 24, 1982, the tribunal handed down its decision on the case between the Government of Kuwait and American Independent Oil Company.

When it comes to the methodology for assessing fair compensation, the tribunal was thus not constrained in any way by the arbitration agreement. As such, it was left to determine the meaning and method of fair compensation. Aminoil wanted "prompt, adequate and effective compensation"; a paradigm that has widespread recognition or approbation by many distinguished and authoritative authors in the developed world. Kuwait preferred and urged the tribunal to adopt a less encompassing (flexible) standard that was more appropriate in a case of lawful nationalization. Articles 35 and 36 of the International Law Commission's (ILC's) *Articles on Responsibility of States for Internationally Wrongful Acts* distinguishes between restitution and compensation:

> A State responsible for an internationally wrongful act is under an obligation to make restitution, that is, to re-establish the situation which existed before the wrongful act was committed, provided and to the extent that restitution: (a) is not materially impossible; (b) does not involve a burden out of all proportion to the benefit deriving from restitution instead of compensation.
>
> (Article 35, Restitution, *restitutio in integrum*)

> The State responsible for an internationally wrongful act is under an obligation to compensate for the damage caused thereby, insofar as such damage is not made good by restitution. 2. The compensation shall cover any financially assessable damage including loss of profits insofar as it is established.
>
> (Article 36, Compensation)

Therefore, the law of restitution is the law of gains-based recovery. When lost gains are too burdensome or elusive, a tribunal may settle for the second-best, compensation, based on losses incurred (indemnification). When it comes to compensation, the disputants had deferred to the legal opinion of the *ad hoc* tribunal. The tribunal adopted the term "appropriate compensation" as used in the UN's General Assembly Resolution 1803.[138] By so doing, the tribunal did not leave the matter of compensation entirely within the domain of municipal law as prescribed by later General Assembly Resolutions, including the 1974 Charter of Economic Rights and Duties of States, which purport to weaken the customary international law standard of compensation for expropriation.[139] Hence, the tribunal preferred an enquiry into all the circumstances that were relevant to the case to determine the level of appropriate compensation. The preference of the tribunal created flexibility for what it perceived to be an equitable response to the expectations of the disputing parties and for adjudicating cases on a case by case basis and the established legal relationships of the disputants.

Aminoil estimated its claims based on future profits, interest payments, and expected future profits over the life of the concession, discounted to the present by a discount rate. Projected profits were based on the volume of oil to be produced, including the remaining reserves, the capacity of the facility, the volume of sales, prices at which sales would have been made, operating and capital (long-term) expenditures incurred, and taxes and other payments due to Kuwait.[140] The company based its projection on its operating history with a degree of certainty that is not applicable to other valuation techniques. The tribunal did not accept the projected value provided by Aminoil but it provided an allowance for the legitimate expectation of the investor to a "reasonable rate of return" as provided for in Part 2 of Annex 1 to the 1973 Agreement.[141]

Since the tribunal could not deconstruct the 1973 Agreement, including clauses for which there was no consensus, it relied on contractual clauses that once bound the parties to determine their financial commitments. Implicitly, the parties had agreed to incorporate new financial obligations into their contractual relations. The tribunal valued Aminoil's investment at just over US$206 million while its liabilities to the government were US$123 million, leaving an award in favor of Aminoil of US$83 million. The interest payable on this amount was set at 7.5 percent and it was compounded.[142] An additional allowance of ten percent was made for inflation.

The tribunal concluded that Aminoil had "come to accept the principle of a moderate estimate of profits and that it was this moderation that constituted its legitimate expectation." Consequently, the tribunal set Aminoil's reasonable rate of return at US$10 million per year. The amount due to Kuwait under the Abu Dhabi formula was the estimated amount of profits Aminoil could have earned in excess of this income.[143]

Hunter and Sinclair (2005) identify some notable aspects of the case: (i) the tribunal's decisions on the applicable laws to govern the procedure for the arbitration and the substance of the dispute, (ii) the views expressed by the majority, and by the separate opinion of former ICJ Judge Sir Gerald Fitzmaurice (concurring on the operative part), on the legal effect of so-called "stabilisation clauses" in public international law, and (iii) the effect of changes in market and industry conditions on long-term oil concessions.[144]

CHAPTER SUMMARY

- International economic laws are intricately related to the liberal exchange of goods and assets across international boundaries. That is, goods and financial assets are expected to be exchanged across international boundaries without undue or unfair restrictions that will imperil the welfare of business and consumers.
- Trade restrictions may be unfair policies with discriminatory intentions and effects. As such, they prevent certain businesses and countries from doing business in foreign countries on an even playing field.
- The imposition of a tariff generates at least four outcomes: (i) a transfer effect from consumer to producers, (ii) a production effect (an increase in domestic production and probably employment), (iii) a revenue effect, and (iv) a consumption effect.
- As nations trade to increase their welfare, they can also engage in unfair trade practices. They can dump their goods, discriminate, and subsidize the production costs of domestic firms to create artificial comparative advantages. Dumping occurs when identical or similar goods are sold for cheaper prices in foreign markets relative to domestic markets.
- The scope of international trade law is very broad and evolving, but it generally covers: (i) exemptions, (ii) tariffs (iii) dumping, (iv) RTAs, (v) price discrimination, (vi) subsidies, (vii) product quality, and (viii) a dispute settlement mechanism.
- The dispute settlement system of the WTO is a central element in providing security and predictability to the multilateral trading system. The Members recognize that it serves to preserve the rights and obligations of Members under the covered agreements, and to clarify the existing provisions of those agreements in accordance with customary rules of interpretation of public international law. Recommendations and rulings of the DSB cannot add to or diminish the rights and obligations provided in the covered agreements (Art. 3(2)).
- Nations that plan to grow in the future rely on long-term investment. Long-term investment is particularly significant for developing economies where the paucity of national saving and high levels of public debt inhibit or retard economic growth and development.
- The investment laws governing FDI are largely bilateral, based on what foreign investors can ethically offer and legally adhere to, and the obligations of states to protect the property and returns of foreign investors.

KEY WORDS

• Absolute Advantage	• Dumping	• MFN
• Arbitration	• DSU	• NTBs
• Comparative Advantage	• FDI	• Subsidy
• Confiscation	• Fair and equitable treatment	• RTAs
• Currency manipulation		• Zeroing
• Countervailing duties	• Good business practices	

CHAPTER QUESTIONS

1. Why do nations trade? Explain why freer international trade is welfare-enhancing. Show and explain why trade theories have influenced the evolution and interpretation of international laws.
2. Why are international conventions unequivocal sources of international law? Can nations renege on their treaty obligations? When and why?
3. What is the difference between a dispute settlement understanding and a dispute settlement mechanism? With reference to specific cases, discuss why dispute resolution mechanisms have enhanced cooperation among nations and increased the welfare of consumers.
4. Can nations unilaterally alter the value of their currencies? Why? Explain why arbitrary alterations of the value of currencies could destabilize global economic performance. How have international courts dealt with the issue of confiscatory devaluations?
5. Refer to the Boeing-Airbus dispute. What have been some of the central rulings of WTO panels since the inception of the dispute? Did Boeing have a prime-mover advantage? Why?
6. What is foreign direct investment? How can foreign investors minimize undesirable economic exposures in foreign territories?
7. When is the expropriation of foreign investment illegal? With reference to specific cases, how have international courts dealt with the issue of illegal expropriations of foreign investment?
8. Does foreign direct investment augment the paucity of national saving and innovation in developing countries? Why? How does FDI contribute to global economic growth?
9. Was the Abu Dhabi formula inhibitive and akin to indirect expropriation? Could there have been a public purpose for Decree Law No. 124? Why? What are some of the economic and investment implications of the law?
10. Referring to similarly situated cases, did the Kuwaiti Government engage in unfair and discriminatory treatment to foster an illegal expropriation of the assets of Aminoil?

NOTES

1 See O'Connell (1965, p. 8).
2 See the *Lotus Case* (1927), PCIJ (Ser. A) No. 10; the *Asylum Case* (1950), *Columbia v. Peru*, ICJ Reports (1950), ICJ Rep. 266; the *Paquette Habana Case* (The Lola, 175 U.S. 677 (1900)), and the *North Sea Continental Shelf Cases* (1969), ICJ Rep. 3, involving Germany, Netherlands, and Denmark for the application of customary law.
3 A self-executing treaty becomes judicially enforceable after ratification.
4 See O'Connell (1965, p. 22).
5 Pursuant to Art. 13 of the UN Charter, the General Assembly asked the International Law Commission (ILC) to codify and progressively develop the customary law of

treaties. The ILC concluded its work on May 22, 1969 by the adoption of the *Vienna Convention on the Law of Treaties*. The Convention entered into force on January 27, 1980. RESERVATIONS must be made at the time of ratification, acceptance, or accession in so far as: (i) The RESERVATION is not prohibited by the Treaty; (ii) The RESERVATION is considered to be permissible by the Treaty; and (iii) That the RESERVATION is not incompatible with the object and purpose of the treaty (see *Reservations to the Genocide Convention Case*; ICJ Rep. 15, May 28, 1951).
6 See Vienna Law of Treaties Article 26.
7 Vienna Law of Treaties Article 62; for example, The Hague Convention was terminated because of a fundamental change of circumstance in 1939.
8 See O'Connell (1965, p. 28).
9 See the dissenting opinion of Judge JB Moore in the *Lotus Case*.
10 See League of Nations, Permanent Court of International Justice, Advisory Committee of Jurists, Procès-verbaux of the Proceedings of the Committee, June 16–July 24, 1920.
11 See Weston, Falk, & D'Amato (1990, pp. 118–119).
12 Ibid; see the *Chorzów Factory Case (Germany v. Poland)*, 1928 PCIJ (Ser. A) No. 17 for the application of general principles of law.
13 See the *United States–Norway* Arbitration Award 1922.
14 An MFN agreement is a nondiscrimination agreement, which ensures equal or fair market access to the markets of the participating countries. Provisions are occasionally created for dependent countries. Contemporary trade agreements make provisional exceptions for developing countries; see Irwin (2011) for a comprehensive analysis of pre-1940 trade arrangements with the US. "Acceptance of a MFN clause in its unconditional form occurred in 1922 in the United States, but Europe, France and Spain resisted the application of the unconditional MFN clause until 1927/28. The generalization of the MFN clause over the course of the 1920s did not, however, extend to national treatment of foreign traders or firms. This meant that additional domestic charges or regulations could undermine the value of the tariff commitment, and do so in a discriminatory manner" (WTO, 2007, p. 41).
15 "As a result of Spain's retaliation, US car exports to Spain dropped by 94 percent in three years, while British, German, and Canadian cars were unaffected by the duties and saw their sales surge" (Irwin, 2011, p. 168; see also Jones, 1934, p. 52).
16 See Irwin (2011, pp. 158–169).
17 See Warburton (2018a, pp. 1–12) for a fuller discussion of commodity money and mercantilism.
18 See Kurz (2017, p. 12); see also www.la.utexas.edu.
19 See also Smith's *The Theory of Moral Sentiments* (1759). While Smith's theory of liberalization or freer market operations is often touted as a basis for trade and efficient market outcomes, freer trade or liberalization must not be devoid of the ethical preconditions that are necessary for the smooth operations of markets and efficient outcomes. *The Theory of Moral Sentiments* must be regarded as a complement to *An Inquiry into the Nature and the Causes of the Wealth of Nations* (1776).
20 Consumer surplus is the difference between the per unit price that consumers are willing to pay and the per unit price that they actually pay for a good or service. The consumer surplus is usually estimated as the area under a market demand curve that is above the prevailing market price. Producer surplus is the difference between the

price that will induce a producer to produce a good (usually a sunk or fixed cost) and the per unit price that the producer actually gets from market transactions.
21 Smith refers to the detrimental practice of mercantilism under Mr. Colbert, the French minister of finance under Louis XIV. It is noteworthy that he recognized his great abilities but then proceeded to note that the sophistry (clever lobbying or chicanery) of the merchants promoted monopolistic ambitions rather than competition.
22 Conceptually, economists usually make a distinction between economic growth and development. Economic growth is oriented towards an increase in national income, commonly associated with an outward shift of the transformation curve (production possibilities frontier) of a nation. Development is a broader indicator of progress, encompassing infrastructure, health, human capital, sustainable development, and the levels of poverty and income inequality.
23 There are various simplifying assumptions that are associated with the H-O model over time (the short and long run): both labor and capital can freely move between local industries, the production of one good requires relatively more capital or labor in terms of the labor-capital or capital-labor ratio, labor-capital ratio in one country must exceed that of another, final products should be traded freely, there are no technological differences between or among trading countries, consumers do not have significantly different preferences for goods that are produced, and immigration cannot be allowed to destabilize factor concentration. Ancillary trade theories like factor prize equalization, Rybczynski theorem, and factor intensity reversal have been considered to be beyond the scope of this work.
24 See Pugel (2020, p. 256) for further discussion; see also the 2007 World Trade Report (WTO, 2007, pp. 138–9).
25 The inclusion of Part IV on "Trade and Development," which codified the notion of "non-reciprocity," as well as a waiver for non-reciprocal preferences, which were later made permanent under the 1979 "Enabling Clause." The Enabling Clause is a comprehensive specification of special and differential treatment for developing and least-developed countries, which amounted to a permanent waiver from the MFN clause; see WTO (2007, pp. xxiii & 187).
26 Sales of the like product destined for consumption in the domestic market of the exporting country shall normally be considered a sufficient quantity for the determination of the normal value if such sales constitute 5 per cent or more of the sales of the product under consideration to the importing Member, provided that a lower ratio should be acceptable where the evidence demonstrates that domestic sales at such lower ratio are nonetheless of sufficient magnitude to provide for a proper comparison (Art. 2.2). Sales below per unit costs are made in substantial quantities when the authorities establish that the weighted average selling price of the transactions under consideration for the determination of the normal value is below the weighted average per unit costs, or that the volume of sales below per unit costs represents not less than 20 per cent of the volume sold in transactions under consideration for the determination of the normal value (Art. 2.2.1).
27 For the purpose of paragraph 2, costs shall normally be calculated on the basis of records kept by the exporter or producer under investigation, provided that such records are in accordance with the generally accepted accounting principles of the exporting country and reasonably reflect the costs associated with the production and sale of the product under consideration (Art. 2.2.1.1). For the purpose of paragraph 2, the amounts for administrative, selling and general costs and for profits shall be

based on actual data pertaining to production and sales in the ordinary course of trade of the like product by the exporter or producer under investigation. When such amounts cannot be determined on this basis, the amounts may be determined on the basis of: (i) the actual amounts incurred and realized by the exporter or producer in question in respect of production and sales in the domestic market of the country of origin of the same general category of products; (ii) the weighted average of the actual amounts incurred and realized by other exporters or producers subject to investigation in respect of production and sales of the like product in the domestic market of the country of origin; (iii) any other reasonable method, provided that the amount for profit so established shall not exceed the profit normally realized by other exporters or producers on sales of products of the same general category in the domestic market of the country of origin (Art. 2.2.2).
28. Normally, the date of sale would be the date of contract, purchase order, order confirmation, or invoice, whichever establishes the material terms of sale (Art. 2.4.1).
29. "Like product" (*produit similaire*) or comparable product is interpreted to mean a product which is identical, i.e. alike in all respects to the product under consideration, or in the absence of such a product, another product which, although not alike in all respects, has characteristics closely resembling those of the product under consideration (Art. 2.6).
30. Substantive investigation requires sufficient evidence of either dumping or of injury to justify the continuation of a case. There shall be immediate termination in cases where the authorities determine that the margin of dumping is *de minimis*, or that the volume of dumped imports, actual or potential, or the injury, is negligible. The margin of dumping shall be considered to be *de minimis* if this margin is less than 2 per cent, expressed as a percentage of the export price. The volume of dumped imports shall normally be regarded as negligible if the volume of dumped imports from a particular country is found to account for less than 3 per cent of imports of the like product in the importing country, unless countries which individually account for less than 3 per cent of the imports of the like product in the importing Member country collectively account for more than 7 per cent of imports of the like product in the importing Member country (Art. 5(8)).
31. One example, though not an exclusive one, is that there is convincing reason to believe that there will be, in the near future, substantially increased importation of the product at dumped prices (Art. 3(7)).
32. For the purposes of the Agreement a customs territory must be understood to mean any territory with respect to which separate tariffs or other regulations of commerce are maintained for a substantial part of the trade of such territory with other territories (Art. XXIV(2)).
33. A free-trade area must be understood to mean a group of two or more customs territories in which the duties and other restrictive regulations of commerce (except, where necessary, those permitted under Articles XI, XII, XIII, XIV, XV and XX) are eliminated on substantially all the trade between the constituent territories in products originating in such territories (Art. XXIV(8)(b)).
34. See Pugel (2020, pp. 161–241) for a comprehensive discussion of trade restrictions; see also Salvatore (2010, pp. 247–310), and Feenstra and Taylor (2017, pp. 241–369).
35. Objective criteria or conditions, as used herein, mean criteria or conditions which are neutral, which do not favour certain enterprises over others, and which are economic

in nature and horizontal in application, such as number of employees or size of enterprise.
36 In the case of programmes which span industrial research and pre-competitive development activity, the allowable level of non-actionable assistance shall not exceed the simple average of the allowable levels of non-actionable assistance applicable to the above two categories, calculated on the basis of all eligible costs as set forth in items (i) to (v) of this subparagraph (Art. 8(2)(a) fn).
37 Members recognize that where royalty-based financing for a civil aircraft programme is not being fully repaid due to the level of actual sales falling below the level of forecast sales, this does not in itself constitute serious prejudice for the purposes of this subparagraph (Art. 6.1(d) fn).
38 The duration of the waiting period is unaffected by the choice of voluntary procedures of good offices, conciliation, or mediation (Art. 5(4)).
39 The written request must indicate whether consultations were held, identify the specific measures at issue and provide a brief summary of the legal basis of the complaint sufficient to present the problem clearly. In case the applicant requests the establishment of a panel with other than standard terms of reference, the written request shall include the proposed text of special terms of reference (Art. 6(2)).
40 Each panel shall have the right to seek information and technical advice from any individual or body which it deems appropriate. However, before a panel seeks such information or advice from any individual or body within the jurisdiction of a Member it shall inform the authorities of that Member. A Member should respond promptly and fully to any request by a panel for such information as the panel considers necessary and appropriate. Confidential information which is provided shall not be revealed without formal authorization from the individual, body, or authorities of the Member providing the information (Art. 13(1)). Panels may seek information from any relevant source and may consult experts to obtain their opinion on certain aspects of the matter. With respect to a factual issue concerning a scientific or other technical matter raised by a party to a dispute, a panel may request an advisory report in writing from an expert review group. Rules for the establishment of such a group and its procedures are set forth in Appendix 4 (Art. 13(2)).
41 There shall be no ex parte communications with the panel or Appellate Body concerning matters under consideration by the panel or Appellate Body (Art. 18(1)).
42 When the panel considers that it cannot issue its report within six months or within three months in cases of urgency, it shall inform the DSB in writing of the reasons for the delay together with an estimate of the period within which it will issue its report. In no case should the period from the establishment of the panel to the circulation of the report to the Members exceed nine months (Art. 12(9)). As a general rule, the proceedings shall not exceed 60 days from the date a party to the dispute formally notifies its decision to appeal to the date the Appellate Body circulates its report …. When the Appellate Body considers that it cannot provide its report within 60 days, it shall inform the DSB in writing of the reasons for the delay together with an estimate of the period within which it will submit its report. In no case shall the proceedings exceed 90 days (Art. 17(5)).
43 Where there is disagreement as to the existence or consistency with a covered agreement of measures taken to comply with the recommendations and rulings such dispute shall be decided through recourse to these dispute settlement procedures, including wherever possible resort to the original panel. The panel shall circulate its

report within 90 days after the date of referral of the matter to it. When the panel considers that it cannot provide its report within this time frame, it shall inform the DSB in writing of the reasons for the delay together with an estimate of the period within which it will submit its report (Art. 21(5)).

44 Permissible development subsidies were limited to loans that should be repaid within seventeen years and they were also required to be repaid in that timeframe at an interest rate no less than the cost of borrowing to the government. Benefits to be received indirectly through government contracts were capped at three percent of the industry-wide turnover and four percent of the turnover for each individual manufacturer; see Kienstra (2012, pp. 580–1).

45 The US learned of an explicit export subsidy provided to Deutsche Airbus in the form of exchange rate guarantees worth an estimated $2.5 million on each aircraft delivered in 1990. A second complaint was filed in May 1991, covering subsidies given to each of the Airbus entities by the member governments since its inception, totaling $13.5 billion (op. cit).

46 See the SCM Agreement; see also Kienstra (2012, p. 584).

47 See WTO ANALYTICAL INDEX SCM Agreement–Article 3 (Jurisprudence), 7.

48 Ibid.

49 See the *Chicago Tribune*, March 28, 2019 (retrieved from boeing.com); see also Kienstra (2012).

50 The AB issued its report on DS353 on March 12, 2012 and the DSU adopted the recommendations and rulings on March 26, 2012.

51 See Kienstra (2012, p. 597). The WTO later referred the matter back to the original panel, at the US's request, to determine compliance.

52 Loc. cit.

53 Loc. cit.

54 The investigation was focused on Kawasaki Steel Corporation ("KSC"), Nippon Steel Corporation ("NSC"), and NKK Corporation ("NKK") for individual investigation, since the three companies accounted for more than 90 percent of all known exports of hot-rolled steel from Japan during the timeframe of its investigation.

55 Panel Report, para. 2.6.

56 USDOC established the following margins of dumping: 67.14 percent for KSC; 19.65 percent for NSC; and 17.86 percent for NKK. The "all others" rate was 29.30 percent. (Panel Report, para. 2.7; Notice of Final Determination of Sales at Less Than Fair Value: Hot-Rolled Flat-Rolled Carbon-Quality Steel Products From Japan ("USDOC Final Determination"), United States Federal Register, May 6, 1999 (Volume 64, Number 87), Exhibit JP-12 submitted by Japan to the Panel (p. 24,329 at 24,370).

57 Panel Report, para. 2.8.

58 Ibid., para. 2.9.

59 Appellate Body Report, *US–Hot-Rolled Steel*, para. 165.

60 Appellate Body Report, *US–Hot-Rolled Steel*, para. 147; see also WTO Analytical Index, Anti-Dumping Agreement, Article 2 (Jurisprudence,) p. 10. The US had disregarded sales (exports) to affiliates as not constituting part of trade in the "ordinary course of trade" when the weighted average selling price to an affiliated party is below 99.5 percent of the weighted average price of sales to all non-affiliated parties, thereby repudiating the "arms-length" test. Japan claimed that the alternative test was inconsistent with Article 2.1 of the Anti-Dumping Agreement

because it excluded only low-priced affiliated sales, which inflated normal value, and, second, that the test relied on an arbitrary threshold that did not take account of usual variation of prices in the marketplace. The Panel found that the application of the 99.5 percent test "does not rest on a permissible interpretation of the term 'sales in the ordinary course of trade'" The Appellate Body upheld the Panel's finding, although it followed a different reasoning; see Appellate Body Report, *US–Hot-Rolled Steel*, paras. 137–158, see also WTO Analytical Index op. cit., p. 11.

61 Op. cit., p. 14.
62 Loc. cit.
63 See Mankiw and Swagel (2005, p. 116). The US steel industry was the leading user of antidumping procedures: nearly half of antidumping tariffs imposed since 1970 were on steel imports. Ibid., p. 113.
64 Appellate Body Report, *US–Softwood Lumber V* (Article 21.5–Canada), para 142. Adopted and followed e.g., in Panel Report, US–Shrimp (Viet Nam), para. 7.93; see also WTO Analytical Index op. cit., p. 46.
65 Appellate Body Report, *US–Zeroing (Japan)*, paras. 123–124.
66 Subject to the provisions governing fair comparison in paragraph 4, the existence of margins of dumping during the investigation phase shall normally be established on the basis of a comparison of a weighted average normal value with a weighted average of prices of all comparable export transactions or by a comparison of normal value and export prices on a transaction-to-transaction basis. A normal value established on a weighted average basis may be compared to prices of individual export transactions if the authorities find a pattern of export prices which differ significantly among different purchasers, regions or time periods, and if an explanation is provided as to why such differences cannot be taken into account appropriately by the use of a weighted average-to-weighted average or transaction-to-transaction comparison. (Art. 2.4.2)
67 Appellate Body Report, *US–Washing Machines*, para. 5.160. See also Panel Report, *US–Anti-Dumping Methodologies (China)*, paras. 7.208–7.209.
68 *US–Zeroing (Japan)*, para. 7.159.
69 See Trebilcock et al. (2013, p. 21).
70 See the 2007 WTO World Trade Report (WTO, 2007, p. 132).
71 See WTO ANALYTICAL INDEX GATT 1994–Article I (Jurisprudence), p. 4; see also p. 36, and Panel Report, *Canada–Autos*, paras. 10.55–10.56.
72 See WT/COMTD/W/239 of the WTO. The Enabling Clause is also considered to be the legal basis for regional arrangements among developing countries and for the Global System of Trade Preferences (GSTP), under which a number of developing countries exchange trade concessions among themselves.
73 See WTO ANALYTICAL INDEX GATT 1994–Article I (Jurisprudence), p. 20.
74 A chapeau is the introductory text that broadly defines the general principles, objectives, and background of a treaty. The text alludes to conduct or obligations of members that can minimize or prevent derogations. The obligations of members are broadly characterized to generate the maximum amount of good will, restraint (exceptions), and public morals required to guarantee the functionality of a treaty. In trade treaties, a chapeau is generally intended to prevent discrimination and abuse.
75 See also Chang (2005, p. 30).
76 See WTO (2012, p. 15).

77 The new Regulation violated GATT Art. I.I (MFN treatment) by using the pre-1991 best-ever-volume as a basis for quota allocations. Though the Lomé Convention can legitimately set import limits for the ACP countries some countries were capable of exporting more than their best pre-1991 volume.
78 In an issue not appealed to the Appellate Body, both Panels found that the preference granted by the European Communities of an annual duty-free tariff quota of 775,000 mt of imported bananas originating in ACP countries constituted an advantage, which was not accorded to like bananas originating in non-ACP WTO members, and was therefore inconsistent with Art. I:1. The Panel also found that the European Communities had failed to demonstrate the existence of a waiver from Art. I:1 for the time after the expiration of the Doha Waiver to cover the preference granted by the European Communities to the duty-free tariff quota of bananas from ACP countries (WTO, 2012, p. 16).
79 See 2007 World Trade Report of the WTO (2007, p. xxviii).
80 For a brief history of money, see Miller, Wehnke, Haynes, and Parker, 2000, p. 41).
81 Until the early 1870s, many countries operated under the bimetallic standard in which currencies were defined in terms of gold or silver (not electrum). In the US, the Coinage Act (1792) legalized bimetallism until 1873 when Congress dropped the silver dollar from minting. In the US before the Civil War, 371.25 grains of silver or 23.22 grains of gold could be transformed into silver and gold coins respectively. In effect, the mint parity suggested that at some point the value of gold was 16 times more than the value of silver, when multiples are considered (371.25/23.22 = 16). In Britain, bimetallism was maintained until 1816 (the conclusion of the Napoleonic war). The gold standard ultimately emerged out of the bimetallic standard; see Krugman, Obstfeld, and Melitz (2015, p. 522); see also Resnick and Eun (2015, p. 28), and Warburton (2018a, pp. 1–6).
82 See Warburton (2018a, pp. 6–11).
83 The expression (overvaluation) is contingent on the definition of exchange rates and it must be studied with some amount of precaution. It is misleading to think that the domestic currency has become stronger in this case.
84 See Salvatore (2010, p. 766).
85 See Mishkin (2019, pp. 432–6) for a comprehensive discussion of sterilization.
86 A more modern, financially based, and very conservative criterion is an amount that is equal to all short-term debt denominated in foreign currencies. Of course, unforeseen contingencies and actual and perceived population growth can complicate the analysis.
87 For a very comprehensive analysis of the Mundell-Fleming model see Van den Berg (2017, pp. 259–307).
88 See Eichengreen and Irwin (2010, op. cit., p. 879).
89 The SDR is an international reserve asset that was created in 1969 to supplement or augment the existing reserve assets. SDRs may be used in a variety of voluntary transactions, including swap arrangements, voluntary transfers, forward operations, payments of interest, and repurchases of currencies involving the General Resources Account. However, a general allocation of SDRs requires the threat or existence of general international illiquidity. The daily value of SDR is based on a weighted average of the currencies of the dominant players in global markets. A new weighting formula was adopted in 2015 to assign equal shares to exports and a composite financial indicator, including the sum of outstanding international bank liabilities and international debt securities denominated in currency.

90 In order to prevent an aggravation of the situation [internal or external], the Security Council may, before making the recommendations or deciding upon the measures provided for in Article 39, call upon the parties concerned to comply with such provisional measures as it deems necessary or desirable. Such provisional measures shall be without prejudice to the rights, claims, or position of the parties concerned. The Security Council shall duly take account of failure to comply with such provisional measures (UNC Art. 40). The Security Council may decide what measures not involving the use of armed force are to be employed to give effect to its decisions, and it may call upon the Members of the United Nations to apply such measures. These may include complete or partial interruption of economic relations and of rail, sea, air, postal, telegraphic, radio, and other means of communication, and the severance of diplomatic relations (UNC Art. 41); see also the preambular provisions of the UN Charter and Article 34.

91 … [T]he proposed purchase would be a reserve tranche purchase, or would not cause the Fund's holdings of the purchasing member's currency to exceed two hundred percent of its quota (3(b)(iii)); the Fund has not previously declared under Section 5 of this Article, Article VI, Section 1, or Article XXVI, Section 2(a) that the member desiring to purchase is ineligible to use the general resources of the Fund (3(b)(iv)).

92 The Board of Governors shall adopt regulations under which a member may send a representative to attend any meeting of the Executive Board when a request made by, or a matter particularly affecting, that member is under consideration (Art. XII § 3(j)).

93 See Warburton (2018a) for extended discussions of monetary law.

94 See O'Connell (1965, p. 1099).

95 See the IMF's *Balance of Payments Textbook* (2005, p. 107).

96 See Chapter 2 for the effects of long-term investments in different countries.

97 See Chapter III of the 2019 *World Investment Report* (2019b).

98 Long-term rates of return are measured in terms of the annual FDI income for a given year divided by the average book values of FDI stock for the year and the previous year; op. cit, p. 14.

99 Other forms of foreign investment (relatively shorter period investment) have not been considered here. These include portfolio investment, which covers investment in equity (stocks and shares), and other securities and financial derivatives. Non equity securities are bonds, bills, negotiable certificates of deposits, preference shares, bankers acceptances, and marketable promissory notes.

100 See the *Mavrommatis Jerusalem Concession Case* (*Greece v. UK*) (1924), (1925), (1927) PCIJ., Ser. A. Nos. 2, 5, and 11.

101 OECD (2011).

102 See also UN GA Res. 2625 (XXXV), 1971 (the Friendly Relations Declaration).

103 Subsumed in the National Treatment law is the principle of fair and equal treatment (FET) an equivalent of the MFN clause of the WTO, which has a lot to do with the application of BITs rather than the per se provisions; see also Collins (2017, pp. 124–137).

104 Adhering governments are generally prohibited from using the Guidelines to promote protectionist policies or policies that will call into question their comparative advantages when multinational enterprises make investments (see OECD Guidelines 1.7).

105 Transnationals are also expected to respect consumer privacy and protection of consumer data. Guidelines IX, X, and XI deal with Science and Technology, Competition, and Taxation respectively.
106 See UNCTAD (2012, p. xi); see also Collins (2017, pp. 156–213).
107 Ibid. While the framework for indirect taking has been shaped by customary law, the role of the proportionality approach and the criterion of direct benefit to a state are unsettled. Another unsettled issue is the use of market value for compensation and reparation for unlawful taking.
108 See for example, *Tecmed v. Mexico*, ICSD Case No. ARB (AF)/00/2 (29 May, 2003); see also discussions in Collins (2017, pp. 168–84).
109 See Collins (2017, p. 167).
110 ICSD Case No. ARB/02/8 (17 Jan 2007); see also Collins (2017, ibid).
111 The three conditions are conventionally referred to as the Hull Formula, in recognition of the US Secretary of State, Cordell Hull, who first proposed it; see Collins (2017, p. 188).
112 ICSD Case No. ARB/96/1 (17 Feb 2000) at [78]; see also Collins (2017, p. 190).
113 For varieties of valuation methods see Collins (2017, pp. 198–213); see also valuation methods in Chapter 5 of this book.
114 An economic concession is a license that is granted to an individual or a corporation by a state to undertake works of a public character extending over a period of time, and involving the investment of large sums of capital; see O'Connell's *The Law of State Succession* (1956, 2015, p. 106). Today, it is fashionable to talk about bilateral investment treaties or contracts rather than concessions.
115 See Hunter and Sinclair (2005, pp. 349–50). The small oil company was eventually sold to a major tobacco company, RJ Reynolds Tobacco Company Inc.
116 Op. cit., p. 351.
117 Op. cit., p. 357.
118 Op. cit., p. 352.
119 Op. cit., p. 353.
120 In the 1960s many former colonies regarded nationalizations as part of their decolonization. In 2000, the Zimbabwean Government seized 110,000 square km of land from white farmers and "redistributed" them to black farmers. In less democratic states with coups d'état and state succession problems, foreign investment may be seized to solicit political support and arouse nationalist sentiments.
121 Op. cit., p. 356.
122 GA Res 1803 (1962) 17 UN GAOR Supp (No 17) 15 reprinted (1964) 13 *ICLQ* 400.
123 Ibid; see also Hunter and Sinclair (2005, p. 359).
124 Op. cit., pp. 360–61.
125 Op. cit., p. 362.
126 Aminoil, 584 para 85; see also Hunter and Sinclair (2005, p. 361).
127 See Collins (2017, p. 126).
128 Cited in Collins (2017, pp. 126–7).
129 Loc. cit. It is presumed that the disputing parties are transparent and open and honest about their intentions as reflected in the text of a treaty. That is, FET can be evaluated by good faith measures.
130 See Hunter and Sinclair (2005, p. 379).
131 Op. cit., p. 372.

132 By 1978, it was estimated that one fine ounce of gold cost around US$226; by 1980, the value went up to about US$600 in some markets, op. cit., p. 373.
133 Op. cit., p. 354.
134 See the *Chorzów Factory Case* (1927) PCIJ, Ser. A, No. 17 at 47. Interestingly, the tribunal did not pointedly reference the *Chorzów Factory Case* and its underlying principles, most likely because it did not find reasons to establish that the taking was confiscatory.
135 See the *Lotus Case* (1927), PCIJ, Ser. A, No. 10, the *Asylum Case* (1950), ICJ Rep. 266, and the *North Sea Continental Shelf Cases* (1969), ICJ Rep. 3.
136 Cited in Hunter and Sinclair (2005, p. 365).
137 Op. cit., pp. 354–5.
138 GA Res 1803 (1962) 17 UN GAOR. Supp. (No 17) 15 Article 4.
139 See Hunter and Sinclair (2005, p. 362); see also GA Res. 3281 (1974), 29 UN GAOR. Supp. (No 31) 52 Article 2.
140 Op. cit., p. 365.
141 Loc. cit. The tribunal held that the 1973 Agreement was binding on an interim basis; see p. 352.
142 Op. cit., p. 367; no detailed explanation was provided for the derivation of the value. See Hunter and Sinclair (2005) for an analysis of the implications of the work of the tribunal.
143 Op. cit., p. 366. The tribunal did not specify the remaining number of years that it used to calculate Aminoil's return.
144 Op. cit., p. 348.

FURTHER READING

Bergsten, C. F., & Gagnon, J. E. (2012). *Currency manipulation, the US economy, and the global economic order*. Policy Brief, No. PB12-25. Peterson Institute for International Economics, 1–25.

Bernanke, B. (2013). *The Federal Reserve and the financial crises*. Princeton, NJ: Princeton University Press.

Berry, S., Levinsohn, J., & Pakes, A. (1999). Voluntary export restraints on automobiles: Evaluating a trade policy. *American Economic Review*, 89(3), 400–430.

Bhagwati, J. N. (1969). Optimal policies and immiserizing growth. *American Economic Review*, 59(December), 967–970.

Bloomfield, A. I. (1959). *Monetary policy under the international Gold Standard: 1880-1914*. New York: The Federal Reserve Bank.

Brent, R. J. (1996). *Applied cost–benefit analysis*. Cheltenham, UK: Edward Elgar.

Carbonell, J. B., & Werner, R. A. (2018). Does foreign direct investment generate economic growth? A new empirical approach applied to Spain. *Economic Geography*, 94(4), 425–456.

Chang, H. F. (2005). Environmental trade measures, the Shrimp-Turtle rulings, and the ordinary meaning of the text of the GAT. *Chapman Law Review*, 8(25), 25–51.

Choe, J. I. (2003). Do foreign direct investment and gross domestic investment promote economic growth? *Review of Development Economics*, 7(1), 44–57.

Chowdhury, A., & Mavrotas, G. (2006). FDI and growth: What causes what? *World Economy*, 29(1), 9–19.

Cobet, A. E., & Wilson, G. A. (2002). Comparing 50 years of labor productivity in U.S. and foreign manufacturing. *Monthly Labor Review*, 51–65.

Collins, D. (2017). *An introduction to international investment law.* New York: Cambridge University Press.

Crabbe, L. (1989). The international Gold Standard and US monetary policy from World War I to the New Deal. *Federal Reserve Bulletin, 75,* 423–440.

Crucini, M. J., & Kahn, J. (1996a). Tariffs and aggregate economic activity: Lessons from the Great Depression. *Journal of Monetary Economics, 38,* 427–467.

Crucini, M. J., & Kahn, J. (1996b). Tariffs and the Great Depression revisited. In E. Prescott & T. Kehoe (Eds.), *Great Depression of the twentieth century.* Minneapolis: Federal Reserve Bank of Minneapolis.

Eichengreen, B., & Irwin, D. A. (2010). The slide to protectionism in the Great Depression: Who succumbed and why? *Journal of Economic History, 70*(4), 871–897.

Feenstra, R. C., & Taylor, A. M. (2017). *International economics* (4th ed.). New York: Worth Publishers.

Flake, J. (2017). *Conscience of a conservative.* New York: Random House.

Fusfeld, D. R. (2002). *The age of the economist* (9th ed.). New York: Addison Wesley.

Gaines, S. (2001). The WTO's reading of the GATT Article XX chapeau: A disguised restriction on environmental measures. *University of Pennsylvania Journal of International Economic Law, 22*(4), 739–862.

Haberler, G. (1936). *The theory of international trade.* London: W. Hodge & Company.

Hansen, H., & Rand, J. (2006). On the causal links between FDI and growth in developing countries. *World Economy, 29*(1), 21–41.

Heyman, E. (2007, February 1). Boeing v. Airbus: The WTO dispute that neither can win. *Deutsche Bank Research*, 1–12.

Hoda, A. (2002). *Tariff negotiations and renegotiations under the GATT and the WTO: Procedures and practices.* New York: Cambridge University Press.

Holmes, T. J., & Schmitz, J. A. (2010). Competition and productivity: A review of evidence. *Annual Review of Economics, 2*(1), 619–642.

Hudec, R. E. (1993). Circumventing democracy: The political morality of trade negotiations. *N.Y.U. Journal of International Law & Politics, 25,* 311–322.

Hume, D. (1752). Of the balance of trade. Retrieved from www.la.utexas.edu. Accessed December 28, 2017.

Hunter, M., & Sinclair, A. C. (2005). Aminoil revisited: Reflections on a story of changing circumstances. In T. Weiler (Ed.), *International law and arbitration: Leading cases from the ICSID, NAFTA, bilateral treaties and customary international law* (pp. 347–381). London: Cameron May.

International Monetary Fund. (2005). *Balance of payments textbook.* Washington, .C: International Monetary Fund.

International Monetary Fund. (2011). *Articles of agreement.* Washington, DC: International Monetary Fund.

Irwin, D. A. (2011). *Peddling protectionism: Smoot-Hawley and the Great Depression.* Princeton, NJ: Princeton University Press.

Jackson, J. (1997). *The world trading system—Law and policy of international economic relations* (2nd ed.). Cambridge, MA: MIT Press.

Johnson, H. G. (1967). *Economic policies towards less developed countries.* New York: Praeger.

Jones, J. M. (1934). *Tariff retaliation repercussions of the Hawley-Smoot Bill*. Philadelphia, PA: University of Pennsylvania Press.

Kienstra, J. (2012). Cleared for landing: Airbus, Boeing, and the WTO dispute over subsidies to large civil aircraft. *Northwestern Journal of International Law & Business*, 32(3), 569–606.

Kotkin, J., & Shires, M. (2015, July 23). The cities leading a U.S. manufacturing revival. Retrieved from http://forbes.com/sites/joelkotkin/2015/07/23/the-cities-leading-a-u-s-manufacturing-revival/#44341b431d0a. Accessed December 28, 2016.

Krugman, P. R., Obstfeld, M., & Melitz, M. J. (2015). *International economics: Theory and policy* (10th ed.). Upper Saddle River, NJ: Pearson.

Kurz, H. D. (2017). *Economic thought: A brief history*. New York: Columbia University Press.

Lipsey, R. G. (1957). The theory of customs unions: Trade diversion and welfare. *Economica*, 24(1), 40–46.

Lipsey, R. G. (1960). The theory of customs unions: A general survey. *Economic Journal*, 70, 496–513.

McClenehan, G. (1991). The growth of voluntary export restraints and American foreign economic policy. *Business and Economic History*, Second Series 20, 180–190.

Maddison, A. (1998). *Monitoring the world economy, 1820–1998*. Paris: Development Centre Studies, OECD.

Maddison, A. (2001). *The world economy: A millennial perspective*. Paris: OECD Publishing.

Malkin, E. (2017, June 6). Mexico agrees to sugar trade deal, but U.S. refiners remain unhappy. Retrieved from https://nytimes.com/. Accessed December 31, 2018.

Mankiw, N. G., & Swagel, P. (2005). Antidumping: The third rail of trade policy. *Foreign Affairs*, 84(4), 107–119.

Miller, S., Wehnke, R., Haynes, R., & Parker, C. J. (Eds.) (2000). *World history: People and nations, ancient world*. Austin TX: Holt, Rinehart, and Winston.

Mishkin, F. S. (2019). *The economics of money, banking, and financial markets*. London: Pearson.

Mun, T. (1630 [1664]). *England's treasure by forraign trade or the balance of our forraign trade is the rule of our treasure*. London: J. G. for Thomas Clark.

Nurkse, R. (1944). *International currency experience*. Princeton, NJ: League of Nations.

O'Connell, D. P. (1956, 2015). *The law of state succession*. London: Cambridge University Press.

O'Connell, D. P. (1965). *International law* (Vol. 2). London: Stevens and Sons.

OECD. (2011). *OECD guidelines for multinational enterprises*. OECD Publishing.

Ohanian, L. E. (2014). *Competition and decline of the Rust Belt*. Federal Reserve Bank of Minneapolis, Economic Policy Paper, 14–6, 1–5.

Petersmann, E.-U. (1997). International trade law and the GATT/WTO dispute settlement system 1948–1996: An introduction. In E.-U. Petersmann (Ed.), *International trade law and the GATT/WTO dispute settlement system* (pp. 3–122). London: Kluwer.

Prebisch, R. (1964). *Towards a new trade policy for development: Report by the Secretary-General of the United Nations Conference on Trade and Development*. New York: United Nations.

Pugel, T. A. (2020). *International economics* (17th ed.). New York: McGraw-Hill.

Pyatt, S. (1999). The WTO Sea Turtle decision. *Ecology Law*, 26(4), 815–838.

Reinert, K. A. (2012). *An introduction to international economics.* New York: Cambridge University Press.

Resnick, B. G., & Eun, C. S. (2015). *International financial management* (7th ed.). New York: McGraw-Hill.

Sachs, J. D. (2005). *The end of poverty: Economic possibilities for our time.* New York: Penguin Press.

Salvatore, D. (2010). *International economics.* Hoboken, NJ: John Wiley and Sons.

Singer H. W. (1950). The distribution of gains between investing and borrowing countries. *American Economic Review, 40*(2), 473–485.

Smith, A. (1759 [2000]). *The theory of moral sentiments.* Amherst, NY: Prometheus Books.

Smith, A. (1776 [1994]). *An inquiry into the nature and causes of the wealth of nations.* New York: Random House.

Sykes, O. (2003). *The economics of WTO rules on subsidies and countervailing measures.* University of Chicago Law School Working Paper 415789. Retrieved from http://law.uchicago.edu/Lawecon/index.html.

Trebilcock, M., Howse, R., & Eliason, A. (2013). *The regulation of international trade.* New York: Routledge.

United Nations Conference on Trade and Development. (2012). *Expropriation: UNCTAD series on issues in international investment agreements II.* New York: United Nations.

United Nations Conference on Trade and Development. (2019a). *World trade report 2019.* New York: United Nations.

United Nations Conference on Trade and Development (2019b). *World investment report.* Geneva, Switzerland: UNCTAD.

U.S. Bureau of Labor Statistics (2018, January 1). Manufacturing sector: Real output per hour of all persons [PRS30006092]. Retrieved from FRED, Federal Reserve Bank of St. Louis; https://fred.stlouisfed.org/series/PRS30006092.

USDA, ERS. (2018, January 1). Mexico trade and FDI. Retrieved from https://ers.usda.gov/topics/international-markets-trade/countries-regions/nafta-canada-mexico/mexico-trade-fdi/

Van den Berg, H. (2017). *Economic growth and development* (3rd ed.). Hackensack, NJ: World Scientific.

Viner, J. (1950). *The customs union issue.* New York: Carnegie Endowment for International Peace.

Warburton, C. E. S. (2017a). International trade and industrial recovery in the USA. *Regional and Sectoral Economic Studies, Euro-American Association of Economic Development, 17*(1), 5–22.

Warburton, C. E. S. (2017b). Trade treaties and deglobalization. *Applied Econometrics and International Development, Euro-American Association of Economic Development, 17*(4), 71–88.

Warburton, C. E. S. (2018a). *The development of international monetary policy.* New York: Routledge.

Warburton, C. E. S. (2018b). Positive time preference and environmental degradation: The effects of population growth and environmental degradation on intergenerational equity. *Applied Econometrics and International Development, 18*(2), 5–24

Wessels, W. J. (2018). *Economics* (6th ed.). New York: Barron's.

Weston, B. H., Falk, R. A., & D'Amato, A. (1990). *International law and world order.* St Paul, MN: Thomson-West.

World Trade Organization. (2007). *World trade report*. Geneva, Switzerland: World Trade Organization.
World Trade Organization. (2012). *WTO dispute settlement: One-page case summaries 1995–2011*. Geneva, Switzerland: World Trade Organization.
Zhang, K. H. (2001). Does foreign direct investment promote economic growth? Evidence from East Asia and Latin America. *Contemporary Economic Policy, 19*(2), 175–185.

TABLE OF CASES

Case	Finding
	Consumer class action suit
Am. Pipe & Constr. Co. v. Utah (1974)	Class action suit can be efficient (less costly)
Gen. Tel. Co. of Sw. v. Falcon (1982)	(Efficiency effect)
Eubank v. Pella Corp. (2014)	Class action can be inequitable and scandalous
Ebner v. Fresh, Inc. (2016)	Class action could have insufficient evidence
Kane v. Chobani (2016)	Deceptive labeling
	Conspiracy
Iannelli v. US (1975)	Conspiratorial agreements can be inferred; they don't have to be oral or written
US v. Powell (1984)	Inconsistency is insufficient to overturn a conspiratorial judgment (not everyone may be guilty in a conspiracy)
US v. Schmidt (1991)	Conspiracy must have plurality (more than just the agent)
	The discount rate
Kelly v. Chesapeake & Ohio (1916)	Future value payments must be discounted
Chesapeake & Ohio Ry. Co. v. Kelly (1916)	Total offset does not apply to cases where interest could be earned
Beaulieu v. Elliot (1967) (Alaskan Rule)	Discount rate should be zero
Sierra Blanca Sales Co. v. Newco Industries, Inc. (1975)	Trial judge should determine the appropriate discount rate
Havens v. Tonner (1976)	Inflation and productivity are speculative and inadmissible
Kaczkowski v. Bolubusz (1980)	Future inflation must be equal to future interest rates, with offsetting effects
Doca v. Marina Mercante Nicaraguense (1980)	Trial judges may use 2% real interest rate
Budge v. Post (1981)	Judges should instruct jurors about discount rate without specificity of applicable rate
Westman Commission Co. v. Hobart Corp (1982)	Expert testimony and discount rate of 25%
Jones & Laughlin v. Pfeifer (1983)	Discounting must be based on the best and safest investment
McCrann v. United States Lines, Inc. (1986)	Future value payments must be discounted

TABLE OF CASES

Case	Finding
Monessen Southwestern Ry. Co. v. Morgan (1988)	Discount rate and jury instruction
CHR Equipment Financing, Inc. v. C&K Transport Inc. (1989)	Commercial rates may be considered for discounting
LLECO Holdings, Inc. v. Otto Candies, Inc. (1994)	Expert testimony and discount rate of 25%
Wells v. Wells (1999)	Safe securities must be utilized to control for inflation (British House of Lords)
Ammar v. United States (2003)	Discounting may not always apply
Case	**Finding**
	Scientific evidence
Texas Dept. of Community Affairs v. Burdine (1981)	Under Title VII, a plaintiff can prove discrimination by preponderance of evidence without scientific certainty
Bazemore v. Friday (1986)	Preponderance of evidence may not require scientific evidence
Daubert v. Merrell Dow Pharmaceuticals (1993)	Scientific evidence is admissible in courts of law with judges as gatekeepers
Ted Smith et al v. Virginia Commonwealth University (1995)	Omitted variable bias calls into question external validity
Federal Trade Commission (FTC) v. Staples (1997)	Omitted variable bias can have prejudicial effect
Interflora Inc v. Marks & Spencer plc (2012)	Use of surveys may not be permissible for resolving patent disputes
	Deceptive financial transactions and misappropriation of information
Dodge v. Ford (1919)	Managers cannot abuse their discretion
Chiarella v. United States (1980)	Confidential information can be misappropriated
Securities and Exchange Commission v. Materia (1984)	Beneficiaries should disgorge benefits from misappropriated information
Basic, Inc. v. Levinson (1988)	Material information affects investment decisions
United States v. Mulheren (1991)	Manipulative devices are violation of Rule 10b-5
Central Bank of Denver v. First Interstate Bank of Denver (1994)	Banks may not be liable as indentured trustees under Rule 10b-5 for "aiding and abetting false information"
Software Toolworks Inc. Securities Litigation v. Painewebber Inc. (1994)	Defendants should not be liable for inaccuracies after legally espousing "due diligence"

Case	Finding
Itoba Ltd. v. Lep Group PLC (1995)	US SEC law has extraterritorial effect
US v. O'Hagan (1997)	Lawyers may misappropriate privileged information provided by their clients
Wright v. Ernst & Young LLP (1998)	Auditors may not be liable for press release of unaudited financial information
Wharf (Holdings) Ltd. v. United International Holdings Inc. (2001)	Rule 10b-5 is applicable to oral contracts
Lustgraaf v. Behrens (2010)	To be liable, defendants must exercise general control over their subsidiaries
Janus Capital Group, Inc. v. First Derivative Traders (2011)	A third party cannot be responsible for inaccurate statements under Rule 10b-5
Antitrust and restraint of trade	
United States v. Columbia Pictures Corp (1960)	Assets include intellectual property
United States v. El Paso Natural Gas Co. (1964)	Antitrust activity requires demonstration of intent and ability of targets to compete
Ball Memorial Hosp. v. Mutual Hosp. Ins. (1986)	Antitrust violations can result in deadweight (societal) losses
Eastman Kodak Co. v. Image Technical Services, Inc (1992)	Antitrust causes market imperfection
Cohen v. De La Cruz (1998)	Antitrust damages can be trebled
United States v. Microsoft Corp (1999)	Antitrust (tying products and restraint of trade)
Telecor Communications Inc. v. Sw. Bell Tel. Co. (2002)	Damages can be trebled to offset societal loss
Expropriation of creative rights	
Vitronics Corp. v. Conceptronic, Inc. (1996) and *Phillips v. AWH Corp.* (2005)	Patent litigation must have acceptable methodology for asserting claim construction
Markman v. Westview Instruments, Inc. (1996)	Judges should provide guidance for claim construction
Viskase Corporation v. American National Can Co (1998)	Patents can be infringed when elements are equivalent or identical as a matter of material fact
Siemens Med. Solutions USA, Inc. v. Saint-Gobain Ceramics & Plastics, Inc. (2011)	The accused product or process contains elements identical or equivalent to each claimed element of the patented invention[1] 1 We have assessed the insubstantiality of an alleged equivalent by applying the function-way-result test as set forth in *Union Paper-Bag Mach. Co. v Murphy*, 97 U.S. 120, 125 (1877), which asks whether an element of an accused product "performs substantially the same function in substantially the same way to obtain the same result" as an element of the patented invention. [Preponderance of evidence]

Case	Finding
Global-Tech Appliances, Inc. v. SEB (2011)	Infringer may be liable for willful ignorance and inducement
Rolls-Royce PLC v. United Technologies Corporation (2010)	Patent infringement
Interflora Inc v. Marks & Spencer plc (2012)	Use of surveys can be limited in patent disputes
Mixed Chicks LLC v. Sally Beauty Supply LLC (2012)	Patent infringement (hair line product)
	Tax evasion and avoidance
Pollock v. Farmers' Loan & Trust Company (1895)	Income tax on interest was unconstitutional
Bullivant v. AG (1900)	Definition of evasion (Britain)
WT Ramsay Ltd v. CIR (1981)	Tax avoidance, a scheme to defeat income (capital gains) from investment (Britain)
Eilbeck v. Rawling (1981)	Capital gains are taxable even when schemes are undertaken to generate losses for tax avoidance
Furniss v. Dawson (1984)	Capital gains and avoidance (Britain)
Conner v. Commissioner (2018)	Tax avoidance (sale of real estate)
Felton v. Commissioner (2018)	Tax avoidance (religious contributions)
Simonsen v. Commissioner (2018)	Nonrecourse debts (debts for which lenders assume default risk) may not generate tax liability
IRC v. Willoughby (1997)	Tax laws can be amended to tax offshore financial instruments that once enjoyed tax-free status
Salinas v. US (1997) and *Whitfield v. US* (2005)	Proof of overt acts is not required for Racketeer Influenced and Corrupt Organizations (RICO) and money laundering offenses
	Exchange rates and relevant dates (breach date or judgment date)
Rawlings v. Duvall (1797)	Breach of tort
Cowan v. McCutchen (1870)	Breach of tort
Di Ferdinando v. Sinton, Smits & Co. (1920)	Breach date (Court of Appeal, England)
Hicks v. Guinness (1925)	Date of injury (default) and value of marks in US dollars (two-rule doctrine)
Die Deutsche Bank Filiale Nurnberg v. Humphrey (1926)	The date of breach and application of foreign law
Miliangos v. George Frank Ltd. (1975)	Currency of preference diversified by House of Lords

Case	Finding
Competex v. LaBow (1985)	Conversion rule can be applied
Mitsui & Co. v. Oceantrawl Corp. (1995)	Award in yen
	International law (courts)
Paquette Habana Case (1900)	International law is part of US law and must be ascertained and administered by the courts of justice of appropriate jurisdiction
Mavrommatis Jerusalem Concession Case (*Greece v. UK*) (1924), (1925), (1927)	States can represent the interests of their nationals
Brazil v. France (1929); see also *France v. Serb-Croat-Slovene State* (1929)	Gold clause must apply; devalued currency must not be used for loan payments
Germany v. Poland (1928, Chorzów Factory Case)	General principles of law can be applied to the resolution of international disputes
Columbia v. Peru (1950)	Asylum case: customary law was insufficient (not well developed or established) to provide asylum
Denmark v. Federal Republic of Germany (North Sea Continental Shelf Cases, 1969)	Equity must be considered in international disputes over access to natural resources
Government of Kuwait v. American Independent Oil Company (1982)	States have autonomy over natural resources, but foreign nationals must be compensated for illegal expropriation fairly and expeditiously
Ecuador et al. v. EU (1997, EC-bananas III)	Trade discrimination (WTO, AB)
Shrimp-Turtle Case (1998), *India, Malaysia, Pakistan and Thailand v. US*	Economic activity must consider conservation (sustainable development) (WTO, AB)

INDEX

adjusted gross income (AGI), 274, 277
Airbus 380–382, 409, 411–414; see also Boeing
Alaska 73
Alaskan rule 223; see also Beaulieu v. Elliot
American Insurance Group (AIG) 125–126, 151n100
Aminoil case 449–459, 480
Ammar v. United States 69, 477
Am. Pipe & Constr. Co. v. Utah 46n30, 476
Analysis of covariance (ANCOVA) 208, 212–213
Analysis ToolPak 202
Analysis of variance (ANOVA) 211–213
Andersen, Arthur 116
Annual percentage rate (APR) 59, 217; see also nominal interest rate
annuities 217–218, 228, 230, 232, 250, 311n41
antitrust laws 4–5, 16, 317, 320, 322; see also Cellar-Kefauver Act (1950); Clayton Act (1914); Federal Trade Commission Act (1914); Hart-Scott-Rodino Act (1976); Robinson Patman Act (1936); Sherman Act (1890); Wheller-Lea Act (1938); Williams Act (1968)
Articles of Agreement 76, 397, 431, 434, 436, 438

Balance sheet 96, 99–106, 115–116, 121–122, 127, 130, 134, 142, 147n16, 148n28, 150n86, 153n132, 255n44, 430
Ball Memorial Hosp. v. Mutual Hosp. Ins. 353, 478
Basic Inc. v. Levinson 149n47, 477
Bazemore v. Friday 253n18, 477
Bear Stearns 121, 124, 126, 129
Beaulieu v. Elliot 223, 476
Berne Convention 160, 176, 186n1
Boeing 380–382, 409, 411–414, 461n5
Bretton Woods System 74, 85n27, 85n33, 428, 433–436
Breusch-Godfrey test 209
Budge v. Post 226, 476
Bullivant v. AG 298, 479
business cycle 52–58, 89, 285, 383

capital adequacy 124
capital asset pricing model (CAPM) 221, 246
capital gains tax 277
Cash flow statement 96, 105–109
Cellar-Kefauver Act (1950) 327–330, 338, 357n15
Central Bank of Denver v. First Interstate Bank of Denver 111, 477
Chesapeake & Ohio Ry. Co. v. Kelly 67–68, 224, 476

Chiarella v. United States 112, 149n49, 477
Chicago school 8–9, 11
Chi square 238–244, 251n6, 268–269
CHR Equipment Financing, Inc. v. C&K Transport Inc. 227, 477
Civil Rights Act (1964) 27–30, 43, 213–215; see also occupational discrimination
Clayton Act (1914) 5, 319–322, 327, 329, 332–333, 336, 338, 351, 356n7
Coerced loan theory 59, 84n22
Cohen v. De La Cruz 354, 478
Coinage Act (1792) 81, 85n34, 468n81
cointegration 45n26, 207, 252n8
Colbert 370, 375, 463n21
collateralized debt obligations (CDOs) 125–126
Common Reporting Standards 273
Competex v. LaBow 78, 81, 480
competitive market 8, 16, 38–39, 43, 131, 342, 384–385; see also market concentration
conduct test 119, 145; see also effects test
Conner v. Commissioner 302, 310n30
consumer price index (CPI) 63–65, 69; see also inflation; Producer Price Index (PPI)
consumer surplus 16–17, 39, 42, 353, 359n59, 373, 462n20
cost of capital 246–248
countervailing measures 398–410, 417, 425; see also subsidies
Cowan v. McCutchen 85, 479
cross-sectional data 196–197, 254n19
currency devaluation 80–81, 368, 387, 392, 425, 428, 433, 449, 456
currency manipulation 392, 430–431

Daubert v. Merrell Dow Pharmaceuticals 4, 180, 194–195, 228, 249–250, 252n5, 477
deadweight loss (DWL) 24, 353–354, 356n5
Delaware corporate law 117, 137–139, 141, 143–144, 249, 317, 450
Denmark v. Federal Republic of Germany (1969) 461n2, 480; see also North Sea Continental Shelf Cases
Die Deutsche Bank Filiale Nurnberg v. Humphrey 79, 479; see also Hicks v. Guinness
Di Ferdinando v. Sinton, Smits & Co. 79, 85n30, 479
discretionary spending 273, 285–286
Dispute Settlement Body (DSB) 402–408, 412–413, 416, 460, 465n42, 466n43

Dispute Settlement Understanding (DSU) 5, 161, 402–412, 414, 425, 434, 438, 466n50
Doca v. Marina Mercante Nicaraguense 68, 476; see also *McCrann v. United States Lines, Inc.*
Dodge v. Ford 103, 129–137
dummy variable 35, 208–209, 213
dumping 132, 381, 383–385, 387, 389–395, 408, 414–419, 460, 464n30, 466n56–60, 467n66–67
Durbin-Watson 209; see also serial correlation

Eastman Kodak v. Image Technical 12, 348, 359n52, 478
Ebner v. Fresh, Inc 46n36, 476
Econometrics 1, 4–5, 9, 193–255
effective annual rate (EAR) 59, 217; see also annual percentage rate (APR)
effects test 3, 119
Eilbeck v. Rawling 299, 479
elasticity 16, 24–27, 42, 131–132, 199, 208, 253n14, 294–295, 343, 353–354, 359n64
employment cost index (ECI) 66, 69; see also inflation
Enabling Clause 420–421, 463n25, 467n72
Engle-Granger 252n8
Enron 92, 108, 115–116, 121–123, 136, 150n86
Equal Employment Opportunity Commission (EEOC) 29–30
equilibrium 19–21, 146n3, 379–380, 382, 395, 432
equity 1–2, 7–8, 10, 12–13, 160, 164, 187, 215, 480
equity risk premium (ERP) 246
Eubank v. Pella Corp. 46n29, 476
European Central bank (ECB) 63–64
Eurozone 64–65
Excel 35, 193, 200, 202–205, 211, 213, 219, 228, 230–234, 243, 347
exchange rates 1, 3, 51, 73, 75–79, 83, 85, 89, 285, 305, 368, 392–393, 426–431, 436, 456, 468n83, 479
expropriation 3, 159–190

Fed funds rate 234; see also nominal interest rate
Federal Rule of Civil Procedure 21, 42
Federal Trade Commission (FTC) 93, 253n19, 321–322, 324–326, 330, 332–333, 339–341, 347, 351, 356n9, 477
Federal Trade Commission (FTC) v. Staples 216
Felton v. Commissioner 303, 310n31, 479
Financial Accounting Standards Board (FASB) 101, 147n15
Fisher equation 224, 248
fixed effects 254n19; see also random effects
forecasting 4, 67, 193, 196, 198–207

Foreign Account Tax Compliance Act (FATCA, 2010) 305, 307
Foreign direct investment (FDI) 166–167, 170, 439–442, 460, 469n98
Form 10-Q 115
FTC v. Ruberoid Co. 324
Furniss v. Dawson 299–300, 479
future value 169, 217–218, 220–222, 228, 230–232, 258–260, 476; see also present value of money

General Agreement on Tariffs and Trade (GATT) 161, 368–369, 377, 388–390, 393, 397–398, 400, 404, 410, 417–418, 420–422, 424–425, 467n71–73, 468n77
Generally Accepted Accounting Principles (GAAP) 96–97, 101, 122, 147n15, 148n30, 279
Gen. Tel. Co. of Sw. v. Falcon 46n30, 476
Germany v. Poland (1928) 462n12, 480
Glass-Steagall Act (1933) 124
Global-Tech Appliances, Inc. v. SEB 180, 479
Gold Standard 85n33, 368, 386, 428–430, 433, 439, 468n81
goodwill 100–101, 104, 106–107, 147n24, 148n29, 183–184
Government of Kuwait v. American Independent Oil Company (1982) see Aminoil case
Gramm-Leach Bliley Act (1999) 124
Greece v. UK (1924–1927) see *Mavrommatis Jerusalem Concession Case*
Gresham's Law 428

Harmonized Index of Consumer Prices (HICP) 64; see also inflation
Hart-Scott-Rodino Act (1976) 332–336, 352
Havens v. Tonner 223, 476
Hazelwood School District v. United States 214
Heckscher, Eli see H-O theorem
Herfindahl-Hirschman Index (HHI) 5, 341–343, 345
heteroskedasticity 208–209
Hicks v. Guinness 79, 479
horizontal mergers 337; see also vertical mergers
H-O theorem 379, 463n23
Hume, David 370

Iannelli v. US 149n62, 476
income statement 96–102, 105–106, 147n16, 255n44
Individual Retirement Account (IRA) 274
infant industry 380, 390
inflation 2, 15, 51, 53, 55, 59–69, 72, 75, 80, 82, 83n7, 84n10, 90, 203, 223–226, 248, 293, 308n1–3, 308n8, 457, 459, 476–477
injury 57, 67, 69, 71, 77–79, 81–82, 84n15, 111, 118–119, 145, 193, 195, 223, 237–238, 326–327,

320, 372, 384, 390–391, 393–395, 400, 409–410, 412, 415, 436, 464n30, 479
Intellectual Property Enterprise Court (IPEC) 184, 189n54
Interflora Inc v. Marks & Spencer plc 183, 477, 479
internal rate of return (IRR) 218, 230, 233–234
Internal Revenue Code 301–302, 412
Internal Revenue Service (IRS) 147n15, 279, 281–282, 287–290, 301–307, 309n13–14, 311n42
International Court of Justice (ICJ) 76, 366, 459, 461n2, 461n5, 471n135
international law 1, 5, 159–160, 185, 354, 363–471
International Monetary Fund (IMF) 74–77, 84n26–27, 368, 389, 431, 433–434, 438, 456
International Trademark Association (INTA) 166–167, 186
International Trade Organization (ITO) 369, 388, 390; *see also* General Agreement on Tariffs and Trade (GATT)
intrinsic value 4, 244–245, 426
IRC v. Willoughby 298, 479
Itoba Ltd. v. Lep Group PLC 109, 117–119, 478

Janus Capital Group, Inc. v. First Derivative Traders 149n44, 478
Jones & Laughlin v. Pfeifer 68, 224, 476

Kaczkowski v. Bolubusz 223, 476
Kane v. Chobani 46n36, 476
Keynes, John Maynard 53; *see also* spending multiplier
Kondratiev 52, 168

Laffer *see* tax Laffer curve
Lanham Act (1946) 162, 176–177, 182, 188n48
Lehman Brothers 92, 121, 124, 126–128
Lerner Index 345
LLECO Holdings, Inc. v. Otto Candies, Inc. 227, 477
long-run production cost 36–38, 133, 344
Longshoremen's and Harbor Workers Compensation Act (LHWCA) 84n15
Lustgraaf v. Behrens 149n40, 478

mandatory spending 273, 285–286
marginal tax rate 72, 247, 275, 280, 293, 295, 298
market concentration 328, 339, 341–342
Markman hearings 180, 188n42
Markman v. Westview Instruments, Inc. 478
Mavrommatis Jerusalem Concession Case 402, 469n100, 480
McCrann v. United States Lines, Inc. 69, 476; *see also Ammar v. United States*
Marx, Karl 52–53

Maximum Freight Case 40
mercantilists 370
Microsoft Case 346–349, 359n45, 359n56, 478
Miliangos v. George Frank Ltd. 80–81, 479
Minsky, Hyman 52, 83n1, 91, 93, 140, 146n6
Mitsui & Co. v. Oceantrawl Corp. 81, 85n34, 480
Mixed Chicks LLC v. Sally Beauty Supply LLC 183–184, 189n53, 479
Modified Accelerated Cost Recovery System (MACRS) 98, 148n25, 279–282
Monessen Southwestern Ry. Co. v. Morgan 224–226, 477
monetary rules 61
monopoly 9, 27, 39–40, 162, 169, 294, 315–316, 320, 323, 328, 342–343, 347–349, 353–354, 356n6, 359n56, 375, 381, 383, 391, 409; *see also* market concentration
Mooresville Honda 235–238
Mortgage-Backed Securities (MBS) 117, 125, 127, 281
most favored nation (MFN) 367–368, 388–389, 419, 421, 424–425, 462n14, 463n25, 468n77, 469n103
moving average 200–205
multipliers *see* spending multiplier; tax multiplier
Mundell-Fleming 432, 468n87

Nebraska 40–41, 47n50
net acquisition value (NAV) 234, 344
net present value (NPV) 96, 218, 230, 232–233
net working capital 103, 105
New Haven School 1, 10, 44n1
New York Stock Exchange (NYSE) 117, 147n14
nominal interest rate 60–61, 68, 224; *see also* real interest rate
nonaccelerating inflation rate of unemployment (NAIRU) 66
normative economics 1, 10–12, 42, 129, 134
North American Free Trade Agreement (NAFTA, United States-Mexico-Canada Agreement USMCA) 377, 420
North Sea Continental Shelf Cases (1969) 461n2, 471n135, 480

Ockham's razor 14, 207
Okun, Arthur 55
ordinary least squares (OLS) 198, 201, 207–211, 250, 253n17
Organization for Economic Cooperation and Development (OECD) 55, 56, 167, 278–279, 283, 306, 308n9, 442–447, 469n101, 469n104
over the counter (OTC) 93–94
overt act 111, 114–115, 117

Paquette Habana 461n2, 480
Pareto, Wilfredo 12, 44n5, 45n23
per se rule 5, 315, 349, 359n53
Phillips v. AWH Corp 180, 185, 478
Phillips-Ouliaris 252
Phillips-Perron 200
Pollock v. Farmers' Loan & Trust Company 275, 308n6, 479
pooled data 196–197
positive economics 10–11, 45n11; see also normative economics
post-judgment interest 72–73; see also prejudgment interest
preferential trade agreements (PTAs) 376, 382, 385, 419–420
prejudgment interest 67, 70–71, 350
present value of money 220–221, 223, 232
principal-agent problem 3, 89, 120–145
Producer Price Index (PPI) 63, 65

quick ratio 105
quotas 367, 379, 387–388, 396, 423

random effects 253n19
Rawlings v. Duvall 85, 479
real interest rate 60, 67–70, 72, 83n7, 476
recession 53–55, 83n1, 281, 288, 339
regional trade agreements (RTAs) 382, 385, 387, 389, 397, 460; see also preferential trade agreements (PTAs)
Regression see ordinary least squares (OLS)
Restatement of Conflict Laws 77
return on assets (ROA) 134; see also return on equity (ROE)
return on equity (ROE) 134, 247–248
Revenue Act (1861/1862) 275–276, 278, 308n5
Rhue v. Cheyenne Homes 45n20
Ricardo, David 376
Robinson-Patman Act (1936) 5, 322–324, 332
Rolls Royce PLC v. United Technologies 180, 479
root mean squared error (RMSE) 202, 205–206, 250
rule of reason 5, 315, 349, 359n53; see also per se rule
Rule 10b-5 94, 109–113, 116–117, 119, 145, 477–478
rule utilitarianism 45n16

Salinas v. US 149n65, 479
sampling 4, 193, 241, 329, 351; bias 216; cluster 197–198, 291; error 288; random 250, 288; stratified 198; systematic 198; 216, 241
Schumpeter, Joseph 52, 159, 168
serial correlation 206, 208–209, 236
Securities and Exchange Commission (SEC) 3, 93–96, 109–110, 114, 115–121, 123, 127, 145, 147n15, 152n119, 152n127, 332, 478
Securities and Exchange Commission v. Materia 113, 477
shareholder equity 99–106, 116, 121–123, 127–129, 134, 141, 147n13, 148n34, 152n19, 223, 236, 244–247, 249, 294, 311n41, 331–332, 337, 339, 366, 399, 410, 412–413, 439, 469n99
Sherman Act (1890) 5, 27, 45n22, 317–319, 324, 332, 336, 338, 346–348, 350, 354–355, 359n56
Shrimp-Turtle Case 422–423, 480
Siemens Med. Solutions USA, Inc. v. Saint-Gobain Ceramics & Plastics, Inc. 188n39, 478
Sierra Blanca Sales Co. v. Newco Industries, Inc. 226, 476
Simonsen v. Commissioner 304
Smith, Adam 92, 371–376, 382, 463n21
Smoot-Hawley tariff 367–369, 386
Software Toolworks Inc. Securities Litigation v. Painewebber Inc. 149n42, 477
special drawing rights (SDRs) 75, 434, 468n89; see also International Monetary Fund (IMF)
spending multiplier 283; see also tax multiplier
stare decisis 8, 11, 364
stationarity 4, 196, 198–207
subsidies 18, 292, 379–381, 388–389, 398–402, 410–414, 425, 460, 466n44–45; see also countervailing measures
surveillance 94, 402, 407, 437

taxes 2, 4, 14, 18, 51, 59, 67, 70–72, 82, 97–99, 102, 107, 135, 150n82, 245–246, 273–277, 279–280, 285, 289, 300, 309n17–19; avoidance 275, 283, 289–300; corporate 276, 310n38, 451, 456–459; deferred 104–105; evasion 275, 278, 283, 289–301, 304; excise 289; flight 305–306; progressive 274, 308n4; property 310n30; tariffs 379–380, 387, 413; value-added 64; see also Modified Accelerated Cost Recovery System (MACRS)
tax gap 287–290, 296, 309n14
tax Laffer curve 278, 293
tax multiplier 283
tax wedge 275, 278, 308n4
Taylor Rule 60, 68
Ted Smith et al v. Virginia Commonwealth University 215, 477
Telecor Communications Inc. v. Sw. Bell Tel. Co. 353, 478
Texas Dept. of Community Affairs v. Burdine 215, 477
time series data 196, 198, 201 see also cross-sectional data

INDEX

total offset 69, 84n15, 223–224, 226, 476
trade creation 382–383, 419
trade diversion 382–383
trade-related aspects of intellectual property rights (TRIPS) 161, 163, 186n2, 389
Treasury bills 59
Treasury Inflation Protected Securities (TIPS) 67, 69, 72
Tuna-Dolphin Case 421–423

Unemployment 2, 51, 53–59, 82; frictional 55, 83n2, 89–90, 237, 280, 282, 284, 289, 368–369, 383–385, 430; measurement 54; structural 55, 83n2; see *also* nonaccelerating inflation rate of unemployment (NAIRU)
Union Pacific Railway 41, 47n50
United Air Lines v. Evans. Hazelwood 214
United Nations Conference on Trade and Development (UNCTAD) 440–442, 448–449, 470n106
United States v. Columbia Pictures Corp 329, 478
United States v. El Paso Natural Gas Co. 330, 478
United States v. Microsoft Corp see Microsoft Case
United States v. Mulheren 149n48
unit root 200, 252n8, 252n10
Uruguay Round 161, 388, 399, 410
US v. O'Hagan 113, 149n54, 478
US v. Powell 114, 476
US v. Schmidt 149n64, 476

vertical mergers 317, 338, 341, 356n14

Vienna Law of Treaties 365, 389, 436, 462n6
Viskase Corporation v. American National Can Co. 180, 478
Vitronics Corp. v. Conceptronic, Inc. 180, 478

wages 32–33, 52, 57, 66, 68–69, 97, 151n112, 168–169, 193, 211, 214, 223, 226, 274, 276, 278, 285, 394
Warner Mgmt. Consultants, Inc. v. Data, Gen. Corp 354
Wells v. Wells 69, 477
Westman Commission Co. v. Hobart Corp 227, 476
Wharf (Holdings) Ltd. v. United International Holdings Inc. 149n46, 478
Wheller-Lea Act (1938) 5, 324–327
Whitfield v. US 479, 149n65
Williams Act (1968) 153n142, 331–333
working capital 103, 106, 150n82, 245–246
World Bank 56, 65, 431
World Intellectual Property Organization (WIPO) 160, 171–172, 174, 187n24–25, 189n55
World Trade Organization (WTO) 5, 161, 367–369, 377, 381, 382, 388–389, 402, 411, 413, 414–415, 420–423, 425, 431, 434, 438, 460, 462n14, 463n24–25, 466n60, 468n78, 480; see *also* General Agreement on Tariffs and Trade (GATT)
Wright v. Ernst & Young LLP 149n43, 478
WT Ramsay Ltd v. CIR 299–300, 479

zeroing 417–419
zero interest lower bound 62

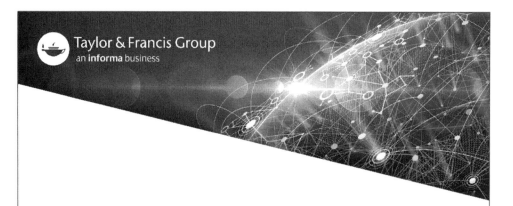